THE NEW
CHILD PROTECTION TEAM
HANDBOOK

GARLAND REFERENCE LIBRARY
OF SOCIAL SCIENCE
(VOL. 380)

THE NEW CHILD PROTECTION TEAM HANDBOOK

Editors:

Donald C. Bross
Richard D. Krugman
Marilyn R. Lenherr
Donna Andrea Rosenberg
Barton D. Schmitt

GARLAND PUBLISHING, INC. • NEW YORK & LONDON
1988

Library of Congress Cataloging-in-Publication Data

The New child protection team handbook.

(Garland reference library of social science; v. 380)
Bibliography: p.
Includes index.
1. Child abuse—United States—Handbooks, manuals, etc. 2. Child abuse—United States—Prevention—Handbooks, manuals, etc. 3. Social service—United States—Team work—Handbooks, manuals, etc. 4. Medical social work—United States—Handbooks, manuals, etc. 5. Social work with children—United States—Handbooks, manuals, etc. 6. Children's rights—United States—Handbooks, manuals, etc. I. Bross, Donald C. II. Series
HV741.N397 1988   362.7'044   88-2542
ISBN 0-8240-8519-1

Printed on acid-free, 250-year-life paper
Manufactured in the United States of America

*Dedicated to the pioneers in child protection
and to those who contribute
to the safe and optimal
development of children.*

Editors

DONALD C. BROSS, J.D., Ph.D.; Associate Professor in Pediatrics (Family Law); Legal Counsel for C. Henry Kempe National Center for the Prevention and Treatment of Child Abuse and Neglect, University of Colorado Health Sciences Center, Denver, Colorado

RICHARD D. KRUGMAN, M.D.; Director, C. Henry Kempe National Center for the Prevention and Treatment of Child Abuse and Neglect; Vice Chairman for Clinical Affairs and Associate Professor, Department of Pediatrics, University of Colorado Health Sciences Center, Denver, Colorado

MARILYN R. LENHERR, M.S.; Coordinator, Child Protection Team, University Hospital; Training Administrator, C. Henry Kempe National Center for the Prevention and Treatment of Child Abuse and Neglect, University of Colorado Health Sciences Center, Denver, Colorado

DONNA A. ROSENBERG, M.D.; Assistant Professor of Pediatrics; Director, Child Protection Team, University Hospital, University of Colorado Health Sciences Center, Denver, Colorado

BARTON D. SCHMITT, M.D.; Associate Professor of Pediatrics, University of Colorado Health Sciences Center, Denver, Colorado; Director of Consultative Services, Children's Hospital, Denver, Colorado

Other Contributors

THOMAS L. BIRCH, J.D.; Legislative Counsel, National Child Abuse Coalition, Washington, D.C.

LISANNE BUDDE-GILTNER, M.S.S.W., A.C.S.W.; formerly with the Kent School of Social Work, University of Louisville, Louisville, Kentucky

HENDRIKA B. CANTWELL, M.D.; Pediatric Consultant, Child Protection Team, Denver County Department of Social Services and Health and Hospitals, Denver, Colorado

CLAUDIA CARROLL, Psy.D.; Clinical Psychologist, private practice; Former staff member of C. Henry Kempe National Center for the Prevention and Treatment of Child Abuse and Neglect, University of Colorado Health Sciences Center, Denver, Colorado

DAVID L. CHADWICK, M.D.; Director, Center for Child Protection, Children's Hospital and Health Center, San Diego, California

ANNE H. COHN, D.P.H.; Executive Director, National Committee for Prevention of Child Abuse, Chicago, Illinois

ROBERT E. CRAMER, JR., J.D.; District Attorney, Huntsville, Alabama

ANNE H. CROWE, M.S.S.W., A.C.S.W.; formerly with the Kent School of Social Work, University of Louisville, Louisville, Kentucky

DAVID B. DENSON, M.S.W.; Social Worker, Child Protection Team, University Hospital and State and Regional Team on Crimes Against Children, C. Henry Kempe National Center for the Prevention and Treatment of Child Abuse and Neglect, University of Colorado Health Sciences Center, Denver, Colorado

DONALD N. DUQUETTE, J.D.; Clinical Professor of Law, Child Advocacy Law Clinic, University of Michigan Law School, Director, University of Michigan Interdisciplinary Project on Child Abuse and Neglect, Ann Arbor, Michigan

ELIZABETH ELMER, M.S.S.; Director, Research and Training, Parental Stress Center, Pittsburgh, Pennsylvania

KATHLEEN C. FALLER, Ph.D.; Co-Director, University of Michigan Interdisciplinary Project on Child Abuse and Neglect, Ann Arbor, Michigan

NANCY GARY, C.H.A., M.S.; Child Protection Team, University Hospital, Clinical Instructor of Pediatrics, University of Colorado Health Sciences Center, Denver, Colorado

GAIL S. GOODMAN, Ph.D.; Assistant Professor and Director, Dual Degree Program in Psychology and Law, University of Denver, Denver, Colorado

DIANA B. GORDON; Assistant Director, Center for Child Protection, Children's Hospital and Health Center, San Diego, California

CANDACE A. GROSZ, M.S.W.; Social Worker, C. Henry Kempe National Center for the Prevention and Treatment of Child Abuse and Neglect; formerly Child Protection Team Coordinator, University Hospital, University of Colorado Health Sciences Center, Denver, Colorado

CAROL C. HAASE, B.A.; Program Coordinator, C. Henry Kempe National Center for the Prevention and Treatment of Child Abuse and Neglect, University of Colorado Health Sciences Center, Denver, Colorado

ANN M. HARALAMBIE, J.D.; President, National Association of Counsel for Children; Lecturer in Psychiatry, University of Arizona School of Medicine, Tucson, Arizona

JOAN SUZUKI HART, M.S.W.; Director, Parents and Children Together (PACT), Association of Retarded Citizens/Adams County, Denver, Colorado

CLARE F. HAYNES-SEMAN, Ph.D.; Developmental Psychologist, C. Henry Kempe National Center for the Prevention and Treatment of Child Abuse and Neglect; Assistant Professor in Pediatrics, University of Colorado Health Sciences Center, Denver, Colorado

DAVID P.H. JONES, M.R.C. Psych. D.C.H.; Child and Family Psychiatrist, The Park Hospital for Children, Oxford, England

BARBARA B. KAMINER, M.S.S.W., formerly with the Kent School of Social Work, University of Louisville, Louisville, Kentucky

MARY CAROLINE KEALOHA, R.N., M.A.; formerly with the National Clearinghouse on Child Abuse and Neglect, Washington, D.C.

ROBERT KEAN; Sergeant, Colorado Springs Police Department, Colorado Springs, Colorado

RUTH S. KEMPE, M.D.; Child Psychiatrist, C. Henry Kempe National Center for the Prevention and Treatment of Child Abuse and Neglect; Associate Professor of Psychiatry/Pediatrics, University of Colorado Health Sciences Center, Denver, Colorado

MICHAEL W. LANIER, M.A.; Child Sexual Abuse Consultant for the State of Florida, Jacksonville, Florida

JON L. LAWRITSON; Attorney at Law, Fortune and Lawritson, P.C., Denver, Colorado

DAVID W. LLOYD, J.D.; Counsel, Division of Child Protection, Children's Hospital National Medical Center, Washington, D.C.

JANET T. MCCLEERY, R.N., B.A., C.P.N.P.; Nursing Coordinator, Child Abuse Program, Columbus Children's Hospital, Columbus, Ohio

COLONEL PETER J. MCNELIS, D.S.W.; Office of the Assistant Secretary of Defense for Health Affairs, The Pentagon, Washington, D.C.; formerly with Medical Service Corps, U.S. Army Headquarters, U.S. Army Medical Research and Development Command, Fort Detrick, Maryland

JANET K. MOTZ, M.S.W.; Child Protection Program Administrator, Division of Family and Children's Services, Colorado Department of Social Services, Denver, Colorado

MICHAEL A. NUNNO, M.S.W.; Senior Extension Associate, Family Life Development Center, New York State College of Human Ecology, Cornell University, Ithaca, New York

MARK PERLMAN, M.A.; President, PeopleWork, Inc., Sarasota, Florida; Training Consultant, Children's Medical Services/Child Protection Teams, State of Florida, Department of Health and Rehabilitative Services, Tallahassee, Florida

BELINDA J. PINYERD, R.N., M.S.; Nursing Coordinator, Clinical Study Center Columbus Children's Hospital, Columbus, Ohio

EDWARD J. RODGERS, JR., L.L.B.; Investigative Consultant, District Attorney's Office, Colorado Springs, Colorado

PAULA ROSENSTEIN, Founder and Past President of Family Outreach of America, Inc., Corpus Christi, Texas

SUSAN L. SCHEURER, M.D.; Assistant Professor of Pediatrics and Human Development, Michigan State University; Consultant to Michigan Department of Public Health, Lansing Michigan

MICHAEL W. SCHULTZ, M.S.W.; Director, Pitkin County Department of Social Services, Aspen, Colorado

BRANDT F. STEELE, M.D.; Psychiatrist, C. Henry Kempe National Center for the Prevention and Treatment of Child Abuse and Neglect; Professor Emeritus of Psychiatry, University of Colorado Health Sciences Center, Denver, Colorado

DANA U. WAKEFIELD, J.D.; Judge, Denver Juvenile Court; Adjunct Professor of Law, University of Denver College of Law, Denver, Colorado

J.M. WHITWORTH, M.D.; Associate Professor of Pediatrics, Child Abuse and Neglect, University of Florida and Statewide Consultant, Child Protection Teams, Jacksonville, Florida

JEANNINE WILLIAMSON, M.S.W.; Social Services Administrator, Child Protection, Denver Department of Social Services, Center, Colorado

Contents

Preface

A tradition of interdisciplinary support for children in need of protection, which began in 1958, continues in *The New Child Protection Team Handbook*. In Barton D. Schmitt's *The Child Protection Team Handbook*, published in 1978, C. Henry Kempe recorded this tradition as follows:

> Hospital-based child protection teams came into being 25 years ago through the efforts of Betty Elmer, M.S.W., of the Pittsburgh Children's Hospital; Helen Boardman, M.S.W., Children's Hospital in Los Angeles; and C. Henry Kempe, M.D., of the Department of Pediatrics at the University of Colorado Medical Center in Denver. In the past 20 years, child protection teams have expanded from having two or three members (generally a social worker, a pediatrician, and a nurse) to include a variety of professionals from the fields of psychology, psychiatry, law, and education. Most importantly, in recent years, representatives from the child protective services of welfare departments have become permanent members of hospital-based teams.[1]

Since publication of the first handbook for child protection teams, additional professionals interested in protecting children, including criminal prosecutors, dentists, and teachers, have begun to participate in child protection teams. The number of teams identified in the United States alone has grown from a few dozen to approximately 1000.

Teams are found from the Atlantic to the Pacific, in rural and urban communities. Teams exist in hospitals, departments of social services, mental health centers, on military installations, and in federal tribal jurisdictions. They have many different perspectives and purposes, but are united by the recognition that children need people who can be trusted to work together on their behalf. Multidisciplinary teams work for children by working for professionals: professionals are continuously cross-trained by colleagues and emotionally sustained. Children benefit from professionals who work in multidisciplinary teams, because teams provide structure, continuity, and institutional "memory" for the various disciplines involved. Children's needs are more likely to be confronted, rather than denied, when teams routinely incorporate different professions, agencies, and, where possible and appropriate, community oversight. Multidisciplinary teams are forced to evaluate the efforts of members from a perspective that cannot be totally self-interested, because the interests of so many are involved. Out of the need to achieve consensus for action, validations based on the best interest of the child are more likely than when a single professional is involved.

Teams are not substitutes for parents, even though they must understand and carefully consider parental views. Teams are not substitutes for careful casework or child protective services investigations and case management. Teams do not make legal decisions, hold hearings, or act like courts. Teams can, however, help assure a thoughtful and reasonable response to a child's and family's possible need for protection. Teams can illuminate a family's problem, support a protective service agency, and provide important, perhaps essential, data to courts.

Team recommendations appear to increase the likelihood that service for a child or family will be carried out.[2] When the team members and caseworkers who consulted with teams were asked to rank eight ways in which the team helped caseworkers, both groups independently ranked "support" as the most valuable aspect of teams.[3] Thus, teams may help alleviate "burnout" and reduce feelings of isolation. Teams can also form the nucleus around which a community identifies the extent of its child abuse problem and develops the socio-political framework to begin to do something about it.

As previously pointed out by one of our editors, not everything about multidisciplinary teams is positive, nor can teams answer all problems:

> First, although most child protection teams are voluntary and, therefore, not costly, multidisciplinary treatment is

expensive.   The salaries of the staff—from lay therapist to psychiatrist—are significant, and, except in extraordinary cases, cannot be supported only by generated fee income.

Second, when many people are involved, the chance of conflict increases over time as team communication becomes more difficult.   Further, the personalities of the individuals must be compatible.   Individuals who are either independent "loners" or at the other extreme not able to work independently and in need of constant support, will interfere with the smooth functioning of the team.

Third, abusive parents of any type are often adept at playing off one therapist against another.

Fourth, without direction and coordination, the multidisciplinary approach can sometimes deteriorate into endless anecdotal "can you top this" discussion with the patient being forgotten.[4]

While fully scientific evaluations remain to be undertaken, professionals are increasingly accepting multidisciplinary team work as the standard of practice, by participating on teams and referring cases for team consultation.[5]   The contributors to this book were largely selected because they serve on child protection teams or have special knowledge that has proven to be topical for child protection teams.   The reader's comments are welcome as a contribution to the growing network of teams and body of knowledge that will support child protection.

With special thanks we acknowledge Janice Frary and Lois Robinson of the Kempe Center for the repeated typing and formatting of the manuscript submitted.   Thanks are also due Lyle Kanee for his review of many of the legal chapters, as well as all of the authors for submitting on time.

It is our hope that *The New Child Protection Team Handbook* will prove useful to all who share in the "extended family" of child protection teams, service agencies, and caring individuals.

The Editors
Denver, Colorado
1987

References

1. Schmitt, B.D. (Ed.) "Foreword." *The Child Protection Team Handbook*, p. xiii. New York and London: Garland STPM Press, 1978.

2. Hochstadt, N.J., and N.J. Harwicke. "How Effective Is the Multidisciplinary Approach? A Follow-Up Study." *Child Abuse & Neglect*, 9(1985):365-372.

3. Pearl, Peggy. "Providing Support to Prevent 'Burn-Out' by Utilizing a Child Protection Team." Unpublished manuscript, 1985.

4. Krugman, R.D. "The Multidisciplinary Treatment of Abusive and Neglectful Families." *Pediatric Annals*, 13(1984):761-764.

5. Lovitz, K.E., et al. "Multidisciplinary Team Functioning." *Child Abuse & Neglect*, 8(1984):353-360.

PART I

Organizing
Case Management Teams

Section Editor: Richard D. Krugman

1. University Teaching Hospital Child Protection Team

Richard D. Krugman

Introduction

This chapter discusses the organization and functioning of child protection teams at university teaching hospitals. The first hospital-based child protection teams were established in 1958 at the Pittsburgh Children's Hospital, the Children's Hospital in Los Angeles, and University Hospital in Denver. Each of these hospitals is a university teaching hospital and their roles have not changed over the past three decades. University hospital child protection teams tend to be diagnostic teams, in contrast to the multidisciplinary teams described in Chapters 3 and 4 which are monitoring teams that are either city or county based. Diagnostic teams grew from the need for a multidisciplinary gathering of data to provide better case finding, assessment, and treatment planning for abused children and their families. This chapter reviews the structure and functioning of university-based teams.

Team Purpose and Structure

A university hospital-based child protection team has three main purposes: first, to review all cases of abuse and neglect that are referred to it; second, to provide training for undergraduates and graduates in medicine, nursing, social work, law, mental health, and related professions; third, to serve as a focus for research efforts in the field of abuse and neglect at the hospital or within the university (see Chapter 36).

In all referred cases, the child protection team has two primary functions: (1) diagnosis and (2) treatment. A hospital-based child protection team is likely to review one or two cases per week, generally the more complex cases or those in which there are disagreements, rather than discussing every single case that is seen at the university hospital. At University Hospital in Denver, the child protection team consults on approximately 1,000 cases a year, files official reports on 400 of these cases, but discusses only 75 to 100 cases at the weekly meeting. These are the more difficult cases, presenting challenges in either medical, social, or psychiatric diagnosis. They may also be cases in which there is disagreement between hospital professionals and the county departments of social services who have responsibility for the case.

DIAGNOSTIC FUNCTIONS

University hospital teams have the following diagnostic functions:
(1) To compile a comprehensive evaluation and data base.
(2) To review cases for errors. A team approach protects members from making individual errors that might result in serious consequences.
(3) To evaluate the safety of the child's home environment.
(4) To reach a consensus on diagnosis and treatment.
(5) To formulate the final recommendations for initial treatment.
(6) To formulate the tentative recommendations for long-term treatment.
(7) To provide consultation services either in person or by telephone regarding the diagnostic questions for physicians or other professionals serving the family.
(8) To provide a referral mechanism for primary practitioners, especially in cases where the practitioner is concerned about abuse but is worried about his or her ability to deal with the family.
(9) To improve communication between professionals and agencies. The team conferences help professionals in various disciplines understand each other better, as well as help the hospital-based team understand the pressures faced by the county workers and vice versa.
(10) To serve as an outlet for any wrath from parents whose child is being examined for abuse. The social worker or pediatrician or mental health worker can then be "on the side of the family" and start treatment.

TREATMENT FUNCTIONS

Among the treatment functions of the child protection team are:

(1) To periodically review and evaluate cases to see whether or not the treatment plan is being carried out.

(2) To revise treatment programs as needed should the physical or social climate of the family change.

(3) To stimulate the effective utilization of community resources.

(4) To prevent the return of a child to an unsafe home. County departments of social services often are anxious to return children to their homes even if a diagnostic or treatment plan has not been carried out.

(5) To prevent repeated child abuse with its concomitant high risk of deatn and disability.

(6) To focus on family rehabilitation but to consider termination of parental rights if the treatment is clearly failing.

(7) To provide telephone consultation services regarding treatment questions as they arise.

(8) To coordinate and improve community services for treatment of the child and the family and to encourage interagency cooperation.

(9) To ensure a day in court for any child who needs it, in case a county department of social services or county attorney refuses to file a necessary complaint.

(10) To provide ongoing monitoring and evaluation of community treatment services if county agencies do not provide follow-up data or outcome data on the families they are serving.

Establishing Internal Structure

In many university hospitals, the task of taking care of child abuse cases is given to the most junior faculty member or is rotated among staff members along with such other tasks as interviewing internship applicants, taking care of the junior student program, or other departmental chores. In many other university facilities there are professionals whose major research and teaching interests are in the area of child abuse and neglect. They are directing child protection teams, not because they were assigned to the task, but because it is their chosen field of work. Each university team will develop its own structure to best meet the conflicting needs of case management, teaching, and research, as well as other duties of department members. For purposes of example only, we describe the following University Hospital Child Protection Team as one type of structure that has worked in one settihg. Readers are encouraged to modify or adapt this approach for their own team in the university hospital.

THE CORE TEAM

The team consists of two primary groups. The core team consists of a pediatrician, a social worker, a child health associate, and a coordinator. These four specialists are involved with each of the 400 reported cases as well as the 500 or more non-reported accidental injury or other "non-cases" for which consultation is requested. The physician and the child health associate act in a primarily diagnostic way bringing their medical skills to bear on whether or not a given injury is likely to be accidental or non-accidental. The social worker evaluates the safety of the home and recommends treatment planning for the families as well as gathers the social information necessary for a team meeting. The coordinator is crucial in hospitals with many child abuse cases and/or many county agencies to deal with. In the Denver metropolitan area, for example, there are six metro area counties each with its own child protective services system and children are admitted to University Hospital from all of these counties. With six child protective services systems, 100 law enforcement jurisdictions, six community mental health programs, and many more school districts, the coordinator's role becomes crucial if all of the appropriate professionals and agencies involved in a case are to be brought to a team meeting. For smaller teams, however, or in areas with few agencies potentially involved, the physician or social worker may also take on the role of coordinator.

THE CONSULTATIVE TEAM

Whereas the core team is involved in every case, the consultative team, which meets with the core team weekly, is involved only in those cases that are discussed at the weekly meeting (75 to 100 per year for our team). The larger team consists of an adult psychiatrist who serves in a diagnostic role for assessing the parents, a child psychiatrist who serves in a diagnostic role for the child, a developmental psychologist who is involved in parent-child interactional assessments, an attorney versed in both civil and criminal law, and a public health nurse. The nurse can link to the public health agencies in the community who may be needed for either diagnosis or treatment planning. As these professionals work with each other over many weeks, months, and years they not only bring their own skills to bear on each case, but are also able to consider the perspective of their colleagues from other disciplines should a colleague not be present. It is this combined core and consultative team that develops an expertise of its own that is larger than the sum of its parts. When this group is joined by case-specific professionals, that is, the child's local physician, public health nurse, teacher, the involved social worker, law enforcement officer, guardian *ad litem*, nurse from the hospital setting, and teacher, all of the information needed to make appropriate decisions for the child and the family will be available.

A further discussion of the clinical purposes of university hospital child protection teams including diagnostic and treatment functions can be found in the literature.[1]

Educational Role

It has been our experience at the University Hospital of the University of Colorado Health Sciences Center that an increasing number of students from the Schools of Medicine and Nursing have been interested in attending child protection team meetings as well as doing elective rotations in child abuse and neglect. This is an encouraging sign. Unlike physicians who trained in the 1940s and 1950s, who had to readjust their thinking to accept that children were being battered, these students have grown up in an era when battered children and other forms of abuse and neglect were reported regularly in the media. Consequently, these younger physicians and nurses in training accept abuse and neglect as fact and as one of the reasons for their being interested in coming to health professional training. The early contact of students with the multidisciplinary team can be important in (1) reinforcing their belief that their professional roles include caring for abused children and their families and (2) modeling interdisciplinary behavior so that they are less likely to resist involvement later in their professional lives.

Each case that is discussed at the child protection team should be an educational experience. Furthermore, each case should be reviewed every three to six months to see what the outcome has been. Many times the University Hospital Child Protection Team's recommendations to the county either are not followed or cannot be followed because of lack of court action or community mental health resources. Unless the University Hospital Team keeps track of the outcome of its cases, it is not likely that anyone else will. In addition, without this type of follow-up information, teams may continue to make unrealistic recommendations and ultimately be perceived by the community as being "ivory towerish" and not understanding the constraints and limitations faced by county child protective service agencies.

The university team can also provide continuing education to professionals who are in practice in the community, either by involving them on a case-by-case basis or by developing a series of conferences that are geared toward the individual professions, such as pediatrics, emergency medicine, nursing, social work, psychiatry, psychology, and others.

It is of course also true that by meeting and discussing cases weekly the members of the team maintain their own continuing education. If they are also involved in caring for children who have been abused and neglected, it is our feeling that their educational skills will be magnified. It is difficult to be dogmatic about how a case should be dealt with, if one is involved in working clinically with abused children and their families.

Research Role

There have been a number of good research efforts that have grown out of university child protection teams. These include studies that have been done on injuries that occur when small children fall out of bed,[2] serious head injuries treated at a university emergency room,[3] the differentiation of accidental versus non-accidental rib fractures,[4] retinal hemorrhages,[5] or sexual abuse.[6,7,8] In a field as complex as child abuse and neglect, good clinical observations and carefully controlled research studies are crucial for the best possible civil and criminal intervention on behalf of the victims. While it is true that the data base on which professionals practice in the field of abuse and neglect in the 1980s is imperfect, it is clearly significantly better than it was a decade ago. One would anticipate that with continued research efforts by university-based teams and professionals working in other settings, that the data base for decision making will be that much better in the coming decade.

Limitations of University Hospital Teams

The major limitation of a university hospital team lies in its lack of legal status. While such teams are invaluable from a risk management perspective for the university hospital, protecting the hospital by minimizing the chance of liability from missed cases or failure to report, from the perspective of the child and the family, university hospital teams have no legal clout. The team can make recommendations to the county department of social services, but except in extraordinary situations, unless the department brings the case to the county attorney for filing and unless the county attorney files a case in juvenile court, it is not likely that there will be any action. In some states, the university team, a physician member, or any concerned individual can ask for a hearing should the team feel that the county and the county department of social services is making a great mistake in not filing the case. This is an avenue that should be traversed rarely. It does not help foster communication and coordination between county departments and university hospitals, if the university hospital brings the county into court. In certain situations, however, such action is necessary if there is legitimate professional disagreement about the safety of the child if returned home. Thus, while the university team has no legal status in itself to protect children and families, it can use the weight of its clinical consensus to bring cases to court that might not otherwise be heard.

A second limitation of university hospital teams relates to their lack of funding. Most teams have part-time physicians with relatively little support for the time that the physician puts into child abuse cases. In an era when university hospitals are finding that they are becoming more reliant on clinical earnings, the pediatrician evaluating abuse cases is likely to be one of the very low earners on the pediatric faculty. At our university hospital the child protection team's current collection rate approaches 29%. It is not easy to support faculty on these clinical earnings alone. Some child protection teams have obtained other funding (see Chapter 2, Private Hospital Child Protection Teams) but for the most part the child protection team will be a low earner in a departmental setting. The hospital, however, may be willing to support much of the team's efforts since the hospital is at substantial risk if abuse cases are missed or improperly handled. The liability issues for failure to report or for missed diagnosis may be greater than many others in the university pediatric setting.

Summary

University hospital child protection teams have the longest history and tradition of any of the multidisciplinary child protection teams in the United States. These were begun in the late 1950s by professionals who recognized the complexity of the cases and the need for medical, social work, psychiatric, law enforcement, and legal information in order to properly assess and treat abused children and their families. As these teams have evolved over the past 30 years, they have also fulfilled significant educational and research roles. It is hoped that during the next decade these teams will be able to form a regional network, similar to what universities did with perinatal and poison control services. The potential for future leadership in the field of abuse and neglect from university-based teams is great, if they take up the challenge. Unlike community-based monitoring teams (see subsequent chapters), most of which are swamped with their service role, university teams can take on the educational and research roles so crucial for the advancement of knowledge in the multidisciplinary assessment and treatment of abusive and neglectful families.

References

1. Krugman, R.D.   "The Multidisciplinary Treatment of Abusive and Neglectful Families." *Pediatric Annals,* 13(1984):761-764.

2   Helfer, R.E., and T. Slovis. "Injuries that Occur when Small Children Fall Out of Bed." *Pediatrics,* 60(1977):533-535.

3. Billmire, M.E., and P. Meyers. "Serious Head Injury in Infants: Accident or Abuse?" *Pediatrics,* 75(1985):340-342.

4   Feldman, K.W., and C.C. Brewer.   "Child Abuse, Cardiopulmonary Resuscitation, and Rib Fractures." *Pediatrics,* 73(1984):339-342.

5. Kantor, R.K. "Retinal Hemorrhage after Cardiopulmonary Resuscitation or Child Abuse." *Journal of Pediatrics,* 108(1986):430-432.

6. Krugman, R.D. "Recognition of Sexual Abuse in Children." *Pediatrics in Review,* 8(1986):25-30.

7. Hunter, R.S., N. Kilstrom, and F.A. Loda. "Sexually Abused Children: Identifying Masked Presentations in a Medical Setting." *Child Abuse & Neglect,* 9(1985):17-26.

8. White, S.T., F.A. Loda, D.C. Ingram, et al. "Sexually Transmitted Diseases in Sexually Abused Children." *Pediatrics,* 72(1983):16-21.

2. Private Hospitals as an Environment for Child Protection Teams

David L. Chadwick and Diana B. Bryson

Introduction: Variations in Private Hospitals

Private hospitals include a very large variety of environments that differ considerably in their suitability for child protection activities. Most of the children's hospitals in the U.S. are private, nonprofit corporations and most serve their communities as referral centers for all sorts of serious health problems of children, including children who may be in need of protection because of abuse. At the other extreme are private hospitals with no pediatric or obstetrical service or minimal pediatric activity in the emergency room; such hospitals have little need for child protection programs. In between are private general hospitals with pediatric inpatient units of varying sizes from 10 to over 100 beds, and outpatient services that vary even more. As a general rule, the larger and the more sophisticated the pediatric services provided, the more desirable and suitable it is that the hospital develop a child protection program.

The existence and nature of an academic affiliation may also influence the development of child protection programs, but this factor is less important than the pediatric service mission of the hospital, which will determine whether or not abused children come to the hospital.

REFERRAL PATTERNS

If the region has organized trauma services and if the hospital contains a pediatric trauma center, then a sophisticated system for recognizing, evaluating and managing non-accidental injury is virtually mandatory.

The activity of the obstetrical service also drives a need for child protection programs. Private hospitals that deliver large numbers of newborns inevitably encounter many situations that are high-risk for abuse or neglect, such as instances of ongoing maternal substance abuse or clear patterns of highly abnormal parent-infant interaction.

ECONOMIC FACTORS

In the present economic environment, hospitals may find socially-oriented services, such as child protection, difficult to establish. Although a hospital-based child protection program may be cost-effective in its overall effects, the benefits do not accrue to the hospital and the costs must be defrayed from non-operating income. This is not a simple task for most private, nonprofit institutions. As a result of these economic factors, there is a great deal of variation in the services that similar hospitals provide to abused children and their families. The variation appears to be related to such factors as leadership and individual hospital missions and policies. In our opinion, it may be that those hospitals with the best view of the future recognize the importance of social/medical programs to the future of health care and are more likely to develop strong child protection programs.

Possible Components, Functions, and Staffing of a Private Hospital-Based Child Protection Program

The pre-existing programmatic structure of the hospital may have a strong influence on its child protection program. Hospitals with existing mental health services, substance abuse programs and departments of social services can incorporate part of these into a child protection team (CPT). The application of sophisticated services for the diagnosis and management of trauma has already been mentioned.

FUNCTIONS

Some of the functions that can be performed in a child protection program in a private hospital are the following:

-Recognition of abuse and neglect.

-Reporting.

-Diagnosis in depth (evidentiary examination).

-Expert testimony about abuse cases.

-Treatment of physical problems of victims.

-Treatment of psychological and developmental problems of victims.

-Treatment and rehabilitation of abusive family members.

-Evaluation and treatment of perpetrators other than family members.

-Professional education—undergraduate, graduate and continuing for medical specialists, social workers, psychologists, and other disciplines.

-Public and community education.

-Public policy work, legislative initiatives, etc.

-Research in many different aspects of child abuse work.

STAFFING

These efforts can be carried out by a variety of hospital staff members who become attached to or associated with a child protection team or program, including, but not limited to the following:

-Pediatrician with training and/or experience in physical abuse and neglect.

-Pediatrician (or other specialist) skilled in evaluation of sexual abuse.

-Social worker(s) with expertise in physical and sexual abuse.

-Pediatric radiologist.

-Pediatric pathologist.

-Psychologist and/or psychiatrist with expertise in child abuse of all types and forms.

-Developmental psychologist.

-Occupational and physical therapist.

-Nursing liaison to inpatient units and outpatient services.

-Nurses involved in child protection clinics.

-Researchers from a variety of disciplines.

A minimum child protection team for any private hospital that offers pediatric services consists of a designated physician (probably a pediatrician) with specially developed expertise at recognizing abuse and a part-time social worker with special qualifications in child abuse work. The "maximum" program need not be defined but might provide all of the specialists and functions listed and more. For the benefit of the courts, law enforcement agencies, state and county social services agencies and other interested entities, it would be useful to define and designate a tangible number of levels of service and allow hospitals to qualify as they can.

Establishing a Child Protection Program in a Private Hospital: A Case History with Generalizations

The case described is that of a children's hospital in a large and growing southwestern community of about 2 million with 14 other hospitals with pediatrics services, including a university hospital, a large armed forces hospital and a large health maintenance organization with its own hospital. In 1984 36,000 reports of child abuse and neglect were filed with the county's child protective services office. During the same decade, while the child protection program was developing, the children's hospital was emerging as the principal community resource of tertiary care.

At about the same time that the child protection program was established, the children's hospital developed an intensive care unit and began to provide care to the sickest and most seriously injured children in the community. This resulted in the institution's being seen as a resource for infants and children with very serious or fatal non-accidental injuries. Although such cases were uncommon in comparison with the vast majority of child abuse cases, their presence in the hospital contributed in an important way to a climate in which the staff was motivated to deal with abuse.

Child abuse services in the community were fairly well-advanced when the children's hospital developed its program. The police department had a special child abuse unit and an active community child abuse council was growing up. These professionals welcomed a strong hospital-based child protection program because it provided diagnostic service in doubtful cases with medical implications. Thus, the climate in the community favored the development of a locus of medical expertise in child abuse.

The medical director of the children's hospital had a prior interest in child abuse before assuming that position, and was committed to the development of a child protection program. In addition, a person was available who had assisted in the development of an older hospital-based child protection program in another city and who had considerable experience in organizing such an entity. Thus, the children's hospital had a member of top management committed from the beginning, and had expertise to develop the program. These may be the essential ingredients for the development of a multifaceted and sophisticated child protection program.

As the program developed, it was frequently used by the parent institution as a public relations asset, demonstrating the hospital's commitment to helping children. The hospital's board of trustees and its auxiliary developed a special interest in the program, and were vital in providing the required significant subsidization. The difference between the cost of the child protection program and the income it could generate from fees-for-service has been substantial and grants have not been consistently available for many essential components. Charitable donations by the hospital's auxiliary and other sources have made the program possible and would not have been obtained without support from the hospital's top management and governing body.

Because the hospital had developed a program for physical abuse and neglect, it was well-positioned to develop one for sexual abuse. The agency and community connections needed were much the same and reputation and credibility were very important. Although the methods employed for the evaluation of physical and sexual abuse have significant differences, there are also important similarities that make these programs fit together well. The passage of a state law requiring local governments to provide or to contract for high quality, humane medical evaluations of victims of sexual assault proved to be extremely helpful since it allowed much of the sexual abuse program to be self-sustaining from fees-for-service.

Ten years after the first formal designation of a child protection program, the parent institution defined an entity called the Center for Child Protection (CCP) and established a goal of providing a multigenerational effort to deal with the problem of child abuse. In the process of doing this, the hospital, using trustee-controlled capital funds, guaranteed a three-year subsidy of the CCP of up to $500,000, and facilitated fund-raising so that the CCP could develop its own endowment.

The parent institution also contains a child guidance clinic which for two decades has been a principal resource in the community for ambulatory mental health services for children and their families. This component has provided much of the mental health treatment needed by child abuse victims and their families, and the CCP is the largest source of referrals to the child guidance clinic.

In 1985, the CCP is engaged in a number of activities. The following describes each activity briefly and indicates how each is supported.

SEXUAL ABUSE OUTPATIENT EVALUATIONS

These consist of a detailed age-appropriate interview conducted by an experienced social worker. The interviews are done in a special room with one-way glass, allowing both videotaping and observation by another person, usually a police officer or CPS worker. After the interview, the child has a physical examination by a physician of whichever sex the child prefers. Laboratory studies for both evidence and treatment are obtained as necessary. Detailed reports are prepared and these and the video tapes are made available as evidence. All cases are referred for mental health treatment, either internally or externally, depending upon the nature of the case, the availability of service and location of residence. Almost 1200 of these exams were conducted in 1984. The costs of these exams are paid by law enforcement agencies at a negotiated rate that covers direct expenses of the program.

INPATIENT PHYSICAL ABUSE EVALUATIONS

These are performed by a social worker who conducts an interview with the family, often under very trying conditions, and a physician who evaluates the child and sometimes the family. Reports are prepared and made available as evidence. Various opinions from specialists, such as orthopedists, neurosurgeons and intensive care physicians are correlated and incorporated into the reports. In fatal cases, the clinical findings are communicated in detail to the coroner's office. About 100 of these evaluations are conducted each year. Social work costs are paid from hospital operating income and the medical costs by a combination of fees-for-service and the board subsidy.

OUTPATIENT PHYSICAL ABUSE AND NEGLECT EXAMS

These are conducted by a physician at the request of a CPS worker and are usually limited to evidentiary issues, although some of these infants and their families are treated at the CCP. Infants with non-organic failure to thrive are usually seen in this clinic, and are now rarely admitted to the hospital. About 100 of these exams are conducted per year and costs are covered by fees-for-service and the board subsidy. (Editor's Note: This represents a savings of approximately $500,000 in hospitalizations annually.)

THE PARENT-AIDE PREVENTION PROGRAM

Forty to fifty families considered to be at high risk for abuse and neglect are provided with ongoing services of volunteer parent aides. The parent-aides are supervised by the program coordinator and by social workers. This program is paid for by donations.

OTHER EFFORTS

Some sexual abuse victims are provided with ongoing support by volunteer child advocates supervised by a social worker. Once grant-supported, this program is now supported by donations.

A program to provide sexual abuse prevention education to school children from kindergarten to the sixth grade, called "STOP" was developed over the last three years using volunteers and donated funds. At present, funding has been provided by the National Center on Child Abuse (NCCAN) to "export" this program to three major school districts and to reach about two-thirds of all children in these grades in the county.

The state office of criminal justice planning has approved a grant to evaluate the "STOP" program over a two-year period beginning in late 1985. The evaluation will consist of the cognitive and behavioral testing of 600 children comparing those who receive two different sorts of preventive education with those who receive none.

The CCP provides play therapy for groups of children from four to seven years of age who have recently been evaluated in the diagnostic service. Some of these children may be receiving or awaiting individual therapy. Five groups are meeting weekly under the supervision of social workers. This program is supported by donations.

Because the county being served is large, a satellite office for the sexual abuse evaluation program has been opened forty miles north of the main center.

The CCP provides professional education by bringing in physicians and other specialists for intensive experiences from one day to one week long. The staff frequently lecture to professional groups of many disciplines and have provided programs over a wide area. These programs are typically funded on a case-by-case basis and fees and honoraria are charged to cover the staff costs.

Summary

The extensive clinical and support systems available in private hospitals, including their volunteer and auxiliary groups, make them excellent sites for child protection teams. In many communities, private hospitals have become the center of community wide activities designed to prevent and treat all forms of child abuse and neglect.

References

1.   Schmitt, B.D. (Ed.) "Foreword." *The Child Protection Team Handbook*, p. xiii. New York and London: Garland STPM Press, 1978.

2   Hochstadt, N.J., and N.J. Harwicke. "How Effective Is the Multidisciplinary Approach? A Follow-Up Study." *Child Abuse & Neglect*, 9(1985): 365-372.

3.   Pearl, Peggy. "Providing Support to Prevent 'Burn-Out' by Utilizing a Child Protection Team." Unpublished Manuscript, 1985.

4.   Krugman, R.D.   "The Multidisciplinary Treatment of Abusive and Neglectful Families." *Pediatric Annals*, 13(1984): 761-764.

5.   Lovitz, K.E., et al. "Multidisciplinary Team Functioning." *Child Abuse & Neglect*, 8(1984): 353-360.

3. The Child Protection Team in a City

Jeannine Williamson

Introduction: A Brief History

The Denver Child Protection Team (DCPT) held its first organizational meeting in late February of 1974. It was then known as the Inter-Agency Child Abuse Committee. It was organized by the Honorable Orrelle Weeks, Presiding Judge of the Denver Juvenile Court. Initial membership consisted of representatives of the Denver Department of Social Services, the Denver Police Department, the Denver Juvenile Court, and Denver General Hospital. A lay member and a city attorney were also included in the initial membership. Subsequently, additional members were added from the Denver Public Schools and the Visiting Nurse Association. A psychiatrist from Denver General Hospital was also added to the committee.

The primary functions of the committee were: (1) to review weekly all abuse complaints received by Denver Social Services; (2) to share all knowledge that the participating agencies might have about specific abused children; (3) to determine whether court action was indicated if a filing had not already been initiated; and (4) to give special consideration to the "gray area cases" where a child's life might be threatened but the parent is teachable and the child is accessible.

Effective July 1, 1975, House Bill 1482 known as the "Child Protection Act of 1975" became part of the Colorado statutes. This act provided for the creation of a child protection team in any county which reported 50 or more cases of child abuse to the State Central Registry in the previous year. Thus, what had been known as the Inter-Agency Child Abuse Committee became known as the Denver Child Protection Team. The local director of social services was designated the coordinator of DCPT and that responsibility was delegated to a member of the children and youth staff. Team membership remained essentially the same except for the addition of lay members representing significant minorities in the community. The Visiting Nurse Association withdrew its membership because their budget was cut severely, leading to a staff shortage.

The duty of DCPT, as outlined in the law, was to "review the files and other records of the case including the diagnostic, prognostic, and treatment services being offered to the family in connection with the reported abuse; and [to] make a report to the county department with suggestions for further action or [state] that the Child Protection Team has no suggestions."[1]

In the early phases of the legally sanctioned Denver Child Protection Team, an average of 27 cases per week were presented. New cases were presented by the supervisors of intake workers and the ongoing cases, when new reports were received, were presented by the coordinator.

The Media, the Public, and Litigation

From the beginning of the child protection team the issue of confidentiality was of major concern. In Denver, a reporter from a local paper attended all team meetings and wrote a synopsis of DCPT discussions for the newspaper the following day. His presence and ongoing coverage of DCPT presentations probably had more impact on how DCPT procedures evolved than any other single factor. An early district court ruling in the case of *Gillies and the Denver Post v. Schmitt et al.*[2] allowed for the presence of the "public" attending DCPT meetings in a non-participatory role; this attendance by the public was sanctioned in the Colorado Children's Code.[3]

Although the law specifically allowed DCPT to go into executive session for discussion of confidential medical and psychiatric information,[4] this procedure was utilized infrequently. It was the legal opinion of the Denver Assistant City Attorney that for the most part the actions of the Department should be discussed publicly, with the staff cautioned not to reveal names, addresses, agencies, or other identifying material.

Procedures

Since the inception of the Denver Child Protection Team all cases involving suspected or known abuse in Denver County have been presented. Neglect cases are presented if the neglect is life-threatening or if a pattern of serious neglect is present. Over the years the "unfounded" complaints have been handled differently. They originally were presented by name only by the coordinator of DCPT; now they are screened by the social worker and supervisor and are not presented to DCPT. Individual members of DCPT can ask the worker to present more details about such "unfounded" cases.

DCPT has seen a significant change in procedures, with a gradual shift of the presentation of cases from the supervisor to the investigating social worker. This change resulted from increased volume. As questions were asked about the details of the case, and the presenting supervisors who might not have the answer would request a review so that the questions could be addressed by the workers, these were added to the next week's schedule. It seemed logical to ask that the workers attend DCPT meetings. The questions of team members could then be answered on the spot and the number of cases to be reviewed that week could be reduced. Although this procedure is tedious for line staff, particularly for intake workers, it ensures accuracy in reporting and workers' accountability to the team.

Although the reporting of child abuse and neglect has increased dramatically over the years, the state statute mandates reporting of all referrals on a weekly basis. Thus the procedure for preparation for the weekly team review has not changed significantly since 1975.

SCHEDULING AND TRACKING CASES

The clerk for the Denver Child Protection Team has the ongoing responsibility to keep a file of all referrals of suspected abuse and severe neglect reported during the previous week, to clear with all staff the cases which need to be reviewed by DCPT, to schedule appointments for team presentation, to prepare packets on each case containing the referral, police reports and any other significant information for each team member, to prepare all of the CWS-59's (reporting form to the State of Colorado Central Registry identifying incidents involving child abuse and child neglect), and to send these to staff and track their completion for state recording. To ensure that all cases are identified and reviewed, it is the clerk's task to clear cases with the Denver Juvenile Court and the Denver Public Schools. These agencies keep their own records and serve as a check and balance system for Denver Social Services in terms of timely reporting. The Denver Juvenile Court, which employs a full-time secretary to manage team business, receives all referrals from social services as well as all police referrals. The Denver Public School System keeps a record of all referrals made by their teachers and staff and clears them for actions taken on a weekly basis.

RECORDS OF PROCEEDINGS

The coordinator states publicly the non-identifying information before a worker presents a case. This information includes date, source and nature of referral, degree of abuse or neglect, age of the victim, whether or not the child was hospitalized, and whether or not medical records were checked. The social worker then discusses the specifics of the investigation. All of the team meetings are taped and the tapes are kept on file for one year. The juvenile court secretary keeps written notes on the general discussion and disposition of each case. The Denver Department of Social Services keeps ongoing statistics on the volume of cases presented.

Membership

The current composition of the Denver team is as follows: a representative of the Denver Juvenile Court (and secretary) who has served as team chairman for several years; representatives from Denver Police Department, Denver Public Schools, Ft. Logan Mental Health Center, Denver General Hospital, and Denver Department of Social Services; a pediatrician; a member of the lay community; and a coordinator and an Assistant City Attorney from Denver Department of Social Services.

Problems

The most pervasive problem for the Denver Child Protection Team since its creation in 1974 has been the steady increase in volume. In the beginning of DCPT there was an average of 27 cases each week; in 1985, 70 to 100 cases. To do justice to a review of so many cases in a half day, with the same legal mandate, is virtually impossible. The social workers are under pressure to present cases quickly, and DCPT members struggle to concentrate on each case knowing that other social workers wait, and other cases remain to be heard.

Over the years, DCPT has evaluated options available for reducing the volume and the time spent by DCPT. DCPT has wished for more in-depth discussions on particularly complex cases and has recognized the more routine aspects of the very mild cases of child abuse. Although members are aware of the complexities of scheduling workers to present the cases, they value the opportunity to question the worker who has done the actual investigation and are reluctant to have the presentation delegated to a supervisor or an administrator from the Department.

The law does not mandate the presence of investigating workers at team presentations. Other metropolitan counties have in-depth written material prepared with a paper review by team members. This approach is not feasible in Denver County because of the volume of referrals to the team. In particular, it would be difficult to prepare written material and Denver team members would view this kind of review as lacking spontaneity and impeding their opportunity to ask questions of the worker involved in the decision-making. On the positive side, written material insures the uniformity of facts brought to the attention of DCPT and saves the workers' time at DCPT.

In Denver many cases need to be rescheduled. Reasons for rescheduling are many: the investigation is not completed, the worker is not available for scheduling, or emergencies have prevented the worker from being present. The sexual abuse cases are particularly cumbersome to schedule and to bring to a timely disposition. The number of referrals for sexual abuse has risen dramatically, now averaging 25-30 cases per week. The very nature of sexual abuse referrals precludes a rapid disposition. Facts emerge slowly, often involving extended family members. While facts are being gathered cases are set and reset for review culminating in a perpetual and increasing backlog of cases on DCPT's weekly agenda. Even though some of these referrals were ultimately "unfounded," DCPT and the worker went through a repeated review process in order to arrive at this conclusion.

The reporting of neglect to DCPT has always been less clear-cut than physical or sexual abuse, and involves a greater degree of discretion by the worker and supervisor. Staff has been asked to take into consideration the age of the child, the severity of the incident, and the explanation of the parent or caretaker when deciding whether a case should be presented. If a child has been removed from home and placed three times within the past year due to neglect, the case must be reviewed by the Denver Juvenile Court before the child can be returned to the parents. This case situation must be brought to DCPT for review.

The cases which are "unfounded" do not need to come to DCPT; however, "unfounded" does not always mean "untrue" and often the investigation is not complete. Some cases are set for presentation and are then "unfounded" by DCPT. These cases also increase volume of presentations and often result in considerable discussion before they are "unfounded."

Policy Issues

Since 1975 when the Children's Code set forth the right of the public to attend the meetings of DCPT, the need to protect the anonymity of the client has been an issue for DCPT. In the early days of DCPT with constant scrutiny by the press, DCPT felt constricted in its ability to have a free flow of discussion. There was concern that with disclosure of facts leading up to an incident of abuse, the client would recognize newspaper accounts of his family situation, and set up even more resistance to treatment planning. Years later, though, public participation is more likely to be by professionals new to the field of child abuse and neglect, who are present primarily to learn about the investigatory process rather than to identify gaps or delays by the various agencies. Today, no news reporter attends the meetings, and the freedom of discussion is constricted by the volume of cases and the resulting time constraints, not by worries over confidentiality.

REPORTING AGENCY ACCOUNTABILITY

It is the task of DCPT to review the responses of public and private agencies to each report of abuse or neglect, to assess whether the responses were timely, adequate, and in compliance with the law, and to publicly report any inadequate responses, specifically indicating the public and private agencies involved.[5] The team by law was meant to be an overseer of timely reporting, investigating and appropriate actions taken to protect children, as opposed to in-depth staffings on individual cases.

DCPT takes seriously its mandate to identify agencies who do not report situations in a timely manner or who fail to report. Failure on the part of agencies to follow the mandates of the law results in a verbal or written reminder; however, DCPT does not have the power to do anything other than to bring its concern to the attention of the offending agency. As the role of the child protection team has become institutionalized in the community, many more professionals are aware of the reporting laws. This has been particularly true for therapists, both in the public and private sector. Therapists had been more concerned about the erosion of the therapeutic relationship and the possiblity of upsetting the client, as a result of reporting abuse.

VOLUME OF CASES

Although the volume of cases to be reported has quadrupled since 1975, there has been no acknowledgement by the legislators or from the agencies (social services, court, police, schools, public hospital) that what was once a manageable task is now a cumbersome, tedious, and draining function. (See Table 3.1.) Funding constraints and cutbacks in staff have led to fewer agencies sending representatives, although cases are growing in volume and complexity. The drastic cutbacks suffered by the Visiting Nurse Service in Denver some years ago and their limitations of services to clients active with the Denver Social Services system are a prime example.

LEGAL COUNSEL

Another loss to the Denver Child Protection Team has been the inability of the city attorney's office to send an attorney to DCPT meetings. Although many of the case presentations do not require legal expertise, it is impossible to predict when a case will be presented where legal advice is helpful and necessary to DCPT and the social worker in arriving at a joint decision. This is particularly true in discussing the merits of filing a case with the Denver Juvenile Court.

MINORITY REPRESENTATION

Of ongoing concern, also, is the inability of the Denver team to recruit and maintain, as a team member, a representative of the Hispanic community. Because the Children's Code strongly urges that any significant minority group in the community be represented, this void in membership is significant. Over the years members of this group have been recruited but have had to withdraw due to personal or agency constraints.

TABLE 3.1 *Child Abuse and Neglect Reporting in Denver*

	Abuse	Neglect	Sex Abuse	Total Cases Presented to Child Protection Team
1978	1,752	345		2,097
1979	1,832	224		2,056
1980	2,185	196		2,381
1981	2,369	242		2,611
1982	1,563	456	586	2,605
1983	2,458	327	746	3,531
1984	2,110	253	1,256	3,619
1985*	1,952	258	1,503	3,626

1. Sex abuse referrals were not tabulated separately until 1982.

2. This chart tabulates all of the cases presented to the Denver Child by the Team. Although a weekly percentage of cases is "unfounded" by the Team, this chart gives a graphic picture of the time commitment necessary by Team members and staff to review all cases presented.

HOW DENVER SOCIAL SERVICES STAFF VIEWS DCPT

Does DCPT provide any benefit to the staff who investigate child abuse and neglect? Are their investigations more thorough and timely because of the need to report to DCPT? Do they ever get any help from DCPT?

A questionnaire was sent out to 140 social services staff members in mid-April 1985. Seventy-five staff members responded to the questionnaire:

(1) DCPT is helpful to me:
                                         sometimes 35
                           doesn't matter 20
                             is not helpful 15
                               no response 5

(2) I think the way I investigate abuse/neglect is:
                                             better 19
                                       worse --
                                       same 56

(3) My response time in investigations is:
                                         quicker 10
                                       same 65

(4) On occasion I have received helpful information from team members.
                                       True 58
                                       False 17

(5) I believe that having a CPT is an additional safeguard in the practice of child protection work.
                                       True 65
                                       False 8

(6) I believe that going to the CPT provides me with some support and backing for my actions in child protection.
                                       True 65
                                     False 8

In asking how they would change DCPT if they could,

26 said they would like a worker on DCPT
10 would like a psychiatrist
24 would like a more in-depth discussion
14 wanted more praise for well-done work

5 wanted more criticism for actions taken
8 did not want to have a team

In a public agency there is considerable turnover and many of the respondents to the questionnaire may not have worked at the department before the advent of the child protection team, and their investigations have always been subjected to the scrutiny of DCPT. Some individual remarks give some sense of the variety of views expressed:

> "The support of DCPT is good as well as keeping workers on their toes and doing their work."
> "Some goals and expectations should be provided for those who report to DCPT."
> "Information should be given as to how DCPT can provide support to those reporting to DCPT."
> "I'd like more support, more and better resources, more training, more ideas, etc."
> "Team is not as supportive as it should be."
> "Not enough alternatives are discussed."
> "DCPT shares the liability for worker and sometimes improves the quality and speed of work for the client."

For those staff members whose tenure with the Department precedes DCPT, there is no doubt that the investigation of abuse and neglect is more timely and thorough.

The members of the child protection team were also given a questionnaire to complete on how they viewed DCPT function. This was a small sample, but in certain areas team members were in agreement. They all felt that they personally were more knowledgeable about the handling of abuse and neglect cases, that DCPT had value as an overseer of child abuse and neglect, that their particular agency believed their time spent on DCPT was worthwhile, and that DCPT was of benefit to social work staff. All agreed that their attention level decreased with too many cases, yet most felt they could give the agency no more time to do the job. Most DCPT members were opposed to a pre-screening team, believing this change would not comply with the law. Most felt the response to abuse and neglect referrals by Denver Social Services had improved. Their responses were split on whether the Child Protection Team had made the community more responsive/knowledgeable about abuse and neglect. One member said, "More so when a newspaper reporter attended."

STRUCTURAL PROBLEMS

Team members are more aware than the general public of the lack of resources in the community, such as the lack of foster homes and treatment resources. Although members are sympathetic, they do not have solutions to these problems.

On occasion a team member has been able to help the social work staff by searching for some facts through his or her agency to aid the disposition of a case. Sometimes a member has been able to get the necessary help for a family or a child. However, on the whole all agencies are overburdened and cooperation among agencies to benefit the community is negligible.

TEAM AUTHORITY AS AN ADVANTAGE

A skilled worker can use the authority of the Child Protection Team to advantage in dealing with the resistant, non-motivated parent. This is particularly true in "gray-area" cases, where the worker can present the facts to DCPT and report back the conclusions to the parents. Such an approach is probably not used to its full advantage but can provide leverage for the worker and remove some of the individual responsibility for social work actions.

OTHER AGENCIES

The Denver Juvenile Court, which has a mandate to oversee actions of the Department of Social Services and the law enforcement agency, benefits because DCPT facilitates its supervisory role.[6]

Because the Denver Public Schools refer many children who are suspected of being abused and neglected, the attendance at the child protection team by a school representative ensures an orderly means of achieving an appropriate disposition on a case referred by the Denver Department of Social Services.

All of the agencies represented at the child protection team are concerned about prompt reporting and actions taken by their agencies and all react to criticism and delay in their systems. When the agencies can work together to help the families and children brought to their attention, the result is a good, working child protection community system. On occasion the various agencies and their representatives have been commended publicly. It is important to recognize examples of sensitive work with children on the part of police officers, social workers in the Denver Department of Social Services, hospital, and school and to re-affirm the difficult work of child protection. Regrettably these moments of recognition for well-done work do not come often enough with the pressures of work to be completed.

As the Denver Child Protection Team has progressed from a beginning concept mandated by law to an institution, there has been increased reporting from the private sector. More recently, institutional abuse in day care homes, foster homes, shelter and residential facilities, and schools is being reported and addressed by DCPT. Although the increase in reporting puts additional strain on DCPT, it also indicates that abuse and neglect in these institutions is not being overlooked or suppressed by the private sector.

Summary

The preparation for and ongoing attendance at a metropolitan child protection team such as Denver's is a tedious task, both for members of the team and child protection staff. There seems to be no easy answer for managing an increasing volume of cases. Although DCPT identifies delays and gaps in reporting, in reality the consequences are negligible for the problem agency or individual. Also, the Denver Child Protection Team would function better with the regular attendance of an attorney, a representative of the Hispanic community, and an assigned social worker from the Department.

On the positive side, staff from Denver Social Services agree that having a child protection team is an additional safeguard in the practice of child protection work. The timeliness and quality of investigations of child abuse and neglect is better, due to the emphasis on investigation in the Children's Code and the "oversight" aspect of the Denver Child Protection Team.

References

1.   Colorado Children's Code, Child Protection Act of 1975, Title 19, Article 10.

2.   *Gillies and the Denver Post v. Schmitt, et al.,* Colorado Court of Appeals, September 2, 1976.

3.   Colo. Rev. Stat. Sec. 19-10-109 (6) (d) (1984).

4.   Colo. Rev. Stat. Sec. 19-10-109 (6) (g) (1984).

5.   Colo. Rev. Stat. Sec. 19-10-109 (6) (f) (1984).

6.   Colo. Rev. Stat. Sec. 19-10-113 (1) (1984).

4. Rural Child Protection Teams

Janet K. Motz and Michael W. Schultz

Introduction

This chapter reviews the value of the child protection team approach in rural areas and provides information regarding resistance to the concept as well as a practical approach to the development and maintenance of a rural team. Much of the information contained in this chapter is based on the Colorado experience with teams, yet it can be easily transferred to other states which may or may not have a statutory mandate. Colorado's statute pertaining to teams (see Appendix 4.1) details team composition, role, function, and public participation.

Colorado has a long history of community-based child protection teams. Dr. C. Henry Kempe, who greatly influenced the development of child protective services in this state, was a strong advocate of the team approach. The first community-based teams were developed in 1973 and more were inaugurated in 1974. In 1975 there was a major revision to the Colorado Children's Code which included the mandating of teams in counties reporting 50 or more cases of child abuse and neglect a year to the state's Central Registry. The statute also encourages the development of teams in other counties. Rural counties began to develop teams as early as 1974 and currently 31 of Colorado's 54 rural counties are served by teams. Of the rural teams, only 10 are mandatory. Colorado has a total of 44 community-based child protection teams. Some counties have more than one team and some teams serve more than one county.

Value of Rural Teams

It is apparent from professional practice and the literature that community- and hospital-based child protection teams enhance service delivery in urban settings. The sophistication of those teams and the amount of expertise and resources available to them suggest that teams can only function well in urban settings. Rural communities might be hesitant to consider the development of a team because they may lack resources and experience or expertise in child protection. However, the factors that appear to make the development of a team an impossibility are, in fact, the very reasons that a team is indicated in a rural community. In many cases, the beneficial impact of the team is even greater in the rural community than in its urban counterpart. The team itself becomes an invaluable resource as it develops a high level of expertise and creates other resources.

Resistance to Rural Team Development

Some resistance to the formation of a team is not uncommon. The most significant points of resistance are: (1) who is to control, (2) time constraints, and (3) perceived lack of need.

CONTROL

Control becomes an issue when the agency responsible for child protection services perceives the advisory nature of the team as a threat, and fears that the recommendation will be inappropriate and detrimental to the child. Such resistance will lessen if the team is well trained and its role relative to the agency is clarified. Even more important in diminishing this resistance, however, is an awareness that the team assists the CPS worker and the agency in helping clients. Especially in small rural CPS offices, the single worker can gain much needed support and professional assistance not available before the team's formation. Issues of control must be addressed as an ongoing task in team maintenance.

TIME CONSTRAINTS

Time constraint issues were of great concern to administrators of county departments of social services when Colorado's law mandating teams was enacted without a fiscal note. The chief concern was that already overburdened staff would have to take on additional responsibilities of coordinating the team and other duties associated with team review of cases. Colorado counties have continued to manage these teams with no additional funding and community agencies and professionals have been most responsive in donating their time. Many teams are voluntary, indicating that county departments have found the team to be worthwhile. In rural counties the team meeting saves the time required to have a staffing on an individual case as the cases are staffed in one team meeting rather than several individual meetings. Rural counties have also realized better cooperation and more participation in treatment by other community agencies as a result of the work of the team. The regular team meeting facilitates better communication between agencies and professionals. Professionals in rural areas sometimes have difficulty accessing each other. The public health nurse, for example, may serve a large area, and is not easily reached by telephone. The necessary communication with that nurse can occur at the team meeting.

PERCEIVED LACK OF NEED

The perceived lack of need for a team generally arises because the number of child protection cases reported in any given month in rural counties is small. Some states mandate teams where reports reach an arbitrary threshold. However, resistance to team formation based on lack of cases may not be valid for two reasons. First, given that the number of cases in a community is low, the services to those cases can be enhanced with a team approach. Second, and perhaps more relevant, the team's existence will stimulate an increase in the number of child abuse referrals to the county. This is primarily the result of increased public awareness of the existence of the problem, how to report suspected or known cases of child abuse and neglect, and the belief that the team can be effective in dealing with the problem. Further, as teams review referrals and assess community needs, it becomes an important professional catalyst in developing needed resources.

Team Development

The first step in organizing a rural team is to stimulate interest and concern about the problem of child abuse and neglect, and to gain acceptance of the fact that child abuse and neglect is a community problem rather than the problem of one agency. Colorado communities have accomplished this by conducting community workshops. Often noted experts from outside the community are called upon to conduct these workshops and the focus is not only on the problem but also on the effectiveness and need for a child protection team and community involvement in working toward solutions. Unless the community *believes* it has a problem, it is unlikely to act.

SPONSORSHIP

Once the interest has been generated, the next step is to consider membership and to determine the role and function of the child protection team and to gain administrative support for the team. The strong administrative support of the agency sponsoring a team is essential. In Colorado, the sponsoring agency is, by statute, the county department of social services. In most rural Colorado counties, the development of the team has been at the initiative of that department. In some cases, the initiative has come from outside the county department. In any case, the support of the director of the department of social services must be enlisted early in the planning. The sponsoring agency must be positive about the team concept and making it work or the team is doomed to fail.

ROLE AND FUNCTION

Those planning to establish a child protection team should have a clear idea of the role and function of the team prior to the selection and appointment of the members. The basic role and function of Colorado teams is prescribed by statute. The statutory provision provides that teams will review all cases within seven days of the receipt of the report and also will make findings regarding the adequacy of response of the various agencies. Colorado teams have expanded their role. All of the rural teams provide consultation and recommendations regarding diagnostic and treatment decisions. Most of these teams serve additional functions such as educating the community, taking stands on system issues, participating in treatment, and making efforts to fill the gaps in service delivery.

The sponsoring agency should make some decisions regarding the role of the team in the review of cases: will the team serve only a monitoring function, be purely regulatory (review adequacy of agency responses) or will it also be asked to assist with diagnostic and treatment decisions. If the team is to assist with these decisions, then it must be decided how team recommendations will be treated. Colorado teams are, by statute, advisory only, but although the county department has final decision-making power, many departments have policies that team recommendations can be overridden only at the supervisory or director level. The team must then be provided with an explanation. Decisions regarding activities other than case review can be negotiated with the team after it becomes operational. Generally, there is a natural progression. As the team reviews cases, the gaps in the system become obvious and team members become interested in additional activities.

Membership

The selection of members is a critical part of team development. Those developing the team must choose the agencies to be represented and also give some consideration to the individuals from those agencies who would serve best on the team. Colorado law suggests that "where possible" the team should consist of a physician, a representative of the juvenile court or the court with juvenile jurisdiction, a representative of the county department of social services, a representative of a mental health clinic, a representative of the public health department, an attorney, and one or more representatives from the lay community. The statute also provides for representation of any racial, ethnic, or linguistic minority groups when those groups constitute a significant portion of the population of the jurisdiction of the team [CRS 1973, 19-10-101 (2)]. The suggested representation has been possible for most of Colorado's rural teams. Many of these teams have representation from other agencies or organizations as well. When the team has been inaugurated and is operational, the original members may determine that additional representation could be helpful.

CHARACTERISTICS OF TEAM MEMBERS

The personality of the individual team members is critical to the successful team. Team members who are most effective have the following characteristics:

Assertiveness—The team member must feel confident to share knowledge and express opinions.

Ability to Function as a Team Person—The mere fact that a person is a recognized expert does not mean that he or she will work well as part of a team. There are some persons who use meetings as a forum to prove that they are the best. Many persons work very well independently but have difficulty with the group process and some are intimidated by groups. They are not good candidates for a team despite their expertise. The team member must be able to listen and be open to differing attitudes.

Supportiveness—The team member must be willing to support colleagues and offer criticism in a constructive manner. Highly critical persons sometimes feel the need to criticize at every turn, and do so in the form of attack and put down. This behavior is very destructive to team functioning. Knowing they will be attacked, workers sometimes are afraid to present information that might leave them vulnerable to criticism. Also, team decisions and recommendations can be discounted or ignored because of worker anger or resentment.

Broad Education—Team members should have some knowledge of the whole system to make good decisions. This can be accomplished through selection, ongoing continuing education and team training.

Commitment and Reliability—The effective team member has a strong commitment to the prevention and treatment of child abuse and neglect as well as to the team approach. Those who are most committed are those who attend and participate. During the selection process, it is important to address the issue of commitment of time and energy. Often persons accept a position on the team and then are unable to attend the meetings. Although the person may have valid reasons for sporadic attendance, it is dysfunctional. The team might consider a different meeting time or replacing those members who cannot attend regularly.[1]

Activating the Team

Choices of members in rural communities are limited. There may be only one person in the public health department, for example. Occasionally, those developing the team have expressed a concern that they have had a poor relationship with the one person who could represent a key agency and have been hesitant to include that person on the team. In most cases in our experience, relationships have improved when the person is on the team. On the other hand, in many rural communities, agency staff already know each other and have worked together effectively in a variety of capacities.

Personnel from the agency sponsoring the team are generally the persons who select the agencies to be represented and do some of the selection of individuals. The heads of various agencies to be represented are the ones who appoint the representatives according to Colorado statute. The individual approaching the agency director about an appointment should be assertive about the type of person needed to serve on the team and should be clear about the time commitment. When the agency makes an appointment, the sponsoring agency and team director should then formalize the appointment in writing. It is useful if this letter addresses confidentiality, time commitment and other ground rules.

The lay member of the team should be carefully selected. Some teams have advertised informally and interviewed applicants. In some communities, advocates who are already in a position of trust are natural candidates for team membership.

TEAM ORIENTATION

The first meeting of the team is very important as it sets the tone. Those conducting the meeting should orient members to the role and function of the team, assess training needs and clearly state the task at hand. Confidentiality and other basic ground rules should be clearly stated. A confidentiality statement should be signed by each member. Prior to beginning case review, there should be a series of training sessions based on the needs assessment, and the team should develop policies and procedures. The training sessions should address legal issues, medical issues, family dynamics, evaluation process, treatment modalities, and efficient and effective case review. It is helpful for each agency to update the team as to the services it provides, the fiscal and legal constraints under which it operates, and any limitations affecting the team. Thorough information regarding the role, function and procedures of the county child protective services unit is necessary.   These presentations are important so that members have a clear understanding of their local child abuse prevention and treatment system. With such data, they are less likely to have unrealistic expectations and will have more appropriate recommendations.

The development of team policies and procedures is a process which some teams have resisted. They are usually anxious to get on with case review. In our experience, teams which ignore or side-step this process in the early stages found it necessary to do it later after some serious struggles. There are also secondary gains derived from the process. By setting policies and procedures together, the group begins to function as a team and is better prepared to begin the difficult work of reviewing cases.

TEAM LEADERS

Coordinators of Colorado's community-based teams are by statute persons from the county department of social services. Often the coordinators chair the meetings as well. Some of the coordinators of rural teams have effectively delegated the role of chairperson to another team member who has strong leadership skills. Many rural teams now have a chairperson and a coordinator who jointly plan the meetings. As new teams develop, selection of a chairperson occurs during the developmental phase. The chairperson should be selected on the basis of leadership qualities rather than willingness alone. Some teams have made a major error in selecting a person who could be coerced into taking the job but was not necessarily an individual with leadership skills.

Many teams are often tempted to take shortcuts during their developmental stage. Training is overlooked because the assumption is made that all team members have the knowledge and experience needed or team members do not express a need for training. Teams which have taken these shortcuts have often experienced problems and then have had to back track.

TEAM MAINTENANCE

Maintaining a well-functioning team requires at least as much work and planning as developing one. Often teams have been so focused on the task at hand that they fail to deal with group dynamics, training needs, and administrative issues. They are then forced to deal with these issues when they have reached crisis proportions.

INTERPERSONAL RELATIONS

The most difficult issues for teams to address are those that are interpersonal. These problems do not often disappear when ignored and usually escalate. Among the more common are turf issues, lack of mutual respect, a domineering or intimidating member, or chronic disagreements between the team and the CPS agency. It is the responsibility of the team leader to recognize and address these problems. Team leaders must respond to these issues by using group process to identify the problem and plan strategies of intervention. For example, "unrealistic expectations" may be an issue which causes team members a great deal of frustration. As noted previously, if each agency explains its services, as well as its limitations in providing these services, unrealistic expectations can be avoided.

It also helps to address the real frustrations resulting from the combination of difficult cases and limited resources on a regular basis. If the team should become dysfunctional for any reason, it may help to have a consultant work with the team to evaluate individuals and team processes. The distinct advantage in child protection team maintenance is that the goals are seldom, if ever, challenged. Working from that base, and believing children are better protected because of this community input can resolve many issues that other groups might find more difficult to resolve.

TEAM TRAINING

Ongoing team training is essential to keep team members abreast of current theory and practice. Training sessions should be held at least quarterly and more often if it becomes clear that team members have insufficient knowledge about an area to make good decisions. Training can be conducted by experts within the community. Rural communities need to acknowledge and utilize their own expertise. For example, a team probably does not need to have an attorney from the metropolitan area to explain the new statutory amendments. Team members should also be encouraged to attend workshops held in other communities. Some rural Colorado county departments of social services have paid tuition and travel for team members to attend major conferences. They have found the expenditure to be cost effective as the more skilled and knowledgeable team members are of more assistance to the department.

ADMINISTRATIVE ISSUES

The team should set aside time periodically to address administrative issues, particularly those problems pertaining to review of cases. It might be determined, for example, that the team is being provided with insufficient information about the cases or that there is not sufficient time to review all cases. The manner in which the team is functioning should be reviewed on an ongoing basis.

Colorado's rural teams have found outside technical assistance most helpful. Sometimes an outsider can get more readily to the heart of a problem because he or she is not enmeshed in the problem. If persons who provide technical assistance are familiar with the practice of many teams, they can share solutions reached by other teams with similar problems.

RECOGNITION

Teams recognized as important and valuable by the sponsoring agencies, the agencies represented, and the community are motivated both individually and as a group to excel in their work. Efforts to publicly and privately recognize the teams foster motivation. Some county departments sponsor and pay for a luncheon or breakfast, and some alert the press of the existence of the team, its membership and the value of the team. The most essential recognition is taking team input seriously.

LEADERSHIP

The effective chairperson can make sure that everyone is included and involved, and can dilute attempts at domination by any one member. The chairperson can keep the team on task, avoid rambling discussions and prevent indecisiveness by bringing matters to a vote when appropriate. Some rural teams rotate the chair on a yearly basis so that extra work does not fall on one person and ownership is given to all members.

Unique Features of Rural Teams

Rural teams are faced with some unique problems but also have many advantages. Rural areas lacking resources and teams have to be creative with treatment plans. Expert consultation is often unavailable within the community and has to be obtained long distance. As a rule, professionals from agencies are generalists rather than specialists in such areas as child protection. Although some rural professionals may not have specialized child protection experience, their knowledge of the whole service delivery system often enables them to offer more services than individual specialists.

Child protection teams in rural areas can usually be more thorough in case review because they have a lower volume of cases. While metropolitan teams may minimize a case because of high volume, rural teams must beware of maximizing a case. Sometimes rural teams have found themselves making a serious case of very minor neglect. Outside consultation may be in order to place a situation into its proper perspective.

CONFIDENTIALITY

Rural teams must be extremely cautious and aware of their responsibility to maintain confidentiality. Sometimes the family to be discussed includes a relative or a friend of a team member. To address this, the team professionals might cite a case example on the importance of maintaining confidentiality, or leave out all identifying details. In a rural community it is difficult to protect client identity and team members have to be extremely cautious. Colorado statutes provide for public attendance at team meetings, although identifying information regarding the family and reporting party are not to be revealed at the public discussion. Rural teams have to recognize that even revealing the age of the child (which is allowed by the statute) could, in a small community, identify the child. Rural professionals must guard against case-related discussions being held in any place where they might be overheard. One precaution is for teams to meet in a very private location.

While it creates some confidentiality problems, the fact that everyone knows everyone in a small community can also be positive for the team. When the department of social services presents a case to the team, nearly everyone on the team is aware of the family and the situation, and can generally fill in any information gaps. Generally, the rural teams can make decisions based on more thorough information often unavailable to a team in a larger community.

PUBLIC SUPPORT AND SCRUTINY

Rural teams are more visible than their urban counterparts, and their work is often more open to scrutiny. In some rural communities, everyone in town knows about the team, when they meet, and who the members are. Although they are more open to scrutiny, they often get positive public recognition which is well deserved. Metropolitan teams rarely get this kind of public accolade.

ISSUES OF PERSONALITY

Team members in rural communities often serve on many of the area's committees, councils and task forces, some unrelated to child protection. They have generally served together on these groups and know each other well. This can be an advantage except in cases where the individuals are hostile toward one another because of a particular issue. Yet, because of limited choices of persons to serve on the team, the same individuals may have to be together on the child protection team. Sometimes teams have had one member who was extremely difficult and caused strife, but because the member was from an essential agency, there was no way to avoid having that person on the team. In some cases, the problems were never resolved, and the persons left the team. In other instances the person became a functioning member.

BROADER FUNCTIONS

Rural teams have often expanded their role and functions. Many rural teams have provided community education. Some teams have a booth at the county fair, members speak to groups of professionals, service organizations, schools, etc. Rural teams have also sponsored prevention campaigns. Members of these teams are often involved in treatment of the families. This is often advantageous as the team members are implementing their own recommendations. Teams in some rural Colorado communities also serve as child advocates to develop resources for all children in the area. In many cases, as services are expanded to meet the needs of abused and neglected children, other children benefit as well.

Rural teams are in a position to identify gaps in service delivery and often work in some capacity to fill those gaps. They often take stands on issues. Some, for example, have written letters to their legislators regarding a bill which might be a detriment to the provision of protective services. Since they represent a group of agencies and professionals who have attained expert status in the community, teams are more effective and have more influence than a single agency or professional.

Summary

All rural teams have the potential of becoming a valuable asset to the communities, the agencies, and the children they serve. Those considering a rural team should focus on the positives and the unique features rather than allowing the potential negative features to become an unnecessary deterrent to the development of the team. The team can be a tremendous support to a rural social services agency, given that staff may have very few professionals within the agency with whom they can discuss a case and from whom they can obtain consultation. Rural child protective service workers are often very alone and find great relief in being able to share decision making with the rural team.

References

1.   Motz, J.K. *Colorado's Community-based Child Protection Teams,* p. 18. Denver: Colorado Department of Social Services, 1984.   The writer corroborates several of the concepts enunciated by B.D. Schmitt & C.A. Carroll, "Human Aspects of Team Work." *Child Protection Team Handbook.* B.D. Schmitt (Ed.), pp. 199-203. New York: Garland STPM Press, 1978.

2.   Motz, *ibid.,* p. 16.

3.   Motz, *ibid.,* pp. 17-18.

Appendix 4.1
Pertinent Sections of Colorado Revised Statutes (1973)

Section 19-10-103 (2) "Child protection team" means a multidisciplinary team consisting, where possible, of a physician, a representative of the juvenile court or the district court with juvenile jurisdiction, a representative of a local law enforcement agency, a representative of the county department, a representative of a mental health clinic, a representative of the public health department, an attorney, a representative of a public school district, and one or more representatives of the lay community. Each public agency may have more than one participating member on the team; except that, in voting on procedural or policy matters, each public agency shall have only one vote. In no event shall an attorney member of the child protection team be appointed as guardian for the child or as counsel for the parents at any subsequent court proceedings, nor shall the child protection team be composed of fewer than three persons. When any racial, ethnic, or linguistic minority group constitutes a significant portion of the population of the jurisdiction of the child protection team, a member of each such minority group shall serve as an additional lay member of the child protection team. At least one of the preceding members of the team shall be chosen on the basis of representing low-income families. The role of the child protection team shall be advisory only.

Section 19-10-109 (6) (a) It is the intent of the general assembly to encourage the creation of one or more child protection teams in each county or contiguous group of counties. In each county in which reports of fifty or more incidents of child abuse have been made to the state central registry in any one year, the county director shall cause a child protection team to be inaugurated in the next following year.

(b) The child protection team shall review the files and other records of the case, including the diagnostic, prognostic, and treatment services being offered to the family in conjunction with the reported abuse.

(c) At each meeting, each member of the child protection team shall be provided with all available records and reports on each case to be considered.

(d) The public in a non-participatory role, shall be permitted to attend those portions of child protection team meetings concerned with mandatory team discussion of public and private agencies' responses to each report of child abuse and neglect being considered by the team, as well as the team's recommendations related to public-agency responses. In all its public discussion the team shall not publicly disclose the names or addresses and identifying information relating to the children, families, or informants in those cases.

(e) At the beginning of the public discussion of each case, a designated team member shall publicly state the following information, arrived at by consensus of the team: Whether the case involves mild, moderate, or severe abuse or neglect or no abuse or neglect; whether the child is an infant, a toddler, a preschool or a school-aged child, or a teenager and the sex of the child; the date of the initial report and the specific agency to which the report was made; and the dates of subsequent reports to specific social service agencies, law enforcement agencies, or other agencies. In no case shall the informant's name or other identifying information about the informant be publicly revealed. The team shall also state publicly whether the child was hospitalized and whether the child's medical records were checked.

(f) At this public session, and immediately after any executive session at which a child abuse or neglect case is discussed, the child protection team shall publicly review the responses of public and private agencies to each report of child abuse or neglect, shall publicly state whether such responses were timely, adequate, and in compliance with provisions of this article, and shall publicly report nonidentifying information relating to any inadequate responses, specifically indicating the public and private agencies involved.

(g) After this mandatory public discussion of agency responses, the child protection team shall go into executive session upon the vote of a majority of the team members to consider identifying details of the case being discussed, to discuss confidential reports, including but not limited to the reports of physicians and psychiatrists, or when the members of the team desire to act as an advisory body concerning the details of treatment or evaluation programs. The team shall state publicly, before going into executive session, its reasons for doing so. Any recommendation based on information presented in the executive session shall be discussed and formulated at the immediately succeeding public session of the team, without publicly revealing identifying details of the case.

(h) At the team's next regularly scheduled meeting, or at the earliest possible time, the team shall publicly report whether the lapses and inadequacies discovered earlier in the child protection system have been corrected.

(i) The team shall make a report of its recommendations to the county department with suggestions for further action or stating that the team has no recommendations or suggestions. Contiguous counties may cooperate in meeting the requirements of this subsection (6).

(7) Each member of the team shall be appointed by the agency he represents, and each team member shall serve at the pleasure of the appointing agency; except that the county director shall appoint the representatives of the lay community, including the representatives of any ethnic, racial, or linguistic minority, and shall actively recruit all interested individuals and consider their applications for appointment as lay-community representatives on the team.

(8) The county director or his designee shall be deemed to be the local coordinator of the child protection team. In those counties in which the child protection teams meeting the requirements of this article are currently functioning, they shall be recognized, with the consent of all members, as the functioning child protection team for that county.

(9) The local coordinator in each county shall forward a copy of all reports of child abuse to the child protection team. The coordinator shall forward a copy of the investigatory report and all relevant materials to the child protection team as soon as they become available. The child protection team shall meet no later than one week after receipt of a report to evaluate such report of child abuse. The local coordinator shall make and complete, within ninety days of receipt of a report initiating an investigation of a case of child abuse, a follow-up report, including services offered and accepted and any recommendations of the child protection team, to the state central registry on forms supplied by the state department for that purpose.

(10) In the event that the local department or the child protection team initiates a petition in the juvenile court or the district court with juvenile jurisdiction on behalf of the child who is the subject of a report, the coordinator shall notify, in writing, the guardian ad litem appointed by the court under section 19-10-113 to represent the child's interest. Such notice shall include:

(a) The reason for initiating the petition;

(b) Suggestions as to the optimum disposition of this particular case; and

(c) Suggested therapeutic treatment and social services available within the community for the subject child and the responsible person.

PART II

Diagnostic Tasks of Team Members and Consultants

Section Editor: Donna A. Rosenberg

5. Physical Abuse: The Medical Evaluation

Barton D. Schmitt

Introduction

Physical abuse, or nonaccidental trauma is one of the most common types of child abuse. The yearly incidence in the United States of injuries inflicted by parents or caretakers is generally 1,200 new cases per million.[1] At least 4,000 children die each year from physical abuse. Approximately 10 percent of children less than five years of age seen by emergency room physicians for trauma have injuries that were inflicted.[2] A review of the diagnostic acumen necessary for the recognition of inflicted injuries is of paramount importance to physicians.

Histories Given for Inflicted Injuries

Although many child abuse diagnoses can be based on physical findings alone, the history of how the injury occurred is helpful when a child presents with multiple, nondescript injuries.[3] The following histories are diagnostic or extremely suspicious for nonaccidental trauma.

Table 5.1
Histories Offered for Inflicted Injuries

Eyewitness history
Unexplained history
Implausible history
Alleged self-inflicted injury
Delayed seeking of medical care

EYEWITNESS HISTORY

When a child readily states that a parent or caretaker caused an injury, the history is likely true. When one parent or caretaker accuses the other of injuring a child, the story is usually accurate, if the parents are not engaged in a custody dispute or an analogous situation. Partial confessions by a parent or caretaker are not uncommon and are often as diagnostic as complete confessions. For example, a parent or caretaker may admit causing one of the injuries but not the others, or may state that intent to injure was present but action upon these impulses did not occur.

UNEXPLAINED INJURY

Some parents or caretakers deny knowing that their child had any of the injuries discovered. Other parents or caretakers notice the physical findings but can offer no explanation as to how the injury happened. These parents would like to have it believed that the injury was spontaneous. When pressed, they may become evasive, offer a vague explanation, or become hostile. These responses are revealing. Most nonabusive parents know exactly how, where, and when their child was hurt. They also show a complete willingness to discuss the accident in detail.

IMPLAUSIBLE HISTORY

Many parents offer an explanation for the injury that is implausible and inconsistent with common sense and medical judgment. If the parents offer a blatantly phony history, diagnosis is rather easy. For example, a minor accident is described, yet the injuries are major (e.g., a child reportedly has fallen on to a thick carpet, but has multiple body bruises). Or, the behavior described as leading to the accident is impossible for the child's level of development (e.g., a 10-month-old child who allegedly climbed into a tub and turned on scalding water).

ALLEGED SELF-INFLICTED INJURY

An alleged self-inflicted injury to a baby is most serious. These children can be seriously reinjured or killed if the correct diagnosis is not established. In general, the child who cannot crawl cannot cause a self-inflicted accident. Fractures before this stage of development are almost always inflicted. Absurd stories should be considered highly unlikely and acted upon accordingly. Histories implying that the child is masochistic should always raise questions (e.g., the child who hurts himself badly during a temper tantrum or repeatedly pokes the inside of the mouth with an eating utensil).

DELAY IN SEEKING MEDICAL CARE

Most nonabusive parents seek immediate care when their child is injured. In contrast, some abused children are not presented for care for a considerable length of time, even when there is a major injury. Commonly, in the abusive situation, the adult who caused the injury to the child does not come to the health care facility with the child. Naturally, an assessment as to delay in seeking medical care must be made with the cultural background of the family in mind, as cultural practices may vary.

INFLICTED BRUISES

Inflicted bruises occur at typical sites and/or fit recognizable patterns (e.g., human hand marks, human bite marks, strap marks, or bizarre shapes). Bruises of different vintages may point to multiple beatings.

TYPICAL SITE

Inflicted bruises are so common at certain body sites that discovering them there is diagnostic of abuse.

Table 5.2
Typical Sites for Inflicted Bruises

Buttocks and lower back (paddling)
Genitals and inner thighs
Cheek (slap marks)
Earlobe (pinch marks)

Upper lip and frenum (forced feeding)
Neck (choke marks)

Bruises that predominate on the buttocks, lower back, and lateral thighs are almost always related to punishment (i.e., paddling). Likewise, genital or inner-thigh bruises are usually inflicted for toilet mishaps. Injuries to the penis may include pinch marks, bruising, cuts, abrasions, amputation, or burns.[4]

Bruises on the cheek are usually secondary to being slapped. The outlines of fingers can be evident within the bruise. Accidental falls rarely cause bruises to the soft tissues of the cheek, but instead involve the skin overlying bony prominences such as the forehead or cheekbone. Bruises on the earlobe are usually due to being pinched. Children who are pinched or pulled by the earlobe often have a matching bruise or petechiae on each surface. A child occasionally will suffer a ruptured eardrum from a blow to the ear, though the most common cause of a ruptured eardrum is middle ear infection. Bruises of the upper lip, labial frenulum, and floor of the mouth in a child too young to sit up by himself and inadvertently fall forward are usually caused by impatient, forced feedings or by forcing a pacifier or bottle into the child's mouth. Pharyngeal injuries, tears, or diverticulae may be caused by angry thrusting of a spoon, dropper, or similar object into the child's mouth. Bruises of the labial frenulum may remain hidden unless the lip is carefully everted. A history of inconsolable crying often can be obtained in these cases.

Bruises or cuts on the neck are almost always due to being choked or strangled by a human hand, cord, dog collar, or other such instrument. Other children receive neck marks from sudden traction on a shirt or bib. Accidents to this site are extremely rare, and should be looked upon with suspicion. Choke marks may erroneously be attributed to a resuscitation attempt when in truth they are due to lifting a child off the ground by the neck while slapping him in the face or battering him against a wall. Resuscitative attempts do not leave bruises on the face or neck.

HUMAN HAND MARKS

The human hand can leave various types of pressure bruises.

Table 5.3
Human Hand Marks

Grab marks or finger-tip bruises
Linear marks or finger-edge bruises
Hand prints

Slap marks
Pinch marks

The most common types are grab marks or squeeze marks, oval-shaped bruises that resemble fingerprints. Grab marks are usually due to being held during violent shaking. The most common site is the upper arm or shoulder. Grab marks of the lower extremities are also common until the child learns to walk. Grab-mark bruises can occur on the cheeks if an adult squeezes a child's face in an attempt to get food or medicine into his mouth. This action leaves a thumb mark bruise on one cheek and zero to four finger-mark bruises on the other cheek.

Linear grab marks are caused by pressure from the entire finger. The outline or the entire hand print is sometimes seen on the back or at other sites. The hand leaves outline bruises when capillaries at the edge of the injury are stretched enough to rupture. In slap marks to the cheek, two or three parallel linear bruises at finger-width spacing will be seen to run through a more diffuse bruise. The hand can also leave pinch marks, two crescent-shaped bruises facing each other. The shape of the pinch-mark bruise is primarily due to the fingernails. Poke marks from being jabbed with the end of a straight finger leave small, lunar bruises. Often, 3 or 4 bruises are found in a cluster because the child has been jabbed with the finger tips.

HUMAN BITE MARKS

Human bite marks leave distinctive, paired, crescent-shaped bruises that contain individual teeth marks. Sometimes, the two crescents meet to form a complete ring of bruising. The most common dilemma facing the practitioner is to decide if a single bite on a child is from a playmate or from the parents. The point-to-point distance between the center of the canines (third tooth on each side) should be measured in centimeters. If the distance is greater than 3 cm., the child was bitten by an adult or someone, at least, with permanent teeth (i.e., over age eight). If the distance is less than 3 cm. the child was bitten by another young child with primary teeth.[5] In serious injuries with several suspects, the perpetrator can be determined by having a dentist make wax impressions of each suspect's teeth and compare them to photographs of the bite mark.

STRAP MARKS

Strap marks are variably wide, sharp-bordered, rectangular bruises of various lengths, sometimes covering a curved body surface.

These are often caused by a belt; sometimes the eyelets or the buckle can be discerned. Lash marks are narrow, straight-edged bruises or scratches caused by a thrashing with a tree branch or switch. Loop marks are secondary to being struck with a doubled-over item such as a lamp cord, rope, or fan belt. The distal end of the loop strikes with the most force, commonly breaking the skin and leaving loop-shaped scars.[6]

BIZARRE MARKS

Bizarre-shaped bruises with sharp borders are nearly always inflicted. When a blunt instrument is used in punishment, the resulting bruise or welt will resemble it in shape. For example, a hairbrush leaves multiple punctate bruises and a comb leaves linear bruises or abrasions from being dragged across the skin. The wide assortment of instruments used to abuse children suggests that the caretaker who loses his temper grabs whatever object is handy.[7] Circumferential tie marks on the ankles or wrists can be caused when a child is restrained. (Often, caretakers will try to explain these as caused by high top shoes.) If a narrow rope or cord is used, the child will be left with circumferential cuts. If a strap or piece of sheeting is used to restrain a child about the wrists or ankles, a friction burn or rope burn may result, usually as a large blister that encircles the extremity. The rope marks will not be entirely circumferential if the child is tied directly to something. For example, rope burns on the thighs can result from tying the child to a potty seat. Gag marks may be seen as bilaterally symmetric abrasions that appear near the corner of the mouth. Children may be gagged because of too much screaming.

Accidental Bruises

A thorough knowledge of common and unusual accidental bruising will help in differentiating these from inflicted injuries. Understanding unusual customs or practices that leave bruises is also helpful. Lastly, it is important to remember that all bluish discolorations of the skin are not bruises.

Most children periodically acquire one or two bruises during falls or rough activity. The most common site for multiple, easily explained bruises in children of an age to be mobile (that is, crawling and beyond) are on the knees and lower legs. These bruises are due to normal falling or bumping into objects while running or crawling. Bruises on the forehead are frequent when a child starts to cruise along furniture and when he or she is acquiring walking and climbing skills.

While bruises from falling usually are circular with irregular borders, so are grab marks, ring marks, or blows with a fist. Accidental bruises, however, usually occur on the skin overlying bony prominences (e.g., chin, elbow, forehead, spinous process, greater trochanter, etc.). Nondescript bruises are suspect as abuse when they occur on the soft parts of the body (e.g., cheek, fleshy part of the arm, buttocks, abdominal wall, etc.). Most falls give one bruise on a single surface. Bruises on multiple body planes are usually inflicted unless there is a history of a tumbling accident. True tumbling accidents also give bruises and abrasions over bony prominences.

The caretakers of any child who has multiple bruises should be asked if the child has a tendency to bleed or bruise easily. If the answer is positive, a laboratory assessment for a bleeding disorder should be done.

UNUSUAL BRUISES

Some common ethnic practices can result in bruises that should not be confused with child abuse. The Vietnamese can induce symmetrical, linear bruises from coin-rubbing (Cao Gio). For symptoms of fever, chills or headaches, the back and chest are covered with oil and then massaged in downward strokes with the edge of a coin.[8]

Some teenagers cause multiple petechiae on their arms by direct sucking or on their chins by sucking on a cup until they create a vacuum and then sliding the cup onto the chin.[9] Tourniquets can also cause petechiae, especially in children who already have an erythematous rash.

A passionate and prolonged kiss can lead to an area of purpura on the skin. Vigorous sucking on hard candy can leave an area of purpura on the soft palate. Purpura at this site has also been reported with fellatio. Multiple petechiae of the face and neck can occur following vigorous crying, retching, or coughing, due to a sudden increase in superior vena cava pressure. Petechiae and purpura have even been seen in the conjunctiva or mouth as a result of this mechanism.

PSEUDOBRUISES

Some skin conditions may be mistaken for bruises. The most common is the Mongolian spot. This birth mark occurs in 95 percent of blacks, 81 percent of orientals and American indians, 70 percent of chicanos, and 10 percent of caucasians.[10] Lasting usually from two to three years, they are grayish-blue, do not change color, and have clear-cut margins. Although they commonly occur on the buttocks and back, they can be found anywhere. Localized brown splotches (phytophoto-dermatitis) can result from melanin production in areas inadvertently rubbed with lime, lemon, fig, celery, or parsnip.[11]

Allergic periorbital discoloration is due to long-standing venous congestion from allergic rhinitis and eye allergies. These pseudobruises are usually more brownish than blue, and the discoloration is mainly seen on the lower medial eyelid. The presence of allergies and the duration of the finding points to the correct diagnosis. *Hemophilus influenzae* can give a bluish cellulitis of the cheek. Afflicted children are sick, febrile, and their cheek areas are quite tender to palpation. Bruises from Henoch-Schoenlein Purpura have been mistaken for child abuse. This condition causes symmetrical purpuric lesions of the legs and feet that can be easily differentiated from abuse injuries.

Inflicted Burns

Approximately 10 percent of physical abuse cases involve burns.[12] Burns from hot solid objects are the easiest to diagnose. These are usually second-degree, sometimes without blister formation, and usually involve only one surface of the body. The shape of the burn often resembles its agent and is pathognomonic for child abuse. Abused children are often held against a heating grate or electric hot plate. Cigarette burns give circular, punched-out lesions of uniform size and are often found on the hands or feet. Bullous impetigo should be considered in a differential diagnosis of burns of this nature.

Hot water burns, normally indicated by blistering, are the most common inflicted burns. Immersion burns occur when a parent holds the child's thighs against the abdomen and places the buttocks and perineum in scalding liquid as punishment for enuresis or "resistance" to toilet training. This results in a circular type of burn restricted to the buttocks. With deeper, forced immersions, the burn extends to a level on the thighs and waist. The hands and feet are spared, which is incompatible with falling into a tub or turning the hot water on while in the bathtub. Forcible immersion of a hand or foot as punishment can be suspected when a burn extends well above the wrist or ankle. Scalded skin syndrome (caused by an infection) should be considered in a differential diagnosis of scalding burns.

Inflicted Bone Injuries

Most inflicted fractures are due to wrenching or pulling injuries that damage the metaphysis.[13] The classic early finding is a chip fracture where a corner of the metaphysis of a long bone is torn off, along with the epiphysis and periosteum. From 10 to 14 days later, calcification of the subperiosteal bleeding becomes visible at the periphery. Within four to six weeks after the injury, the subperiosteal calcification will be solid and start to smooth out and remodel. Inflicted fractures of the shaft are usually spiral rather than transverse. Spiral fractures of the femur of a pre-mobile child are usually inflicted. The most diagnostic radiograph shows injuries to multiple bones at different stages of healing. Such findings imply repeated assaults. Medical disorders that predispose to easy fracturing of bones are generally readily seen on radiographs.

Inflicted Eye Injuries

Inflicted periorbital bruising is more common than serious eye injuries. Children who have been hit about the eyes with an open or closed hand present with massive swelling and bruising of both eyelids. Most periorbital bruises caused by accidents involve only one side. A child can acquire bilateral periorbital bruises from a single accident, or more precisely from striking a single object. Bilateral periorbital bruises can occur from blood infiltrating from a large bruise on the forehead or from a skull fracture, since blood moves with gravity. However, these children have minimal lid swelling and no lid tenderness. In addition, the onset of the periorbital bruise is delayed one or two days from the time of the injury. Therefore, these situations should not be confused with those where the child has been struck about the head and eyes.

Ocular damage in the battered child syndrome includes acute hyphema, dislocated lens, traumatic cataract, and detached retina.[14] More than half of these result in permanent impairment of vision affecting one or both eyes. Retinal hemorrhages are also found with subdural hematomas in children with unexplained central nervous system findings. The differential diagnosis of retinal hemorrhages is direct head trauma, shaking injuries, increased intracranial pressure, hypertension, bleeding disorders, sudden compression of the chest, and gymnastic twirling on a horizontal bar. Retinal hemorrhages usually last 10 to 14 days.

Inflicted Head Injuries

Inflicted head injuries include subdural hematomas, subarachnoid hemorrhages, scalp bruises, traumatic alopecia, and subgaleal hematomas.

SUBDURAL HEMATOMAS

Subdural hematoma is the most dangerous inflicted injury, often causing serious sequelae or death. Over 95% of serious intracranial injuries during the first year of life are the result of abuse.[15] These children present with irritability, vomiting, a decreased level of consciousness, breathing difficulty and apneic episodes, a bulging fontanelle, and/or convulsions. The classic case of subdural hematoma is associated with skull fractures. These fractures are secondary to a direct blow from the parent's or caretaker's hand or from being thrown against a wall or door. Numerous other bruises are often present.

Inflicted subdural hematomas can also occur without skull fractures, scalp bruises, or scalp swelling. In fact, more than one-half of the cases have no fractures. Evidence clearly points to a violent, whiplash shaking mechanism.[16] Rapid acceleration and deceleration of the head as it is in motion leads to tearing of the bridging cerebral veins with bleeding into the subdural space, often bilaterally. Most of these cases occur in babies less than one year old, who are shaken in an attempt to make them stop crying. The erroneous concept of spontaneous subdural hematoma in young infants must be discarded to prevent further reinjury or death. Likewise, the diagnosis of chronic subdural hematomas secondary to birth trauma must be viewed with skepticism. Subdural hematomas due to birth injury will often produce acute signs and symptoms within 24 to 48 hours after delivery or be silent. Subdural hematomas may be diagnosed by computerized axial tomography (CAT) scan or by magnetic resonance imaging (MRI) scan of the head.

ACCIDENTAL HEAD INJURIES FROM FALLS

A study of 246 young children who accidentally fell from cribs or beds found that in 80 percent there were no physical injuries.[17] Most of the remainder had single bruises or lacerations. Only one percent of the children had skull fractures, and these were single, linear, non-depressed and not associated with neurologic complications. Another one percent had fractures at other sites, usually the clavicle or humerus. None of the children had subdural hematomas, epidural hematomas, or any serious life-threatening injury.

Inflicted Abdominal Injuries

Intra-abdominal injuries are the second most common cause of death in abused children.[18]   Unlike the contents of the chest, the abdominal organs are not protected. Table 5.4 lists inflicted abdominal injuries in the approximate order of frequency. Most of the injuries are caused by a punch or kick that compresses the organ against the anterior spinal column.

Table 5.4
Inflicted Abdominal Injuries

Ruptured liver or spleen
Intestinal perforation
Intramural hematoma of duodenum or proximal jejunum
Pancreatic injury
Ruptured blood vessel
Kidney or bladder injury
Chylous ascites from injured lymphatic system
Foreign bodies (swallowed or percutaneous)

In all these conditions, trauma to the abdomen is usually denied. Bruises of the abdominal wall (when present) help to establish the correct diagnosis. Unfortunately, there are no visible bruises or marks on the abdominal wall in over half of these cases. The abdominal wall is usually relaxed at the time of the injury, and the energy from the blow is mainly absorbed by the internal organs. The physician must consider child abuse in any abdominal crisis of undetermined etiology.

Medical Management of Physical Abuse

The pediatrician, family physician or emergency room physician should take the following actions if he suspects a case of child abuse.

ELICIT A DETAILED HISTORY OF THE ABUSE

A complete history should be obtained as to how the injury allegedly happened (date, time, place, sequence of events, people present, height of the fall, surface of impact, time lag before medical attention sought, etc.). The parent's explanation for each and every positive physical finding should be sought and recorded. The parents can be pressed for exact details when necessary. No other professional should have to repeat this probing interview. If the child is old enough to give a complete history (usually over age 3 or 4), it should be elicited in a private setting and compared to the parent's version.

PERFORM A THOROUGH PHYSICAL EXAMINATION

All bruises should be listed by site and recorded by size, shape, and color. If they resemble strap marks, grab marks, slap marks, bite marks, loop marks, tie marks, choke marks, cigarette burns, marks of a blunt instrument, or any identifiable object, this should be stated. Special attention should be paid to the retina, eardrums, oral cavity, and the genitals for signs of occult trauma.

ORDER BONE SURVEY X-RAYS ON SELECTED CASES

Every suspected case involving children under two years of age should receive a radiologic bone survey. Between 2 and 5 years, most children should also receive a bone survey unless the child has very mild injuries or is in a supervised setting (e.g., preschool). Over age 5, x-rays should be obtained only if there is any bone tenderness or limited range of motion on physical exam. A recent study on routine skeletal surveys found that 11.5% had evidence of trauma.[19] Of these, 21% were occult fractures (i.e., not suspected clinically). If films of a tender site are initially negative, they should be repeated in 2 weeks to pick up calcification of any subperiosteal bleeding or non-displaced epiphyseal separations that may have been present. (Spine and pelvis films are not required unless the initial bone survey is positive.) The radiologist can be asked to date positive x-ray findings.

ORDER A BLEEDING DISORDER SCREEN ON SELECTED CASES

Indications for bleeding tests are when (1) the physician suspects a bleeding disorder, (2) the case will definitely be going to court because of severe injuries, or (3) the parents deny inflicting the injuries and claim "easy bruising."   A bleeding disorder screen includes a platelet count, bleeding time, partial thromboplastin time, prothrombin time, thrombin time, and fibrinogen, fibrin split products, and monomer (the last four are optional in some cases).

OBTAIN COLOR PHOTOGRAPHS ON SELECTED CASES

Color photographs are required by law in some states.[20]   A ruler and a tag with the date and child's name should be visible in each photograph.   In most juvenile court cases, photographs are not essential to the primary physician's testimony.   In cases where an expert witness who has not actually examined the child is to testify, photographs are nearly mandatory.   In cases where criminal court action is anticipated, they usually will be necessary and will be taken by the police photographer. Whether or not medical photography is available, the physician should carefully diagram the body-surface findings in the official medical chart and carefully date and sign the entry.

SCREEN THE CHILD FOR BEHAVIOR AND DEVELOPMENTAL PROBLEMS

Abused children frequently have associated behavior problems (e.g., negativism or attention deficit disorder) and developmental delays.   The pediatrician should attempt to obtain a Denver Developmental Screening Test (DDST) and record observations on the children's behavior and parent-child interactions.   If this screen is positive, the child should be referred for a more complete assessment and treatment (e.g., to child psychiatry, psychology or a developmental clinic).

INFORM PARENTS OF THE DIAGNOSIS AND THE NEED TO REPORT IT

Tell the parents your diagnosis and the need to report suspicious findings. One can state: "Your explanation for the injury is insufficient. Even though it wasn't intentional, I an concerned that someone may have injured this child.   I am obligated by state law to report all worrisome injuries to Child Protective Services." The physician should do this since the case is reported on the basis of his medical findings. In fact, after all diagnostic studies are completed, the physician should review his interpretation of the cause of each specific injury in as supportive a way as possible. This convinces the parents that he knows what actually happened, and permits them to turn their attention to therapy. The physician should be willing to discuss the general content of the medical report, emphasizing that the problem is treatable and everyone's goal is to help the parents find better ways of dealing with their child, not to punish them. If the parents become argumentative, they can be advised to seek legal counsel, but it is also incumbent upon the physician to be patient with the parents.

REPORT ALL CASES TO CHILD PROTECTIVE SERVICES BY PHONE AND IN WRITING

The case should be reported to CPS by phone immediately. Reporting should secure evaluation, treatment, follow-up and access to the Juvenile Court when necessary. The official written medical report is required by law within 48 hours. As it may be used in court, the accuracy and completeness of this report is very important. A copy of the admission work-up to the hospital or the discharge summary will not suffice, because the evidence for the diagnosis of child abuse is often difficult for nonmedical people to locate in these highly technical documents. A well-written medical report often convinces the parents' lawyer that his clients' case is in question, and he accepts on behalf of his clients ("stipulates to") the petition before the court and agrees to therapy for his clients. Therefore, a well-written medical report may keep the physician out of court and save him or her time in the long run. The report should include: (a) a history—the alleged cause of the injury (with date, time, place, and so forth), (b) a physical exam—a detailed description of the injury using nontechnical terms whenever possible (e.g., "cheek" instead of "zygoma," "bruise," instead of "ecchymosis"), (c) results of lab tests and x-ray films, (d) a conclusion—a statement that this incident represents nonaccidental trauma, the reason behind this conclusion, a comment on the severity of the present injury (e.g., probable sequelae or estimated number of blows the child endured), and an estimate of the danger for serious re-abuse.

HOSPITALIZE SELECTED CASES

In large metropolitan areas, Child Protective Services (CPS) caseworkers are on call 24 hours a day. Children with suspected abuse legally cannot be discharged from the clinic without consulting the county. The worker will either concur with the physician's recommendation that the child can safely be released to the parent, or come to the hospital and evaluate the family regarding the safety of the home. The 20% or so of children at risk for serious re-abuse can be placed in emergency receiving homes. The others can be sent home with services and close follow-up. At this time, the only patients requiring admission are those with major trauma requiring ongoing medical care, those from an outlying county or young children where the diagnosis is unclear. If in doubt, err on the side of protecting the child.

EXAMINE ALL SIBLINGS WITHIN 12 HOURS

There is approximately a 20% risk that a sibling of a physically abused child has also been abused at the same time. Therefore, all siblings under the age of eighteen should be brought in for an examination of the total body surface within twelve hours of uncovering an index case. If the parents say they cannot bring the child in because of transportation problems, the protective service agency can accomplish this. If the parents refuse to have their other children seen, a court order can be obtained and the police sent out.

Summary

Since physical punishment is commonplace in our society, physicians need guidelines as to when corporal punishment is excessive and, therefore, equivalent to physical abuse.[21,22] Corporal punishment that causes bruises or leads to an injury that requires medical or dental treatment is outside the range of normal punishment. Bruising implies hitting without restraint. A few bruises administered in the name of discipline can easily escalate into a more serious injury the next time. Even when there are no signs of injury, an incident that includes hitting with a closed fist or kicking the child represents physical abuse. All of the preceding examples of corporal punishment should be reported to CPS so that these families can learn safer ways of managing their children's behavior. Corporal punishment in the schools contradicts optimal child-rearing practices and should be eliminated altogether.

References

1. American Humane Association. *National Study of the Incidence and Severity of Child Abuse and Neglect*, May 1, 1979 to April 30, 1980, American Humane Association, Denver, 1981.

2. Holter, J.C., and S.B. Friedman. "Child Abuse, Early Case Finding in the Emergency Department." *Pediatrics*, 42(1968):128.

3. Schmitt, B.D. "The Child with Nonaccidental Trauma." *The Battered Child*. C.H. Kempe and R.E. Helfer (Eds.), pp. 128-146. Chicago: University of Chicago Press, 1980.

4. Slosberg, E.J., S. Ludwig, J. Suckett, and A.E. Mauro. "Penile Trauma as a Sign of Child Abuse." *American Journal of Diseases of Children*, 132(1978):719.

5. Levine. L.J. "Bite Marks in Child Abuse." *Clinical Management of Child Abuse and Neglect: A Guide for the Dental Professional*. R.G. Sanger and D.C. Bross (Eds.), pp. 53-59. Chicago: Quintessence Publishing Co., 1984.

6. Sussman, S.J. "Skin Manifestations of the Battered Child Syndrome." *Journal of Pediatrics*, 72(1968):99.

7. Johnson, C.F., and J. Showers. "Injury Variables in Child Abuse." *Child Abuse & Neglect*, 9(1985):207.

8. Yeatman, G.W., C. Shaw, M.J. Barlow, and G. Barlett. "Pseudobattering in Vietnamese Children." *Pediatrics*, 58(1976):616.

9. Lovejoy, F.H., E.K. Marcuse, and P.J. Landrigan. "Two Examples of Purpura Factitia." *Clinical Pediatrics*, 11(1971):183.

10. Jacobs, A.H., and R.G. Walton. "Incidence of Birthmarks in the Neonate." *Pediatrics*, 58(1976):218.

11. Coffman, K., W.T. Boyce, and R.C. Hansen. "Phytophotodermatitis Simulating Child Abuse." *American Journal of Diseases of Children*, 139(1985):239.

12. Lenoski, E.F. ,and K.A. Hunter. "Specific Patterns of Inflicted Burn Injuries." *Journal of Trauma*, 17(1977):842.

13. Merten, D.F., M.A. Radkowski, and J.C. Leonidas. "The Abused Child: A Radiological Reappraisal." *Radiology*, 146(1983):376.

14.   Gammon, J.A. "Ophthalmic Manifestations of Child Abuse." *Child Abuse and Neglect: A Medical Reference*. N.S. Ellerstein (Ed.), pp. 121-139. New York: John Wiley and Sons, 1981.

15.   Billmire, M.E., and P.A. Myers. "Serious Head Injury in Infants: Accident or Abuse?" *Pediatrics*, 75(1985):340.

16.   Caffey, J. "The Whiplash Shaken Infant Syndrome." *Pediatrics*, 54(1974):396.

17.   Helfer, R.E., T.L. Slovis, and M. Black. "Injuries Resulting When Small Children Fall Out of Bed." *Pediatrics*, 60(1977):633-635.

18.   D.R. Kirks. "Radiological Evaluation of Visceral Injuries in the Battered Child Syndrome." *Pediatric Annals*, 12(1984):888.

19.   Ellerstein, M.S., and E.J. Norris. "Value of Radiological Skeletal Survey in Assessment of Abused Children." *Pediatrics*, 74(1984):1075.

20.   Ford, R.J., and B.S. Smistek. "Photography of the Maltreated Child." *Child Abuse and Neglect: A Medical Reference*. N.S. Ellerstein (Ed.), pp. 121-139. New York: John Wiley and Sons, 1981.

21.   Wessel, W.A. "The Pediatrician and Corporal Punishment." *Pediatrics*, 66(1980):639-640.

22.   Christophersen, E.R. "The Pediatrician and Parental Discipline." *Pediatrics*, 66(1980):641-642.

6. Sexual Abuse of Children

Donna A. Rosenberg and Nancy Gary

Introduction

Child sexual abuse is "the involvement of dependent, developmentally immature children and adolescents in sexual activities that they do not fully comprehend, to which they are unable to give informed consent, or that violate the social taboos of family roles."[1]

Sexual abuse of children can occur in intrafamilial and/or extrafamilial settings. The types of abuse that may be perpetrated are extremely variable: children may be the victims of voyeurism; they may be enticed or forced to pose for photographs or videotaping in a sexual context; they may be fondled; they may be penetrated orally, genitally and/or anally; they may be forced or induced to perform all sorts of sexual acts upon the perpetrator; they may be induced to participate in prostitution; they may be involved in ritualistic or demonic activities including torture, bestiality or animal slaughter; they may be paid or unpaid; the activities may take place within the context of a group of adults and/or children or they may take place only with individual perpetrators; the children may be anywhere in age from newborn or infancy to late adolescence; they may be coached to perpetrate sexual abuse; they may survive and they may not.

The function of the child protection team with respect to a child who has been sexually abused is to integrate the data about that child and his or her situation, with a view to protection and treatment. Inasmuch as child protection teams exist in many different contexts (e.g., county departments of social services, hospitals, etc.) the team must also recognize its own limitations vis-a-vis its experience in diagnosing sexual abuse and its capabilities in protecting and treating children. Therefore, the team must have ties to the community resources that can fill the needs of these children.

Demographics

According to data compiled by the American Humane Association from their National Study on Incidence of Child Abuse and Neglect, the estimated incidence of child sexual abuse in the United States was 100,000 cases in 1984. There was a stable increase of 30-35% per year for the years 1982-1984. Based on this rate of increase, the estimated incidence for 1986 was 160,000 new cases of child sexual abuse. One randomized, retrospective, methodologically sound study[2] found that the prevalence of intrafamilial sexual abuse in females was 16% by the age of 18 years, and that the prevalence of extrafamilial sexual abuse in females was 38% by the age of 18 years. Surveys of men in the general population reveal that 2.5% to 8.7% of males were sexually victimized as children.[3] We assume that these figures are low because of unreported cases.

Sexual abuse of children occurs in all socioeconomic strata, and in all races; the perpetrators and victims are both male and female.

Characteristics of Sexually Abused Children

Although the specific circumstances of child sexual abuse vary, in all cases the children are helpless—bribed, exploited or forced.

The effects of sexual abuse on children are varied and the factors that determine the harm are multiple: how a child is related to the perpetrator, the nature, duration and frequency of the abuse, the child's chronologic age and developmental stage, the degree to which the child has been threatened, the degree of associated physical abuse and neglect; and the support available to the child, both from the family and the community, once disclosure has occurred. One or several of the following behavioral characteristics[4] in the sexually abused child are commonly observed: fear, anxiety, shame or guilt. The child may blame himself for participating in a secret activity or for the disruption of the family (after disclosure) in both intrafamilial and extrafamilial cases. He or she may be ashamed when others become aware of the situation, or may feel guilty about sensations of sexual pleasure he may have experienced. The child may also feel responsible for any charges brought against the perpetrator.

The child may appear depressed or withdrawn, possibly even suicidal. The withdrawn child keeps to himself, has no friends, and spends little time with other family members. The suicidal child may be self-destructive, extremely "accident-prone" or may attempt suicide. He may complain of being tired, anxious, unable to concentrate, feeling inadequate or he may exhibit a decreased interest in usual activities, a changed appetite and often has sleep disturbances. Almost all sexually abused children exhibit some sort of change from usual behavior, though this may be subtle.

Because sexually abused children may feel that their lives are subject to outside controls and that they have no control themselves, they often lack assertiveness and are overly compliant.

Sexually abused children are frequently forced to behave as the parent and the spouse in the family. They take on responsibilities well beyond their years including household chores, care of siblings, working to contribute income, buying gifts for birthdays and holidays. The child is in an environment where generational lines and traditional family roles have been blurred.

Sexually abused children often learn seductive behavior from the perpetrator. The child with a seductive manner smiles, cuddles up to, rubs against, and otherwise tries to win evidence of affection from an adult. He may make sexual advances toward the adult because he associates nurturance with sexuality and feels he must offer sexual gratification to receive love. The child is often blamed for initiating the assault and, having learned to be seductive, is a candidate for further abuse.

Lack of impulse control in the sexually abused child may also have been learned from the sexual contacts he has had. The child may have difficulty in delaying gratification or in resisting impulses.

The sexually abused child is sometimes restricted from playing or talking with other children outside of the school environment. This lack of opportunity to participate in out-of-home activities may be one of the reasons for poor peer relationships. Also, because his peers are more naive about sexual matters, it may be difficult for the sexually abused child to relate to age-appropriate conversations. He may also have angry feelings which make him aggressive toward his peers. His fear and anxiety may also cause him to be a loner. When an interviewer learns that a child is not participating in school or social activities, the interviewer should consider the possibility of abuse.

Other symptoms that the sexually abused child may exhibit are wetting or soiling of underwear, nightmares, unusual masturbation, headaches, abdominal pains, phobias, a change in academic performance or symptoms of a sexually transmitted disease.

One of the most pervasive, long term consequences of sexual abuse for the child is that the child develops a poor self image.

Many children will exhibit characteristics of what Summit[5] has described as the "Child Sexual Abuse Accommodation Syndrome": secrecy, helplessness, entrapment and accommodation, delayed, conflicted and unconvincing disclosure and retraction.

It is obvious that not all of these characteristics or behaviors will be present in one sexually abused child, but it is important to be aware of the range of disturbances that sexually abused children may exhibit.

Adolescent perpetrators of sexual abuse have, very commonly, been or are being sexually abused themselves. These youngsters need help desperately so that their behaviors do not solidify into lifetime deviant practices.

Taking a History

Every effort must be made to insure that all concerned professionals (social worker, doctor, police, etc.) are present, so that the history does not have to be repeated.

The three major purposes of the initial interview are as follows:

1. To evaluate the allegations;

2. To assess the need for immediate protection of the child; and

3. To determine the need for other evaluations, as well as appropriate future living arrangements and referrals.

The interviewer must not be rushed and should be prepared to stay with the child until the child finishes. The evaluation may be preceded or followed by an interview with the parents or other professionals involved in the case, but it is preferable to interview the child alone to minimize any outside influence. Also, the child generally may feel more inclined to confide the details of the "secret" if there is a one-to-one relationship with the interviewer. The interviewer must be careful not to promise confidentiality since the information will have to be shared with other professionals who are developing the care plan for the child.

If the parent insists on accompanying the child or if the child is not easily separated from the parent or if another adult is present, ground rules need to be established about the nature of his or her participation. The child should not be aware of, or influenced by, the adult's reactions to his comments. The interviewer should ask the adult to sit next to the child, thereby being in a physically supportive position but out of the child's view. The interviewer should sit opposite both of them.

While it is true that the setting of the interview is important, in terms of privacy and comfort, it should be emphasized that the most important environmental feature is the tone which the interviewer sets. When possible, the other observing professionals should be behind a one-way glass. In evaluating the victims of child abuse, the interviewer must take into account the chronological age, the developmental stage, and the emotional status of the child. For example, a child may be 6 years old but developmentally delayed to the level of a 3 year old and also emotionally disturbed. The method of questioning must be varied accordingly.

The interview can be divided into three phases:

1. The first phase is devoted to establishing rapport with the child so that the child may be put at ease and the interviewer may assess the developmental level of the child. Establishing a good relationship with the child depends on the interviewer's ability to demonstrate interest and sincerity as well as to convey warmth and respect for the youngster. To begin, the interviewer should introduce himself and tell the child his name. The more gentle and non-threatening the demeanor, the better. A young child can be engaged and put at ease by drawing, stringing beads, playing with clay, doing puzzles, or playing a game. One way of putting the child at ease and assessing the development of language skills at the same time is to draw a picture together.

With the older child, it is reasonable to explain the interviewer's job, thereby demonstrating experience with the problem and indicating that he or she is not the only child who has ever been sexually abused. Questions that show an interest in the school-aged child concern his school, his teacher, his best friend, what he wants to be when he grows up, his favorite TV shows, his favorite rock group, what the family likes to do together, what games the child plays with mother and father, what he likes and doesn't like about his parents. Ask the child to describe his parents: what do they do when they are upset? how do they show affection? These questions should be asked in a conversational manner and in words the child can understand. The interviewer should listen carefully and respond appropriately to the child's answers.

2. The second phase of the interview is devoted to eliciting the details of the abuse. With very young children, one often has to change pace to keep the attention of the child. Remember that to elicit details of the abuse, one must speak the child's language and sometimes hunt for the particular word that the child understands. Also, it is often necessary, when one sees that the child is becoming embarrassed, to

reassure the child. Almost all child victims of sexual abuse have been threatened by the perpetrator and are frightened to tell. Many children are threatened with extreme violence or with abandonment. In this phase of the interview, concerned with eliciting the details of the abuse, the interviewer should concentrate on *who* the perpetrator was, *what* happened, *where* the sexual abuse happened, *when* and *why* it happened. To elicit details in interviews with children, one must first understand how children at different ages comprehend and express the concepts of *who, what, where, when* and *why*. This permits the interviewer to have a reasonable expectation of a child's ability to answer given questions and to pose questions that are appropriate to the developmental stage of the child. As a general guideline, children cognitively learn these items in the following order: *what* and *who* are learned first, then *where*, then *when*, then *why*.

In the following brief discussion pertaining to these cognitive developmental milestones, the ages mentioned at which a child achieves them are approximate and refer to a cognitively normal child. Adjustments need to be made in the expected age of development of these milestones in children who are cognitively abnormal.

What happened? The interviewer should not expect a child who is under 4 years old to be able to answer an open-ended question, although this may vary somewhat depending on the child. It is normal for a child at ages 2 or 3 to be unable to answer an open-ended question, such as "tell me about what happened." These children can answer only close-ended questions, that is, questions that require a "yes-or-no" or one word answer. Examples of close-ended questions are: "Did he touch you here?" or "Did she kiss you on your mouth or nose?" It is, therefore, acceptable practice, once the interviewer has established that the child cannot answer open-ended questions, to proceed with close-ended questions. In doing so, the interviewer is asking questions in a developmentally appropriate way and should not be thought of as asking leading questions. One must be cautious, however, in interpreting "yes" or "no" answers from a 2 or 3 year old. Sometimes, the child will answer an entire string of questions with either "yes" or "no," because the child isn't thinking about the questions or is being playful. Therefore, the interviewer should ask several other "yes" or "no" questions to which he or she already knows the answer. This may help to assess the reliability of the child's first answers. By the time a child is about 5, the answer to an open-ended question about what happened may be quite explicit. By the time a child is 7 years old, his answers to the *what happened* question may be graphic. The child of this age should be able to answer open-ended questions easily, although such ability may be limited by embarrassment or guilt feelings. Therefore, the interviewer may gently encourage the child, generally through reassurance.

Who did this? When cases of child sexual abuse enter the court system, either civil or criminal, the question that often arises is, "How do we know that the child isn't confusing the person he is alleging to be the perpetrator with someone else?" Young children of 3 or more can usually easily and correctly identify the people in their lives who have either had *significant* chronic or acute relationships with them. Children who are closer to 2 years of age need to have the question asked several times, and perhaps in several ways to check for consistency. Remember that many children call several people "daddy" or "mommy" etc.

Where did this happen? Developmentally, the next question that children can appreciate and express, after *what* and *who* is *where—where did this happen?* Generally, children can express where they are in the present at an earlier age than they can express where they were in the past when a certain event occurred. By age 1 1/2 or 2 a child may be able to tell the interviewer where he is now, but it is very unlikely that he would be able to tell the interviewer where he was at another time. Children are usually over 3 years old before they can describe where they were, and the younger they are, the poorer the description. To identify the place of the sexual abuse, it is best to ask the questions of children about age 3 or younger without the use of colors or numbers, because many children at that age don't have colors or numbers firmly learned. The interviewer should not ask, "Was it the room with the blue walls?" or, "Was it the room with the two beds?" Questions to young children should be more general such as, "Were you at grandma's house?"

By the time a child is 4 or 5, he should be able to describe the scene of the sexual abuse by telling the interviewer what it looked like, but possibly not by the actual location. For example, the child may be able to tell the interviewer that the event occurred near water, but be unable to tell him whether it was a lake or a stream or a river. Remember that chronic sexual abuse may be occurring at multiple locations, for instance the bathroom, the family truck, a roadside or a bedroom. If the events were multiple, with multiple locations, the child is generally older than 5 or 6 before he can describe which events took place in which locations. By the time a child is 7 or 8 years old, he often can describe not only the site of the sexual abuse, but also the location of other family members at the time.

When did it happen? It is not until children are about 8 years or older that they are able to tell the interviewer with any accuracy when an event occurred in terms of day or date, although children younger than 8 years may be able to relate the event of sexual abuse to daytime or nighttime or major events in their lives, such as birthdays or holidays.

A child of 3 1/2 or 4 may be able to tell the interviewer whether an event occurred during day or night, assuming the child was outdoors at the time or, if indoors, that there was a window in the room. A child closer to 8 years may be able to distinguish between one time and more than once, but his conceptualization of time would probably not extend to knowing exactly how many times, if incidents were multiple.

Why did it happen? Understanding why certain events occur is a very complicated issue, involving the merging of cognitive and moral development. Children under age 5 or so generally respond to the question *why* by answering with either, "I don't know" or "because." In children approximately 5 or 6 to 8 or 9 years, the answers to the why question may be very concrete, and may in fact reflect what the child has been told by the perpetrator of the sexual abuse. If a 6 or 7 year old is asked, "Why did he do that to you?," typical answers would be, "Because he's going to marry me" or, "Because I'm pretty" or, "Because I'm a good boy and he's going to buy me a radio." Older children's answers to the *why* question tend to be more abstract rather than concrete, although this is not always the case.

3. During the third and final phase of the interview, the child should be told that the sexual abuse was not his or her fault. The interviewer should communicate to the child that he will try to make sure that the child is protected. This is also a good time to answer any questions the child may have. Children of both sexes and all ages worry about pregnancy. Some children worry that the sexual abuse has consigned them to a certain sexual orientation in the future. Others worry that the sexual abuse has precipitated development of secondary sexual characteristics. It is not necessarily appropriate to tell the child that no one will be angry with him for telling about the sexual abuse, because there may indeed be others who are very angry. The interviewer may, however, reassure the child that he himself is not angry and he should tell the child what he may expect to happen next. In addition to the history specifically concerning the sexual abuse, a family history, social history, past medical history, and review of systems should be obtained from the most reliable historian. Table 6.1 summarizes the questions that should be specifically included as are age and gender-appropriate, on review of systems. No one of these symptoms, however, is diagnostic of sexual abuse.

Table 6.1

The review of systems should, minimally, include inquiry as to:

-enuresis
-dysuria
-frequency
-recurrent urinary tract infection
-encopresis
-bowel habit dysfunction

-vaginal discharge
-anal abnormalities/pain/itching/bleeding
-genital pain/itching/bleeding/abnormalities
-history of rash/sore (chancre)
-menstrual history
-contraceptive history
-history of last intercourse
-abdominal pains
-headaches
-school problems/phobia
-behavior change(s)
-masturbation habits
-sexualized play
-sleep disturbance
-dramatic weight change
-depression
-suicidal attempt/ideas
-drug abuse/alcohol abuse

Physical Examination

All children in suspected sexual abuse cases should have complete physical examinations, no matter how remote the alleged events. Many sexually abused children live in an atmosphere of pervasive neglect and, as such, may have other previously undiagnosed but treatable disorders, such as dental problems or hearing impairment. Physical examination, while being complete, should also be directed to those positives uncovered on history (e.g., rash, discharge, etc.).

It is best to explain the course of the physical examination to all pediatric age patients. It is generally a good idea for the examiner to try to clarify for the child the reasons for the exam, so that the child understands that he is not being re-abused. Some children may need to be hospitalized for medical and/or social reasons.

A normal physical examination, including a normal genital and anal exam, is compatible with many forms of child sexual abuse.

(a) Physical Examination of Girls

Special attention should be paid, during the course of the complete physical examination, to assessment of the throat and mouth, the breasts, and the genital and anal areas. The Tanner stage and all abnormalities must be recorded. Girls are easily genitally examined in the supine frog-leg position. They may also be examined in the knee-chest position, though many find this more awkward. The genital area may be exposed for adequate inspection by gently spreading the labia majora inferiorly and laterally. All parts of the genital anatomy should be examined, and the presence of any lesions noted. One study[6] suggested that vaginal openings of greater than 4mm in girls under 13 years, examined in the supine, frog-legged position, may be enlarged and that enlarged openings in the absence of known perineal injuries correlated in 75% of children with a positive sexual abuse history.* Toluidine Blue application may elucidate posterior fourchette lacerations.[7] An internal examination is indicated only when there are specific indicators, such as ongoing abnormal bleeding from the vagina or suspicion of an enlodged foreign body. An internal examination may require either oral sedation or general anesthesia. The vaginal examination under general anesthesia reveals an extremely dilated opening compared with that in the unanesthetized state. Anal inspection is necessary, and if there are positive findings found during the history or physical examination related to anal or rectal dysfunction or abnormality, then a rectal examination should be done.

(b) Physical Examination of Boys

Again, a complete examination needs to be done and all abnormalities documented. The penis, testicles, perineum, and anus should be inspected for any lesions or abnormalities and the Tanner stage noted. The same criteria as mentioned for girls for rectal examination apply to boys. It is our impression that even in children who have been chronically anally penetrated, the anal and rectal exams are often normal.

(c) Colposcopy

The colposcope is an instrument which may be used to examine the external genitals and anus. It provides a light source and magnification. Once the range of normal anatomy, as seen through the colposcope, has been established, it may prove to be a useful adjunct in the delineation of abnormal anatomy.

Laboratory Investigations

GENERAL

Depending on the history and physical findings, the following laboratory tests should be considered:

(1) Gonorrhea culture—throat/vagina/urethra/rectum/cervix

(2) VDRL—at the time of examination and in 6 weeks

(3) Chlamydia culture or chlamydia florescent antibody—
vaginal/urethral

(4) Culture for other vaginal organisms:
-Gardnerella vaginalis (may also do whiff test/wet prep
for clue cells)
-Mycoplasma hominis
-Ureaplasma urealyticum
-Group A,B Streptococcus
-Staphlococcus
-Candida albicans
-Enteric flora

(5) Trichomonas vaginalis—wet preparation

(6) Herpes simplex culture—genital/anal/mouth

(7) Viral culture of genital warts

(8) Pregnancy test

(9) Urine analysis and/or urine culture

(10) Human Immunodeficiency Virus (HIV) Test

Insofar as both gonorrhea and syphilis may be asymptomatic in the pediatric age group, it is most prudent to test for these infections.[8] Nonsexual transmission of sexually transmitted diseases is an infrequent occurrence.[9]**

RAPE KIT

If indicated by a history of penetrating sexual abuse within the previous 48-72 hours, a rape kit may be necessary.

All specimens must be carefully identified with the patient's name and then placed in a sealed envelope. The sealed envelopes are usually given to the investigating police officer for delivery to the police laboratory. Typical procedures and specimens to be collected in a rape kit are presented in Table 6.2.

Table 6.2
Rape Kit Instructions

1. VAGINAL SMEAR FOR SPERMATOZOA:
Using a sterile swab, make a smear (approximately 1 cm.) of vaginal pool on a microscope slide. Allow to air dry and place back into slide container. Place this swab into the vacutainer labelled "smear."

2. VAGINAL FLUIDS FOR PROSTATIC ACID PHOSPHATASE:
Take a saturated swab of the vaginal pool. Place this swab into the vacutainer labelled "acid p'ase." (This vacutainer contains 1.0 ml. of saline.)

3. MOTILITY OF SPERMATOZOA:
Using a sterile swab, prepare a wet mount of vaginal pool on microscope slide and examine IMMEDIATELY for motile spermatozoa. Place this swab into the vacutainer labelled "motility."

4. SALIVA FOR SECRETOR STATUS OF VICTIM:
Have victim saturate two swabs with saliva. Have VICTIM place each swab into a vacutainer labelled "saliva." (Victim should have nothing in mouth prior to the collection of this sample.)

5. BLOOD TYPE OF VICTIM:
Withdraw approximately 2-5 cc. of whole blood from victim using the vacutainer labelled "blood."

6. HAIRS:
Using the packaged comb, comb the pubic area of the victim to remove any loose hairs. Place the comb and the hairs into one white envelope and seal.
Pull (DO NOT CUT) 10 to 12 pubic hairs of the victim and place these into the second white envelope.

7. SEAL:
Using the numbered metal seal, seal all items in one compartment of the wood locking box. Record the number of the metal seal on the report form. Place the report form in the same compartment.

8. CLOTHING:
Place all garments worn by the victim at the time of the assault into separate paper bags. Do not use plastic bags. These items should be submitted to the Police Property Bureau by a police officer. If necessary, tampons or other sanitary articles should also be submitted for analysis by a police officer. DO NOT place these in the wood locking boxes!

A single sexual assault kit may be used if both vaginal and oral intercourse have occurred. Use SEPARATE sexual assault kits if both vaginal and anal intercourse have occurred.

LABEL ALL SPECIMENS. DO NOT USE THE SEXUAL ASSAULT KIT IF THE TAPED SEAL HAS BEEN BROKEN.

If pregnancy is a possibility and the assault took place within the previous 72 hours, the health care provider must discuss the option of pregnancy prevention with the patient within 12 hours.

Ongoing Follow-up

The child who has been sexually abused generally needs to be seen in ongoing therapy individually and, depending on the situation, within the context of his family. The psychiatric and psychological assessment of the child and family are covered elsewhere in detail in this Handbook (see chapters by Carroll and Jones, Steele and Kempe) as well as extensively in other references.[10,11]

Reliability of Children's Histories

Little evidence exists in the literature that reports of children are unreliable. *No* evidence supports the theory that children often make false accusations or misunderstand innocent behavior by adults.[12]

In the rare instance when children do make false accusations, it is generally for one of the following reasons: (1) to protect themselves from things that incriminate them when they perceive themselves to be in trouble, (2) to obtain an objective (secondary gain) that is important to the child (dating privileges, custody change) often within the context of marital separation or divorce between the parents, or (3) to please or anger the parent(s).

False accusations are more commonly generated by parents than by children. The reasons for this may be related to child custody issues in the case of a divorce, harassment of a noncustodial parent, or the desire to terminate a partner's parental or visitation rights. Such accusations may be made by the parent (usually when the child is semi-verbal) or by parental coaching of the child.

To the experienced interviewer, instances of parental coaching are not difficult to uncover. The child is unable to repeat the same facts or details in different words and cannot corroborate the history through play. Another evidence of parental coaching is the use of a precocious sexual vocabulary by the child. The child who uses words he can neither pronounce nor explain may have been coached, though he also may have heard these words during actual abuse.

Criteria that are useful for the assessment of reliability include the following:

(1) The ability of children to answer questions consistently in their own words or using different words in a non-mechanical way. It is always desirable to get a spontaneous statement from the child, but for the very young child (2 to 4) who is developmentally unable to answer open-ended questions, the information will have been elicited by direct questioning, such as: "Did he touch your privates?," "Did he put something inside you?," "With what did he spank you?"

(2) The statements of the child are associated with the appropriate affect; that is, the emotional response is consistent with the child's vision of the nature of the abuse that is being related.

(3) The child is able to give, in a developmentally appropriate fashion, specific details about what took place, including details about the sexual abuse and surrounding events. Young children who consistently give the same facts, using their own words, have a personal experience in mind. It is true that young children may fantasize, but fantasy rarely produces an event with the same specific and repeated detail.

(4) The play with "anatomically correct" dolls, drawings or other concrete retrieval props (puppets, doll house, etc.) is consistent with the child's verbal history.

Documentation

This material is covered elsewhere in this Handbook (see the chapter on the Expert Witness by Haralambie and Rosenberg).

Conclusions

The major problem confronting child protection teams responsible for attending to the needs of sexually abused children is the paucity of services available to these children and their families. The extent, in terms of prevalence and variety, of child sexual abuse was never imagined by those pioneers who first brought the issue to popular attention. At this stage, our collective ability to treat these children and their families certainly lags behind our ability to diagnose the problem. Finally, primary prevention[14] should be encouraged though we must not forget that ultimately, it is the adults, not the children, who are responsible for preventing sexual abuse.

Notes

*   A follow-up study showed an even higher correlation.[14]

**   Routine testing for Acquired Immunodeficiency Syndrome (AIDS) is not currently recommended. Since the issues of legalities, ethics, and confidentiality with respect to AIDS are highly complex, it would be prudent in cases where the perpetrator is in a high-risk category to consult a multidisciplinary group of experts.

References

1.   Kempe, C.H. "Incest and Other Forms of Sexual Abuse." *The Battered Child*, 3rd edition. C.H. Kempe and R.E. Helfer (Eds.). Chicago: University of Chicago, 1980.

2.   Russell, D.E.H. "The Incidence and Prevalence of Intrafamilial and Extrafamilial Sexual Abuse of Female Children." *Child Abuse & Neglect*, 7(1983):133-146.

3.   Finkelhor, D. *Child Sexual Abuse: New Theory and Research*. New York: The Free Press, 1984.

4.   Sgroi, S. *Handbook of Clinical Intervention in Child Sexual Abuse*. Lexington, Mass.: Lexington Books, 1982.

5. Summit, R. "The Child Sexual Abuse Accommodation Syndrome." *Child Abuse & Neglect*, 7(1983):177-193.

6. Cantwell, H. "Vaginal Inspection as It Relates to Child Sexual Abuse in Children Under Age 13." *Child Abuse & Neglect*, 7(1983):171-176.

7. McCauley, J., R.L. Gorman, and A. Guzinski. "Toluidine Blue in the Detection of Perineal Lacerations in Pediatric and Adolescent Sexual Abuse Victims." *Pediatrics*, 78(1986):1039-1043.

8. White, S.T., F.A. Loda, D.L. Ingram, et al. "Sexually Transmitted Diseases in Sexually Abused Children." *Pediatrics*, 72(1983):16-21.

9. Neinstein, L.S., J. Goldenring, and S. Carpenter. "Nonsexual Transmission of Sexually Transmitted Diseases: An Infrequent Occurrence." *Pediatrics*, 74(1984):67-76.

10. Mrazek, P., and C.H. Kempe, eds. *The Sexually Abused Child and His Family*. Oxford, England: Pergamon Press, 1981.

11. MacFarlane, K., and J. Waterman, eds. *Sexual Abuse of Young Children*. New York: The Gilford Press, 1986.

12. Jones, D.P.H., and J.M. McGraw. "Reliable and Fictitious Accounts of Sexual Abuse in Children." *Journal of Interpersonal Violence*, 2(1987):27-45.

13. Jenny, C., S.E. Sutherland, and B.B. Sandahl. "Developmental Approach to Preventing the Sexual Abuse of Children." *Pediatrics*, 78(1986):1034-1038.

14. Cantwell, H.B. "Update on Vaginal Inspection as it Relates to Child Sexual Abuse in Girls Under 13." *Child Abuse & Neglect*, 11(1987):in press.

7. Failure to Thrive: The Medical Evaluation

Barton D. Schmitt

Introduction

Failure to thrive (FTT) refers to an underweight condition in a young infant. The organic and environmental causes that must be considered are many. If the etiology is neglect, the child protective services agency must be notified. Overall, the assessment and management of FTT provides a medical challenge of the highest order.

Definition of Failure to Thrive

An infant with FTT has a weight percentile that is significantly less than the height percentile or a weight age that is significantly less than the height age. The present best operational definition of FTT is an actual weight that is 20% or more below the ideal weight for an infant's height (Table 7.1). Profound FTT or marasmus is defined as an actual weight that is 40% or more below the ideal weight for height. Ideal weights for heights can be obtained more accurately from standardized tables than by estimating them from the growth curve.[1]

Table 7.1
Definitions of Failure to Thrive

1.   Actual weight 20% or more below the ideal weight for height.
2.   Poor weight gain: 15 gm (0.5 oz)/day or less during first six months of life.
3.   Triceps skinfold thickness of 4 mm or less.

Another workable definition of FTT is an actual weight that is 10% or more below ideal weight *combined* with a poor weight gain.   This definition requires the availability of growth measurements at 2 or more ages. Poor weight gain in young infants can be defined as 15 gm. (0.5 oz.) or less of weight gain per day. No weight gain over a one month period would clearly meet this definition.

A measurement of the triceps skinfold thickness can help clarify which underweight infants have FTT. A measurement of 4 mm. or less correlates with FTT in the young infant (see Table 7.2).[2] This measurement reflects the infant's state of nutrition and is as important to the precise definition of FTT as are measurements of height and weight. The small, inexpensive plastic calipers provide accurate measurements.[3] Unfortunately, at this time, mild FTT is not associated with any laboratory marker.

FAILURE TO THRIVE IMITATORS

The three main impersonators of FTT are short stature, normal shifting linear growth and normal leanness.

SHORT STATURE

In former years, the most common error in this field was the misdiagnosis of short stature as FTT. Of the 3% of children under the 3rd percentile in height (i.e., short children), the majority are well-nourished.   The height and weight are at a similar percentile. Likewise, the triceps skin fold thickness is normal.   Most of these children have familial understature as evidenced by a positive family history for shortness, a height and weight equally below the 3rd percentile and serial heights that follow a specific growth trajectory.[4] The following heights define the 5th percentile for adults: 5 ft. 6 in. for men and 5 ft. 1 in. for women.

TABLE 7.2 *Triceps Skinfold Thickness (mm)*

Sex	Age (months)	5th	15th	50th	85th	95th	(Percentiles)
Males	0-6	4	5	8	12	15	
Males	6-18	5	7	9	13	15	
Females	0-6	4	5	8	12	13	
Females	6-18	6	7	9	12	15	

(Frisancho, 1974)[2]

SHIFTING LINEAR GROWTH

Most of the infants who are currently referred for FTT and do not have this diagnosis have shifting linear growth. During the first year of life, 60% of normal infants shift to a different growth channel or percentile than the one at which they are born.[5] Birth lengths relate mainly to maternal size, whereas length by two years of age correlates best with the midparent height. In infants with this change, the height and weight "lag down" simultaneously. The heights and weights at various ages never demonstrate a discrepancy. Children who "lag down" usually do so between 6 and 12 months of age. The few children who have organic short stature continue to fall away from their growth channel rather than re-establishing a new one. They usually have underlying endocrine or skeletal disorders.

NORMAL LEANNESS

A lean child can be defined as one who has a recorded weight 10 to 20% below the ideal weight for height, but is adequately fed and has no disease. Unlike the two preceding types, lean children are underweight. In fact, slender children are almost as common as obese children. A physician can be comfortable with this diagnosis if a child has a normal triceps skinfold thickness, is not hungry when offered food in the physician's office, has normal development, is happy, has normal parent/child interactions, and the parents regularly seek medical care. In most cases, the family history confirms the tendency towards slender somatotypes.

Types of Failure to Thrive

Non-organic or environmental FTT accounts for 70% of the total infants with FTT (Table 7.3).

Table 7.3
Types of Failure to Thrive

A. Nonorganic FTT 70%
    1. Neglectful FTT 50%
    2. Accidental FTT 19%
    3. Poverty-related FTT <1%

    4. Deliberate starvation <1%

B. Organic FTT

    1. Recurrent diarrhea (e.g., cystic fibrosis or Giardia)

    2. Recurrent vomiting (e.g., gastroesophageal reflux or peptic ulcer)

    3. Dysphagia (e.g., palatopharyngeal disorders)

    4. Weak suck (e.g., microcephaly or other central nervous system disorder)

    5. Hypermetabolic state (e.g., congestive heart failure or muscular hypertonia)

Neglectful or psychological FTT is the most common type. In these cases, the mother does not spend enough time with her baby and neglects feeding the baby because she is busy with external problems (e.g., overwhelmed with work), preoccupied with inner problems (e.g., depressed), and/or doesn't like the baby. A second type of non-organic FTT can be called accidental FTT or FTT due to errors in formula preparation or feeding techniques. Breast fed babies comprise a large number of these cases. Accidental FTT is discussed in depth in the section on the outpatient management of FTT. A third type of non-organic FTT is poverty-related. The unavailability of food or the lack of money to purchase food accounts for most of the malnutrition in the world today. In this country, however, poverty-related FTT occurs rarely and usually involves families that are transient or isolated. A fourth type of non-organic FTT is deliberate starvation and food restriction. This type usually involves an older child who is confined to his room, not fed, and also physically abused. This premeditated deprivation of food accounts for less than 1% of the total children seen with FTT.

    Approximately 30% of infants with FTT have an organic cause. A list of all the possible organic causes of FTT could contain 200 diagnoses. Infants with an *acute* weight loss of less than one month's duration usually have acute viral gastroenteritis or pneumonitis. The most common *chronic* causes of organic FTT are neurological and gastrointestinal disorders. The chronic disorders can be classified into five major groups (see Table 7.3).

Frequency and Age Distribution

    At the University of Colorado University Hospital, approximately 5% of the total evaluations performed by the Child Protection Team involved infants with alleged FTT. At the New York

Hospital, 1% of all pediatric admissions were for FTT.[6] In a primary care setting in an economically depressed area in North Carolina, 9.6% of infants seen in the first year of life had FTT.[7]

At our hospital, the causes of FTT are approximately 30% organic, 20% accidental and 50% neglectful. Only 18% of the infants with FTT at Buffalo Children's Hospital had organic causes.[8] While most studies combine all the non-organic causes, one study found that 30% of the non-organic FTT cases were due to ignorance or misunderstanding and the other 70% due to neglect.[9]

Most infants with FTT are under one year of age. Those infants with neglectful FTT have an onset under six months of age in 90% of the cases. Neglectful FTT is highly unusual after 2 years of age because older children can obtain food for themselves. Organic weight loss can be present at any age.

Evaluation of Failure to Thrive

The assessment of FTT requires a multidimensional evaluation. In most cases, the home is not dangerous and the evaluation can be scheduled by appointment (unlike abuse evaluations).

FEEDING HISTORY

A detailed feeding history may clarify the factors that have caused an inadequate weight gain. The feeding history is instrumental in diagnosing accidental FTT which is usually based on feeding errors. The interviewer must discuss formula preparation, amounts offered per feeding, amounts left over per feeding, feeding frequency and total amount of formula consumed per day by the baby. The most common errors occur in the preparation of the formula, especially with powdered milk which normally is mixed one scoop per two ounces of water (one of our mothers was mixing 1 scoop per 4 oz. bottle). Sometimes even liquid formulas (normally mixed one-to-one with water) are combined with a higher proportion of water. Occasionally, a child who has been placed on a 4 to 1 ration of water to formula for diarrhea is mistakenly kept on this weak dilution after the gastroenteritis is resolved.[10] Diluted formulas can be suspected by an additional history of polydipsia, polyuria and a voracious appetite.

The primary physician should be able to calculate nutritional intake for infants without consulting a nutritionist. During the first three months of life, most babies need 150 ml. per kg. per day (5 oz. per kg. per day) given at approximately three hour intervals while the baby is awake. All formulas contain 20 calories per ounce if properly mixed and most solids contain about 15 calories per ounce.

Accidental FTT can also occur with breast feeding, food fads, or nipple problems. Accidental FTT occurs more commonly in breast fed babies than bottle fed babies. Food fads such as Zen macrobiotic diets or fruitarian diets can lead to kwashiorkor.[11] Kwashiorkor has also resulted from elimination diets for suspected food allergies.[12] Kwashiorkor can also occur in babies who are given a non-dairy creamer as a milk substitute, since these products contain minimal protein.[13] Occasionally, a baby won't receive adequate calories because the holes in the rubber nipples are too small or clogged by dried milk. Such a baby will be described as always hungry, having a good suck but not taking much milk. For testing purposes an inverted bottle of formula normally will lose 1 drop of milk per second.

The feeding history is less helpful in babies with neglectful FTT. In most cases, the mother will claim that the baby is taking more than enough formula. If details are pursued, however, the intake repeatedly changes. The feeding interval also lengthens if one asks how long a baby can go without acting hungry. In some cases, the mother will report that her baby has significant vomiting and diarrhea. The child's subsequent course in the hospital will disprove most of these diet and feeding histories.

PREVIOUS HEALTH CARE

Prenatal care, immunization status, and health maintenance visits should be reviewed. Most infants with neglectful FTT have not been brought to a physician for their weight problem or any routine medical care. They are often behind schedule with regard to immunizations.

GROWTH CHART

The physician should obtain all available past heights and weights on the patient and carefully plot them on a growth chart. The growth chart in infants with FTT should show a weight gain that is much less than the corresponding height gain. Head circumference limitations occur only with severe malnutrition. Microcephaly usually points to a CNS cause of the FTT. From the growth chart or standardized table, (7.1), the patient's ideal weight can be estimated and then the percentage of underweight can be calculated.

PHYSICAL EXAMINATION

The infant with FTT usually has thin extremities, prominent ribs, and wasted buttocks. A triceps skinfold thickness should be measured. The thickness is usually 4 mm. or less in young infants with significant FTT. Evidence for hygiene neglect would include a rampant diaper rash, unwashed skin, untreated impetigo, uncut fingernails, or filthy clothing. A flattened occiput may suggest minimal handling, though may be normal in some babies. The absence of hair in the occipital area may also suggest neglect but can occur in some normal infants with headrolling habits. Signs of physical abuse should be searched for, especially a tear of the upper labial frenulum due to a forceful bottle feeding. If the infant has been deprived of fluids, signs of dehydration may be present.

LABORATORY STUDIES

An infant with FTT and a normal physical examination requires few baseline laboratory tests. A complete blood count, erythrocyte sedimentation rate, urinalysis, urine culture, serum electrolytes, blood urea nitrogen, sweat chloride, and tuberculin tests if epidemiologically indicated will suffice. If the infant has diarrhea that is confirmed by medical observers, stool for culture, pH, reducing substances and blood are indicated. Infants who are managed as outpatients probably only require a hematocrit, serum electrolytes, urinalysis and tuberculin test (if indicated) as baseline studies. If there is any suspicion of underlying renal disease, a blood urea nitrogen, creatinine and urine culture should be done.

The most common error in the laboratory evaluation of an infant with FTT is to perform elaborate endocrine tests, malabsorption tests and gastrointestinal radiologic studies before attempting a trial of adequate calories for at least a week. Special tests for reported vomiting or diarrhea should not be ordered unless the symptoms are verified in a hospital setting. A recent chart review of 185 patients with FTT found that they received an average of 13 tests per patient. Only 1.4% of the tests were positive and all of these positive tests had specific indications for ordering them present in the clinical evaluation.[8]

OBSERVATION OF BABY'S FEEDING PERFORMANCE

Much can be learned by personally feeding the baby with FTT. Vomiting, regurgitation, dysphagia, a weak suck, a disinterest in feeding, or resistance to feeding can be delineated. The hours that have passed since the last feeding should be determined. An underfed baby will eat voraciously even if less than 2 hours have passed since the last feeding. Babies who have been underfed will usually eat quickly and often consume 8 to 12 ounces.

DEVELOPMENTAL EVALUATION

An infant's development will eventually be stunted by an adverse environment and understimulation. Social delays and speech delays are the most common findings. These delays are rarely observed by the primary care physician before 4 months of age, although they may be present earlier. Findings include an avoidance of eye contact, an expressionless face, and the absence of a cuddling response. Posturing of the arms in a position with the elbows bent 90 degrees and the hands held beside the head can be seen in some infants with neglectful FTT.[14] The frequency of these deprivational behaviors or delayed social interactions in infants with neglectful FTT is unknown. Whitten, et al. stated that deprivational behaviors were present in only 50% of infants with marasmus or severe FTT.[15] Infants with mild FTT probably do not manifest deprivational behaviors. Since mild FTT is much more common than severe FTT, these behaviors are probably the exception rather than the rule. Further research is needed to clarify some of these questions.

Gross motor delays and hypotonia are also found in FTT. Cupoli found that these findings were due to the reduced muscle mass and weakness associated with malnutrition.[16] Therefore, they occur equally in organic and nonorganic FTT.

OBSERVATIONS OF MOTHER-CHILD INTERACTIONS

The medical and nursing staff should make unintrusive observations of the mother-child interactions as frequently as possible. The strengths and weaknesses of the interactions should be carefully recorded in the patient's chart. The amount of time that the mother spends holding, playing with and talking to her baby should be noted. Observations of the mother-child interactions during a feeding may be especially revealing. It is important to observe not only how the mother relates to the baby, but also how the infant responds to the mother. The normal mother or the somewhat overextended mother will usually encourage the baby during feedings and make it a pleasant time. Conversely, the emotionally disturbed or disabled mother will often feed her baby with disinterest or a lack of awareness of the baby's needs. A rejecting mother will often feed her baby with anger and unnecessary force.

PSYCHOSOCIAL EVALUATION OF THE MOTHER

If the child is admitted to the hospital, the mother should be evaluated by the hospital or Child Protection Team social worker. By the end of the psychosocial evaluation, the social worker should be able to categorize the mother into one of the three groups described by Evans.[17] Those three groups are: (1) exhausted and acutely depressed, (2) chronically emotionally disturbed, and (3) violent. Mothers suspected of having serious psychopathology should be referred to a psychiatrist for additional evaluation.

RADIOLOGIC BONE SURVEY

Any child who has both FTT and physical abuse should have a radiologic bone survey. Likewise, any infant with FTT and a limited range of motion or other bone findings deserves this test. While all infants with nonorganic FTT do not need bone surveys, those who demonstrate a rapid weight gain in the hospital and in addition have a parent who is angry or seriously disturbed should probably receive this added investigation.

Guidelines for Hospitalization

Five years ago we admitted nearly every infant with organic FTT, neglectful FTT, or FTT of unknown etiology. The only infants we managed as outpatients were those with accidental FTT. We now manage most infants with mild neglectful FTT as outpatients on a one month trial. The following factors must be present to safely warrant an outpatient feeding trial: the mother-child interaction seems good, the child has normal development, and there are no deprivational behaviors or inflicted injuries.

Outpatient Management of FTT

Accidental FTT usually responds to outpatient management. Occasionally, neglectful FTT will also respond to a home management program, if the mother is cooperative and wants help or if the neglect is situational and transient. The main thrust of outpatient management is a new feeding program, new support systems for the mother, and a method of monitoring progress.

FEEDING ERRORS

The appropriate diet or way to mix the formula so that it contains 20 calories per ounce should be explained to the parent. Many of the mothers who have made these simple errors are mentally retarded or have a borderline intellect.[9] Therefore, the feeding instructions should be carefully written down or explained in detail to friends or relatives who provide support to the mother.

BREASTFEEDING PROBLEMS

Breastfed infants with FTT usually come under medical concern at the 2-week visit when they have not regained birth weight or at the 4 or 6-month visit when their caloric needs begin to surpass the mother's milk supply. Table 7.4 lists the differential diagnosis for poor weight gain with breastfeeding. The most common problems are inadequate letdown reflex and inadequate milk supply.[18] Exhaustion or anxiety in the

Table 7.4
Accidental FTT with Breast Feeding:
A Differential Diagnosis and Treatment Plan

1.   Infrequent or brief feedings

   Rec: Feed q 2 hours minimum
   Nurse 10 minutes minimum each side

2.   Milk suppressant drug (e.g., pyridoxine, ergotamine, birth control pills, anticholingergics, diuretics, excessive alcohol)

   Rec: Discontinue, reduce, or replace drug

3.   Sick baby

   Rec: Admit to hospital

4. Baby with inadequate suck (e.g., thrush, stuffy nose, chronic problem)

    Rec: Specific treatment

5. Nipple problems (e.g., sore nipples, flat nipples)

    Rec: express some milk manually to provide a perch, breast shields, etc.

6. Inadequate letdown reflex (i.e., no dripping of milk or tingling in breasts by history; minimal weight increase when weighed before and after feedings)

    Rec: increased sleep and naps, increased fluid intake, relaxation techniques during feedings, increased support from husband and friends, referral to another mother who has successfully breastfed.

7. Inadequate milk supply (i.e., poor weight gain despite obvious letdown reflex)

    Rec: Supplement with formula after every other feeding (not during first two weeks of life, except to provide dextrose water during first three days of life)

mother most commonly causes the former. Improvements in sleep and support systems usually bring positive results. Some mothers have an inadequate milk supply on a biological basis. Dogmatic statements that baby should receive nothing but breast milk until six months of age have resulted in some FTT babies.[19] In mothers with a good milk supply, most babies need supplements or solids by six months of age. In a mother with an inadequate milk supply, supplements are needed by one month of age or earlier.[20]

ORGANIC FEEDING PROBLEMS

Infants with a cleft palate or swallowing difficulties due to a neurological problem (e.g., Werdnig-Hoffman disease) are difficult to feed. Because of a poor suck, gagging, or regurgitation, they commonly are unable to take adequate calories without special feeding techniques. These special techniques must be taught to the mother in the hospital before the newborn is discharged. After discharge, close follow-up by a public health nurse is essential for re-emphasizing the feeding techniques. Although some of these babies may develop FTT because they are unwanted and neglected by their parents, more commonly the FTT is related to inadequate teaching by the nursing and medical staff.

MILD NEGLECTFUL FTT

The overextended, overwhelmed mother who clearly likes her baby can usually be helped on an ambulatory basis. The baby should be placed on an intake of greater than 150 calories per kg. per day. The baby should be encouraged to feed during the waking hours at 2-2 1/2 hour intervals minimum. The caloric value of the formula may be increased to 24 calories per ounce by adding a glucose polymer (Polycose) at a rate of 2 tsp. of powder per 4 ounces of formula. All solid foods that have fewer calories per ounce than milk should be discontinued. Overall, babies who are malnourished need extra calories rather than extra protein for maximal weight gain. A public health nurse should be informed about the mother's situation and attempt to visit the home at least twice weekly. The baby should be seen weekly for weight checks by the primary physician. The most common error in the management of these cases is following them too long as outpatients. If no weight gain occurs by two weeks on this regimen or the weight gain at four weeks is inadequate, the infant should be admitted to the hospital.

Inpatient Management of Failure to Thrive

Comprehensive inpatient management of an infant with neglectful FTT requires a feeding program, stimulation program and parent counseling. This level of intervention requires a multidisciplinary team approach.

FEEDING PROGRAM

The infant with FTT should be offered unlimited feedings of a regular diet for age. The daily intake must approach 150 calories per kg. per day (ideal weight), or weight gain will not occur. (Normal caloric intake for infants is 110 from birth until 4 months, 100 from 4 to 8 months of age, and 90 from 8 to 12 months of age.) Since the normal baby requires 150 ml. (5 ounces) of formula per kg. per day, the FTT baby requires approximately 225 ml. (7 1/2 ounces) per kg. per day. The baby can be fed on demand, but at least 6 feedings should occur per day (8 feedings for babies under 3 months of age). The formula should be identical to the one reportedly provided at home. Rapid weight gain on a special formula free of cow's milk protein or lactose will not prove that a baby was underfed in the home setting.

STIMULATION PROGRAM

If deprivational behaviors are present in the baby, a stimulation program should be initiated in the hospital setting. The most important time to stimulate the baby is during feedings. Preferably, this extra stimulation should be provided by the mother. If the mother does not visit or visits rarely, the hospital staff should try to provide the nurturing environment these infants need. A foster grandmother and/or primary care nurse can act as mother substitutes for this baby, providing extra cuddling, verbal and visual stimulation. The infants need a minimum of 6 hours per day of being held.

PARENT COUNSELING

The ultimate goal is to have the baby adequately cared for at home by the mother. Therefore, the mother should be encouraged to visit her baby frequently and to provide the care of her baby during these times. The ward nurses should be supportive and teach her more appropriate feeding methods. The ward social worker should seek the mother out and begin helping her with the problems she has at home. The ward staff should offer to help the mother, compliment her on her efforts, and in general build her confidence in herself as a mother. The mother and baby should be treated as a unit from the beginning. The optimal approach provides a rooming-in arrangement. The results of a treatment program directed both at feeding and stimulation of infants with FTT were: 55% of the mothers made major positive changes in their attachment behavior, 25% made small improvements, and 20% continued their negative interactions.[21] The average hospital stay was 14 days.

MONITORING PROGRESS

The physician can follow daily weights, developmental assessments, observations of mother-child interactions, and the mother's visiting patterns. The baby should be weighed daily without any clothing. A nutritionist should be consulted to document the intake in calories per kg. per day. Both daily weights and caloric intake are easier to interpret if these data are plotted on graph paper. The mother-child interactions should be noted and recorded by the ward nursing and medical staff. Hopefully, the staff will see increased holding, cuddling, eye contact and talking to the baby. Since the appropriate disposition may depend on the mother's involvement with the infant on the ward, exact records should be kept of the number and length of visits.

Diagnostic Criteria for Neglectful Failure to Thrive

Diagnosis of underfeeding requires subsequent documentation of a rapid weight gain and the improvement of any deprivational behaviors. Rapid weight gain is the most consistent finding in treated infants with neglectful FTT. This can be defined as a gain of over 2 oz. per day sustained for a one week period (approximately 1 lb. per week), a gain of greater than 1.5 oz. per day sustained for 2 weeks, or a gain that is strikingly greater than achieved during a similar time period at home. Most of these infants also display a ravenous appetite. Average weight gains for normal children vary according to age: 1.0 oz. per day in the first three months of life, 0.7 oz. per day from 3 to 6 months, 0.5 oz. per day from 6 to 9 months, and 0.4 oz. per day from 9 to 12 months of age.[1] A recent report on 57 infants with non-organic FTT found that those less than 6 months of age began to gain weight in 2 to 3 days.[22] All infants less than 18 months old began this weight increase in less than 2 weeks. The authors concluded that hospitalization beyond a 2 week period of observation was not justifiable. Another study reported on 100 infants with FTT who demonstrated a rapid weight gain after 48 to 96 hours in the hospital.[21] Most of them had a gain greater than 90 grams (3 oz.) per day. Any infant who gained less than 45 gms. (1.5 oz.) per day was eliminated from the study.

Most infants with organic FTT will not gain in the hospital. An exception to this rule is an infant with a combined problem of organic and non-organic FTT. An example would be a child with congenital heart disease, feeding problems and a depressed mother. Such a child will probably gain in the hospital setting. Combined etiologies are not uncommon, occurring in 23% to 55% of infants with FTT.[23,24]

Sometimes, infants who gain poorly in the hospital may be labelled non-organic FTT if no evidence of an organic etiology is found. For example, an infant with feeding difficulties who achieves a small weight gain in the hospital due to heroic efforts on the part of the nurses may occasionally be placed in the non-organic category. Some of these infants may be more appropriately referred to as having organic FTT, probably due to a central nervous system disorder or dysphagia. Follow-up studies of these infants are needed.

Weight gains are often delayed in infants with pervasive deprivational behaviors. These children are usually beyond 6 months of age and live in severely depressed or hostile environments. Initially, such infants may be anorexic rather than voracious feeders. Their rapid weight gain may be delayed 1 to 2 weeks until they can tolerate close social interactions.[25]

Reporting to Child Protective Services

By law, all cases of FTT due to underfeeding or maternal neglect must be reported to the child protective services (CPS) agency in the patient's county of residence. The only exceptions are organic FTT or where the underfeeding was due to ignorance on the parents' part which is easily remedied by office advice (accidental FTT). If the parents are fanatic about a particular diet (e.g., Zen macrobiotic) and unwilling to change it, however, CPS should be asked to intervene. The reason for reporting all cases of neglectful FTT to the appropriate agencies are many. A small risk for future physical abuse or starvation is present.[26] Most importantly, CPS can enforce follow-up and counseling for the family. If the family becomes uncooperative about the treatment plan, the early involvement of CPS may help to overcome this.

The CPS agency may be distressed that the medical report of neglectful FTT is delayed. Interdisciplinary meetings may help to clarify that confirmation of this diagnosis requires a trial of feeding and documentation of a rapid weight gain. Sometimes this diagnostic trial requires two weeks. Infants who are emaciated or have a parent with obvious psychopathology can be reported on the day of admission. Telephone reports should be followed by a written report.

We believe that infants with neglectful FTT who are managed as outpatients should also be reported to CPS. While these infants rarely have any significant risks for morbidity or mortality, their families often need help with reducing environmental stresses or obtaining day care services. If no services are needed beyond visits by a public health nurse, the report can state that treatment is going well, the family is cooperative, and CPS investigation is optional from our standpoint.

Guidelines for Placement in a Foster Home

From the experience of our Child Protection Team, there are three dispositional options for babies with documented underfeeding. Approximately 75% of babies go home with added services for the family, 20% go into temporary foster care while the parents receive therapy, and 5% enter long-term foster care with plans for relinquishment or termination of parental rights. Of the 100 children followed in one study, 23% were placed in foster care, 9% initially and 14% when the FTT worsened in the home.[21]

The guidelines for foster placement for a child with neglectful FTT are the following:

1. Associated non-accidental trauma.
2. Danger of non-accidental trauma.
3. Severe emaciation without seeking medical care.
4. The baby is severely disturbed or fearful.
5. The mother-child interaction is overtly hostile.
6. The mother is severely disturbed (e.g., psychotic, alcoholic, drug addicted, suicidal or other condition requiring intensive therapy).
7. Hospital observations find that the mother doesn't visit or if she visits, she cannot learn child care on the ward.
8. The family refuses intervention and services *or* the family is crisis-ridden and can't benefit immediately by services.

Of the 25% of FTT infants who are placed in foster care, approximately 60% are returned home whereas 40% remain in foster care, are relinquished, or have parental rights terminated. These 40% are approximately equally divided between homes with a serious danger of injury or death and homes where the chaos has not improved with intervention. Some of the changes that can lead to returning an infant to the natural home are that the mother has become able to care for herself, she is no longer dangerous, she recognizes the needs of her baby, she keeps all visits with the baby and interacts positively with the baby at these times.

Treatment Plan for Infants Discharged to Their Natural Home

Most infants with neglectful FTT can safely be discharged home. The main requirements are that the mother is treatable, the parents have accepted follow-up services within the home, and the parent-child interaction is positive. In addition, the mother must have demonstrated her ability to care for her baby's needs in the hospital setting. The fact that the baby gained weight while under the care of the nurses on the ward doesn't mean that the baby will gain weight while under the care of the mother. At a minimum, the mother must successfully care for her baby for the 24 hours prior to discharge. Feeding instructions, stimulation instructions, a therapy program for the mother, and a follow-up system should be delineated before discharge.

Close medical follow-up is needed to monitor weight gain. Most infants are appointed weekly until they attain ideal weight. Older infants can be seen less often. Ideal weight is usually reached in 6 to 8 weeks and thereafter, rapid weight gain can no longer be expected. The infant should be re-admitted to the hospital or a medical foster home if there is no weight gain for 2 weeks or a poor weight gain for 4 weeks following discharge. Before making this decision, however, the baby should be weighed again, since a weighing error is the most common cause of weight loss in a clinic setting.

Summary

The diagnosis of non-organic failure to thrive implies that there is a disturbance in the parent-child relationship that must be addressed. The severity of the disturbance is variable and may range from situations in which there is only a minor, temporary problem to situations where the mother has been a lifelong victim of neglect herself and is chronically depressed. Discovering the etiology and depth of the disturbance is crucial to treatment of families in which a baby has nonorganic failure to thrive.

References

1.   Hamill, P.V., T.A. Drizd, C.L. Johnson, et al. "Physical Growth: National Center for Health Statistics Percentiles." *American Journal of Clinical Nutrition*, 32(1979):607.

2   Frisancho, A.R. "Triceps Skinfold and Upper Arm Muscle Size Norms for Assessment of Nutritional Status." *American Journal of Clinical Nutrition*, 27(1974):1052.

3. Jung, E., J.J.M. Kaufman, D.C. Narins, and G.E. Kaufman. "Skinfold Measurements in Children." *Clinical Pediatrics*, 23(1984):25-28.

4. Rimoin, D.L., and W.A. Horton. "Short Stature: Part II." *Journal of Pediatrics*, 92(1978):697.

5. Smith, D.W., W. Truog, J.E. Rogers, et al. "Shifting Linear Growth During Infancy." *Journal of Pediatrics*, 89(1976):225.

6. English, P.C. "Failure to Thrive Without Organic Reason." *Pediatric Annals*, 7(1978):774.

7. Michell, W.G., R.W. Gorrell, and R.A. Greenberg. "Failure-to-Thrive: A Study in a Primary Care Setting: Epidemiology and Follow-up." *Pediatrics*, 65(1980):971.

8. Sills, R.H. "Failure to Thrive." *American Journal of Diseases of Children*, 132(1978):967.

9. Jacobs, R.A., and J.T. Kent. "Psychosocial Profiles of Families of Failure to Thrive in Infants——Preliminary Report." *Child Abuse & Neglect*, 1(1977):469.

10. Kaplowitz, P., and R.B. Isely. "Marasmic Kwashiorkor in an 8-Week-Old Infant Treated with Prolonged Clear Liquids for Diarrhea." *Clinical Pediatrics*, 18(1979):575.

11. Forbes, G.B. "Food Fads: Safe Feeding of Children." *Pediatrics in Review*, 1(1980):207.

12. John, T.J., J. Blazovich, E.S. Lightner, et al. "Kwashiorkor not Associated with Poverty." *Journal of Pediatrics*, 90(1977):730.

13. Sinatra, F.R., and R.J. Merritt. "Iatrogenic Kwashiorkor in Infants." *American Journal of Diseases of Children*, 135(1981):730.

14. Krieger, I., and D.A. Sargent. "A Postural Sign in the Sensory Deprivation Syndrome in Infants." *Journal of Pediatrics*, 70(1967):332.

15. Whitten, D.G., M.G. Pettitt, and J. Fischhoff. "Evidence that Growth Failure from Maternal Deprivation Is Secondary to Undereating." *Journal of American Medical Association*, 209(1969):1675.

16. Cupoli, J.M., J.A. Hallock, and L.A. Barness. "Failure to Thrive." *Current Problems in Pediatrics*, Vol. 11. Chicago: Year Book Medical Publishers, September 1980.

17. Evans, S.I., J.B. Reinhart, and R.A. Succop. "Failure to Thrive: A Study of 45 Children and their Families." *Journal of American Academy of Child Psychiatry,* 2(1972):440.

18. Neifert, M.R. "Returning to Breast Feeding." *Clinical Obstetrics Gynecology,* 23(1980):1061.

19. O'Conner, P.A. "Failure to Thrive with Breast Feeding." *Clinical Pediatrics,* 17(1978):833.

20. Davies, D.P. "Is Inadequate Breast-Feeding an Important Cause of Failure to Thrive?" *Lancet,* 1(1979):541.

21. Ayoub, C., D. Pfeifer, and L. Leichtman. "Treatment of Infants with Non-Organic Failure to Thrive." *Child Abuse & Neglect,* 3(1980):937.

22. Ellerstein, N.S., and B.E. Ostrov. "Growth Patterns in Children Hospitalized Because of Calorie-Deprivation Failure to Thrive." *American Journal of Diseases of Children,* 139(1985):164-166.

23. Homer, C., and S. Ludwig. "Categorization of Etiology of Failure to Thrive." *American Journal of Diseases of Children,* 135(1981):848-851.

24. Casey, P.H., B. Wortham, and J.Y. Nelson. "Management of Children with Failure to Thrive in a Rural Ambulatory Setting." *Clinical Pediatrics,* 23(1984):325-330.

25. Rosenn, D.W., L.S. Loeb, and M.B. Jura. "Differentiation of Organic from Nonorganic Failure to Thrive Syndrome in Infancy." *Pediatrics,* 66(1980):698.

26. Koel, B.S. "Failure to Thrive and Fatal Injury as a Continuum." *American Journal of Diseases of Children,* 118(1969)565.

8. Neglect

Hendrika B. Cantwell

Introduction

Child neglect is overwhelmingly the most frequently reported type of child maltreatment. By definition, neglect is the responsible caretaker's non-provision of care essential to a child, such as food, clothing, shelter, medical (attention), education or supervision. Seventy percent of long-term services provided by departments of social services are for situations in which there is "emotional maltreatment" and/or "deprivation of necessities."

Reported neglect is often only the tip of the iceberg in many dysfunctional, physically or sexually abusive households. For example, neglect may be reported because of a child's absence from school. Upon investigation, it is discovered that none of the child's siblings have gone to school regularly either, even though some are in their teens. When contacted, authorities in other states of past residence report serious medical neglect, and that the family repeatedly disappeared from past residences as soon as a social worker became involved with them. When the children are interviewed and medically evaluated, sexual abuse is discovered to be another major problem in this family. The parents' fear of discovery meant that the children were not allowed to attend school. Therefore, other forms of maltreatment must always be considered in neglectful situations.

The Context of Neglect

Poverty is found in neglect situations more commonly than in other types of child maltreatment situations.[1] It is not always the poverty that causes neglect, though the poverty is sometimes a product of neglect in the previous generation. The parents, because of maltreatment in their childhood, may suffer from developmental inadequacies which leave them inept at providing adequately for their children. In other situations, however, through no fault, a parent's loss of job with resultant eviction from his home may cause the children to be temporarily without shelter. Financial assistance, although available, often takes months to be set in motion. Families which are temporarily in dire need of help can usually be readily distinguished from those whose poverty and child neglect are related to the parents' chronic inability to provide.

The cultural context in which events are taking place should be considered before an assessment of neglect is made. The Native Americans of the Southwest expect fairly young boys to herd sheep and so the boys are not supervised closely on an all-day basis. Generally, this is on a reservation, outdoors, and the children are carefully taught what is expected. Adults are close by if needed. The dangers to which the city child is exposed are absent, such as cooking stoves, traffic, or people who might harm them. Sometimes the failure of a child to make eye contact is given as an example of neglect. However, the experience with some populations of Hispanic origin, for example, is that the culture encourages a modest demeanor, which includes downcast eyes. Children of Eskimo or Native American descent may appear to be delayed in language development due to lack of stimulation. However, their language skills may not be readily apparent since it is considered very impolite to talk too much around people whom one does not know well, and silence is a cultural virtue.[2]

Clearly, it is important to have some knowledge of cultural differences. Most important, however, when neglect is a consideration, is the recognition of those practices that impair children's health and well-being, place them in danger, or threaten to deprive them of a competent adulthood.

Crisis Evaluation and Intervention

When a case of child neglect is reported to the agency designated by the child protection law of that state to receive such reports, an investigative process is set in motion. When first approaching the task, the most important issue is the safety of the children. If they are in imminent danger, emergency removal has to be undertaken. Young children who are left alone must be taken into custody if no adult can be found to care for them. Sometimes a relative or neighbor will assume that responsibility, but as more women are at work, fewer can be found to give emergency care. Sometimes children who are quite young are locked into a home alone and no one can get to them. Unattended children are at risk for many reasons, including accidental fires (often during attempted cooking), falls from windows or other high places, poisonings, or rape by an intruder. Death may result from such neglect.

Even when parents are at home, emergency removal of children may be necessary because the parents are incapable of caring for them as, for example, when the parents are very intoxicated or drugged or severely mentally ill, and unable to keep their children safe. Imminent danger to the child is not necessarily present because a parent is delusional. However, when the parental delusions involve the child, the danger to the child may be grave. If a parent hears voices that say that the child is demonic and demons must be killed, or if the parent's delusion is that all food is poisoned and, therefore, the parent does not feed the child, danger is imminent.

Imminent danger may also result from the physical environment of the house. The house in which there is no heat in cold months, no functional plumbing, which has broken windows, broken stairs, or is otherwise severely damaged, clearly is not habitable. If at all possible, temporary alternative housing for the entire family should be arranged. Removal of the children would need to be undertaken only if the parents refuse to see the condition of the house as a threat to the children's well-being. The severity of the dilapidated housing has some relationship to the children's ages, being possibly less hazardous to the older ones. This relationship to age is also a consideration when encountering formerly adequate housing which, by neglectful housekeeping, has become dangerous. The danger of broken glass scattered about, alcohol in glasses and bottles left on floors and tables is much greater for toddlers and preschoolers than for infants in cribs or for older children. Especially if it can be seen that the children are happy, relate well to the parents, and seem healthy, it may be appropriate to set a time for a second visit to the house, with the expectation that cleaning will be adequately accomplished. The dilapidated house and the very dirty house, therefore, must be evaluated as to the dangers they pose to the children who live there before deciding that imminent danger requires their removal to a safer place.

Various forms of family violence result in emergency placement of children. When the adults are using weapons (or even threatening to do so), children can get in the way and get injured. Some custody disputes reach such a level of uncontrolled fury that the children are in imminent danger.

The issue of school-age children being left alone is much disputed. Most counties do not have a law which states at what age children may care for themselves, though in Denver, with the support of the juvenile court and the police, it is expected that children under 12 years of age not be left alone. Aside from children's potentially dangerous lack of judgment, the danger from predatory adults is higher when it is common knowledge that the children are home alone. It is not safe to leave a younger child in the care of a nine year old for several reasons which include the nine year old's undeveloped judgment and his or her lack of training and maturity in responding to emergencies. A nine year old is entitled to participate in peer activities and not be prematurely burdened with an adult supervisory role. Furthermore, when a child who has been self-governing becomes a teenager, difficulties may arise when the parents attempt to set limits on dating, bedtime, and school attendance.

When dealing with a handicapped child, the degree of limitation in cognitive or physical development is a more salient issue than chronologic age, when assessing the child's safety in being alone.

Usually, medical care for children is consistently sought by the parents. Reports of medical neglect, however, are not infrequent. It is preferable if parents can be persuaded to come with an ill child to the medical facility, though if a child is seriously ill and the parents refuse medical intervention, the child may need to be treated against the parents' wishes.

Child protective agencies are also called when a child with a chronic disease such as asthma, diabetes or congenital heart disease, is being medically neglected.[3] If the condition represents imminent danger to the child, this needs to be clearly communicated by the reporting doctor to the child protection agency. The medical neglect of chronic illnesses often needs to be brought to juvenile court because such neglect may have a fatal outcome. Of course, the dilemma often is that even with court supervision, which can order the parents to bring the child in for clinic appointments, one cannot be at home with a family to observe the ongoing care of the child.[3] An assessment must be made as to whether the medical neglect of the child is the result of a parental situation that might be ameliorated by some intervention by social services; for example, parental mental retardation, transportation problems, fear or denial of the child's illness, or misunderstanding as to the seriousness of the condition.

Symptoms and Signs of Neglect

INFANTS AND TODDLERS

Very early in life, the effects of lack of attachment and lack of nurturance are observed in the child whose mother refuses to hold her infant and who interacts with the baby only in accordance with her needs rather than the child's. The baby's needs are chronically unmet. When one sees this in combination with rather unpredictable behavior in the mother, the child may soon begin mothering the mother.[4] This role reversal may begin surprisingly early and is easily confused with healthy attachment. If such a child is removed from her home, in the toddler years, she may not trust caretaking adults, may not allow them to care for her (or her siblings) and may miss her mother, worrying about who will care for mother in her absence. Tragically, this behavior may follow the child into adult life, so that when she herself becomes a parent she expects to be cared for and nurtured by her young children. There is, therefore, a generational repetition of the neglect.[5]

The neglectful parent expects the infant to consider parental wishes, or the infant is expected to anticipate and respond to parents' needs; neglected infants are often expected to behave at a level years beyond their developmental capabilities. If they do not, they may be punished or ignored. Often one hears these children referred to as "spoiled," "stubborn," "not minding," or "doing it just to get me." For example, a 15-month old child incurred an extensive burn on his back while his mother stood nearby as the child was burned on a hot water heater. Her explanation was, "I told him it was hot and to stay away. If he wanted to go near it anyhow, that's his fault." The unreasonable expectations and the lack of supervision keeps these children at high risk for accidents and injuries.

Toddlers, in neglectful homes, who behave age appropriately may be considered "bad" or "hyperactive" (a term often misused by neglectful parents, reflecting their attitude about a normally active child).[6] Unfortunately, professionals sometimes agree that the child is "the problem" when the young child is out of control. The problem is usually not in the child but in the parents' misparenting, in their inability to set boundaries in a caring and appropriate way. Signs of neglect in the infant and toddler may include developmental delays (gross motor, fine motor, language, and personal-social interaction), growth failure, behavioral abnormalities or psychiatric disorders.

SCHOOL AGE CHILDREN

Neglected children are rarely, if ever, praised for school work, activities, or chores well-done. The neglectful parent typically says that he is not praised at work for doing his job correctly and his children should not expect to be treated otherwise. The children's failures, however, are readily pointed out by the parent with belittling, teasing, name-calling, and persistently telling the children that they are worthless. This emotional abuse, so often a part of pervasive neglect, interferes with the child's development of a sense of competence. Instead of positive nurturance, the parent-to-child message is a continually negative one, creating and then exacerbating the sense of failure which secondarily causes poor school performance. The neglected child feels he "cannot do anything right."

The neglected school age child with a poor self-image is also often delayed in language development. The neglectful household fosters only minimal interactive language. The child is addressed in short, command sentences such as, "Stop that," "Don't do that," "Come here," "Sit down," "How come you're so stupid?" There is no effort to teach language in the naming of things around the house and neighborhood, in talking about experiences or discussing what the child may feel. This paucity of language skills, if not remediated early, seems to remain lifelong. Not only does it hamper school performance pervasively, but it may also lead to the labeling of the child as mildly retarded.

The neglected school age child may have poor self-discipline and, therefore, be disruptive in the classroom. This child, prior to the school years, has been exposed to erratic, inconsistent and unexplained discipline at home which prevents the child from developing self-discipline. Furthermore, the neglected child, uncared for at home, may be unreceptive to concepts of caring and respect for others (peers and teachers) at school.

Other home problems of neglected children interfere with performance at school. Abuse of alcohol and/or drugs by adults at home, often accompanied by violent and unpredictable behavior, does not foster an atmosphere that helps the child concentrate on homework or school projects. (Incidentally, children may be encouraged or forced to participate in drug and alcohol abuse by the adults in the home, often from toddlerhood.) When the child's family changes school districts frequently, the child may have a difficult time attaching and re-attaching to schoolmates. Some children stay home from school in an effort to make sure that they don't lose home and parent(s) while away, or to protect a parent from drug (alcohol, glue-sniffing, etc.) abuse.

LONG-TERM PLANNING

Children removed from the home because of imminent danger need to have resolution of their "in limbo" status. One of the most difficult assessments in this evaluation is the parents' psychological and emotional status.

Sometimes, child neglect is a reiterative issue that arises with psychiatrically ill parents who have recurrences of serious problems and may be on medications. When well-monitored and appropriately medicated, all may go well for months; then, what appeared to be an adequate situation for the children may abruptly deteriorate. It is very difficult for children to be placed repeatedly in foster care because their mothers or fathers have to be hospitalized.

Most neglectful parents were themselves seriously damaged through various types of abuse and neglect in their own childhoods. They are often depressed, have poor self-esteem, and have been left with such deficits of nurturance and guidance from their own childhoods that they do not comprehend their children's needs. They cannot provide a normal childhood experience for their children since they never experienced it; they have never had the opportunity to internalize how parents and children interact healthily.

Some children taken out of the home may not be able to return home for a protracted period or ever, and it is very important to find suitable relatives who will and can raise the children, temporarily or possibly long term. If no relatives are available, especially young children may benefit from placement in a foster home which will adopt them if they become free for adoption. This, hopefully, will protect the children from disruption of attachment (multiple foster homes). It is painful for foster parents who are hopeful for adoption if they have to give up a child, but it is worse for children to suffer repeated losses.

With less severe disability in the parents, specific tasks and expectations can be outlined; for instance, that they seek employment or that they apply for subsidized housing (once the children are removed from the home the monies from Aid to Dependent Children, of course, cease). In the instance when adequate housing is found, the children may begin weekend visits. The appearance of the children after the weekend and their comments may be very valuable in judging the progress being made by the family. If inadequate feeding was an issue, the children can be weighed before and after visits. (This is more valuable in infants than in toddlers or older children). Drug and alcohol treatment may be a prerequisite to the return of children to what was a chaotic household. In short, the specific condition which precipitated removal of the children from the home must be corrected within a reasonable time frame. Some tasks might be expected to be accomplished in three months (or at least the parents must show that improvement is being made), with six months as the time period by which parents must be ready for the return of the children into an improved environment. It should be noted that it is often necessary for agencies to provide services to neglectful families for long periods of time and to monitor the situation on a protracted basis as there is commonly, in the neglectful family, a regression to chaos.

Documentation of neglect must refer, not only to the conditions of the children's lives, but also to how the conditions are causal in affecting the children adversely. For example, dirty or old clothing may reflect poverty, rather than neglect. The situation becomes neglectful when financial assistance is squandered and not used to help the children from being ostracized by peers as a result of being dirty or smelly. When a clear picture is put together of all the elements in the parenting which are harmful to the child and exactly how the child's development and well-being are adversely affected, then a program of remediation can be developed.

The apparent effects of intervention must also be documented well. Some parents superficially appear to be compliant with the treatment plan, but the child is, in fact, not being helped. Record keeping of progress must contain three elements: first, the parents' cooperation and compliance in doing that which was requested vis-a-vis their problems (i.e., go to the doctor; send the children to school on time, regularly, in a reasonably acceptable condition of cleanliness; prepare meals for the children; speak politely to the children; make them come inside before dinner, sit down to eat with them; send them to bed at a reasonable hour; attend psychological counseling, accept visiting nurse in the home, or go to parenting classes; be home when social worker has an appointment, etc.). Secondly, the child's progress must be noted. It is the child who is the one in need of protection. Despite some parents' efforts, the treatment of the children may not be better or improved enough to meet a minimally adequate standard. Thirdly, any other concerned professionals must be consulted to assess whether they have seen improvement in the child's situation.

The involvement of the court is usual if a child is removed from the parents. When court action is considered, observations which indicate deficits in the child must be shown to be causally related to the neglect by the parent. Sometimes court involvement becomes imperative by the sheer accumulation of incidents of neglectful parenting. When such a presentation is brought before the court, all efforts which have been made to correct the parents' omissions should be well documented. If this is not done, courts can easily dismiss the neglectful behavior as ignorance by inexperienced young parents. The court's involvement frequently is instructive when dealing with a family that resists intervention and believes no one should interfere. The emphasis to the parents by the societal authority—the court—that some change in their parenting behavior is necessary may improve the parents' efforts to do so.

The court process establishes a record that is probably the most valuable documentation. A treatment program that is court-ordered will also be reviewed by the court. The court must know if there has been adequate improvement by the parents or not. If there has been adequate improvement, and the children had been placed outside the home, the children must be returned to the family home without delay. On the other hand, some seriously neglectful parents do not participate in, or cannot benefit from, any known intervention.

Legal termination of the parent-child relationship must be set in motion when parents are unable to learn to parent minimally adequately. The legal process to accomplish this is slow. Emphasis must be on accurate, clear documentation of the efforts made to remediate the unsatisfactory response by the parents, and the harm that their parenting inflicts on the children.

AVAILABLE TOOLS FOR TREATMENT/REMEDIATION

Clearly, before a treatment plan can be designed, it is necessary to evaluate the type and severity of the neglect. When developmental delays in young children are prominent, remedial nursery school experience may be valuable. Payment for this may be a problem, but many counties have some funds for protective or therapeutic day care. The purpose of these day cares is to help children who need more environmental stimulation, to teach families how to help their children and sometimes to provide adequate supervision when the parent is unable to do so. Problems are most commonly encountered when night care is needed. In most communities, it is difficult to arrange; it may be unavailable. Employers need to be approached in a community where night care does not exist so that night time child care for their employees' children may be developed.

Older neglected children may benefit from special programs in the schools to ameliorate their delays in cognition and personal-social development. Some children need psychiatric counseling. Transportation to counseling and payment are often problems for parents, and public agencies may not have funding to provide these supports.

Volunteers have been successfully utilized to help children.[7] Many communities may be able to identify adults who are talented at spending time with neglected children. These adults may be able to give the children some experiences of "normalcy" otherwise denied them. Experiences which are quite ordinary such as an outing with a picnic, a trip to a zoo or baking cookies in an orderly home, having conversations about self-image and hygiene, discussing problems, helping with homework, or reading stories, can all be helpful.

For parents, the needs may be extremely broad. The family may need a full-time "parent figure" to be in the home. Social service agencies, in general, cannot provide this. Homemakers, though, may be assigned to be in the home several half days per week to teach the family to organize housework, to care for the home and the children, to keep appointments, and often to help them find their way through the maze of obtaining financial assistance, food stamps and food supplements for young children. (Dealing with organizations that are large, full of rules and papers to be signed may be too bewildering for many neglectful parents who are depressed and damaged by their own childhoods.) Homemakers or parent aides may be able to give more time, be available as friends, and do a lot of "re-parenting."

Parenting classes may be useful. There are successes with this modality, but not in a short time. Those who benefit generally remain with a group for about two years by which time some of the information has gradually become internalized and may be used at home. For more damaged parents, parenting classes may be helpful insofar as these parents see that they have not been singled out and labeled as "inadequate" parents. Some of the nonverbal parents improve their ability to verbally communicate.

Formal psychotherapy is more useful for people who have adequate verbal skills.[8] It may be especially helpful in sorting out the relationship between these parents' childhoods, characterized by rejection, abuse, and neglect, and their current parenting difficulties. A therapist who works with both the parents and children together may be helpful in altering the parents' neglectful responses to the children. This method, if at all successful, is slow, since it requires the parents to internalize new behaviors.

When indicated, drug and alcohol rehabilitation is most important. Alcohol abuse is surprisingly often missed as the primary problem in the entire spectrum of child protection. One should consider the possibility of drug and/or alcohol abuse in all cases, and then rule it in or out. Parental alcohol and/or drug abuse is present in 70-80% of all neglect cases.

Summary

Intervention may need to be considered prenatally if neglect of the fetus is evidenced by such activities as severe drug or alcohol abuse, denial of the pregnancy, failure to seek medical care or other activities covered in the next chapter. In the natal period, neglect may be evidenced by rejecting behavior toward the newborn, in actions and words. It must be remembered that significant elements of neglect often also exist in the categories generally seen as abuse: failure to thrive, psychological abuse, sexual and physical abuse.

The objectives of intervention in child neglect are to improve the parents' skill sufficiently so that the children's rights are protected. This means that the children must have adequate food, clothing and shelter, have reasonable access to medical care, partake of public education, and grow up healthy in body and spirit.

References

1.   American Humane Association. *Trends in Child Abuse and Neglect: A National Perspective.* Denver: American Humane Association, 1984.

2   Carrighar, S. *Moonlight at Midday.* New York: Pyramid Publications, 1967.

3.   Cantwell, H.B. "Child Protective Services Indicated in Parental Mismanagement of Childhood Diabetes." *Diabetes Educator,* 9(1984):41-43.

4   Egeland, B., and L.A. Stroufe. "Attachment and Early Maltreatment." *Child Development,* 26(1981):44.

5.   Polansky, N., et al. *Damaged Parents: An Anatomy of Child Neglect.* Chicago: The University of Chicago, 1981.

6.   Wood, S., et al. "Differences in Abusive, at Risk for Abuse, and Control Mothers' Descriptions of Normal Child Behavior." *Child Abuse & Neglect,* 19(1986):397-405.

7.   *Report on Parent Aide Intervention of Child Abuse Prevention Volunteers, Inc. (CAP).* Denver: Writer for Policy Research, 1985.

8.   Cantwell, H.B. "Psychiatric Implications of Child Neglect." *The Harvard Medical School Mental Health Letter,* 3(December 1986):5-6.

9. Recent Issues in Child Maltreatment

Donna A. Rosenberg

Introduction

This chapter focuses on two areas of child maltreatment that have received relatively recent attention and which will, no doubt, be further clarified in the years to come. The two areas are: (1) Munchausen Syndrome by Proxy and (2) Disregard for Fetal Development (Fetal Abuse).

Munchausen Syndrome by Proxy

DEFINITION AND BACKGROUND

A syndrome may be defined as a cluster of symptoms and/or signs which are circumstantially related. In Munchausen Syndrome by Proxy the following constitute the syndrome cluster:
   (1) There is illness in a child which is simulated (faked) and/or produced by a parent or someone who is *in loco parentis and*
   (2) There is presentation of the child for medical assessment and care, usually persistently, often resulting in multiple medical procedures *and*

(3) There is denial of knowledge as to the etiology of the child's illness *and*

(4) The acute symptoms and signs of illness abate when the child is separated from the perpetrator.

The definition specifically excludes physical abuse only, sexual abuse only, and non-organic failure to thrive only.

Munchausen Syndrome by Proxy was first formally described by Meadow[1] in 1977. He referred to it as "the hinterland of child abuse." The name of the syndrome is derived from Munchausen Syndrome, originally outlined by Asher[2] in 1951, when he described adults who gave "dramatic and untruthful" medical histories, accompanied by "apparent acute illness" most of which was ultimately found to be "made up of falsehoods . . . (the patients) having deceived an astounding number of other hospitals." Baron K.F.H. von Munchausen was an eighteenth century mercenary who, like the patients Asher described, had peripatetic habits and told vastly imaginative tales of his exploits. Thus, "the syndrome is respectfully dedicated to the baron and named after him."[2] In Munchausen Syndrome by Proxy, by contrast, the children become the victims of this type of adult behavior.

SAMPLE CASE

A case history will help to give the flavour of this syndrome. N.L. is a 9-year-old white male admitted to hospital because of a five day history of fever, chills and vomiting. His physical examination reveals a febrile child with a central venous catheter (Broviac) in place. His blood cultures, drawn at time of admission to the hospital, are positive for two enteric (bowel) organisms (*Enterobacter cloacae* and Group D *Enterococcus*). (This means that bacteria from the bowel somehow got into the bloodstream.) The child responds well to intravenous antibiotics, and no organic cause for the blood infection (polymicrobial bacteremia) can be established, despite thorough medical investigations. The Child Protection Team is consulted and extensive review reveals the following:

Past Medical History: N.L. was an only child with a history of 13 hospitalizations. He had been taken into this adoptive home at 8 weeks of age. The adoptive parents had waited seven years on a waiting list for a child.

The perinatal course was unremarkable. At age 1 3/4 years, there was an accidental ingestion of one of his mother's antihypertensive medications. He was observed as an outpatient and did well. However, 5 days later, there was "persistent lethargy" and multiple investigations were undertaken. No etiology for the lethargy was discovered.

At age 2 1/4 years, there was another drug overdose, where the mother said the child accidentally got into two other of her antihypertensive medications.   Mother gave the child Ipecac (an emetic) at home, without successfully inducing vomiting. She then took the child to hospital where he was again given Ipecac, this time vomiting 4 or 5 times. The child was briefly admitted to the hospital and did well.

At age 4 1/2 years, the mother began reporting episodic rapid heart rate in the child.   All medical investigations were repeatedly normal. Because of reported persistence of episodic, rapid heart rate, the child was eventually started on medications to control this (diagnosis was paroxysmal atrial tachycardia).   The mother kept daily records for months as to the severity, frequency, and duration of the rapid heart rate episodes in the child. He had them almost daily. At five years of age, he had a scheduled Holter monitoring (24-hour home heart monitor with a print-out) and mother's records reflect no rapid heart rate the day before, the day after, and the day of the Holter monitoring. There is no other time in 4 months of the mother's records examined that this length of symptom-free time occurred.

At 5 1/3 years of age, N.L. was admitted to hospital because of digoxin (the patient's heart medication) toxicity. The child had an electrocardiogram abnormality from very high levels of the drug in his blood. There was no explanation for this. Two weeks prior to this hospitalization, the child had been on the same prescribed dose of digoxin and his blood level, when routinely tested, had been in the therapeutic range. During the hospitalization, the child was successfuly treated, and the drug level in the blood fell to a low range.   The electrocardiogram returned to normal. Just prior to the time when he was meant to be discharged from hospital, he again suddenly developed those electrocardiogram abnormalities specifically from toxic levels of digoxin.

At 5 1/2 years of age, N.L. developed intermittent vomiting. The vomiting eventually took on a pattern of occurring every ten days to two weeks and was violent and unresponsive to powerful anti-emetic medications. Vomiting became an increasingly prominent symptom. The "episodic rapid heart rate" soon was mentioned only rarely by the mother.

By age 7 1/2 years, the vomiting had became a major chronic problem, causing significant school absence. The medical diagnosis was "cyclic vomiting." Prescription drugs for the episodic rapid heart were stopped without any problems ensuing. The "rapid heart rate" never recurred.

At age 9 1/3 years, after multiple hospital admissions because of a *history* of recurrent vomiting (only actually seen to vomit once), a central venous catheter was surgically implanted. (The child had poor peripheral venous access because of multiple peripheral intravenous lines.)

At age 9 1/2, the child was again re-admitted because of fever and found to have polymicrobial bacteremia with enteric organisms. (Multiple types of bowel organisms growing from the blood cultures.)

The Mother: Mrs. L. is a mid-thirties, attractive, pleasant and devoted-appearing mother. She is middle class, and is a Certified Medical Assistant working part-time in an obstetrics office. She herself was infertile as a result of a hysterectomy at age 18 (reason not known). Initially, she easily related details of the child's complex medical history. When the subject of impact of the child's illnesses on the family was broached by the interviewer, the mother's manner changed dramatically, from one of affability to one of distress, tearfulness and anger. She said she got little help from her spouse and would like a "trade-in" on her adoptive child.

The Father: Mr. L. is a 35-year-old man who works full time as a printer occupying himself otherwise with marathon running. He described the child's illnesses very vaguely, saying that he found them "annoying" and "sometimes trying."

The Child: N.L. is (when not acutely ill with sepsis) physically and developmentally normal. He says he feels best when he is in the hospital and is very familiar with medical terminology.

Assessment: N.L. was the victim of Munchausen Syndrome by Proxy. Falsefied illnesses include the "episodic rapid heart rate" (paroxysmal atrial tachycardia). Produced illnesses probably included digoxin poisoning, poisoning with various antihypertensives, polyuria from diuretic poisoning, chronic vomiting from poisoning with an emetic and blood infection (polymicrobial bacteremia) from injection of feces into the child's intravenous (IV) line. Some of the produced illnesses were potentially fatal.

In all, N.L. had had prescribed for him twenty-two different medications for the above fabricated and produced illnesses, had multiple investigations including spinal tap, multiple blood and urine tests, electroencephalogram, electrocardiograms, plain x-rays (chest, skull) x-rays with contrast (lower and upper gastrointestinal series, intravenous pyelogram), and computerized axial tomography of the head. He had 13 hospitalizations and had surgery twice for central venous catheter placement, as well as innumerable peripheral intravenous lines.

In hospital, the child recovered from his last episode of polymicrobial sepsis. The central venous catheter was removed. The parents were informed of the report to the county Department of Social Services.

The mother refused to discuss the situation any further and refused psychiatric care, as did the father. He denied believing anyone, including himself or his wife had produced the child's illnesses.

Neither criminal or civil court action was undertaken. The Department of Social Services, however, did try to work with the parents on a voluntary basis. This was not accepted by the parents.

The child, at home after discharge from hospital, remained entirely medically well. Months after his last hospitalization, his mother commented, "I want you to know that he doesn't have to go to foster care because nothing is going to happen to him."

Although N.L. has remained medically well, it is not always the case that attack on the child ceases after confronting the parents with the medical opinion as to the etiology of the child's illness.

FEATURES COMMONLY ASSOCIATED WITH MUNCHAUSEN SYNDROME BY PROXY

To date, the following are the features that have been noticed sufficiently in these cases as to make them items worthy of inquiry or observation.[3]

(1)   The perpetrator is in a medical-related line of work or has been medically trained.

(2)   The perpetrator is almost always the mother.

(3)   There is a history of Munchausen Syndrome in the perpetrator.

(4)   The perpetrator has a history of symptoms and signs similar to those which she simulates or produces in the child.

(5)   The perpetrator spends a lot of time on the hospital ward, and is "confidentially friendly" with hospital staff. She sometimes exhibits unusual familiarity with medical terminology.

(6)   The perpetrator may insist that she is the "only one" for whom the child will eat or swallow medicines, etc.

(7)   The perpetrator may be paradoxically calm in the face of the child's illness.

(8)   Most victims are infants and toddlers. The older the child, the more likely the possibility of the child knowing what is transpiring or actually colluding (consciously or unconsciously) with the perpetrator.

(9)   The diagnostic possibilities for the child's signs and symptoms become, with time, limited and of the rare type. Even then, the child's illness fits no known diagnostic possibility well. The doctor thinks he may be seeing a "never-before-described disease."

(10)   If the child's symptoms and signs appear to be consistent with a particular diagnosis and appropriate therapy is begun, the

"disease" may be refractory to conventional therapy for no apparent reason.

(11) In reviewing the child's medical records, multiple subspecialty consultations have been requested. Rarely is an unreserved organic diagnosis made.

(12) The spouse of the perpetrator is only peripherally involved.

(13) It is probably rare to find associated sexual abuse or "conventional" physical abuse. Failure to thrive may co-exist, but is usually the result of chronic illness produced by the perpetrator.

(14) Morbidity is 100%. (Either parent-induced or as a complication of medical intervention.)

(15) A perpetrator who starts out by simulating illness may then go on to produce illness in the child.

(16) Male and female children seem to be equally affected.

(17) There may be a history in a sibling of the child under investigation who has also been a victim of Munchausen Syndrome by Proxy.

Recommendations for the Medical Approach When the Diagnosis of Munchausen Syndrome by Proxy Is Suspected

(1) Take steps to protect the child immediately (considering there are reported deaths associated with the Syndrome, with death generally preceded by a protracted illness; there is a parent-induced morbidity rate of about 80%).

(2) Recognize that methods of simulating or producing illness are virtually limitless. Almost nothing is ridiculous or far-fetched. Especially when substance poisoning is suspected, "routine" laboratory toxicological screens will miss many offending agents. Decide which substances are suspected and obtain specific assays on the appropriate body fluid and/or exogenously administered fluid.

(3) Perform whatever diagnostic tests are possible to confirm diagnosis. This is useful medically and when subsequently working with the families and in court. Other professionals (crime labs, veterinarians, etc.) might be useful in aiding diagnosis.

(4) The hospital is a good place for a diagnostic evaluation. Have a specific strategy planned and coordinated with the rest of the medical, nursing and ancillary staff. Remember that child is not free of

risk merely by being in hospital (there is about a 70% chance of an illness being produced by a parent while the child is hospitalized).

(5) If the child is verbal, interview him or her individually. Diagnostic clues, "secrets" and the question of collusion if the child is older, should be sought.

(6) Scrupulous and legible documentation is vital. Attention to handling of laboratory specimens (chain of evidence) is most important.

(7) Check out the family medical history from other *medical* sources (do not just accept the history proffered by the family). Look for unusual illnesses in siblings of the patient, unusual illnesses in parents, etc. Check out the social and work histories, too.

(8) It is not recommended that the parents be permitted to change doctors when they don't accept the diagnosis. "Doctor-shopping" inevitably disrupts or terminates effective and consistent intervention. The parents will say to the doctor, "How can we work with you when you don't even trust us?" and then keep moving on until they find a doctor, ". . . we like. He tries to find out what's wrong with Mathilda, instead of blaming it on us just because he can't figure this out, like you did."

(9) If visits by the parents to the hospitalized child are to be supervised, the supervision should be by a medically experienced person. No food or drink should be brought in by the family.

(10) Psychiatric care should be made available to the parents immediately after disclosure because there is significant risk for maternal suicide attempts and emotional decompensation.

(11) The child should be psychiatrically and psychologically evaluated.

(12) Because of their complexity, cases are often referred to major medical centers. Ongoing communication with the referring doctor and with the department of social services in the referring location is most important.

(13) Be prepared to put in a lot of time. Major expenditures of time go to the family, social services, courts, police, coordinating medical staff and sorting out medical staff conflicts. Families are known to engage sympathies of medical personnel.

Working with the Social Services Department
and the Court in Cases of
Munchausen Syndrome by Proxy

(1) Report the suspected case immediately.

(2) When a diagnosis is made of Munchausen Syndrome by Proxy (MSBP), request ongoing, court-ordered supervision of the case. Trying to rehabilitate these situations without court order is fraught with pitfalls.

(3) Out of home placement of the child is prudent. The attack on the child does not necessarily cease following confrontation with the parents. There are at least a couple of reports where the parents have been confronted and the child sent home, only to be further attacked or killed.

(4) Request court-ordered, long-term psychiatric or psychologic evaluation and treatment. Limited evaluations give limited results, especially in patients with occult psychopathology who are highly sophisticated at deception. An evaluation by a developmental psychologist of the child-adult relationships may be useful. The DSM-III does not have a diagnostic code for MSBP. The underlying psychopathology of the perpetrator is not yet well characterized.

(5) Be prepared to go to court. Discuss the case with counsel before court convenes. Give attorneys, social workers, and judges articles on MSBP. Write the medical reports intended for courtroom use in lay language.

(6) If the mother is the perpetrator and the father is "uninvolved," recognize that returning the child home to both parents, with the father "supervising the situation" is an inadequate plan.

(7) Make it clear that the perpetrator who, so far, has only simulated illness in the child may go on to produce illness in the child, if there is no protection of the child. Simulation of illness and production of illness are not mutually exclusive.

Conclusion

Though Munchausen by Proxy has been characterized syndromatically, there is still very little clarification as to the underlying psychopathology in the perpetrator. Hopefully, this area will be better developed in the near future.

Disregard for Fetal Development (Fetal Abuse)

BACKGROUND

Although for a long time there has been recognition that some pregnant women undertake lifestyles or activities that may be harmful to the growing fetus, it is only recently that this issue has been seen as a facet of child abuse and neglect. Now, social workers, health care providers and the legal profession are becoming increasingly involved in these types of cases. There is, however, vast variability as to how these cases are assessed and handled by the involved professionals.

While recognizing the rights of the pregnant woman, including the right to privacy, one may still encounter situations in which the assault upon the developing fetus, either through substance abuse, mental illness, or medical neglect may appear so potentially morbid as to draw into analysis the issue of neglect of the unborn child and the rights of the unborn child.[4] The legal precedents to date as to a pregnant woman's rights when they are in opposition to the rights of an unborn child are summarized elsewhere.[4,5,6,7]

There has been limited civil court involvement in this matter to date, but it has included court-ordered Caesarian sections, court rulings that *in utero* drug exposure can be a form of child neglect, including a ruling that a child born addicted to heroin presents a *prima facie* case of abuse or neglect, a ruling that a child has a right to bring a negligence action against the mother for taking drugs during pregnancy, and a ruling that a child, who was a 5-month old fetus at the time of her prenatal injuries, was a legal person for purposes of maintaining, after her birth, an action against her mother for negligence during a driving incident.[4] We are also aware of a case in which the juvenile court has appointed a guardian ad litem to represent the best interests of a fetus. We are aware of only one case in which criminal (misdemeanor) charges were filed against a pregnant woman who allegedly abused amphetamines and caused her full-term newborn to be born brain-dead as a result.[8] Charges were subsequently dismissed.

Medical Approach to the Issue of
Disregard for Fetal Development

DEFINITIONS

In constructing an approach to this issue, the following definitions are pertinent:

fetus—A developing human, placenta-dependent for basic life requirements.

abuse—Disruption of structure and/or function (with respect to the fetus).

disregard for fetal development—*Risk of* disruption of structure and/or function in a developing human, placenta-dependent for basic life requirements.

"Disregard for fetal development" is considered a term preferable to "fetal abuse." Implicit in the definition of "Disregard for Fetal Development" are (a) that the fetus doesn't have to actually suffer the problem, but just has to be at great risk for it and (b) that cases of first trimester substance abuse or self-harming behavior, when the woman doesn't know she's pregnant, are not included if the woman desists from such activity when the pregnancy becomes known to her.

CASE ANALYSIS

Given that therapeutic abortion is a legal and a private matter, the flow-chart for case analysis begins there (Figure 9.1).

EVALUATING THE SIGNIFICANCE OF THE DANGER TO THE FETUS

Certainly, cases of possible disregard for fetal development fall along a broad spectrum of significance. Because of the consideration of the rights of the pregnant woman, only those cases that can truly be said to pose *significant* risk of *substantial* harm to the fetus should necessitate civil court involvement. Examples of substantial harm would be, but are not limited to, profound organ system anomaly or dysfunction including central nervous system disorder.

When assessing the significance of the risk to the fetus, these questions should be asked, with respect to *both* the fetus and the pregnant woman:

(a) What is the severity of the untreated outcome?

(b) What is the probability of that outcome?

Figure 9.1 Algorithmic Approach to Medical Decision-Making in Cases of Possible Disregard for Fetal Development

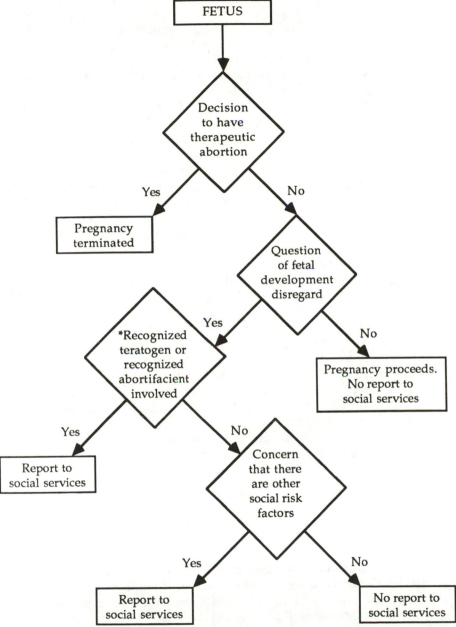

*Evidence that substance or activity in which woman is partaking causes significant fetal abnormalities or fetal death. Evidence must be established scientifically in peer review journals. Methodology of studies must be sound.

(c) What is the probability of success with the proposed intervention?

(d) What are the risks and consequences of the proposed intervention?

e) What are the alternatives?

Bross describes the interventions, based on an analysis of least restrictive alternatives which protective services may attempt in cases of disregard for fetal development. "All of the steps assume that adequate attempts at voluntary compliance have been undertaken:

1. Document prenatal behavior harmful to the child as a method of establishing a syndrome or pattern of conduct justifying immediate court action as soon as the child is born.
2. Ask the court to take jurisdiction over the unborn child, and to appoint a guardian ad litem for the unborn child.
3. Ask the court to order a social investigation of the family.
4. Ask the court to order a medical or psychiatric examination of the mother (or father).
5. Ask the court to order a medical regimen, following the application of informed consent principles and considering primarily procedures benign or beneficial to the mother.
6. Ask the court to order fetal monitoring or other intervention if, and only if, relatively benign to the mother.
7. The most restrictive alternative possible is an order of confinement. Involuntary confinement or restriction of physical activities creates special problems of right to travel, and special concerns of due process under law. While such a step could occur only under the most extraordinary of circumstances, involuntary evaluation and treatments do occur rather frequently in mental health cases and cannot be ruled out in some prenatal abuse cases."[4]

Conclusion

Disregard for fetal development is a relatively new concern for professionals in the area of child abuse and neglect.[9] Even if social service or court intervention is not undertaken, it must be remembered that the social situations of the pregnant women are often, though not invariably, very distressed and that these women have themselves often been victims of chronic abuse and neglect. Furthermore, the disregard for fetal development may foreshadow a diminished ability of the pregnant woman to care for the baby, once born.

References

1. Meadow, R. "Munchausen Syndrome by Proxy: The Hinterland of Child Abuse." *Lancet*, 2(1977):343-345.

2. Asher, R. "Munchausen Syndrome." *Lancet*, 1(1951):339-341.

3. Rosenberg, D.A. "Web of Deceit: A Literature Review of Munchausen Syndrome by Proxy." *Child Abuse & Neglect*, 11(1987):in presss.

4. Bross, D.C., and A. Meredyth. "Neglect of the Unborn Child: An Analysis Based on Law in the United States." *Child Abuse & Neglect*, 3(1979):643-650.

5. Bross, D.C. "Court-Ordered Intervention on Behalf of Unborn Children." *Children's Legal Rights Journal*, 7(1986):11-15.

6. Doudera, E.A. "Fetal Rights? It Depends," *Trial*, 39(April 1983):38-39.

7. Myers, J.E.B. "Abuse and Neglect of the Unborn: Can the State Intervene?" *Duquesne Law Review*, 23(1984):1-76.

8. "Mom's Drug Use Killed Baby, DA Charges," *Denver Post*, October 2, 1986:11A; "Emotional Debate Erupts in Charge of Drug Abuse to Fetus." *Denver Post*, October 5, 1986.

9. Landwirth, J. "Fetal Abuse and Neglect: An Emerging Controversy." *Pediatrics*, 79(1987):508-514.

10. Nursing Evaluation and Treatment Planning*

Janet T. McCleery and Belina J. Pinyerd

Introduction

The nurse assumes a vital role as a member of the multi-disciplinary child protection team. Due to the nurse's presence in both health care institutions and social services, the nurse is in an ideal position to assess the parent-child dyad. Detection of child abuse and/or neglect depends upon the nurse considering that diagnosis whenever children are seen for health care in any practice setting.[1] Prevention and early detection are two of the nurse's major roles in addressing the problem of child abuse.[2]

Nurses who care for children and their families must be knowledgeable about theories that explain relationships between social events in the environment and subsequent health status.[3] When there are abusive or neglectful elements in the child's life that are detrimental to the child's well-being, the nurse must intervene. The nurse may be responsible not only for identification and treatment of the abused child and the family but may also be involved in the coordination of care provided. As a member of the multidisciplinary team, the nurse assists in planning and implementing the health care, based on the nursing assessment, the medical diagnosis, and the needs of the child and family.

As all 50 states have enacted legislation mandating reporting of abuse, the nurse has a legal as well as an ethical responsibility to communicate suspicious findings to the proper authorities. He or she is required to share normal and confidential information needed for the investigative process with child protection and law enforcement agencies. To ensure a healthy and honest relationship with the family, the nurse must inform them of the dual role: that of family advocate as well as a child protector.

It is important that the nurse not allow personal attachments or prejudices to interfere with reporting of the incident or evaluation and treatment of the child. This may be in conflict with cultural attitudes that make it difficult to believe that parents would harm their children.[4] When the nurse has identified the suspected abuse, referral must be made to the local child protection agency. The agency may then suggest an extensive evaluation by a local physician or child protection team. On the other hand, the nurse who is a member of an organized child protection team will function somewhat differently with respect to the level of involvement. Responsibilities may include developmental assessment or observations of family interaction. The following guidelines will be helpful.

Establish Suitable Environment for Evaluation

The nurse is often the first professional to interact with the abused child and the family. Despite the extent of the injuries and one's possible inclination to an emotional reaction, it is imperative that the nurse be calm, objective, and prudent.

The child and family should be made to feel physically and emotionally as comfortable as possible during the evaluation process. Find a room that is private and quiet, preferably separate from the emergency room or acute care setting. If the suspected abuse situation is identified during a routine check-up or at the time of unrelated emergency treatment, an attempt should be made to transfer the family to a more suitable environment. This area should provide adequate space for all members of the family to be comfortably seated and the children to have space to play. The nurse should also be seated during the evaluation process so as not to appear hurried.

Explain Assessment Process to Child and Family

Whether the child has been a victim of physical or sexual abuse or neglect, the child and family should be prepared for the evaluation. Explain your concern about the child's injuries and that a physical exam is necessary, just as in any visit for routine health care. The term "abuse" should never be used to justify the evaluation. As these events are being explained, it is recommended that the child remain fully clothed and not be undressed and gowned until the physical exam is imminent. The child may see and manipulate the equipment to be used and be encouraged to ask questions. Explain that certain laboratory tests may be needed to diagnose any possible problems. These may include blood, urine or stool samples, cultures, or x-rays. The nurse is usually the professional in charge of collecting and transporting all specimens to the laboratory. The specimens must clearly be labeled and the name of the person transporting the specimens must be documented. This information may be later needed for court.

Collect Past Health Information

General health information should be obtained at the time of the evaluation. Sources of information include the parents, medical records, or the child. This data should include the following information on the family:

-name of current primary health care provider
-current and past health status of parents and siblings
-prior visits of siblings for trauma
-history of prior contact with community agencies such as public health, child protection service, public welfare, law enforcement, etc.

A medical history of the child being evaluated should include:
-known allergies
-chronic illnesses
-acute illnesses
-recurrent illnesses
-developmental status
-current medications
-history of previous trauma
-history of previous hospitalizations
-immunization status

This information will provide a profile on how the family utilizes community resources and values health. Future intervention can be directed to and coordinated with the agencies already involved with the family. Furthermore, this information will assist the nurse in the identification of additional care needs of the child that are not directly related to the abusive incident. For example, a child who has a developmental delay may need an extensive developmental assessment with possible referral for specialized education.

Observe Interaction of Family Members

While collecting the health data, valuable information can be obtained through direct observation of the family. The nurse should note the behavioral patterns of those present, non-verbal communications, and abilities for conflict resolution. Note should be made regarding:
    (1) the child's reaction to parents and other adults, to procedures, and to developmentally appropriate toys;
    (2) the parents' reaction to health professionals, to the child, and the interview process;
    (3) parent-child interaction, with the focus being on the assessment of parental empathy toward the child and appropriateness of expectations.[5]
Note who is the main historian and if the information provided by various family members is consistent. Note any conflict between the parents, and the child's reaction to it. The nurse must also be aware of his or her own non-verbal cues to the family which interfere with or influence the interview.

Perform Physical Examination

The nurse may encounter an abused or neglected child in any of the following circumstances:
    -As a public health nurse during a routine home visit.
    -As a clinic, office, or emergency room nurse when a child presents with an injury.
    -As a nurse practitioner during a well-child visit.
    -As a staff nurse providing care to a hospitalized child.
    -As a school nurse.

The nursing assessment in these situations may or may not include a physical examination. Often the nursing role is limited to an interview, because a complete medical evaluation will be conducted subsequently. Summaries of physical findings relevant to different forms of abuse are found in this section in the chapters on physical abuse, sexual abuse, neglect, non-organic failure to thrive, and recent forms of child maltreatment.

Document Information Obtained and Observations Made

Clear, accurate, and comprehensive observations about the child and family should be included in the medical record and in the report sent to the child protection agency. Many abused children are also neglected and socially deprived. Therefore, each child should be formally evaluated for developmental status and physical growth, and a summary of these findings should be a part of the record. A growth chart (including weight, length, head circumference, and weight/length ratio) should also be completed, with all known past measurements also plotted. In measuring the children, all equipment should be properly calibrated on a regular basis. A diagnosis of failure-to-thrive or short stature could be overlooked or a medical evaluation conducted needlessly because of inaccurate measurements or erroneous plotting on the growth charts.

All information should be recorded formally for the medical record, but in clear, non-technical terms for the community professionals. Record details of observed events, rather than simply an overall impression. For example, instead of recording "the mother is inappropriate," record exactly what you observe: "Mother places infant on exam table, props the bottle, and leaves room to smoke cigarette."

It is recommended that standardized forms be used in the collection and documentation of information (see sample in appendix). Use of such forms may be helpful in obviating the need for appearances in court. They also help to delineate the roles of the various team members and ensure that all information is included, especially since the nurse may not be required to testify for many months. There should also be an institutional protocol for the reporting of suspected child abuse and neglect. The protocol information should be disseminated in both written form and through in-service education. Nursing should take both an active role in the development of the protocols and act as a resource for both institutional staff and community agencies.

Reports and Testimony

Reporting statutes very clearly state that all health care professionals are mandated to report suspected cases of child abuse and neglect. Occasionally there may be disagreement between professionals as to whether or not the situation should be reported to the child protection agency. For example, a child is left in a bed next to an open window without screening and falls out of the window and sustains a skull fracture. Is this neglect? Or, a child allegedly falls off the couch and sustains a spiral fracture of the humerus. Is this abuse? If there is suspicion in the mind of any one of the professionals, the family should be reported to the child protection agency, despite disagreement among the team members. It is wiser to report and find that abuse was unsubstantiated than to fail to report and potentially have the child return with a more serious injury. Before any report is made, however, there should be ongoing communication between all the professionals involved.

The nurse may be required to appear in court and provide testimony concerning cases of child abuse or neglect. If the nurse is to be admitted as an expert witness, he will need to provide testimony about his professional qualifications, the details of the case, and his opinion.

If subpoenaed to court for the first time, the nurse is advised to follow the guidelines below in presenting as a witness:

1. Review one of the many educational films available to health care professionals regarding court testimony.
2. Contact a nurse with experience in court procedures who can provide advice.
3. Review the medical records and other data, such as photographs and x-rays.
4. Review all the information with other team members who are also involved in the case.
5. Contact the attorney who issued the subpoena to discuss the testimony.
6. Tour the courtroom prior to the court date and become familiar with the setting.

Treatment and Follow-up Care

Depending on the practice setting, the role of the nurse in treatment of child abuse cases may vary. For example, the nurse practitioner in a small community health department may gather social and health information, perform the physical assessment, report the incident, and coordinate the treatment plan. The nurse practitioner in a large regional pediatric center may act as a liaison and educator for parents and community professionals.

During the treatment of the acute injuries related to the abusive incident, the nurse:

-provides emotional support to the child and family during the interview and physical examination.

-assists in the treatment of the acute injury.

-clarifies procedures that may have been ill-explained or confusing to the child and the family.

The nurse may also have a central role in coordination of care, referring the family to such agencies as Parents Anonymous, Head Start, infant stimulation programs, food and formula supplement programs, mental health agencies, child care facilities, and medical facilities for well-child care. The nurse may actually assist the family in making these appointments, as these procedures may be complex or intimidating.

At follow-up visits, the treatment plan should be reviewed and modified, if necessary, based on the current status of the child and family. Siblings may need to be included in the treatment plan as well, even if they were not identified victims. The nurse practitioner on the team may become the primary health care provider for the siblings while the physician cares for the identified abused child who may have moderate to severe health problems subsequent to the abuse.

A major component of the treatment and follow-up plan is the prevention of further injury to any child in the family. The nurse is in an ideal position to educate the community. Some program suggestions include:

-Child care classes at local junior and senior high schools.

-Opportunities for junior and senior high school students to work, with supervision, in local child care centers.

-Workshops on child care to community groups.

-Participation in preceptorship programs for nursing and medical students.

-Organization of local and regional parenting fairs.

-A column in the local newspaper on child care.

-Interviews over radio and television on child care issues.

-Visit with families one to two weeks after the birth of a baby, with ongoing support of new parents and parents under stress.

-Establishment of neighborhood respite care centers for children at risk for abuse.

-Initiation of child assault prevention program.

-Participation in the legislative process on child health and welfare issues, locally and nationally.

Research

The nurse on the child protection team may initiate research based on questions raised in the practice setting or collaborate on research projects with other members of the multidisciplinary team. Consulting an experienced researcher is always useful while devising the study design. The nurse must keep abreast of current trends in practice and research. When reviewing journal articles that suggest a change from current practice, it is prudent to first assess the soundness of the study's methodology.

Summary

The nurse as a result of training and experience in physical and emotional disabilities brings unique skills to the child protection team. Furthermore, because child abuse and neglect are ubiquitous problems but there is currently not an adequate number of multidisciplinary teams to assess these problems, the nurse may certainly take on the role of organizing and administering the local child protection team.

Note

* The time devoted to the development of this chapter was funded in part by the Columbus Children's Hospital Abuse Program and the Clinical Study Center, grant number 74366. The authors also wish to thank Theresa Honnold for her clerical support.

References

1.   Thomas, J.N. "Yes, You Can Help a Sexually Abused Child." *RN,* 43(1980):23-29.

2.   Bridges, C.L. "The Nurse's Evaluation" in: *The Child Protection Team Handbook.* B.D. Schmitt (Ed.). New York: Garland STPM Press, 1978.

3.   Withrow, C., and J.W. Fleming. "Pediatric Social Illness: A Challenge to Nurses." *Issues in Comprehensive Pediatric Nursing,* 6(1983):261-275.

4.   Walles, J. "Non-Accidental Injury" *Nursing Mirror,* 10(1983):20-22.

5.   Bridges, C.L.   "The Nurse's Evaluation." *The Child Protection Team Handbook.* B.D. Schmitt (Ed.). New York: Garland STPM Press, 1978.

Further Readings

Bergerson, S. "Charting with a Jury in Mind." *Nursing Life,* 2(1982):30-37.

Burgess, A., A.N. Groth, L. Holmstrom, S. Sgroi. *Sexual Assault of Children and Adolescents.* Lexington, Mass.: Lexington Books, 1982.

Campbell, J., and J. Humphreys. *Nursing Care of Victims of Family Violence.* Reston, Va.: Reston Publishing Co., 1984.

Committee on Standards of Child Health Care. *Standards of Child Health Care.* Chicago: American Academy of Pediatrics, 1972.

Foster, P.H., A. Davis, J.M. Whitworth, R. Skinner. "Medical Foster Care—An Alternative Nursing Practice." *Maternal-Child Nursing,* 7(1982):245-248.

Heilberg, J. "Documentation of Child Abuse." *American Journal of Nursing,* 83(1983):236-239.

Heindl, M.C. "Symposium on Child Abuse and Neglect." *The Nursing Clinics of North America,* 16(1981):101-188.

Rosenberg, N.M., S. Meyers, and N. Shackleton. "Prediction of Child Abuse in an Ambulatory Setting." *Pediatrics,* 70(1982):879-882.

APPENDIX 10.1

Child's Name _____

Medical Record # _____

CHILD ABUSE PROGRAM

EDUCATION · SERVICE · RESEARCH · PREVENTION

NURSING ASSESSMENT—NON-ORGANIC FAILURE-TO-THRIVE

Observation of parent*-child interaction—Observed for _____ minutes

_____

Observation of parent care of child _____

Observation of parent feeding skills _____

Parent's reaction to diagnosis

_____ hostile   _____ demonstrates willingness to
                                                 cooperate

_____ denial   _____ demonstrates concern for baby's
                                                 well-being

_____ other _____

Parent's response to teaching

_____ eager to learn   _____ verbalizes understanding

_____ disinterested—ignores suggestions   _____ demonstrates skills well

_____ available for teaching   _____ "Helping Hands" provided

_____ unavailable for teaching   _____ other _____

Additional information

_____ welcomes P.H.N.   _____ parent can read and write

_____ refuses P.H.N.   _____ parent cannot read or write

_____ other _____

Recommendations _____

_____

Guidelines for Completing Form

Include observations such as those listed below
under each heading.

1. Observations of parent-child interaction
   —name by which parents refer to baby
   —name by which parents call baby when visiting
   —when visiting together, describe behavior of
     both parents toward baby and toward each other
   —baby's response to parents
     eye contact
     verbalization   number of times during
     touching   given time period
   —if not visiting, does the parent call to obtain
     information regarding the child

2. Observation of parent care of child
   —length of visit
   —frequency of visit
   —where is baby during visit (most of the time)
     ____bed ____out of bed (explain) ____physical
     contact with parent
   —parent volunteers to give care
     ____feed ____change diapers ____bathe
   —parent refuses to provide care (i.e., leaves room
     when meal time)

3. Feeding skills
   —position parent holds baby during feedings
   —eye contact during feedings
   —burps—when and how (explain techniques)

*or primary caretaker

Signature _____ Title _____ Date _____

Print Name _____

Confidential: For Professional Use Only

Use Black Ink

APPENDIX 10.2

Child's Name _____

Medical Record # _____

NUTRITIONAL SUMMARY OF NON-ORGANIC FAILURE-TO-THRIVE

NUTRITIONAL STATUS UPON ADMISSION

				Date	**Test**	**Result**
Adm Wt (kg)	_____	,	_____ %			
Adm length (cm)	_____	,	_____ %	_____	Hgb (gm/dl)	_____
Head Circ (cm)	_____	,	_____ %	_____	Hct (%)	_____
Desirable Wt (kg)	_____	(50% for length)		_____	Alb (gm/dl)	_____

*Chronological age corrected for _____ months of prematurity?

DIETARY HISTORY PRIOR TO ADMISSION

Source of Information _____

Description of Diet _____

_____

ESTIMATED INTAKE PER DAY

Total _____ ,   Kcal/kg _____ ,

Gm Protein/kg _____ ,   Ml Fluid/kg _____

Feeding Problems or Intolerances _____

FEEDING TECHNIQUES

_____

HOSPITAL COURSE

Description of Diet and Tolerance in Hospital _____

_____

Estimated Energy needs (kcal)/kgm/day _____   Protein Needs (gm)/kgm/day _____

Actual Energy Intake (kcal)/kgm/day _____   Protein Intake (gm)/kgm/day _____

Expected Rate of Weight Gain (gm/day) _____

Actual Rate of Weight Gain (gm/day) _____   Days Averaged _____

ASSESSMENT

_____

_____

NUTRITION EDUCATION PROVIDED

_____

Confidential: For Professional Use Only

Use Black Ink Only

Signature _____ Title _____ Date _____

Print Name _____

APPENDIX 10.3

Child's Name_____

Medical Record #_____

CHILD ABUSE PROGRAM

EDUCATION · SERVICE · RESEARCH · PREVENTION

DEVELOPMENTAL SUMMARY OF NON-ORGANIC
FAILURE-TO-THRIVE

Patient's developmental status upon admission:

_____Denver _____Bayley _____Michigan Assessment _____Portage

_____Other_____

Gross motor_____   Language_____

Fine motor_____   Social/Emotional_____

Cognition_____   Self-Care_____

Bayley mental_____   Bayley motor_____

Comments_____

_____

Chronological age corrected for _____ months of prematurity?

Changes noted in patient's development during hospitalization:

_____Denver _____Bayley _____Michigan Assessment _____Portage

_____Other_____

_____Gross motor   _____Language

_____Fine motor   _____Social/Emotional

_____Cognition   _____Self-Care

_____Bayley mental   _____Bayley motor

Summary of Changes_____

_____

Discharge Plans

_____Referral to community program

　　　specific program_____

_____Home instruction with parent

_____Parent did not participate in developmental stimulation

_____Reassess Development_____

_____Refer for Additional Psych. Services_____(date)_____

Comments_____

_____

_____ _____ _____
Signature   Title   Date

_____
Print Name

Confidential: For Professional Use Only
Use Black Ink

11. Social Work Evaluation and the Family Assessment

Elizabeth Elmer and Barbara S. Schultz

Introduction

The social worker has a pivotal role on the child protection team. The purpose of this chapter is to define this role. The setting determines to some extent how the team and each of its members functions. Nevertheless, a generic core is discernible that seems to apply to the social work role whatever the outer differences in setting. This chapter focuses on this core of activity in the context of the team.

Not all cases of suspected abuse are reviewed by an multi-disciplinary team. In a large metropolitan area where reported abuse cases number in the hundreds, such review is almost impossible. (As noted by Motz,[1] some counties have developed a system of mini-teams that review cases and select those to be presented to the full team membership.) Other cases may not come up for team evaluation because they are dismissed at intake. The opposite situation may occur when the child appears to be in such immediate danger that a court hearing is sought at once leaving no time for team consultation. Finally, reluctance to report suspected abuse is unfortunately still a common reason that cases are not discussed at team meetings. This is especially true of abused children who are patients of private physicians, but private social agencies also have been known not to report. The agency may continue to provide regular services or may pull in additional services once abuse is suspected. While the quality of service may be acceptable, even excellent, the situation loses the advantages of consideration by a group of uninvolved professionals from a variety of backgrounds. In general, the cases commonly reviewed by child protection teams are the critical ones that present knotty problems of diagnosis, management, or community involvement.[2]

Hazards Confronting the Social Worker

Before proceeding, we need to be aware of certain obstacles in the performance of assigned social work duties. In working with child abuse, the worker may encounter a series of double binds and some reactions to status.[3] As used in this chapter, the double bind refers to contradictory but fairly equal constraints on the individual, permitting no clear-cut resolution and no escape from the dilemma. A perennial example drawn from child abuse work is the social worker's conflict between revulsion toward the caretaker who inflicts injury on a helpless child and the need to understand and empathize with the human being within the parent shell. The double bind is made more potent by the realization that we cannot really help the child without helping the parents, and this requires a genuine feeling of respect and affection. Until we learn the act of caring, as so well delineated by Perlman,[4] this dilemma is ever ready to engulf even the most seasoned social worker.

The service network gives rise to another kind of double bind. Although officially we deplore the redundancy of certain customs or regulations, in actuality little effort may be addressed to eliminating the repetitions. Instead, we allow the clients to shoulder the burden of the double bind. An example is the private agency that has developed a relationship with a client, discovered abuse, and reported it to the designated public protective agency. The information collected by the private agency over several weeks or months may then be gathered all over again, this time by the worker from the public agency. This may also work in reverse, as when the public agency refers a case to the private agency and information is again re-gathered, this time by the social worker in the private agency. Very often, a case is allowed simply to drift into a new format without the thoughtful planning and interpretation that could ease the transition and make it a positive experience for the clients.

Along with double bind dilemmas, the social worker, probably more than members of other professionals, may be sensitive to questions of professional status. Especially this is true of the worker from a purely social work agency such as child protection services who serves on a multidisciplinary team that includes physicians. Hand in hand with learning medicine the student physician learns how to exercise authority, a role that has been reinforced by society's willingness to confer on the doctor the status of final authority in many matters. Small wonder that the social worker from the one-discipline agency may worry about his or her standing in the group. When the trepidation spills over into hesitation to express an opinion, the utility of the team may be reduced.

Regardless of the social worker's perceptions of status differences, a worker may be so intent on group cohesion that he or she cannot express an opinion contrary to that of the majority.[5] Although the authors note that any member of the group may act in this manner, the social worker appears an especially likely candidate. We perceive the traditional social work role as more focused on healing than on confrontation, more on comforting than on raising questions.

The obstacles mentioned by no means exhaust the list. The purpose in presenting them is to alert the social worker to some of the difficulties that will affect vigorous participation in the team unless they are brought under the conscious control of the individual worker.

Theoretical Model

In addition to obstacles and double binds, the social worker attached to a team will find many rewards. One gratifying experience is to help team members relate to a theoretical model that has been previously selected. A model can provide an integrative system for weaving together the masses of data that are often accumulated in the assessment of just one situation. When used consistently over time, a model can highlight areas where knowledge is thin, for example, reliance on folk medicine among certain ethnic groups. Since the practice of folk medicine may be counter to traditional health practices in majority groups, it is important for the team to have access to such knowledge when dealing with child abuse.

There are other values in finding and utilizing an acceptable theoretical model: (1) it can help the members organize around a set of known, inter-related concepts; (2) the model implies the nature of information to be gathered; (3) it suggests avenues for possible intervention or treatment; and (4) it provides data useful for preventive efforts. Strangely, although much good material exists in the area of team (or group) process, there is little evidence to suggest adoption of a theoretical model by teams. We believe that using such a model could facilitate group process by reconciling, in an interactional system, divergent viewpoints as to etiology, e.g., psychological disturbance in the parents, the abuse-eliciting child, stressful forces in society, cultural values such as emphasis on violence, etc.[6]

The social worker's role in relation to the model is to be familiar with its elements and to keep it alive with the other team members as cases are discussed. This is compatible with one of the established roles of the social worker, which is to be in touch with a variety of resources such as legal, educational, housing, in order to help the system "reach out and incorporate the client."[7]

Current interactional models[8,9,10] stem from Bronfenbrenner;[11] which model is chosen is less important than the use of one to guide team activities. For purposes of illustration we will briefly discuss Parke's social interactional framework. As shown in Figure 11.1, variables at different levels of abstraction—family, community, and culture—interact with each other and also with the child victim. The older concept that child abuse is a unidirectional phenomenon has given way to a multifactoral explanation. Effects may be direct as when a father who believes strongly in corporal punishment disciplines his son with more than usual vigor and the child is injured. Or the effects may be indirect as when a father berates his wife, who takes out her anger on the three year old.

An example of how the culture influences the community, then the family, concerns the provision of day care in the United States. Prior to World War II, day care was almost non-existent. Cultural beliefs held that women's place was in the home, and that young children belonged strictly with their mothers. With the onset of World War II, thousands of women began working outside the home; the need for day care became acute and communities had to provide this resource, helped along by various governmental units. When the war ended, most of the day care resources evaporated and the old beliefs regarding the place of women and young children again took hold. But then, the element of communism was introduced: if government had a hand in rearing young children, we would be shifting in the direction of communistic groups and our traditions would be wiped out. Thus, families who had come to depend on outside child care (community resources) were forced to find makeshift arrangements because of the lack of resources caused by the fear of communist influence (the culture). Knowledge of how family, culture, and community have interacted over time can help team members catch current trends important for enlightened case management.

For an interactional model to be useful to the members of the team, each should take responsibility for gathering and presenting information in specific areas. Depending upon the professional make-up of the team and the complexity of a particular case, this responsibility may shift, but generally, it is the social worker who provides material

Figure 11.1 A Social Interactional Model of Child Abuse

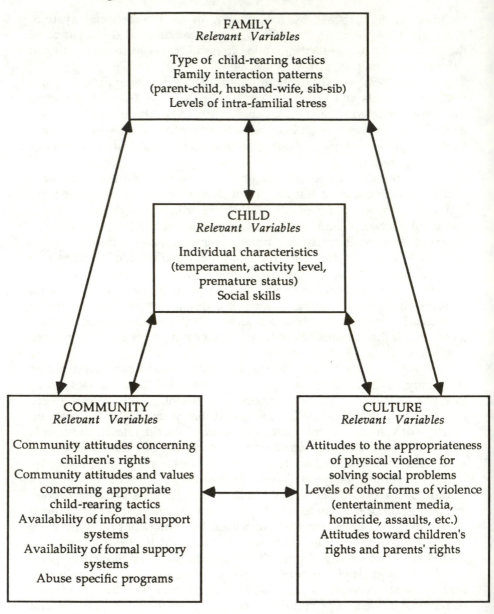

FAMILY
Relevant Variables

Type of child-rearing tactics
Family interaction patterns
(parent-child, husband-wife, sib-sib)
Levels of intra-familial stress

CHILD
Relevant Variables

Individual characteristics
(temperament, activity level,
premature status)
Social skills

COMMUNITY
Relevant Variables

Community attitudes concerning
children's rights
Community attitudes and values
concerning appropriate
child-rearing tactics
Availability of informal support
systems
Availability of formal suppory
systems
Abuse specific programs

CULTURE
Relevant Variables

Attitudes to the appropriateness
of physical violence for
solving social problems
Levels of other forms of violence
(entertainment media,
homicide, assaults, etc.)
Attitudes toward children's
rights and parents' rights

about the parents and the child. Following are suggested guidelines for securing that information. Considering the current increased reporting of child abuse and neglect and the concomitant financial restraints on hiring staff, these tasks may be somewhat burdensome. The goal should be funding adequate to carry out the job without compromising quality.

Evaluating the Parents

The immediate concern in beginning any family assessment is the safety of the child. In cases reported to a public child welfare agency, it is the responsibility of that staff to assess the child's safety. Removal of the child from the parental home will be determined by data from the referring source, consistency of explanation of injuries with medical evidence, acknowledgement of abuse or neglect, parent willingness to accept service, and the child's viewpoint (when age appropriate).

Since the mid 1960s, when recognition of child abuse and neglect as a national problem accelerated, there has been debate as to the viability of one social worker doing the investigation of the report, the family assessment, and the treatment.[12,13,14] It is not the purpose of this chapter to take a position on that issue but to give some suggestions to any social worker whose responsibility it is to complete a family assessment in a suspected child abuse case.

The social worker's first meeting with the parent(s) can occur in a variety of settings, for example, at the parents' home or an office. The worker's ability to refrain from accusing the parents of abuse but to clearly delineate the concerns about the child is more important than the setting. Parents will have a wide range of responses to this initial meeting but it seems safe to say that they will, in one way or another, be fearful of what is to follow. An exploration with the parents, and where age appropriate, the child, of the initial complaint is needed. The discussion must move beyond this point, if not in the initial interview, in subsequent ones, to gain sufficient information to develop the treatment plan. Where more than one caretaker exists it may be advisable to have separate interviews as well as a joint session.

State child abuse laws have defined time periods in which investigations must be completed. Meddin et al.[15] remind us that the assessment period, one of crisis, is a crucial one for giving service. This is an important point since it is possible under the pressure of investigatory issues to neglect to offer help.

The willingness and ability of parents to share their life story will vary but the worker needs a foundation, a place to start understanding. The process of sharing information can be the first step in establishing a trusting relationship, albeit under difficult circumstances for both parties. The mutual impression made at this point will be remembered as the case work proceeds. Many good psychosocial history outlines exist, but there are certain basic categories to be covered:

> *Identifying Information*: names, birth dates, race, religious affiliations, marital status, household composition.
>
> *Family of Origin*: factual and affective description; genogram with or without participation of parents; separations and placement out of home; patterns of discipline; nurturing atmosphere; education and work history; finances and accessibility to resources; social patterns and cultural influences; chemical abuse; psychiatric problems; conflict with the law.
>
> *Nuclear Family*: All of the areas suggested under "Identifying Information" and "Family of Origin" plus friendship patterns; social activities; nature of relationships; available support including individuals and organized and informal groups; willingness to use support; skills and hobbies; physical description, dress, mannerisms, eye contact; verbal skills and body language; affect during interviews; how parents impress the worker.

HEALTH HISTORY

A comprehensive health history of the parents and the children is another necessary component to completing a family assessment. Maltreating families are known to have poor physical health, and economic strains cause personal health care to deteriorate. A birth and pregnancy history for each child in the family but especially for the index child should be taken.

> *Details of pregnancy and delivery*: planned or unplanned pregnancy; mother's feeling about, and support by the biological father, prenatal care; preparation for childbirth, parenting classes; drug use during pregnancy, either prescribed or not; nutritional status, and smoking; labor: duration, complications, medication, support; where was baby delivered; special care required for infant.
>
> *Information about post-partum*: when did parent(s) see, hold the child; how did baby look, seem to parent(s); where did mother go upon discharge; any available support, familial or agency; when was mother able to return to normal activities; anything the parent(s) might recall about this period of their life that is significant to them.

ENVIRONMENTAL ASSESSMENT

A home visit will add additional valuable data about the family's environment, including the adequacy and quality of housing, neighborhood description, transportation availability, and recreational opportunities.

COLLATERAL INFORMATION

The legal mandate of the social worker's agency will determine the capacity to gather collateral data. Where written permission of the parents is required to secure information from other agencies or individuals, it should, of course, be secured. Even if written permission is not required, it would seem responsible, except in unusual circumstances, to inform the parents of these contacts. A professional judgment must be made as to the appropriateness of the contact where neighbors, other family and friends are involved. Generally, contact with schools, mental health agencies, family agencies, and private therapists are advisable. A good rapport with these resources during the assessment period will be helpful as a multi-service treatment plan is developed for the family.

Evaluating the Child

The family affair of child abuse and neglect reminds us that the child brings certain characteristics and complications to the situation. Evaluations from child specialists are helpful during the assessment period but the reality is that they may not be available. Social workers, through academic work and in-service training, need to equip themselves with knowledge about child development. A sense of the child's growth will have been learned from the parents and collateral sources, but the social worker must add his or her own impressions. For children under age five, plotting height and weight progress on a standardized chart is recommended.

Most of the factual information about the young child will come from adults but the social worker's interviews directly with the child will add another dimension. Depending upon the severity and nature of the crisis, the initial interview with the child may, of necessity, focus on the incident that precipitated the report. Even in these difficult circumstances, it will be possible for the social worker to gather some impressions about the child's development. Is he pseudomature, delayed in language, accelerated in gross motor skills, or perhaps a survival child who seems developmentally on track despite living in adverse circumstances? With subsequent contacts, the worker will be able to increase the depth of his or her knowledge of the child and perhaps find it necessary to rethink initial impressions.

Temperamental characteristics of the child are factors to consider in the context of abuse and neglect. Is there a match between the parents and the child, or do they seem out of step with each other? We all know young children who are difficult to care for from the outset because of colic, high energy levels, piercing cries, fussy food preferences. The worker's sense of the child and of the parents' reaction to his temperament helps put the worker in the parents' shoes and adds a sense of reality to the situation. If the child has physical handicaps or intellectual limitations the parents will be faced with additional demands on their personal and social resources.

For the older child, peer relationships and extended family relationships should be examined as well as the role of significant others in the child's life. Information about the child's school experience can yield data in these areas as well as an estimate of intellectual development and hobbies, interests, and special skills. For the adolescent a number of areas in the psychosocial history that are relevant to adults are applicable. One should especially note chemical abuse of any kind, difficulty with the law, and truancy. As with the parent evaluation, the child's evaluation material should be brought to the team discussion as a course of treatment is devised.

Family Interaction

If circumstances permit, an interactional session with parent(s) and child is advisable. Even when a child has been placed in protective custody, it may be possible to hold such a session. From this session the worker will begin to identify both positive and negative ways the parents relate to one another, how they relate to the child, and how siblings interact.

Burgess[16] reports that abusive mothers react less positively with other family members than mothers in control families and that their responses are more negative. Abusing fathers were found to direct verbal and physical responses in a more positive fashion than abusing mothers. "Abuse and neglect do not occur in a vacuum. They happen within a social matrix and that social matrix consists largely of the recurring transactions taking place between various members of the family. While it is certainly true that abuse and neglect occur within a broader historical and cultural context tolerant of aggressive behavior, these dysfunctional patterns are more immediately traceable to contingency histories within the family itself."[17]

Knowledge of Interacting Variables and Effects

On the whole, mental health professionals are more familiar with family dynamics than with the identification and interplay of community and cultural influences with each other and with the family. This is probably a matter of selective inattention, as the essential elements of both community and culture are far from novel. We recommend that the social worker on the team ensure that these elements are included in case discussions.

With reference to the community, the following variables are relevant in evaluating individual cases: the prevailing economic situation, which affects the quality and reliability of employment; and attitudes concerning the rights of children and institutionalized ways to carry these out, e.g., protected play space and child-size equipment in public housing. The lack of these may mean that children are inadvertently exposed to danger through alleged parental neglect. Other questions concern the accessibility and affordability of health care facilities and the availability of informal support systems such as mothers' groups or organizations of single parents. How does the community promulgate its child-rearing values—through law enforcement or through education and outreach? These kinds of general influences form the context of child care in the community; the team needs to know the specific ways these influences interweave with the needs and characteristics of the family and the prevailing cultural beliefs and values.

Compared to community influences, the evaluation of cultural influences is more difficult, if only because of the higher level of abstraction that is required. Our main concern is to be sensitive to the generosities, prejudices, and inconsistencies of our own culture. It is indeed helpful to be acquainted with the customs of other societies; for the purposes of the team, however, the particular value of such knowledge is to highlight some of our own beliefs which, accepted uncritically, may become our standard for child care. Although the basis for such beliefs may be fragile, the acquired standard can be iron-like in its rigidity. To spot this kind of cultural trap one should be alert to any statement beginning, "They say . . . (or "Everybody agrees . . ." or "Nobody should . . ."). Such dicta often reinforce old wives' tales that are contrary to empirical or scientific evidence.

An example of an unproven popular belief is that young children should not be cared for by their older siblings. In some other cultures such caretaking arrangements are standard. Further, young caretakers appear to acquire an increased capacity for empathy and nurturing which is good preparation for parenting. According to Korbin,[18] determining whether caretaking by siblings is evidence of adult neglect should be a matter of context, i.e., whether such caretaking is valued by the group or is imposed on an unwilling older child with no recognition of his or her contribution. How much responsibility is involved? Are adults readily available in case the young caretaker needs help? A similar line of reasoning in relation to customary practices can help establish team decisions on a thoughtful rather than an arbitrary basis.

Matters of culture affect team functioning in yet another fashion: the entire service network of which the team is a part is a miniature culture which becomes a model for the family.[19] The model may be one of exemplary organization as when procedures are clearly explained; a reasonable time schedule is in effect; responsibility among different services is defined; overlaps and gaps in services are quickly identified and addressed; and decisions are rational. Or, the opposite may be true: the service network may reflect the disorganization of the family. In either case—tight organization or sloppy disorganization—the network acts as a powerful force upon the family and its capacity to solve its problem.

The service network may likewise mirror the pathology of the family. This happens, for example, when one service component is made the scapegoat for all others to blame when anything goes amiss. Again, two or more network agencies may be in collusion for their own purposes, which may be in conflict with the collaborative plan of the network.

All team members bear a responsibility to help minimize possible service network dysfunction. The team social worker, however, is in an advantageous position in this regard. He or she can assume a liaison role between the network and the team and become the "central switchboard" for the involved community groups.[20] The successful execution of this role can help keep dysfunctional tendencies under control and can help augment useful collaboration within the service network and between providers and the family.

Treatment Planning

Treatment planning flows naturally from the comprehensive assessment of the family, its problems, strengths, and supports. In a few cases, this assessment points up the apparent futility of attempting any kind of treatment currently available because the scales are weighted so heavily against the slightest positive movement on the part of the parents.

Decisions that may be required are: will treatment be long-term or short-term? Are the family's needs mainly for concrete services, e.g., health care, job training, housing, transportation; or are the chief needs in the clinical area, e.g., marital or individual counseling, psychotherapy, etc.? What community resources can provide the required service(s)? How emergent are the family's needs?

Another vital consideration in treatment planning must be the abused child's needs. Again, each team member should be aware that the abused child may well have special needs that are not necessarily met through treating the adult caretakers. In relation to the child, the social worker may function again as the scorekeeper—one who keeps track of each player and makes sure nobody is lost.

Summary

In closing this chapter, we have to be impressed with the multiple demands on the team social worker. It should be borne in mind, though, that one purpose of the team is to offer support to each other and to share responsibilities that are often oppressively heavy. Each member, not only the social worker, must deal with multiple demands, and each offer and receive support through other team members. Experience with the team method has shown over and over that it outshines any other method for handling the serious and puzzling phenomenon of child abuse.

References

1. Motz, J.   "Colorado's Community Child Protection Teams."
    Multidisciplinary Treatment for Mistreated Children. Donald C. Bross,
    (Ed.). Denver: National Association of Counsel for Children, 1984.

2. Bennett, H., S. Collins, G. Fisher, S. Hughes, J.B. Reinhart. "SCAN: A
    Method of Community Collaboration." *Child Abuse & Neglect,* 6(1982):81-
    85.

3. Elmer, E. "Social Workers' Double Bind: Conflicting Roles of the Social
    Worker in Working with the Child, Parents, and the Community."
    Approaches to Health Care. Roger B. White (Ed.), pp. 1-17. Baltimore: The
    Johns Hopkins University School of Hygiene and Public Health,
    Department of Maternal and Child Health, 1976.

4. Perlman, H.H. "On the Art of Caring." *Child Welfare,* 64(1985):3-12.

5. Bourne, R., and E. Newberger. "Interdisciplinary Group Process in the
    Hospital Management of Child Abuse and Neglect." *Child Abuse &
    Neglect,* 4(1980):137-144.

6. Belsky, J. "Child Maltreatment: An Ecological Integration." *American
    Psychologist,* 35(1980):320-335.

7. Compher, J.V. "The Case Conference Revisited: A Systems Review." *Child
    Welfare,* 63(1984):411-418, esp. p. 412.

8. Belsky, J. "Child Maltreatment." *American Psychologist,* 35(1980):320-335.

9. Garbarino, J. "An Ecological Approach to Child Maltreatment." The *Social
    Context of Child Abuse and Neglect.* L. Pelton (Ed.). New York: Human
    Sciences Press, 1979.

10. Parke, R. "Theoretical Models of Child Abuse: Their Implications for
    Prediction, Prevention, and Modification." *Child Abuse Prediction.* R.H.
    Starr (Ed.). Cambridge, Mass.: Ballinger, 1982.

11. Bronfenbrenner, U. *The Ecology of Human Development.* Cambridge,
    Mass.: Harvard University Press, 1979.

12. Hegar, R.L. "The Case for Integration of the Investigator and Helper Roles
    in Child Protection." *Child Abuse & Neglect,* 6(1982):165-169.

13. Faller, K.C. "Unanticipated Problems in the United States Child Protection
    System." *Child Abuse & Neglect,* 9(1985):63-69.

14. Meddin, B.J., and I. Hansen. "The Services Provided During a Child Abuse and/or Neglect Case Investigation and the Barriers that Exist to Service Provision." *Child Abuse & Neglect*, 9(1985):175-182.

15. Meddin, *ibid*.

16. Burgess, R.L. "Project Interact: A Study of Patterns of Interaction in Abusive, Neglectful, and Control Families." *Child Abuse & Neglect*, 3(1979):781-791.

17. Burgess, *ibid*., esp. p. 789.

18. Korbin, J. "The Cultural Context of Child Abuse and Neglect." *Child Abuse & Neglect*, 4(1980):3-13.

19. Compher, J.V. "The Case Conference Revisited: A Systems Review." *Child Welfare*, 63(1984):411-418.

20. Compher, *ibid*., esp. p. 412.

12. Psychological Testing of the Parent and Child and Treatment Planning

Claudia A. Carroll

Introduction

Psychological testing and evaluation with abusive parents and abused children are valuable adjuncts in understanding the combination of factors that occurred to cause the abuse and the factors that are needed to remedy the family difficulties. From this we can fairly well hypothesize what will likely occur in the future. The assessment of psychological findings of abuse and neglect cases is less pure than clear-cut medical findings. Nonetheless, psychological testing lends significant insight to assessment of abuse cases and the difficult decisions that must be made.

Unequivocally, what is most needed at the beginning of every new case is a complete data base about the family. In this way, a realistic treatment plan can be formulated with the seriousness of the case assessed, and a course of action developed. These data are needed as soon as possible following disclosure, before psychological defenses are re-established by the individual. Several months into the case, the treatment team will then know if any progress has been made compared to the baseline information and data organized at intake. When mistakes are made on child protective cases, it is often because we have not had a complete data base, and are trying to make serious decisions without benefit of adequate information. It is the composite of information from many sources that gives us the best insurance that we are taking a reasoned course of action.

Psychological Tests

GENERAL

Psychological tests are structured interviews in which one is able to glean more information in less time, with the added benefit of some degree of verifiable reliability and validity. The psychologist in testing gathers often seemingly disparate information in an organized way. Psychological tests should not replace a well conducted clinical interview. The results of the battery of psychological tests contribute toward constructing a theory about a person's inner world. Testing gives us some ideas about how the person's behavior is regulated, what his self-image and self-esteem are, his general intelligence, his ability to think abstractly and integratively, how he views others and his relationships with them, the degree to which he sees the world as others do, what the person's ability is to plan and hope, what adaptive and defensive mechanisms he uses, and his perceptions or basic assumptions around which his world is organized (e.g., "something is rotten in me or I wouldn't have been treated poorly by others"). In summary, what one looks at in testing are the following: personality conflicts, ego function and structure, defense structure, thought process, affective integration, intellectual functioning, and how the person puts them together and experiences his life and world.

INDICATIONS FOR PSYCHOLOGICAL TESTING REFERRAL

Typical clinical questions in abuse and neglect cases that should initiate a referral for psychological testing include the following:
1. Lethality—what is the degree of dangerousness of this parent? Clinical example: Mr. C. denied abusing his six month old son who had several fractures including a skull fracture. The father's claim was that the baby was accidentally dropped while being bathed. Psychological testing revealed that Mr. C. had a character style of being evasive, guarded and smooth. All of the testing pointed to serious problems with impulse control. A diagnosis of anti-

social personality disorder was consistent with all test findings.

2.   Culpability—Although one can't be infallible in this assessment, one can often deduce culpability through adequate data collection and evaluation. Profiles emerge that can be seen as consistent or inconsistent with perpetration of the abuse. Clinical example: both Mr. and Mrs. S. denied knowing how their 13 month old daughter, Alicia, incurred a second degree burn on her upper arm. Psychological testing found Mr. S. viewed the baby as an intrusion and threat to his dependent relationship with his wife.   He had a lack of empathy for the baby's developmental needs, and a distorted perception of her normal development, viewing it as "infractions of the rules." He was seen to have little capacity to regulate his feelings, especially aggressive, angry ones, and carried a view of life as "an eye for an eye." It was later determined that Alicia had accidentally spilled a cup of coffee on him, so he did the same to her from the coffee pot. Mrs. S. was seen to have a non-abusive profile, though she lacked many internal resources that would permit her to ask for help from others, because of feeling concerned about her husband's violent temper and her tendency to leave the baby with her husband only infrequently because of this worry. Alicia was left in her mother's custody and her father was court-ordered out of the home.

3.   What is the diagnosis of the parent? The diagnosis should be considered both in terms of a possible Diagnostic and Statistical Manual (DSM III) diagnosis and a psychodynamic diagnosis.   First, vis-a-vis a DSM III diagnosis, one is looking at considerations such as whether the parent is schizophrenic, has a major affective illness, has a substance abuse problem or simply is experiencing an adjustment disorder.   Secondly, for the psychodynamic diagnosis it is essential to have an idea of the life story and accompanying major traumas, often from early childhood, that need to be treated.   In short, how sick and incapacitated is the parent, and what strengths might he have to remedy the situation and grow psychologically?

4.   What is the prognosis?   Insofar as the past is the best predictor of the future, if one has some understanding of how and why a person has coped in a certain way in the past, one is in a better position to ascertain how intractable or amenable to change the parent's behavior may be.

MAKING THE REFERRAL TO THE PSYCHOLOGIST

For the psychological evaluation to be most useful, it is important for the referring person to formulate his questions specifically. The following are useful referral question areas:

1. An assessment of risk of abuse by the parent in the future.
2. Strengths and weaknesses of the parent/child interaction.
3. An assessment of the level of stress which may have precipitated the abuse and ability of the parent(s) to handle future stresses differently.
4. Treatability of the parent.
5. Issues of placement of the children.
6. Whether termination of parental rights is indicated.
7. Interaction between siblings.
8. The impact of separation from the parent on the child.
9. Impulse control.
10. Ability to modulate effect.
11. Identification of the child with the parent.
12. Capacity for empathy by the parent for the child.
13. Diagnosis of the parent.
14. The degree to which the parent experiences a coherent sense of self.
15. Which repetitive problems of the parent's past are being repeated with the child in the present.

TYPICAL TEST BATTERY

There are four kinds of tests: the projective test, the objective test, the intelligence test, and the assessment of neurological damage.

1. Projective tests present ambiguous visual stimuli (e.g., inkblots, pictures). The assumption is made that to some degree the stimuli will evoke unconscious and conscious components of the person's personality. They tap such areas as the person's organization and perception of events, his interactions with others, impulse control, emotional tone, identification and repetitive issues. Examples of projective tests are the Rorschach Inkblot Test, Thematic Apperception Test, Incomplete Sentences Blank, Draw-A-Person, Draw-A-Family, and The Child Apperception Test.

2. Objective Tests are tests in which standardized questions are posed to which a person indicates "true" or "false," or "agree" or "disagree." These tests can be more vulnerable to faking than the projective tests as their validity is somewhat dependent on the willingness of the subject to self-disclose. Examples of Objective Tests are

the California Psychological Inventory (CPI) and the Minnesota Multiphasic Personality Inventory (MMPI).

3. Intelligence Tests are structured tests which measure a person's basic intelligence—how the individual learns, what cognitive strengths and weaknesses are present, what capacity the individual has to integrate and organize information, plan ahead, and think abstractly. Intelligence tests can be useful indices of how a person approaches a task, the degree of anxiety present and the likelihood of impulsive versus planned behavior. Examples of Intelligence Tests include the Stanford Binet (for children up to 16 years), the Wechsler Adult Intelligence Scales, the Wechsler Intelligence Scale for Children-Revised (for children ages 6-16 years), the Wechsler Preschool and Primary Scale of Intelligence (WPPSI) (for children ages 4-6 1/2 years). Intelligence testing with abusive parents can be particularly helpful in those cases where it is unclear if the parent is having difficulty because of limited I.Q. or a severe character disorder, such as sociopathy.

4. Tests that assess neurological deficit establish the degree, if any, of brain damage from either injury or disease. Examples of neurological tests include the Halstead-Reitan, Object Sorting Test, and the Bender Visual Motor Gestalt Test. These tests are rarely needed in assessment of abusive parents unless there is serious consideration of cerebral impairment of the parent.

While structured tests such as the intelligence tests (WAIS and WISC-R) have good reliability and validity, the projective tests such as the Thematic Apperception Test and Rorschach have been criticized in these areas. (Reliability is the consistency and stability of test scores by the same person when re-tested with an identical test or an equivalent form of the test. Validity is the degree to which a test measures what it is supposed to.) Each test brings with it another piece of the puzzle, and it is the combination of a good diagnostic interview, a full psychodiagnostic testing battery, review of past history, and information from other sources that yield the most reliable and useful understanding of the patient. Recurrent themes tend to be interwoven across the tests. For example, one loose or distorted Rorschach response should not be used as confirmatory information about an individual. It must be viewed and integrated in the context of all the available information and themes seen in the battery.

Characteristics of Abusive Parents
as Seen in Psychological Testing

Generalizations about how abusive parents present in psychological testing are difficult, as abusive parents represent a wide range of personality types. Certain themes, however, present themselves recurrently. No single diagnostic category or description fits all abusive parents, with the exception of Dr. Brandt Steele's description, "abusive parents are abused children grown up."

Abusive parents may be deeply troubled, joyless individuals. They are emotionally impoverished, developmentally arrested adults who have experienced in their formative years the same or similar lack of "good enough mothering" from which their children now suffer. The reason abusive, neglecting families end up in the child protective system stems generally from a flaw or schism in the original mother-child relationship. It is an early developmental failure that causes a serious problem in the parent's current functioning.

Parents tend to encounter difficulties with their children at that stage of development at which they themselves were experiencing difficulty. Many abusive parents have had significant difficulty with separation from their own parents, having not gotten enough from them to truly separate. The residua of this leave them with deficits in the essential "mirroring role" of the parent. Thus, they are unable to adequately mirror back to their children their children's own separate identities. Having not been truly "seen" by their parents, they now suffer from being unable to give this recognition to their children. Therefore, they have serious difficulty with object constancy (which Mahler described as requiring the ability to tolerate separation from the object, remember the object in its absence, and have the ability to experience ambivalence toward the object). They may tend to inappropriately look to the children for fulfillment of their own needs. They cannot see the children as entirely separate and, in essence, are unconsciously saying, "I only like you for what you give me, not for what and who you are." One of the central ideas of the development of object constancy is that it must be completed for one to have the capacity to develop empathy or altruism for others. With the most severe child abuse cases, the child's separate identity from the parent is non-existent and a merger occurs in the parent's psyche between parent and child. For example, when a 13 month old baby girl, who had serious failure to thrive was placed in the hospital, the mother said, "How will you know when to feed her as she's only hungry when I am?" In less dramatic cases, the child becomes, at best, a need-fulfilling part-object. In these cases, the child is not a whole person in his own right; he is part-self and part-object with the parent.

The parent relies on the child to supplement his own inner incompleteness. As a result of this developmental arrest of fixation, abusive parents do not have a good sense of identity or truly know who they are. They characteristically experience acute senses of aloneness, loneliness, helplessness and depression. In an attempt to survive their own impoverished childhoods, they usually have identified with their own parents' distorted views of themselves, and these identifications tend to be punitive, highly critical, and unempathic.

The following themes are characteristic of an abusive parent's psychological testing evaluation:

1. *Poor sense of self.* Revealed by incomplete, impoverished figures on the Draw-A-Person and Draw-A-Family tests, often characterized by missing parts and appearing "broken." Significant identity problems are paramount.

2. *Expecting and longing for a constant supply of love.* A desperate wish to be liked and loved presents itself in a variety of ways. For example, in TAT stories, some themes are prominent: the conviction that it is hopeless that the subject will ever be loved, the subject having no one to turn to for comfort or safety, or on the other hand, exploitive use of others for self-gain. Incomplete Sentence examples from two sexually abusive fathers were: "I am best *when I am around loving people;*" "I suffer *when no one can feel the love I want to give.*"

3. *Overwhelming feelings of loneliness and abandonment.* Interpersonal relationships as seen on the projective tests are fraught with conflict and create anxiety; TAT stories may end defensively with `happy ever after' qualities or with total loss, alienation and themes of death. An Incomplete Sentences example was, "When I was a child, *I loved to talk to the animals for they seemed to understand me better than my parents.*"

4. *Difficulty modulating strong affect.* What one sees clinically in this area are two extremes: either extreme constriction of affect or significant aggressive drives. In the former, the parent presents with a very bland, empty, flat affect. In the latter, the aggressive drives often become prominent in the protocol. The aggression tends to be expressed crudely and directly, relatively untouched by repression. Poor form level and "raw aggression" are often seen on the Rorschach. Examples are: "Two lizards pulling apart a fish on the bone," or "blood dripping." The TAT stories have a quality of revenge and justification for impulsive, out-of-control behavior such as "He's raging mad

and wants to get even." There may also be difficulty in tolerating ambivalence in relationships.

5. *Maladaptive Defenses.* Defenses of abusive parents include, but are not limited to, denial, rationalization and projection of responsibility. On the other hand, one often sees an excessively rigid superego with primitive masochistic guilt, the abusive parent feeling that his parents were justified in treating him badly, and that he deserved no better.

6. *Feelings of emptiness and looking to others to define his own sense of self.* In cases of sexual abuse, the sexually abusive father's self-image is so fragile that he tends not to have the ego strength to seek an adult relationship for need gratification and instead looks to a vulnerable child by whom to be nurtured. Sexually abusive fathers often have related drug and alcohol problems. Feelings of emptiness are often correlated with elevated scores on the Social Introversion Scale and on the Depression Scale on the MMPI.

7. *Performance on structured tests is non-problematic compared to performance on projective tests.* By and large, abusive parents fall within the normal range on the structured tests, yet their projective tests show many of the themes mentioned.

8. *Difficulty suspending his own needs.* This difficulty often becomes apparent on the Rorschach and the TAT. For example, on the TAT, instead of telling a story about the person in the picture, the subject over-identifies with the stimulus. For example, on Card 1 of the TAT, instead of saying, "This looks like a little boy worried about his violin lesson," the subject might respond, "This is me when I was his age. . . ." and proceed to tell about something that had happened to him.

9. *Separation conflict.* Rorschach responses which are merged, such as "one person coming out of another" or "two dogs connected at the hips," may indicate separation conflict.

10. *Distorted object relations.* Abusive parents have difficulty trusting others, and there is evidence in their projective tests of the residua of the unhappiness and unresolved loss. One might see their wariness of others in a Rorschach response such as "peering eyes." They also tend to see more part objects than whole objects on the Rorschach. For example, a person might be seen but with missing parts. When people are seen, both on the Rorschach and TAT, they tend to be in conflict.

Indications of areas of strength in the subject include a sense of self that remains well-defined throughout the testing despite the inherent stress of the situation, the capacity for empathy for others, a sense of responsibility for the subject's own behavior, the ability to appropriately turn to others for help with a sense of positive identification with others, and finally, the ability of the subject to have contact with his own inner world.

Characteristics of Abused Children as Seen in Psychological Testing

Abused children often suffer silently. Psychological testing often helps better define and understand these children's problems, especially insofar as they commonly display a superficial adaptability that helps them survive their feelings of helplessness, anxiety and loneliness. Thus, their need for help is often overlooked.

It is important to quickly assess the way in which the child can be best understood. Some children are more comfortable in play activity, whereas others prefer to communicate through drawings. Children often express themselves more spontaneously through actions rather than through words. The evaluator must feel comfortable with this and not need the child to describe feelings in explicit words.

A useful projective story to tell a child to see how he finishes the story is *The Bird Fable*. It is a standard story about a mother, father and baby bird in a nest that falls in a windstorm. The mother and father can fly but the baby cannot. The child is asked, "What do you think happens?" This story provides a good clue as to the child's relationships, the sense of safety, rescue and trust. Abused children often give stories in which the baby bird falls to the ground and dies.

Children's drawings may be a particularly rich way of understanding the child. For example, the Draw-A-Person is widely held to represent a person's perception of himself and his body image. The projective elements in children's drawings often represent their buried concerns and worries, while at the same time giving an idea of the structure of the child's personality organization, how he copes with his anxieties, and what his current capacity is for autonomy.

It is highly illuminating to compare pictures drawn by normal children with those drawn by our abused and neglected population. What one sees in pictures drawn by non-abused or neglected children are relatedness and a sense of object connectiveness, life and richness. These children also provide essential details of the subject matter they are drawing, often adding a few details that are not essential. In abused children's drawings, one sees impoverished, empty, often non-completed figures. There are usually feelings of depression, helplessness, emptiness and loneliness.

The testing battery is similar to that given an adult. For a child, one may want to use an intelligence test, the Child Apperception Test, Rorschach, Draw-A-Person, Draw-A-Family, and an Incomplete Sentences Blank. The testing should be done in conjunction with the clinical interview of the child and the observation of the child's play.

The following factors are likely to become apparent on testing with abused or neglected children:

1. Nurturance is conditional and dependent upon the child meeting the needs of the parent; for example, a six-year old child's Incomplete Sentences Blank was, "What I want to happen most is *that I will call my momma a sweetheart, and I'll buy her food when I grow up.*" This statement may suggest that this child, in order to gain affection, needs to meet the mother's needs.

2. Difficulty tolerating affect or anxiety: Abused or neglected children demonstrate a lack of affect tolerance and have a tendency to become quickly flooded by any strong emotion.

3. Extremely poor and distorted self-image and self-esteem.

4. The use of more primitive defenses and primary process magical thinking.

5. Impaired cognitive abilities. Abused children tend not to have the same curiosity and exploratory behavior as other children. They range from being hypervigilant to having a poor attention span, have difficulty concentrating, and fear trying for fear of failing.

6. Lack of a true sense of self.

7. Indices of chronic depression; these are often children who are chronically depressed. This depression may be either a low-grade sadness in which the child seems not very spontaneous, or the depression may be quite apparent. They have internalized the feeling that they must have done something wrong for their parents to have treated them in this way, blaming themselves. It is difficult for the child or adult victim of abuse to reach the point in treatment where they can truly be angry with the parent. After all, it is this parent upon whom they are still dependent for love.

8. For children who have been sexually abused, there will often be a confused sexual identity, i.e., preoccupation with sexual themes in their play, or sexual percepts on the Rorschach, and/or asexual Draw-A-Person figures because

any expression of sexuality might be experienced as dangerous.

9. Autonomous functioning is problematic: These children have a definite limitation in their own regulatory systems with a high reliance on external controls or they are too controlled and become vulnerable to decompensation when their controlling defenses cannot be maintained.

10. Abused children are at higher risk to develop primitive ego states, either as children or as adults. This could be characterized by dissociative episodes or amnesia, for example.

11. Many abused children demonstrate poor impulse control. They tend to act out their impulses rather than being able to successfully sublimate drives or substitute words for actions.

12. Self-observing functions will be brittle, and tend to weaken when the child is severely stressed.

13. One of the most consistently damaged areas of abused children's lives is in object relations. The capacity for true empathic feeling is less likely to be seen in them as their needs have not been regarded empathically by others. They develop a variety of defenses such as cautiousness, hypervigilance, emotional inhibition, and superficiality, to survive the unpredictable and often dangerous world in which they live. Such children, for example, on TAT stories, may go to no one for help and nurturing. Such self-containment is a hollow substitute for the development of a true sense of trust and confidence in others. These children are affectively constricted. They show little curiosity in playing and are likely to come into the playroom and line the toys up, cautiously taking one out at a time; on the other hand, the disorganized child loses himself in the play, often becoming very aggresive and out-of-control. By and large, what one sees in the children's play is that they aren't really having fun. Play to them is yet another burden. Even after successful treatment with an abused child, we as therapists and evaluators must come to grips with the fact that we can never give back to the child his childhood. Even with the most successful treatment, the child will likely have some psychological scars. The residua one might see include reservation in sharing feelings, less emotional elasticity and more stereotyped responses than non-abused children.

14. Abused children will likely be unable to verbally express their anxieties yet they harbor intense feelings of anxiety

and anger. They have enormous fear that something dire will happen if their anxieties and anger are expressed.

Indicators of a positive prognosis for a child include the following: evidence that he hasn't as yet fully given up on the adults in his world, and can acknowledge his wish to be taken care of; evidence that the child can gradually give up his pseudo-mature world and become a child; evidence that he can begin to tolerate the full range of his own emotions; and the evaluator can see during the evaluation some glimmering in the child of what can be described as "a twinkle in his eye."

The parent-child observation session may be conducted by the psychologist. Much helpful information can be gleaned from observation, and is covered in some detail in the chapter by Clare Haynes-Seman et al. in this book.

Access to Records

It is imperative for the psychologist to have an interpretive session with the parents following the evaluation, sharing with them the results of the testing evaluation, answering questions they may have about the findings, and personally sharing with them one's recommendations. One should try to communicate one's trustworthiness, even though there will be times when they strongly disagree with or are disheartened by what the psychologist recommends. There are conditions under which a parent should not have direct access to the report: when the parent has a past history of violence to others and has felt justified in those behaviors, or when it would be too overwhelming to someone who is fragile emotionally to read the report. These parents should be given a verbal interpretation.

Conclusion

Psychological testing of abused and neglected children and their families may be a useful tool in assessment, and supplements, but does not substitute for, more long-term, open-ended evaluation. The testing may also provide direction for a treatment approach.

Bibliography

Adler, Gerald. "The Borderline Narcissistic Personality Disorder Continuum." *American Journal of Psychiatry,* 138(1981):46-50.

Adler, Gerald, and D.H. Buie, Jr. "Aloneness and Borderline Psychopathology: The Possible Relevance of Child Development Issues." *International Journal of Psychoanalysis,* 60(1979):83-96.

Anastasi, Anne. *Psychological Testing,* 4th Edition. New York: Macmillan Publishing Co., 1976.

Burns, Robert C., and S. Harvard Kaufman. *Kinetic Family Drawings and Introduction to Understanding Children Through Kinetic Drawings.* New York: Brunner-Mazel, 1970.

Fraiberg, S. "Libidinal Object Constancy and Mental Representation." *The Psychoanalytic Study of the Child,* pp. 2419-47. New York: International University Press, 1969.

Goodwin, Jean. "Use of Drawings in Evaluating Children Who May Be Incest Victims." *Children and Youth Services Review,* 4(1982):269-278.

Halpern, Florence. *A Clinical Approach to Children's Rorschachs.* New York: Grune-Stratton, 1953.

Kagan, Jerome. "Thematic Apperception Techniques with Children." *Projective Techniques with Children.* A.I. Rabin and M.R. Hayworth (Eds.), pp. 105-112. New York: Grune & Stratton, 1960.

Mahler, M.S., F. Pine, and A. Bergman. *The Psychological Birth of the Human Infant.* New York: Basic Books, 1975.

McDivitt, J.B. "Separation-Individuation and Object Constancy." *Journal of the American Psychiatric Association.* 23(1975):714.

Pine, F. "On the Pathology of the Separation-Individuation Process as Manifested in Later Clinical Work: An Attempt at Delineation." *International Journal of Psychoanalysis,* 60(1979):225-241.

Lerner, Howard, P. Lerner, and A. Sugerman. *Phenomena in the Rorschach Test.* J. Kwawer (Ed.). New York: International University Press, 1980.

Tallent, Norman. *Psychological Report Writing.* Englewood Cliffs, N.J.: Prentice-Hall, Inc., 1976.

13. The Psychiatric Evaluation and Treatment Plan

David P.H. Jones, Ruth S. Kempe,
and Brandt F. Steele

Introduction

Psychiatrists are often members of the multidisciplinary team responding to child abuse and neglect. Adult and child psychiatrists who involve themselves with child abuse cases undertake a variety of activities, including evaluation of children, families and adult individuals, treatment, research, teaching, court and forensic work, managing staff groups for "battered professionals,"[1] and liaison with other professionals. In this chapter, the focus is upon the diagnostic evaluation and the subsequent formulation of a treatment plan directed toward adult, child or both.

Purpose of the Evaluation

The purpose of the adult psychiatric evaluation is to develop information about the patient's early life history and development, especially in relation to abuse and neglect.

Abusive, neglecting behavior is not considered to be purely haphazard or impulsive, but rather to be understood as a particular constellation of emotional states and specific adaptive responses that have their roots in the earliest months of life.[2] As reported in previous studies[3,4,5] it is common for abusive or neglectful caretakers to give a history of having experienced some significant degree of neglect, with or without accompanying physical abuse. Some caretakers who abuse children may show characteristic symptoms of major psychiatric disorders (e.g., schizophrenia, depression) or any of the neuroses or character disorders. In general, it seems to be useful to consider child abusive behavior as a group of abnormal patterns of caretaker-child interactions related to psychological characteristics that may exist concurrently with, but quite independently of, any psychiatric disorder or even in otherwise relatively healthy personalities. However, recent investigations have pointed to a relationship between abuse or neglect experienced in childhood and certain adult psychiatric disturbances.

In evaluation, data are developed about the adult's relationships with parents, spouse, children, and other important individuals. The questions are aimed at discovering how these relationships bear upon an individual's sense of self, identity, and patterns of behavior, especially when these involve parent/child relationships. The psychiatrist also develops ideas about the depth and seriousness of any psychopathology, and predicts the likelihood of a response to treatment.

With children, the psychiatrist aims to discover the child's perspective on life within his/her family from as far back as can be remembered. The quality of the child's relationships with caregivers, siblings, friends and teachers is assessed. The child may be interviewed about a potentially abusive experience to obtain details of the event as well as his/her emotional response to it. A further purpose is to understand how abuse has psychologically affected the infant or child. An understanding of the family's functioning, concurrently as well as historically will be the prime focus in some cases.

Who Should Be Seen?

It is unrealistic to recommend a psychiatric evaluation of every child and parent, but who should be selected? To a large extent, this depends upon the availability of local resources and different professionals who can contribute to the evaluation and treatment of abused children and abusive adults. The recommendations offered below require adaptation, dependent upon local circumstances.

ADULTS

A psychiatric assessment may be helpful with parents who exhibit one or more of the following problems:
  (a) Signs of emotional distress or illness (severe anxieties, depressions, hallucinations, delusions, "blackouts," aggressive outbursts, poor impulse control, alcohol and/or drug abuse);
  (b) History of psychiatric illness, criminal activity, or violent behavior such as spouse abuse;
  (c) Lack of awareness or denial of the seriousness of their child's condition, despite compelling circumstantial evidence to suggest their causal role in that condition;
  (d) History of the parents themselves having been abused or neglected, especially sexually abused as children.
  (e) History of serious or repeated abuse or neglect, especially of children under three; history of inflicting cruel or bizarre injuries upon a child;
  (f) Suspected history of inflicting Munchausen Syndrome by Proxy[6] (fictitious illness) in a child;
  (g) Current fanatic involvement with a cult that sanctions child abuse or neglect;
  (h) Mental retardation.

CHILDREN

Children who exhibit one or more of the following problems will likely require a psychiatric assessment:
  (a) Aberrant relationships including: little or no attachment toward their parents, or anxious attachment[7] with excessive clinging behavior (resisting minor separations from their parents); abnormal vigilance; indiscriminate affection, forming immediate, unreserved relationships with any adult; preschool children who display excessive fearfulness or aggressiveness toward their parents;
  (b) Developmental delay or symptoms of emotional or behavioral conduct problems;
  (c) Depressive symptoms including sadness, apathy, sleep disturbances, weight changes, withdrawn social behavior with peers or adults, decreased learning, or self-harming behavior;
  (d) Behavioral symptoms of abuse including a runaway history, prostitution, alcohol or drug abuse, anorexia nervosa, bulimia, or bizarre ideation; psychosomatic; dramatic or

histrionic symptoms, sexualized play or precocious sexual knowledge or language or a marked change in school and social behavior which is not obviously explained by other circumstances.

ASSESSMENT—GENERAL CONSIDERATIONS

The aim of psychiatric assessment is to find psychological explanations of etiology rather than to search for guilt or criminal responsibility. The examiner attempts to relinquish stereotypes, biases and preconceived notions and adopts a "don't yet know" attitude.[8] The emphasis should be on listening, yet within the framework to be outlined below. The reason and circumstances of the psychiatric referral and what specifically is requested are noted by the examiner. Who referred the child, adult or family, and for what purpose? Was it to discover if abuse had occurred? To develop a treatment plan? To decide if termination of parental rights is the only solution; or to aid in the preparation of a defense for an accused parent in criminal proceedings? In some instances, the psychiatrist might consider it unethical to agree to a request for a one-sided evaluation, for example, to examine an adult accused of assault without either seeing the child or carefully examining the child's statement.

Most psychiatrists like to have prior records before starting an evaluation. These records include the statement of the child or victim and prior biographical details from police, psychological and psychiatric assessments, social work and medical reports, and juvenile records, if available.

At the beginning, the patient's understanding of the reason for his referral to a psychiatrist should be explored. The psychiatrist may be well advised to make a statement to the patient such as "I may need to talk to other people about this. I will not need to talk about irrelevant material. I will try not to do anything to hurt you."

The five main areas of interest can now be examined in more detail. They consist of three major areas of family functioning and the examination of the child and parent individually. The three main areas of family functioning are the family as a whole, the marriage, and the parenting capacity of the adults.

THE ASSESSMENT OF THE WHOLE FAMILY

The family evaluation consists of gathering information concerning the development of the family and its current functioning. One approach to this is to draw a family tree with the family members present. How the parents met and where they have lived is explored. The parents are asked, "How many pregnancies did you have? (did your wife have?)" This is a more reliable question than asking, "How many children do you have?" and draws out information regarding lost and abandoned children as well as child deaths. Similarly, the construction of a family tree allows discussion of losses and deaths of important people. The families of origin (grandparental generation) are discussed together with questions about the type of childhood the parents themselves experienced. Information is gathered about psychological and physical health of family members. Has the current family unit separated from the family of origin? How much, and what quality of contact occurs and what is the quality of that relationship currently? Questions aimed at the development of attachment between each parent and each child may be asked in a family evaluation or when the parents are seen separately. (This depends upon the age of the child). In assessments of families containing infants inquiry about attachment can occur more readily within the family session (see Chapter 14). The clinician decides how appropriate such questions would be in front of the child.

The family's current level of functioning is assessed from its emotional tone and capacity to communicate effectively. The structure of the family is explored by considering such issues as who makes the rules in the family. Are adults and children in their appropriate roles, or do children have responsibilities and duties which, in most families would not be required of them? Is the family a chaotic one with little privacy or control over who comes and goes? Polansky and coauthors emphasized how neglectful families are different from their neighbors and unrepresentative of their locale.[9] Thus, inquiry should be made concerning neighbors, friends, and local relations. Is the family isolated, friendless or argumentative?

Sometimes when abuse allegations are made in the context of a custody or visitation dispute between the parents, the allegations may not be true. Such cases require extensive time by a professional team to evaluate all the different family perspectives effectively.   Much depends upon the assessment of the family and parenting capacities as well as observations of the interactions between parents and children in the two families who are at war. Only on the basis of full evaluation can conclusions be drawn; otherwise, a one-sided view is obtained. Sometimes, the very first statements that the child makes to anyone concerning the possibility of child abuse can be helpful to the validation process.

Some parents are so hostile, belligerent and verbally aggressive, that it is difficult to obtain any useful information. These parents may respond to genuine interest in their grievances, complaints and opinions. Usually, after a period of letting off steam, some form of evaluation is possible. It may be necessary to have police or security present, either just outside the door or in the room for certain interviews, and the time-honored technique of sitting between the patient and door, should not be forgotten.

ASSESSMENT OF THE MARRIAGE

In this section, the evaluation of the marriage or cohabitation is outlined. The examiner is interested from an historical perspective to discover how the couple first met and courted. This will lead to an inquiry as to their expectations of their relationship. How have things changed during the time they have been together? The examiner is interested in each partner's work patterns and interests outside the home. Does each have individual friends and relationships? What is the attitude of the other towards this? The couple's sexual relationship both currently and over the course of their marriage is documented. What about their ups and downs? Details are elicited on these as well as any separations or extra-marital relationships. A history of spouse abuse or violence is sought with details obtained of any incidents that are vividly recalled. The exact nature of any injuries or hospital attendances is essential, with appropriate releases sought for obtaining medical records. Ideally, some of this inquiry is conducted with the couple, and the same information should be gathered from the individual interview.

The interviewer also inquires about current marital functioning. Here, the technique of inquiring in detail about a typical day can give useful information on this area of the family's functioning, as well as the parenting area. The interviewer is interested in the extent and quality of contact and communication between the couple. For example, in an incest family, the husband and wife may hardly ever communicate or see each other with one working the night shift and the other the day. In abusive and other dysfunctional marriages, communication sometimes consists of shouting and verbal abuse, sometimes with overt physical violence and battering. The degree of emotional support that one spouse provides the other is inquired into, and also inferred from the way one partner describes the other's role. Inquiry is made into each spouse's participation in household chores and involvement in child care. What are the current feelings for each other, criticisms, dissatisfactions, disagreements? What area of life would each wish most to change? As with all these questions, self-report and the expression of feeling while answering are equally important. Feeling may be expressed through words, loudness, pitch and rhythm of speech, and through non-verbal cues such as facial expression, gesture and bodily posture. The interviewer adopts a relatively bland style so that emotion is not unduly influenced while at the same time making it clear that the interviewer wishes to know about the couple's feelings.[10] Some important areas to be observed include the degree of emotional warmth and affection displayed, the balance of power between the couple, how often one spouse intrudes upon the speech of the other, how often they look at each other, and in what context. Is the account to the interviewer *exactly* the same as the partner's, or are there the expected differences which reflect that two individuals usually see the same event in a slightly different way.

PARENTING

The couple's capacity and aptitude for parenting can be evaluated, though surprisingly few psychiatrists inquire into this very important area of an individual's functioning. Perhaps as a reflection of this situation, the topic of parenting is seldom discussed in the standard texts of child or adult psychiatry. There are, however, other authoritative references on parenting.[11,12,13] What qualities does the concept of parenting include? The following are aspects of parenting that are considered to be fundamental to its proper operation and success.[14,15] The most important elements are the provision of adequate food, shelter, and basic medical care; insuring security of emotional relationships, with an emphasis on continuity and the provision of a secure emotional base from which to explore the world; a responsiveness to the child's changing emotional needs at different developmental stages; a capacity for empathy, and an ability to see the child as a separate being with needs distinct from those of the parent. The parents must help the child develop moral values by providing a framework for the development of standards, showing and modeling to the child appropriate behavior. Discipline must shape behavior effectively, but also in a harmonious manner that ultimately can be expected to increase the child's own inner sense of control. Another parenting function is to provide an education that is culturally appropriate. Cutting off the child's exposure to all life experiences may represent deprivation of important life experiences that could provide a springboard for a child's growth and development. A parent should also be able to aid the child to develop coping skills and become skilled at social problem-solving.

How might parenting qualities be evaluated? First, evidence concerning such qualities may be gathered from the history of parenting. Here, the focus is on the development of each child from the moment the mother thought she was pregnant to the present time. From this biography the development of mother/child and father/child attachment is gauged. A permission-giving style of questioning may be helpful here and a question searching for a post-partum feeling of attachment could be phrased "Not everyone feels close to her baby straightaway; how long did it take you to feel close to yours?" Events on the child's path to the present are inquired about, especially concerning ill health, perceived or actual difficulties, and problems with feeding, sleeping, urinary and bowel control, emotions and behavior. Full detail is needed here, including how the child's earlier fears and episodes of distress were viewed and handled by the parents.

There are certain nodal points around which conflict and abuse tend to arise: crying, messiness, perceived disobedience, and toilet training. For example, a mother may be asked how the baby's crying makes her feel or if it recalls feelings from her past. A response such as "It makes me feel that I'm no good; it reminds me of my mother screaming at me" or "I got smacked when I cried too much" may be a pivotal clue to the psychiatrist in understanding the mother's response to her baby, eventually helping her to understand and mitigate it.

If not previously asked, the question, "How would you like to bring this child up differently from how you were brought up?" can be very useful at this stage. Similarly, the parents should be asked their perspective on recent problems in their parenting, or about a recent suspected episode of abuse or neglect. As in all psychiatric evaluations, the response to specific inquiries is important, but the psychiatrist is also concerned with making observations about how and at what point or in what context particular responses are made.

Second, inquiry is made as to the current functioning of the parents, and how each parent handles each child's current fears or episodes of distress. While the parent describes the handling of these episodes, the parent's empathy and response to the child as a separate individual can be assessed. This area of inquiry itself will initiate an account of each child's behavior, and lead to a discussion of what behavior is expected of the child, and what is prohibited for that child. Inquiry will also be made about current disciplinary practices by both parents. The areas of note here are the consistency of discipline, e.g., does the child receive the belt one day and laughter the next for stealing items within the house? What methods are used to discipline—belt, stick, hand, standing in the corner (how long?), grounded to bedroom or house (how long and is food provided?), loss of privileges? What reward is available for positive, desired behaviors, and can privileges be earned? Lastly, how effective is the discipline? Does it achieve its end but without harmony, e.g., by instilling fear? A typical day may be inquired about in detail and provides useful information regarding who is in contact with the children and what is the father's role in this family. It will also provide information concerning any disagreements between the parents over the care of the children.

Parents should be asked how they like being a parent—what they particularly enjoy and what they dislike. Lack of pleasure in their child's company may be a feature of an abusive parent's make-up.

While these subjects are being discussed, the psychiatrist will be making observations about the parent who is talking about his or her child.   Observations can be enhanced by viewing the parent/child interaction *while* the parent is being asked about that child's development. Different but similar observations can be made while the parent is involved in some activity with the child, *without* the interviewer present in the same room. Usually the interviewer is behind a one-way glass or videotaping the interaction session. Examples of situations that may be used to make such observations include feeding, explaining recent events, planning a vacation or trip together, or simply playing together.

We have considered the psychiatric assessment of the family and aspects of family life, and will now turn to the assessment of the individual adult and child.

ASSESSMENT OF THE ADULT

When interviewing a potentially abusive adult, it is usually clear that the reason for referral is either an acknowledged abusive incident or an alleged one. Thus, inquiry into the adult's recent history will include an inquiry into his or her account of the abusive incident or history of neglect. The psychiatrist will look for inconsistencies in the statement. However, more commonly there are significant omissions from an otherwise plausible story. For example, one father described how he and his 18 month old son were lying on the bed and suddenly the child became rigid, pale, and began to vomit.   Next, the father, quite truthfully, described how the child was brought directly to the hospital emergency room. However, he omitted relating the critical period which preceded these events. He had become so enraged at his son's persistent crying that he had hurled him against the wall and then laid him down on the bed beside himself and continued to watch TV as if nothing had happened. After a period of time, his son's cerebral edema and subdural bleeding led to seizures and the remainder of the father's story was true.

The psychiatrist will also look for evidence of empathy for the child in question and draw inferences about the understanding and feeling that the parent has for that child. Many parents deny their complicity in an abuse incident, but sometimes admissions are made during a psychiatric interview. If an admission to an episode of abuse or neglect does occur, then the psychiatrist must discover what is being admitted to and how often the abuse occurred. Where did it occur? How was the cooperation of the child obtained if it was sexual abuse? What was the degree of violence involved? What was the response of the child? Sometimes admissions are repentant with the adult expressing remorse and sorrow at the event in question. Often, however, admissions are unrepentant and accompanied by such statements, as "Well, it happened to me and it didn't do me any harm." It is quite common for partial admissions to be obtained whereby adults will say that they did something but then minimize the event. For example, an adult who sexually abused his daughter, said, "Well, I was only educating her."

The family history has been mentioned in the preceding sections but the adult's view of the children in the family will be important together with aspects of the development of adult relationships and child-rearing practices. It is quite common in situations of abuse and neglect to find the caretakers expecting their infants and small children to behave and perform tasks with unusual efficiency much too early in the child's life while, at the same time, disregarding the child's own feelings and wants. This phenomenon has been well described by Morris and Gould[16] as role reversal. The child is treated as if he were an adult while the caretaker expects satisfaction of his or her own desires.

It is also possible to see significant neglect occur as a result of a child's failure to perform well enough to satisfy caretaker expectations. An infant who fails to respond to mother's inept or inappropriately timed feedings or other caregiving procedures is perceived as being defective, negativistic, generally unfit or no good, and is then deemed not worth caring for, resulting in failure to thrive or other forms of neglect. Thus, although abusive and neglectful parents have the same pattern of high expectations of the child, their responses to the child's failure to meet expectations are quite different. In the one case, the child is perceived as failing to follow through to his full capabilities and, therefore, is punished to make him "shape up" and do better. In the other case, the child is seen as incapable of proper response, is worthless and, therefore, is given only cursory, inadequate care or almost totally disregarded.

In assessing the adult, personal history should be explored in some depth including the adult's history of physical and psychological health. The psychiatrist is interested in any losses or deaths that have occurred to friends or relatives of the parent, and will also wish to explore the parent's own childhood history and record recent crises or life changes. Many adults who present for psychiatric evaluation are aware that there is a connection between abuse and violence in the family of a child, and the later development of parenting difficulties when that child becomes an adult. Therefore, many adults will be on the defensive against revealing a history of childhood misuse. Furthermore, it is not uncommon for adults who were abused and neglected as children to have so adapted to their unfortunate childhood experience that they have come to believe there was nothing wrong with it, that perhaps they deserved such treatment, or have formed other ways of rationalizing or forgetting their childhood experience. Thus, simple questions such as "Was your childhood happy?" are of little help. A more detailed exploration along the lines of "Where did you live as a child?," "In what sort of house?," "What did your parents do for a living?," "How many siblings were in the family?," "Who made the rules?," and "Who did the disciplining?" can enable a picture of an adult's childhood to be recovered by the evaluator. As mentioned, inquiries about which things were most liked and most disliked about key figures in the adult's childhood can be useful areas of inquiry, as well as "In what ways do you want to bring up your child differently from how your parents brought you up?" It is important to supplement this history of the parent's childhood with a history of school progress. School difficulties are very common in abused and neglected children, and this can be another indirect way of finding out what the adult's early childhood was like.

The inquiry into adolescence leads on to questions about first sexual experiences. When and from whom did the parent learn about sexuality, and what was the quality of early relationships? Were any early experiences abusive? Further inquiry is made into drug and alcohol abuse. Here again, questions along the line of how much do you drink, rather than do you drink, are more valuable. Questions also need to be asked concerning violence both outside the home and within the home. Was the adult in trouble as a juvenile—whether apprehended or not. Additionally, the adult's interests should be explored. Is babysitting enjoyed? When evaluating a potential perpetrator of incest, is he or she involved in supervising community children's groups or coaching the local team?

The adult's social history must also be explored, investigating the living situation, housing, overcrowding, and employment. Lack of employment and housing and living circumstances may cause important stress, and be very relevant to the issue of abuse and neglect. The adult's response to these stresses is important to note.

A mental status examination may be necessary in certain circumstances, but general observations of emotional state and capabilities are made while the cited areas of inquiry are being explored. For example, mood changes may be evident when describing certain events in childhood or memories of particular disappointments in the adult's marital relationships. Similarly, observations should be made concerning evidence of anxiety or depression. Any suspicion raised by the personal history or obtained from staff as to the presence of mood change, or psychological symptoms necessitates a more formal mental status examination. Similarly, a history suggestive of an organic brain disorder, such as lack of general knowledge, forgetfulness, problems with orientation or memory lead to a mental status examination. In older men or women accused of sexual abuse, a mental status examination should be performed. The examiner should be alert to paranoid delusions that may involve the child because such individuals may attempt to act upon their delusions and kill or severely harm the infant. The morbid delusions of a psychotic depression may be hard to uncover. Parents with a chronic psychosis can provide adequate care for their children at least part of the time, especially if they are linked with a mate who is not similarly affected. The worst situation is when the chronically psychotic parent meets another parent with a major personality disorder, and then attempts to bring up children. Besides the wider family situation, the character of the illness, its fluctuations, and the psychotic parent's perception of his child and his parenting role are essential. The content of any delusions or hallucinations is especially important; if the psychosis actively involves the child, then the child may be placed at high risk for death or injury. In this regard, evidence from previous psychotic episodes can be useful. Hence, the restriction of a psychiatric assessment solely to the mental status of the parent is totally inadequate and must be expanded to include family functioning and parenting capacity in order to provide an accurate assessment of the risk of abuse and neglect. Naturally, an acutely psychotic parent should not be responsible for a child. Visitation should be arranged if at all possible, but supervision is necessary. In any event, the illness and course of treatment in a psychotic parent needs to be monitored.

Post-traumatic symptoms may be evident from the history but dissociative episodes or periods of significantly raised anxiety may be evident in the session when painful events are being recalled. An attempt should be made to describe the adult's defensive mechanisms when areas such as these are explored.

Individuals who meet the criteria for borderline personality disorder need to be assessed carefully, particularly with respect to their emotional availability to the child, and their ability to parent in a *consistent* manner. In these cases, the previous track record of the individual and family, as well as the monitoring of progress over time is the yardstick by which the safety of the child can best be measured, in contrast to a one time diagnostic assessment, because the assessment of borderline states is an especially difficult one.

Physical examination should either be performed or arranged when there is any suspicion of organic disease, when the adult's physical history suggests it, or if there is a history suggestive of a physical disorder that may have an influence over the person's psychological status. Similarly, in the case of an infant with non-organic failure to thrive, the height and weight of the parents should be obtained, if this has not already been done by the pediatrician, to investigate the possibility of constitutionally small stature.

Psychological testing may be useful when the adult appears to have a limited intellectual capacity, when there is suspicion of organic disease, in those with paranoid ideas or those with significant evidence of character or personality disturbance.

The psychiatric formulation will be more helpful than the provision of a diagnostic label. The formulation must take into account psychological, social and physical factors, as well as past and present influences upon the individual, and provide a more appropriate framework with which to understand the individual than a diagnostic label. In a minority of those adults who abuse children, a formal psychiatric diagnosis is made, and even in these cases the most important assessment is the one concerning family functioning and parenting capacity. Thus, even if a formal diagnosis of major psychiatric disturbance such as schizophrenia is made by the psychiatrist, the more pertinent consideration is to what extent this adult's schizophrenia affects his or her capacity to empathize with and care for the child.

THE ASSESSMENT OF THE CHILD

When children are being seen, the reason for their referral has to be clarified in order to avoid re-interviewing children unnecessarily.

It is necessary to have full prior records relating to the child's development, whether these are looked at before evaluating the child psychiatrically or after the child has been seen. These records will include any developmental assessments, records of physical health and disease, including immunization records, psychological reports, school reports, and any reports of special placements the child may have had in foster care or group home.

Whether the child is interviewed and talked to about his situation or whether the interview consists primarily of a play session or developmental assessment will depend upon the age and developmental status of the child. At any rate, the interviewer needs to have the flexibility necessary for conducting effective child interviews. In this chapter emphasis is placed upon the psychiatric interview with the child in cases where abuse and neglect are at issue. However, it is assumed that the interview will also address the more general areas of a standard psychiatric assessment.

Inquiry should be made into the child's perspective and direct recall of any physical, sexual abuse or neglect to which the child may have been subjected. The psychiatrist also should be interested in the circumstances of any disclosure of abuse, and what was the precipitant for that disclosure. Prior to disclosing abuse to authorities, the child may have tried to tell a friend, relative or neighbor that he was in trouble, and the psychiatrist can inquire about these attempts. Older children may be able to talk about recent stresses, losses and disappointments in their lives, whereas younger children may reveal such matters only through their play.

Physically and sexually abused children have often been threatened not to tell any authority figure about their experiences. If the abuse has been going on for a long time, the children adapt to this state of affairs and become equally suspicious of outside inquiries. Such children will need a lot of reassurance in order to be able to talk about abuse, and may need more than one evaluation session. It is in these circumstances that the psychiatrist, or any interviewer, has to be cautious to avoid employing leading and suggestive questioning as a means to overcome the child's fear and silence. It is especially tempting to do so because the interviewer may be very well aware that if the child does not talk about his difficulties, the child may have to return to the abusive situation without protection. Mentioning to the child how difficult it is to talk about feelings, and letting him know that his silence is respected and understood by the interviewer can be very helpful. Equally, avoiding a more bombastic and overpowering approach is important.[17]

The older child can relate aspects of his personal history: school, home life, friends of both sexes, and his perspective of the discipline to which he has been subjected. An older child must be asked about his sexual attitudes and behavior, and some younger children who have been prematurely engaged in sexual activity may also be talked to about this area of their life. Any involvement with police or juvenile authorities, as well as drug and alcohol abuse needs to be established. With the older child, his own perspective on his psychological health, anxieties, feelings of depression, sadness, loss, disappointments, and feelings of guilt and remorse can be directly explored. History of physical health, past and present, should be obtained.

The family history has been considered under the assessment of the family above, but if the child alone is being seen, the evaluator is interested in the child's view of his family, any special alliances or relationships with other individual family members, and what tasks or special roles the child has in the family. The child's perspective on his own neighborhood can provide useful information.

The type of mental status assessment depends upon the child's age. In young children, general observations are made from the play interview, and the context in which the child expresses emotion. For example, one child was quite content talking about many of the areas described until the interviewer asked an open-ended question concerning touching. At this point, she suddenly became extremely sad and began to cry stating that she just couldn't talk about that. Children should be talked to directly about feelings of depression, suicidal or even homicidal impulses or thoughts, as well as any anxieties or fears that they may harbor. Caregivers and teachers are often not aware of the extent of a youngster's psychological distress, despite their close contact. The psychiatrist will usually make an assessment of the child's cognitive level in order to determine whether formal psychological testing is appropriate.

The physical status of abused or potentially abused children will probably have been assessed by the pediatrician. In particular, height, weight and head circumference records are necessary on children for whom abuse or neglect is suspected. Specific laboratory investigations may be necessary in cases of suspected sexual abuse. Additionally, a physical examination is needed if there is a history suggestive of physical disorder.

A psychological or developmental assessment is required because abused children have problems in this area. The problems include general intellectual impairment, language and speech delays and these may have a significant impact upon the overall psychological status of the child.

As in the situation with adults, the final formulation of the child's problems should not be made along a single dimension but rather, in a multi-axial manner. The formulation needs to include psychological disorder, cognitive functioning, specific delays in development if present, physical condition, and the child's psycho-social situation. When making a formulation in this sub-specialty area, particular emphasis has to be placed on the child's view, role, and relationships within the whole family. The formulation should also take into account the likely effect of removing the child from the family home, based on a family assessment and the type and quality of attachment between child and parents, as well as between child and siblings. In sexual abuse, the formulation addresses the effect upon the child of the perpetrator's removal from the home, where the position of other family members, especially the non-abusive parent may be crucial.

Treatment Planning

The treatment plan is based upon the assessment outlined above and also addresses the original referring problem. It takes into account both the cooperation of the various parties, as well as their previous record and attempts at therapy. However, the parents' cooperativeness early on in the assessment process may not correlate very well with outcome, and conversely, even the most uncooperative parents may do well in therapy. Any plans for treatment must be realistic with respect to personal and local resources; it is of little use to suggest daily psychoanalysis at huge expense to the unemployed, and the goals of treatment must take into account limited treatment facilities.

The treatment plan may include individual or group psychotherapy, self-help groups such as Parents Anonymous, the use of volunteers for both adults and children, and the use of health visitors, lay or professional. Additionally, the approach should include reaching out to the abusive family and all abusive families should not be expected to attend a central outpatient office or hospital.

The psychiatrist must not act alone, but be able to work in a multi-disciplinary fashion with other professionals who provide different treatment approaches. Consequently, a staffing of the various professionals is essential for coordinating treatment efforts. A treatment plan that emerges from this process should contain clear expectations as to the areas of family functioning that must change to produce a safe home for the child. Mere attendance at treatment or therapy sessions is not sufficient, and neither is the maintenance of a clean and tidy house. These are insignificant compared with altering the degree of emotional availability within a household.

If the family members reveal particularly dangerous qualities, either within an individual or within the chemistry of the family, then the treatment providers, the social services agency, and the court that is responsible for overseeing the protection of the child, must all be clearly aware that the family in question may find it difficult or even impossible to participate in treatment. In a similar vein, when the parents continue to fall beneath a minimally adequate standard vis à vis their parenting, and there has been no discernible change in them despite treatment efforts, termination of parental rights should at least be seriously considered by the involved professionals. The time frame for this consideration is not by any means established, but it has been suggested that no more than twelve months should go by when the involved child is under three, and no more than eighteen months when the child is over three. If all local resources are consumed in providing treatment for hopeless cases, then there will be nothing left for those families who *can*, with help, undergo sufficient change to become safe.[18]

Preparation of Reports

The psychiatrist's report should be prepared in a timely fashion and in accordance with the usual methods. Insofar as the report may be used during court proceedings, four areas deserve to be highlighted.

(a) Relate the diagnoses of the family, marital, parenting, individual adult(s) and child to the child's welfare and prognosis within the context of the family. Assignation of diagnostic categories alone is virtually useless.

(b) Practical suggestions by the psychiatrist are important. The psychiatrist may wish to suggest, for example, that individual therapy should be undertaken simultaneously with family therapy, or that there is a need for pharmacologic intervention for a family member, etc.

(c) Ongoing progress reports from the involved psychiatrist are vital.

(d) Estimates as to prognosis, together with the clinical basis for such a judgment, are helpful to the court.

Summary

Psychiatric assessment of abusive and neglectful parents and their children may be rather time-consuming but for many families may be the optimal way for an effective treatment plan to be developed.

References

1.   Fletcher, L. "Battered Professionals." *Child Abuse; A Community Concern.* K. Oates (Ed.), pp. 239-245. New York: Brunner/Mazel, 1982.

2.   Steele, B.F. "Psychodynamic factors in Child Abuse." *The Battered Child,* 3rd edition. C.H. Kempe and R. Helfer (Eds.). Chicago: University of Chicago Press, 1968.

3.   Kempe, C.H., F.N. Silverman, B.F. Steele, W. Droegemueller, and H.K. Silver. "The Battered Child Syndrome." *Journal of American Medical Association,* 181(1962):17-24.

4.   Steele, B.F., and C. Pollock. "A Psychiatric Study of Parents Who Abuse Infants and Small Children." *The Battered Child,* 1st edition. C.H. Kempe and R. Helfer (Eds.). Chicago: University of Chicago Press, 1968.

5.   Steele, B.F. "Parental Abuse of Infants and Small Children." *Parenthood: Its Psychology and Psychopathology.* E.J. Anthony and T. Benedek (Eds.). Boston: Little, Brown, 1970.

6.   Meadow, R. "Munchausen Syndrome by Proxy: The Hinterland of Child Abuse." *Lancet*, 2(1977):343-345.

7.   Vaughn, B., B. Egeland, A. Sroufe, and E. Waters. "Individual Differences in Infant-Mother Attachment at Twelve and Eighteen Months: Stability and Change in Families Under Stress." *Child Development*, 50(1979):971-975.

8.   Goodwin, J., D. Sahd, and R.T. Rada. "False Accusations and False Denials of Incest: Clinical Myths and Clinical Realities." *Sexual Abuse: Incest Victims and their Families*, pp. 17-33. J. Goodwin (Ed.). Boston: John Wright, 1982.

9.   Polansky, N.A., J.M. Gaudin, P.W. Ammons, and K.B. Davis. "The Psychological Ecology of the Neglectful Mother." *Child Abuse & Neglect*, 9(1985):265-271.

10.   Brown, G.W., and M. Rutter. "The Measurement of Family Activities and Relationships." *Human Relations*, 19(1966):241-263.

11.   Anthony, E.J., and T. Benedek (Eds.). *Parenthood: Its Psychology and Psychopathology*. Boston: Little, Brown, 1970.

12.   Brody, S., and S. Axelrod. *Mothers, Fathers, and Children*. New York: International Universities Press, 1978.

13.   Cath, S.H., A.R. Gurwitt, and J.M. Ross (Eds.). *Father and Child*. Boston: Little, Brown, 1982.

14.   Steinhauer, P.D. "Assessing for Parenting Capacity." *American Journal of Orthopsychiatry*, 53(1983):468-481.

15.   Dowdney, L., D. Skuse, M. Rutter, D. Quinton, and D. Mrazek. "The Nature and Qualities of Parenting Provided by Women Raised in Institutions." *Journal of Child Psychology and Psychiatry*, 26(1985):599-625.

16.   Morris, M.G., and R.W. Gould. "Role Reversal: A Concept in Dealing with the Neglect/Battered Child Syndrome." *The Neglected/Battered Child Syndrome*. New York: Child Welfare League of America, 1963.

17.   Jones, D.P.H., and M. McQuiston. *Interviewing the Sexually Abused Child*. Denver: Kempe Center Publications, University of Colorado School of Medicine, 1985.

18.   Jones, D.P.H. "The Untreatable Family." *Child Abuse & Neglect*, 11(3)(1987):409-420.

14. Interactional Assessment: Evaluation of Parent-Child Relationships in Abuse and Neglect

Clare F. Haynes-Seman and Joan Suzuki Hart

Introduction

The purpose of this chapter is to describe a videotaped assessment procedure for evaluation of parent-child relationships in cases of alleged abuse and neglect. The term "interactional assessment" describes an assessment procedure that uses observations of parent-child interaction patterns with both the target child and siblings and interview with the parents to reconstruct the children's experiences within the family. It is also useful as a tool to determine the specific psychological conflicts or social factors that resulted in the maltreatment or allegations of maltreatment of the target child.

The interview is conducted in the presence of the children, and the entire session is videotaped for subsequent review and transcription. The videotaped record allows unlimited review of interactions and transcription of the entire session. The transcribed record includes the parents' responses to specific interview questions; it also records the children's behaviors toward the adults and the parents' behaviors toward the children in various interactive contexts during the session.

Reviewing and transcribing the videotape of the session prior to drawing any conclusions about the nature of the relationship provides the objectivity that is essential to interpreting the meaning of behaviors observed and identifying the themes revealed during the interview with the parents. Recurrent themes and repetitive patterns of interaction may show not only the nature of the parents' relationship with each child but also the nature of the parents' own relationship with their parents, unresolved psychological conflicts, and current social problems that are affecting parenting capacity.

Theoretical Framework

Such an approach to the assessment of parent-child relationship is based on the theoretical work of Sander, Fraiberg, Kohut, Steele and Spitz. Sander[1] conceptualized the parent-child relationship in terms of a series of developmental issues to be negotiated. With each biological change in the infant a new issue arises in the parent-child relationship that requires changes in the social environment. For the successful negotiation of each developmental issue, the parents must be sensitive to the child's states and needs as well as demonstrate their understanding of the child's developmental needs, capabilities, and limitations. The parents' sensitivity to the child as a unique person is the primary criterion for assessing the quality of the parent-child relationship. Sensitivity refers to the parents' capacity to see the child as a separate individual and to respond to the child in a way that enhances the child's developmental competence and sense of self. The balance the parents are able to achieve between empathy and objectivity determines, in the words of Sander, "the unique combination of areas in which [the child's] needs may be met by appropriate response or further intensified by inappropriate stimulation or lack of response (p. 132)."[2]

Fraiberg and her colleagues[3] described the infant as the "catalyst" that evokes the parents' own memories of what it was like for them to be infants and leads to repetition of the parents' own experiences with their child. The influence of the parents' own experiences of being parented as reflected in their response to their infant's signals has been characterized as "ghosts in the nursery."[4] The inclusion of the child in the session allows the clinician to see not only the parents' experiences of being nurtured repeated in their interactions with their child, but also enhances the parents' recall of their own memories of what it was like to be a child.

Kohut,[5] Spitz,[6] and Steele[7] emphasized the importance of both observation and interview in understanding the development of adaptive or maladaptive behavioral patterns. Kohut[5] described the role of the child's interactions with primary nurturing figures in the development of a sense of self.

I have in mind the specific interactions of the child and his self-objects through which, in countless repetitions, the self-objects empathically respond to certain potentialities but not to others. ... This is the most important way by which the child's innate potentialities are selectively nourished or thwarted. The nuclear self, in particular, is not formed via conscious encouragement and praise and via conscious discouragement and rebuke, but by the deeply anchored responsiveness of the self-objects, which in the last analysis, is a function of the self-objects' own nuclear selves. (p. 100)[5]

Steele[6] described observing in parent-infant interactions the kinds of experiences that have produced the behavior of the adult being observed.

In the maltreatment situation we believe we can see in the parent-infant interaction the experiences that instigate in the infant the psychological patterns that produce the behavior of the very adult we are simultaneously observing. Thus, in this "experiment of nature" we are seeing a much foreshortened longitudinal study. (We observe in a single scenario the infantile beginnings and the adult outcome without having to do twenty-year-long follow-up studies.) To be sure, many other things have entered into the adult's psychic development and modified it, but the thread of continuity in psychic function between infant and adult are astonishingly clear. (p. 235)[6]

The pioneering work of Steele[7,8] showed this "thread of continuity," as parents who abused and neglected their children gave histories that indicated inadequacies in their own rearing.

Spitz[9] demonstrated the crucial role of both observation and interview in understanding the parents' behavior to the child and the ontogeny of maladaptive behaviors. Of particular relevance is Spitz's work on the effects of intense overstimulation in an environment of deprivation. The child who experiences deprivation of stimulation in most areas and intense stimulation in selected areas is particularly susceptible to the development of maladaptive behavioral patterns. Spitz described the case of Jerry diagnosed as failing to thrive at eight months of age who was observed to push his fingers into his throat to gag himself during feedings. This behavior could not be understood until observations of feeding showed his mother pushing the bottle, as well as a hard biscuit, deep into his throat. Because of the deprivation in other aspects of the relationship, these behaviors had become associated with his mother's attention and reciprocity and thus were being repeated by the child, although painful and contradictory to survival. The mother's own history with a sadistic, opinionated father provided an understanding of her intrusive feeding behaviors and her neglect of Jerry at other times.

Observations of parent-child interactions in the context of the parents' report of their own childhood experiences and experiences with the child provide insight into the disturbances in the parent-child relationship. Parents are not themselves aware of their behaviors to the child or of the conflicts from their own childhood histories that are being repeated with the child. The interactional assessment procedure provides a vehicle for the evaluator to observe the disturbances in the parent-child relationships and to identify the parents' unconscious conflicts that are being reenacted in their relationships with the child.

Overview of the Interactional Assessment

Transcription and analysis of the videotaped record of parent-child interactions and of the interview with the parents are essential features of the interactional assessment as described in this chapter. The entire process of review and transcription of the videotaped record, as well as analysis of the transcribed notes must be completed before conclusions can be drawn about the level of adequacy of parental care and the psychosocial factors that may be interfering with the development of a healthy attachment relationship. This process gives objectivity in assessing the child's experiences without undue influence of the parents' perspective or social presentation during the interview. It also helps the viewer see behaviors that are outside the range of normal even though they occur within a normal interactive context, e.g., a father tickling his three month old son's genitals while he smiles and talks to him as the mother watches, apparently oblivious to the unusual behaviors of the father to the child.

Recurrent patterns of the parents' responsiveness or of the child's behaviors in various interactive contexts are identified to determine the normal or deviant aspects of the relationship. To focus on isolated positive or negative behaviors that may have little relevance to understanding the nature of the relationship is misleading. Behaviors that appear positive on the basis of observed interactions during the session may have a different meaning when the videotaped records are reviewed and transcribed. In the analysis of observed parent-child interactions, a number of questions should be asked: What behaviors do the parents direct to the child? Are they appropriate or inappropriate in terms of the child's state, the interactive context, the child's age, or as judged by the child's response? Which clusters of behaviors consistently evoke the parents' attention and lead to reciprocity versus which behaviors are consistently ignored or evoke a minimal response? What behavior does the child consistently direct to the parents or act out with toys or in play with dolls? Are these behaviors unusual or bizarre (e.g., in the case of the child having been orally sexually abused, the child's ritualistic incorporation of oblong objects and her repeated approaches to her father with her head to his crotch followed by avoidant behavior when picked up).

Themes in the interview often give meaning to the interactive patterns or observed behaviors.   A parent who has unresolved psychological conflicts related to her parents' responses to her own injuries as a child may give attention primarily when her child is hurt but is unable to empathize with the child's pain at such times. Both observation and interview may reveal that the child is often the target of the parent's aggression and has a history of serious accidental injuries resulting from the parent's failure to anticipate and protect him from dangers in the environment. A parent who has unresolved issues related to being sexually victimized as a young child may unwittingly engage in sexually provocative play with one child who is perceived to have the characteristics that made the parent a victim as a child.   The integration of observation and interview provides information about the disturbances in the parent-child relationship not available from either observation or interview alone, or without the analysis of the transcribed record of the videotaped session.

Assessment Procedure

The assessment procedure includes a protocol for observation of interactions in different interactive contexts and for interview of the parents about their experiences with the child, their own experiences as children, and their current situation. The parents should be interviewed in the presence of the children unless the parents themselves express discomfort in talking about some topics with the children in the room or the evaluator recognizes the child's anxiety in response to the parents' insensitivity to the child (e.g., their talking openly and continuously of their dislike of the child). Portions of the interview, however, should always be conducted with the children present.

Observation in Different Interactive Contexts

Parent-child interactions are observed both when the parents are alone with the child and when they are distracted by the interview process. The parents are left alone to play with the child at the onset of the session, and then later for lunch or feeding of the child.   A separation-reunion sequence may be included to assess the child's reaction to separation from the parents, to being alone with the strange evaluator, to being alone in the room, and to reunion with the evaluator first, then with the parents. For the children who are already in foster placement and come to the evaluation separately from the parents, a reunion at the onset of the session is often diagnostic of the relationship and the effects of separation. A videotaped separation sequence as the child prepares to leave to return to foster care provides another opportunity to assess the nature of the child's attachment relationship with the parents. The attachment relationship is broadly classified as healthy or unhealthy following the original classification scheme of Ainsworth and Wittig[10] for year old infants and the more recent work of Egeland and Sroufe[11] with an abused and neglected population at twelve and eighteen months of age.

Observation of interactions in different interactive contexts shows different aspects of the child's relationship with the parent that would not be available in a shorter or less varied observation sequence. For example, a child may experience intense stimulation in the play period when alone with the parent and may be ignored when the parents are distracted by the interview process. This observation provides an understanding of the deprivation the child often experiences when the parents are distracted by other matters during the course of a normal day, in contrast to the brief periods of intense stimulation when the child is the focus of the parents' attention. Similarly, the parents' attention and reciprocity during sexually provocative play while changing a diaper may sharply contrast with the lack of eye contact and minimal interaction during lunch or at other times when the child is not fulfilling the needs of the parent. The child's capacity to play when the parents are distracted, as well as his or her initiated bids for the parents' attention during the interview, provide another dimension for understanding the nature of the parent-child relationship.

Interview Style and Protocol

The interviewer uses open-ended questions and a conversational style to enhance communication with the parents. The basic interview protocol includes topics to be addressed rather than specific questions. The interview protocol for the interactional assessment has been adapted from the protocol for the assessment of failure-to-thrive infants and toddlers developed by Kempe, Cutler, and Dean[12] and used by Haynes, Cutler, Gray, and Kempe[13] in a clinical research study of hospitalized failure-to-thrive infants. The adapted protocol includes eight major areas of inquiry:

1. Parents' View of Allegations of Maltreatment
2. Feeding Experiences from Newborn to Present
3. Prior Illnesses or Accidents
4. Prenatal and Newborn Experiences
5. Present Experiences with the Infant
6. Life Style Issues
7. Parents' Memories of their Childhood Experiences
8. Present Life Satisfaction

PARENTS' VIEW OF ALLEGATIONS OF MALTREATMENT

The overall purpose of the interview is to gather information that will enable the evaluator to determine the veracity of the allegations of abuse or neglect, the nature and severity of the maltreatment of the child, the underlying psychological or social problems that resulted in the maltreatment or the allegations of maltreatment of the child, the kind of intervention most appropriate for parent and child, and the prognosis for change in the parents' motivation and capacity to provide adequate care within a time frame appropriate for the child. To answer these questions, it is important to know how the parents see the problem that has brought them to the attention of protective services. The parents are encouraged to give their view of the allegations of maltreatment, their concerns about the child, and their experience of restricted contact with the child as a result of the allegations of maltreatment. The parents' responses to this line of questioning show their understanding of the concerns of others about parenting, their denial or acceptance of a problem in their relationship with the child, their role in the alleged abuse or neglect, their recognition of the impact of such experiences on the child, and their openness to therapeutic intervention to resolve the difficulties that led either to allegations of maltreatment or to actual maltreatment of the child.

FEEDING EXPERIENCES

In cases of growth failure with suspected underfeeding the parents are asked to describe feeding experiences since early infancy. Feeding is the primary caregiving activity in which the infant experiences a predictable relationship between his signals and the responses of the caregiver. It is also the primary context for social interactions and for the child and parent to get to know each other. Questions about the feeding history, what the child was like to feed, how he was fed, and how he let the parents know he was hungry in infancy and at present, provide an understanding of the adequacy of care and the parents' capacity for interpreting accurately and responding appropriately to their child's signals of basic needs. The parents' report may be discordant with observed feeding interactions or with the poor physical growth of the child. Their responses may convey a negative perception of the child who as an infant willfully rejected their caregiving efforts, or show the deprivation of interpersonal stimulation and the emotional abuse the child experiences in interactions with the parents. The content and style of the parents' responses become crucial in reconstructing the actual experiences of the child and in determining the effect of these experiences on the child's present or future physical growth and social emotional development.

HISTORY OF ACCIDENTS AND ILLNESSES

A history of prior accidents or illnesses is not uncommon in cases of maltreatment. The parents' description of accidents or illnesses provides insight into the child's vulnerability, the parents' failure to provide adequate protection for the child or to anticipate danger, the parents' responses to the child's injuries, and the parents' attitude toward what may be an unusual course of accidents or recurrent illnesses. Consistent kinds of physical injuries, illnesses or infections may corroborate other information in the evaluation that suggests the nature of the disturbances in the parent-child relationship.

PRENATAL AND NEONATAL EXPERIENCES

The parents are asked to recall their reaction to the pregnancy, feelings during labor and delivery, reactions to the first sight and sound of the new baby, and experiences with the baby during the newborn hospitalization and in the first months of life. Their descriptions of these experiences provide an understanding of the meaning of these events to the parents, their readiness to develop a relationship with the new baby, and their capacity to achieve a balance between empathy and objectivity in their interpretations of the baby's behaviors. The parents' description of their feelings when they first learned of the pregnancy may show their conflicts about the pregnancy which, in some cases, led to consideration of abortion or, in other cases, to consideration of suicide, to avoid delivering the unwanted child. The descriptions of the baby's first smile and the circumstances surrounding that event, as well as their perception of whether the infant cried a lot as a baby or whether he cried more or less in comparison to other babies gives a sense of their interpretation of and response to the infant's social signals, both positive and negative. The choice of a name and the wish for a boy or girl may provide an understanding of the unconscious conflicts that have interfered with the development of an attachment relationship with this baby. The parents' perception of what was hard or easy about taking care of the baby in early infancy may indicate unrealistic expectations for the baby, show the disappointment they have experienced with the baby and in their parenting role, or indicate the negative identification of the baby with another family member.

EXPERIENCES WITH THE CHILD AT PRESENT

The parents' description of recent experiences with the child gives a sense of what the relationship is like at present, as this relates to the problem that brought the child to the attention of protective services. Attitudes and behaviors that were present in the descriptions of the early experiences may continue to be expressed in the description of the child as he or she is now. The description may be unrelated to the child as observed during the session, but may reflect the parents' idealized selves or show their negative perception of the child who is not valued as a unique person. The parents' description of what kinds of things the child is doing now not only gives a sense of the child's developmental progress, but may show also the parents' disappointment in a child who does not fulfill their unrealistic expectations. Their description of what is hard or easy about taking care of the child at his or her present age shows their understanding of the needs of the child at this developmental level and their willingness to adapt to these changing needs. The description of a typical day provides some insight into how the parents spend their time, and shows the degree of the parents' involvement with the child during a normal day. Questions to assess the reasonableness of the parents' expectations for the child and their acceptance of age-appropriate behaviors include what the child does when they say "no" to him, what they do when the child says "no" to them, and what they think it is important to teach the child as he or she grows up. Responses to these question often show what the parents perceive as problems in their own growing up as well as what they think is required to be a competent member of society.

CURRENT LIFE STYLE ISSUES

The parents' responses to questions about their life style in relation to support systems, the marital relationship, substance use, leisure activities, and current problems reveal external stresses on the family that may have interfered with their parenting capacity in general or with their ability to develop an attachment relationship with the target child. The questions should be framed in a way that suggests it is socially acceptable to have problems in these areas. For example, the parents can be asked what kinds of things they argue about, on what occasions and how often they drink or use drugs, what kinds of things they like to do for fun, and what help they have in taking care of the child.

THE PARENTS' MEMORIES OF CHILDHOOD EXPERIENCES

The parents are asked to reflect on their childhoods in relation to present parenting as they are asked if they wish to raise their children the same way they were raised. If the answer is "no", they are asked what things they would like to be different, and if the answer is "yes", what they would like to be the same. This form of questioning in the presence of the child evokes memories of what it was like to be a child and shows the inadequacies in their own experiences of being parented that are being reenacted in their relationship with their children. Other probes may be used to enable the parents to recall the significant experiences of their childhood, including which parent they felt closer to when growing up, favorite siblings, where they fit in their family, significant deaths or other losses they experienced. Their memories of being children even when they believe the experiences to have been normal may show the inadequacies in their own rearing that are being unconsciously repeated in their interactions with the child. The work of Kohut (5) described earlier regarding the role of "countless repetitions" of specific interactions in the development of self and the work of Buxbaum (14) that describes the repetition of one's own experiences of being nurtured in the earliest years in terms of "body memory" provide explanations of the processes of such repetition. The cycle of maltreatment may be broken, however, with appropriate therapeutic intervention on behalf of child and parents. Fraiberg and her colleagues[4] described parent-infant psychotherapy that is directed toward enabling the parents to ". . .re-experience and remember [their] childhood anxiety and suffering." When therapy is successful, the parents ". . .become the protectors of their children against the repetition of their own conflicted past(p.196)."

CURRENT LIFE SATISFACTION

Current life satisfaction is assessed in terms of responses throughout the interview process; however, this issue may be specifically addressed by asking the parents what they would like to change in their lives right now if they were able to change anything. The response to this question not only reveals unfulfilled dreams, but gives a clear sense of their satisfaction or dissatisfaction with their parenting role and with their life at present.

Clinical Analysis of the Videotaped Session

The clinician, ideally with a multidisciplinary team, reviews the videotape of the session and makes notes of the parents' behaviors and responses to the interview questions. Based on the review of the videotape and the clinical notes, the clinician should be able to identify themes in the interview and patterns of parent and child behaviors that show the nature of the parent-child relationship and the conflicts or problems that are interfering with a healthy parent-child relationship. Recurrent themes in the interview and patterns of interaction may not be apparent until after careful review and analysis of the videotape are completed. Reviewing the videotape without repeated viewing or careful attention to patterns of parent and child behaviors may yield erroneous results as significant behaviors or verbal statements are missed or their meaning misinterpreted. As with interpretations of the parents' verbal statements, the verbal statements of the child must be interpreted within the context of clinical observations of the child's behavior during a play assessment and in interactions with the parents or other caregivers. The child's experiences with the parent are manifested in the child's behavior both in the presence and the absence of the parents. A brief synopsis of the case of Annie illustrates the use of the interactional assessment in evaluation of a failure-to-thrive child and her mother.

THE CASE OF ANNIE

Background Information: Annie was hospitalized at seven months of age because of poor weight gain. A diagnosis of non-organic failure-to-thrive and concerns about her mother's ability to provide adequate feedings or stimulation after discharge from hospital led to her placement in foster care. Two weeks after her placement in foster care, Annie was referred with her mother for an evaluation of the parent-child relationship and the mother's parenting capacity.

Themes in Interview: Ms. B. described a rejecting relationship with her mother that was unconsciously being repeated in her relationship with Annie. She was adopted soon after birth, and when she was two years old, her parents adopted a second child, a little boy. She believed her adoptive mother favored her little brother and encouraged his aggressive behavior toward her. Ms. B. described her relationship with her adoptive mother as one of mutual dislike: "My mother never liked me, and I never liked her. It worked both ways."

Ms. B. had demonstrated her inability to provide care for an older child while she was serving in the armed forces overseas. Her oldest child had also been diagnosed as failing to thrive and was removed from her care two weeks after his birth. The paternal grandparents had custody of this child, now five years old.

Ms. B.'s description of her reaction to the pregnancy with Annie showed her rejection of Annie prior to birth. She said if she had known she was pregnant, she would have miscarried as she had done with prior pregnancies. She focused on her own inconvenience when the baby was born on Thanksgiving, but noted that things worked out because her neighbor brought food to the hospital for her to eat. In her description of experiences with Annie, Ms. B. portrayed Annie as a hostile, rejecting, even aggressive baby who victimized her. When the evaluator commented on Annie's smile, Ms. B. warned her to watch for Annie's teeth, noting that Annie had bitten her once. When asked to say how Annie let her know when she was hungry, she said most of the time she cried; then she noted that "sometimes she won't, sometimes I catch her before she cries, and sometimes she cries before I'm ready to feed her." This account graphically showed the asynchrony that characterized their relationship and provided an understanding of the problems that had led to inadequate feedings for Annie. When asked why Annie cried, she said most of the time she had a wet diaper, but that sometimes she wanted to eat. She then complained that recently Annie had been sleeping through the night and waking up soaked because the child didn't let her know she was wet.

Ms. B. denied she had ever hurt Annie, but described instances in which Annie's father, from whom she was currently separated, had become upset with Annie's crying and she had had to protect Annie from his abuse. She said there were times when she did get frustrated with Annie's crying and wanted to throw her against the wall, but would vent her anger by throwing a toy instead. Ms. B.'s interpretation of Annie's crying showed her projection of her own feelings onto Annie: She said Annie threw temper tantrums when she wanted to sleep on the water bed and was not allowed to do so, and that she got mad when her favorite television program was discontinued by the network. Her mother's description of her frustration with Annie suggested Annie was at risk for abuse as well as neglect if returned to her mother's care.

Ms. B. showed little insight into the inadequacies in care that had led to Annie's poor weight gain. She said she believed weight gain was related to genetics and not to intake. She was a very obese woman who had had problems with weight since elementary school. However, she denied that eating had anything to do either with her obesity or Annie's failure to thrive. She said, "I eat like a bird and look at me, she eats like a horse and look at her."

Patterns of Interaction: Ms. B. held Annie in her lap facing away during most of the session even when left alone to play with her at the beginning of the session. Her comments were consistently negative and degrading, and her actions punishing and rejecting. Annie avoided eye contact with her mother. She did not smile or vocalize to her mother, although she did make eye contact and smile at the evaluator whom she did not know. Hence, she showed a differential avoidance of her mother not observed with others.

Observations of feeding showed Ms. B.'s active interference with Annie's ability to feed even when she was hungry. The session had been scheduled at a regular feeding time and food was brought from the foster home. At the onset of the session, Ms. B. was reminded that it was close to Annie's feeding time and that she should feel free to feed her whenever she thought Annie was hungry. About 30 minutes into the two-hour session, Annie began to give intermittent signals of distress as she fussed briefly, rubbed her eyes, rubbed her ears, chewed her hand, and showed a general restlessness. Ms. B. ignored these signals until Annie's fussiness escalated to a cry, at which point she offered her a pacifier that Annie rejected. When the evaluator's discomfort led her to suggest that Annie might be hungry, Ms. B. said she thought she was tired, but that she would see if she were hungry. As Ms. B. prepared the bottle, Annie's attention remained on the bottle. When her mother placed her in a reclined position and moved the bottle toward her mouth, Annie did not relax but maintained her visual attention on the proffered bottle. Just as the nipple was approaching Annie's mouth, Ms. B. withdrew the bottle and placed it aside as she accused Annie of wetting on her again and said she would have to change her. Annie cried and reached toward the bottle, but did not persist in her distress when her signals were ignored by her mother who spent a prolonged period in dressing, changing, and redressing her before starting the feeding. The difficulty her mother had in giving her the bottle was reflected in her statement that she would feed her if she "could find the bottle." After the feeding was in progress, Ms. B. looked at Annie and apologized for the delay; she said she was sorry but she had to change her diaper.

At the onset of the feeding, Annie sucked vigorously as she maintained her visual attention on her mother. She would briefly release the nipple to burp herself. When Ms. B. removed the bottle to burp Annie, she waited until Annie began to fuss before resuming the feeding. When Annie closed her eyes during the feeding, her mother demanded that she open them if she wanted more food. Annie went to sleep after taking only a small amount of formula and slept snuggled up against her mother's chest until her mother awakened her for play toward the end of the session.

When Ms. B. was left alone to play with Annie after the completion of the interview, her play was aggressive and withholding. She pushed toys into Annie's face or offered a toy and then withdrew it just as Annie reached for it.

Summary of Results: The results of the evaluation showed severe disturbances in the parent-infant relationship, a poor prognosis for Ms. B. to be able to provide adequate feedings for Annie, and a potential for her to abuse or further neglect Annie. It was recommended that Annie should remain in foster placement while her mother began a treatment program. The court-ordered treatment plan included parenting classes, counseling for the mother, and supervised weekly visits with Annie.

Reevaluation One Year Later: Annie was reevaluated with her mother one year after the initial evaluation. Ms. B. had completed her counseling, attended parenting classes, and had had supervised visits with Annie. The evaluation indicated a lack of positive change in the mother-child relationship. Annie responded to her mother's social initiations by screaming at her, hitting her, and running away from her. Although Annie appeared to be hungry, she was unable to eat when her mother's attention was on her or when in physical contact with her mother. Once, when she was covertly eating food behind her mother's back, she responded to her mother's attention and speech by crouching and facial grimacing. She was focused on food and eating throughout the session, but could not feed herself or pantomime-feed the doll. She would place the doll on various surfaces around the room and try to feed it the bottle. She could occasionally feed the doll with the bottle directly to the stomach, or put the bottle in the doll's hand. However, she was unable to feed the doll with the bottle directly to the mouth. She would start moving the bottle toward the doll's mouth, and then interrupt her action to scream at the doll and hit it. She would then pick the doll up, hold it *en face* and talk softly as if apologizing for her actions. At other times, she would deliberately place the doll on its stomach or facing away. She would set up the table and chairs for the small doll figures to eat, but would move them to another location and repeat the activity before anyone was "fed."

Ms. B. showed the same withholding of food as observed during the bottle feeding at eight months. She offered the bag of chips to Annie with, "See what I've got." When Annie hesitantly approached and reached toward the bag, Ms. B. moved it out of reach, took a chip for herself, and then offered a chip to Annie directly to her mouth.

Ms. B. showed no insight into the problems in her relationship with Annie that had led to the failure-to-thrive or to Annie's avoidant behavior with her. She gave the same account of her mother's rejection of her as a child, and her anger toward her husband whom she believed to be a danger to herself and to society. She had made no progress in resolving conflicts related to her experiences with a rejecting mother who encouraged her brother's aggression to her. These conflicts were now affecting her capacity for relationships of intimacy not only with Annie but with others. She had no understanding of the psychological needs of Annie or of the importance of her maternal role. She believed Annie was now old enough to play with other children on the street and needed very little attention from her except to feed, bathe, or dress her.

Because of the lack of positive change in Ms. B.'s relationship with Annie and the poor prognosis for her to be able to develop a relationship of intimacy with Annie, termination of parental rights was recommended. Tragically, the child died one month after the evaluation, while in foster care.*

Summary and Implications

This approach to the assessment of parent-child relationships in cases of alleged maltreatment has been found to provide information not available through interview with the parents alone or through direct observations of interactions. The relationships that have developed in day to day interactions, whether healthy or unhealthy, are reflected in the behaviors of both parents and children even when they are aware of being videotaped. In some cases, parents may make every effort to present themselves well and may attempt to inhibit behaviors that they believe others might view as inappropriate; however, patterns of the parents' behaviors to the child, as well as the child's behaviors to the parents, reveal the experiences of the child within the family, and, in many cases, the parents' own experiences of being parented.

The interactional assessment provides an understanding of family dynamics, unresolved conflicts from the parents' own experiences of being parented, and external social factors that have resulted in the abusive or neglectful parenting. A feedback session with the parents after completion of the interactional assessment may enable the parents to recognize problems in their relationship with the child which resulted in the maltreatment and make them amenable to becoming involved in appropriate treatment programs. If psychotherapy is indicated, progress in therapy may be enhanced when the therapist has access to the results of the interactional assessment and begins therapy with some insight into the parents' psychological conflicts and how these conflicts are reflected in their interactions with the child.

As Alice Miller[15] has so poignantly described, the parents rely on the therapist to help them see what they cannot see for themselves:

> Because this process does not begin in adulthood but in the very first days of life as a result of the efforts of often well-meaning parents, in later life the individual cannot get to the roots of this repression without help. It is as though someone has had stamped on his back a mark that he will never be able to see without a mirror. One of the functions of psychotherapy is to provide the mirror. (p. 7)[15]

In cases of severe and early maltreatment in which the parents survived by repressing their pain and anger, even as infants, psychotherapy for both parents and the infant may offer the only hope for the parents to overcome childhood tragedies and to avoid repeating them with their children. Parenting classes, weekly visits by a social worker, or other supportive services may provide some relief to the stressed parents, but are unlikely to help the parents resolve psychological conflicts that are interfering with empathic parenting. Parents who have no history of good relationships with nurturing parenting figures or with significant others have a poor prognosis for establishing a relationship with their child or with a therapist. The goal of all treatment programs is to help the parents resolve the problems that are interfering with empathic parenting while modifying the child's experiences within the family to avoid further psychological damage to the child. When the prognosis is extremely poor for the parents to be able to develop a good relationship with the child, we need to give the child the opportunity to establish relationships of trust with empathic and nurturing adult caregivers.

Notes

* Review of autopsy results indicated Annie died from early pneumonia and streptoccal sepsis (bacterial infection in the bloodstream). At the time of death, Annie's weight was still significantly below the 5th percentile. Whereas normally behavioral signs have predictive value for severity of febrile illness as early as the second month of life, this may not have been the case for Annie even at 20 months of age. Roberts (*Contemporary Pediatrics* 4(1987):14-30) noted that physicians when evaluating the significance of fever in infants are "heavily influenced by such signs as social eye contact and playfulness."(p.16) When these normal signs of physical health are not a part of the child's repertoire because of early social deprivation, one speculates that illness may go undetected until fatal.

The authors express appreciation to Diane Baird, M.S.W., for her editorial comments on this chapter and to both Diane Baird and Michele Kelly, Psy.D., for their contributions to the content through their use of the interactional assessment in evaluation and treatment of at-risk children and their families.

Jane Gray, M.D. provided the synopsis of the death of Annie.

References

1. Sander, L.W. "The Longitudinal Course of Early Mother-Child Interaction: Cross Case Comparison in a Sample of Mother-Child Pairs." *Determinants of Infant Behaviors*, Vol. IV. B.M. Foss (Ed.), pp. 189-227. London: Methuen & Co., 1969.

2. Sander, L.W. "Issues in Early Mother-Child Interaction." *Infant Psychiatry: A New Synthesis*. R.N. Rexford, L.W. Sander, and T. Shapiro (Eds.), pp. 127-147. New Haven: Yale University Press, 1976.

3. Fraiberg, S., V. Shapiro, and D.S. Cherniss. "Treatment Modalities." *Clinical Studies in Infant Mental Health: The First Year of Life*. S. Fraiberg (Ed.), pp. 49-77. New York: Basic Books, 1980.

4. Fraiberg, S., E. Adelson, and V. Shapiro. "Ghosts in the Nursery: A Psychoanalytic Approach to the Problem of Impaired Infant Mother Relationships." *Clinical Studies in Infant Mental Health: The First Year of Life*. S. Fraiberg, (Ed.), pp. 164-196. New York: Basic Books, 1980.

5.   Kohut, H. *The Restoration of Self.* New York: International Universities Press, 1976.

6.   Steele, B.F.   "The Effect of Abuse and Neglect on Psychological Development." *Frontiers of Infant Psychiatry.* J.D. Call, E. Galenson, R.L. Tyson (Eds.), pp. 231-244. New York: Basic Books, 1983.

7.   Steele, B.F. "Psychodynamic Factors in Child Abuse." *The Battered Child,* 3rd edition.   C.H. Kempe and R.E. Helfer (Eds.), pp. 49-85.   Chicago: University of Chicago Press, 1980.

8.   Steele, B.F. "Generational Repetition of the Maltreatment of Children." *Parental Influences on Health and Disease.* E.J. Anthony and G. H. Pollock (Eds.), pp. 121-133. Boston: Little, Brown, 1985.

9.   Spitz, R. "The Derailment of Dialogue: Stimulus Overload, Action Cycle, and the Completion Gradient." *Rene A. Spitz: Dialogues from Infancy: Selected Papers.* R.N. Emde (Ed.), pp. 161-178. New York: International Universities Press, 1983.

10. Kempe, R.S., C. Cutler, and J. Dean. "The Infant with Failure to Thrive." *The Battered Child,* 3rd edition.   C.H. Kempe and R.E. Helfer (Eds.), pp. 163-172. Chicago: University of Press, 1980.

11. Haynes, C.F., C. Cutler, J. Gray, and R.S. Kempe. "Hospitalized Cases of Non-Organic Failure to Thrive: The Scope of the Problem and Short Term Lay Health Visitor Intervention." *Child Abuse & Neglect,* 8(1984):229-242.

12. Ainsworth, M.D.S., and B.A. Wittig. "Attachment and Exploratory Behavior of One-Year-Olds in a Strange Situation." *Determinants of Infant Behavior,* Vol. IV. B.M. Foss (Ed.), pp. 111-136. London: Methuen & Co., 1969.

13. Egeland, B., and A. Sroufe. "Attachment and Early Maltreatment." *Child Development,* 52(1981):44-52.

14. Buxbaum, E. "Vulnerable Mothers—Vulnerable Babies." *Frontiers of Infant Psychiatry.* J.D. Call, E. Galenson, R.L. Tyson (Eds.), pp. 86-94. New York: Basic Books, 1983.

15. Miller, A. *For Your Own Good: Hidden Cruelty in Childhood and the Roots of Violence.* Toronto: McGraw-Hill Ryerson, Ltd., 1983.

15. The Law Enforcement Officer as a Member of the Child Protection Team

Robert Kean and
Edward J. Rodgers, Jr.

Introduction

The abused child is an individual who is truly beleaguered by his environment. He is like a person standing in a rising tide who is unable to move.

The job of the child protection team is to erect a caisson around this child to hold back the tide until it recedes. The walls of this caisson barrier comprise the four basic components of child protection: medicine, social work, law enforcement, and the legal profession (including the courts). If any component fails in its task, the team fails and the child is left to fend for himself in his hostile environment.

This chapter discusses the role of law enforcement in child protection and the application of the specialized skills that only law enforcement has to offer the abused child.

Law enforcement officers are often resistant to becoming involved in child abuse investigations. This is unfortunate. Our belief is that this problem arises from two basic areas of confusion. The first area is based on the belief that law enforcement should not become involved in any *civil* court action. Since, on average, less than 10% of all child abuse investigations will result in the filing of criminal charges, officers often feel that this is an area not worthy of their time.

While it is true that officers should strive to remain uninvolved in *private* civil disputes, such as breach of contract or damage actions, this is not the case in dependency and neglect actions. These actions are brought by the state on behalf of the child. They are not private disputes, but are state actions just as criminal prosecutions are state actions. The main differences are that the goal is not punishment and the burden of proof is *less* than that needed for a criminal action.

The second area of confusion arises out of the fact that child abuse investigations should not be approached in the manner of the classic investigative models used, often unconsciously, by law enforcement officers to investigate other types of crimes. This leaves the officers feeling uncomfortable and uncertain as to what steps to take.

Reasons for Law Enforcement Involvement

There are, however, compelling reasons for law enforcement officers to become involved in child abuse cases.

First, child abuse is a crime. Law enforcement agencies should not refuse to investigate it solely because it has not been traditionally investigated or because some other non-law enforcement public agency also investigates it.

Second, law enforcement agencies have skills and resources that are highly applicable to child abuse investigations. In many places, law enforcement is the only agency available 24 hours a day to respond to calls for help.

Third, law enforcement is also the only agency empowered to take children into protective custody without a court order in most jurisdictions.

Fourth, officers have tremendous experience in recording detailed information uncovered during investigations for later use in court.

Fifth, they have the resources to do crime scene examinations for the collection of physical evidence and the preservation of that evidence for later use in court. All evidence that would be useful in criminal court would also be useful in civil court to determine custody of an abused child.

Sixth, law enforcement agencies are solely empowered to obtain search warrants to look for this evidence.

Finally, law enforcement agencies have the broadest access to their community of any public agency. In the course of daily interactions, the officer on the street will come across evidence of previously unreported abuse. Agencies should encourage officers to pursue these investigations.

Traditional Law Enforcement Models

While police skills are highly applicable to child protection investigations, the two traditional investigative models used by officers are not.

In the first model, the officer receives a report of a crime from a citizen, who requests the officer to take action on the report. The officer then takes a formal report, gathers evidence, interviews witnesses, and starts a search for the perpetrator.

In the second (officer initiated) model, the officer sets out to look for a specific criminal action. When the officer sees a certain activity, he makes a preliminary determination of whether or not it fits the definition of a crime. If it does, the officer stops the perpetrator and questions him (a Terry stop). He then arrests the subject.

Child abuse investigations do not fit these models for a number of reasons. First, in both cases criminal activity is presumed at the initial stage of the process. In child abuse cases, a great deal of investigation must often be undertaken prior to a determination that a crime has been committed. Also, in each of the prior models, the officer is either a direct witness to the crime or he has a complaining witness pressing for action. Child abuse victims rarely complain to the police and child abuse is even more rarely committed in front of witnesses or law enforcement officers. This means the officer must continue an investigation without the traditional perceived support for his actions.

An Alternative Law Enforcement Model

We would propose an alternative investigative model specific to child abuse. In this model, the officer receives a report of a child who has suffered an injury of unknown origin. The officer responds and identifies the injuries *in detail*. The officer then determines the mechanism of injury (exactly what type of actions could cause the injury, e.g., a twisting force to a leg for a spiral fracture or immersion in a hot liquid for a stocking burn pattern).

The officer then establishes who had custody of the child at the time the injury was received and interviews the custodian of the child about the *reported* mechanism of injury. A comparison is made between the reported mechanism of injury and the known mechanism of injury. If they are inconsistent, child abuse is then presumed.

If the known mechanism and the reported mechanism of injury are consistent and the reported mechanism of injury is accidental in nature, then the injuries are presumed to be accidental.

Use of this model will avoid needless trauma to families in incidents that turn out to be accidental and will insure that non-accidental trauma is properly investigated.

Documentation of Observations

Once a potential child abuse case has come to the attention of the officer, he should immediately determine what type of injuries the child has suffered.   While extremely small injuries may not have any direct significance to the child's health, they can be of extreme importance in determining the mechanism of injury. Therefore, no injury is too small to be documented.

Officers should be extremely aware of small injuries on planes of the child's body other than the major area of trauma. Children normally suffer one injury per action. Multiple injuries on various planes indicate multiple actions.

Some types of injuries are normal for active young children such as bruising over bony surfaces (e.g., shins, knees, elbows). On the other hand, bruises to the stomach, backs of the thighs, buttocks and other soft tissue areas are less likely to be accidental.

Circumferential ("wrap around") injuries are indicative of a blow inflicted by a flexible object, such as a cord or belt. In such a case, if the explanation offered is that the child fell onto a coffee table, the reported mechanism of injury is obviously not the known mechanism of injury, and must be deliberately inflicted (non-accidental).

Medical Examinations

When serious injuries occur, the child will be examined by a physician. The officer should interview the examining physician, obtaining a *detailed* statement of the medical findings. The officer should specifically ask about all major and minor injuries that the child has suffered. The officer should document in detail what history was given to the physician by the custodian of the child. The officer should find out if all the injuries are of the same relative age. The officer should ask the physician what would cause such injuries, both major and minor, in one incident.

Finally, in a case of serious injury to a small child, it can be helpful if the officer provides the physician with a doll and asks him to chart on it the injuries the child has suffered. Such a three-dimensional record becomes the doctor's "original notes" and may be relied upon at a trial to explain the case. This procedure also gives the trier of fact a better understanding of the relationship between the various injuries on the child than does a verbal explanation.

This record will assist the officer in attempting to reconstruct the incident which caused the injuries to the child. Such a reconstruction can be extremely important in discovering the actual process of an injury such as an immersion burn.

Detailed color photographs should also be taken of the child, both with and without a scale.

Interviewing Children

All children who are able to talk should be interviewed regarding what happened to them. Various states handle the question differently of whether or not these statements can be later admitted into evidence. Regardless of how the courts rule on this question, the child's statement is vital to the investigative process.

This statement should always be taken outside of the parents' presence. The officer should not only be alert to indications of who injured the child and how but also to statements that indicate the location of the scene and the existence of possible physical evidence.

The officer should also be alert to signs of coaching in the child. The exact words the child uses in his or her statement are all important in determining reliability and should be documented as such. A child who speaks normally for his age but then uses terms beyond his years to describe his injuries as accidental may have been coached.

At the initial stages of the interview with a child, an officer should identify himself and explain, in terms that the child can understand, his purpose for investigating the injuries. Children, as adults, have a sense of privacy. If this is not respected, the child may decide not to tell what happened.

Too much of an explanation can be as bad as none. Children do not need a detailed explanation of the legal process. Something along the following lines should suffice. "Hi, I'm Officer Smith. I'm a policeman. One of my jobs is to protect children. I'm worried about how you got hurt.

Sometimes grown-ups do things that hurt kids and my job is to make them stop. Before I can make them stop, I have to know what they did. I want to talk with you to find out if someone did something to hurt you so I can make whoever did it stop. OK?"

When interviewing the custodian of the child who has been abused, it is recommended that the Miranda warning be given, even in a non-custodial setting. There are several reasons for this. First of all, the perpetrator expects it. He or she has been conditioned by the popular media to think that this is the way it should be. When given along with an explanation as to why the investigation is being conducted, the officer can express a professional, detached, impartial attitude, that is essential to a successful interview. Rather than alarm the custodian of the child, the officer can impress the individual with his fairness.

It is preferable and very easy to interview a suspect or witness without accusing him of child abuse. The media has popularized the notion that certain types of injuries to *adults* have to be investigated by the police, (e.g., all gunshot wounds, traffic accidents, etc.). When a parallel is drawn between these cases and a case of a child who suffers certain types of injury, the custodian will normally be much less sensitive to the fact that an investigation is being conducted.

Second of all, if the court were to rule that the interview was custodial in nature, the statements would still be admissible. Care should be taken to point out to the subject of the interview that he is not under arrest just because he has been advised of his rights. All potential perpetrators should be interviewed separately so that it is more difficult to cover up inconsistencies.

The interview with a potential abuse perpetrator should be prioritized so that if the interview is cut short, essential information has not been omitted. Normal biographical information common to all police interviews should be obtained first. The next information needed is the custody status of the child at the time the injuries were apparently inflicted. This should be followed by recording a *detailed* explanation of how the child received all of the injuries discovered in the examination, both new and old. At this stage, the perpetrator should not be confronted. The officer should document these statements in a matter-of-fact manner and then obtain a detailed statement of the child's activities in the period of time in question. The officer should be alert to unusual perceptions or unrealistic expectations on the part of the interviewee towards the child. Examples are a parent who thinks an infant doesn't "like" him, or one who thinks a one year old wets his pants because he is "mad" at his caretaker.

The officer should specifically ask about common discipline used with the victim. He should also discuss .the custodian's childhood history. Where the interviewee was raised and by whom, and what common discipline was used can all be useful. The subject should also be asked if he considered himself abused as a child.

Evidence at the Scene

The officer should ask to see the scene where the child was injured. This extremely basic step in the process is often overlooked by even the most experienced investigator. The officer should always keep in mind the possible existence of physical evidence when examining the scene. Blood stains, semen stains, hair, and fiber evidence may be found at the scene and support or refute the claims of the caretaker. An instrument used to inflict a characteristic shape of bruises may be found. The physical characteristics of the premises may preclude the possibility of the injury having been received in the manner reported. An example is a child who sustains a subdural hematoma and the reported mechanism of injury is a fall from a crib to the floor, but an examination reveals the crib is only 24 inches off a thickly carpeted floor.

At this point, if the reported mechanism of injury, the scene of the injury, and the known mechanism of injury are not consistent, this should be pointed out to the caretaker in a firm, logical, and non-judgemental manner. The interviewer should then ask the subject for a response to these inconsistencies. Even if the officer believes the party to have lied, he should end the interview on a positive note and indicate a willingness to explore the subject's explanation further. The officer might ask if it would be all right to contact the subject later to clarify these differences.

Nonexpert Witnesses

Lay witnesses are often overlooked in child abuse investigations, although officers realize that most other police investigations would be impossible without them. Friends or neighbors, especially those who accompany a caretaker to a hospital, can be the source of important information, even if they are hostile to the idea of an investigation being conducted.

Lay witnesses can be a source of information about versions of events given previously by the caretaker, prior injuries, and unusual attitudes on the part of the caretaker towards the child. All of these things can be of importance in follow-up interviews conducted with the suspected perpetrator. They can also be of importance in establishing battered child syndrome later in court.

One investigative aid that many law enforcement agencies have at their disposal is the polygraph. However, the use of the polygraph is very controversial. As with any tool, it is quite useful if properly used by a skilled examiner and ineffective or even dangerous if applied inappropriately or used by an untrained individual.

A child abuse investigator should observe some basic points when using the polygraph. First, the polygraph is an investigative aid, not a trier of fact. Neither is it a substitute for a complete investigation. The more information the examiner has when designing his questions, the better the results will be. The polygrapher needs to have an understanding of the mechanism of injury to do a valid test. The test subject should not be interviewed in an accusatory manner on the day of the test. If the case involves a major emotional trauma such as a death or serious injury, the test should not be conducted for about two weeks after the funeral or incident. Test questions should be designed in a factual, non-emotional manner. Emotional terms, such as rape, sexual assault, abuse, assault, beat, etc., should be avoided. Rather than these terms, unemotional descriptions of the acts should be used. Tests should take between 60 and 90 minutes, minimum, including the pre-test interview. The reliability of the test declines proportionately with a decrease in time allotted to the test. Finally, polygraph tests on children under the age of 14 years are difficult.

The Court Process

As previously stated, there is a tendency on the part of law enforcement officers not to get involved in civil matters. Most officers believe that if they do a thorough job investigating a crime and can prove that a criminal act has been committed, then the perpetrator should be punished. However, child abuse investigations are not fully understood by many law enforcement officers because in most jurisdictions there are two investigations going on at the same time, evolving from the same set of facts.

The department of social services conducts an investigation concurrent with the police investigation to determine whether civil action needs to be taken to safeguard the child. Their investigation may involve obtaining a court order to remove a child from the custody of one or both parents. If the child is removed from the home, the parents must be notified of this fact. Depending on the jurisdiction, a custody hearing is held within 24 to 72 hours. These hearings are usually held before family courts, juvenile judges, referees, or commissioners.

The court, after hearing testimony concerning the case, makes a decision as to whether both the legal and physical custody of the child should be vested in the department of social services or in the parents. Hearsay is usually allowed in such hearings. As in criminal cases, parents are given an opportunity for representation by an attorney. A guardian ad litem, usually an attorney, may be appointed to protect the interests of the child or children. A child can be placed in foster care as a result of such a hearing or be returned to the parents.

As part of this legal inquiry, the court may order psychological evaluations, issue restraining orders, and order various types of therapy to be provided for members of the family. The process can go on for years with periodic reviews. It can also result in termination of parental rights. The role of the social worker in these cases is to be supportive to the family and the ultimate goal is to keep the family intact, whenever possible. The paramount consideration, however, is the safety of the child.

The evidence required for adjudication of a civil court procedure is a preponderance of evidence, whereas, in the criminal court, proof beyond a reasonable doubt is the standard, even though the case may be based on the same facts. In a few jurisdictions, the civil standard may be clear and convincing evidence, which is still well short of beyond a reasonable doubt.

Many law enforcement officers, as a result of their training and philosophy, often shy away from the civil side of the case. With experience in child abuse investigations, they eventually realize that because of the nature of these cases, it is neither always possible, nor desirable, to convict a perpetrator of abuse. Such a situation will lead the officer beyond the normal parameters of his criminal investigation. Then, as a member of the community multidisciplinary team, he can help the department of social services in safeguarding the child. The usefulness of the law enforcement officer in the civil court process lies in his ability to collect and preserve evidence to support the civil case. He should not view himself as a case-worker. He is to safeguard the peace, health, and welfare of the community by use of his police powers.

Testimony

In either the civil or criminal action, the law enforcement agency can be the central depository for all evidence utilized in the case. The officer should be called for testimony in the civil case, as his training and experience have prepared him to be an effective witness.

The following is a list of suggestions for successful court testimony:

1. Be direct, brief, and have a judicious yet pleasant demeanor.
2. Respond to the question and avoid extraneous matter.
3. Don't go beyond the subject matter of the question.
4. Avoid going into medical-legal issues.
5. Explain your investigation sequentially.
6. Explain, in layperson's terms, the medical injuries you observed.
7. Avoid police or legal jargon.
8. Don't become argumentative on cross examination.
9. If, on cross examination, the attorney misquotes you, straighten it out right away and without emotion, e.g., "that is not what I stated. What I stated was _____ ." (And here you have an opportunity to repeat your testimony again.)
10. Avoid nervous mannerisms.
11. Avoid gestures.
12. When you respond to questions, look at the judge or jury.

Lastly, in preparation for court, the law enforcement officer should review all pertinent reports; determine that all evidence to be introduced is readily available. If at all possible, a discussion of the officer's testimony prior to trial should be undertaken with the attorney who will handle the people's case.

The officer, to be effective and credible in testifying, should avoid excessively referring to his notes or reports.

Medical Testimony

Frequently, the term "battered child syndrome" comes up in the course of a child abuse trial. It is a medical diagnosis introduced usually by a pediatrician, medical examiner, pathologist or other medical expert and is admissible in court in most states. There are several elements that establish the criteria for the battered child syndrome. Courts have recognized the following factors in making this diagnosis:

1. The child is usually under three years of age.
2. There is evidence of bone injury at different stages of healing.
3. There are subdural hematomas, with or without skull fractures.
4. There is evidence of soft tissue injury.
5. There is evidence of neglect.
6. The aforementioned injuries are inconsistent with the explanation given by the custodian as the mechanism of injury.

The officer's testimony is normally the source of the *detailed* explanation of the mechanism of injury given by the custodian. It is up to expert medical witnesses to explain to the trier of fact why the explanation given is not plausible and to propose an alternate explanation. Related types of medical evidence can be offered for children of any age and with other injuries, as described in the medical chapters of this book.

The officer should be aware that medical physical findings are just one type of expert testimony that is available. Other forms of expertise which may be relevant include child development, child psychiatry or psychology, and forensic odontology.

Special Law Enforcement Officer Problems

Often, law enforcement officers are confronted with events in the field that represent special problems in the area of child protection. One of these is the discovery of a dead child who is the possible victim of sudden infant death syndrome (SIDS), more commonly called crib death. Sometimes, a child abuse homicide resembles a SIDS case. The problem for the officer then becomes one of how to perform a minimally intrusive investigation while still preserving the case for further follow-up should the autopsy reveal that the child died as a result of abuse.

All deaths of children that occur outside of medical care should be investigated. This is important for two reasons: it keeps a potential homicide from eluding investigation, and it creates a precedent so that there is no question that these cases are a routine non-criminal matter handled by the law enforcement agency. This removes the necessity to administer a Miranda warning.

The routine report in sudden death cases should include:

1. The last time the child was seen alive and well.
2. When and what the child last ate.
3. Any illness, deformation or other medical problems.
4. Any pre-death symptoms.
5. Who discovered the child and when.
6. What actions were taken upon discovery of the child.
7. Who was the child's custodian during the time in question.
8. A description of the scene at which the child died.

The officer should also look at the victim for any signs of trauma. Care should be taken not to confuse lividity with bruising.

If possible, depending upon local practice, the investigator should attend the child's autopsy. If the autopsy reveals the child died of SIDS, the investigator should re-contact the parents. They should be provided information on SIDS and referred to one of the many support groups for parents who have lost a child in this manner. The key point is sensitivity. These parents, and particularly the final caretaker of the child, are likely to be experiencing a great deal of unfounded guilt over the child's death.

The parents may have moved, dressed, cleaned or otherwise changed the child's final position prior to calling the authorities. These actions may have been a reflection of this unfounded guilt over perceived neglect rather than an attempt to destroy evidence.

If, on the other hand, the autopsy reveals that the child died as a result of a trauma, the parents should be re-contacted, the Miranda warning given, and the parents re-interviewed with these findings in mind. The investigation should then proceed as any other child abuse homicide investigation.

"Chicken Hawk Pedophiles" and "Home Movie Pornography"

Another special law enforcement problem is dealing with the "chicken hawk" type of child molester or other producer of "home grown" types of child pornography. These cases normally have not involved other agencies since the perpetrators live outside the home.

Investigators should involve other members of the child protection team in these cases, especially the social service agency.

In these cases, the victims are quite different from victims of other crimes. They are often willing participants in their own victimization. They have been seduced into these activities by the perpetrators and are at high risk for re-victimization if intervention is not undertaken.

Officers who deal with runaways should be alert to signs that the child has been sexually exploited by an adult. A child who has been "kept" and supported by an adult while on the run should be gently questioned about how he was able to survive while on his own.

Officers should also be alert to signs of child pornography. "Kiddie porn" is contraband, per se, and may be seized whenever an officer lawfully comes into contact with it.

It is not uncommon for a victim of a "chicken hawk" or homosexual pedophile to turn around and burglarize the chicken hawk's home after the relationship has ended. The victim may feel safe in committing the crime. Officers who see evidence of a preoccupation with children of a specific age and sex in the home of a single burglary victim should be aware of this possibility. When the burglar is caught, this possibility should be explored.

Officers should keep in mind that individuals who take sexually explicit pictures of children usually keep this material forever. It is their most prized possession. Thus, information of the existence of homemade "kiddie porn" does not grow stale for the purposes of a search warrant.

The untreated victim of a "chicken hawk" or "chicken," as these perpetrators refer to their victims, is at great risk of becoming a perpetrator himself in later life if intervention is not undertaken. While therapy is well outside of the role of the law enforcement agency, for the case to be properly handled it should be brought to the attention of the child protection team.

Summary

The "lone ranger" type of investigation is fine for most police work. Child protection is different. The law enforcement community claims to "serve and protect." Yet, law enforcement cannot protect children and serve their interests unless it is done through coordinated efforts with other professionals. The officer should become familiar with those who also serve and protect children in the community and attempt to gain an appreciation for their role.

Law enforcement, generally, must come to grips with this problem in all of its myriad dimensions and join the multidisciplinary effort on behalf of these victims. By the same token, the other members of the team should seek out the law enforcement officers who deal with children so they are aware of what law enforcement can do to help their efforts.

We must all find a way to stand in the tiny shoes of these precious members of society whom we are sworn to protect.

PART III

Case Conferences

Section Editor: Marilyn R. Lenherr

16. Program and Case Coordination

Marilyn R. Lenherr, Carol C. Haase,
and Janet K. Motz

Introduction

The need for coordinated community resources to address the complexity and volume of child abuse and neglect cases has resulted in the emergence of child protection teams throughout the nation. The purpose of these teams is to foster a coordinated interdisciplinary team approach to diagnosis, treatment, consultation and prevention of child abuse. Teams have evolved into several basic forms according to community needs, state statutes, and funding allocations. They may differ according to definition, structure, purpose, and uniqueness of community needs and resources; however, as a requisite, program coordination guidelines must be developed. This chapter concentrates on aspects of coordination that are relevant to implementation of any type of interdisciplinary team. These include external factors to be considered, as well as specific internal tasks necessary for effective team management. For purposes of discussion, material is organized into two main segments: Program Coordination and Case Coordination. On a practical level, however, there is no arbitrary division as these are interrelated program components. Figure 16.1 is a graphic representation of a coordinated planning model for a comprehensive community child protection program.[1] Protocols, forms, and other materials developed by many types of teams are also referenced. However, each group should modify such guidelines in accordance with the specific function and community setting of their team.

Figure 16.1 Community Child Protection Program Planning Model [1]

PENNSYLVANIA MODEL

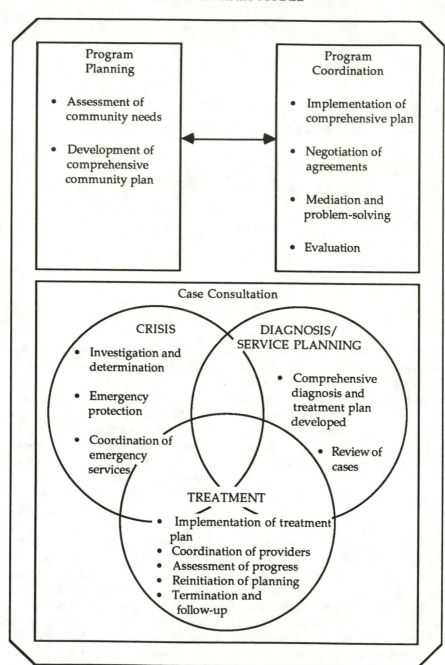

Community Coordination: Getting Started

The potential establishment of a team often begins when professionals in the community express the need for a coordinated interdisciplinary effort in resolving child abuse issues. A strategy meeting should be initiated which involves those professionals who have indicated an interest and willingness to participate in the formation of a multidisciplinary team. In these early steps of organization, experience has shown that child protective services, law enforcement, juvenile court, medical, and mental health representatives should be invited to join planning meetings. Once these participants endorse the concept of a team, they can become strong advocates for its formation. Inclusion of civic and political leaders and agency directors into this forum establishes a beginning foundation for intercommunity coordination of a multidisciplinary program. Often, this group of interested individuals forms a community action committee that provides the impetus for the development of a consultation team. In many instances, this committee identifies a smaller core group that eventually functions as a diagnostic or treatment team.

Role Definition and Purpose

A key element in the formation of a team is to have a precise purpose for the team's existence and a clear definition of goals. Teams may serve a variety of functions that range from serving as a regulatory body, collaborating with child protective service agencies in diagnostic and treatment decisions, to providing other services such as community education, development of community resources, and legislative advocacy. It is important, therefore, that such groups identify specific roles and activities. However, teams should not supplant the services of existing agencies but function as adjuncts with Child Protective Services (CPS) and other professionals within the community mandated to diagnose, report, and treat child abuse.

A review of the organization and functions of the four most prevalent types of teams is suggested during this initial process of team formation.[2] These will be discussed in more depth to clarify the difference between service delivery and advisory roles.

REGULATORY TEAMS

The goals and objectives of these teams emanate from statutory requirements and policies. In the pure sense, these teams have no direct service responsibilities. Members representing various community agencies and groups are appointed to serve on the team, often as designated by state statute. Responsibilities are focused on monitoring and accountability of agencies and professionals involved in child abuse cases. These teams review such issues as the timeliness of the investigation by the responding agency, the adequacy of the assessment regarding the degree of risk to the child, the appropriateness of placement decisions, and the progress of the treatment plan.

CONSULTATION TEAMS

These teams are multidisciplinary in nature and provide advice either by telephone or by meeting on an ad hoc or regularly scheduled basis with professionals responsible for carrying out child protective services. These teams do not provide direct services or face-to-face contact with the families. Their purpose is to offer support during the various stages of case investigation. Consultation may be available from the initial referral and intake process (usually up to 30 days), during development of treatment plans, or until case resolution. Also, some teams are established solely to deal with specific issues such as institutional abuse, permanency planning, "Baby Doe" cases or child death.

TREATMENT TEAMS

Treatment teams provide direct services such as psycho-social and medical evaluations for the abused child and family. They may be involved in the intake phase of a case on a short-term basis, or continue services until case resolution. Some teams offer a broad spectrum of expertise, while others provide help with specific types of cases such as child sexual abuse or failure to thrive. Treatment teams are often distinguished by affiliation with a single agency such as a hospital, psychiatric or mental health facility, or social services. In some communities, CPS provides a permanent representative or maintains a coordination role.

COMBINATION TEAMS

Combination teams provide consultation as well as direct services. It is common for teams to have some level of overlap in functions, such as treatment and consultation, and any regulatory requirements established by statutes. Some groups also incorporate advocacy activities; however, teams that have sole responsibility for community needs assessment, planning resource development or community education are frequently referred to as advocacy teams or community councils.

Initial Team Development

Once a core group has convened to discuss team development, a plan of action should be instituted to define more specifically the type of team needed in a community, as well as identify available resources. A preliminary community analysis must be undertaken to identify the existing service delivery system, significant gaps or overlaps, and obstacles to the development of a coordinated program.[3] Respondents should include organizations and individuals currently providing services as well as other potential participants in prevention or treatment efforts. In addition, recommendations should be sought from any existing client groups, such as Parents Anonymous chapters. An assessment should also reflect the community context in which abuse occurs (i.e., indigenous cultural values and child rearing traditions). This long-range planning is essential to establish the overall priorities among goals, reduce confusion as to which activity is most important, and outline the interdependence of various program functions. The following steps for initial planning should be considered:

1. Send a brief needs assessment to all agencies, community organizations, hospitals, and professionals that may have contact with child abuse cases (Appendix 16.1). Suggested questions for this needs assessment are:
   a. Should there be a multidisciplinary team in this community?
   b. What services should a team provide?
   c. Would your organization designate a person for participation on a team?
   d. What services or resources could your organization offer?

    e.   What additional community programs are needed?
    f.   What questions, anticipated problems or barriers should be considered?

2. Arrange a regularly scheduled meeting time. Consider breakfast or luncheon meetings that can accommodate participants' busy schedules.
3. At the first meeting, provide the opportunity for getting acquainted with one another and each person's affiliated area of service.
4. Elect a chairperson and a recorder.
5. Prepare an agenda that includes responses from the needs assessment.
6. Develop a preliminary definition of purpose, objectives, and action plan.
7. Summarize discussions of each strategy meeting, record issues that surface, list responsibilities for participants, and identify time frames for task completion.

Program Coordination

The establishment of a comprehensive multidisciplinary child protection program is an ongoing process. Many factors influence the coordination of these four basic types of teams. As a task force continues program development meetings, attention should be given to the following areas:

1. Child Protective Services Policy.
2. Service Area.
3. Team Sponsorship.
4. Community Agency Endorsement.
5. Team Composition.
6. Membership Qualifications.
7. Team size/Membership Terms.
8. Community Resources.
9. Logistics/Operational Policy.
10. Legal/Legislative Issues.
11. Staff Development.
12. Media/Public Awareness.

CHILD PROTECTIVE SERVICES POLICY

A thorough understanding of child abuse and neglect guidelines of the county department of social services is critical. It is important to know the general and operational policies of the Child Protective Services agency mandated to investigate all child abuse reports, including criteria for acceptance or denial of high risk or gray area cases that are potential abuse situations. Cases not accepted for services by CPS will significantly influence team decisions for management and referral. It is often the county CPS agency that assumes the leadership role in establishing a multidisciplinary team; however, when another agency initiates such a project, the need for close collaboration with CPS from the onset cannot be overemphasized.[4]

SERVICE AREA

One of the first decisions a team must make is to define the service area. This may be a single county, a district within a large metropolitan city, public or private hospital, or, in the case of rural areas, all or part of several counties. Most teams function in a single county but a community-based team may define the service area differently.[5] Many factors will affect this decision, such as:

1. Size of population needing services.
2. Necessary financial resources and staffing.
3. Existing service delivery catchment area.
4. Political boundaries.
5. Other linkages through business, social interests, transportation systems, or similar problems amenable to solution through joint efforts.

TEAM SPONSORSHIP

Multidisciplinary team programs may be part of a specific unit of an agency, joint agencies, or an autonomous service group. Any of these alternatives requires some degree of structure to establish sanction for the team, funding sources for team members and operational budget, in-kind staff participation, meeting space, etc. Following deliberations regarding service delivery area, groups should formalize a plan for team sponsorship. Possibilities include:

1. *Single Agency Sponsorship*

An appropriate community organization sponsors and plans for the team's activities as one of its programs. This is often the local CPS unit or perhaps a large hospital pediatric department or mental health facility. In these situations, the agency provides direct support for team members or contributes staff time as well as meeting space and other operational needs.

2. Joint Agency Sponsorship

More than one group may commit staff and operational assistance for a team, but the team itself usually plans and monitors its own activities.

3. Joint-County Sponsorship

Some counties, particularly in rural areas, may have a limited case volume or lack of multidisciplinary representation to establish a functioning team. A joint or multi-county model may be considered. This arrangement, however, requires careful planning with regard to geographical distances, travel time, potential differing community standards, or county guidelines for management of abuse.[6]

4. Independent Sponsorship

Some groups function in an autonomous manner with no formal affiliation with an agency. This modification may be adopted by Advocacy Teams that do not have the role or responsibility for provision of direct services. These teams, however, need to work closely with other agencies in determining focus for prevention, community awareness, or political activities. They secure meeting space, operational funds, and volunteer staff on an independent basis.

COMMUNITY AGENCY ENDORSEMENT

Whether a team comprises members from existing community groups, or is newly formed and established with a single agency or hospital, a key element to its success is active support and administrative endorsement *from* and *within* each affiliated organization. For example, with a hospital-based team, it is critical that hospital administrators communicate with the medical staff, the designated medical director of the team, and all departments on which the team would impact.

Each organization represented should assess internal service capability, administrative procedures, staff and funding resources, and level of commitment to the team. The team, in turn, should obtain appropriate written agreements from agencies and organizations within the service delivery system that specify responsibilities and clarify how they will interface with each other. These interagency agreements should be signed by team and agency directors. It is also useful to encourage quarterly conferences among cooperating agencies to revise agreements as necessary.

Another important reason for obtaining a broad base of community agency endorsement is funding. Support may come primarily from the budget of a sponsoring agency, but combined resources might guarantee a broader and more stable financial base. Time and services may be donated by core team members or consultant resource representatives from several agencies. Organizations that wish to participate at a more peripheral level may provide meeting space, clerical assistance, postage, telephone service, etc. A planning group of multiple community agencies committed to a Child Protection Program can also establish cooperative efforts between the public and private sectors for exploring other sources of revenue which may be necessary to provide salary for team members, or for expansion of potential service options.[7]

TEAM COMPOSITION

Since the purpose of a Child Protection Team is to provide a multidisciplinary, multi-agency approach to child protection and to make intervention a function of the entire service delivery network, team composition should include representatives from social services, medical and public health, mental health, education, law enforcement, the legal profession, and any military installations within the area to be served. Some state laws also support lay citizen participation, particularly if any racial, ethnic, or linguistic minority group constitutes a significant portion of the population within a team's service jurisdiction.

This configuration of multidisciplinary membership was suggested by a Colorado statute which first mandated teams in 1975, though there was no fiscal budget appropriation for such teams. Figures 16.2 and 16.3 denote agencies and professions represented on 42 county teams in Colorado based on a survey completed in 1984.[8] The data reflect that broad representation recommended by statute was possible for most teams. It is a positive indicator of individual and community response and an impressive effort if volunteer time is translated into dollar contributions.

MEMBERSHIP QUALIFICATIONS

A treatment or diagnostic team should comprise members with experience and professional expertise in the management and intervention with abuse cases. This group is often termed a "core" team whose membership remains relatively permanent. It is also important that individuals representing agencies have sufficient stature and authority to make decisions or commitments on behalf of their organizations. Where possible, core team members should be drawn from

Figure 16.2
Agencies Represented:
Colorado Community-based teams

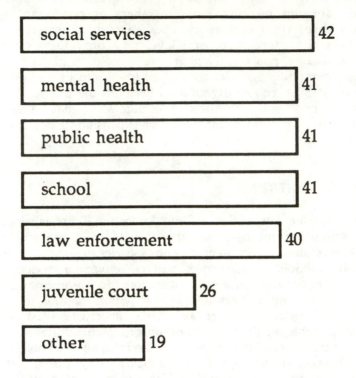

social services	42
mental health	41
public health	41
school	41
law enforcement	40
juvenile court	26
other	19

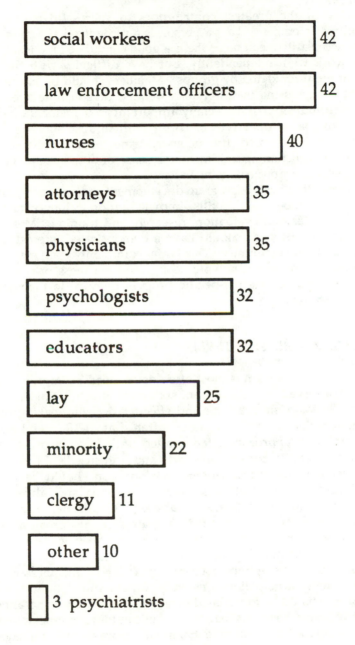

Figure 16.3
Professionals Represented:
Colorado Community-based teams

social workers 42

law enforcement officers 42

nurses 40

attorneys 35

physicians 35

psychologists 32

educators 32

lay 25

minority 22

clergy 11

other 10

3 psychiatrists

local treatment agencies to encourage a referral network between a team and an agency.

One of the greatest contributors to successful teams is the personality of members. That a person is a recognized expert in a field does not necessarily mean he or she is a good candidate for a team. Some persons work well independently, but have difficulty with the group process or are intimidated by groups. Members should be assertive and confident in expressing their opinions, yet also demonstrate openness to differing attitudes. It is especially important that members have the capacity to be supportive of their colleagues and deal with disagreements in a constructive manner. Other personal characteristics vital to a well functioning unit include a sense of humor, reliability, and commitment to serve on an ongoing basis.

Teams that include program development and advocacy functions may recruit members with skills, knowledge, or influence related to program organization, evaluation, research, and training. Members of this broader constituency should have a demonstrated interest in child abuse within their community. This larger community team may include representatives from civic and volunteer groups, business, or government who agree to participate in specific projects relevant to their areas of skill or knowledge.

TEAM SIZE/MEMBERSHIP TERMS

The size of a team is most often determined by its purpose, case volume, area served, and the level of staff commitment by individuals or agencies. To establish a realistic and effective decision-making process, a permanent or core team most often has 3-10 members. A multidisciplinary approach is too limited with fewer representatives; larger groups tend to become unwieldy and unfocused. If case volume exceeds capacity for management, consideration should be given to establishment of an additional team or perhaps specialized teams dealing with particular types of abuse. Additional associate or consultant members may participate in team meetings on an as-needed basis, usually determined by issues involved with specific cases.

Term of membership may be set for one year or longer after which individuals have the option to terminate and new members can join. Since consistent participation is essential for the functioning of a team, clear policies should be formulated concerning attendance and alternates when a regular member must be absent. Policies for recruitment, selection, and ongoing identification of potential members are also recommended.

COMMUNITY RESOURCES

Knowledge of community resources is imperative. Existing diagnostic and treatment services should be utilized in establishing a multidisciplinary network. In the planning stage, the group should review any available pamphlets on community programs or develop an abbreviated reference list. Such summaries can be useful to new members unfamiliar with the range of options, and provide guidelines for making *realistic* treatment recommendations, or the identification of programs or services lacking in the community. A variety of referral, consultative, or support services may be available in a community. For example:

1. Medical specialists in radiology, neurology, surgery, pathology, etc.
2. Community health centers.
3. Physical and occupational therapists/developmental specialists.
4. Nutritionists.
5. Mental health centers and private practitioners.
6. Social service units for foster care, adoption, AFDC, and food stamps.
7. Hospital social service and nursing departments.
8. Community visiting nurse programs.
9. School nurses, counselors, administrators, teachers.
10. Translators of foreign languages.
11. Day care providers and Head Start staff.
12. Photography and audiovisual services in some agencies and hospitals.
13. Community and civic programs such as Parents Anonymous, Battered Women's Shelters, Junior League, etc.
14. Professional schools in universities/community colleges.

LOGISTICS/OPERATIONAL POLICY

Basic logistical arrangements such as meeting location, frequency, and duration can be important contributing factors to team productivity and should not be overlooked or regarded as insignificant. Privacy, comfort, and a centralized location are priority considerations for meeting space. Determining a conference schedule that accommodates all members can be difficult. Team meetings may be held weekly, bi-weekly, monthly, or an on on-call basis. The type of team, volume of cases and requirements of statute will influence this decision. Some states, for instance, require conferences within one week of a case report. As a general rule, attendance is more consistent if meetings are held on a permanent basis and become part of members' regular schedules. When there are no new cases for discussion, this time may be used for reviews, training, or other administrative matters. Also, a meeting of 2 to 2 1/2 hours is usually as long as people can be expected to work effectively. Although there are exceptions, teams may note more reliable participation and productive work when conferences are convened during morning hours.   Professionals are often tied up with patient appointments, court schedules, or emergencies later in the day. Energy levels seem to be higher in the morning than in late afternoon. Monday morning/Friday afternoon times are less desirable (i.e., long weekends, flexdays, emergencies). In summary, teams need to establish a meeting schedule that most realistically accommodates members' needs and the work to be accomplished. Failure to do so may result in disruption, confusion, and dysfunctional groups.

Teams should also prepare guidelines for standard operational procedures and fiscal policies.   Such by-laws provide written clarification of ground rules and structure for decision-making. These statements might include:

1. Role, responsibility, and term for team members.
2. Role, responsibility, and term for team director.
3. Method of electing chairperson or director.
4. Recruitment, selection, or termination of members.
5. Process for conduct of meetings.
6. Plan for fiscal accountability.

LEGAL AND LEGISLATIVE ISSUES

Teams should exercise vigilant attention to legal guidelines and liabilities related to child protection cases. More in-depth discussion of legal matters is the focus of Section Four of this book, but a few general policies will be addressed here because of their significance to program and case coordination.   Careful review of state laws is *critical* for beginning teams; established programs should review any revised legislation pertinent to any area of case management.[9]

Three of the most common questions relevant to teams are (1) Is the team mandated or sanctioned by law? (2) What are the standards for access to case information and confidentiality?   and (3) What is the liability for a team or individual members? Some states address these questions in child abuse statutes. Excerpts from Colorado and Florida law follow:[10,11]

Colorado Children's Code 19-10-109 (6)

(a) It is the intent of the general assembly to encourage the creation of one or more child protection teams in each county or contiguous group of counties. In each county in which reports of fifty or more incidents of child abuse have been made to the state central registry in any one year, the county director shall cause a child protection team to be inaugurated in the next following year.

(b) The child protection team shall review the files and other records of the case, including the diagnostic, prognostic, and treatment services being offered to the family in connection with the reported abuse.

(c) At each meeting, each member of the child protection team shall be provided with all available records and reports on each case to be considered.

Florida Statutes 415.511

Immunity from liability in cases of child abuse or neglect. Any person, official, or institution participating in good faith in any act authorized or required by Sect. 415.502-415.514 shall be immune from any civil or criminal liability which might otherwise result by reason of such action.

Careful review of child protection statutes is also necessary for development of other team guidelines such as: releases to obtain information, policies on public attendance at team meetings, and distribution of reports and recommendations including the appropriate restrictions and liabilities of any case materials shared with the media. When the law does not clearly address the issue of multi-disciplinary teams, an attorney general's opinion may be requested.

Further, as interdisciplinary groups convene to address the problems of child abuse, they can influence governmental officials in the development of standards for state laws that create, and in some instances mandate, multi-disciplinary teams. They should assist political leaders in understanding the complex problems of child abuse and proposing realistic appropriations for services to families.

Consideration should be given to the wording, intent, and the level of flexibility in proposed legislation creating teams, as these factors provide the legal framework for the team's philosophy, structure, policies, and, most importantly, its authority. Rigidly structured statutes have a tendency to narrow the team's scope and create unique problems for some communities, yet work well in others. In contrast, a loosely constructed statute may have varied impacts on the team's authority and responsibility depending upon the community's interpretation. For example, the word "advisory" in the definition section of the Colorado Statutes on Child Protection Teams may create a feeling of impotence for a team in one community, and be interpreted as empowering in another.

In some areas, specific agencies are charged with the development, maintenance, and coordination of services of multi-disciplinary teams throughout the state. In other states these teams are independent entities with advisory or mandated authority. Flexibility in laws regarding teams is important so that a child protection program can be tailored with consideration of community needs.

MEDIA/PUBLIC AWARENESS

Another important external factor is the team's relationship with the media. Teams should be actively involved in public awareness campaigns to raise child abuse issues and to inform the community of their services (Appendix 16.2). Several methods may be used: radio and television appearances, as well as interviews in print media such as newspapers and newsletters of professional or service organizations. It is not uncommon, however, that an active public awareness campaign and media exposure will result in a staggering increase of referrals made to the team, which in turn, must be prepared to respond with concrete services, consultations, and carefully established networking resources. Thus, the media can be important for a team, but should be used in a timely and judicious manner.

Review of legal guidelines pertaining to release of information must be stressed. Professional judgment is important when sharing cases, photographs, and other materials with the media. Often, information solicited by local television networks or newspapers may involve serious, unusual, or dramatic situations. Teams should consider proactive development of news releases that balance and communicate the full range of dynamics and problems associated with child abuse.

Another benefit of media exposure is public recognition that the team is worthwhile. Teams perceived as important and valuable by the community are generally far more motivated both individually and as a group to excel in their work.

STAFF DEVELOPMENT

Staff development is an integral part of a team's responsibility. Groups inaugurating a team should plan orientation and ongoing education. The professional growth and development of each member is essential and should include pre-service, in-service, and formalized training on a periodic basis. Team members are not effective if they do not have current information on all aspects of the prevention and treatment of child abuse and neglect. Poor decisions are often made out of ignorance.

Once planning for a team is completed, it is necessary to provide orientation for team members as well as for those who will be referring cases. All involved must understand the functions and responsibilities of the team. Clarification and definition of terms and procedures are important. This process should be continued for new team members and referral sources as needed. Basic orientation should focus on:

1. Purpose and function of the team.
2. Team composition and roles of members.
3. Team management protocols.
4. Legal guidelines: definitions of child abuse and neglect, police holds, reporting mechanism, court process, evidentiary standards, testimony.
5. Perspectives on child abuse: national scope and history, local programs, problems, statistics.
6. Referral and consultation process (i.e., who can refer, referral criteria, forms, reports, etc.).
7. Format for case staffings to include case selection, content, methods for presentation.
8. Group process, decision-making, and conflict resolution.
9. Other concerns of members related to the team.

Continuing in-service training should include opportunities for members to observe child abuse evaluations and treatment of the child and parents by specific disciplines; i.e., social work, medicine, law enforcement, psychiatry. Familiarity with the various components of the legal process may also be effectively acquired by attending detention hearings, court reviews, adjudicatory and termination proceedings.

Informal training may include case presentations by team members, review of current literature and research in the field. Formal training such as conferences, workshops, and seminars that provide information on a wide range of topics or focus on specific discipline/interdisciplinary clinical skills should be encouraged. Responsibilities for updating knowledge and state-of-the-art expertise in the field should be standard requirements for each team member. Providing a manual that includes all team protocols is recommended for use by new members and as an ongoing reference source.

Case Coordination

Each team will need to prioritize and develop operational procedures for case coordination that correspond to stated purpose and function. A newly established team should draft guidelines and necessary forms *prior* to the provision of service or consultation that address day-to-day management procedures. Numerous case management protocols are provided in another chapter; however, some general policy areas and other components integral to coordination of consultation and treatment/diagnostic teams are as follows:

1. Confidentiality Waivers/Agreements.
2. Case Selection Criteria.
3. Specialized Treatment Components.
4. Consultations.
5. Referral Assessment Criteria.
6. Initiation of Referrals/Case Evaluation.
    a. Acute/Emergency Referrals
    b. Non-Acute Referrals
    c. CPS/Law Enforcement Notification
    d. Diagnosis/Documentation Guidelines
    e. Legal/Reporting/Placement Issues
7. Case Staffing Guidelines.
    a. Mini-Staffings
    b. Case Conferences
8. Conflict Resolution.
9. Case Review and Follow-up.
10. Criteria for Case Disposition and Closure
11. Data Collection.
12. Team Evaluation.
13. Coordination Tasks.

CONFIDENTIALITY WAIVERS/AGREEMENTS

Development of confidentiality waivers specific to release and sharing of case information is crucial. Team members or other professionals involved in the diagnosis and evaluation of a case may be reluctant to share critical information without written clarification of legal guidelines (see Appendix 16.3 and 16.4 for examples of such agreements). Groups should be especially cognizant of the need to protect the rights of children and parents during presentation of cases. Any information shared should be safeguarded to the greatest extent possible.

One or more of these methods may further insure confidentiality of case material:

1. Members may sign an agreement form regarding confidentiality.
2. Clients may be informed that their case is being referred to a team.
3. Referring professionals may try to obtain the clients' permission prior to submitting case for team consultation.
4. Cases may be presented to the team in an anonymous manner or coded for identification.
5. Team members may be limited only to representatives of agencies allowed by law to investigate and share information.
6. All case materials received during a team meeting are returned.

While a team must be guided by existing law and regulations, careful consideration should be given to a method for informing and involving families in the decisions made and securing cooperation in a treatment plan. Case management teams should be aware of increased legislative activity and litigation concerning the individual's right to privacy and freedom of information as well as parents' rights and professional malpractice.

CASE SELECTION CRITERIA

Newly formed teams have a tendency to encourage community agency referrals of every potential or abuse case. Also, acceptance of *all* case consultations is sometimes dictated by state statute. This would be ideal; however, the effect could be devastating. As staffing and funding resources often remain constant with little or no increase in relation to the burgeoning increase in serious abuse referrals, a team could soon be overwhelmed with cases. Additionally, it should be noted that as soon as the team is well established within the community, case referrals will almost automatically increase. To avoid the potential result of accepting more consultations than can be adequately and thoroughly handled, a brief needs assessment should be completed during the first months of operation to formulate a realistic estimate of expected cases within a given year. If substantial volume is projected, criteria for selection should be established (unless a team is otherwise mandated by law to review all cases). It should be understood these criteria are not carved in stone and should be reviewed periodically as changes occur in the capacity to provide service. The following types of cases are considered appropriate referrals:[12]

1. Unexplained or implausibly explained bruises, burns, head injuries, or fractures in children of any age.
2. Sexual abuse in which vaginal or anal penetration is alleged or reports involve fondling, oral sex and child pornography.
3. Venereal disease in prepubescent children.
4. Malnutrition and failure to thrive.
5. Prenatal, medical, developmental, and educational neglect.
6. Suspected emotional abuse in which the child is exhibiting symptoms of severe emotional problems.
7. Child is at risk for suspected child abuse and neglect.
8. Child is dead on arrival due to suspicion of abuse or neglect.
    The condition and risk to siblings should be of special concern.
9. When there is a need for medical documentation of abuse.
10. When several agencies and professionals are involved with a multiproblem family and there is a need for coordination of services.
11. When multiple agencies and professionals are in conflict about diagnosis and treatment recommendations or legal action.
12. When a decision to remove or return children to the parental home or terminate parental rights must be approved by the courts and deliberate preparation is possible and needed.

Some teams may establish case acceptance criteria that permit referrals from only certain agencies, for example, Child Protective Services. The optimal situation is an intake policy that also includes referrals from other individuals and organizations in the community:

1. Referrals may be made by any agency or individual having legitimate concern or involvement with the case.
2. Cases may be limited to those in which the child or family is a resident of the county or team service delivery area.
3. Referrals may be made from outside the immediate service area if there is a sound rationale for team consultation.

Since teams are intended to serve as adjuncts to existing agencies, they should avoid the position of a "go-between" for reporting abuse cases to CPS. The team should provide consultation to community professionals regarding the appropriateness, necessity, and procedures for reporting suspected and known cases of child abuse to the authorities mandated to investigate these concerns.

SPECIALIZED TREATMENT COMPONENTS

Teams may also provide specialized services or treatment with some types of cases. This function is assumed for a variety of reasons such as the unavailability of services elsewhere in the community, immediate access to an array of medical personnel and resources, interest in research, or need for an interdisciplinary focus. These referrals may include:

1. Child sexual abuse by a non-family member.
2. Abuse in out-of-home care which involves some form of physical or sexual injury to a child inflicted by a person responsible for the child's welfare such as a foster parent, administrator or employee of a program, public or private school, etc.
3. High-risk newborns.
4. Medical neglect requiring extensive ongoing medical care or involvement in foster home program.
5. Child death cases in which fatalities are the result of non-accidental injury to the child.
6. Ingestions which involve illegal drugs or common toxic substances in a household, or ingestion of alcohol under certain circumstances.
7. "Baby Doe" cases in which an infant is chronically and irreversibly comatose.
8. Sensitive cases involving community leaders, professional colleagues, or cases receiving media attention.

CONSULTATIONS

Consultations are defined as referrals in which there is an exchange of information but no direct services are provided. The team member responding to a consultation should document pertinent case data, services requested, recommendations, and action taken. Information requested or questions regarding physical abuse, sexual abuse, emotional abuse, or neglect may be of a medical, social, legal, or psychological/psychiatric nature. Also, cases that are high risk should be referred for discussion about the degree of danger and the appropriateness of intervention. (Appendix 16.5 is a sample referral/consultation form.)

REFERRAL ASSESSMENT CRITERIA

For a team to function efficiently, promote communication, and avoid misunderstandings, a consistent process for case referrals should be developed. This involves alerting community agencies about information needed:

1. Child's name and birthdate.
2. Parents' or custodian's name, address, phone number, and information as to how they can be reached (work address and phone number, close relative, etc.)
3. Siblings' names and ages, if available.
4. Type of alleged or suspected abuse.
5. Seriousness of the injury and the child's present condition.
6. Degree of risk for further abuse for the identified child and the child's siblings, if available.
7. Information surrounding the abusive incident; i.e., precipitating factors, family stresses, etc.
8. History of previous abuse or high-risk incidents, including information from CPS records/Central Registry.
9. Information about the alleged perpetrator; i.e., name, address, relationship to child, if there is still contact with the child, etc.
10. Name, address and phone number of the referring source.

Appendix 16.6 is an example of a referral sheet which incorporates most of this suggested data and questions to be covered during the intake process. However, many variations of forms can be designed for recording pertinent information, including a checklist or brief narrative format. Teams dealing with a substantial volume of some types of cases, such as sexual abuse, or collecting additional information for statistical purposes may develop materials specific to those objectives (Appendix 16.7, 16.8).

INITIATION OF REFERRALS/CASE EVALUATION

A process for screening and prioritizing cases must be established. For some teams, the determination of case acceptance, referral to other sources of intervention, or the need for additional information and evaluations is left to the discretion of the team coordinator. Other teams may use screening committees. It is important that team members and referring sources understand the process, sequence, and other necessary action required such as:

a. Acute/Emergency Referrals

Some member of the team should be available to accept referrals and consults on a 24-hour basis. It is recognized that this service may not be readily available in some small or rural communities; however, if at all possible, an experienced team member should be assigned after regular work hours (perhaps on a rotating basis) to provide consultation, at the minimum. This team availability is a necessary service to CPS for providing support or evaluations during case investigation.

b. Non-acute Referrals

Referrals to teams should be made in a timely manner, ideally when the family is at a point of crisis, as this affords the greatest opportunity for obtaining case information. However, referrals to either consultation or treatment teams may be made during any phase of case involvement.

c. CPS/Law Enforcement Notification

Referrals from any type of team to Child Protective Services should be made immediately upon suspicion of abuse. Additionally, in cases where criminal charges are possible, law enforcement should also be notified. (Appendices 16.9 and 16.10 are sample CPT notification summaries. Some states and counties have standard reporting forms—these should be developed in conjunction with CPS or law enforcement agencies.)

d. Diagnosis and Documentation Guidelines

The following questions should be considered at the time of case intake:

1. Has as much information as possible been elicited from the referring source?
2. Has a psychosocial history been completed for the family?
3. Should a medical history, examination, and interview be scheduled for child and siblings?
4. Which additional professionals should be notified?
5. Which professional is responsible for interviewing the child?
6. Which professional is responsible for interviewing the parents?
7. Should the interview be videotaped?
8. Should photographs be taken?
9. What additional diagnostic tests, radiological films, or laboratory screenings are necessary?

e. Legal, Reporting/Placement Issues
1. What legal issues or actions should be addressed?

2. Has the case been referred to the appropriate authorities: i.e., child protective services and/or law enforcement?

3. Is an official written report to the county CPS or state abuse registry indicated?

4. Is a team staffing and report necessary?

5. What immediate decisions or recommendations can be made?

6. Is a temporary court hold order necessary?

7. Is placement of the child necessary?

8. Is a court order needed for consent to treat?

9. Is hospitalization required?

10. If child is hospitalized, has discharge planning been coordinated with medical and CPS staff?

11. What additional services or referrals are appropriate for the child or family?

12. What follow-up services will the team provide?

Case Staffing Guidelines

MINI-STAFFINGS

To promote communication between team members and other professionals, "mini-staffings" may occur periodically throughout the initial assessment and diagnostic stages of the case. The purpose is to share information and develop a mutually acceptable plan of action throughout the evaluation process, particularly prior to the established date for full review by a team. Mini-staffings are generally brief and *ad hoc* in nature and may be convened at various stages during the initial delivery of services such as prior to the child being seen, for information sharing purposes, after family members have been interviewed, after the medical exam, or when it is important to manage any specific problem on a case. Such meetings may involve two or more of the following professionals: team social worker, coordinator or physician, physician treating the child, referring agency representative, law enforcement officer, hospital staff, attorney, or any other appropriate consultant.

In some instances, the mini-staffing process has evolved into establishment of mini-teams or core groups which function as adjuncts with the larger established team. Generally, these mini-teams are composed of three to four multidisciplinary professionals who are available for consultation during the diagnostic phase and throughout case disposition. They may also screen cases and refer only the more serious or other designated cases for full team review. Whichever process is most functional for a team, summary reports are advised (Appendix 16.11).

CASE CONFERENCES

The child protection team conference is the focal point for the team's primary function of multidisciplinary case assessment and integration of treatment services for the child and family. Because effective management of these meetings is so vital, a separate chapter includes discussion about the multiple components involved in organizing staffings such as type and number of cases scheduled, process for presentation, attendance, confidentiality, etc. Other guidelines for formulating treatment plans are outlined in some of the chapters in Part II of this book.

The following comments will provide elaboration of two areas: (1) the case data base and (2) methods and formats for summarizing information.

The most critical factor in case review is a comprehensive assessment and summary of the family's problems and strengths. For a team to adequately provide recommendations for intervention, information must be available in *each* of the following categories:

1. The specific CA/N diagnosis (e.g., physical abuse, failure to thrive, sexual abuse, medical care neglect, intentional drugging or poisoning, emotional abuse, abandonment, lack of supervision, severe physical neglect, high-risk child, true accident, etc.)
2. Patient's physical/emotional/developmental status.
3. Sibling's physical/emotional/developmental status.
4. Mother's physical/emotional status/strengths.
5. Father's physical/emotional status/strengths.
6. Perpetrator's (other than parent's) emotional status.
7. Marital status/problems (e.g., discord, separation, desertion, divorce).
8. Involvement of relatives/others.
9. Environmental situation/current crisis (e.g., inadequate home, financial stress, loss of job, etc.)
10. Summary/safety of the home (e.g., composite data from above that relate to degree of risk and legal decisions).

This master list was developed and discussed in the first team handbook.[13] Continued utilization by many teams has confirmed its relevancy; circumventing any segment of data has most often resulted in the need for re-scheduling case discussion until information is obtained, or errors in dispositional planning due to inadequate or incomplete knowledge. For example, incidents of previous abuse to patient or siblings, history of death of another child due to abuse by parents or perpetrator, multiple accidents or questionable injuries noted in review of medical records, numerous concerns about neglect, psychiatric problems or assaultive criminal activity of parents/perpetrator, often suggest very complex and high-risk factors. Obviously, access to such past and current information can significantly influence team decisions about prognosis for remediation and current intervention.

Following review of case material condensed in the above categories, team deliberations should address five main questions:

(1) What is the safety of the home for this child?
   -Confirmed NAT, suspected, accident
   -Seriousness of injury, degree of risk for re-abuse
(2) What action has been taken?
   -Report filed
   -Evaluations completed
   -Criminal investigation
   -Court involvement
(3) What are the optimal treatment recommendations?
   -Type of treatment or other services indicated for each individual (child, parents, siblings, perpetrator, other)
(4) Which persons or agencies are responsible for carrying out treatment recommendations?
   -Social services, medical, legal, law enforcement, mental health, other
(5) Have any problems, evaluations, or recommendations been overlooked?
   -Suggested time for review.

Teams use a variety of methods and formats for presentation of case material. These may consist of verbal summaries by the caseworker, supervisor, team coordinator, or referring professional. Other options are forms that contain only identifying information and nature of the report. Sometimes narrative reports include content of interviews/evaluations, medical findings, and tentative case plan.

The materials for case review may also correspond to the comprehensive data base previously outlined, with addition of pertinent questions. An example of a report consolidated in this format is provided (Appendix 16.12). A suggested aid for listing identified problems, community resources to be utilized, and time frame for implementation and review is illustrated (Appendix 16.13). Abbreviated forms may be used for case reviews that reflect the status of intervention, progress, and current questions for consideration (Appendix 16.14).

Many reasons influence the choice of method and depth of case material presented for team review. For example, the type of team may be a decisive factor. Teams that function as regulatory groups must review large volumes of cases in limited time. Abbreviated reports may be the only practical option; however, prior screening of all case material should be completed by a committee or professional assigned to the case. Some teams may have representation from the public sector or media at meetings, and use brief summaries to ensure confidentiality. Narrative presentations may be preferred by teams with very limited numbers of cases for consultation.

It is optimal, however, that teams have access to written reports that summarize significant problems and information about the child and family constellation in *all* the categories outlined. The advantages of this method are numerous. A team's effectiveness and efficiency can be increased by:

1. A comprehensive data base that encourages a long term view of family problems and strengths.
2. Synthesis of multiple, lengthy evaluations.
3. Formulation of diagnosis and tentative treatment recommendations by all evaluators in advance of meeting.
4. Structure for presentations that limits unproductive digression.
5. A point of reference for latecomers or those not in attendance that reduces time-consuming repetition of details.
6. Focus on primary questions and priorities for case decisions required.
7. Clarification of other information or evaluations needed.
8. Focus on realistic recommendations and resources available.
9. Identification and role of service providers.
10. A systematic approach for follow-up, review of progress, and documentation for permanent case records.

Various tasks are required in preparing comprehensive case agendas for team review. The first step is prioritizing cases to be scheduled for in-depth consultation. Next, information about the child and family should be synthesized in the ten categories outlined. This requires identification of multiple professionals and agencies with previous or current involvement such as: social services, physicians, private or public mental health facilities, visiting nurse service or hospital staff, law enforcement, school counselors, etc.

Those contacted should be apprised of the reason for inquiry, how the information will be used, and invited to the case review, if appropriate. Summaries from each source, problems noted, and questions are then recorded for the team report. However, obtaining pertinent records (i.e., medical and psychiatric charts) may also entail securing parental permission for release whenever possible.

The question remains as to *who* prioritizes cases and prepares the agenda for conferences. These functions are best managed by a designated team coordinator who is familiar with community agencies, is knowledgeable about legal statutes on access to information, has skill in determining and synthesizing the most relevant information, and the availability of all open cases in the intake and follow-up system. The coordinator then works in close collaboration with an individual CPS social worker assigned to a specific case. Some teams rotate these responsibilities among members. This system may have benefits for sharing the workload, but drawbacks in terms of continuity. Also, some teams depend primarily on the assigned caseworker to provide all the information. Though social work evaluations should incorporate a comprehensive data base, this is not always the outcome, or material may be written in lengthy reports. Thus, workers should be familiarized with team expectations and case review forms prior to presentation at team conferences. Inevitable frustrations on the part of referring workers and team members may be ameliorated by advance clarification of these guidelines.

The following concerns are frequently expressed about the use of written team reports. One of the foremost *perceived* disadvantages is the time required for assimilation of data base. Clearly, this method necessitates extensive preparation prior to case conferences. However, since use of comprehensive records results in faster and more effective reviews, the work completed in advance is preferable to inefficient use of time scheduled by multiple team members and consultants.

Confidentiality is another prevalent issue raised about such documentation. Legal requirements for access to records by child protection teams and treatment providers, and methods of protecting identity of clients are discussed in Chapter 21. Adherence to legal guidelines about distribution of materials is again emphasized. Some teams have provisions that only allow duplication of team agendas for the CPS worker and guardian ad litem who have *participated* in the case staffing. With the exception of medical evaluations or other official reports substantiating abuse, permanent charts such as hospital records may have only a notation that the case has been reviewed by a child protection team, the name of caseworker assigned, and the source of further information. Other professionals, such as the parents' attorney or other individuals who might be involved in ongoing medical or mental health services, can access records from social service or team files. This policy provides important safeguards: (1) information abbreviated for the purpose of team discussion is less likely to be misinterpreted or used out of context; (2) the report per se is not inappropriately submitted as a document for court proceedings.

Some teams have expressed reluctance to list all professionals involved because of potential court subpoenas. Clearly, random requests for court involvement based on the team conference record is inappropriate. Rather than omitting this information, such problems may be addressed by clear assignment of one or two professionals who will be available for court testimony.

A final observation relates to professional accountability and exposure. One of the advantages of written materials is the identification of the types and thoroughness of evaluations provided, as well as progress of the treatment plan. This is a positive development. Written documentation promotes an internal check and balance for group and individual accountability and shared responsibility for case decisions and outcome.

CONFLICT RESOLUTION

Child protection team staffings may not always result in a consensus regarding case recommendations or plan of action. When there are critical differences of professional opinion, such as the advisability of foster care placement, it is helpful to have guidelines for communicating divergent views. For example, if there are disagreements about case management among members of the team, a letter of clarification may be sent to the CPS social worker, supervisor, guardian ad litem, and court personnel. This summary could clarify the recommendations proposed by the majority of team members as well as identify those team consultants who are not in agreement.

There may be situations in which team members are unanimous in recommendations, but agreement for all or part of the case plan cannot be established with the social worker or county attorney from the CPS unit. Written protocols for conflict resolution may be necessary. There are several ways in which differences can be resolved, such as additional communication via meetings, phone calls, or written clarification of the team's position. The following is a recommended sequence for conflict resolution. The first communication should be between the team social worker or coordinator and the CPS social worker with direct responsibility for the family. The next step should involve supervisory personnel from the team and the agency. If no resolution is possible, the final step should be discussions between team and agency directors. If there is no agreement, both the team and an agency may "agree to disagree" on a professional basis with the decisions made on the case, with each providing separate recommendations. A team may also have alternatives for taking some form of legal action, such as submitting a motion or petition to the juvenile court, depending on statute and case law. If this recourse is necessary, it is advisable to have legal counsel from the team attorney and guardian ad litem representing the child. It is important that teams make every attempt to resolve conflicts and avoid polarization with other agencies as much as possible. On the other hand, *a child's best interest should never be compromised just to avoid an adversarial position.*

CASE REVIEW AND FOLLOW-UP

Each team should create a mechanism for case review and follow-up. This often involves extensive coordination with many outside agencies. Because these families have multiple problems within their family system, various disciplines may have responsibilities for services and treatment of the child and family. Child protective and criminal investigations, juvenile and criminal court proceedings, treatment and rehabilitation options involve social work, medical, psychological, psychiatric, legal, and criminal justice professionals. Therefore, interagency coordination and cooperation is essential. A team can provide the impetus to identify the progress of the child and family in this extensive community network as well as note inadequacies in provision of services.

Systems for management of case follow-up and review may be extremely variable and are most often influenced by the type of team and case volume. Most teams, however, provide these services to some degree. For example, the 1983 Colorado survey reflected team review of some or all cases (Figure 16.4). Figure 16.5 illustrates criteria for review.

Other stages of a case that might necessitate case review or monitoring are:

1. During the dependency investigation phase with CPS.
2. During the criminal investigation phase with law enforcement or prosecuting attorney's office.
3. When requested by medical personnel called upon to document, testify, or treat the child's injuries and provide any ongoing medical care.
4. When legal action is warranted to ensure the child's protection or to review the court order and treatment plans.
5. When necessary to determine the child's status, adjustment, and behavior while in temporary or permanent foster care.
6. During treatment for the child and family.
7. When the child changes foster homes.
8. When the child is to return to the parental home.
9. When there is re-abuse.

10. When a permanent placement plan is being considered for the child.
11. When termination of services is being considered for the family.
12. When there is no case progress or the family has fallen between agency gaps.
13. When the case is to be closed.

Once a team has determined baseline criteria, some logistical mechanism needs to be designed for case review/monitoring. Several methods might be considered:

1. Card files of serious cases or those that meet other criteria for re-staffing. These may be organized in monthly categories.
2. Monthly or annual calendars listing each case staffed, significant court dates, or other recommended times for review.
3. Looseleaf notebooks that contain brief one-page summaries of case treatment plan and other notations about necessary monitoring.
4. Computer systems that incorporate data specific to case follow-up.

Development and maintenance of a functional follow-up system is a challenging task with no simple solutions, and should be regarded as an ongoing process. Teams should institute a plan that, at minimum, ensures follow-up of serious cases, but with enough flexibility to address the many other variables that influence the need for team review.

CRITERIA FOR CASE DISPOSITION AND CLOSURE

Because of the long-term treatment necessary for many abusive families, these cases can potentially remain in the CPS, Child Protection Team, or legal systems *ad infinitum*. This consequence may be counterproductive for the child and family as well as for the agencies involved. The systems may get overloaded with ongoing cases, resulting in ineffective case management, inability to provide the kind of services needed, and distraction from focused attention on the more serious situations. Therefore, teams should establish criteria for case disposition and closure. Guidelines for determining safety of the home and termination of parental rights are discussed in Chapter 19. Other factors that affect these decisions include:

Figure 16.4
Number of Cases Reviewed
Colorado Community-based Teams

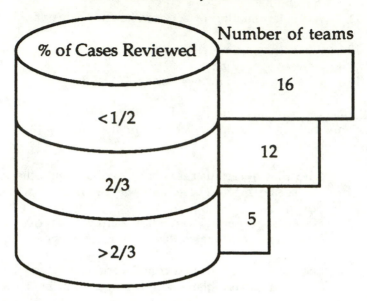

Figure 16.5
Criteria for Rereview
Colorado Community-based Teams

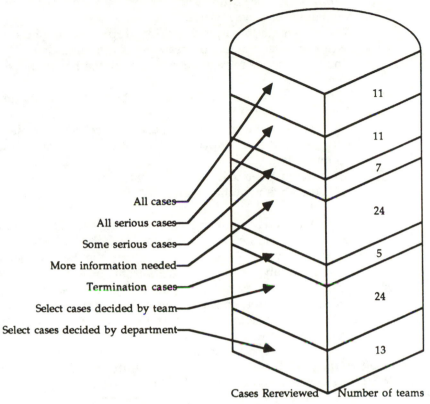

All cases
All serious cases
Some serious cases
More information needed
Termination cases
Select cases decided by team
Select cases decided by department

11
11
7
24
5
24
13

Cases Rereviewed   Number of teams

1. Death of the child (with no siblings at risk for abuse).
2. Mobility of the child and family (moving from one community, county, or state).
3. When parents have learned appropriate methods of discipline or termination of treatment is recommended.
4. When the abuser is permanently out of the home and the home appears safe.
5. When there is positive interaction between parents and child.
6. When other agencies also support the decision that there has been positive improvement within the family and recommend case closure.
7. When the responsibility for case management or treatment rests solely with another agency.

Prior to discussions regarding closure, teams should initiate multidisciplinary staffings to determine if other referrals or services are indicated. For example, though ongoing monitoring may be impossible due to mobility of the family, or there is a death from abuse but currently no other siblings, these cases may still be potentially high risk cases. In such circumstances, every effort consistent with the law should be made to alert other appropriate agencies and transfer team assessments, records, and recommendations.

If consideration for case closure is based on lack of specific resources for the child and family, this should be documented. Identification of community needs and other barriers in the service delivery network is critical to future program development.

DATA COLLECTION

A mechanism for data collection is another important element of coordination. Case files should be maintained for each referral or consultation to include all significant data, team recommendations, and final case outcome. Information can then be summarized in monthly or annual reports that may include:

1. Number of cases referred.
2. Number of cases investigated.
3. Type of evaluations or services provided (i.e., medical, social work, psychiatric, etc.).
4. Number of cases founded, unfounded.
5. Diagnosis—type of abuse/neglect.
6. Severity of abuse.
7. Number of deaths.

8. Number of re-abuse cases.
9. Age/sex of child.
10. Identification of perpetrator.
11. Source of referrals.
12. Geographic area of referrals.
13. Number of children hospitalized.
14. Number of out-of-home placements.
15. Number of cases court involved.
16. Number of cases open for CPS services.
17. Number of cases terminated.

This type of data collection is crucial for team planning and can provide the statistical base for objective assessment of prevention, diagnosis, and treatment needs in a community. The team or other individuals may also utilize this information for specific research projects. Cooperation with research professionals may result in valuable planning and evaluation assistance to the team. Any research project, however, should be carefully reviewed to determine purpose, validity, and potential use; that a researcher is following acceptable research standards such as those governing the protection of human subjects; and that information released is in compliance with statutes regarding confidentiality or other legal guidelines.

TEAM EVALUATION

One important factor in attainment of a successful team is continuous self-evaluation. Some systematic approach should be developed to ensure that the team is meeting the needs for which it was created, to assess intervention in terms of benefits to the child/family, and to evaluate costs and feasibility of goals. Several areas may be considered:

a. Team Members
Records should be kept on team membership, disciplines represented, length of service, participation and attendance at team meetings, difficulties in recruitment, members' degree of satisfaction with the team or problems encountered.
b. Team Meetings
Data should reflect the number of meetings scheduled, number of new cases staffed, number of cases reviewed for follow-up, attendance by other professionals involved with a case.
c. Team Recommendation Patterns
Periodic checks should be made to review the type and quality of team recommendations. This can be accomplished by the

selection and follow-up on a random basis of a representative sample of cases. The process may highlight certain dangers in team decision-making. For example, one of the pitfalls common to teams is "rubber stamping"; i.e., situations in which the team rarely adds to the diagnostic or treatment plan presented by the CPS caseworker. At the other extreme are teams that make too many recommendations or ones that are unrealistic or not feasible. Equally significant in team evaluation is information regarding the effectiveness of the treatment plan for the child and family.

d.   Implementation of Team Recommendations

Many teams operate in an "advisory only" capacity as designated by law or stated purpose. Therefore, the CPS unit is often the pivotal factor in implementing team recommendations. Some departments have formal policies. In some counties, only the director has the authority to reject team recommendations, following discussion of reasons with the team. In other counties, the process is much more informal and is left to the discretion of the assigned worker. Thus, it is important teams know about such departmental guidelines. The variability of such policies in Colorado teams, for example, is represented in Table 16.1.

Table 16.1
Colorado Community-Based Teams

Implementation of Recommendations	Number of Teams
Supervisor and Worker decide	20
Mandatory implementation	7
Supervisor decides	6
No policy	5
Worker decides	4
Other	1

Follow-up on the status of case decisions is necessary and may be critical to team continuity. When few, if any, team suggestions are incorporated in the CPS case plan, the result can be frustration, decreased morale, or even team disbandment. At the other extreme, some courts mandate case review by child protection teams and accept team recommendations as priority considerations in lieu of the case plan submitted by CPS. This may result in similar frustration and conflicts among protective service workers. Information in this area can provide the basis for discussion and problem-solving between the team and CPS unit when necessary.

e.   Referring Workers

Since a team is designed to function as a resource for the service provider, some attempt should be made to document utilization of its services, degree of satisfaction with team recommendations, and problems encountered from the perspective of referral sources. Informal discussion about team management may be initiated with various professionals who have requested consultation (physicians, nurses, psychiatrists, law enforcement officers, etc.). A more in-depth study of evaluations by social workers is suggested since these professionals are most often frequently and consistently involved with a team on child abuse cases. A form designed for social work comments on the team process, help provided, and response to case recommendations is suggested (Appendix 16.15).

f.   Cost Benefit

It is important that hours of consultation provided by team members and the approximate value of services be shared with community agencies, CPS, and the legislature. This should include diagnostic, treatment, and court time.

g.   Training/Public Awareness Activities

The number and types of training programs conducted for team members and other professional service providers should be documented. This summary can be useful in developing a comprehensive training plan as well as highlighting gaps in clinical offerings. The number and types of public awareness programs should also be recorded.

h.   Team Assessment

Periodically, an internal assessment is recommended to determine members' understanding of the team function and policies; and to identify problems, benefits, needs, and future projects. Appendix 16.16 is a *Multidisciplinary Team Survey Instrument* which may be a useful aid for this purpose.[14]

These are only a few suggested components for team evaluation. The results, however, may be significant to a team's effectiveness, acceptability and sense of accomplishment; and secondly, have a major impact on the overall service delivery system in a community.

COORDINATION TASKS

Coordination is a pivotal function in the operation of a team. Specific needs will vary with the type and purpose of a given team, but may include responsibilities for both program and case coordination as follows:

-Coordinate the multiplicity of services on cases referred to the team.

-Provide case consultation and crisis counseling.

-Obtain and compile medical and psychosocial histories and evaluations on case referrals.

-Maintain records, files, and regular progress notes on assigned cases.

-Prioritize cases appropriate for mini-conferences and full staffings.

-Schedule case conferences/mini-staffings, including notification of all professionals involved in a specific case.

-Facilitate preparation of agendas for staffing or review.

-Coordinate distribution of team reports and recommendations.

-Classify cases for level of follow-up required.

-Initiate periodic reviews of cases involving the team and community agencies.

-Identify breakdowns in provision of services and lack of resources within the team or community systems involved in assessment, diagnosis, treatment, and legal proceedings.

-Compile statistical information for monthly/annual summaries and data for research purposes.

-Provide annual report of activities, services rendered, and other information related to team evaluation.

-Participate in development of team protocols and guidelines.

-Oversee management of logistical needs such as meeting space, audio-visual equipment, etc.

-Develop fiscal budget; maintain and control expenditures.

-Implement and maintain recruitment process of team members.

-Provide orientation and program services information to all new team members.

-Provide supervision of team members.

-Coordinate in-service training programs.

-Provide educational material for review by team members; i.e., information pertaining to conferences, reports, and publications related to child abuse and neglect.

-Maintain the team's cooperative working relationship with community agencies, individuals, and hospitals.

-Function as liaison representative with multiple community agencies.

-Participate in speaking engagements, community education seminars, and other public relations activities for professionals and other individuals in the community.

Once a team has identified the coordination needs specific to its program management and operation, several alternatives might be considered for the allocation of these tasks:

1.   *Team Coordinator*
Ideally, a full- or part-time salaried team coordinator position is established, subsidized by one or more sponsoring agencies or through external funding such as grants. Also, some county teams have assigned employees who have other responsibilities. Persons responsible for coordination of community-based teams in Colorado are listed in Table 16.2.

Table 16.2
Colorado Community-based Teams

Coordinator Identity	Number of Teams
Line Social Services Supervisor	13
Social Services Director	9
Other Social Services Staff	8
Line Worker	7
Social Services Administrator	5

2   *Team/Sponsoring Agency*
Coordination tasks may be shared. A designated team member may manage functions such as screening and scheduling cases, facilitating meetings, follow-up, etc. A sponsoring agency may contribute staff time for clerical assistance with typing and distribution of records, maintenance of files, and compiling of statistics.
3.   *Team Members*
Responsibilities for coordination may be prioritized and assigned to various members of a team, either on a permanent or a rotating basis.

With any of these arrangements, however, it is important that coordination responsibilities be clearly defined and assigned to prevent misunderstanding and confusion.

Summary

Many types of multidisciplinary Child Protection Teams have been developed and implemented since the inception of the concept thirty years ago. Thorough and planned coordination is a significant factor in the success of these teams. Conversely, lack of coordination may be one of the most prevalent reasons for a group's demise.

Improved coordination of services to families and communication between agencies were the two most frequently cited benefits of team utilization noted in a survey conducted by the American Public Welfare Association.[15] Other advantages of a coordinated team listed were:

1. The group is a source of personal and professional support that builds expertise, confidence, and prevents burnout.
2. The team provides opportunities to learn the strengths and limitations of other agencies and is a forum for the communication and development of policies and programs.
3. The team approach facilitates a more consistent, coordinated response with clients, promotes efficient use of resources, and avoids duplication of efforts.
4. Effective team coordination results in more accurate case reporting, in-depth evaluations, comprehensive treatment planning, and earlier detection/prevention of high risk situations.
5. A multi-disciplinary group shares the burden of difficult decisions.
6. A coordinated program helps keep the focus on child abuse as a community problem requiring a comprehensive commitment to the identification and development of needed resources.

Some disadvantages of a team approach may in reality be the result of inefficient coordination. For example, the APWA Survey (Selinske, 1981) identified several factors that were impediments to successful team functioning. These included: (1) Absence of role delineation or misperception regarding the function of a team; (2) Absence of authority; (3) Irregularly scheduled team meetings; (4) Problems with recruitment of team members; (5) Too few or too many referrals; (6) Too time consuming/costly. Some of these problems can be minimized by improved coordination, as discussed in this chapter.

Three concerns commonly cited about teams warrant final comment. Teams may be perceived as threatening by CPS agencies; i.e., that the agency will lose control of cases, become accountable to professionals outside the CPS system, or need to meet expectations of team members. Clearly defined and mutually established guidelines about the purpose and role of a team are critical in avoiding this outcome. Team members should also be aware of the "ivory tower syndrome"; i.e., making recommendations perceived as too idealistic, unavailable, too costly, and with the expectations that these can and will be implemented by the caseworker. Power struggles frequently emerge between a team and CPS staff over these issues, including who has the authority to see that recommendations are followed. Again, effective program coordination is instrumental in dealing with these concerns.

The cost and time involved in a multidisciplinary approach is often regarded as a prohibitive factor. Demonstration of cost effectiveness is critical; the State of Florida, for example, developed methods in which comparative costs of using multidisciplinary teams and long-term impact could be evaluated.[16] Other alternatives for team management, coordination, and resources developed by many kinds of teams have been discussed. However, additional research, analysis of costs vs. benefits to the child and family, and exploration of untapped resources is indicated.

Finally, the advantages of using teams would appear to far outweigh the problems. Many communities have been successful in producing a service that is responsive to the needs of children and their families. However, a mechanism for sharing ideas about what works and what doesn't is needed. Perhaps the establishment of a national Child Protection Team Network to provide opportunities for teams to contribute their experiences and reduce isolation would be a timely goal in the further development of the multidisciplinary approach.

References

1.   Department of Health, Education, and Welfare. *Multidisciplinary Teams in Child Abuse and Neglect Programs.* DHEW publication No. (OHDS) 78-30152, Washington, D.C., August 1978, p. 5.

2   Chamberlain, W.A. "Multidisciplinary Child Abuse and Neglect Team Models." *Multidisciplinary Child Abuse and Neglect Manual.* Athens, Ga.: Regional Institute of Social Welfare Research, 1978.

3.   Jenkins, J.L., R.A. MacDicken and N.J. Ormsky. *A Community Approach: The Child Protection Coordinating Committee.* DHEW publication No. (OHDS) 79-30195, Washington, D.C., 1979

4.   Faller, K.C., and M. Ziefert. "The Role of Social Workers in Multidisciplinary Collaboration." *Social Work with Abused and Neglected Children.* K.C. Faller (Ed.), pp. 207-218. New York: Free Press, Inc., 1981.

5.   Department of Health, Education, and Welfare. *Multidisciplinary Teams.* Washington, D.C., August 1978.

6.   Department of Health, Education, and Welfare. *Child Abuse and Neglect Prevention and Treatment in Rural Communities.* DHEW publication No. (OHDS) 78-30154, Washington, D.C., 1978.

7.   Vecchiolla, F. *Connecticut Children's Protection Project.* Hartford, Conn.: Connecticut State Department of Children and Youth Services, Hartford Division of Children and Protective Services, 1981.

8.   Motz, J. *Colorado's Community-Based Child Protection Teams.* Denver, Colo.: Colorado State Department of Social Services, 1984.

9.   Department of Health and Human Services. *Child Abuse and Neglect— State Reporting Laws.* OHDS publication No. (OHDS) 80-30265, 1980.

10.   Colo. Rev. Stat. 19-10-101 et seq. (Supp. 1984).

11.   Fla. Stat. Ann. Sec. 415-511 (Supp. 1983).

12.   Haase, C.C., G.R., Marden, J. Goldsmith, et al. "District VII Children's Medical Services Child Protection Team Operational Policies and Procedures." Manuscript developed for Florida State Department of Health and Rehabilitative Services, District VII, Orlando, Florida, 1983.

13.   Schmitt, B.D. "Problem-Oriented Record and Team Reports." *The Child Protection Team Handbook.* B.D. Schmitt (Ed.), pp. 176-177. New York: Garland STPM Press, 1978.

14.   Selinske, J. *A Survey of the Use and Functioning of Multidisciplinary Teams in Child Protective Services, pp. 17-21.* Washington, D.C.: National Professional Resource Center on Child Abuse and Neglect, American Public Welfare Association, 1981.

15.   Selinske, J. *A Survey of the Use and Functioning of Multidisciplinary Teams in Child Protective Services.* Washington, D.C.: National Professional Resource Center on Child Abuse and Neglect, American Public Welfare Association, 1981.

16.   Whitworth, J.M., M.W. Lanier, R.G. Skinner, Jr., and N.L. Lund. "A Multidisciplinary Hospital-Based Team for Child Abuse Cases: A Hands-On Approach." *Child Welfare,* 60(1981):236-237.

Appendix 16.1 Preliminary Community Analysis

PRELIMINARY COMMUNITY ANALYSIS

I. When a family is in crisis, which agency(s) do they call?

_____

_____

II. Who is responsible for Child Protective Services in your community?

Legally responsible_____

Other_____

III. Which agencies receive reports and referrals?

Department of Public Welfare _____
Juvenile Court _____
Police Department _____
Other (specify)_____

Number of reports received per month
Families_____ Children_____

Number of referrals to/from other agencies per month
Families_____ Children_____

Number of children on whom neglect/dependent petitions are filed per month____

Number of children placed in temporary shelter care per month____

IV. What kinds of services are now available?

Service	*Agency Providing*
( ) Foster Family Care (long-term)	_____
( ) Emergency Foster Family Homes (24 hour)	_____
( ) Homemakers (Teaching)	_____
( ) Emergency Homemakers (24 hour)	_____
( ) Emergency Caretakers (24 hour)	_____

( ) Answering Service (after normal work hours)   _____

( ) Emergency Intake Service (24 hr., weekend, holidays)   _____

( ) Child Protective Service Intake (8 a.m.–4:30 p.m., Mon.-Fri.)   _____

( ) Outreach and Follow-up   _____

( ) Emergency Shelter for Adolescents   _____

( ) Institutional Care   _____

( ) Group Homes   _____

( ) Treatment Facilities (Older Youth)   _____

( ) Counseling for Parent-Child Conflicts   _____

( ) Neighborhood Crisis Centers   _____

( ) Twenty-Four Hour Walk-In Day Care   _____

( ) Other (specify)   _____

V. Are available services for children in crisis coordinated in your community? Describe:

_____

_____

Are there agreements between agencies? written( ) or verbal( )
List, such as:

Dept. of Social Services--Juvenile Court   _____
Dept. of Social Services--Police Department   _____
Dept. of Social Services--Other child caring agencies   _____

_____

_____

How do the agencies relate, both positive and negative? Describe:

_____

_____

Are there formalized (written) referral procedures? List:

_____

_____

Are there regular meetings for review of agreements, procedures, and problems?

_____

_____

Are there specific individuals within the agencies designated to receive and process referrals? List agencies and describe procedure briefly:

_____

_____

VI.   What gaps in services are there in your community for providing emergency services? List:

_____

_____

Could some services now being provided be shifted to include additional services for a more complete system? *THINK*: then describe what shifts or changes *might* be possible and estimate additional cost, if any.

_____

_____

_____

If additional monies would be needed, from where would they most logically need to come?

        State_____
        Local_____
        Private_____
        Other_____

List individuals and/or groups, both political and nonpolitical, who would need to be contacted to begin discussion. What would this need to include?

_____

_____

Children's Hospital and Health Center
Center For Child Protection

CHILD PROTECTION PROGRAM

This program provides for the identification, treatment, and rehabilitation of neglected and abused children using multiple medical, social, and therapeutic approaches. Approximately 800 new patients are seen each year through the Child Protection Program. Special focus is placed on early intervention and prevention services to "at risk" families and specialized support programs for victims of sexual abuse.

* Child Protection Team: Twenty professional CHHC staff members as well as liaisons from Sharp Hospital, San Diego Police Department Child Abuse Unit, and San Diego County Child Protective Services.

* Parent Aide Program: Intervention and support services to families in crisis utilizing trained volunteer paraprofessionals supervised by the Child Protection staff. Primary goals are to reduce isolation, enhance parenting skills, and reduce stress levels that may lead to abuse. A Mothers' Group providing the opportunity for socialization and parent education is provided.

* Child Sexual Abuse Program: Medical evaluation, crisis intervention, and evidentiary examinations are provided for victims of sexual abuse. A comprehensive play interview and use of anatomically correct dolls are among the tools utilized by the treatment team.

* Child Advocate Program: Support services to child victims of physical and sexual abuse utilizing trained volunteers. Focus is on friendship and socialization, to determine the advocacy needs for each child and develop recommendations for the victim's participation in court proceedings.

* Play Therapy Groups: Several groups supervised by CPT social workers provide abuse victims a consistent cohesive group environment which serves to reduce isolation and anxiety as well as increased self confidence and expressive skills. A Mothers' Group is also available for parents whose children are referred to the Play Therapy Groups.

* Physical Abuse Evidentiary Exams: CPT physicians provide physical examinations and medical evaluation services for victims of physical abuse or neglect. Social service evaluations and play interviews are available on request.

****

All intervention and child abuse prevention programs are supported by the Children's Hospital Auxiliary and community organization contributions.

****

Appendix 16.3 Confidentiality Agreement

Client_____ Date _____

AGREEMENT ON CONFIDENTIALITY

We, the undersigned, on behalf of our respective agencies or interests agree:

(1) That the purpose of this conference is to bring together staff from local and state public, private, and quasi-private agencies, involved in serving children and families, and private individuals who have a direct, tangible, legitimate interest in the case to be brought before this conference;

(2) That cooperation between these individuals and sharing of case information is necessary to enable each family to receive the maximum benefits of the services of each agency;

(3) Each agency and individual signatory below agrees to keep confidential all information obtained from this case conference;

(4) The individuals whose names appear below attest that they are authorized to represent an agency with a direct tangible, legitimate interest in the individual who is the subject of this case conference or his immediate family, and that they are authorized to commit that agency to the transmittal of information relating to this case and will maintain confidentiality of any matters relating to the case; Private individuals below attest that they too have a direct, tangible, legitimate interest in the individual who is the subject of this case conference and will maintain confidentiality of any matters relating to the case.

(5) Termination of services to the above named individual by any agency and/or individual will discontinue any further mutual information flow, herein authorized, beyond provision of a termination summary when requested.

Subsequent sharing of information will then be regulated by standard release of information procedures in effect for the requesting agency and/or individual.

Name   *Agency*

Appendix 16.4

CHILD PROTECTION TEAM
Orlando Regional Medical Center

CONSENT FOR RELEASE OF INFORMATION AND RECORDS

I,_____hereby grant permission to
(Parent, Guardian, or Patient if over 18)
The Child Protection Team to release information contained in the
medical, social, psychological, and psychiatric records and other
information, including substance abuse information, of the
child (ren) and family of_____

_____

to physicians, hospitals, health consultants, public and private
agencies involved in the treatment of the child (ren) and family
and further grant permission to physicians, hospital, health consultants, public and provate agencies involved in the treatment
of the child (ren) and family to provide medical, social psychological, psychiatric and alcohol and drug information to the
Child Protection Team.   In regards   to alcohol   and drug
information, if present, that information has been released in
accordance with Federal Law which prohibits making any further
dislosure of it without the specific written authorization of the
undersigned, or as otherwise permitted by such regulations.

_____

Signature of Parent, Guardian, or
Patient if over 18

_____

Date

_____

HRS Counselor or Witness

85 W. Miller, Suite 304 ▪ Orlando, Florida 32806 ▪ (305) 841-5111, Ext. 5940
HRS Children's Medical Services of Orange, Osceola and Seminole Counties

Appendix 16.5

CHILD PROTECTION TEAM
🦢 Orlando Regional Medical Center

CONSULTATION FORM

CHILD`S NAME:_____D.O.B.:_____

DATE OF CONSULTATION:_____REQUESTED BY:_____

REASON FOR CONSULTATION:_____

_____

DISCUSSION/ASSESSMENT:_____

_____

_____

_____

_____

_____

_____

_____

RECOMMENDATIONS: RESPONSIBILITY:

1._____   1._____

2._____   2._____

3._____   3._____

4._____   4._____

5._____   5._____

_____
CASE COORDINATOR   DATE

85 W. Miller, Suite 304 ■ Orlando, Florida 32806 ■ (305) 841-5111, Ext. 5940
HRS Children's Medical Services of Orange, Osceola and Seminole Counties

CHILD PROTECTION TEAM
⚚ Orlando Regional Medical Center

REFERRAL FORM

CHILD'S NAME_____ DOB_____

DATE OF REFERRAL_____ REFERRED BY_____

MOTHER'S NAME_____ ADDRESS_____

FATHER'S NAME_____ ADDRESS_____

CARETAKER_____ADDRESS_____ REL. TO CHILD_____

REASON FOR REFERRAL_____

_____

Records Check: (Is family known to?)		Services Requested		Date Rendered
HRS	_____	Telephone Inquiry	_____	_____
State Atty	_____	On-siteAssessment	_____	_____
Public Health	_____	Consult	_____	_____
Hospital	_____	Team Staffing	_____	_____
CMS	_____	Medical D&E	_____	_____
School	_____	Psychological	_____	_____
Police	_____	Psychiatric	_____	_____
Mental Health	_____	Legal Evaluation	_____	_____
Counseling	_____	Social Evaluation	_____	_____
Other(specify)	_____	Med. Records Check	_____	_____
		Other (specify)	_____	_____

Mini-staffing Recommendations/Treatment Plan   Date of Staffing_____

Staffing Members	Recommendations	Responsibility
CACC_____	1._____	1._____
HRS_____		
Dr._____	2._____	2._____
LE_____		
Other_____	3._____	3._____
	4._____	4._____
	5._____	5._____

85 W. Miller, Suite 304 ■ Orlando, Florida 32806 ■ (305) 841-5111, Ext. 5940
HRS Children's Medical Services of Orange, Osceola and Seminole Counties

Children's Hospital and Health Center
Center For Child Protection

CHILD PROTECTION TEAM PATIENT REFERRALS
PHYSICAL ABUSE/NEGLECT/OTHER

MONTH_____

No. of Referrals - Current Month_____

Fiscal Year Total_____
Year to Date Total_____

Sex of Victim	Race of Victim	Age of Victim	Time Seen
Male_____	Caucasian _____	0-3 yrs. _____	Reg. Hrs _____
Female_____	Black _____	4-6 yrs. _____	After hrs _____
	Hispanic _____	7-10 yrs. _____	
	Am. Indian _____	11-14 yrs. _____	Inpatient _____
	Asian _____	15+ yrs. _____	Outpatient _____
	Other _____		
	Unknown _____		

Referral Source

CHHC Referral Source		Outside Referral Source	
Child Protection	_____	San Diego Police Dept.	_____
Medical	_____	Other Law Enforcement	_____
Neonatal ICU	_____	Camp Pendleton Agreement	_____
Pediatric ICU	_____	Child Protective Services	_____
Special Care	_____	Hospital/Private Physician	_____
Surgical	_____	Family/Victim	_____
Trauma	_____	Other	_____
Other_____	_____		

Handicapped   Alcohol/Drug

Pre-Injury _____   Known History of Alcohol Use in Family/Incident _____
Post-Injury _____   Known History of Drug Use in Family/Incident _____

Known History of Abuse/Neglect to Victim_____

Reason for Referral

Multiple Injuries	_____	Addicted Newborn	_____
Bites	_____	Failure to Thrive	_____
Bruises	_____	High Risk Newborn	_____
Burns	_____	Ingestion	_____
Fractures: Skull	_____	Near Drowning	_____
Fractures: Other	_____	Neglect: Medical	_____
Trauma: Abdominal	_____	Neglect: Physical	_____
Trauma: Head	_____	Other	_____
*Number of Deaths*_____			

Appendix 16.8

Children's Hospital and Health Center
Center For Child Protection

CHILD PROTECTION TEAM PATIENT REFERRALS   MONTH_____
SEXUAL ABUSE

No. of Referrals - Current Month_____   Fiscal Year Total   _____
                                                Year to Date Total   _____

Sex of Victim	*Race of Victim*		*Age of Victim*	*Time Seen*	
Male_____	Caucasian	_____	0-3 yrs. _____	_____ Reg. Hrs	_____
Female_____	Black	_____	4-6 yrs. _____	_____ After hrs	_____
	Hispanic	_____	7-10 yrs _____		
	Am. Indian	_____	11-14 yrs. _____	_____ Inpatient	_____
	Asian	_____	15+ yrs. _____	_____ Outpatient	_____
	Other	_____			
	Unknown	_____			

Referral Source

CHHC Referral Source		Outside Referral Source	
Child Protection	_____	San Diego Police Dept.	_____
Medical	_____	Other Law Enforcement	_____
Neonatal ICU	_____	Camp Pendleton Agreement	_____
Pediatric ICU	_____	Child Protective Services	_____
Special Care	_____	Hospital/Private Physician	_____
Surgical	_____	Family/Victim	_____
Trauma	_____	Other	_____
Other_____	_____		

Handicapped   *Alcohol/Drug*
Yes_____   Known History of Alcohol Use in Family/Incident   _____
No_____   Known History of Drug Use in Family/Incident   _____

Known History of Abuse/Neglect to Victim

Reason for Referral/Type of Abuse
In Home/Family   Penetration _____   Molest _____
Out of Home/Non-Family   Penetration _____   Molest _____
Unknown   Penetration _____   Molest _____

Suspected Perpetrator		*Suspected Perpetrator/Sex*	
Father	_____	Male	_____
Mother	_____	Female	_____
Both Parents	_____	Both Male and Female	_____
Stepfather	_____	Unknown	_____
Stepmother	_____		
Other Family Member	_____	*Suspected Perpetrator/Age*	
Significant Other (Parent)	_____		
Significant Other (Patient)	_____	Adult	_____

8001 Frost Street, San Diego, CA 92123 • (619) 576-5803   TTY 576-5831

Known to Family	_____	Juvenile	_____
Stranger	_____	Both Adult and Juvenile	_____
Unknown	_____	Unknown	_____
More than one category	_____		

History Obtained		*Physical Findings*	
Positive for Abuse	_____	Positive Physical Findings	_____
Negative for Abuse	_____	Negative Physical Findings	_____
Inconclusive	_____	Inconclusive	_____

History of Pornography___ Child Photographed by Suspected Perpetrator___

Appendix 16.9

CHILD PROTECTION TEAM
Orlando Regional Medical Center

MEDICAL REPORT   **ATTACHMENT IX**

NAME:

D.O.B.:
D.O.E.:
H.R.S.:
C.P.T.:

HISTORY: This section includes social information and
                               history provided by the child, family and
                               other involved people, those pertinent to the
                               problem presented for medical evaluation.

PHYSICAL EXAMINATION: This section includes information obtained
                               from the physician's examination of   the
                               child.

ASSESSMENT: This section includes the physician's
                               assessment and diagnosis of the presenting
                               condition, based on physical and historical
                               information obtained.

PLAN: This section includes the physician's
                               recommendations for treatment, diagnostic
                               testing and recommendations for protection of
                               the child.

                               Signature_____
                                         Title

85 W. Miller, Suite 304 ■ Orlando, Florida 32806 ■ (305) 841-5111, Ext. 5940
HRS Children's Medical Services of Orange, Osceola and Seminole Counties

Appendix 16.10

CHILD PROTECTION TEAM
Orlando Regional Medical Center

SOCIAL SUMMARY

ATTACHMENT VIII

NAME:

D.O.B.:
D.O.R.:

PRESENTING INFORMATION:

This section includes physicial And social information presented to the Child Protection Team by the referral source.

CHILD'S STATEMENT:

This section includes what the child tells the CPT case coordinator about the presenting problem.

PARENT'S STATEMENT:

This section includes what the parents or other caretakers tell the CPT case coordinator about the presenting problem.

FAMILY HISTORY:

This section includes information concerning the present family dynamics, history and life situation, including information concerning parents's or caretaker's families of origin.

IMPRESSION/RECOMMENDATIONS:

This section includes the case coordinator's case assessment and recommendations for further CPT services and to the referral source.

Signature _____
Title

Appendix 16.11

CHILD PROTECTION TEAM
Orlando Regional Medical Center
CPT MINI STAFFING RECOMMENDATIONS

Child's Name_____D.O.B.:_____

Mother's Name_____Father's Name:_____

Address:_____Address:_____

Siblings_____D.O.B.:_____

_____D.O.B.:_____

_____D.O.B.:_____

_____D.O.B.:_____

Date of Referral:_____Referred by:_____

Date of Medical D&E:_____Physician:_____

MEDICAL D & E ATTACHED   _____Yes   _____No

Reason for Referral: _____

_____

_____

Mini Staffing Recommendations: Responsibility:

1._____   1._____

2._____   2._____

3._____   3._____

4._____   4._____

5._____   5._____

6._____   6._____

Mini Staffing Dates: Staffing Members Signature:

_____   CPT:_____

_____   DR:_____

_____   HRS:_____

LE:_____

OTHER:_____

85 W. Miller, Suite 304 ■ Orlando, Florida 32806 ■ (305) 841-5111, Ext. 5940
HRS Children's Medical Services of Orange, Osceola and Seminole Counties

Appendix 16.12

 University of Colorado Health Sciences Center

Department of Pediatrics

The C. Henry Kempe National Center for the Prevention and Treatment of Child Abuse and Neglect

1205 Oneida Street   University Hospital
Denver, Colorado 80220   School of Medicine
(303) 321-3963   School of Nursing
                           School of Dentistry

SAMPLE CASE - ALL NAMES, DATES, AND OTHER IDENTIFYING INFORMATION HAVE BEEN CHANGED TO INSURE CONFIDENTIALITY

CASE CONFERENCE AGENDA

Child Protection Team Case Conference
University of Colorado Health Sciences Center
September 1, 1986

Patient: R.F.   *Professionals Involved*
BD: 8/10/84 (2 years)   SW-Denver County SS
Hospital # 5841   SW-Arapahoe County SS
County: Denver   Psychiatrist-MHC
                                 PHN Coordinator
                                 RN - Tri-County Health
                                 MD,RN,SW-University Hospital

#1. *Child abuse and neglect diagnosis*

-emotional abuse/high risk potential
-*current status*: very disturbed, unconsolable child observed during 8/19 UH clinic appointment. Self-assaultive behavior for 1 1/2 hours (i.e., repeatedly scratched, pinched, grabbed at his eyes, arms, legs, banged head on floor). Self-inflicted injuries include bite marks on left arm
-recoiled from comforting efforts of R.N. but would not go to anyone else
-mother handed child to hospital staff saying she couldn't handle anymore
-day care services offered, refused by mother until l month ago. Set up 8 hours/day, 5 times/week
-currently in voluntary foster care as of 9/18/86
-*past history*: documented concerns by hospital staff at time of birth regarding potential for CA/N, particularly with child's father who threatened to hurt baby and mother. Tri-County, PHN and Mental Health Center referrals
-Mental Health Center referral to Arapahoe Social Services 9/84 regarding potential CA/N
-no documentation of abuse from 9/84 to present
-unsubstantiated complaint regarding neglect. Arapahoe County planned on filing in court with recommendation for custody and foster care. Family moved: case not filed
-case transferred to Denver Social Services 6/85 to present
-child in voluntary foster placement 4/85 to 6/85 following mother's TAB. Child described by SW as adjusting well. Child returned home when family moved to different county
-stepfather has observed child banging head, rocking behavior, not talking at home. Fears child will develop serious emotional problems

-mother says child "always wants his way and hurts himself if he doesn't get it." Has stated
several occasions not being able to manage and control child, has expressed fears of losing cor
and hurting child
-mother and current husband talk of adopting R.F.

Recommendations: 9/1/86

-continue foster care
-thorough evaluation of emotional and developmental status—UH Family Evaluation Clinic
-carefully document child's behavior and adjustment in foster care—SS
-counseling with foster mother regarding management of child—SS

#2 Patient's physical/developmental status

-DDST completed at Tri-County 10/85. Results: no delays
-UH documents growth parameters declining on curve 4/86: weight 50th percentile, down 40th
percentile; head circumference 75th percentile, down 10th percentile
-regular medical follow-up at Tri-County up to date, no missed appointments, no reports of abus
(two incidents considered accidental were self-inflicted: 5/86 black eye and abrasions on cheek
with history of fall on coffee table, 8/86 bite marks on underskin of forearm—self inflicted)
-episodic care at UH ER 9/85. Evaluated for possible fracture of left foot with history of child
falling out of crib. Results: normal (no trauma survey)

Recommendations: 9/1/85

-continue medical follow-up at Tri-County
-developmental evaluation — UH Family Evaluation Clinic

#3 Sibling's physical/emotional/developmental status

-sibling: new baby due 9/15/86, prenatal care, UH
-planned pregnancy. Mother now upset, multiple complaints—"feels bad all over"
-husband excited about baby but both express some concern to UH SW of not being ready for baby
-mother wanted this baby "taken out of her" since 26 weeks' gestation
-mother wanted to be hospitalized medically during this pregnancy

Recommendations: 9/1/86

-document parent/child interaction at birth; determine what parents think of this baby—UH
SW/RN/MD staff
-referral to enhance mother/child interaction—PHN coordinator
-medical follow-up at Tri-County
-provide as much support as possible to mother during hospitalization to encourage bonding—U
staff
-encourage 3-to-4 day stay in hospital post-partum—UH MD/RN/staff

#4 Mother's physical/emotional status (age 21)

-has been in psychiatric treatment 1 1/2 years at MHC, recently terminated. Diagnosis: borderline personality, borderline MR, hysterical dependent, considered high risk for CA/N. Impression: not able to utilize therapy
-new therapist assigned, mother refused continuing individual therapy, did not keep appointments
-described as manipulative; involves multidisciplines, splitting
-says she has "been in a shell" since age 13, received psychiatric care but none has helped. Feels no one understands or meets her needs
-admits to difficulty with RF; feels he deliberately does things to irritate her; feels things will be better with new baby
-suicidal in past, twice when pregnant with R.F. Psychiatric hospitalization one week in 1/86 following OD on Librium, slashed wrist slightly; threatened to stab self with knife
-multiple ER visits with physical/emotional problems
-TAB few months prior to current pregnancy
-has signed papers for tubal ligation following this pregnancy
-multiple treatment services offered from time prior to R.F.'s birth to present (i.e., individual psychotherapy, group counseling via Social Services, Mental Health Center, PHN and Tri-County)
-no treatment currently
-strengths: has frequently recognized crises and sought services

Recommendations: 9/1/86

-close follow-up—SS and PHN
-continued involvement with MHC
-consider relinquishment counseling of R.F.—SS

#5 *Father's physical/emotional status:* (age 24)

-biological father has requested visitations with R.F. Plans to contest any adoption plans. Has psychiatric history. Diagnosed as schizophrenic by psychiatrist at MHC.
-according to mother's history, has been assaultive with her and R.F.

Recommendations: 9/1/86

-if visitations approved, must be on supervised basis with SS

#6 *Stepfather's physical/emotional status* (age 23)

-limited information available
-admits he doesn't relate well with R.F.

Recommendations: 9/1/86

-interview stepfather to obtain better history, his interest in R.F. and new baby—SS
-observe parent/child interaction with new baby—UH RN/SS/staff

#7 *Marital status*

-mother married to R.F.'s father 8/83, divorced 10/85. States marriage happy until child's birth when "all became bad." Mother reports previous husband tried to beat/kill R.F. and was assaultive with her
-custody of R.F. awarded to mother after divorce
-remarried 3/83 to present
-she and current husband have been involved in group marital counseling until recently at MHC

Recommendations: 9/1/86

-re-involve in group therapy if possible

#8 *Involvement of relatives/others*

-mother's family lives in area. Mother and sister have provided some help with child care and transportation
-no further information available about her family or current husband's family

Recommendations: 9/1/86

-further assessment of both families, particularly to determine if supportive services available

#9 *Environmental situation/current crisis*

-unstable home
-new baby due soon

Recommendations: 9/1/86

-same as #3

#10 *Safety of the home*

-two-year old boy with serious emotional trauma due to extremely poor mother/child relationship, mother with significant psychiatric difficulties, an unstable environment. Has been placed in foster care twice. Also, has recently been in day care five days per week
-growth parameters declining
-both parents have expressed concerns about managing child, fears of hurting child
-new baby due
-multiple services and intervention have already been tried

Questions for the Team:

1. What does R.F. need in terms of evaluation, services and intervention?
2. Should there be court filing on R.F. and new baby?
3. If so, on what basis?
4. Are there other services that are needed for the entire family, new baby, etc.?

Case Review (after new baby is born and any further evaluations completed):

APPENDIX 16.13 *Multidisciplinary Team Report of Recommendations*

CASE NAME _____ DATE OF INITIAL REVIEW _____ TEAM ID _____

WORKER NAME/AGENCY _____

Specific Problems in This Case (Letter each consecutively)	Team Recommendations/ Intervention Plan (Letter each recommendation consecutively)	Suggested Community Resources to Be Utilized and Referral Plan (Letter each consecutively)	Suggested Time Frame for Implementation

Appendix 16.14

 University of Colorado Health Sciences Center

Department of Pediatrics

The C. Henry Kempe National Center for the Prevention and Treatment of Child Abuse and Neglect

1205 Oneida Street
Denver, Colorado 80220
(303) 321-3963

University Hospital
School of Medicine
School of Nursing
School of Dentistry

Case Review Agenda

Case Identification:

Date of Review:

Date of Previous Staffing:

Social Worker Assigned:

County:

Professionals Currently Involved:

Summary of new or additional information, evaluations, legal action, treatment plan, and questions should be completed in the following categories.

1. *CA/N diagnosis*

   -Recommendations/Previous staffing
   -Current Status
   -Recommendations/Case Review

2. *Patient's physical/emotional/developmental status*
   -Recommendations/Previous Staffing
   -Current Status
   -Recommendations/Case Review

3. *Sibling's Physical/emotional/developmental status*
   -Recommendations/Previous Staffing
   -Current status
   -Recommendations/Case Review

4. *Mother's physical/emotional status/strengths*
   -Recommendations/Previous Staffing
   -Current status
   -Recommendations/Case Review

5. *Father's physical/emotional status/strengths*
   -Recommendations/Previous Staffing
   -Current status
   -Recommendations/Case Review

6. *Perpetrator's emotional status (other than parents)*

        -Recommendations/Previous Staffing
        -Current status
        -Recommendations/Case Review

7. *Marital status/problems*
        -Recommendations/Previous Staffing
        -Current status
        -Recommendations/Case Review

8. *Involvement of relatives/others*
        -Recommendations/Previous Staffing
        -Current status
        -Recommendations/Case Review

9. *Environmental situation/current crisis*
        -Recommendations/Previous Staffing
        -Current status
        -Recommendations/Case Review

10. *Summary/safety of the home*
        -Recommendations/Previous Staffing
        -Current status
        -Recommendations/Case Review

Questions for the Team

Appendix 16.15

MULTIDISCIPLINARY TEAM SUMMARY REPORT

The multidisciplinary team is a resource for the service provider. Your evaluation of the recommendations made on your referral will be helpful in our discussion of other referrals.

Date_____ Worker_____
Case Identification_____ Agency_____
Date of Initial Review_____ Supervisor_____

Status of Recommendations

Please indicate the status of the recommendations made by the team by completing the following information. Use letters corresponding with the Team's Report of Recommendations.

I. In your opinion, do you think the recommendations made by the team were helpful in reaching a resolution or achieving positive movement in this case?   Yes_____   No_____

II. Indicate which recommendations you were able to implement:
    A   B   C   D   E   F   G   H   I   J

III. For each recommendation, were there any barriers encountered?

A B C D E F G H I J   None

A B C D E F G H I J   Waiting list for service

A B C D E F G H I J   Service not available

A B C D E F G H I J   Inadequate resources/income

A B C D E F G H I J   Uncooperative parents/substitutes

A B C D E F G H I J   No transportation

A B C D E F G H I J   Change in family living arrangements

A B C D E F G H I J   Changes in family composition

A B C D E F G H I J   Insufficient time to implement plan

A B C D E F G H I J   Time/effort required of worker too extensive

A B C D E F G H I J   Worker's caseload/responsibilities changed

A B C D E F G H I J   Other (please specify)_____

_____

IV. Worker's evaluation/comments regarding the case at this time:

_____

_____

_____

_____

_____

V. Worker's evaluation/comments regarding the team process:

_____

_____

_____

_____

_____

Appendix 16.16

American Public Welfare Association
National Professional Resource Center
on Child Abuse and Neglect

Multidisciplinary Team Survey Instrument

1. What *initial* factor or combination of factors led to the creation of your multidisciplinary team (please check all that apply)?

_____ Community action
_____ Legislative mandate
_____ Department policy
_____ Other (please specify below)

2. Please provide a brief description of the factor(s) leading *to the formation of your team*:

3. Approximately how much time was involved in getting the team started (from conceptualization to the first team meeting)?

_____ Under one month
_____ 1 to 3 months
_____ 4 to 6 months
_____ 7 to 12 months
_____ Other (please specify below)

4. Did the initial efforts to establish a team lead to the formation of the current team (current team in terms of structure and responsibility, not membership)?

_____ Yes
_____ No
(If yes, go to item #5.)

    4.a If no, please explain (e.g., how many efforts were required to get a team started, over what period of time, what were the major impediments, etc.).

5. What is the approximate population size of the geographic area covered by your team?

_____ Predominantly urban
_____ Predominantly rural
_____ Other (please specify below)

7. What is the number of reported cases of child abuse and neglect per year within this geographic area?

8. What are the functions of the team (please check all items that apply):

_____ Identifying service gaps and developing and/or improving programs and services
_____ Case consultation to child protective service personnel
_____ Diagnosis and treatment
_____ Other (please specify below)

9. Does the team make binding case decisions?

_____ Yes
_____ No

(If no, go to item #10.)

9.a. If yes, what is the basis for this decision-making authority?
_____ Legislation
_____ Department policy
_____ Other (please specify below)

9.b. If yes, in what areas does the team make binding decisions?
(check all that apply)
_____ Removal of children from their homes
_____ Initiation of court action
_____ Development and implementation of a treatment plan
_____ Other (please specify below)

9.c. If yes, how has the authority vested in the team affected the authority of the child protective service agency in case-related matters?
_____ Increased the agency's authority
_____ Decreased the agency's authority
_____ No change

9.d. If yes, does the CPS agency have a mechanism/procedure for appealing the decision of the team?
_____ Yes (please describe below)
_____ No

10. What cases are handled by the team?
_____ All CPS cases
_____ Selected CPS cases
_____ Other (please explain below)

(If all cases, go to item #11)

10.a. If selected cases, please describe the criteria used for selection, including who makes the decision.

11. With what frequency does the team meet?
_____ Weekly
_____ Twice monthly
_____ Monthly
_____ Quarterly
_____ Other (please specify)

12. Does the team have regularly scheduled meeting times (e.g., every other Tuesday)?
_____Yes
_____No

(If yes, go to item #13)

13. What is the *average* length of a team meeting?
_____ One hour
_____ Two hours
_____ Three hours
_____ Other (please specify)

14. What is the average number of cases conferenced during a team meeting?

15. What is the average number of cases conferenced during a three-month period?

16. Does the team participate in the following activities (please check all applicable items)?
_____ Case assessment
_____ Case monitoring and review
_____ Case closure decisions
_____ None of the above (please explain)

17. What professionals are included as standing members of your team (please check all that apply)?
_____ Social workers/caseworkers
_____ Physicians
_____ Nurses
_____ Psychiatrist/other mental health personnel
_____ Attorneys
_____ Judges or court staff
_____ Police officers
_____ Educators/teachers
_____ Other (please specify)

18. Have you had difficulty recruiting representatives from any discipline/profession?
_____ Yes
_____ No
(If no, go to item #19)

18.a. If yes, please indicate those disciplines/professions within which you have had recruiting difficulties.

19. Please list, by type, the agencies represented on the team (e.g., public mental health center, local hospital):

20. Which of the following categories best describes the composition of your team?
_____ Predominantly direct service personnel
_____ Predominantly mid-level supervisory personnel
_____ Predominantly administrative personnel
_____ Mixture (please describe briefly)

21. Please describe briefly the selection criteria and procedures used for team membership (i.e., who is eligible and how are they selected?)

22. How is membership structured?

_____ The total membership is permanent (i.e., all members are expected to attend each meeting for the duration of their terms)

_____ Only a core group of the membership is permanent with other members attending meetings as indicated by case circumstances

_____ Other (please describe below).

If you did not check the core group response, go to Item #23)

22.a. If a core group serves as the permanent team, which members serve on an "as-needed" basis (please specify these members by both agency affiliation and profession)?

23. How many members comprise your total standing team?

24. What is the average attendance at each team meeting?

25. Who currently chairs the team (please specify by profession and agency affiliation)?

26. Please describe the procedures used for selecting a chairperson.

27. Who is eligible to serve as chairperson?

_____ Any team member

_____ Only CPS personnel

_____ Only non-CPS personnel

_____ Other (please describe below)

28. Does the team have procedures for handling conflicts in professional judgment among team members?

_____ Yes

_____ No

(If no, go to item #29)

28.a. If yes, please describe these procedures briefly.

29. How is client confidentiality handled (please check all applicable items)?

_____ Team members sign an agreement to protect client confidentiality

_____ Client permission is obtained before a case is presented to the team

_____ Cases are handled in an anonymous manner by the team (i.e., no client names are used)

_____ Other (please describe below)

30. How does state legislation impact on the team's handling of confidentiality?

_____ Legislation empowers the team to handle confidential information
_____ Legislation restricts the team from handling confidential information
_____ There is no applicable legislation
_____ Other (please describe below)

31. Are there controls on the flow of written case information among agencies and team members?

_____ Yes
_____ No

(If no, go to item #32).

31.a. If yes, please briefly describe these controls.

32. Are clients invited to participate in team meetings?

_____ Yes
_____ No

(If no, go to item #33).

32.a. If yes, in approximately what percentage of cases brought before the team are clients invited to participate?

32.b. If yes, what percentage of clients invited to participate actually do so?

32.c. If yes, please describe the criteria used to determine when clients should be invited to participate.

32.d If yes, please describe briefly the client's role in the team meeting.

33. With regard to legal liability, have lawsuits been brought or threatened against individual team members for their participation in decisions made by the team?

_____ Yes
_____ No

(If no, go to Item #34).

33. a If yes, please briefly describe the lawsuit or threatened lawsuit and the outcome (if known).

34. Are there previous court decisions in your state which indicate whether individual team members are liable for their participation in decisions made by the team?

_____ Yes
_____ No
_____ Do not know

(If no or do not know, go to item #34).

34.a. If yes, briefly describe these precedents.

34.b. If yes, can a copy of the court decision be obtained?

_____ Yes
_____ No

35. Have team members raised concern about their own legal liability?

      _____ Yes

      _____ No

(If no, go to item #36).

      35.a. If yes, please cite specific concerns and indicate any measures taken to address these concerns.

36. Are new team members given orientation training?

      _____ Yes

      _____ No

(If no, go to item #37).

      36.a. If yes, please briefly describe the content and duration of the training and indicate the title of the agency(ies) and/or person(s) who organizes and provides the training.

37. Does the team have a program of ongoing training for its members?

      _____ Yes

      _____ No

(If no, go to item #38).

      37.a. If yes, please briefly describe the content and frequency of training and indicate the title of the agency(ies) and/or person(s) who organizes and provides the training.

38. Please list, by category, the types of expenses associated with operating your team (e.g., personnel, supplies, telephone, travel, etc.)

39. What is the team's source(s) of funding (please check all that apply)?

      _____ NCCAN grant

      _____ State/county budget

      _____ Other (please specify below)

40. Please list the factors that have most impeded the team's progress.

41. Please briefly describe how these inhibiting factors have been dealt with.

42. Please list the factors that have most facilitated the team's progress.

43. Please cite the primary benefits of using the team.

44. Has your agency attempted to measure/quantify these benefits (e.g., has the cost-effectiveness of providing services via the team been studied)?

    _____ Yes

    _____ No

(If no, go to item #45).

44.a. If yes, please briefly describe how benefits have been measured/studied.

44.b. If yes, has your agency attempted to disseminate information about the benefits of multidisciplinary team use?

    _____ Yes (please describe the dissemination effort below)

    _____ No

45. Please cite the primary disadvantages of using the team.

46. Please briefly describe how these disadvantages have been dealt with.

47. Do you have written documents describing the team and its operations that you could share with us?

    _____ Yes

    _____ No

48. Are you willing to serve as a resource person for other states and locales interested in forming multidisciplinary teams?

    _____ Yes

    _____ No

17. Conducting Effective Team Meetings

Candace A. Grosz and David B. Denson

Introduction

A crucial component of team functioning is the multidisciplinary team conference. The multidisciplinary conference of every team requires ground rules if it is to be effective and efficient. The immediate goals of the guidelines in this chapter are:
1. To increase the team's competence and decision-making skills; i.e., effectiveness; and
2. To minimize the time required; i.e., efficiency.
We will focus on helping the team be task oriented through structuring the team, case presentation, and decision-making.[1]

Team Structure and Expectations

MEMBERSHIP

The team needs to require that agencies send representatives with decision-making power. Team members can then negotiate the agency's position, commit resources, and follow through on recommendations made for the family. If a member cannot attend on a regular basis, establish when he or she will come; e.g., the first meeting of each month.   Core team members should avoid alternating because this diminishes group cohesion.   It can become particularly disruptive if several members alternate so that each meeting has a new cluster of core members in addition to those persons working with a specific case. Members also need to express a strong commitment to participate for at least one year. Turnover of members is both a cause and result of poor team functioning.

LOGISTICS

Child protection teams need to set a regular meeting time that is part of the members' schedules. Meeting weekly or early in the day has been shown most effective in minimizing absences and increasing the effectiveness of meetings.[2] Canceling a few meetings is much easier than scheduling each meeting on an ongoing basis. Any "extra" time can be used for in-service education of team members, administrative duties, socialization, or special projects.

A convenient, comfortable location is an obvious need, but may be difficult to arrange.   If possible, accessible parking, a seating arrangement that allows good eye contact, and some refreshments can help to get things going.   Most important is a location that provides privacy and freedom from interruption.[3]

Meetings should be limited to two hours maximum, if at all possible. Systems review teams with a large volume of cases may find this time insufficient, but going longer fatigues members and jeopardizes effectiveness and efficiency. If meetings must be longer than two hours, then a fifteen minute break after ninety minutes is recommended.[4]

ATTENDANCE

When all team members are present, it maximizes the dissemination of information and allows more competent decision-making. Therefore, teams should openly state the expectation that all members will be there. When members are absent, they can be expected to bring the case back to the team for review, if team recommendations cannot be followed. If team recommendations are disregarded, members become frustrated and disinterested, feeling their time is wasted. Both advisory and compulsory teams need feedback about inappropriate recommendations or changes in the cases that require modification of plans. Members should notify the coordinator or other designated person of an absence as much in advance as possible, so the agenda can be modified as needed. The key for team functioning is predictability and reliability. No-shows seriously disrupt the team's ability to get its work done. Keeping a team calendar and recording planned absences, attendance, and tentative agency items will help to minimize disruption. When an absence is anticipated, the coordinator should collect data and recommendations from that member prior to the meeting. An alternate member can also be considered, such as the person's supervisor or colleague. A speaker phone can be used to consult an absent member, or several members, at another location. This is especially valuable to persons in private practice who may be unwilling to leave their practice and attend the meeting, or where long distances prohibit attendance.

It is crucial to start meetings on time. Waiting for late arrivals or no-shows wastes time and may perpetuate this problem. Teams can use a written summary to help late members catch up, rather than orally reviewing the discussion they missed. It is also important to ask members not to leave the team meeting for phone calls. This disrupts the team's decision-making process and wastes everyone else's time. It is just as important to end on time and avoid losing members who must leave during decision-making. When this happens, it increases the frustration and fatigue for members remaining.[5] It can be very difficult to end on time if the case presentation is too lengthy or if the team gets bogged down in decision-making. Both of these issues will be considered in later sections of this chapter.

AGENDA

An agenda provides the essential focus for content (which cases) and process (what order and time parameters). Each team needs to establish a regular pattern for team business. This is an agreement by members of how they will approach problem-solving and decision-making.[6]

The agenda should also list time limits for each case or each section of the meeting. The amount of time varies according to the function of the team. Systems review teams may do many cases briefly; i.e., less than five minutes each. In-depth review teams may take up to an hour for each case. Many teams combine these functions with an agenda that includes:

1. quick review of new intakes
2. full review of investigated cases
3. brief reports (but not discussions) of follow-up on previous cases.

Many teams have developed systems to handle large volumes of cases that include the use of a mini team or coordinator to screen and prioritize cases before the meeting. If the team is not reviewing all cases, it is best that cases from the full spectrum of child abuse and neglect, as well as accidents, be selected to help the team maintain a good base. Additionally, any team member, or other community professional, should be able to request a team review of a case by contacting the designated person to place the case on the agenda.

Members may try to pressure the team to review serious cases immediately during a crisis; e.g., a fatal re-abuse case. Such crisis meetings are usually unproductive. The team should not permit itself to be rushed into reviewing the case until a complete data base is available. This usually takes several days. The team does not need to be a forum for crisis counselling of individual professionals, for this can be provided through other channels. Grief or anger around a particular case is better worked through at a different time and place.

CONFIDENTIALITY

It is standard for team members to consider all case information confidential and to use strict professional standards to safeguard the client's privacy. It is prudent to include reminders of this and to clarify the information sharing team members will do among agencies. There may be provisions for this in state laws regarding reporting of child abuse or establishing child protection teams. Safeguards can include gathering all written material at the end of the meeting. Revised summaries are then sent only to the direct service providers for each family. Initials or numbers can also be used rather than names, especially if media or public persons are observing the meeting. If the identity of a child or family is known, public discussion may have to be much more restricted. Developing trust and cohesion among the members can resolve many issues of confidentiality. This takes some experience in working together, guidelines for discussing cases, and policies for sharing reports.

VISITORS

Child protection teams should establish an ongoing policy before visitors attend meetings so that members are not surprised. The team's policy may differentiate participation according to the type of visitor. Other professionals or lay workers involved with cases of the team are not considered visitors; although they attend infrequently, they are team members for the discussion of that family. Professionals or professionals in training can gain much from observing, often without serious disruption, if the frequency and number of these visitors are limited. Guidelines for allowing media or public persons to attend may depend on state laws. These visitors generally are appropriate only for systems review teams, and with careful safeguards for confidentiality. An alternative can be to schedule a time for visitors to talk with team members rather than include them in a case discussion.

All visitors need a brief orientation and feedback session. To minimize disruption to the team, seat them away from the discussion table, and help them to understand that they are observers and non-participants.[7] When possible, alert the team prior to the arrival of any visitors. Be certain to introduce all visitors so members know who they are and why they are there.

We have summarized the essential elements for structuring the team in Table 17.1.

Table 17.1
Team Structure

Enlist regular members with decision making power.
Schedule weekly meetings at a comfortable, private location.
Limit meetings to two hours. Start and end on time.
Use a team calendar to record attendance and plan ahead.
Prepare an agenda for content and process within time limits.
Plan for confidentiality and visitors.

Case Presentations

BEFORE THE MEETING

Individual evaluations should be completed prior to team review to make maximum information available for decision-making. Each professional must think through his or her assessment, and reach initial conclusions and make tentative recommendations prior to the meeting. Supervision, mini-conferences, and phone calls can be used to share information and make decisions that cannot wait for the meeting. The team then has more time for critical decisions. An exception to this is a systems review team, which must make a timely and adequate initial response.

Prior to the meeting, a written summary should be prepared of the essential elements of the case. Most teams have a form, outline, or problem-oriented approach that is also a checklist for comprehensive evaluation. This written summary condenses the extensive case information and quickly gives members a basis for case discussion.

Each professional directly involved with the case needs to prepare for the meeting by considering:

1. The diagnosis of child abuse and neglect (what we have).
2. Action taken to this point (what has been done).
3. Prognosis for individuals and the family (the professional's opinion).
4. Tentative recommendations (where we go from here).
5. Gaps in information.
6. Primary questions for the team.

Individuals who will present case information should spend a few minutes preparing the report to avoid rambling narration. These oral presentations must give a capsule view of the data, and add only enough detail to share the dilemmas, emotional responses, and opinions. A few brief anecdotes can be an effective addition to portray the essence of the situation. A long discourse on family history or quoting dialogues with family members is not effective. The goal is to relate succinctly both the family development and the current situation.

Before the meeting, three or four primary questions should be listed for each case.[8] This is the key to focusing and prioritizing team decision-making. Commonly, primary questions for child protection teams include those listed in the preceding chapter on team coordination.

Each presenter needs to know how much time is allotted for presenting the case material in the meeting. Usually, it is five minutes or less. Often members will need reminders of these time restraints before and during the meeting, as well as some practice in giving concise case material. Case presentation must remain concise to allow the team to move on to decision-making.

New participants need a clear description of the team process, guidelines for oral presentations, and the purpose of the team's review, prior to the meeting. It is best to provide an outline for preparing written information at the time of invitation. The new participants may need help in formulating the primary questions they have for the team. They should be seated next to experienced members who can answer questions, help them feel more comfortable, and encourage their participation in the meeting.

AT THE MEETING

Case material should be presented in a logical sequence. Often teams follow this pattern: initial report of suspected child abuse and neglect, medical/social work psychiatric evaluations, legal or other

Table 17.2 Family Tree*

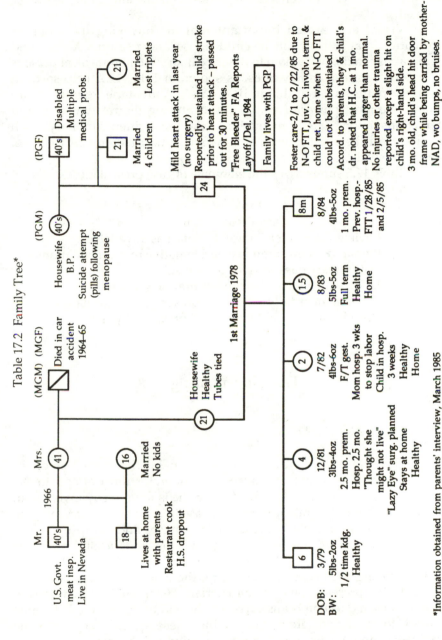

*Information obtained from parents' interview, March 1985

specialty opinions and reports on actions taken, and other agencies involved.

Visual aids are an important tool in conveying the complex information that is common in child abuse and neglect. X-rays and photographs can do much more to describe injuries to non-medical persons than medical terms. Family trees, as shown in Table 17.2, help sort out histories, patterns, and the individuals. Videotape segments are perhaps the most powerful visual aid, capturing the relationships and interactions among family members. Like the written summary, each visual aid can be another way of conveying information concisely yet comprehensively.

Table 17.3 summarizes the elements of case presentation.

Table 17.3
Case Presentation
Review cases after complete data base available.
Prepare written summary and tentative recommendations.
List primary questions for team discussion.
Enforce time limits for concise oral presentations.
Develop an orderly pattern to present case information.
Use visual aids: videotapes, photos, family tree.

Decision-making

ROLE OF THE MODERATOR

The role of moderator can be taken by the same person or alternate among members. Because the moderator must attend to the process of the meeting, it is helpful if he or she is not directly involved in evaluation or has only a minor portion of case information to present. The moderator has four tasks: focus, direct, pace, and wrap-up. The moderator uses the agenda and primary questions to *focus* and prioritize team discussion. He begins the meeting by reviewing the overall agenda and introducing each case. If necessary, the primary questions can be revised during presentation of case material. The moderator then tries to assure that each question is answered by the end of the review. He must be alert to irrelevant items and table these quickly or both the effectiveness and efficiency of the team meeting will be lost.

The moderator *directs* the meeting. He maintains an atmosphere of open expression to allow all opinions to be heard. Humor may be of great help. He must try to prevent attacks and defensiveness, yet foster the expression of differences in perspective that are so crucial in a multidisciplinary approach. When possible, the moderator should have other members present case information, and openly acknowledge personal opinions and biases. It is essential to ensure that members voice their views, questions, and recommendations. The moderator may need to interrupt and tactfully silence a dominating member or call on less forceful people. Failure to do this seriously undermines the team's work.[9]

Pacing the meeting is crucial. It must start and end on time, with time allotted to balance a variety of tasks. Teams that spend too much time on case presentation are then hard-pressed to end during decision-making. Conversely, inadequate case presentation can result in premature decision-making, increasing the frustration and futility the team may experience.[10] A written summary listing primary questions and concise oral reports greatly aids successful pacing. The moderator must continually keep a close eye on the clock while monitoring the consensus for tentative recommendations.

To *wrap-up*, the moderator summarizes the assessments and recommendations for the case. This assures understanding among members, and makes clear who will do what and when. The moderator checks that primary questions have been adequately addressed and spells out follow-up plans, subsequent team review, and the name of the case coordinator. However, summarizing should not be done too soon, so that it cuts off the discussion and suggestions prematurely. The timing of this task is all important, as the wrap-up, by highlighting the good work they have done, can significantly diminish the frustration or down mood a team feels during difficult decisions.

RECORDING TEAM DISCUSSION

Discussion and recommendations should be recorded by someone who is not a primary presenter of case material. This record should consist of the content and process of the meeting. Additions and revisions can be recorded on the written case summary or another form. If a secretary is not available, this task can rotate among members. The recorder must be careful to list the recommendations in detail, as often these become the baseline to measure case progress in treatment or in court.

CONSENSUS

Most case management teams try to arrive at their decisions by consensus. This means that every member has an opportunity to influence the final decision and determine what is best for all.[11] When no consensus is possible, the team may be able to agree on some short term recommendations, with another team review soon. This allows for more assessment, and a trial at intervention, and will increase the information base for decision-making. When further assessment, such as a psychiatric evaluation is recommended, the specific concerns and questions should be listed to help avoid unnecessary referral.

It may be necessary to look at differences that prohibit consensus, including issues beyond specific cases. Sometimes differing professional beliefs, agency turf battles, or identifying with particular family members give team members such a strong bias that consensus is difficult. The group may need to look for issues underlying a conflict that are not the direct result of the case at hand. Private differences of opinion are an asset of the multidisciplinary approach that can yield more effective decision-making. Public arguments, however, outside the team meeting, may seriously disrupt intervention for the family, and be confusing to all.[12] A team which can constructively work through conflict is strengthened and experiences success for the group.[13] The ideal for the team is to arrive at a consensus through successful use of conflict and scrutiny of alternatives.

When the team is faced with no good choices, they may find it necessary to consider the least detrimental plan for ensuring the safety and welfare of the children. Here, a team review in a few weeks or months may be beneficial by providing information after a trial of the treatment approach. These seem to be the cases where extended team review is especially necessary to share the decision-making and risk-taking.

Teams must be certain to plan for implementation of their recommendations, carefully outlining who will share in the specific tasks for intervention. It can become too easy for members to agree on a plan and then think that only the decision-making is their job; doing it is someone else's.[14] Table 17.4 provides a summary of the components of decision-making.

Table 17.4

Decision-making

The moderator must focus, direct, pace, and wrap-up.

Carefully record findings and recommendations.

Seek a consensus through the constructive use of conflict and review of alternatives.

Consider the least detrimental plan for the children.

When no consensus is possible, obtain further assessment or a trial at treatment.

Summary

Attention to the development of a structure for conducting team meetings cannot be overemphasized. The guidelines suggested are intended to help groups maintain focus on the primary task of multidisciplinary decision-making about case management. Productive team meetings not only affect the intervention necessary for a child and family but may subsequently contribute to the professional satisfaction and continuity of the team itself.

References

1. Schmitt, B.D., and C.A. Grosz. "Ground Rules for Effective Team Conferences." *The Child Protection Team Handbook.* B.D. Schmitt (Ed.), pp. 169-174. New York: Garland STPM Press, 1978.

2. Motz, J. *Colorado's Community-Based Child Protection Teams,* p. 6. Denver: Department of Social Services, 1984.

3. Holland, G. *Running a Business Meeting,* p. 14. New York: Dell Publishing Co., 1984.

4. Newman, P.J., and A.F. Lynch. *Behind Closed Doors: A Guide to Successful Meetings,* p. 19. Englewood Cliffs, N.J.: Prentice-Hall, 1983.

5. Doyle, M., and D. Straus. *How to Make Meetings Work,* p. 108. New York: Jove Publications, 1976.

6. Doyle, M., and D. Straus. *How to Make Meetings Work,* pp. 91-94. New York: Jove, 1976.

7. Doyle, M., and D. Straus. *How to Make Meetings Work,* p. 122. New York: Jove, 1976.

8. Newman, P.J., and A.F. Lynch. *Behind Closed Doors,* p. 47. Englewood Cliffs, N.J.: Prentice-Hall, 1983.

9. Doyle, M., and D. Straus. *How to Make Meetings Work,* p. 107. New York: Jove, 1976.

10. Bradford, L.P. *Making Meetings Work,* p. 35. La Jolla, Calif.: University Association, 1976.

11.   Bradford, L.P. *Making Meetings Work*, p. 45. La Jolla, Calif.: University Association, 1976.

12.   Bourne, R., and E.H. Newberger. "Interdisciplinary Group Process in the Hospital Management of Child Abuse and Neglect." *Child Abuse and Neglect*, 4(12)(1980):137-144.

13.   Bradford, L.P. *Making Meetings Work*, p. 12. La Jolla, Calif.: University Association, 1976.

14.   Bradford, L.P. *Making Meetings Work*, p. 17. La Jolla, Calif.: University Association, 1976.

18. Group Process and Interprofessional Communication: The Human Aspects of Teamwork

Mark Perlman and J.M. Whitworth

Introduction and Rationale

For many years it has been recognized that child abuse and neglect is a multidisciplinary problem involving medical, psychological, legal, social work, law enforcement, and other disciplines. It follows that since all of the above disciplines are often involved in a given child abuse case, it is unreasonable to assume that any one person or professional can provide the total observations, assessment, and planning that such a case may demand. Thus, to choose professionals of high quality from each of the aforementioned disciplines would be the logical approach to comprehensive, thorough, and high-quality casework planning. It is within this conceptual framework that the popularity of multidisciplinary child abuse teams has grown in recent years throughout the country. Those of us who have been fortunate enough to create and/or participate in such multidisciplinary teams, are more convinced than ever of the validity of this approach.

By definition, a "group" is two or more people who interact through a common focus or interest. It is different than an "aggregate" which may involve two or more people, but without the purposefulness, or mutual interest that a group shares. Thus, the members of a group have a shared reason for being together, and this reason serves to define the nature and purpose of the group. A "therapy group" joins together for the mental health and growth needs of the participants; a "training or supervision group" joins together for the professional growth and learning experience of its members. A child protection team may be referred to as a "task-oriented group" with a specific goal to accomplish. The goal often involves information gathering and sharing, creative discussion, case-planning, and interagency cooperation for successful service delivery. The goal of the task-oriented child protection team is to bring together the vast amount of diverse professional information and knowledge through a harmonious, comprehensive process that will directly benefit the client by providing case assessment and planning that reflect the full utilization and integration of the multidisciplinary team approach. It is through the awareness of group dynamics and successful application of group process techniques that this goal can be realized. Group process theory gives a framework for understanding both positive and negative aspects of the team approach.[1]

Defining Group Process

Defining group process is not an easy task. Although it affects the experience of being part of a group or team, as well as the group's work product or case outcome, it is not often consciously noticed or constructively utilized. It may be useful to approach a definition of group process by first making clear what is not.

It is important to clarify that content does not equal process. Team staffings involve a great deal of important content or data upon which all members are focused. Examples of this content material are: type and severity of abuse or neglect, the child's physical and behavioral indicators, conditions of siblings in the home, environmental conditions in the home, data on the mother and father and their marital relationship, resources and strengths within the family, safety of the home, law enforcement and legal considerations, as well as other pertinent information. This content material is highly relevant and should occupy a central focus in team staffings, but should never be confused with process.

What is this "mystical" group process that has to be superimposed on the content material and is so relevant to how the team staffing and case may turn out? If content is the "what" of team staffings, group process is the "how." For example, how is the content information communicated and has it been heard by all members of the group? How are the various team members feeling about being at the staffing and their roles? Do they feel encouraged and free to participate and share their knowledge and information, or are they shy and intimidated? Is there an atmosphere of competition where one professional is trying to prove another wrong, or is there an attitude of cooperation and respect in which all people feel validated and encouraged to participate? Group process involves the interaction between people. Therefore, it is referred to as the "human aspects of teamwork." Group process is to the team what fuel and a tune-up is to the automobile. It enables high-quality and finely honed parts to work together as a smoothly functioning whole.

The group process is governed by certain predictable laws that are influenced by the use of certain skills. We can utilize this knowledge and these skills to create more functional and harmonious group process. We have all asked ourselves the following questions from time to time, and these questions point to the need and relevance of consciously utilized group process techniques for successful group or team work:

> Why do team staffings sometimes work so well, and why at other times do they work so poorly?
> Why is it difficult for professionals from different disciplines to understand each other and reach agreement?
> Why do some group members seem to dominate and take up so much time at group meetings, while others are so quiet and rarely have input at all?
> What can I, as group facilitator, do to make these staffings more efficient and effective?

The answers to these and similar questions and the corrective possibilities point to the relevance of interprofessional communication and group process skills.

The Relationship Between "Process" and "Content"

People join together in "task-oriented" groups because, as the old saying goes, "two heads are better than one." We hope to get improved task performance from the team compared to a single person performing the same task. Specifically, the team creates a broader information base upon which to make assessments, a more thorough decision-making process, a broader range of creativity or case-planning, and a service plan that is truly multidisciplinary and multi-agency in nature. In complex and sensitive cases of child abuse and neglect, it is in these ways that a team approach leads to higher task performance than an individual approach. As stated before, it is the major goal of a child protection team to be a "task-oriented group."

There are other reasons why professionals join and become part of the multidisciplinary team. These reasons may be considered secondary gains, and are often stated as follows:

-Increased professional contact and support.
-New learning and ongoing training from contact with other team members at team staffings.
-A shared caring for the client and quality of service.
-Increased interagency cooperation and communication.

No one questions the value of these primary and secondary goals, but it is important to acknowledge that these goals are not automatically achieved by convening a child protection team. This is where a fundamental law of group process must be restated clearly and simply--process affects content. Whether any or all of the goals can be achieved depends upon the nature of the group process at work in the specific group. When group process is "functional," the elements of communication, influence, decision-making, and cooperation are all working in such a way as to achieve the primary and secondary goals. At this point, it is critical to acknowledge that when the group process is "dysfunctional" in any one or all of these areas, not only may the goals not be reached, but they may be sabotaged with negative results. Dysfunctional group process can result in prejudicial or extreme case decisions, negative feelings on the part of group members, and greater separation and discord between agencies involved. Each of these major group process elements shall be discussed more fully in this chapter.

As we proceed to look at group processes and dynamics, it is important to think of the group as an organism that grows and changes with time. It is not created in static and unchanging form. With appropriate understanding and use of group process, we can influence the growth of our teams in a desirable direction. For maximum team effectiveness, it is necessary to view the team and its functioning as a fluid, open process that encourages growth and change.[2]

We suggest a proactive approach in utilizing this knowledge and these skills, namely, to begin utilizing what we know at the earliest possible stages of team selections and team development, and to continue by employing group process training and techniques as the team matures and develops. This positive approach to creating and maintaining "functional" team dynamics prevents the erosion of team spirit and function.

A group that has just been formed typically has the following characteristics:[3]

1. Each member has some assets and liabilities relative to the the group's purpose. These include control over resources, individual talents and hangups, information and ignorance.
2. Some members are not aware of the group's objectives, or these objectives may have yet to be established.
3. Some members are antagonistic toward the group's objectives.
4. Some members are not aware that certain of their assets are relevant to the group's objectives.
5. Most members are not aware of all of their liabilities. Those who recognize that they have some deficiencies in resources, personality, or information are probably defensive about them.
6. Some members tend to guard their assets jealously—particularly information.
7. Most members are unaware of the assets and liabilities of each of the other members.
8. Some members will be attracted to or already friendly with other members and will form cliques within the group.
9. One or more members will be left out of these cliques.
10. Most or all members are uncertain about the operating structure of the group, procedures that will follow, and where the real power lies.
11. Some of the members are not wholly in agreement with the leadership of the group, whether the leader is elected or appointed.
12. More than one member would like to influence the group's activities.
13. Most members are uncertain about the kinds of relationships they will develop with other members.
14. At least one member is apathetic or indifferent.

In contrast, consider the characteristics of a mature group that can be both effective and efficient:

1. Members are aware of their own and each other's assets and liabilities vis-à-vis the group's task.
2. These individual differences are accepted without being labeled as good or bad.
3. The group has developed authority and interpersonal relationships that are recognized and accepted by the members.
4. Group decisions are made through rational discussion. Minority opinions and/or dissension are recognized and

encouraged. Attempts are not made to force decisions or a false unanimity.
5.   Conflict is over substantive group issues such as group goals and the effectiveness and efficiency of various means for achieving those goals. Conflict over emotional issues regarding group structure, process or interpersonal relationships is at a minimum.
6.   Members are aware of the group's processes and their own roles in them.

This overview of the maturation process of a group's development offers useful guidelines in defining where we begin and where we would like to evolve over time. Because of space limitations, we will not be able to provide a total blueprint for facilitating group development and maturity.   The nature of good process skills necessitates direct, experientially based training for the desirable learning to take place. Within these realistic limitations, we will provide some tools and guidelines that are useful in guiding the group process toward functional maturity.

Interdisciplinary Communication

In general, communication facilitates most kinds of group outcome. Other things being equal, improvements in the quality and frequency of intragroup communications should be reflected in improvements in external outcomes such as productivity and group decisions and in internal outcomes such as cohesiveness, satisfaction, and influence.[4]

As that statement indicates, communication may be the single most important factor influencing the group process. The key function of communication is to transmit information. In a task-oriented group such as a child protection team, the successful transmission of information within the group is central to the accomplishment of the task at hand. The communication process can be broken down into three distinct parts:

a. Sending information (speaking)
b. Receiving information (listening)
c. Feedback

We will address each of these three "communication skills" in the context of a team staffing.

SENDING (SPEAKING)

This is the major method for transmitting data, facts, and information regarding a child abuse case. Since many professionals attending the staffing have relevant information to present, it is necessary to monitor the time of each presentation. We have found that two to three minutes is a sufficient amount of time for most presentations; a maximum of five minutes may be allowed. It is the responsibility of the person presenting the information, as well as the group facilitator who is monitoring the group process, to monitor the time of presentation. Adequate preparation is another important factor in the clear, thorough, and succinct presentation of information to the group. Reading directly from a report is a somewhat bland approach, although certain people who are intimidated or "frozen" within group settings may have to rely on this means in order to convey information. It is helpful to prepare an outline of the presentation. By this method one can control the order and flow of information while maintaining eye contact with the group. Attention to the data and to the group is important for successful communication. It is also important to be aware that feelings or emotions may be communicated. If one has strong feelings about the case or data being presented, it is very useful to communicate such feelings to the group. The direct approach often works best, e.g., "I have strong feelings in the case for these reasons." If one determines that this emotional component is better left out of the communication, it takes special preparation beforehand to become clear about one's emotions and to conscientiously omit them from the presentation. This is sometimes more easily said than done. In a later part of this chapter, closely related issues such as influence and power as part of group process will be discussed.

At this point, it is useful to mention non-verbal communication as part of the transmission process that can be utilized to one's advantage. Awareness of body position and body language in relationship to the group, tone of voice, eye contact, and perception of the listener are all relevant to successful transmission of information.

RECEIVING (LISTENING)

Listening is a communication skill that completes the other half of the transmission of information process. Effective listening is an active rather than a passive process. It is one in which we actively open our eyes, ears, and minds to the person who is sending the information so that we become open and receptive. Active attention and eye contact to the speaker not only assure us of receiving the full range of a communication, but it also signals respect and interest to the speaker. One cannot be formulating his own ideas or responses while listening actively to another.

FEEDBACK

This is the third communication skill that is most often ignored in analyzing the communication process. Feedback is an active completion of the communication loop between sender and receiver. It can be initiated by the sender with such questions as "Have I made myself clear?" or "Is there any part of what I've said that you would like me to repeat or amplify?" The listener can also initiate important feedback with such questions as "Could you put Section C in simpler terminology?" or "Thank you for the thorough and relevant information." This feedback between sender and listener ensures the success of the communication but it also provides validation both to the sender and the receiver, thereby encouraging communication as a positive group process function.

Maximizing opportunity for communication in the group setting by increasing the communication flow facilitates successful task completion, decisions by the group, positive feelings and learning in a child protection team staffing. Practicing successful communication is the responsibility of each team member with special help from the group facilitator.

Attention to the physical setting in the room can aid the communication process. Simple comforts such as the room temperature, lighting, and comfort of the chairs in which the team members sit can all affect communication and the group process. A seating arrangement with a round or oblong conference table so that the group members can see one another and write or take notes as needed, is desirable. Attention to such detail can affect the psychosocial atmosphere within a group and lead to a more positive group process.

Practicing communication skills leads to cohesiveness in a group and facilitates a spirit of mutual respect and cooperation. These elements are conducive to productivity and positive feelings among group members. Since a group is an organic whole, attention to or change in any one element tends to affect many other elements in the group process. Attention to improving communication skills will have a positive effect on communication.

When considering members for a multidisciplinary child protection team, we naturally think of professional expertise and knowledge as the dominant factor in making such a choice. In considering these "human aspects of teamwork," it is advisable to consider certain personal characteristics or styles along with the professional credentials of the team members, for it is these personal characteristics that will impact upon group process.

Being an expert in one's field in no way assures successful communication of the knowledge that person possesses, or a harmonious and positive impact on the group as a whole. Examples of this phenomenon are common. In general, people who are aggressive, critical, highly competitive, dogmatic and narrow, pedantic, domineering, and control-oriented will usually make dysfunctional group members. Group members with these characteristics tend to waste great amounts of time and energy, set up distractions and discord within the group, adversely affect the morale of other members, and negatively affect productivity. A proactive approach through careful initial screening and selection of group members can save great difficulty and stress. Experts who have been group members in other settings and have functioned well in those settings are likely to be assets to a team. Characteristics such as reliability, cooperativeness, trust, supportiveness, the ability to listen, a clear and direct style of communication, humor, and the kind of caring attitude that keeps the needs of the child and family as the highest priority (as opposed to personal power or influence) indicate team members with potential for excellence.

Since a child protection team is a multidisciplinary group by nature, certain elements are indigenous to this group. Such a group can suffer from a language barrier in that professional jargon and terminology can get in the way of successful interpersonal communication. Once group members are made aware of this factor, they can be encouraged to simplify their language to facilitate communication. This is a legitimate feedback technique that promotes interdisciplinary learning. This process is an exciting part of the continuing interdisciplinary training and cross-fertilization that constantly take place in successful team settings. A team member who cannot cross this "language barrier" may be too narrow in his or her disciplinary orientation or may be using the professional language in the service of influence, power or insecurity.

Another potential problem in the multidisciplinary setting is related to professional degrees and the status they represent. People who perceive each other as similar in status usually have a shared respect and experience, and therefore, ease of communication. By virtue of differences in degrees, education, credentials, and professional experience, group members may perceive each other in terms of "higher" or "lower" status, and this may hinder communication. Choosing group members who reflect the aforementioned positive personal characteristics, along with preparation and training in team-building exercises, can narrow the gap and facilitate successful communication among all team members. The team members' and group facilitator's efforts toward a cohesive and respectful atmosphere in the group will also help in this area. It is useful to view each team member as wearing two hats. One hat represents their discipline and professional expertise, for which they should be listened to and respected accordingly. The second hat represents the human characteristics that bind the people in the group as a whole, including: caring for the children and families; dedication to quality, service, and responsible decisions; and the knowledge that we can do so much more in working and cooperating with each other than anyone can do alone. The recognition of this second hat assists in overcoming the status differences that professional degrees sometimes tend to bring out, and facilitates interprofessional communication.

Although this section on communication skills and interdisciplinary communication is focused on the team staffing setting, all of the elements discussed here can be applied to any group or interagency activity or meeting. Attention to these basic elements can assist in interagency coordination and positive community relationships. They serve to build linkages that enable us to perform our interdependent tasks more successfully and with more personally rewarding relationships.

Group Process and Dynamics

TRAINING: A MODEL FOR LEARNING GROUP PROCESS SKILLS

The methodology of choice for learning group process and communication skills is experientially based training (learning by doing). This is an educational model that sees learning as an active process of engagement. It goes beyond classroom-styled learning that relies on reading or lecturing as the major teaching tool. The process of experientially based learning can be summarized as follows:

a. The trainer presents the group with simple and direct instruction.
b. The group interacts on the instruction, getting involved in doing, practicing or experiencing.
c. The participants then engage in a period of discussion and analysis of what they have just experienced based on the interaction. The guidance of the trainer during this section is extremely important to help the participants express their experience clearly and appropriately.

d. The trainer guides the participants to formulate insights, conclusions, and new learning based on their analysis and experience.

e. The trainer will then summarize the learning, give "feedback" to the specific participants and highlight applications for this new learning.

The need for a professional trainer is essential to the success of experientially based learning. Such a person with group process and training skills can create a relaxed and open learning environment, help guide the group through meaningful structured experience, and in doing so, facilitate new learning and skill building. Again, the proactive approach of working with the team in a training format, prior to ever staffing a case, is highly desirable. This pre-service training will help team members get acquainted and comfortable with one another; begin the team-building process toward a cooperative and cohesive group; highlight and practice communication skills; and begin working with group process so that the desirable roles, goals, and norms can be established from the outset.

PROCESS OBSERVATION SKILLS

Process observation and intervention skills are an essential role and responsibility of the group facilitator. Groups tend to function best when these skills are also learned by group members, and responsibility for maintaining functional group process is shared.

The following list of questions help to direct attention and focus awareness on certain group processes that enable us to see group interactions in a new light.

1. In what kind of psychological "atmosphere" did the group work?

2. Was it democratic in that it encouraged everyone to participate spontaneously and freely, or was it autocratic in that a single person or small group of people took control of the decision-making process?

3. Was sympathetic consideration given to all contributors? If not, why?

4. Was there any evidence of the exertion of social pressure against any member of the group?

5. Did all of the members of the group have an equal opportunity to participate?

6. Did the group make the best use of its resources?

7. At what points did interpersonal tension exist? Why? What brought it about? Was it released? If so, why or why not?
8. Were some members frustrated at any point in the process?
9. Did leadership of the group rest with one individual, or was it shared among the group members?
10. Were any members of particularly high influence, or particularly low influence?
11. Was there rivalry or competitiveness in the group?
12. Were members of the group satisfied with their decision? Satisfied with their leadership? Satisfied with their own contributions to the group?

These are just a few examples of process observation questions. Practicing such observation in a group setting sharpens our awareness. Such observation can be used to give feedback to specific group members or to the group as a whole, with the goal of encouraging positive and productive interactions.

Two cautions about such feedback:

1. These observations should be behaviorally descriptive and specific and are not meant to be judgmental.
2. A skilled trainer or group leader is often necessary to insure that such feedback is clear, constructive, and supportive.

ROLES IN A GROUP

Roles in a group refer to certain styles of being/acting that a group member may perform, or certain expectations placed on group members by the group as a whole. In the multidisciplinary team setting, the discipline that one represents most likely brings with it certain role identifications and expectations such as "medical expert," "legal expert," and "psychological expert." These are necessary and appropriate roles, but if they are our only roles to the exclusion of all others, they may become self-limiting and narrow.

Group process roles, unlike the leadership and professional roles discussed above, can be practiced by all group members at one time or another. These roles may be divided into two general categories—task roles and maintenance roles.

Task-roles can be defined as functions required in the selecting and carrying-out of the group's task. Examples of these roles are: initiating activity, proposing solutions or suggesting new ideas, seeking information, asking for clarification, seeking opinion, giving information, giving opinion, elaborating, coordinating or summarizing.

The second general category of roles is maintenance roles. These serve to strengthen and maintain group vitality and activities. Examples of maintenance roles are: encouraging (being friendly, warm, responsive to others); gate-keeping (trying to activate participation of silent group members); standard setting (expressing or reminding the group of standards regarding content, procedures, or evaluation of decisions); expressing group feeling (summarizing the emotional tone of the group); relieving tension (use of humor or other mechanisms for relieving tension in the group context); mediating (harmonizing differences or suggesting conciliatory alternatives).

These task and maintenance roles are all functional in groups, and they serve as behavioral reference points for group members to practice and/or observe.

GROUP NORMS

Group norms (sometimes referred to as rules) are standards for behavior. These rules of process and procedure are agreed to by the group either overtly or implicitly. We believe that the overt recognition of these norms by the group is the most functional and gives all group members objective standards for reference. Norms should be openly and democratically discussed and agreed upon, and reflect the group's purpose and membership. Some examples might be: treating other group members with respect, beginning staffings no later than five minutes after an agreed upon time and ending staffings no later than five minutes after an agreed upon time, two to three minutes for each presenter, and practicing good communication skills. Specific norms are derived from the group and reflect its uniqueness.

THE GROUP FACILITATOR OR GROUP LEADER

The role of group facilitator is important and necessary for successful group interaction and teamwork. This role is best performed by a person who has training and experience in group process and dynamics, and group leadership skills. It is a role that can be learned with appropriate training and experience, and one that grows and improves with practice. The role of group facilitator is so central to successful group functioning that we feel it should not be mixed or diluted with other roles. Therefore, it is preferable that the group facilitator not be one of the professional/disciplinary experts such as those in the medical or legal field.

Likewise, the person serving as group facilitator should not be the case coordinator or social worker with the responsibility for presenting and recording the case information at the staffing. Blending of these roles tends to be dysfunctional, not only because it fragments the attention of this person, but also because role conflict and power confusion may arise. The group facilitator is the expert in group process, and it is toward this function that his or her leadership, influence, perceptiveness, and intervention must be directed. An effective, efficient, highly participatory and democratic group process should result. Combining the roles of group facilitator and disciplinary expert runs the risk of confusing leadership with one specific discipline, thereby creating a power issue in which that disciplinary expert may exert undue authority, leading to autocratic decision-making.

Whatever the unique style of the facilitator, he or she should serve as a model of a functional group member, practicing good communication skills, utilizing the functional roles in a group, reflecting the norms of a group, and practicing those behaviors that lead to positive and productive group interaction. This modeling, along with skilled process intervention, is where the group leader's strengths and influence lie. Therefore, the leader's status and function in the group is derived from his or her skills along with the acknowledgement and respect of the other group members.

Successful group performance is both a function of individual group member participation and leadership by the group facilitator that results in successful task completion. Although the focus and responsibility of the facilitator is on group process as opposed to content (case details), successful outcomes such as case-plans, agency cooperation, and so on are very much a function of good process-oriented leadership. Such process-oriented leadership should involve: helping the group with successful communication, providing clear instructions and task overview, seeking information, stimulating participation and action, handling crises such as hostility, competition and pressure, watching time, summarizing, testing for group consensus, and leaving the group with a positive feeling or perspective at the end of the staffing. This partial list of group leader roles and responsibilities indicates why this role in a group must be maintained as specialized and separate from other roles.

CONSENSUS DECISION-MAKING

Consensus decision-making refers to a process through which a group arrives at a decision based on maximum participation and input from all group members. This high level of group participation and respect and fairness devoted to each group member can be called democratic, but it is not a process that involves voting or averaging. Instead, it is a decision-making process in which "members of the group reach substantial agreement, rather than unanimity."[5]

Basic group problem solving can be outlined in the following steps:

a. Definition of the problem
b. Gathering of information
c. Combing and recombing information into new patterns (discussion, brainstorming, etc.)
d. Decision as to the best solution/plan
e. Verification, reality testing, barrier identification

These basic decision-making steps reflect a sound group process recommended for task-oriented groups such as child protection teams. To ensure this process in consensus decision-making, the following guidelines should be respected: maximum participation of all group members so that a complete airing of facts and data can occur; maximum time allowed for complete discussion; exploration of alternatives; and allowance for creative solutions to the problems at hand. Substantial agreement is reached by relying on facts, logic, and the influence that these bring to bear on the problem. The weight of the evidence and viability of the decision must be strong enough so that the opposition will not stand in the way of implementing the decision.

This process takes more time, attention, and energy than other decision-making processes such as voting or averaging, but the benefits of the investment on the group are evident in the results. Decisions are more reliable built upon a complete data base and high level of participation, and the resultant feelings in the group are more positive. In this process, conflict is seen as a creative statement of difference, and it is helpful to the process of seeking consensus. All group members feel that the problem received a full airing, that each group member had the opportunity to be heard, and there is no sense of defeat or loss. The consensus decision-making process maximizes the use of the group's resources through encouraging full participation of its members and proves with functional group process that the whole can truly be greater than the sum of its parts.

INFLUENCE, POWER, AND CONFLICT

Part of the group decision-making and the "sending" function of communication is the intent to influence others. Influence can be exerted by the strength of one's professional knowledge and expertise, along with clear presentation, careful planning, and thoroughness. When facts shade into opinions or judgments, it is important to identify them as such. This maintains an honesty and clarity in communication. Not to separate facts from opinions is to exert covert influence or manipulation. This leads to dysfunctional group interaction. If influence or power is exerted in an indirect or manipulative fashion, other group members will eventually react. They may retreat into passivity or defeat, or they may react by fighting back. The latter type of interaction is dysfunctional because it results in a power-conflict or power-struggle. This should not be confused with a disagreement of fact which is perfectly functional in a group and can be useful to decision-making. A power-conflict takes the focus of the group away from substantive issues (the data, treatment plan) and shifts to a purely interpersonal arena. Someone is "pushing," someone feels "pushed," and reacts. A battle of egos is being waged in which someone stands to win and someone stands to lose. In reality, it is often the client being discussed and the group process that lose.

What to do? Drawing attention directly to the fact that a power struggle has occurred and suggesting refocusing on the data at hand can work, but it is a high-risk intervention. Both parties may feel hurt or defensive, resulting in a "lose-lose" outcome which is undesirable. Another possible intervention which may bring better results would be for the group facilitator to say something like, "Psychologist A and Psychologist B have different positions on this issue. Let me try to state each position clearly so that the group can benefit from both of these positions in trying to reach the best possible solution." The facilitator may even stand up and summarize on a blackboard; the act of standing up changes the focus from the combatants to the facilitator. With a little luck, the focus is shifted back to the case, and Psychologists A and B both feel legitimized and heard. This is "win-win" (or no lose) intervention which is desirable whenever it can be accomplished. Therefore, another critical role of the group facilitator must be to remain aware of such power issues, especially when high-powered professionals from different disciplines are working (or trying to work) together.

Power struggles are bound to arise but with proper attention to group process, they can be constructively managed. As the group matures, there should be fewer of these conflicts. If a particular group member is chronically and habitually communicating in a manipulative, authoritarian, or other power-oriented way that disrupts the group, it may be necessary for that issue to be discussed privately with the group member. If not dealt with, such a dynamic can seriously harm the group's ability to function both in terms of group feeling or experience and in terms of the quality of a work product. Left unresolved, this problem can lead to unpleasant time-wasting discord, or to the group giving its power over to a single authority, in which case, the group decision-making process will have been abandoned. If the group member in question cannot or will not alter this disruptive form of communication, he or she may have to be replaced by another authority who can share knowledge in such a way that the team (and the clients) can benefit.

One more word on power, as it relates to child abuse and group process. "Seek the power that is in everyone and over no one." (Gandhi) It is vitally important to keep this in mind in professional and personal dealing with each other, whether it be at team staffings, group meetings, or one-to-one contact. This is particularly important in the context of work with child abuse. Both physical and sexual abuse involve abuses of power—an adult using physical and emotional power over and against a child. This orientation to power is "power over." If we relate to each other in overbearing or manipulative ways, we are, in more benign form, utilizing the same "power over" orientation. We either create submission in others or we create antagonisms and power struggles. The use of power in this way in the team setting results in an environment of fear and intimidation. The alternative style of power discussed in this section leads to more fulfilling interpersonal and group contact and has a unifying rather than a divisive function. It is more consistent with caring for the child and families who suffer from abuse, and it grows from professional knowledge, honesty, and integrity; not from a context of personal gain or loss. The result is a supportive, encouraging environment in which the full power of the group can be utilized.

Barriers and Difficulties

In this section, some barriers or difficulties that may be encountered when attempting to implement group process awareness and skill building in a team setting will be outlined. These barriers, in generic form, emanate from the very nature of group process activity, teamwork, and interpersonal communication. These barriers are, in a sense, proof of the importance of the group process, in that they point to the "human aspects of teamwork" elucidated in this chapter. As we shall see, these barriers are: resistance, denial, avoidance, fear and threat felt by group members. Those persons who are most resistant to discussing and learning from the group process may very well be those team members who need it most. With patience and perseverance, along with a strong group facilitator and consistent feedback from the group itself, these barriers can often be eliminated.

SUSPICION OF GROUP PROCESS ITSELF

Group process may be new to many team members and, initially, may be viewed with suspicion. It may be seen as something amorphous, mystical, and intangible. Team members who work within the disciplines of the physical sciences may have difficulty in this area and question its relevance. "Nothing but the facts" and "let's go back to what really matters" are reactions that might be expected from members who are unfamiliar with process-oriented information. However, the group process offers an excellent opportunity for new learning, interdisciplinary cross-fertilization, and personal and professional growth.

THE THREAT OF SELF-AWARENESS

Group process focuses on qualities within team members that affect their ability to function in a group setting, and on interpersonal dynamics that affect both productivity and relationships within the group. This area of discussion and analysis is threatening to some. It is one thing to look at the problems of "others" (the clients whose cases we are staffing); it is another matter altogether to look at our own strengths and weaknesses with openness, honesty and integrity.

HOW EQUAL ARE WE, REALLY?

We have discussed issues of status in the group, and the desirability of a democratic and consensus decision-making process. This may be more easily said than done. Some professionals may be more accustomed to hierarchical and power-status oriented professional relationships, such as found in hospital and courtroom settings. Although the group will respect and call upon individuals for their professional knowledge and expertise, they will not have unilateral or autocratic decision-making authority. Preparation, training, and team building exercises offer an opportunity to practice new ways of relating. It takes a special person, one who is comfortable with power and authority, to relinquish some status and role-orientation for the sake of teamwork and a truly multidisciplinary decision-making process.

DEALING WITH FEELINGS

Working in groups and learning group process skills involves dealing with feelings, along with content and data. This may bring reactions ranging from shyness to reluctance or avoidance and refusal, depending upon one's discomfort level with this area. Feelings are part and parcel of interprofessional and group communication, and can be constructively utilized only if dealt with consciously.

BRINGING DYNAMICS TO LIGHT

An active awareness and utilization of group process brings to light dynamics and interpersonal realities that might normally remain hidden or avoided. Feedback provides team members with specific information that can lead to self-awareness and change in such areas as power, conflict, anger, competitiveness, and dominance. This is vitally important to a healthy and functional group process. If constructively rendered, it is an excellent opportunity for personal growth. Resolution depends on the skill of the group facilitator and participants willing to face the threat of discovery.

Benefits

In this section, we will summarize in outline form some of the benefits that may be derived from the application of group process knowledge to the team setting.

IGNORANCE IS NOT NECESSARILY BLISS

Much of what has been discussed in this chapter will be manifested in any team or group. Knowledge and conscious application of group process skills is a critically important factor in reaching team goals.

PROBLEM-SOLVING CAPABILITY

A delineated decision-making, problem-solving strategy, accompanied by practice in application, leads to improved problem solving capability by the group.

WORK PRODUCTS

Reports, assessments, treatment plans, and direct services to clients tend to be of higher quality because they are the product of increased data and information, the synergy and creativity of interprofessional communication, and the result of cooperative efforts.

POSITIVE FEELINGS

Group members feel a higher level of satisfaction, commitment, excitement, and pride from positive group encounters. There is also a sense of shared responsibility, and again, the personal benefits from cooperation.

FEWER UNRESOLVED ISSUES

Barriers, difficulties, and unresolved feelings can be openly discussed and resolved by attending to group process. Without it they can drain life from the group and sabotage productivity.

PARTICIPATION AND OWNERSHIP

Successful use of group process leads to maximum levels of input and participation. This leads to feelings of more ownership in the work product, better implementation and follow-through, and increased commitment.

POSITIVE OVERFLOW

Successful team experiences lead to positive effects outside the team setting.

PROTECTION AGAINST "BURNOUT"

The shared responsibility, support, positive input, congeniality and networking that come from teamwork serve as excellent protection against "burnout."

HUMOR AND FUN

Humor and fun should be perceived as a benefit. Humor is healing, especially when a group must deal with painful and difficult content week-in and week-out. Shared humor, never at the expense of a group member or client, is an uplifting and important aspect of teamwork. We are never embarrassed by the team that takes a moment to see the lighter side; we are more concerned by the team that never does.

It should be a goal of the team to take some time out for fun together on a regular basis. Inviting local Child Protection Services workers and perhaps other closely related agency staff to a social get-together is an excellent idea. An overall beneficial effect on group process comes from relaxed fun, recreation, and meeting one another outside professional roles.

Summary

Proper attention to the group process and dynamics and the elements of interprofessional communication has wide-reaching benefit to the individuals, the agency, and the community. Functional group dynamics lead to positive feelings, along with personal and professional growth that benefit both the individual and the agency. People practice and model qualities such as caring, respect, and good communication that have benefits among staff members, as well as between professional and client. The positive meeting ground for different community agencies at a team staffing or group meeting can develop interprofessional relationships and interagency networks that can lead to cooperation, creativity, and overall improved services. This recycles back into positive personal feelings. In this way, functional group process is like a "grow-light" that stimulates and regenerates personal, professional, and interagency growth.

Individual team members should be encouraged to complete the Group Process Self-Evaluation Sheet (Appendix 18.1) so they can assess their own participation in the group. This self-evaluation sheet can also be used to facilitate discussion and feedback. More extensive written materials, including a Group Facilitator Manual and Team Staffing Participants Manual, along with an accompanying videotape on the group process are available for teams wanting to focus training on this critical area of team functioning.[6]

References

1.   Bourne R., and E. Newberger. "Interdisciplinary Group Process in the Hospital Management of Child Abuse and Neglect." *Child Abuse & Neglect*, 4(1980):139.

2.   Schmitt, B.D, and C.A. Carroll. "The Human Aspects of Teamwork." *The Child Protection Team Handbook*. B.D. Schmitt (Ed.), p. 203. New York/London: Garland STPM Press, 1978.

3.   Jewell, L.N., and H.J. Reitz. *Group Effectiveness in Organizations*. Glenview, Ill.: Scott, Foresman, 1981.

4.   Jewell, L.N. *Group Effectiveness in Organizations*. Glenview, Ill.: Scott, Foresman, 1981. p. 147.

5.   Pfeiffer, W., and J.E. Jones. "Synergy and Consensus Seeking." *1973 Annual Handbook for Group Facilitators*. Pfeiffer and Jones (Eds.), pp. 108-110. San Diego, Calif: University Associates, Inc., 1973.

6.   Perlman, M., and V. DeCoslan (Instructional Designer). *Group Process and Teamwork for Multidisciplinary Teams*. Tallahassee, Fla.: State of Florida, Department of Health and Rehabilitative Services, 1986.

APPENDIX 18.1 *Group Process Self-Evaluation Sheet*

Scale: Poor   Fair   Avg.   Good   Excellent
         (1)   (2)   (3)   (4)   (5)

GROUP AS A WHOLE:

_____ Communication (listening and expressing)

_____ Staying on task (focused)

_____ Setting priorities (what needs attention first)

_____ Discovering new information through teamwork

_____ Openness to changing points of view

_____ Group feeling of mutual respect

_____ Use of appropriate humor

_____ Usefulness of group moderator/facilitator

YOU AS A GROUP MEMBER:

_____ Willing to express views/share information

_____ Willing to ask questions (explore/probe)

_____ Listen to others

_____ Willing to reconsider/change views

Do you normally leave the Team meetings feeling good—
a sense of accomplishment?

Are you sensitive to the group process—how are we
interacting with each other?

Of which of the above do you feel you could do more?
(Please circle for your own reference)

On what do you feel the group as a whole could improve?

Choose three words that best describe your feelings about
being part of this group.

Additional Comments:

Developed by: Mark Perlman, Training Consultant
Children's Medical Services/Child Protection Teams
State of Florida Department of Health and Rehabilitative
Services, Tallahassee, Florida

19. Guidelines for Team Decisions and Case Management

Barton D. Schmitt and Susan L. Scheurer

Introduction

The purpose of this chapter is to discuss the decision making process in team management of cases and to provide sample guidelines for making many of the difficult decisions.

Decision-making Process

Before decisions can be made information needs to be shared. Many professional specialists may evaluate the child's and family's needs and this represents a multidisciplinary approach. Once the child and his family have been assessed by all, the group gathers, shares findings and ideas, and formulates a plan. This then becomes the interdisciplinary process.[1] Sharing of information becomes the primary task and this implies a mutual trust between team members. The range of information and resources is expanded dramatically for the child and family. The sharing of information in a trusting environment and the processing of this information contribute to the team members' personal and professional growth and make decision-making easier.

Key Questions Addressed

Decisions in general are easier to make if the key decision questions are focused on repeatedly. Key questions to be asked in child abuse and neglect cases are: Do the injuries constitute abuse or neglect? Is the home safe? What must be done to make the home safe?

Adoption of Guidelines

The adoption of guidelines or standards for a community often includes qualifiers. For example, each team will have to adjust to the nature and extent of community resources. Communities with few resources may have to use the Court more frequently, because the children are not safe at home without certain services. (Communities must identify these deficits and attempt to provide the needed services.) Application of the guidelines also requires a close linkage with the juvenile/family court, to develop a coordinated plan for the child and family.

Ideally, the plan for foster care includes a statement of the reason the child is being placed, the goals for the placement and a proposed timetable. Martin's delineation of goals for foster care (protection, diagnosis, and treatment) provides a useful framework for such statements.[2] Protection and diagnosis are short-term goals, during which a decision is made about whether and under what circumstances the child could return home. Three months is usually enough time to complete an evaluation of the child and the family, and decide either to return the child home with a treatment plan, or maintain the child in foster care, also with a treatment plan and a revised timetable.

Treatment itself, for both child and family, may be accomplished in three months to one year, to a degree that allows reunion of the family, if such a goal is possible. If treatment will require significantly longer periods of time (any more than a total of two years), a petition for permanent wardship should be considered. Prolonged temporary removal is not fair to the child and is very damaging to all parties.

Occasionally when a team makes the difficult decision to petition, some courts deny the case for unsatisfactory reasons, leading some professionals to avoid requests for custody. Avoiding the courts in this situation is intolerable; it leaves a child at great risk. When a community has developed criteria for removing a child from home and these criteria are met in a particular case, the court must be petitioned. The responsibility then lies on the court, to intervene or to assume the risk for the child. While often there are problems in working with the court, in most situations a satisfactory relationship is possible, if the community and the court agree on guidelines and acknowledge each other's roles.[3]

Definitions of Child Abuse and Neglect

Team members need to agree on definitions of the types of child abuse and neglect. (The definitions adopted must correspond to the county, state, and/or federally stated laws.)

SAMPLE DEFINITIONS

Physical Abuse: Non-accidental physical injuries inflicted by a caretaker, sibling, or babysitter. The extent of the injury can be rated as mild (a few bruises, welts, scratches, cuts, or scars); moderate (numerous bruises, minor burns, or a single fracture); or severe (large burn, central nervous system injury, abdominal injury, multiple fractures, any life threatening abuse, or, in the extreme, death). It must be remembered that the severity of the injury does not always correspond to the severity of the family problem; i.e., one episode of shaking in a newborn can lead to permanent central nervous damage or death. Since physical punishment and spanking are acceptable in our society, communities must have guidelines as to when punishment becomes excessive and, therefore, unacceptable. Corporal punishment that causes bruises or leads to an injury that requires medical treatment is outside the range of normal punishment. Bruising implies hitting without restraint. Even when there are no signs of injury, an accident that includes hitting with a closed fist or kicking the child represents physical abuse.

Neglect: Harm to a child's person or development through failure to provide adequate food, clothing, shelter, medical care, education, or adult supervision.

1. *Failure to Thrive (FTT):* FTT is failure to gain weight adequately. Most of these infants are less than one year of age. Underfeeding (caloric deprivation) causes over 50 percent of cases of failure to grow (underweight) in infancy. Rapid weight gain out of the home (greater than 2 oz./day sustained in one week or

striking gain compared to similar intervals at home) is diagnostic. Other causes of failure to grow include medical illness related causes (30 percent) or a feeding error on the parents' part (20 percent). However, approximately three percent of normal children are short but well nourished.

2.   *Medical Care Neglect*: Serious acute diseases where the parents refuse treatment can usually be dealt with by a court order, rather than the child abuse laws. When a child with a chronic disease has a serious deterioration in his or her condition or there are frequent emergencies because the parents repeatedly ignore medical recommendations for treatment, reporting and/or foster care placement may be indicated.

A gray zone arises when considering children with incomplete immunizations, recurrent diaper rashes, flea bites, missed medical appointments, and other types of suboptimal health care. These situations are best handled by a public health nurse or school personnel. Only if repeated offers to help are not accepted should the case be referred to child protective services.

3.   *Educational Neglect*: Laws to guarantee school attendance for children have long been in effect. If parents do not respond appropriately to counseling regarding school phobia or keep a child home for housework or babysitting, full investigation is required. (Note: Truancy should not be included here, unless the parents are promoting it.)

4.   *Lack of Supervision*: Young children under age 12 are left without an adult or babysitter in attendance. Also included are children over age 12 continually left alone overnight. Abandonment, or when parents leave the child with no obvious intentions of reclaiming him, is the end of the spectrum.

5.   *Failure to Provide Adequate Clothing, Shelter, and Food*: These categories are easily confused with poverty and ignorance and are initially best approached in a helping way by public health nurses, school personnel, or department of social services. Flagrant cases of neglect should be assessed promptly and the child protected. Most cases are of a chronic nature and many factors need to be considered (i.e., severity of neglect, chronicity, age of child, child's physical and developmental status) before determination can be made of the severity of a situation. Mild cases of so-called "neglect" often are "value judgments" and need to be recognized as such. The following do not usually constitute neglect:

a.   Clothing: torn pants, no raincoat, etc.
b.   Food: unbalanced meals or cultural food preferences.
c.   Hygiene: dirty face, or hair lice.

    d.   Home environment: messy and/or unclean home, poorly washed dishes.

    e.   Cultural deprivation or intellectual stimulation neglect: not enough creative toys or children not talked to enough.

    f.   Emotional: child not given enough parental time or love.

Emotional (Verbal) Abuse: Can be defined as an interaction or lack of interaction on the part of a caretaker inflicting damage on the child's personality, emotional well-being, or development. Continuous scapegoating, berating, or rejection of the child are common behaviors having damaging effects on the child's personality. Psychological terrorism can be present in some cases, such as locking a child in a dark cellar or threats of mutilation, or threats of mutilating someone or something close to the child. The severity of these types of abuse can be ascertained by:

-Nature of the disturbed behavior or psychopathology of the child.

-Knowledge regarding the age of the child along with intensity and frequency of the abuse occurring.

-Willingness of the parents to cooperate with and make progress in treatment.

Sexual Exploitation or Sexual Abuse: "The involvement of dependent, developmentally immature children and adolescents in sexual activities that they do not fully comprehend, are unable to give informed consent to, or that violate the social taboos of family roles."[4] Sexual exploitation of a child for sexual gratification of an adult can include a spectrum of abusive behaviors. Sexual activity between an adult and child may range from exhibitionism to intercourse, often progressing through the following spectrum of behavior:

1.   Nudity: The adult parades nude around the house in front of all or some of the family members.

2.   Disrobing: The adult disrobes in front of the child. This generally occurs when the child and the adult are alone.

3.   Genital Exposure: The adult exposes his or her genitals to the child. Here the perpetrator directs the child's attention to the genitals.

4.   Observation of the Child: The adult surreptitiously or overtly watches the child undress, bathe, defecate, or urinate.

5.   Kissing: The adult kisses the child in a lingering and intimate way. This type of kissing should be reserved for adults.   Even very young children sense the

inappropriateness of this behavior and may experience discomfort about it.

6. Fondling: The adult fondles the child's breasts, abdomen, genital area, inner thighs, or buttocks. The child may similarly fondle the adult at his or her request.

7. Masturbation: The adult masturbates while the child observes; the adult observes the child masturbating; the adult and child observe each other while masturbating themselves; or the adult and child masturbate each other (mutual masturbation).

8. Fellatio: The adult has the child fellate him or the adult will fellate the child. This type of oral-genital contact requires the child to take a male perpetrator's penis into his or her mouth or the adult to take the male child's penis into his or her mouth.

9. Cunnilingus: This type of oral-genital contact requires the child to place mouth and tongue on the vulva or in the vaginal areas of an adult female or the adult will place his or her mouth on the vulva or in the vaginal area of the female child.

10. Digital (finger) Penetration of the Anus or Rectal Opening: This involves penetration of the anus or rectal opening by a finger. Perpetrators may thrust inanimate objects such as crayons or pencils inside as well. Pre-adolescent children often report a fear about "things being inside them" and broken.

11. Penile Penetration of the Anus or Rectal Opening: This involves penetration of the anus or rectal opening by a male perpetrator's penis. A child can often be rectally penetrated without injury due to the flexibility of child's rectal opening.

12. Digital (finger) Penetration of the Vagina: This involves penetration of the vagina by a finger. Inanimate objects may also be inserted.

13. Penile Penetration of the Vagina: This involves penetration of the vagina by a male perpetrator's penis.

14. Dry Intercourse: This is a slang term describing an interaction in which the adult rubs his penis against the child's genital-rectal area, inner thighs, or buttocks.[5]

Guidelines for Common Team Decisions and Case Management

This section is divided into 3 major sections: initial case assessment, follow-up case review if the child remains in the natural home, and follow-up case review if the child is placed in foster care.

INITIAL CASE ASSESSMENT

1. Sample Criteria for Accepting Cases for Team Assessment or Review
    a . The primary problem is one of child abuse, neglect, failure to thrive, or sexual abuse.
    b. There is a need for multidisciplinary evaluation or review of the family by a team composed of professionals in a variety of fields, including medicine, psychology, social work, nursing, etc.
    c. There are no other resources that could better provide the type of evaluation needed (i.e., more relevant to the particular problem or closer in terms of geographic distance).
    d. Priority will be given to cases of abuse and neglect that are more serious and/or complex. For example:
        (1) Chronic neglect families (large dysfunctional families, substance abuse families, families with generational abuse).
        (2) Mentally ill/mentally retarded parents.
        (3) Sexually abused children and their families.
        (4) Children with emotional/psychological disorders.
        (5) Children exhibiting failure to thrive.
        (6) Children with moderate to severe physical injuries.
        (7) Physical abuse in any child under one year of age.
        (8) Death of child.
        (9) Reabuse cases, after initial report and intervention.
        (10) Parents are resistant or uncooperative.
        (11) Foster care is considered or indicated.
        (12) Termination of parental rights is considered.
        (13) Specific questions exist regarding diagnosis or treatment.
        (14) The recommendations of different professionals or agencies are in conflict.
2. Guidelines for Completing the Evaluation
    a . Baseline Data Helpful in Completing an Evaluation

Referral   Information:
  (1)   Referral source and the reason for referral; what does the referring person ask for and what concerns do they have.
  (2)   Identify professionals and/or resources currently being utilized by the family.
  (3)   Identify pertinent records that might be useful to review (i.e., medical records, school reports, psychological testing, police reports, etc.).

Family   Intake   Information:
  (1)   Family's understanding of the referral and current concerns.
  (2)   Description of events leading up to team involvement including the history of the present complaint or incident.
  (3)   Description of the present family composition, living arrangements, and daily routine.
  (4)   Describe logistical needs and current crises.
  (5)   Describe the interactional and communication patterns between family members and the prevailing problem-solving style.
  (6)   Describe previous agency involvements and the outcome of previous treatment attempts, including how the family perceives outside agency involvements.

Child   Interview   and   Examination   Information:
  (1)   Interview child about current incident, taking into account the child's developmental level.
  (2)   Describe current and past medical problems, including perinatal history, well child care, school progress, etc.
  (3)   Physical examination to include estimate of growth pattern and development.
  (4)   Highlight the child's performance and abilities in play, testing, etc., including major presenting affect, significant behavior problems or psychopathology, special education needs, extreme reactions to parents or strangers, and sibling relationship.   Identify major coping defenses.

Adult   Interview   Information:
  (1)   Describe current and past medical problems including current problems, substance abuse history, mental illness, medications, birth control methods, special education needs, etc.
  (2)   Describe how the subject perceives his rearing, current and past relationships with parents, siblings, mate. Also, include perceptions of children, history of

pregnancy and newborn period, expectations of children.

   (3)   Describe the behaviors that were observed by the team during the evaluation, as well as the interactional and communication patterns between adults, and adults and children.

b.   Indications for Formal Psychiatric or Psychological Assessment

   (1)   Severe abuse, especially if premeditated or sadistic.

   (2)   Reabuse cases after initial report and intervention.

   (3)   Parent suspected of being dangerous:

      (a)   Psychotic (for example, bizarre ideas, paranoid ideas, fanaticism, inappropriate affect).

      (b)   Suicidal, or past suicide attempts.

      (c)   Homicidal.

      (d)   Sociopathic (i.e., prison record, multiple arrests, violent temper outbursts, or threats with a weapon).

      (e)   Drug addiction or severe alcoholism.

      (f)   Past psychiatric hospitalization.

      (g)   Past intensive psychotherapy without improvement (Note: A psychiatrist is mainly required in cases that are going to court and need an expert witness regarding the parent's prognosis, especially if termination of parental rights is being considered).

   (4)   Parent suspected of having intellectual limitations (obtain psychometrics).

   (5)   Perpetrator: uncertain (evaluate both parents).

   (6)   Child:

      (a)   Appears severely emotionally disturbed.

      (b)   Recipient of longstanding, profound child abuse/neglect regardless of symptoms.

      (c)   Claims sexual abuse or other severe child abuse/neglect without any evidence.

      (d)   Parent claims child is severely disturbed without any evidence.

      (e)   Psychometrics when intellectual limitations are suspected in the child.

c.   Indications for Police Consultation

   (1)   Accusations of abuse and parents refuse to cooperate.

   (2)   Parents refuse to admit the child to a hospital or threaten to remove him from the hospital.

   (3)   Child is under legal custody and is unexpectedly removed from hospital or foster home by the parents.

          (4)   Majority of sexual abuse cases.

      d.   Indications for Legal Consultation

          (1)   Serious accusation of abuse, and parents refuse entry, and police refuse to help.

          (2)   Parents refuse treatment for child with life-threatening disorder, and court order to treat is needed (most expeditious approach is to talk directly to juvenile court judge).

          (3)   Interpretation of state laws is needed for complex case.

          (4)   Consider taking the case to juvenile court.

          (5)   Consider request for criminal investigation.

          (6)   Consider recommending termination of parental rights.

3.   Guidelines for Case Selection for Indepth Conferences

The following types of cases should be routinely reviewed by a multidisciplinary team. If the team reviews all cases, the cases on this list should be allotted the most time (for example, 30 minutes to 1 1/2 hours). Cases not on this list may only require a few minutes of discussion each.

      a.   Severe physical or sexual abuse (for example, homicides, life-threatening abuse, multiple injuries, large burns, sadistic injuries, incest, severe malnutrition, or deliberate poisoning).

      b.   Reabuse cases, all failures.

      c.   Severe emotional cases—child severely emotionally disturbed and totally rejected/unwanted by parents.

      d.   Child less than one year old with any physical abuse.

      e.   Parent suspected of being dangerous.

      f.   Cases requiring police consultation.

      g.   Cases requiring legal consultation.

      h.   Considering foster care placement, or foster placement has been accomplished.

      i.   Considering returning a child home from foster care.

      j.   Considering termination of parental rights.

      k.   Specific questions exist regarding diagnosis or treatment.

      l.   The recommendations of different professionals or agencies are in conflict.

      m.   An unusual number of professionals and agencies are involved in a multiproblem family situation.

      n.   Educational cases (present briefly).

4.   Guidelines for Safety of the Home

In determining the safety of the home, drawing up a problem list with strengths and weaknesses of each family member and the family as a whole will organize the data base into a useful framework. The family's processes for solving problems and coping with crises are also important indications of the child's safety in the home. Questions to ask regarding these areas include:

a. How effective is the family at problem-solving?

b. What is the style of problem solving?

c. How chronic are their current problems?

d. How motivated is the family toward change?

The following in combinations are usually indications of a safe home:

a. Child is over age 2 (reason: child can run away or tell others what is happening to him/her, or the child can usually change his behavior in a self protective manner).

b. Child has many lovable qualities in the parents' viewpoint, and is not seen as unduly provocative or obnoxious.

c. The perpetrator is openly remorseful about loss of control and is not judged a dangerous person by initial evaluation.

d. Both parents have good health and normal intelligence.

e. At least one parent has a stable job.

f. The marriage is stable (e.g., the parents are supportive of each other and can relieve each other in child care and housework).

g. Lifelines are available, preferably in the home. Ideally, each parent has a friend or relative to whom they can turn.

h. Other professionals, agencies, or relatives provide collateral confirmation that the home is safe.

i. The perpetrator admits to problems and is willing to accept counseling and close supervision by Child Protective Services Agency (especially if the parents have accepted and utilized help in the past).

j. No major home crises (according to the initial evaluation) and any crisis that precipitated the abusive incident is resolved.

k. Cases involving confined physical injuries (buttocks, back or legs) inflicted, in the name of discipline for specific misbehaviors, and occurring only once or twice.

l. The nonperpetrator is appropriately protective of the child and will not leave the child alone with the perpetrator parent (i.e., angry at perpetrator parent).

m. Perpetrator removed, lives elsewhere, or has definitely left town (must be more than promises not to let a boyfriend in). This is particularly true if the nonperpetrator parent is appropriately protective of the child and angry that the situation occurred.

5. Guidelines for Placement Outside the Home

a. *If the child presented as*:

        (1)   Deserted child: Lack of contact by the parents or lack of suitable arrangements for the child's care.

        (2)   Seriously physically abused child. In judging the seriousness of abuse to a child, the extent of injuries and the child's age are the key factors. The lack of an adequate explanation for the injuries is enough reason to petition the court. The extent of injuries is not predictive of how the family will respond to treatment.

   b.   *If the parent presented as:*

        (1)   Seriously emotionally disturbed resulting in dangerous and unpredictable behavior with the child. There is reason to be concerned if the psychological assessments have labeled behavior as psychotic, sociopathic, suicidal, or homicidal. A child may be at a particularly high risk if he is looked upon as evil or possessed.

        (2)   The parent refuses or is unable to guarantee the safety of the child. The parents may deny the existence of a serious problem, refuse intervention, or justify serious injury to the child.

        (3)   The parent or family with serious problems that reoccur and/or do not respond to treatment. These families acknowledge the problems, or at least cooperated with the development of a treatment plan. However, with time, their lack of progress and the serious impact of the problems in the children become apparent. Sometimes these parents want the child placed after inappropriate counseling.

   c.   *Special situations warranting foster care:*

        (1)   Child is extremely fearful to be with parent or to return home.

        (2)   Adolescent refuses to return home and is beyond parent's control.

        (3)   Sibling had severe abuse in the past or was murdered.

6.   Guidelines for Criminal Investigation of the Perpetrator

   a.   Severe physical abuse (that is, assault and battery).

        (1)   Death.

        (2)   Life-threatening injury (for example, abdominal injuries or brain injuries not due to shaking).

        (3)   Numerous fractures.

        (4)   Beating with a weapon (aggravated assault).

        (5)   Gunshot wound.

b.   Premeditated physical abuse (for example, numerous cigarette burns or serious hot water burns) or torture (that is, mutilation or sadism).

c.   Nonsevere physical abuse, but where previous sibling was killed or died under suspicious circumstances.

d.   Most sexual abuse cases.

e.   Deliberate poisoning with intent to kill (premeditated murder) Note: Criminal filing should be strongly considered as a way of enforcing treatment when the offender is an unrelated adult (for example, boyfriend, day care center worker, teacher).

7.   Guidelines for Case Conferencing

a.   All relevant information exchanged, within legal limits.

b.   Discussion of needed additional information and plans to obtain it.

c.   Careful consideration of each discipline's perspective.

d.   Family-focused perspective, with attention to needs of all family members and environmental factors.

e.   Review of all community resources relevant to immediate client needs.

f.   Provision of emotional support to worker(s).

g.   Solicitation of client family input, if present.

h.   Discussion of safety of child(ren) in home.

i.   Solicitation of input from involved service-providers.

j.   Full participation of each discipline in decision-making.

8.   Guidelines for Formulating a Treatment Plan

Each Child Protection Team can generate a written plan that takes into consideration the problems, strengths, and weaknesses of each family member, any current environmental crises and matches these needs to services available in the community. This plan could be organized in the following way:

a.   *Referred child*:

(1)   Type of abuse with extent of injuries.

(2)   Follow-up required for these injuries.

(3)   Listing of other physical problems including dental needs.

(4)   Follow-up and treatment required for physical problems might include:
-further evaluation
-obtain releases of information for evaluations done elsewhere
-routine child health care by private MD, resident MD, neighborhood clinic, etc.
-public health nurse visits

        -special instructions for diet, weight gain expectations, etc.

        -special instructions for parents regarding home medical care if the child has chronic disease (e.g., cerebral palsy)

        -parent room-in with child for 24 to 48 hours prior to discharge to learn details of special care (especially in failure-to-thrive cases or when the mother visits infrequently)

(5) Listing of developmental problems.

(6) Recommendations for follow-up and treatment of developmental problems. Options might include:

        -further developmental screening and testing (DDST, Bayley, etc.)

        -speech therapy, physical therapy, etc.

        -infant stimulation program, day care center or nursery school (especially for children with developmental delays)

(7) Listing of emotional problems.

(8) Recommendations for treatment of emotional problems might include:

        -further evaluations by specialists; i.e., projective testing, referral for individual psychotherapy or play therapy

        -referral to group psychotherapy

        -therapeutic playschools, day care, or Head Start

        -foster grandparent program referral

        -child companion, Big Brother, or Big Sister program

        -recreational activities (e.g., community recreational center, youth group)

        -give phone number of crisis center or lifeline to adolescent patients

        -ongoing counseling relationship with CPS worker

b.   *Siblings* (same as a.)

c.   *Mother*

(1) Listing of physical problems.

(2) Follow-up and treatment required. Might include:

        -referral to specialist

        -dental services

        -locating primary care physician or clinic

        -family planning options

(3) Listing of emotional problems.

(4) Follow-up and treatment required might include:

        -continued counseling by Child Protective Services social worker

-Public Health Nurse service (PHN)

-parent aide/lay therapist counseling

-group therapy, (e.g., Parents' Anonymous, drug abuse group, Alcoholics' Anonymous, or other self-help groups)

-psychological testing and/or psychiatric evaluation (outpatient vs. inpatient)

-individual psychotherapy (clinic vs. inpatient unit)

-family therapy

-crisis outlets: 24-hour hotlines, crisis nursery, emergency babysitting services, install a phone, provide CPT members' home phone numbers, suicide hotline, battered women's shelter

-job training/have the mother return to work/volunteer activities

-homemaker services/babysitters

-recreational activities

-vocational counseling

-psychotropic drugs

-child-rearing or discipline counseling with parent by CPS worker, pediatrician, PHN, young mother's group sessions, parent education classes, PET, etc.

d. *Father* (same as c.)

e. *Marriage*
    1) List marital problems.
    2) Treatment might include:
      -marital and/or divorce counseling
      -sexual dysfunction therapy

f. *Extended family*
    (1) List problems.
    (2) Recommendations might include:
      -counseling parents about independence and autonomy from relatives
      -therapy geared to working through real or perceived family losses
      -enlisting extended family in cooperation with treatment plan
      -evaluation of relatives to determine feasibility of temporary placement in their homes or potential for adoption
      -enlisting extended family in cooperation with treatment plan
      -evaluation of relatives to determine feasibility of temporary placement in their homes or potential for adoption

g. *Environmental situation/crises*
   (1) List problems.
   (2) Recommendations might include:
       -environmental crises intervention; i.e., financial assistance, legal assistance, emergency funds, food stamps, food, shelter, transportation, housing and tenant assistance, telephone service, etc. (Note: These items should have first priority in order to restore some equilibrium to the home.)
       -training in utilization of appropriate community services
       -home improvements to remove safety hazards
       -assertiveness training

h. *Options for guaranteeing safety of the child*
   (1) CPS supervision with the child in the home utilizing monitoring via the school, day care, PHN, MD, and CPS worker as required.
   (2) Voluntary foster home.
   (3) Encourage voluntary relinquishment for adoption.
   (4) File a dependency and neglect petition.
   (5) Appoint a guardian ad litem.
   (6) Adjudicate juvenile court petition as soon as possible.
   (7) Court-ordered supervision, child in home.
   (8) Court-ordered supervision, child with relatives.
   (9) Court-ordered foster home (short-term vs. long-term).
   (10) Court order of above treatment plan (monitor for lack of cooperation or inability of parent to care for self).
   (11) Initiate termination of parental rights petition.
   (12) In-depth CPT review before any return to parents' home.
   (13) Deferred prosecution (most common in sexual abuse cases).
   (14) Restraining order.

i. *Coordination of treatment plan*

The final step in the treatment plan may be the most important and should include:
   (1) Team members to share their understanding regarding future caregiver roles.
   (2) Identification of team members who will review team findings with parents and negotiate a final treatment contract.
   (3) Team members meet with family to review findings and treatment recommendations and formulate a treatment contract.

(4) Written summary circulated to all involved, within legal limits.

(5) Verbal referrals/feedback to caregivers involved in case but not present during staffing.

(6) Date set for case review conference within 6 weeks after case assessed.

FOLLOW-UP CASE REVIEW IF THE CHILD REMAINS IN THE NATURAL HOME

1. The team needs to consider several questions during periodic case reviews:

   a. Does the child continue to be safe in the home?

   b. Has the treatment plan been followed?

   c. Is progress being made?

   d. Are adjustments needed in the treatment plan?

   e. Can the case be closed?

2. Documenting improvement may include the following areas:

   a. The parents have been cooperating with CPS and utilize therapy (e.g., keep appointments, fulfill treatment contracts, talk about their problems, use less denial, consider therapy helpful).

   b. The parents requested additional help during crises or in further dealing with problems.

   c. The parents and the professionals involved with the family note improvements in coping such as:

      (1) The parents can talk about alternative ways of dealing with their anger.

      (2) The parents have demonstrated impulse control around some frustrating childhood behaviors.

      (3) The parents can tolerate expression of some negative feelings toward them (e.g., "I hate you").

      (4) The parents use discipline techniques that are fair, non-punitive, and consistent.

      (5) The parents have asked for advice regarding child rearing and were able to implement some of this advice.

      (6) The parents begin to recognize the child as an individual with needs, desires, and rights of his own.

      (7) The parents begin to understand the concept of age appropriate behavior and have more realistic expectations of their child.

(8) The parents speak in positive terms about their child.

d. The perpetrator of the abuse can recognize potentially dangerous situations and has to plan for removing himself from the child at these times.

e. The non-perpetrator has demonstrated an ability to recognize potentially dangerous situations and can intervene on behalf of the child.

f. The parents and/or professionals involved with the family document specific improvements in the family's ability to cope with crises:

(1) The parents no longer live in an ongoing, overwhelming, chaotic environment.

(2) The parents are more supportive of each other and can relieve each other in child care or housework.

(3) The parents can talk about alternatives to dealing with crises.

(4) The parents have solved specific crises.

(5) The parents have recognized and resolved specific stresses before they turned into major crises.

(6) Interpersonal relationships have increased; isolation has decreased. The parents have a friend or relative who is supportive and available.

g. The parents and/or professionals involved with the family document improved functioning of the child.

(1) Medical care and child health visits have been kept.

(2) No further documentation of injuries.

(3) Growth and development follow predictable parameters.

(4) Appointments for treatment and therapy have been kept.

(5) Child reports no further abusive treatment.

(6) The child is able to recognize potentially dangerous situations and has a plan for protecting himself or getting help.

(7) The child is no longer fearful of his parents.

(8) The professionals involved with the child, including the schools, note specific improvements in the child's behavior, school work, relationships, self image, etc.

FOLLOW-UP CASE REVIEW IF THE CHILD IS PLACED IN FOSTER CARE

1.   Guidelines for Returning a Child Home from Foster Care

The most serious decision that a child protection team is called upon to make is when to return a child from a foster home to the natural home. This decision is much more difficult than the one for removal from the natural home. The return of the child to the natural home requires clear-cut behavioral changes in the parents and should not be tied to any set time schedule. This plan should be clarified with the parents at the time of placement.

Prerequisites. Changes in all of the following areas are essential before return:

      a. If either parent was diagnosed as severely disturbed or dangerous on a previous evaluation—this person is permanently out of the home or a recent evaluation has been done and a mental health professional finds major improvement has been made in impulse control and that no homicidal risk factors are present.

      b. If the *child* was unduly provocative or demanding, his behavior has markedly improved.

      c. The parents are cooperative and have made documented improvements in child rearing and crisis management (see previous section).

      d. A multidisciplinary team conference considered and recommended the decision for the child to return home after answering the following questions:

          (1) Has the treatment plan been followed?

          (2) Is progress being made?

          (3) If the child returns home, what adjustments are needed in the treatment plan?

          (4) If the child returns home, what supervision is needed?

      e. Court approval has been obtained in any situation where the child was initially removed from the natural home by court order.

2.   Guidelines for Termination of Parental Rights

Not all abusive families are treatable and termination of parental rights becomes a necessary alternative. Only in this way can these children be freed up for adoption, rather than endure a life of endless foster homes. Major indications include alone or in combination:

      a. Serious injuries or repetitive moderate injuries.

      b. Untreatable psychopathology in one or both parents leading to abuse to the child.

      c. Untreatable substance abuse in one or both parents leading to abuse to the child.

    d.   Treatment of parents leads to better independent functioning (i.e., self-care), but the prognosis for improvement in ability to parent remains bleak.

    e.   Abandonment of a child.

    f.   Voluntary placement of a child without visits, correspondence, or other contact for one year.

    g.   Both parents institutionalized for mental illness, mental retardation, or criminal conviction with no possibility of release for over one year.

Child Protection Teams can serve a critical function by becoming knowledgeable about the process and information required to terminate of parental rights. Suggestions include:

    a.   The team should consider this outcome early in their deliberations.

    b.   Convincing agreements to the court will include:

        (1)   Strong professional evaluations.

        (2)   Clear-cut treatment plans that have been appropriately negotiated with and communicated to the family.

        (3)   Solid documentation of lack of progress.

    c.   Professionals from the team must support termination:

        (1)   The physician's evaluation must document with certainty the types of physical abuse, nutritional deprivation, or sexual abuse that have occurred.

                Severe emotional abuse of a child should be confirmed by a child psychiatrist or psychologist.

        (2)   Have written statements from both a psychiatrist and an experienced social worker that the parents are relatively incurable, and that abuse is likely to continue in their home.

        (3)   Have written statements from professionals treating the family regarding extent of contacts with the family, outreach attempts, condition of the home on visits, and specific examples of chronic unacceptable behaviors.

    d.   Document treatment attempts and failures. This can be done by outlining in contract form a treatment plan with outcome objectives, time frames, and responsibilities of families and professionals. Review hearings can then be made at regular intervals (e.g., three months) to monitor and document progress or lack of progress.

    e.   In some states, adoption planning has to be completed before the court will consider termination of parental rights.

    f.   Parents in counsel with their lawyers may opt for voluntary relinquishment for adoption if approached with an honest appraisal of the situation, including the conclusions reached by the professionals involved in the case.

Summary

The guidelines discussed are viewed as resources for diagnostic and treatment teams. Multiple protocols are outlined; however, since teams vary considerably in purpose and function, each group should adapt or develop an operational plan that is relevant to specific needs, state law, and community standards.

References

1. Helfer, R.E. "Interdisciplinism in the Field of Child Abuse and Neglect." Unpublished Report, October 1978.

2. Scheurer, S.L., and M.M. Bailey. "Guidelines for Placing a Child in Foster Care." *The Battered Child*, 3rd Edition. C.H. Kempe and R.E. Helfer (Eds.), pp. 291-305. Chicago: University of Chicago Press, 1980.

3. Martin H.P. *The Abused Child*. Cambridge, Mass.: Ballinger, 1976.

4. Schechter, M.D., and R.L. Roberger. "Sexual Exploitation." *Child Abuse and Neglect*. R.E. Helfer and C.H. Kempe (Eds.), pp. 127-142. Cambridge Mass.: Ballinger, 1976.

5. Sgroi, S.M. *Handbook of Clinical Intervention in Child Sexual Abuse*. Lexington, Mass.: D.C. Heath, 1982.

PART IV

The Legal System and Child Protection Teams

Section Editor: Donald C. Bross

20. The Legal Basis for Child Protection Teams

Donald C. Bross

Introduction

In a sense, there is no need to discuss the legal basis for child protection teams. Teams simply represent free association to meet the needs of participants for support and consultation. On the other hand, teams operate within political and legal systems. Analyzing the legal basis of teams means looking at powers and limitations of teams, and the sources for these powers and limitations. By analyzing the legal aspects of child protection teams, some of the practical ways in which teams should be managed, what problems are solved by team activities, and which parameters should govern team activities can be highlighted.

Multidisciplinary Consultation *Within* Agencies

Common law recognizes the difference between officials, managers, employees, or agents of state and private organizations and those outside the same organizations. The contractual relationship existing between an organization and those hired encompasses reciprocal obligations and privileges. These obligations and privileges can be unwritten or expressed by regulations, policies, and by-laws. An organization typically creates groups of employees or agents to meet certain tasks, and child protection teams are just one type of task force. The parent organization can limit the powers and duties of the child protection team, or delegate to the limit of the powers of the particular hospital, protective services agency, or other institution. Child protection teams were created in hospitals and protective services agencies long before they were mandated or even recognized by statute.[1]

Child protection teams serve important functions for agencies which create them, including facilitation of information exchange and better accountability. Each agency is in a position to establish, maintain, and supervise teams in the manner most consistent with overall goals, because the team concept is intrinsically flexible. All the agency must do is to examine assumptions about duties of the team and assure these duties are carried out in a manner consistent with the parent organization's policies.

INSTITUTIONAL BYLAWS, POLICIES, AND RULES

Whether meeting as a team or not, individuals are expected to be aware of and adhere to institutional rules. Depending on the flexibility and openness of an organization, the use of teams and teamwork may be prevalent or even be the standard of practice. "Teaming" may not be subject to any rules beyond those applied to individuals. No individual may act beyond the scope of his or her authority, but an individual's scope of authority and activities may be quite broad in some settings. If not prohibited by written policy or the culture of the work setting, teams can easily be established on a formal or informal basis.

DELEGATION OF AUTHORITY

In hierarchical organizations, authority tends to be guarded and delegated with care. However, even less structured organizations must address the question of delegating authority to members. If members from outside the organization are used, a letter of appointment setting out the powers, duties, and responsibilities of the team members can be useful in avoiding misunderstandings. A letter of appointment may also be used to clarify the coverage of insurance, as well as to establish the term for the team members when appointed to the team.

INTRA-DEPARTMENTAL AND INTER-PROFESSIONAL CONSULTATION

Most professions are bound by duties of confidentiality with respect to clients. Yet within their own office setting, professionals, employees, and colleagues commonly share confidential data because this sharing is essential if clients are to be served well. In a hospital, for example, laboratory technicians, nurses, secretaries, and maintenance personnel may all be aware of some of the private details of a patient's presence and treatment. Unless this information is "published" to the public with resulting harm, this common exchange of essentially confidential data is rarely considered or even noted. Staffing of cases by individuals of different departments and professions should not raise legal issues unless a statute, rule, or the special nature of the activities calls into question the practice of consultation.

Rather than restrict the sharing of information between professionals, the law actively encourages sharing by creating a potential liability for those who fail to seek a second opinion when extra experience or expertise might change the view of a client's case. The sharing of data, of course, does not necessarily mean the sharing of identifying information, so that a case often may be discussed without an identified individual being discussed. On the other hand, the identity of the person or persons involved may be essential for proper discussion of the situation. Additional information may be forthcoming from team members, and mistakes as to whose tests and records belong together are more likely to be avoided when mistakes of identity are lessened. A good rule of thumb is always to ask about the "need to know" identifying information in discussing a case.

COMPARABLE CONSULTATION AND REVIEW ACTIVITIES

When an organization or profession reviews its members' activities, access to individual client records may be essential. Audit committees in financial institutions, tissue and morbidity committees in hospitals, and bar grievance committees are among those groups with a recognized "need to know" in many review situations. Child protection teams can also be seen as operating within a review framework in protective services.

Hospital ethics committees are an example of a recently developed approach to illuminating difficult matters through structured interdisciplinary consultation.[2] The membership of hospital ethics committees commonly includes representatives from more than one department and profession, and often involves individuals from outside the hospital.[3] The activities of ethics committees will be worth monitoring for those concerned with legal issues involved in the use of internal consulting groups. For example, the use of ethics committees has been categorized into four approaches:

(1) mandatory-mandatory
(2) mandatory-optional
(3) optional-mandatory
(4) optional-optional.[4]

The first word in each pairing refers to whether or not use of the team is required. The second word refers to whether or not the team's recommendations must be followed. Thus, a mandatory-optional policy by a hospital would mean that referral to the team of certain ethical issues would be required, but following the committee's recommendations would not be. The decision to follow one of these four policies with respect to the role of child protection teams will vary by institutional setting. A team's recommendations in a protective services agency might be discounted by the agency director, if it was felt that other factors had to be given greater weight. Absent a statute requiring an agency to comply with a child protection team's recommendations, agency directors retain discretion and overall responsibility. In contrast, a child protection team based in a hospital which indicates that a report of suspected child abuse should be made cannot be ignored without flying in the face of existing mandatory reporting laws. Thus an agency's policy with respect to child protection team referrals merits careful thought and might be analyzed in part by applying the ethics committee paradigm.

The value of looking around for other examples of multidisciplinary team practice is also evident from a risk management perspective. An ethics committee which staffed a "right to die" situation was sued by the patient whose wish not to have certain procedures continued was refused.[5]

Multidisciplinary Consultation *Between* Agencies

Consultation between professionals, even from different agencies, need not affect or involve duties of non-disclosure. A situation can arise, on the other hand, that does carry such a risk. For example, if a lawyer were to call a specialist in another law firm for consultation, the client's problem and identity should be breached, if at all, with care, given the possibility that the other firm already may be involved in the case directly or remotely. The very nature of two agencies or their governing laws may also create obstacles to joint staffings.

Agencies providing treatment for alcohol and drug abuse are covered by specific federal laws.[6] Interpretation of these laws has led to at least one litigated case in which suspected prenatal child neglect was reported. Even before federal laws were amended, a court upheld the reporting as not in violation of federal drug treatment confidentiality laws.[7] To decrease arguments even further, some facilities and governmental entities have reached interagency agreements for sharing data when child neglect and drug abuse are both involved.[8] In an unreported trial decision, a public health department was required to provide information on relatives of a child who had tested positive for a sexually transmitted disease.[9]

As long as an agency's own powers and duties are not exceeded, the appointment of a person outside an agency to serve within the agency, with or without pay, may be a good way for agencies to staff a team. Cross appointments, contribution of in-kind services, and interagency agreements are all approaches frequently utilized by nonprofit and governmental agencies creating child protection teams.[10]

Statutes Creating, Authorizing, or Recognizing Child Protection Teams

Statutes can serve to enumerate the duties and powers of child protection teams, recognize or require their establishment, and clarify potential conflicts with respect to confidentiality or jurisdiction. In 1975 one state mandated teams.[11] By 1978, however, Fraser identified ten states recognizing or mandating child protection teams.[12] This number has grown to 26 states, as indicated in Table 20.1 The results of the survey of child protection teams reported in Chapter 33 vary from Table 20.1. Regulations rather than specific statutes may account for "mandated" teams in some states. Other states have mandated teams by statute since the survey was completed.

Fraser identified three approaches to child protection teams:

> The first is the creation of an advisory team at the community or state level. The advisory team is a passive participant in the resolution of a child abuse case. The agency worker who is ultimately responsible for the case is given the option of utilizing the team's expertise. . . .
> The second type of team is one organized on a county level, with fixed responsibilities. The team reviews each case of

TABLE 20.1 *The Legal Basis for Child Protection Teams*

STATE STATUTES MANDATING OR RECOGNIZING CHILD PROTECTION TEAMS

State	Reference	Mandates	Recognizes	Defines	Powers/Duties Enumerated	Prescribes Membership	Other
Alabama	None found						
Alaska	None found						
Arizona	None found						
Arkansas	None found		X	X	X	X	
California	Cal. Welf. & Inst. Code Sec. 18951(d); Sec. 18960(f)						See Chapter, 4 Appendix I
Colorado	Colo. Rev. Stat. Sec. 19-10-109(6)(a) et seq.	X		X	X	X	
Connecticut	Conn. Gen. Stat. Sec. 17-446(a)		X				Makes grants available for teams
Delaware	None found						
Florida	Fla. Stat. Ann. Sec. 415.503(4), Sec. 415.5055	X		X	X	X	Detailed statute
Georgia	None found						
Hawaii	Haw. Rev. Stat. Sec. 321-38		X				Advisory to Dept. of Health
Idaho	None found						
Illinois	Ill. Stat. Ch. 23 Sec. 2057.1(b)	X				X	Demonstration teams thru 1985
Indiana	Ind. Code Ann. Sec. 31-6-11-14, 15	X	X	X	X	X	
Iowa	Iowa Code Ann. Sec. 235A.13(9)		X	X			
Kansas	None found						
Kentucky	None found						
Louisiana	R.S. 46:51(16)	X*					*Child Protection Centers
Maine	None found						
Maryland	Md. Ann. Code Art.		X		X		
Massachusetts	Mass. Gen. Laws Ann. Ch. 119 Sec. 51	X			X	X	Detailed section
Michigan	Mich. Comp. Laws Ann. Sec. 722.629(1)	X				X	
Minnesota	Minn. Stat. Ann. Sec. 626.558		X		X	X	
Mississippi	None found						

State	Citation				Notes
Missouri	Mo. Rev. Stat. Sec. 210.145(6), 150(1)	X			Team may have access to data
Montana	Mont. Code Ann. Sec. 41-3-108	X	X		
Nebraska	None found				
Nevada	None found				Team may have access to data
New Hampshire	N.H. Rev. Stat. Ann. Sec. 169-C:III(a)	X			
New Jersey	N.J. Stat. Ann. Sec. 24:4a-76,77				Establishes "crisis units"
New Mexico	None found				
New York	None found				
North Carolina	None found				
North Dakota	N.D. Cent. Code Sec. 50-25.1-04.1	X	X		Creates one state team
Ohio	None found				
Oklahoma	None found				
Oregon	None found				
Pennsylvania	Pa. Stat. Ann. Sec. 2216	X	X	X	Vague with respect to multidisciplinary aspects; creates "crisis teams"
Rhode Island	R.I. Gen. Laws Sec. 42-72-5(4)				
South Carolina	S.C. Codes Sec. 20-10-120	X			
South Dakota	S.D. Codified Laws Ann. Sec. 26-10-16	X	X		
Tennessee	Tenn. Code Ann. Sec. 37-1-407	X	X	X	
Texas	None found				
Utah	Utah Code Ann. Sec. 78-36-8(4), (7), (8)	X	X	X	
Vermont	Vt. Stat. Ann. tit. 33 Sec. 687	X	X		
Virginia	Va. Code Sec. 63.1-248.6	X	X		
Washington	None found				
West Virginia	W.Va. Code Sec. 49-1-3(f)	X	X	X	
Wisconsin	Wis. Stat. Ann. Sec. 48-981(7)(a)6	X	X		
Wyoming	Wy. Stat. Ann. Sec. 14-3-212	X	X		

suspected child abuse and has some decision-making powers. The second type of team, unlike an advisory team, is an active participant in the resolution of child abuse cases. . . .

The third type of team is one on a regional level, with fixed responsibilities which include the receipt and the investigation of reports of suspected child abuse, the review of each case on a regular basis, and ultimate decision-making power.[13]

Fraser suggested that by 1978 California, Massachusetts, Michigan, Missouri, Pennsylvania, and South Carolina utilized the first approach. Colorado, Wyoming, and Tennessee had the second approach. Virginia had taken the third approach.[14] Also commenting in 1978, Besharov observed that "five states specifically mandate and three others specifically permit the creation of such interdisciplinary child protection teams."[15] The discrepancy in figures between Fraser and Besharov may be explained in part by the ambiguity of language concerning the creation of teams and other special units. Table 20.1 can be used to compare current statutory approaches from state to state.

MANDATORY CHILD PROTECTION TEAMS

Twelve of twenty-six states with provisions that have been interpreted to recognize child protection teams also *require* the establishment of teams under certain conditions. The number or density of teams, the person responsible for establishing the team, and the issue of compensation are handled differently from state to state. Massachusetts requires regional directors, in cooperation with district attorneys, to establish one or more teams in each region of the state. The statute specifies that no compensation will be paid to members above any state compensation already received.[16]

North Dakota requires the director of children's services to create only one state team, with funding not mentioned.[17] Florida funds team activities, and requires the department to "develop, maintain, and coordinate the services of one or more disciplinary child protection teams in each . . . of its service districts."[18] Colorado is unique in setting a threshold for mandating a county director of social services to establish a team when 50 cases of suspected abuse or neglect are reported to the agency in a given year. Colorado's legislation does not include an appropriation for teams.[19] Among the more complete legislative schemes are the Florida, Tennessee, Colorado, and Massachusetts laws, as referenced in Table 20.1.

The better statutes are clear about at least four factors:

1. When child protection teams must be established.
2. Which agency or individual is responsible for creating the team and acting as host agency.
3. The powers, limitations, and duties of the team.
4. Protections for the teams, agency, and team members.

Most language with respect to incentives and protections for child protection teams must be read *in pari materia*, that is, with other sections of the protective services legislation. Specific incentives and protection often are not incorporated specifically into team creation and management sections.

OPTIONAL CHILD PROTECTION TEAMS

Even when a state does not require that teams be established, language defining, empowering, limiting, and protecting team activities can be very useful. In Montana, "the county attorney or the county welfare department may convene one or more temporary or permanent interdisciplinary child protection teams."[20] The statute also establishes membership, duties, and the team coordinator. South Dakota permits the establishment of teams by the secretary of social services, permits information exchange with teams, and immunizes team activities.[21] California encourages creation of teams through the funding of pilot projects.[22] Among fairly detailed permissive statutes are those of Indiana, Minnesota, and West Virginia, as cited in Table 20.1. Where state statutes have not worked out the details of child protection team operations, litigation can be expected to fill in many details. Well-structured and thoroughly thought-through statutes are an efficient instrument of predictability. Good statutes can be very usefully applied to reducing the uncertainty that seems inevitable in responding to chaotic or disturbed parent-child relationships.

Summary

Child protection teams can be created legally without statutory authority. Statutes can provide clarity and resolve actual and perceived conflicts of authority, confidentiality, and liability with respect to the operation of child protection teams. In about one-half of the United States, there are statutes concerning teams, although the well-developed statutes are much fewer in number.

References

1. See the Preface of this work. Colorado's Child Abuse Reporting Act of 1975 was the first legislation mandating child protection teams. The 1975 statute required that teams be established the year following in any county receiving 50 or more reports in one calendar year. Much of the information on early teams and the Colorado Reporting Act is found in J. Davies, "Colorado's Child Abuse Reporting Act: A Review of Its History." *Colorado's Children*, 2(2)(1983):3-5 (Colorado Department of Social Services).

2. Crawford, R.E., and A.E. Doudera. "The Emergence of Institutional Ethics Committees." *Law, Medicine, and Health Care*, 12(1984):13-18.

3. Youngner, S.J., C. Coulton, and B.W. Juknialis. "Patients' Attitudes Toward Hospital Ethics Committees." *Law, Medicine, and Health Care*, 12(1984):21-25.

4. Robertson, J. "Committees as Decision Makers: Alternative Structures and Responsibilities." *Institutional Ethics Committees and Health Care Decision Making*. R.E. Crawford and E.E. Dondera (Eds.). Ann Arbor: Health Administration Press, 1984.

5. *Medical Ethics Advisor*, 2(12)(1986):153-155.

6. 42 C.F.R. Sec. 2.63 (1982); 42 C.F.R. Sec. 2.12 (c)(4); Sec. 2.11 (1983).

7. *Matter of Baby X*, 97 Mich. App. 111, 293 N.W.2d 736 (1980).

8. *In the Interest of C.*, No. 83JV330, District Court of Mesa County, 8-27-84, cited in *The Guardian*, 6(1984):3-4.

9. Fraser, B.G. "A Glance at the Past, a Gaze at the Present, a Glimpse of the Future: A Critical Analysis of the Development of Child Abuse Reporting Statutes." *Chicago-Kent Law Review*, 54(1978):641-686.

10. Fraser, *ibid.*

11. Fraser, *ibid.*

12. Fraser, *ibid.*

13. Fraser, *ibid.*

14. Fraser, *ibid.*

15.   Besharov, D.J. "The Legal Aspects of Reporting Known and Suspected Child Abuse and Neglect." *Villanova Law Review*, 23(1977-1978):458.

16.   *Mass. Gen. Laws Ann.* Ch. 119 Sec. 51D.

17.   *N.D. Cent. Code*, Sec. 50-25.1-04.1.

18.   *Fla. Stat. Ann.*, Sec. 415.5055.

19.   *Colo. Rev. Stat.*, Sec. 19-10-109(6)(a) et seq.

20.   *Mont. Code Ann.*, Sec. 41-3-108.

21.   *S.D. Codified Laws Ann.*, Sec. 26-10-16.

22.   *S.D. Codified Laws Ann.*, Sec. 26-10-16.

23.   *S.D. Codified Laws Ann.*, Sec. 26-10-16.

24.   *Cal. Welf. and Inst. Code*, Sec. 18960(f).

21. Liability of Agencies, Child Protection Teams, and Individuals

Donald C. Bross

Introduction

While liability for failure to protect children has developed slowly, recent court decisions are a measure of change towards greater accountability through law on behalf of children. Legal and social services commentators have remarked on the trend towards greater liability.[1,2,3] In a variation of an old debate, concern is expressed for professionals exposed to personal liability while optimism is heard about the value of lawsuits for improving protective practices for children.

Liability lawsuits can be a learning device utilized by those not directly affected for anticipation, reform, and prevention of harm to children. While lawsuits for negligence cannot be ruled out in protective services, at least not without denying children important protections, a proper program of risk management will examine examples of documented error or adjudicated liability as basis for changing hiring, training, supervising, consulting, and other essential practices and policies. In order to arrive at a risk management strategy,[4] illustrative types of liability should be reviewed.

Basic Types of Liability in Child Protection Practice

Three basic types of liability for child protection can be readily identified and presented in the order in which a child proceeds through a protective services system. Failure to identify, diagnose, and report suspected child abuse and neglect can result in criminal or civil liability under statutes or case law throughout the United States.[5] No response or inappropriate response to reports of suspected child abuse and neglect have been litigated and have led to damage suits in a number of states with varying results,[1,3] including dismissal, settlement, and final damage awards. If a child is placed, a number of additional issues arise with respect to selection, training, and monitoring of the child in placement. Each of these areas can be discussed with special consideration for the role of child protection teams.

FAILURES OF DIAGNOSIS AND EVALUATION

Cases in which either "false positive" or "false negative" evaluations have occurred can result in loss of confidence, recriminations, and even liability. A false negative can occur when a child is abused or neglected but the professional rules out child abuse or neglect. A false positive case, in which child abuse or neglect is suspected but later shown not to be a problem, can lead to complaints of negligence, slander, defamation, or outrageous conduct. In one reported case,[6] the attending physician accused parents of child abuse, and then reported them without taking a complete medical history of the child or ordering indicated lab tests such as bleeding screens. The child was later diagnosed as being a hemophiliac. Had information been released to the public, additional complaints of breach of confidentiality, slander and defamation might have been justified. A therapeutic approach to child and family, even when a false positive occurs, should minimize any emotional trauma caused. In a child protection team (CPT) setting, the physician would have been more likely to give full weight to another doctor's reported view that this child was suffering from a blood disorder before reporting.

The risk of a "false negative" diagnosis carries with it all of the risks of child abuse and neglect, such as physical injury, death, impaired development, and emotional trauma. A "false positive" report can affect a family emotionally with more vulnerable families perhaps at greater risk for harm than more healthy families. Nevertheless, the case in which child abuse or neglect is occurring but not diagnosed, carries the greatest risks, including death, serious injury, and severe emotional harm equivalent to or greater than emotional harm caused by intervention.

Until now, this view is supported by the greater number of substantial awards reported for underreaction rather than overreaction to a report of suspected harm. Lawsuits are most commonly initiated by guardians *ad litem* and noncustodial parents for failure to intervene.

FAILURE TO CONSULT, REFER, OR REPORT

An important safeguard against both false positive and false negative decisions is additional information, especially when a case remains troubling. Child protection teams encourage and provide the resources for additional case data. Additional information can be obtained by retesting, new evaluations, consultations, second opinions, or even a third approach. While sometimes costly initially, this thoroughness is often cost-saving because of reduced delays over the long term. Specialists and non-specialists alike should be especially wary of assuming total responsibility for any complicated case, and child abuse and neglect is intrinsically a complicated issue.

The imposition of reporting laws throughout the United States, Canada, and Australia explicitly recognizes the need for more than one individual and more than one agency to evaluate and respond to possible child abuse or neglect. Few would argue that, within limits, the larger the number of qualified individuals, techniques, and longer period of time employed, the more reliable the results. Given that intervention can itself be overwhelming and that resources are limited, there is rarely justification for proceeding in isolation in matters of child abuse and neglect. There must be both additional knowledge and emotional support available to those involved in child protection cases. The child protection team increases second opinions and decreases the likelihood of complaints of failure to consult or refer.

FAILURE TO ESTABLISH AND OPERATE A CHILD PROTECTION TEAM

The greater inherent reliability of using more than one discipline, obtaining second opinions, and utilizing agencies with different resources for responding to harm and risk of harm means that those not using such approaches have to overcome the implication that "splendid isolation" is per se inadequate in child protection. The plight of some rural professionals and socially isolated professionals in many areas needs to be recognized and overcome by referral networks.

Child protection teams epitomize the concept that children's problems of abuse and neglect do not "belong," paraphrasing C. Henry Kempe, to any agency or profession, and their problems require a multidisciplinary and coordinated approach to resolution.   Child protection teams include representation from different professions, different experiential backgrounds, and sometimes different agencies or departments.   Second opinions are largely "built in" or intrinsic to a properly constituted child protection team. To the extent that a team is composed of one discipline or does not allow the possibility that other agencies' departments will be included in staffings where appropriate, it is not what has been classically considered to be a child protection team.[7]

The need for what a child protection team provides is so manifest that the failure to practice in this way can now be seen as malpractice in itself. With the existence of over 900 child protection teams nationally as demonstrated by B.B. Kaminer and her colleagues elsewhere in this book, CPT's are arguably the professional standard of practice in child protection. In states which legislatively recognize or require CPT's, the failure to have a team or to use it to staff cases as appropriate, can be litigated as statutory *negligence* per se when a child is harmed by failures of evaluation.   As discussed later in the section on risk management, instead of being threatened, most professionals and the public have welcomed the partially immunizing effects of child protection teams.

FAILURE TO MONITOR THE CHILD'S SAFETY AFTER INTERVENTION

The role of a particular multidisciplinary team will govern the degree to which issues of selection, training and monitoring of foster parents and institutional staff are a primary concern. While an intake, evaluation, and diagnostic team should be aware of placement issues, especially as these relate to the importance of any initial placement for the long-term effects of placement on the child,[7] other teams may have statutorily imposed duties to monitor children in placement.[8]

To the degree that a team is established for "permanency planning" or other forms of oversight, the liability is primarily a function of the degree to which the team is "on notice" of harmful or high risk conditions and does nothing.[9] If a team, however, has a primary duty to seek out data through visits, routine evaluations, or other proactive methods, and fails to actively seek this data, it may also be held accountable or even legally liable for failures to assure the child's safety in placement.[10] Had a child protection team staffed the case described in *Doe v. New York City Department of Social Services*,[11] the disagreements between the agency psychologist and child psychiatrist should have been highlighted. The foster father's continuing resistance to evaluation would have been noted. The child would have been much less likely to remain in a sexually abusive home for 2 1/2 years.

TREATMENT FAILURE

As in the example of failures of monitoring a child in placement, the degree of liability for a team depends on the degree to which the team's primary *raison d'être* is direct treatment of a child or family or monitoring of treatment. While there may be value in multiple approaches to complicated treatment problems, as discussed with respect to diagnosis and evaluation, some separate concerns can also be raised in the treatment area.

Teams based in departments of social services must be aware of the treatment afforded children in foster care. In particular, the time a child stays in foster care may be litigated under common law principles,[12] Titles IV and XX of the Social Security Act,[13] and perhaps Section 1983 of the Federal Civil Rights Act. Only one case to this time has led to damages partially based on a right to permanency, and this occurred through an out-of-court settlement.[14]

Teams based in institutional and residential care facilities have more treatment concerns. Minimally adequate treatment may be required,[15] including (1) a humane and therapeutic environment, (2) a sufficient number of qualified staff, (3) individualized treatment plans, (4) planned therapeutic programs and activities. It must be clear that placement in a residential program is the least restrictive alternative for the child.[16,17] Improper aversive techniques are an invitation to a lawsuit,[18] whether these include corporal punishment, physical or mechanical restraints, seclusion or emotional abuse.[19] Informed consent is a core issue in all treatment areas, and must also be considered in foster placements and adoptions.

Confidentiality

In their comprehensive review of confidentiality and child protection, Weisberg and Wald[20] analyze the balance between the need in modern society to assure as much privacy as possible and the need to know enough to make good child protection decisions. Child protection teams experience both sides of the confidentiality equation. Teams are in the position of needing to know enough to act wisely and may have to try and override attempts to keep vital information about a child's safety from team consideration. Teams are also in the position of having to maintain a protective stance towards releasing information about a child and family while assuring the appointing authority or the public that team members are carrying out the task of child protection in an adequate manner.

RIGHTS OF PRIVACY, NON-DISCLOSURE, AND PRIVILEGE

As seen in common law protections against trespassing, constitutional restrictions on unauthorized searches, cultural and legal opposition to eavesdropping, and numerous other examples, it is commonly understood in the United States that individuals have a general right of privacy. The usual right to have privacy in one's own home, to confidentially through non-public avenues like the mail and telephone, and to enjoy privacy with respect to sexual and family matters can be outweighed by other considerations of health and safety, if the stakes of life and health are high enough. The obligation not to disclose private matters is an essential element in the web of rules assuring privacy, and the privilege to prevent certain types of testimony in the face of formal, compelled proceedings is another. Nevertheless, either may have to give way depending on a number of circumstances.

Mandatory reporting statutes encapsulate the consensus of public opinion that suspected child abuse or neglect should be evaluated by an independent entity, even at the risk of embarrassing a caretaker or finding that no further intervention is justified. The child abuse reporting laws, like laws requiring reporting of some infectious diseases, are, of course, not a general abrogation of privacy rights. Each of the reporting statutes implicitly or explicitly differentiates between disclosure between agencies and individuals with a need to know for assuring adequate child protection, and any disclosure to the public at large. These rules against disclosure are modified, but not abandoned in child protection.

Many of the reporting statutes also abrogate some of the privileges not to testify, often including patient-physician, husband-wife, and client-mental health professional privileges. The team is most likely to be concerned about testimonial privileges in cases presenting difficult evidentiary problems, especially if a civil or criminal action is deemed necessary to protect a child. Access to data from others is a much more frequent concern.

RELEASES

Good clinical evaluation practitioners obtain consent for procedures, such as permission to release clinical data obtained. If video or audiotapes are to be made of the evaluations, participants are generally informed that this will be done, and that copies will be available at cost with a proper release. An evaluation ordered by a court, it should be clear, will be released to designated parties at the court's order, absent substantiated objections which must be made by the party opposing release. At the earliest time, perhaps through a letter in advance of the evaluation, participants should be made aware of the basic nature of the evaluation. Before the evaluation, adults being evaluated should be asked to sign releases clarifying their understanding, acknowledgement, and willingness to have data about their case shared with other individuals with a need to know. If the individual does not wish to have information shared, this is the time for objections to be raised and court action to be sought if appropriate. Even if statutory provisions make a release technically unnecessary, clarifying that some data can and perhaps must be shared under the law should contribute to trust or at least a shared understanding between the evaluator and the evaluated individual.

WAIVERS

Waivers for the release of normally confidential data can occur through practice, case law, or statute. Duties of nondisclosure do not prevent fairly large numbers of hospital personnel, law firm employees, bank employees, and other institutional personnel from knowing about and handling confidential information. The specific professional dealing with a client is usually not the only person with access to confidential data. It is quite a different matter if this information is "published" or made accessible to the public at large.

There are other explicit or implicit waivers of the usual restrictions on release of confidential information. By participating in a court-ordered evaluation, an individual may waive the right to object to the release of information in the civil court setting.[21] The mere fact of participation in a lawsuit exposes an individual to some loss of privacy through procedural rules of discovery.

Some child protection statutes expressly require the sharing of data between the police and child protective services. One of the important potential advantages of legislation recognizing child protection teams is the opportunity to establish a framework for gaining access to data without carelessly exposing the same data to unnecessary dissemination. For example, one statute provides:

[T]he child protection team shall go into executive session . . . to consider identifying details of the case being discussed, to discuss confidential reports, including but not limited to the reports of physicians and psychiatrists. . . . [A]ll relevant materials [shall be forwarded] to the child protection team as soon as they are available.[22]

Data normally confidential and restricted within an agency may sometimes be shared with other agencies under express statutory waivers.

While Federal law requires confidential handling of all educational records,[233] exceptions contained within the act permit disclosure if a prior state statute requires disclosure,[24] if there is a health or safety emergency,[25] or in response to a court order, including a subpoena.[26] Since this law governs records only, what a teacher can testify to based on direct observation or knowledge should not be covered.

To reduce the conflict between federal mandates in the area of child abuse and neglect and drug and alcohol treatment, qualified service agreements can be arranged between protective services agencies, and drug and alcohol treatment centers.[27] By operating within specified circumstances or seeking a court order,[28] release of some drug and alcohol-related information may be obtained. As Weisberg and Wald[20] discuss, however, confidentiality remains a technical area of the law of protective services requiring that competent legal counsel be readily accessible.

ACCOUNTABILITY TO THE PUBLIC AND CONFIDENTIALITY

Protecting the confidentiality of child protection data without reservation or limitation cannot be the only goal of an agency. Courts may require that certain data be made public in individual cases, and there is the broader issue of general accountability to the public. At the same time that some statutes require confidentiality of child protection records, other statutes require open records on public meetings, even when the issue is sensitive.

The breadth and specificity of overlapping statutes, the purposes of the different laws, and the degree to which data are identifying may determine which information is to be provided to the public through meetings or the news media, and which data must be withheld.[29] After a court ruling clearly restricting the release of data from a child protection team,[30] one state legislated elaborate criteria for the sharing of information with the news media and the public, as well as limiting the release of *identifying* information.[31] A distinction is drawn in the legislation between public meetings, at which the response of private and public agencies to reports of abuse and neglect must be discussed along with nonidentifying information about specific cases, and executive sessions during which identifying data, evaluations, and treatment details are discussed.

Under the statute, information not considered to be "identifying," and, therefore, required to be released to the public, includes:

> whether the case involves mild, moderate, severe abuse or neglect, or no abuse or neglect; whether the child is an infant, a toddler, a pre-school or school-aged child, or a teenager, and the sex of the child; the date of the initial report and the specific agency to which the report was made; and subsequent reports to specific social service agencies, law enforcement agencies, or other agencies.[32]

What remains unclear is whether a specific item of information required to be released would still have to be released if it could be shown that the particular item would be "identifying," as in the instance of a small town.

In a federal case in Texas, the judge struck down a statute allowing almost total access to a central registry.[33]   A balanced approach, based on a need to know, a need to protect children and parents from unnecessary exposure to publicity, and careful attention to the sometimes competing interests of law and policy, can be helped by referral to the few precedent cases available.

LIABILITY OF THE ENTIRE TEAM

The laws, regulations, or letter of appointment establishing a child protection team provide the clearest standards for team performance. A failure to follow reasonable team procedures with a directly resultant and significant harm to an individual, would provide a basis for liability, but no successful lawsuit has been brought to date.

Successful suits against a team and its members may be difficult, to the extent that membership is multidisciplinary. Each discipline has its own standards, and if the team has followed its own guidelines, a plaintiff would have to show that many different professional standards were failed in order to establish team liability.

Risk Management

Risk management is a prospective and preventive approach to liability. It requires examination of lessons learned within one's own agency and practice, and monitoring liability developments in similar settings. Attention is directed to preventing specific acts of negligence, including the hiring and retention of inadequate personnel, recognizing and ameliorating developing liability, and tracking problem areas over a sufficient length of time and breadth of concern so that risk can be adequately assessed.

By their intrinsic nature, child protection teams are a risk management tool. Built-in second opinions, at least partly heterogeneous composition, the structured exposition of conflict, and review of CPT practice all decrease the chance of error for the agency which employs teams properly. The job of a plaintiff's attorney will always be more difficult, given a problem of ordinary negligence, to the extent that a failure of many different professional standards must be demonstrated. Child protection teams, of course, can be badly managed, composed of inept individuals, or controlled so tightly that the natural checks and balances are destroyed with resultant vulnerability to mistakes.

ACCOUNTABILITY ON BEHALF OF CHILDREN

Everyone who cares for children wishes that any services for a child be competent and appropriate. Experienced individuals, probably without exception, know of situations in which a child has not received reasonable or even minimal care by an agency or professional. Without the possibility or reality of court orders and damage awards, children will have greater vulnerability and less chance for redress of wrongs than others. Thus every child care professional must support reasonable accountability.

Sophisticated child care professionals are aware that some reforms, such as setting caseload structures,[34] requiring medical care, dental care and other services for children in foster care,[35] and even increased numbers of protective services workers, may result from litigation. These reforms, results of attempts to assure accountability for children, may also directly benefit child care professionals.

Finally, it is unprofessional not to learn from the mistakes of others. Lawsuits for damages and injunctions, as well as complaints about services, clinical reviews, and research dealing with both successes and failures of practice are indispensable to progress within any discipline.

INTERNAL REVIEW

Retrospective review of services is built into many professions. Physicians use tissue committees, post-mortems, grand rounds and other devices to learn from patient losses. Lawyers are required to study prior case decisions, in which at least someone invariably fails to prevail, to guide future legal practice. Error finding must also be built into child protection. Since supervisors may often share liability for the work of a caseworker, protective services agencies must assure the independence of error review. Incident report systems, a risk manager, and a child protection team are all approaches to review that must be considered in any modern system of child protection.

The child protection team that periodically reviews case outcomes for cases it has staffed decreases the chances for future error. The degree to which certain types of cases or individuals are challenging a solution may be highlighted only through periodic review.

Team Liability Versus Individual Liability

The distinction between liability for an individual, a team, or an agency has not been emphasized until now because the types of action that might produce liability are basically the same for all three entities. Given that an individual is found liable, the hiring or supervising entity may also be liable under the doctrine of *respondant superior*. Since teams rarely are established as separate entities, but exist rather as an instrument of a parent organization, the practical approach to suing a team will be to sue individuals *and* the parent organization to reach the locus of responsibility and funds. Because teams have represented "good practice per se" as they have developed, questions of standards of team practice have been slow to emerge. It is nevertheless conceivable that all or most members of a team could take a flagrantly wrong approach to a case with resultant harm. While working in teams may help members practice better, teams cannot immunize members against deliberate evasion of the law.

Public policy should favor teams, however, and only willful and wanton negligence or overreaching should be culpable. It is in the interest of children, families, and the public at large to encourage consultation and coordination between child protection services. Many considerations will affect liability. For example, the degree to which a team is liable may depend on the degree to which its actions are supervisory as contrasted to educational or advisory.

As mentioned before in this chapter, ethics committees may offer useful analogies to child protection team practice. In late 1986, the first lawsuit naming as defendant an ethics committee was filed in California, but later dismissed. The case was filed on behalf of Elizabeth Bouvia, a quadriplegic, who wished to exercise a right to die which she claimed was denied by the committee. Child protection teams will benefit from following this and similar cases.

Summary

The intrinsic advantages for the use of CPTs in modern child protection practice are numerous and include many that relate to liability. Use of a team can avoid negligence per se claims when errors are made. There is less chance that a failure to meet standard practice can be successfully alleged. The complainant may be forced to prove that many different standards of care have been failed. Most of all, for children and the professionals that serve children alike, the prospects for error and repeated error will be reduced.

References

1. Besharov, D.J. *Criminal and Civil Liability in Child Welfare: The Growing Trend*. Washington, D.C.: American Bar Association, 1984.

2   Spearly, J.L. "Caseworker Indictment—A Closer Look." *National Child Protective Services Newsletter*, 3(1981):6-10.

3. Bross, D.C. "Professional and Agency Liability for Negligence in Child Protection." *Law, Medicine, and Health Care*, 11(1983):71-75.

4. Freeman, L. (Ed.). *Managing Risks While Protecting Children*. Denver: National Association of Counsel for Children, 1986.

5. *State Statutes Related to Child Abuse and Neglect: 1984, Volume 1.* Complete Version in State Order. Washington, D.C.: Clearinghouse on Child Abuse and Neglect, OHDS, ACYF, Children's Bureau, 1985.

6. *Austin v. French*, No. 80-114, (D) (W.D.Va. March 23, 1981).

7.   Schmitt, B.D. *The Child Protection Team Handbook*, pp. 1-13. New York and London: Garland STPM Press, 1978.

8.   Goldstein, J., A. Freud, and A. Solnit. *Beyond the Best Interests of the Child.* New York and London: Free Press, 1973.

9.   42 United States Code Annotated, Section 675(6)(West Supp. 1975-1982).

10.   *Koepf v. York*, 251 N.W. 2d 866 (Neb. 1977).

11.   *Doe v. New York City Department of Social Services*, 649 F. 2d 134 (2d Cir. 1981); *Johnson v. City of New York*, 440 N.Y.S. 2d 529 (1985).

12.   *Bradford v. Davis*, 626 P.2d 1376 (Or. 1981); but see *Smith v. Alameda County Social Services Agency*, 90 Cal. App. 929, 153 Cal. Rptr, 712 (1979).

13.   *Joseph and Josephine A. v. New Mexico Department of Social Services*, 8 Family Law Reporter 2188 (U.S. District Court, N.M. 1982).

14.   *Bradford v. Davis*, Settlement reported in *Youth Law News Journal*, October 1982.

15.   *Wyatt v. Stickney*, 344 F. Supp. 373, 379-386 affirmed in separate decision 344 F. Supp. 387, 395-407 (M.D. Ala., 1972).

16.   *Lake v. Cameron*, 364 F. 2d 657 (D.C. Cir. 1966).

17.   *Lessard v. Schmidt*, 349 F. Supp. 1078 (E.D.Wis. 1977).

18.   *Wheeler v. Glass*, 473 F. 2d 983 (7th Cir. 1973).

19.   VanBiervliet, A., and J. Sheldon-Wildgen. *Liability Issues in Community-based Programs.* Baltimore: Paul H. Brookes, 1981.

20.   Weisberg, R., and M. Wald. "Confidentiality Laws and State Efforts to Protect Abused or Neglected Children: The Need for Statutory Reform." *Family Law Quarterly*, 18(1984):143-212.

21.   Matter of Edward D., 132 Cal. Rptr. 100 (1976). See also *Werner v. Kliewer*, No. 57612, Kansas Supreme Court, December 6, 1985.

22.   Colorado Revised Statutes, Sections 19-10-109(6) and (10).

23.   20 United States Code, Section 1232g (1982).

24.   20 United States Code, Section 1232g (b) (1) (E) (1982).

25.   20 United States Code, Section 1232g (b) (1) (I) (1982).

26.   20 United States Code, Section 1232g (b) (2) (B) (1982).

27.   45 Code of Federal Regulations, Part 2.

28.   45 Code of Federal Regulations, Sections 2.61-2.67-1.

29.   *Gillies and the Denver Post v. Schmidt et al., Colorado Court of Appeals,* September 2, 1976.

30.   *Ibid.*

31.   Colorado Revised Statutes Section 19-10-109(6)(1978) and 1985 Supplement.

32.   *Ibid.*

33.   *Sims v. State Department of Public Welfare,* 438 F. Supp. 1179 (1977), reversed sub nom Moore v. Sims, 442 United States 415 (1979).

34.   *Lynch v. King,* 550 F. Supp. 325 (D. Mass. 1982), affirmed sub nom *Lynch v. Dukakis* 719 F. 2d (1st Cir. 1983).

35.   *G.L. Zumwalt,* 564 F. Supp. 1030 (W.D. Mo. 1983).

22. The Attorney's Role with the Child Protection Team

David W. Lloyd and Donald C. Bross

Introduction

The complexity of legal issues that can arise for a multi-disciplinary team makes it a necessity for the team to have access to legal counsel. For example, in a single case there may be questions about whether informed consent for diagnosis and treatment has been obtained or is unnecessary, whether specific concerns rise to the level of neglect and, therefore, require reporting to authorities, whether confidential information may be disclosed to other professionals involved with the family without a signed release, what information must be developed to bring a case to court, whether concurrent legal proceedings will have an effect upon proposed treatment plans, and whether proposed actions by the team members are in compliance with federal, state, local and agency laws and policies.

Relatively few attorneys are specialists in child protection team (CPT) work. Most attorneys involved in child protection teams bring skills and interests from other areas such as health law, domestic relations, corporate practice or criminal law. More importantly, however, an American Bar Association informal survey[1] suggests that the quality of agency representation, and presumably the quality of CPT representation, is a function of the importance attached to receiving quality legal advice by the agency or team. Developing expectations and standards for lawyers on child protection teams is an important task for lawyers and non-lawyers alike. Since it is extremely rare for a state to address the role of the attorney for a CPT legislatively,* lawyers and their colleagues must work for consensus on the attorney's role as they practice together. A self-assessment instrument for evaluating agency legal representation, available from the National Legal Resource Center for Child Advocacy and Protection of the American Bar Association, is an important contribution to better practice.

Types of Child Protection Teams and Attorney Preparation

As documented throughout this book, there are many different types of child protection teams. Two types of teams, the public agency based team and the medical facility based team will be briefly discussed in this chapter to illustrate similarities and differences in the role of the attorney in each type of team. For example, the attorney for the public agency CPT must be well informed about the myriad state and federal rules governing child protection services, whereas the attorney for the hospital-based team is likely to be especially well-versed in such areas as informed consent and medical issues. However, it is advisable that on either team, the attorney be available on a full-time basis. Because problems requiring immediate legal attention can occur at any time, preventive legal efforts are more likely with the attorney always available. The availability of a full-time lawyer helps educate and sensitize the staff to varied legal issues, and full-time availability assures that the attorney, in turn, will be well-versed in the business of his colleagues and the business of children and families. Attorneys in any child protection team setting should have some background in risk management and careful consideration should be given to his/her knowledge of juvenile and criminal law, domestic relations law, mental health law, constitutional law, torts, and administrative law.

THE PUBLIC AGENCY TEAM (PAT)

Attorneys in PATs are typically volunteers from the community, county attorneys, or attorneys contracted by the agency specifically for child protective services work. The source of funding for the attorney can affect the perception of all as to whether the attorney acts with the independence of a criminal prosecutor or acts as a representative of the agency or the client, much as any civil lawyer represents a client. Given a choice, most agencies should prefer an attorney specifically responsive to their instructions in a classic attorney-client relationship. This avoids role confusion for the attorney and clarifies that the attorney should act in response to team requests unless it is unethical or illegal to do so.

THE MEDICAL FACILITY TEAM

In his article on the role of attorneys in child protection teams,[2] Richard Bourne identified several roles for the attorney in a child protection team based on his experience in a hospital setting. Bourne states that the primary role of the lawyer is to inform the staff of legal obligations, to spend time urging other institutions to fulfill their responsibilities, and, if necessary, to help initiate legal actions where appropriate. Bourne believes there are a number of differences in the perception of lawyers and other team members of the value of court intervention, as discussed in the section on case reviews. In general, it may be noted that most CPT attorneys in medical facilities are hired by doctors or the agents of physicians, and these attorneys clearly work for the team. Since attorneys, like members of other professions, have varying perspectives with respect to any issue, including the value of court proceedings, the hospital child protection team should take the attorney's philosophy with respect to court intervention into consideration during the hiring process. A review of ethical considerations relative to directions by clients to lawyers may be helpful in understanding the role of the team lawyer.[3]

Legal Consultation

FACTUAL ASSESSMENT

One of the most important roles of the attorney is to help in evaluating a case for the need to report or to proceed in court. As the attorney for the team hears the clinical presentation of data, he/she must assess factual material at hand against statutory and case law standards.

Equally as important, the lawyer must be prepared to assist the clinician in identifying methods for obtaining and documenting evidence that will be admissible in court. Whether evidence at hand is already sufficient, whether members or colleagues are likely to be required as witnesses in court, and the degree to which information must be obtained through court orders to assure that an adequate basis for the case exists are all frequent issues of consultation. The lawyer performs an important function in helping all team members understand when minimal standards for either reporting or proceeding in court have not been met, as well as the extent to which it would be premature to give up on a case without trying various available legal procedures.

CONFIDENTIALITY AND DISCLOSURE OF INFORMATION

Issues of confidentiality and child protection can be quite complicated.[4] In many instances, the discussion between team members and the team attorney may be treated as coming within attorney-client relationships, but exceptions may arise as when persons from outside the team are involved in case conferences. The law with respect to privilege and non-disclosure, and exceptions to both privilege and non-disclosure laws, should be routinely analyzed and discussed where appropriate during meetings. Additional discussion of these issues is contained in the chapter on the liability of child protection teams.

IMPLEMENTATION OF TEAM RECOMMENDATIONS THROUGH OUTSIDE AGENCIES

Whether the team is public agency based or hospital-based, there are many circumstances in which lack of communication, lack of resources or other less acceptable reasons may prevent action on behalf of a child who needs protection. One of the least acceptable reasons is a lack of knowledge of the legal options available. A public agency based team might find itself recommending that a lawsuit be brought against a local school system in order to assure that Public Law 94-142 benefits are provided to children in protective services. A hospital-based team might have to file its own action in court for the protection of a child when a responsible public agency has failed to do so. and a child remains at substantial risk of harm. The team attorney assures that practical legal options are prosecuted. Often, by maintaining good relationships with legal colleagues in other agencies, lawyers also can help avoid unnecessary agency conflicts.

LIABILITY ISSUES

No public agency or hospital, nor a CPT working for these institutions or similar institutions, can be entirely immune from the possibility of lawsuits for failure to properly evaluate and respond to cases of harm to children. Historically, the best response to liability has been one of risk management. Risk management identifies those areas of greatest potential harm to clients, and through a program of review and training reduces the likelihood that such harm will occur. The reader is referred to the chapter in this book on liability issues. Prevention of lawsuits and the mitigation of harm where lawsuits are possible are significant responsibilities of the CPT attorney.[5]

Case Reviews

SUMMARY OF LEGAL PROCEEDINGS

CPTs can become involved in preparation for either civil or criminal proceedings. The differences in the criminal and civil court systems, including different evidentiary standards, different rules for investigations, and different purposes and results of proceedings, are all areas in which the attorney for the CPT must be well-versed. The CPT attorney must enable team members to understand their role in these different kinds of legal proceedings, and their rights as professionals and witnesses in such cases. The likelihood or advisability of either criminal or civil proceedings may be an issue for any case brought before the team. Understanding the difference in preparation and outcomes in criminal and various types of civil proceedings can help the team make appropriate recommendations for disposition of the case. The team lawyer must help colleagues understand legal issues from a legal perspective, how to work within the legal framework, any limitations on the many legal devices available, and "solutions" offered by the legal system. Given that adjudication may be an important therapeutic tool in addressing child maltreatment,[6] the team attorney must seek and prepare appropriate, even creative, evidentiary and other legal solutions to problems presented.

EVIDENTIARY AND PROCEDURAL PROBLEMS

Two brief examples illustrate the value of immediately available consultation. In the first example, there was a fair amount of information about a possible sexual abuse perpetrator's background, prior acts, and personality. Information from the physical examination and various statements by the child strongly corroborated the likelihood of sexual abuse. The attorney was able to help sort out which parts of this case documentation would be likely to be admitted for the purposes of adjudication, and how it would have to be prepared for admission into evidence.

As another typical example, the parents were the only two individuals with access to a child who had suffered from a shaken infant or whiplash syndrome. In some jurisdictions, both civil and criminal law precedents provide some guidance as to the types of information that will probably be required to prove either that the child needs a protected status or that a crime has been committed or both. The principle of *res ipsa loquitur* has been successfully applied in abuse cases, by statutory interpretation, and has been supported in at least one law review article that argued that a child with unexplained injuries may need to be adjudicated as neglected or abused.[7,8,9]

DUE PROCESS FOR CHILDREN AND PARENTS

Throughout the activities of a CPT, the availability of the attorney is essential to help assure that due process considerations are kept in mind for both children and parents. Issues of confidentiality are discussed elsewhere in this book, but many other issues remain. The adequate representation of children and parents, proper information to courts and various legal representatives in a case, considerations of the coordination of criminal and civil processes, and legal options on behalf of the child, parent or family are all properly considered under the general heading of "due process." As an example, the attorney can be helpful in identifying ways in which the clinician can use various public systems to benefit a child and a family. The case of a child injured because of unsafe conditions may reveal a landlord-tenant issue rather than an issue of parental neglect. If exploration of a case reveals that a family has been evicted for non-payment of rent, that they had been withholding their rent because the apartment had numerous housing code violations, that the father has recently become unemployed, or that one of the other adults in the apartment to which the family moved is responsible for physically abusing the child while babysitting, the attorney may help explain the procedures for applying for public housing, and how to use the landlord-tenant court to help remedy the family's situation. Another possibility is to help the child abuse investigation caseworker push for quicker application for public assistance benefits, and to work with district attorneys in the investigation or prosecution of the "outsider" who injured the child.

A specific question that may arise with respect to CPT meetings is whether or not attorneys for the child or parent should be involved. Child protection team meetings traditionally have not been "hearings" or any type of proceeding which could be construed as a hearing and thus warrant the attendance of attorneys for interested parties. Most teams exist to help professionals and agencies understand what has happened in a case, and what should happen next. Since recommendations by teams may lead to court filings or other activities of a formal nature, it is understandable why some parties would argue for a more formal "hearing" approach to CPT meetings. In particular, respondent's counsel may wish to decrease the likelihood that a case will be tried by challenging the nature of the information considered, and perhaps the process used, by the CPT.

The policy arguments against converting CPT meetings into hearings include the likelihood of:

(1) greater costs to CPTs;
(2) reduced "give and take" between different agencies and professionals; and
(3) reduced prospects for a thorough examination of a child's or a family's situation.

Among the specific legal principles that might be related to this issue are questions of the right to consult with agency attorneys and have work-product rules apply when judicial proceedings might be anticipated, and the degree to which court jurisdiction is usurped if adjudicatory matters are not presented because of overly complicated preliminary investigations. Practically, the issue may be approached by allowing only team members and outside consultants to participate at the evaluative stage. Limited participation is justified to the degree that work-product issues or perhaps the degree to which a case should be litigated are discussed. Once team opinion is fairly firm, even if there are majority and minority views, the involvement of lawyers for all parties to the case may more efficiently reveal the total evidence available and the opinions held. This can avoid surprise in court and avoid inefficient discovery. Another practical issue of when to involve an attorney relates to the likely adversarial position being taken. If the attorney sees the case as one in which the team being "right" about some issue means the client's interests are necessarily harmed, then the attorney is more likely to challenge or disrupt the proceedings in ways more suitable for court hearings. If the attorney sees the case as one in which the team is appropriately trying to discover what has happened and what must happen to benefit the attorney's client, then the attorney may be able to participate without great disruption, and even improve the chances for a suitable result. Quite often, the attorney who can most easily assume a role of using the team for the client's benefit is the attorney for the child. The team attorney must consider all of these issues when the decision is being made whether to allow participation or not, as well as during the time other attorneys are allowed to participate in team staffings.

COMPLIANCE WITH ADMINISTRATIVE REQUIREMENTS

As a legally trained individual, the team lawyer should be more aware than other members of the legal relationships between different entities within the same institution or between different institutions. There may be more than one group, for example, with some responsibility for oversight in possible cases of child abuse or neglect. With the advent of hospital ethics committees, some formed an "Infant Care Review Committee" to deal specifically with handicapped newborns. Thus, as one example, issues of medical care neglect may need to be reviewed by more than one group. A CPT in a public protective services agency may need to share data with the foster care review or permanency planning committee. As child protection continues to develop as a field within the social and health services, further complexity can be anticipated. The basic questions to be answered will continue to include choices of who should be at this meeting or know about it, and who should be informed of the results.

With respect to outside agencies, statutes as well as regulations must be followed to the extent possible. A great deal of time and annoyance often can be avoided by maintaining current contacts with the many agencies involved in child protection, and logging changes in protocols and personnel.

Policy Preparation and Implementation

A child protection team should consider having a policy manual to provide all staff with guidance for their daily team activities. The range of policies might cover general administrative issues, such as personnel matters, use of office equipment, security, public relations, case management guidelines, and special guidelines for specific types of cases. It is possible, of course, that the parent institution has policies covering most CPT concerns.

INTERNAL MANAGEMENT

The lawyer can be helpful in identifying the need for policies and guidelines to control such issues as risk management. Broader policy implications may follow from case consultations, for example, with respect to authority for acting on behalf of an agency, in concert with an agency or independently of an agency, and these broader implications may need to be addressed.

When internal management issues are to be addressed by written policies, the starting point will normally be a review of existing program mandates from statutes, regulations, and other constraints. The parent agency may already have written policies that can or should be adapted to team management. It is usual to set forth the mission statement for an agency or for a team in a policy manual. All subordinate policies of the team should be congruent with the desired goals and objectives of the parent agency.

The process by which a policy is written will contribute to or undermine the perception of members that they are functioning as a team. The attorney should either draft policies in conjunction with other team members who represent the other disciplines, or should review, in a supportive manner, the drafts of those team members who initially prepare them. The process of review, comment, and revision can be an important learning experience for staff as they grapple with the need for clarity and flexibility, advocacy for the child, respect for the constitutional or other legal rights of all involved, and attention to the accountability of staff.

Once it is created, the manual must be maintained and periodically reviewed for possible revision. As new statutes and regulations are promulgated, it may become necessary to withdraw, revise, or add new policies and guidelines. Policies, even though optional when adopted, can become mandatory and lead to legal liability if not followed. Not having a manual is preferable to having an erroneous, dated, or unclear manual.

POLICIES WITH RESPECT TO OTHER AGENCIES

A process of study, consultation, and cooperation is also needed in interagency meetings, whether on a city, county or state basis. For example, in Washington, D.C., the Mayor's Advisory Committee on Child Abuse and Neglect has several subcommittees, one of which focuses on interagency cooperation and reviews the various public and private agencies' policies and procedures for their impact on each other and on children and families. One of the major tasks of this subcommittee has been to stimulate the development of memoranda of agreement between agencies, including one between the public agencies from all jurisdictions in the District of Columbia, Maryland, and Virginia encompassed by the Washington, D.C., metropolitan area. The team lawyer can be called to draft, negotiate, and review interagency agreements, interrelating statutes and regulations, in ways that enhance rather than restrict cooperation.

Professional Education

Some of the issues of training and education are treated elsewhere in this book. The attorney's specific role is briefly reviewed in this section.

ORIENTATION OF NEW STAFF

Team members learn a great deal from each other merely by participating in case staffings. When new members join a team, they may or may not have had ready access to a lawyer whose responsibility it is to be available for meeting with them whenever the attorney is needed. The attorney will want team members to become good consumers of the law, meaning that each team member will develop a basic understanding of the variety of legal options usually available in a case, and the degree to which attorneys in the case appear to be performing competently.

The team attorney will also want team members to be in contact early when an important legal issue arises. This approach reduces the chances of error, increases the legal options that are likely to be available, and allows the lawyer to act "preventively" in a risk management sense. By reaching out to new team members with a chance to sit down and talk or even join classes and orientations that the lawyer may be teaching, each of these areas can be comfortably addressed for the new team member.

IN-SERVICE REVIEWS OF PROCEDURES

Changes in statutory and case law should be routinely brought to the attention of team members by the lawyer. Similarly, if it becomes clear that certain areas are presenting difficulty, for example, confidentiality, civil-criminal coordination, cooperation with other committees or teams, or court preparation, the attorney should provide in-service reviews of these procedures. If such reviews of important legal developments already take place routinely, for example, by participation in journal clubs or grand rounds, the need for special reviews will probably decrease.

CIRCULATING ARTICLES FOR INFORMATION

Depending on the number of formal presentations, staff meeting presentations, journal club activities, grand rounds and similar activities carried out by the team lawyer, it may be appropriate simply to circulate new cases, statutes or other developments, with or without commentary. This will alert staff members to query the lawyer if the materials are not clear or to raise questions about current procedures.

FORMAL PRESENTATIONS

Much can be said for a setting in which scholarship that is linked to practice is the norm for all professionals. The child protection team attorney who has the opportunity to give formal presentations should present cogent updates of developments within the law. Questions that arise in research for, or presentation of, such materials will increase the chances that the team attorney will have anticipated new or complicated developments. Child welfare law, health law, and malpractice, to mention just a few areas, are rapidly developing as specialties. No team attorney should miss bringing the importance of new developments in children's law to team members and help them apply the new knowledge to their work.

PUBLICATIONS

There is a need for those involved in representing over 900 child protection teams in the United States to share their experiences, failures and successes. Publication is one of the few methods for sharing professional experience in a nation the size of the United States. Even a single publication will encourage contact from colleagues and a chance to share ideas, approaches and trends.

Research

Research on child protection intervention is greatly needed, and indeed outcome assessment should become routine within the field. The rarity of this form of monitoring is such that outcome assessments may constitute an important source of insights.

REVIEW OF RESEARCH PROTOCOLS

Many legal and ethical concerns are raised when research on human subjects is undertaken. If the child protection team or its sponsoring agency applies for federal funds, whether or not the funds are specifically for research purposes, the agency must comply with federal regulations for the protection of human subjects. The attorney should be consulted both for a review of current requirements, and to review the research protocol for compliance. For example, the informed consent of parents and the assent of a child old enough to understand the research will have to be obtained. If the child is no longer in parental custody, a number of complex issues may arise. A guardian *ad litem*, guardian, or court may or may not be required to provide informed consent to the child's involvement.

LEGAL OUTCOME RESEARCH

Since the court process is often an important variable in child protection cases, the team lawyer is helpful in analyzing the meaning of certain legal outcomes. The possibility of monitoring legal outcomes may depend on such variables as state requirements for maintaining pertinent information. For example, the state central registry may or may not permit feedback about the case outcome to a reporter. If the harm to the child was caused by nonfamiliars, the tracking mechanism will necessarily be different.

The attorney may be the individual assigned the role of collecting outcome data, as is true for the team at Children's Hospital National Medical Center in Washington, D.C. The data are entered in the child's record and statistically aggregated in formats that identify the jurisdiction and type of maltreatment. Other data recorded include whether or not a case was reported to authorities, the reason if not reported, the outcome of the official investigation, and the outcome in the family and criminal courts.

Witness Preparation

Since many of the cases before the child protection team are eventually presented in court, the attorney can be of great assistance in preparing testimony. The attorney may need to determine whether the guardian *ad litem* has prepared the child victim and any child witnesses for the trial, including a tour of the courtroom and a general role play of testimony. If not, the CPT attorney can meet with the child and team clinician and prepare the child. Frequently, young children have no idea what court is like. The attorney may be able to draw analogies to situations with which the child is familiar. For example, a child may be told that court is comparable to an adult trying to find out what caused a dispute between two children at school or at home, except that the judge wears a robe, the attorneys ask questions, there is a person keeping a record of what is happening, and other formalities. Older children may have distorted ideas of court from popular television shows and dramas, or may be fearful of court. The attorney must assess the child's cognitive and emotional functioning, perhaps with the help of an expert, prior to engaging in role play.

Young children usually have to demonstrate competency to testify. This involves questions from the lawyers or the judge seeking answers that indicate that the child can understand questions, respond in an articulate and accurate fashion, recall facts from memory, know the difference between "telling a lie" and "what really happened," and understand the obligation of telling the truth. The attorney for the team may be able to help the child establish competency without requiring the child to relate factual details of events that are the subject of the court proceeding. Coordinating with other attorneys will prevent unnecessary contact with the child and avoid confusion.

The CPT lawyer may also have to help prepare a team member who has been called to testify. The team member can be taught a number of skills for witnesses, such as refreshing one's memory from notes, how to be clear in testimony, and how to alert the court and other attorneys if a question may create confusion or mislead the factfinder. The possible tactics of opposing attorneys, what to do during objections and discussions between lawyers at the judge's bench, the approach to qualifying the witness as an expert, or other relevant events at trial can be explored in anticipation. Again, role play is one way of working with the less experienced witness.

One of the most important roles the attorney has with respect to team witnesses is in responding to inappropriate use of the professional. Improperly served subpoenas have special significance if the attorney seeking the witness has been non-supportive. The CPT attorney may have to help the team member alert the appropriate lawyers that they have not prepared a witness on the factual or legal issues, have not formed a working relationship with the witness, or have failed to give the witness a reasonable opportunity to provide the testimony or other expected evidence at court.

Summary

The essence of teamwork in child protection is for each professional to recognize the importance of other disciplines for assuring the safety of children at risk.   Working together daily produces individuals with expert skills, and the ability to help colleagues raise issues and ask questions outside one's own specialty. This increases the thoroughness and accountability on behalf of the children and families served, colleagues, and employing institutions.

Notes

* However, one state provides that the team attorney can be neither guardian ad litem for the child nor counsel for the parents in a case before the team. Moreover, Colorado Revised Statutes Sect. 19-10-103(2) provides that the team attorney can be neither guardian ad litem for the child nor counsel for the parents.

** Of 42 county-based child protection teams in Colorado in 1983, 35 had volunteer lawyers also representing the child protective services agency.[10]

References

1.   "Legal Representation of Child Welfare Agencies." *Legal Response: Child Advocacy and Protection,* 3(1983):1, 14-15.

2.   Bourne, R. "The Role of Attorneys on Hospital Child Abuse Teams." *Chicago-Kent Law Review,* 54(1978):773-784.

3.   Code of Professional Responsibility, Ethical Considerations 7-5, 7-7, 7-8 and 7-9.

4.   Weisberg, R., and M. Wald. "Confidentiality Laws and State Efforts to Protect Abused or Neglected Children: The Need for Statutory Reform." *Family Law Quarterly,* 18(1984):143-212.

5.   Besharov, D. *Criminal and Civil Liability in Child Welfare Work: The Growing Trend*. Washington, D.C.: American Bar Association, 1984.

6.   Wolfe, D.A., et al. "The Importance of Adjudication in the Treatment of Child Abusers: Some Preliminary Findings." *Child Abuse & Neglect*, 4(1980):127-136.

7.   *In re S.*, 66 Misc. 2d 683, 322 NYS 2d 170 (Fam Ct. 1970).

8.   *In the Matter of Tara H., New York Law Journal*, Friday, October 19, 1984.

9.   Miller, L.M. "Principles of *res ipsa loquitur* Apply to Proof of Child Abuse and Neglect." *Texas Tech Law Review*, 9(1977-78):355.

10.   Motz, J. *Colorado's Community-Based Child Protection Teams*. Denver: Colorado Department of Social Services, 1984.

23. Team Recommendations and the Courts

Dana U. Wakefield and
Jon L. Lawritson

Introduction

Child protection teams staff cases with many legal implications. The team may be asked to submit a report or provide testimony relevant to civil or criminal matters. Just as individual expert witnesses must be aware of courtroom considerations, team members must understand and prepare to support the court's decision-making role.

Types of Legal Proceedings

Issues surrounding the care and custody of children are presented in several types of court actions. While courts with jurisdiction over matters of probate may be concerned with children's issues, e.g. when a parent or guardian of a child has died, the vast majority of court orders affecting children are issued in criminal, domestic relations, or dependency and neglect cases. All three of the latter types of cases can occur at the same time, involve the same child, and be in different courts, yet each action differs from the others in significant ways. Each action proceeds largely independently of the others, although an issue of custody will ultimately be decided by the court having jurisdiction over the child. The criminal court does not have jurisdiction to enter custody orders and the domestic relations court must forego its jurisdiction over custody aspects of a case if dependency and neglect action is also pending in court. If no dependency and neglect action is pending in court involving the same child, then the domestic relations court possesses the authority to enter custody orders. In the following chapter, Table 24.1 summarizes the distinctions between civil and criminal proceedings.

CRIMINAL CASES INVOLVING WRONGS AGAINST CHILDREN

A criminal case is initiated through a law enforcement agency and by a prosecutor, such as a district attorney. In order for a criminal court to have jurisdiction, a wrong against a child must have been committed which violates the statutory proscriptions against specified conduct. When the perpetrator is arrested, he will be advised of his rights by a judge or other judicial officer and bond will be set to ensure that the perpetrator, if released, will return for court hearings. Before the defendant is required to plead either guilty or not guilty, he is entitled to force the prosecution to show its hand and to produce to the court sufficient evidence to establish probable cause that the defendant committed the offense. At this preliminary hearing, the defendant has his first opportunity to hear the testimony of witnesses who may be called to testify against him at trial; the child may or may not have to be one of the witnesses at the preliminary hearing. If the prosecution is able to establish probable cause, the defendant will then be called upon to plead either guilty, in which case the matter will be set for sentencing without further evidentiary hearings, or not guilty, in which case the matter will be set for a full trial.

The court may be requested before trial to make rulings concerning what evidence will be allowed at trial or consider other preliminary matters. These preliminary motions hearings may involve testimony of witnesses or only legal argument. Because the sentence for violating the criminal laws may include a deprivation of the defendant's liberty, the defendant cannot be convicted of the offense unless the prosecution is able to produce so much evidence that the fact finder, the judge or the jury, is convinced beyond a reasonable doubt of the defendant's guilt. The burden of proving the case beyond a reasonable doubt is one which is especially difficult for the prosecution in cases involving wrongs to children. Wrongs to children are usually not committed in the presence of anyone other than the child, and there may be little or no physical evidence available to corroborate the child's testimony, assuming the child is old enough to testify or communicate effectively. The defendant cannot be called as a witness nor made to testify against himself. He may, however, be required to give what is called non-testimonial evidence such as his fingerprints, handwriting, blood samples, hair clippings, bite mark impression, or other physical evidence.

While society's interest in protecting children is the impetus for the passage of criminal laws against abusing, molesting, or otherwise wronging a child, it is the "mere fact" that the criminal law has been broken that is the focus of the criminal case. Society, the "people," whose laws have been broken, is the only party in the case other than the defendant—the perpetrator of the wrongdoing. The wronged child is not even a party to a criminal case, and generally is not represented by his own legal counsel; the victim child is but a witness in the case just as any victim of a burglary, robbery, etc. As with any other witness, the child usually can be protected on the witness stand only by the prosecuting attorney who calls the child as a witness or by the court, which has the authority to protect any witness from abuse on the witness stand.[1] Victim advocates and therapists, however, may be able to ease the child's anxiety before, after and sometimes during the trial.

If the defendant either pleads guilty or is found guilty at trial of committing the offense against the child, the court must determine and order the appropriate sentence. A criminal sentence is designed to deter the conduct which the violated law proscribes, to rehabilitate the perpetrator, and to punish the perpetrator when the interests of the public protection so require. The interests of the child are considered in criminal sentencing only to the extent that those interests may interplay with one of the purposes for which criminal sentencing is designed. The sentences may range from long prison terms to probation with terms and conditions requiring the defendant to participate in rehabilitative therapy, etc. The sentencing court does not have authority to order treatment for the child, who may have suffered as a result of the defendant's conduct, nor to order participation in treatment by any other family members whose conduct or condition may have played an integral part in the dynamics that gave rise to the criminal act or its aftermath.

Any commentary is left to the reader in pondering the fact that in criminal cases, the child is not a party and is almost never represented by his own legal representative even though the child's interests may be affected substantially by having to testify, or by having his parent or some other significant person in his life sentenced to prison for years.

DIVORCE

In domestic relations cases, also known as divorce or dissolution of marriage, parents are basically disputing their own relationship. The law protects the child's interests by allowing him to be represented by a legal representative, a guardian *ad litem*, if the court determines that such representation would be appropriate.[2] The purpose of a domestic relations action in court is the settlement of the dispute between the parties who are separating; the child's custody may be only one of several matters in dispute. The court's authority will be limited to resolving contested issues of custody, visitation, and support of the child. The best interests of the child are the guiding test for the court in determining issues of custody and visitation.

A child's custody and visitation may be determined temporarily by the court at a temporary orders hearing when the parties first separate and initially bring the contest to the court; thereafter, permanent orders will be entered when the dissolution of marriage is approved at a later hearing. In determining custody and visitation at the permanent orders hearing, the court is not bound by its temporary orders entered earlier in the proceedings. Even after the permanent orders hearing, a change of custody and/or visitation can be ordered by the court if a motion requesting such change is filed with the court and if sufficient changes can be shown to the court to warrant a modification.

Even where no marital dispute is at issue, the court can be asked to enter a custody order, but only by certain people who have significant involvement with the child. In any domestic relations court action, it is the choice of custodian and surrounding issues of visitation and support that are within the power of the court to effect and not any issues of treatment for either the child or other family members.

DEPENDENCY AND NEGLECT

Unlike domestic relations or criminal cases, actions in dependency and neglect focus specifically on the child and his status, needs, and best interests. However, if it cannot be shown by at least a preponderance of the evidence that the child is in the status known as dependent or neglected, then the court has no further involvement and the case is dismissed.

Because the dependency or neglect of a child is considered in law to be a matter of state interest, it is the state or its agent which must bring the court action. Usually, the petitioner is a state or local social service department of the government which brings the action and which serves as the plaintiff.[3]

Because the sole question in the case is the status of the child, there is no defendant in the action. The child's condition or status may not be the fault of any particular person; therefore, no person is on trial for wrongs to the child. Where there is fault that could be assessed for causing the dependency or neglect of the child, the perpetrator may be a party to the action so that the court can control that person's activities vis-à-vis the child. Parents, of course, because it is their child who is being subjected to court intervention, are necessarily parties to the action. The child, too, because he or she is the central focus of the action, is an indispensable party to the action as well. Any other person with a significant interest in the welfare of the child, or who sufficiently impacts on the child, may be required to be or may request to be made a party to the case. In short, anyone over whom the court believes it is necessary to have authority in order to carry out the court's obligations to act in the child's best interest may be included as a party to a dependency of neglect action.

A court may only act to order involved persons to do or to refrain from doing certain things if it has been proven to the court that the child is dependent or neglected. As plaintiff, the social services department has the burden of presenting evidence to the court to prove that the child is a dependent or neglected child. In order for the court to continue to be involved, a preponderance of the evidence presented must establish the dependency or neglect of the child. There will be a trial to establish whether the child is dependent or neglected only if the parties to the action do not agree that the child is dependent or neglected. Any party to the action who disagrees with the claim that the child is dependent or neglected may request a trial.

The guardian *ad litem* is the legal representative of the child who is charged with the responsibility of seeking through court action that which will best serve the interests of the child. The guardian *ad litem* aligns himself with either the plaintiff who believes the child to be dependent or neglected or with the party opposing that position. The guardian may even participate in the trial without having made a determination of whether the child is dependent or neglected or with the party opposing that position. The guardian may even participate in the trial without having made a determination of whether the child is dependent or neglected until he has heard the evidence presented at trial. The guardian may approach the case independently, for example, by seeking to introduce a different evidentiary or discovery basis for legal proceedings with respect to the child's interests.

Dependency and Neglect Procedures

A trial does not take place immediately after a dependency or neglect action is filed. Before the parties can take a position in the case, it may be necessary for them to "discover" what each of the other parties has for evidence. As with any civil court action, the parties may engage in discovery proceedings to ascertain the evidence of the other parties.

Before trial, a pretrial conference is usually held at which the parties can discuss and attempt to resolve preliminary matters, and at which the court can rule on various evidentiary matters and direct the parties in the conduct of their discovery and of their preparation for trial. The only parties involved at the pretrial and trial stages are, usually, the plaintiff department of social services, the child through his guardian *ad litem*, and the parents or custodians of the child. Other interested parties may be permitted to participate after it has been determined that the child is a dependent or neglected child.

Before a determination at trial is reached as to whether or not a child is dependent or neglected, it is almost always necessary for the court to enter interim orders concerning the child's custody and other matters relating to the child's care. These temporary orders may include the removal of the child from the home and the placing of custody of the child with the department of social services or with some other agency or person.

Once it has been determined, either by trial or by agreement or admission of all of the involved parties, that the child is dependent or neglected, the court is obligated by law in many states, to approve a treatment plan designed to correct the circumstances that gave rise to the dependency and neglect of the child. The goal of treatment planning is to provide proper care for the child, preferably in his own home. If that is not possible, then the child should be in the most appropriate out-of-home placement while the court continues to assist the child's parents or former custodians to become better caretakers themselves. A child may not be removed or retained away from his home unless it can be shown to be necessary, not just advisable. "Necessary" in this context is usually not specifically defined by law and is considered a legal "term of art."

When treatment planning is unsuccessful the court may be asked to order the termination of the parent-child legal relationship. Fundamentally fair process is due the parents in such proceedings. This due process usually includes, among other things, the right to be represented by a lawyer, to have a full hearing before the court, and in at least some states, to employ an expert to independently evaluate the situation. Because the remedy being requested of the court is so much more drastic in a termination hearing than at the hearing to determine whether the child is dependent or neglected, termination of the parent-child legal relationship can be ordered by the court only if the party requesting termination can convince the court by clear and convincing evidence—evidence which is substantially more convincing than a preponderance of evidence but less than proof beyond a reasonable doubt.[4]

If termination of the parent-child legal relationship is ordered by the court, the child may be placed for adoption. In no other involuntary court action does any court have the authority to terminate parents' rights. In domestic relations actions, the court can change custody, but the legal relationship between the parent and child cannot be severed, except in some instances of stepparent adoptions. In criminal cases involving wrongs against children, the court does not even have the authority to enter or change custody orders.

Information Common to Civil and Criminal Proceedings

The cardinal rule for teams when communicating with the court is to share *all* relevant information. The quality of the decision by a judge is directly related to the quality and quantity of information given to the judge. If there is any doubt, an error in favor of sharing rather than withholding information should be made.

To prepare properly for the number of hearings scheduled in one day, most judges in busy courts will at a minimum be required to read 50 to 100 pages. Therefore, a much appreciated format for reports to the court is a succinct summary with supporting details attached as a supplement to the summary report. The judge can then quickly grasp an overall view of the situation and also have readily available detailed information to support conclusions or opinions. The manner in which a report is provided to the court will depend on many factors. A team may be court-ordered to provide the report. The team may work for an agency which is a party or has statutory authority to move a case. The team may be requested by an attorney, individual or agency to staff a case, and then the attorney, individual, or agency will have the responsibility of trying to introduce or block introduction of the team's report. The team which has a report to give which will not be offered into evidence should explore its options with legal counsel.

In all proceedings when abuse or neglect are issues, the judge or prosecuting attorney at some stage of the proceeding will need certain information. The information contained in Table 23.1 is common to all such proceedings and should be considered minimal.

Table 23.1
Information for the Court

A. If there has been *physical injury* to a child:
    1. Results of physical examination;
    2. Results of x-rays;
    3. Results of laboratory tests;
    4. Color photographs;
    5. Injury history given by:

        a. Mother
        b. Father
        c. Child
        d. Witnesses
        e. Police

B. History of each parent or adult household member
1. Was parent abused or deprived as a child? When and how?
2. Record of mental illness. When diagnosed? Prior hospitalizations?
3. Difficulties with the law. When? Type (assaults, drug abuse, alcohol related)?
4. Prior reports of abuse or neglect.
5. Violent temper outbursts toward child or other family members.
6. None of the above.

C. How do parents view child or children?
1. Inappropriate or rigid expectations;
2. Harsh or unusual punishments;
3. Child seen as difficult or provocative;
4. Child unwanted;
5. Very appropriate view of children.

D. Crisis or stress in family at present
1. Type.
2. Length of presence of stress.

E. Socially isolated family or socially active family?
1. Give example to support conclusion.

F. Name, address, phone number of all witnesses with information and a summary of their probable testimony.

INFORMATION SPECIFIC TO DIFFERENT TYPES OF LEGAL PROCEEDINGS

Some data are more relevant to one type of legal proceeding than another. Again, the information found in Table 23.2 should be considered minimal information. One of the best methods for determining the best format and most useful information for a particular judge is to ask that judge. A judge with whom you deal frequently may welcome the opportunity to provide you with an outline similar to that contained in this section of the handbook or you might use these outlines as discussion springboards.

Table 23.2
Proceeding-Specific Information for the Courts

A. Dependency and Neglect
    1. Why safety of child can't be insured in home.
        a. Crisis situation needs to be calmed;
        b. Severe mental illness in home;
        c. Will not allow anyone in home;
        d. No one to care for child;
        e. Violent person in home needs treatment commenced;
        f. Parent needs to obtain parenting skills, i.e., failure to thrive;
        g. Child needs special care not available in home;
        h. Age of child;
        i. Other.
    2. Available alternative methods of insuring safety of child other than by removal from home.
    3. Length of child's probable stay away from home.
    4. Other children in home and their probable safety.
    5. Treatment plan for all members of household.
B. Domestic
    1. Comparison of parents.
        a. Strengths;
        b. Weaknesses;
        c. Practical ability to care for child;
        d. Actual caretaker if awarded custody;
        e. Interaction with children.
    2. Recommendation regarding custody.
    3. Need for dependency and neglect filing.
C. Criminal
    1. Specific information regarding alleged perpetrator:
        a. His statements;
        b. Why he did abuse;
        c. Criminal history
        d. Physical surroundings of abuse;
        e. Implements used during abuse.
    2. Statement of child and others.
    3. Name, address and phone number and summary of all witnesses;
    4. Appropriate sentence, if convicted.

Additional Issues

Teams are often faced with specific problem areas when dealing with courts. Possible issues include the following:

MINORITY REPORTS

Because, by their very nature, teams represent many individuals from various disciplines, it is not unusual to have a disagreement about conclusions and opinions that should be expressed to the court. If there are, for example, five team members, it certainly would not be particularly helpful to a judge to receive five separate reports with five separate opinions. However, if three team members favor one conclusion and two favor another, there is certainly no reason why both of those divergent views should not be expressed. Obviously, the team member writing the summary report should be a member of the majority opinion. That person should be very careful, however, to point out specifically the differing minority view. A caveat should be made at this point. It is very likely that if the majority and minority view are presented in a report, each of the team members will be subpoenaed into court to testify individually.

ATTORNEYS AT STAFFINGS

Not infrequently, there is a request by a guardian *ad litem* or by an attorney representing the parents to be present either during the evaluation or at a staffing following individual evaluations. While it is certainly appropriate for a team to indicate to an attorney that his presence during an evaluation could disrupt the evaluation and make it invalid, it is generally best to accommodate reasonable requests. The use of one-way mirrors or the use of videotapes may be helpful in meeting requests to view the individual evaluations. If the presence of an attorney is inhibiting the free discussion by all members of the team at a staffing, this should be brought to the attention of the attorney and there is certainly nothing wrong with asking him to leave during a particularly sensitive discussion. Generally, requests from attorneys should be accommodated because the attorney in most instances will be able to obtain a court order to attend both the evaluation and the staffings.

TESTIMONY

Whether acting as individuals or representing a team, witnesses should be completely familiar with the considerations stated in the following chapter on the expert witness.

Summary

Team documents and procedures should reflect the possibility of courtroom presentations. Just as an individual prepares for testimony, a team must be prepared to offer reports that are objective, detailed and relevant to the specific legal issues to be determined. Clear, focused reports will usually have the greatest impact.

References

1. See, however, *State of New Hampshire v. Walsh*, 495 A.2d 1256 (N.H., 1985). The New Hampshire Supreme Court ruled it was not reversible error for the guardian *ad litem* for a child-victim-witness to sit at the prosecutor's table during a criminal sexual assault trial.

2   The states of Wisconsin and New Hampshire require appointment of a guardian *ad litem* in divorce custody disputes.

3. Some states provide that *any* individual may bring a matter of possible child abuse or neglect to the court's attention by merely requesting a hearing, as distinct from commencing a formal legal proceeding through the filing of a petition. See, for example, Colorado Revised Statutes, Section 19-3-101(2).

4. The Indian Child Welfare Act imposes a higher standard of proof in adjudications and terminations affecting Native American children.

24. The Expert Witness: Social Work, Medical, Psychiatric[1]

Ann M. Haralambie and
Donna A. Rosenberg

Introduction

Expert opinion testimony is admissible where the expert's specialized knowledge will assist the trier of fact (the jury, or in a non-jury case, the judge) in understanding the evidence or determining a fact in issue.[2] The witness may be qualified as an expert by knowledge, skill, experience, training or education.[3] To be effective the expert needs to be skilled in the substantive area of the witness's expertise and in the art of testifying. In addition to these skills, the expert needs adequate data concerning the case and adequate communication with the attorney.

While it is the attorney's job to elicit testimony from the witness, an expert who relies on the attorney to know what is relevant and to ask the right questions may leave the courthouse with great frustration at not having communicated the most important information to the court. Attorneys ought to contact and prepare their witnesses before trial, but often they do not. The witness's irritation at the attorney should not be allowed to hamper the testimony, which is generally offered in support of the child's welfare. Therefore, the expert should not hesitate to take the initiative in contacting and educating the attorney, and to insist upon an explanation by the attorney of the legal issues and procedures involved.

RESPONSIBILITIES OF THE EXPERT WITNESS

The expert witness, in contrast to the non-expert witness, is permitted to render an opinion (interpretation) based upon a foundation (data). This privilege is accompanied by certain responsibilities. An expert may testify in cases where he has first-hand, in-depth, knowledge of a child and/or his family, or, at the other extreme, may testify in cases where his knowledge of those cases is limited to a review of other people's records. In either situation, it is the responsibility of the expert to familiarize himself as thoroughly as possible with the facts of the case, but the expert testifying on the basis of other people's records alone is especially cautioned that he may not be able to ensure that the records are complete or, indeed, accurate.

The responsibilities of the medical expert have been aptly stated by Brent,[4] apply to other experts, and are summarized here:

1. The testimony provided should be similar whether one is testifying for the plaintiff or defense, otherwise one is presenting partisan testimony.
2. The expert witness should be a scholar in that field or related fields, and be familiar with and have contributed to the literature in that field.
3. He should be an active or recently active investigator in a field, if testifying on research matters. He should be an active or recently active clinician in a field, if testifying on clinical matters.
4. His role as an expert witness should be a minimal part of his professional activity. One cannot be a professional expert witness, inasmuch as the main activities of an expert witness should be those of a scholar, clinician, teacher, or investigator in the field of his expertise.
5. He should be aware of the legal and ethical impact and importance of his testimony.
6. He should be aware of the basic elements of the law and the legal procedures with which he will be involved.
7. He must understand that it is not his job to win the case and, therefore, he must avoid becoming consumed by the adversarial atmosphere of the legal process.
8. He is obliged to obtain all the facts from the attorneys and clients so as not to be surprised by information late in the legal process. Frequently, attorneys are reluctant to provide expert witnesses with damaging information. It is important that the expert witness makes it clear to the attorney that he must have all the information.

9. He must avoid being manipulated by the attorney into becoming a partisan. It is the attorney's role to win a case by any legal means. The expert witness must refrain from becoming involved in this process.

10. He must remember that his testimony will affect the outcome of the trial and may prevent injured parties from receiving compensation, may ruin the lives of innocent defendants and their families, may destroy the reputations of individuals or families, or may financially destroy an individual or a family. The expert witness should never forget this burdensome responsibility.

11. Above all, he must remember that he is an expert, a scholar—not a lawyer, not a judge, and not a jailer.

Understanding the Issues

The expert witness in a child abuse case may be called to testify in a civil and/or criminal proceeding. Table 24.1 outlines the basic differences between these two court settings.

Table 24.1
Comparison of Civil vs. Crimal Child Abuse Proceedings

	Civil	*Criminal*
Purpose	Protect child and treat family	Punishment Rehabilitation Deterence
Law	State Child Protection Law; Case Law	State Criminal Codes for Specific Crimes (example: Misdemeanor or felony child abuse, etc.); Case Law
Issue	The child was dependent and neglected or abused	That a specific individual injured the child at a particular time
Lawyers Present	1) County or District Attorney (represents the Department of Social Services)	1) Prosecutor aka District Attorney (prosecutes cases; represents "the People")

	2) Guardian *ad litem* (represents best interests of the child; may or may not be a lawyer)	2) Defense Attorney— either a Pubic Defender or privately hired counsel
	3) Attorney(s) representing parent(s) (grandparents, etc.)	3) Guardian *ad litem* (representing best interest of defendant if a juvenile)
Trier of Fact	Judge (may have jury for adjudication hearing)	Judge (preliminary hearing); Judge and/or jury (trial)
Burden of Proof	Preponderance of evidence (dependency and neglect petitions); Clear and convincing evidence (termination of parental rights)	Evidence beyond a reasonable doubt
Maximum	Removal of the child from the parents; termination of parental rights	Imprisonment (or death, if defendant convicted of first degree murder in certain states)

To determine what is relevant to the attorney, the expert will need to know something about the legal issues involved. For example, in a custody case, the best interests of the child are of paramount importance. However, in a termination of parental rights case, the parents' constitutional rights, the public policy favoring family integrity, and the statutory requirements must all be balanced against the child's best interests. Therefore, testimony that the child's adoption by a third party would best serve the child's interests is not relevant, while testimony of the parent's inabilities or abusive actions are relevant. Similarly, a diagnosis alone of the parent's mental illness will not prove anything; it is necessary to show the *effect* of that mental illness on the parent's caretaking abilities and treatment of the child and the resultant or anticipated adverse outcome on the child. The prognosis for the family is usually very important, and the availability of supplemental and rehabilitative services may affect the outcome of the case. Where the parent and the state, or some other third party, are litigating the issue of parental unfitness, the expert needs to evaluate the situation based on fairly low standards of adequacy, rather than on clinical standards of good parenting.

The expert must understand what must be proven legally and what options are available. Sometimes there are factual issues: whether a parent has sexually, physically, or emotionally abused or neglected a child, with whom a child desires to live, or whether a party is mentally retarded. Sometimes there are diagnostic issues: whether an injury could have been sustained in the manner described by the parent, how a parent's mental or physical disability affects his or her parenting skills or whether a parent is mentally ill.

The attorney will usually know the factual issues and some of the diagnostic issues. The expert should ask the attorney to clarify these so that the witness will know the legal posture of the case, what must be determined, and how the expert's testimony fits into the entire scheme of the case.

Preparation for Court

DOCUMENTATION

When a professional who is going to be called as the expert witness has seen any or all members of a family in which abuse or neglect is suspected, the single most important way for that witness to prepare for court is to ensure that complete documentation has been undertaken. Any professional who becomes involved in a possible child abuse/neglect case must assume that court involvement is a possibility and should, therefore, prepare his records in accordance with that assumption. This means that the record must contain all the information gathered (subjective and objective), an assessment, and a plan.

The professional's document should be planned with the following construct in mind:

(1)   Letterhead stationery is preferable.
(2)   All reports should be dated with the time, the day, the month and the year. If there is a difference between the time the patient or client was seen by the professional and the time the report was made, this should be noted.
(3)   The person(s) seen and/or examined by the professional should be identified by as many of the following as possible: name (given name and surname, any known aliases); date of birth; address; phone number; hospital or clinic number.
(4)   The place at which the patient or client was seen and the mode or reason for the professional's examination should be

noted. If a child suspected of being abused or neglected is seen, any accompanying adults should be identified in the report.

(5) The body of information will vary depending upon the professional preparing the document. Medical documentation may include some or all of the following: chief complaint, the history of the present illness, the past medical history, the review of systems, the family history, the social history, the physical examination findings, laboratory data (including blood tests, x-rays, or other tests). Psychiatric data may include the findings on a mental status examination and/or other observations about the patient. A social worker's document may include data concerning the structure and function of the family or any of its members.

(6) An assessment based upon the data outlined in the document is indicated, including the professional's reasons for coming to any conclusions.

(7) The professional's actions taken and recommended plan should be noted.

(8) The identification of the professional should be clear from the document.

In addition to written documentation, audiotapes, videotapes and photographs may be part of the formal record. Written documentation must be legible. Audiotapes, videotapes and photographs must be of sufficient quality to permit comprehension by other parties. Any laws on the confidentiality of written documents pertain equally to the other forms of documentation aforementioned.

EDUCATING THE ATTORNEY ABOUT THE WITNESS

It is important for the judge or jury to be informed about the witness's qualifications. Since the attorney must ask the questions, the expert must first give this information to the attorney and explain its significance.

It may be helpful to educate the attorney about the profession itself, especially in the case of non-physicians. A judge needs to know what a social worker, a psychiatric social worker, or a psychiatric nurse is. Many courts do not know what kind of training social workers have, especially the types of classes and internships they take. Because the term "social worker" does not necessarily imply a particular degree, social work experts must convey this information to the attorney. The attorney needs to know the differences between psychologists with degrees in psychology, education, or counseling and guidance. It is important to know the requirements of admission to the profession.

If the expert is a member of any professional societies, the attorney should know whether any member of the profession may join or whether more rigorous prerequisites must be met. Similarly, board certification, listing on national registries, and other indications of the witness's standing in the profession should be explained to the attorney.

Questions that are commonly asked to qualify an expert witness are outlined in Table 24.2.

Table 24.2
Qualifying the Expert Witness*

The series of questions that follows are representative of the kinds of questions that may be asked to qualify an expert witness:

Q.   "Please tell the court your name and your occupation or profession."

Q.   "Where are you presently engaged in the practice of (your profession)?"

Q.   "Where do you maintain your offices?"

Q.   "Are you licensed to practice (profession) in this state?"

Q.   "When did you receive your license to practice (profession)?"

Q.   "What professional degrees have you been awarded?"

Q.   "When were these degrees received and from what schools were they received?"

Q.   "Following your graduation from (name of school most recently graduated from), have you received any additional professional training?"

Q.   "Please tell the court when this training was received, the nature of the training, its duration, and the place of the training."

Q.   "Are you a member of any (professional) associations or societies?"

Q.   "Have you ever taught or written any professional articles?"

Q.   "Following your graduation from (name of school most recently graduated from), where have you engaged in the practice of (profession) and for what periods of time?"

Q.   "During this time, how many (evaluations have you performed/ children have you treated) in the practice of (profession)?"

Q.   "When and in what court have you been previously qualified?"

Q.   "In what areas have you been qualified?"

*Courtesy of John MacDonald, M.D., Professor of Psychiatry, University of Colorado School of Medicine

It is often helpful for the witness to supply the attorney with an up-to-date curriculum vitae and publications list. Anything that is particularly noteworthy should be pointed out and explained.

It is helpful for the witness to review his or her publications before testifying, because the opposing attorney may use any inconsistencies between the expert's position in the publications and the trial testimony to impeach the witness during cross-examination.

If the witness has testified in similar cases, the attorney should know that and should also know whether there has been a pattern to the testimony. For example, an expert who generally testifies on behalf of fathers may have diminished impact in another father's rights case, but may have enhanced impact when testifying on behalf of a mother. Similarly, an expert who frequently testifies on behalf of the Department of Social Services may be more persuasive when testifying for a parent than testifying, yet again, for the state agency. Any time a witness testifies contrary to his or her general bias, that fact should be made known to the attorney. On the other hand, the expert should be prepared to explain why a different position is being taken in the current case.

EDUCATING THE ATTORNEY ABOUT THE ISSUES

The expert should familiarize the attorney with the general substantive area involved and with the specific information relevant to the issues of the case. It should be assumed that the attorney knows nothing about the substantive area unless the expert has had prior involvement with the attorney. The attorney should be able to understand the expert's significant findings and conclusions and the general methods by which the expert arrived at them. The reasons for ruling out differential diagnoses should also be explained. The expert should provide the attorney with an analysis of the issues and the relevant facts. For example, where one parent is alleged to be mentally ill, the attorney should understand the nature of the mental illness, how it affects parenting abilities, what treatment is available, how treatment will affect parenting abilities, and the anticipated course and length of treatment.

In contested cases, it is important for the attorney to be aware of treatises, articles, and research studies that support the expert's opinions, as well as any major articles that rebut those opinions. Subjective opinions can be strengthened by showing that there are empirical data to support the opinion. The expert should be prepared to explain why the supporting materials are more persuasive than the opposing materials. Support found in standard texts is particularly helpful.

The expert should provide the attorney with a list of points the expert believes should be made and the significance of those points. It can be very helpful for the expert to prepare a list of questions and answers for the attorney to use at trial. Such lists may ensure that the important information is provided to the court and that the expert understands the questions asked. The expert should always be involved in formulating hypothetical questions.

If the expert cannot *teach* the attorney why certain things are relevant and how they fit together to support the expert's opinions, then it is unlikely that the attorney will be able to persuade the court that the opinions ought to be accepted.

EDUCATING THE ATTORNEY ABOUT THE OPPOSITION

In many cases, each side has its own experts who battle one another in court. In addition to preparing the attorney for making the most out of direct examination, the expert should prepare the attorney for cross-examining the opposing expert.

The first step is the evaluation of the opposing expert's credentials. For example, an expert trained to counsel basically normal clients with family problems may not be sufficiently trained to diagnose or treat clients who are seriously mentally ill. Few therapists have experience or training in working with intrafamilial sexual abuse cases. A family internist may have little experience diagnosing intentionally inflicted injuries in children. An opposing expert who comes from a perspective on the fringes of the profession may not be accorded much credibility by the court. The expert is in a better position than the attorney to recognize such weaknesses.

The expert should also thoroughly review and critique the opposing expert's test data, evaluation methods, conclusions, and reports. The amount of time spent, extent of background information gathered, omissions, and alternative explanations should be covered. The expert may be permitted to be present during the opposing expert's deposition or court testimony. The expert can then suggest cross-examination questions during the testimony and later point out areas which the expert can rebut during his or her own testimony.

COLLABORATION IN DISCOVERY

The attorney has a number of pretrial tools available to obtain records and other information for use in preparing the case and, under some circumstances, to compel a party to submit to an examination or evaluation. These tools are regrouped together under the term "discovery," and a collaborative effort between the expert and attorney during the discovery phase of pretrial preparation can be beneficial for both.

The expert can ask the attorney to obtain additional information. For example, the opposing expert's reports can be subpoenaed along with files, notes, lab reports, or protocols showing the raw data upon which the expert relied. Similarly, school records, police reports, hospital records, and other documents may be obtained for the expert's use.

Frequently one party declines to be evaluated by the expert. The expert can suggest questions to be asked of that individual during a deposition, and some limited statements may be made by the expert based on the responses. A more formalized approach would include "administering" the Parenting Assessment Discovery Form for Attorneys[5] during a deposition.

The expert may also suggest questions to be addressed to a party by way of written interrogatories. Where the expert wants questions to be answered by non-parties, such as the opposing expert, the questions may be posed during an oral deposition.

Whenever the expert desires more information, the attorney should be advised. Frequently, a discovery procedure will exist to enable the attorney to obtain the needed information. Unlike most professionals, the attorney has the ability to summon court assistance to obtain information.

Finally, the expert can assist the attorney in analyzing and evaluating the information produced by the various discovery procedures. Significant admissions or other information should be highlighted, and the significance should be explained. In this way, the attorney will be better able to present the case at trial.

CONFIDENTIALITY OF DATA

The usual professional-patient or professional-client privilege that exists is abrogated when the case concerns possible child abuse or neglect. First, every state in the United States mandates that certain professionals report suspected child abuse or neglect to a designated agency. In most states there is a penalty to the professional for not reporting. The professional is immune from civil or criminal action taken against him as a result of this report if the report was made "in good faith." The law presumes good faith. Second, for the purposes of court testimony, the professional may not cite privilege in order to conceal data to the court. Again, privilege is abrogated. A subpoena itself, which is issued by the court clerk without a ruling by a judge, does not dispense with the rules of confidentiality. The privilege should be asserted if there is any question.

If there is any question in the professional's mind as to who may access the professional's documents concerning the patient or client, then the professional should consult with his hospital, agency or personal lawyer. In general, the legal guardians of a child, the designated department of social services, the investigating police agency and certain attorneys (the county or district attorney, the guardian *ad litem* for the child) may have access the records.

When a professional is subpoenaed by an attorney, the opposing attorney may request that the professional speak with him prior to the hearing. If the opposing attorney has a valid release of information, then it is up to the professional to decide whether or not to grant the interview. He may decide to do so only if the presence of the attorney who subpoenaed him is also assured, as he may be concerned that he will subsequently be misquoted by opposing counsel.

Testifying in General

The expert's role in court is to provide and interpret information for the judge and/or jury who will evaluate that information and, with consideration of the other evidence at trial, make the final decision. Most of this is done during direct examination, when the expert is questioned by the attorney who has called the witness to testify. An expert whose recommendation is not followed has not failed and should not assume that his expertise was lightly regarded. However, there are some things that the expert can do to enhance the testimony and ensure that its full impact will be communicated to the court.

The witness should make eye contact with the jury, or if there is no jury, with the judge. This may be more difficult that it sounds, because one ordinarily addresses an answer to the one who asks the question. In court, the attorney asks the questions, but it is the trier of fact who needs to hear the answers. By directing the answer to the judge or jury, the witness can gauge whether the answer is understood and can ensure that attention is being paid to the answer, even if only because of common courtesy. It is more difficult for a judge's mind to wander when the witness is making eye contact.

The most important attribute a witness can have is objectivity. It is the *attorney's* job to be an advocate based on the testimony given. Trusting the attorney to advocate will relieve the witness of the dangerous feeling that the testimony itself should be given in an advocacy tone. The witness's demeanor should remain the same, regardless of which attorney is doing the questioning. A witness will lose a good deal of credibility on direct examination by appearing to be overly friendly with or solicitous of the attorney doing the direct examination or hostile towards the opposing attorney.

Experienced witnesses acquire a feel for how long an answer to an open-ended question should continue and pause periodically to allow the attorney to pose another question. If an objection is made, the witness should stop the answer immediately, even in mid-word, and await further direction from the judge. If the judge "sustains" or "allows" the objection, the witness may not give the answer. If the judge "overrules" or "denies" the objection, the witness may continue with the answer. If the witness is unsure of the meaning of the judge's ruling, he may ask the judge whether or not an answer may be given. The witness should never offer objections (for example, stating that something is hearsay); that is the attorney's prerogative. The rules of evidence are more complex than they may seem and are full of exceptions. Many attorneys do not understand the proper bases for objections, and the witness should not presume to do so.

As a final note, it is appropriate for the witness to inform the attorney who has subpoenaed him that he prefers to testify on an on-call basis, if that is at all possible. This means that the witness will make himself available and will respond quickly when called, but this helps the witness spend as little time as possible away from his practice, and may help the attorney reduce witness fees. If it is not possible for the expert to be kept on call, most attorneys are willing to schedule an expert for a convenient time and, perhaps, to call the witness out of order if necessary. The witness should always inform the attorney of any time limitations or conflicts to allow for a more convenient and efficient schedule.

Direct Examination

The witness must understand the difference between the purposes of direct and cross-examination. What is permitted to one attorney may not be permitted to the other. Because leading questions (those which suggest the answer to the witness, such as "isn't it true that . . .") are not permitted during direct examination, the attorney may ask what seem to be unduly vague questions. The witness must understand what the attorney needs to prove and what information must be provided through the witness's testimony. If the witness knows what information he or she is expected to provide, the purpose of the questions will be more readily ascertained, and the witness will not need to ask the embarrassing question, "What are you trying to get at?" Direct examination questions are usually open-ended, allowing the witness to elaborate on an answer.

If the witness is unfamiliar with testifying or with an attorney's style of questioning, it is acceptable for the witness to ask the attorney to rehearse the testimony. The witness should not allow the attorney to provide the substantive answers, but there is nothing wrong with going over particular questions to be asked and the techniques involved in testifying.

If hypothetical questions will be posed during direct examination, the expert should assist the attorney in preparing them in advance and should review the questions prior to trial. If the expert cannot form an opinion based only on the facts presented by the hypothetical question, he should not feel obliged to answer the question. Rather, the witness should state that there are insufficient facts upon which to base an expert opinion. Such a witness gains a great deal of credibility with the judge, who will be more likely to listen to opinions which the expert can state. As much as the witness may want to help a particular side, even the child, he must remain true to the standards of his own profession. If the opinion cannot be stated based on the witness's expert standing, then the opinion should not be expressed.

The witness should be careful not to overstate the case. What are merely clinical impressions should not be solidified into firm diagnoses merely because the opinions are being expressed in a courtroom. Sometimes testimony has a way of taking on a life of its own, and the expert goes farther and farther out on a limb trying to justify each new overstatement. The court will respect a witness's opinions much more if the witness refuses to let the attorney make the case stronger at the expense of the expert's professional integrity.

Cross Examination

The witness should understand the purposes and some of the techniques of cross-examination to avoid feeling personally attacked or ridiculed and to avoid being admonished by the judge for giving inappropriate answers.   Unlike direct examination, during cross-examination the opposing attorney is permitted to ask leading questions. It may be the essence of good cross-examination to "put words in the witness's mouth," and the witness must understand that this is a perfectly acceptable technique. Cross-examination is typified by short questions that call for direct, limited answers, often "yes" or "no." The witness should not be defensive about the technique or be lulled into the rhythm of a good cross-examiner, thereby giving an erroneous answer. The witness must listen carefully to the question and give an accurate, but short, answer, unless the attorney or judge requests elaboration. This is in contrast to the more open-ended questions and expansive answers characteristic of much of direct examination.

It is crucial for the witness to remain objective and professional during cross-examination. In addition to understanding the different format of the questions and answers, the witness will be more at ease by understanding the purposes behind cross-examination. During cross-examination the opposing attorney attempts to elicit information helpful to his client or attempts to impeach some or all of the witness's testimony. It is the impeachment function that is most often threatening to the witness; however, understanding the goals and methods of impeachment can neutralize some of the "sting."

There are several areas of impeachment: the witness's training and experience, limited data base, theoretical rationale, choice of treatment methods, bias, or dishonesty. The last category is relatively rare. All of the other categories can be the basis for impeaching the expert's credentials, data, or findings.

The value of an expert's opinions is limited by the data upon which they are based, and inquiry into this area should not be interpreted as a personal attack. The witness should not be defensive about admitting limitations in data. An expert can *always* use more information, and the witness's credibility is severely damaged if he or she steadfastly refuses to concede that any possible combination of new and contradictory data would alter in any way the opinions expressed. The witness should concede weaknesses and claim only so much conviction in the opinions as is warranted *within the standards of the expert's profession*, given the data available. (This is why questions during direct examination are often phrased in terms of "do you have an opinion, to a reasonable degree of medical certainty. . . ?") It may help the witness to imagine a discussion with professional colleagues as delineating the degree of conviction. The witness can certainly testify to the degree of unlikelihood that a certain constellation of known facts, particularly if supported by objective data, would exist randomly.

Since conclusions are only as valid as the underlying data, the attorney can extend the demonstration of limited or faulty data to impeach the expert's conclusions. The expert can feel less threatened by this area of impeachment by keeping in mind that such discussions frequently occur between consulting members of the same profession. By maintaining this perspective, the witness should be able to strike a balance between being unreasonably entrenched and throwing the opinion out the window. The court does not expect certainty from any expert, and the witness should not abandon a reasonably formed opinion merely because certainty cannot be guaranteed.

Some attorneys use a "divide and conquer" technique on cross-examination. This is done by getting the expert to acknowledge the insufficiency of each fact alone to sustain the opinion on its own. Carried to its logical conclusion, the entire opinion is discarded. If the expert has relied on many types and sources of information, which together confirm the opinion, that fact should be pointed out. It is rarely possible to base an opinion on one isolated fact. The expert should make clear that it is the totality of the information that leads to the conclusion. Mental health professionals are frequently impeached during cross-examination because of the subjectivity of their opinions. One way to minimize this is to show that more objective data, such as objective psychological testing, support the conclusions reached.

One common ploy on cross-examination is to say to the witness, "You're being paid by the plaintiff to testify here, aren't you?" The expert should reply that payment is being made for the *time* spent in making the evaluation and for the *time* spent away from the office during testimony. Because judges are well aware that experts paid for their time are not necessarily providing "bought testimony," this ploy reflects more on opposing counsel than on the expert. However, some experts answer the question with such defensiveness and resentment that they never regain an objective demeanor.

Some attorneys engage in expert-baiting, a dangerous tactic for both attorney and expert. The expert who is widely respected in his or her own field may be subjected to insults, innuendo, and demeaning remarks if counsel and the judge permit it. It is extremely important for the expert not to lose control. The witness should not spar with the attorney or engage in debate. The attorney is likely to be attempting to make the expert lose his or her poise on the stand, thereby weakening the impact of the testimony. Such tactics are resorted to most frequently when opposing counsel has no good reply to the substantive testimony.

Once the expert understands the tactic, it will be easier to resist the temptation to become visibly angry or irritated.

One of the most frustrating aspects of cross-examination for experts is the questioning attorney's instruction to "answer the question yes or no." Sometimes a question is easily given to such an answer (e.g., "Did you read the mother's hospital records?"). Other times, it cannot be answered "yes" or "no" at all. In such cases, the witness should explain that such an answer is not possible. Most cases fall somewhere in the middle. If such an answer is possible but misleading, the witness may state that to the judge. Frequently, the judge will direct the witness to explain. If not, the witness has alerted the attorney who originally called that witness to the need to explain on re-direct examination. Used sparingly, one technique witnesses may use is the "but, yes" answer instead of the "yes, but" format, putting the qualification before the dogmatic answer. The two examples below illustrate the differences:

Q. Don't you feel that John, in his mother's custody, is an undisciplined boy?
"Yes, but" format
A. Yes, but—
Q. Thank you, that answers the question.
"But, yes" format
A. To the extent that most adolescents are rebellious, yes.

Witnesses easily become adept at this maneuver, and if the qualification is kept short, the opposing attorney rarely has time to cut off further answer. The witness must not overuse this technique, however, because it then becomes objectionable sparring, which may elicit a direct admonition from the judge to answer the questions "yes or no."

The expert should understand that if he or she acknowledges the authoritativeness of a standard text, article or author, that writing or other works by that author may be used for impeachment. Therefore, the expert should deny, if appropriate, or narrow the scope of the author's agreed upon competence when presented with such an inquiry on cross-examination.

The witness should always understand the question before answering. It is proper to ask the attorney to break down multiple questions or to restate a question to make sure that it is correctly understood. If the attorney misstates the witness's previous testimony or report, the witness should point that out. Similarly, if the attorney misstates a fact in the case, the witness should answer that the facts are understood by the witness to be different.

Sometimes an expert will be asked a hypothetical question on cross-examination. The expert will be asked to assume the truth of various statements and then to form an opinion based on those facts. If the witness is able to form such an opinion, it should be expressed even though the witness does not accept the truth of the facts as presented. However, often the list of facts will leave out other information vital to the formation of an opinion. Under such circumstances, the witness should indicate that no opinion can be expressed without knowing more information, specifying where possible the types of additional information needed.

If the expert is concerned about the prospects of cross-examination, the attorney who calls the witness to the stand should be asked prior to trial to supply a list of potential cross-examination questions, and perhaps, even to do a mock cross-examination with the witness. Since that attorney has a chance to ask questions during redirect examination following the cross-examination, the witness will be able to clarify any misconceptions raised during cross-examination. Hints given during the cross-examination testimony may be sufficient for the attorney to know what areas need to be addressed. Otherwise, the witness may ask to speak to the attorney (although this is sometimes not permitted and should be avoided in any case unless the additional information is vital to the case).

Summary

Testifying can be a much less harrowing experience if the expert takes the time to become prepared on the legal aspects of the case. Good attorney-witness communication and cooperation should ensure this result and enable the witness to educate the judge or jury in a manner that will enhance the likelihood of an appropriate judicial determination.

References

1.   This chapter is based in part on materials first published in A. Haralambie, *Handling Child Custody Cases*. Colorado Springs: Shephard's/McGraw-Hill, 1983, and is used with permission.

2   See, e.g., Rule 702, Federal Rules of Evidence, and the state rules patterned after it.

3.   *Ibid*.

4. Brent, R.L. "The Irresponsible Medical Expert: A Failure of Biomedical Graduate Education and Professional Accountability." *Pediatrics*, 70(1982):754.

5. Baker, J., A. Burkholder, A. Haralambie (1983), reprinted from Appendix I, A. Haralambie, *Handling Child Custody Cases*. Colorado Springs: Shephard's/McGraw-Hill, 1983.

25. The Child Witness: Evaluation and Preparation*

Gail S. Goodman and
David W. Lloyd

Introduction

Anyone who reads the newspaper these days is likely to run into stories such as these:

> Inconsistent testimony by the five young girls he was accused of sexually molesting was the main reason jurors were unable to reach a verdict in the trial of a former South Bay preschool aide, a juror said Saturday. . . . "I think what you come back to is 'do you believe the children or not,'" Wilson (the jury foreperson) said Friday night. . . . "I think the real problem is children testifying in court," Hart (Assistant District Attorney) said after the mistrial was announced on Friday, "It's just difficult for them."[1]
> There are those . . . who tend to believe the children's stories that [Mr.] Nokes, and as many as 76 other adults, were members of satanic child molestation rings that engaged in cannibalistic murders of infants. And, there are those who, citing an admitted shortage of substantial corroborating evidence and obvious errors in the children's stories, tend to believe that Nokes and the others are victims of a massive witch hunt. . . . But the sheriff said that "when you hear things like we heard from those kids you just can't ignore them. . . .

414

What made those kids really credible was when, independently, they began telling the same stories."[2]

These news stories reflect societal concern about the credibility of children's testimony. What do we know about children's abilities to report events accurately? What factors indicate that a particular child should or should not testify? And, when children have to appear in court, how should we best prepare them? These are some of the issues addressed in this chapter.**

The Reliability of Children's Reports

HISTORICAL VIEW

Historically, children's testimony has been viewed with much skepticism. Children were deemed "the most dangerous of witnesses.[3] In the legal profession, clear biases against children, particularly female children, existed. For example, a legal scholar named Gross[4] stated that: ". . . the boy who has passed his first years of childhood is, if well trained, the best observer and witness that can possibly be found, because he watches with interest all that goes on around him, stores it impartially in his memory, and reproduces it faithfully; whereas the girl of like age is often untrustworthy, and even a dangerous witness" (p. 41). The courts, while permitting children to testify, established competency laws so that judges could censor children's appearances. Corroboration laws limited children's testimony to cases in which corroboration of their statements could be obtained.[5] Jury instructions reminded jurors of children's presumed suggestibility and inability to understand the seriousness of a trial.[6]

Psychologists, too, were skeptical of the child witness. Early research, conducted by Binet,[7] Stern,[8] Varendock,[9] and others, led to the conclusion that children are too impressionable to provide accurate testimony.

At the turn of the century, when studies of children's suggestibility were first conducted, the term "suggestibility" included the notion of conformity.[10] Later, laboratory studies employing fairly artificial tasks (e.g., judging the length of lines as in the famous Asch experiments, and counting metronome clicks) generally demonstrated that children were more conforming than adults,[11] although the relation was sometimes curvilinear rather than linear.[12] Thus, young children were at times no more suggestible than adults.

Studies of conformity often relied on having a group of adults or children claim in the presence of a target child that, for example, a short line was longer than it truly was. Studies of children's suggestibility often relied on showing the child a mundane picture for a few seconds, followed by the introduction of misleading questions. In most investigative interviews that we have read, when suggestive questions are asked, they are more subtle than this and concerned less trivial matters than the length of lines or what appeared in mundane, briefly seen pictures. It is unclear whether the findings of these older laboratory studies of suggestibility and conformity can be projected to interviews with child victims or witnesses to criminal acts.

Freudian theory also lent a "scientific" stamp to the notion that children's statements about sexual and physical abuse could not be trusted.[13] Recently, however, Freud's conclusions concerning "sexual fantasies" have been challenged.[14,15] Studies of the prevalence of child sexual abuse[16,17] indicate that it is so widespread as to have probably affected Freud's patients.

Despite its flaws, the work of these early researchers and theorists influenced laws concerning children's testimony and influenced modern views of the reliability of children's statements. Under German law, for example, it became mandated that child victims of alleged sexual abuse be evaluated by psychologists.[18] As another example, Freudian theory had a powerful impact on professionals' and the public's willingness to believe children's testimony, especially when such testimony concerned sexual abuse.   Jean Piaget[19]—the great developmental psychologist whose theory, until recently, provided the dominant framework for interpreting children's cognitive development—was influenced by both Freud and Stern. He claimed that "everyone knows, thanks to the fine work done by Stern and his followers, that until the age of 7-8 the child finds systematic difficulty in sticking to the truth. Without actually lying for the sake of lying, i.e., without attempting to deceive anyone, and without even being definitely conscious of what he is doing, he distorts reality in accordance with his desires and his romancing. To him, a proposition has value less as a statement than as a wish, and the stories, testimony, and explanations given by a child should be regarded as the expression of his feelings rather than of beliefs that may be true or false" (p. 164). As the evidence will show, however, current research indicates that children are more capable of testifying accurately than these theories or the former research indicate.

DEVELOPMENTAL CONCERNS

Free reports. Important changes take place over a person's lifetime in the ability to report events. Children, by and large, tend to recall less information about an event than adults do. When asked to describe what happened, a young child's response can be quite skeletal.[20] For example, a 3-year-old kidnap victim might say, "He told me to take my pants off," but when asked what else happened say, "Nothing." Except for such errors of omission, children's reports to open-ended questions can be just as accurate as adults.[21] At least in laboratory studies of children's memory for real-life, personally significant events, even 3-year-old children can produce virtually error-free reports.[22]

Over time, as forgetting occurs, children's free reports become even less detailed although not necessarily any less accurate.[23] If the event is repeated and similar events intervene before a report is given, certain types of errors might occur, however. For example, Myers-Worsley, Cromer, and Dodd[24] questioned children about what typically happened in preschool five years after the children had attended. Using a recognition task, they found that children confused standard parts of the kindergarten routine with the preschool experience. For example, the children indicated that taking the pledge of allegiance to the flag occurred in preschool when it was actually part of the kindergarten routine. It is not clear from this study, however, whether such errors would have occurred in the children's free reports.

Few laboratory studies have examined the effects of repeated interviewing on children's reports, but in actual criminal cases, repeated interviewing is common. Questions arise as to the effects of such multiple interviews. In a simulation of such practices conducted by Dent and Stephenson,[25] 10- and 11-year-old children watched a film of a man stealing a package from a car. The researchers then interviewed the children immediately, two days, three days, two weeks, and finally two months later. Some of the children were asked to provide free reports, that is, to respond to open-ended questions about what happened. Their responses were just as accurate two months after seeing the film as after two days. If the initial report was delayed, however, the completeness—but not the accuracy—of the report decreased. Other children were asked specific questions and were just as accurate on the immediate and the repeated tests. Fewer errors were produced in free reports than in answers to specific questions, however.

Objective questions. Children's responses to nonleading, objective questions can be quite accurate, especially when the questions concern central actions of an event that involve a child's own body. Even 3 year olds can, in response to such questions, provide most valuable information. For example, in a study by Goodman et al.,[22] 100% of the 48 3- to 6-year-old children questioned about a personally significant event (recorded on videotape) knew that they had not been spanked. In addition, when asked if they had been touched anywhere other than where they actually had been touched, none of the children falsely claimed inappropriate touching. In answering other types of objective questions, however 3 year olds' accuracy sometimes falls short of older children's and adults'.[21,22] And, even 8 year olds may be unable to provide accurate information when asked objective questions about a person's age, weight, and height, if the answers require use of adult units of measurement such as years, pounds, and inches.[26,27]

In general, children's answers to questions about descriptions of people—at least unfamiliar people—and of the room where an event occurred are typically less accurate than their answers to questions about actions that took place.[22,25,28] Interestingly, preliminary data reveal that sometimes, in response to objective questions, children's memory is jarred and they can then spontaneously recall more about what happened.[27]

Suggestibility. While children's free reports are impressively accurate and while even 5 and 6 year olds can be as accurate as adults in response to certain objective questions, it is the extent of children's suggestibility that is currently the subject of most debate. That witnesses' reports—whether made by children or adults—can be altered by misleading information has been convincingly demonstrated by Loftus[29] and others. Under certain conditions it appears, however, that the original, accurate memory can be retrieved.[30] Moreover, studies of the effects of misleading information have largely concentrated on bystander witnesses' reports of brief events and of fairly peripheral detail rather than the main actions involved.

Recent studies of children's suggestibility have concentrated on children's testimony for relatively brief, real-life events. In these studies, age does appear to be a factor that can help predict an individual's suggestibility. Specifically, in studies to date, 3 year olds are often found to be more suggestible than older children and adults;[21] the findings for 5 and 6 year olds are more variable.[21,31,32]

Along with age, the types of information queried can also influence a child's suggestibility. In a recent study of children's memory for a stressful event (e.g., having an inoculation at a medical clinic), 5 and 6 year olds were found to be significantly less suggestible about the actions that took place and the person who gave them the shot than about aspects of the room in which the inoculation was given.[22] These findings are important because in most court cases, the actions that took place and the person involved are of major concern. Unfortunately, many studies that have examined children's suggestibility have not differentiated between the types of information suggested. Finally, there is some evidence that the status of an interviewer can affect a child's suggestibility.[33]

Photo identification. Children's performance on photo identi-fication is currently the cause of some concern, especially when the iden-tification concerns a briefly seen, unfamiliar adult. Research to date indicates that in such situations children tend to make a distressingly high number of false identifications,[22,34,35] as do adults in some similar situations.[36] Nevertheless, when the "culprit" is pictured in the lineup, older children (e.g., 6 year olds) can be as accurate as adults and sometimes more so.[21] Of course, in many cases of child abuse and other assaults on children, the offender is a known adult or is unfamiliar but viewed for longer than a few minutes, raising the chances of obtaining an accurate identification.[37,38]

Increasing the accuracy of children's reports. How can the accuracy of children's testimony be increased? One technique is to present the child with props, such as a replica of the room where the event took place and dolls representing the child and others. The child can then be permitted to act out and at the same time describe what happened using the props. A child's ability to report an event can be increased in this way.[39]

One type of prop—anatomically correct dolls—has been the subject of much controversy. Proponents of the dolls claim that such props facilitate children's reports since young people often do not have terms for sexual acts or may be too embarrassed to describe such acts in words. Critics claim that the sexually explicit dolls may be suggestive in themselves or that interviewers may mistake as descriptions of sexual abuse children's natural curiosity about the dolls. To investigate this possibility, White[40] asked social workers and child developmentalists to interview children with the aid of anatomically correct dolls. Half of the children were suspected victims of sexual abuse, while the other half were not. The interviewers, who were blind to the children's classification, did *not* falsely conclude that the nonabused children were victims.

Returning the child to the scene of the crime can, in theory, also facilitate a report. Research by Price and Goodman[39] indicates that after children have experienced a repeated event in a room, their ability to recount what happened increases if they return to the room and are permitted to act out and describe what went on there. The Price and Goodman study concerned a neutral event, however. We do not know if re-experiencing the trauma of a criminal event would interfere with a child's report.

Researchers have not yet discovered techniques that increase the accuracy of children's photo-identifications. Techniques that help prevent false identifications by adult witnesses may be useful with children, however. Wells[41] found that presenting subject-witnesses with a "blank" lineup (i.e., one that did not contain the culprit of a staged crime) before presenting the culprit-present lineup could be used effectively to reduce the number of false identifications. Practice with blank and target-present lineups for familiar people (e.g., the child's mother) could be explored as a technique to teach children how to respond appropriately. In addition, Lindsay and Wells[42] recently found that sequential presentation of pictures in a lineup can reduce the number of false identifications by adults, a finding that may be true for children as well.

Theories of memory and cognitive development. Current theories of development indicate that a child's ability to remember any event is likely to be affected by the child's familiarity with it and ability to understand what occurred.[43,44] Children are better at recalling concrete events than abstract concepts. Fortunately, testimony generally involves memory for concrete experience. While many mental health professionals and attorneys are familiar with Piagetian theory, this theory tends to underestimate children's ability and has been largely replaced by neo-Piagetian approaches,[44,45] which acknowledge that children's thinking may be more advanced in some areas than others. Thus, even young children are not necessarily "prelogical" and, if questioned properly, may be able to report events accurately.

CONCLUSION

In summary, the type of questioning and memory tasks employed can affect the accuracy of a child's report. Regardless of the type of questioning, children cannot report all types of information equally well. Moreover, while children's free reports can remain reasonably accurate over long periods of time, children may provide what is or appears to be inconsistent testimony for a variety of reasons—a tendency to leave out information and to confuse repeated events, as well as providing some incorrect responses to suggestive questions. Moreover, if the child is frightened, has been threatened, is embarrassed, or is otherwise uncomfortable, the child's willingness to describe an event may be reduced. Nevertheless, children can be quite accurate in reporting the main actions that took place, and at least by 5 to 6 years of age, can be resistant to suggestion about the "culprit's" physical description and the actions involved in a personally significant event.

Unfortunately, little is known about children's *testimony* for repeated events.[20] Because repeated exposure to information can heighten memory, children's testimony about the people and main actions involved in repeated events might lead to even greater accuracy. As long as the child does not have to describe the specifics of each episode but instead is simply required to tell generally what happened, the child's accuracy should be high. While much more research is needed on a variety of topics related to child witnesses, we are particularly in need of work on children's testimony for repeated events and also on ways to optimize the accuracy of children's testimony.

Children's Credibility as Witnesses

As soon as a child reports an event, the child's credibility becomes an issue. Parents, relatives, teachers, police, social service workers, mental health workers, attorneys, and judges may all be placed in a position to evaluate the child's credibility. In custody disputes, the parents' credibility also becomes a matter of debate. This debate is often sparked by the fear that a parent intentionally influenced his or her child to make a false report.

European researchers have attempted to develop "criteria of credibility" in the hopes of distinguishing credible from false testimony. Based on the evaluation of thousands of criminal cases, Undeutsch,[46] for example, asserts that the amount of detail reported and the concreteness of the description produced by a witness can be used to help identify true and false reports. Unfortunately, there is little sound empirical work with children to support these claims. Because one can rarely know what occurred in actual cases, it is difficult to verify what is true and what is false. One might hope to rely on confessions by adults or retractions by children, but false confessions and false recantations undermine these sources of validation.

An alternative strategy—based on scientific experimentation— has recently been employed by Schooler, Gerhard, and Loftus[47] to evaluate the characteristics of adults' real and "suggested" memories. Adult subjects watched a slide show depicting a car accident in which a traffic sign was or was not present. For those subjects who did not see the traffic sign, its presence was suggested in subsequent questioning. Subjects were later asked to indicate if they had seen the traffic sign. Schooler et al. found that real memories generally contained more sensory detail, less reference to cognitive processes (e.g., what the subject was thinking while viewing the original slide sequence), and less verbal hedging (e.g., "I think"). Thus, a number of cues can help distinguish adults' real and suggested memories.

Schooler et al. further investigated how well a new group of adults ("subject-judges") could gauge the accuracy of the original subjects' memories. It was found that they could distinguish real from suggested memories better than would be expected by chance but not as well as one might hope. The subject-jurors did, however, rely on many of the cues found to distinguish real from suggested memories.

While the Schooler et al. study provides an important step in the experimental study of criteria of credibility,[48] it has a number of limitations. First, the suggested information concerned a stop or yield sign. It is thus unclear whether the results would generalize to other types of suggested information. Second, the form of the question affected subjects' responses. For example, the question, "Was the Datsun the same color as the stop sign?" increased the amount of sensory detail reported by subjects who had in fact not seen the stop sign. Finally, since the study included only adults, we do not know if the results would generalize to children.

Jury studies provide additional information about the criteria adults use to judge the credibility of a witness. Mock-jurors often rely on the confidence with which the witness holds to her or his statements[47,49,50] and the amount of detail that can be recalled.[50] Children, however, may appear less credible under these criteria even when giving true reports. For example, children tend to report less detail[21] and, we can speculate, are likely to appear less confident, more likely to have their confidence shaken, and might hedge more than adults.

In general, adults have been found to be hesitant to believe children. Yarmey and Jones[51] found that a high percentage of legal and psychology professionals felt that an 8-year-old child would provide inaccurate testimony either by answering questions in the way an attorney wanted or by saying, "I don't know." Goodman, Golding, and Haith[52] found that mock jurors judge children to be less credible witnesses than adults and, in particular, question children's memory and resistance to manipulation. Even in literature, children's credibility as witnesses has often been attacked. In *The Crucible*, Miller[53] portrayed the adolescent girls of Salem as either hysterical or vindictive. A similar portrait is conveyed by Hellman[54] in *The Children's Hour*.

It is possible, however, that adults' willingness to believe children is changing. In a recent national telephone survey of 2,627 adults conducted by the *Los Angeles Times*,[55] 79% of the respondents indicated that they were "certain" that children under 13 are capable of giving accurate accounts of much earlier events. Moreover—and again relying on the possibility that art mirrors public sentiment—in a recent movie entitled *Witness* a young boy who observed a murder is portrayed as able to make an accurate identification of the killer.

The Child in the Legal Context: Pragmatics

INVESTIGATIVE INTERVIEWING

When a crime against a child is reported, one of the first steps taken is to interview the child. Mental health professionals, police, and others are often attacked for the techniques they use in investigative interviewing. These attacks typically center around whether or not the interviewer was leading the child through suggestive questions. Some mental-health workers, in particular, may be unaware of the types of questions and situations that are considered leading by legal professionals. Moreover, as therapists, they may be trained to use techniques that promote the child's overall adjustment as opposed to techniques that elicit the most accurate testimony.

Laboratory studies often find that the first interview is the most accurate or at least the most complete.[29] These studies have not, however, examined the effects of fear, intimidation, and embarrassment on children's reports. Moreover, for stressful events, there is some evidence—albeit mixed—that the completeness of a report can remain the same or even increase over time with repeated questioning.[56,57,22] The first report—and the questioning used to elicit it—often become of crucial concern in an actual case.

It is important in the first interview to begin by building rapport with the child. Once the actual questioning commences, a free report should be elicited. That is, the child should be asked to describe what happened, without being asked specific questions. It is important, however, to ensure that the child is cued, in a nonleading way, to the incident of interest. If the child starts to talk about another incident and the interviewer does not realize the mistake, communication becomes confused.

While the narratives of adults typically begin with several sentences devoted to orienting the listener to the time, place, people, and behavioral situation involved,[58] young children (e.g., 3 and 4 year olds) tend to provide less information than older children about issues of who, where, why, and when.[59] As a consequence of violating this and other such verbal conventions, young children's narratives can appear somewhat incoherent by adult standards.[60]

The elicitation of free report should be followed by questioning. Children can be expected to be particularly accurate about the actions that took place. Several recent studies have found that children, when questioned anywhere from three to eleven days after an event, are highly accurate in answering questions about whether they were hit, spanked, kissed, touched, or had their clothes taken off.[22,27] The errors that do occur are largely of omission rather than commission. Children's accuracy can be expected to decrease if they are asked about peripheral detail.

The language used in questioning children will have an influence on their accuracy. Children have difficulty with double negatives, passive constructions, and long sentences with embedded clauses, for instance (see 61, for a review of the language development literature). The questions must remain simple and within the child's level of understanding. The child's terms for parts of the body or various acts should be used. Interviewers must also be sensitive to children's tendency to interpret words literally. Thus, a child who has been in a man's apartment may not think of it as a "home" or "house." If asked whether he or she has been to the man's home, the child might, therefore, answer "no."

While recent research indicates that, at least by the age of 5 or 6 years, children who have experienced a personally significant event can resist suggestion about the actions and persons involved[22]—at least to a greater extent than many would have imagined—the use of suggestive questioning should be avoided. Even if the child can resist suggestion, the use of such questioning will do damage to the child's credibility in a court of law.

Through free reports and questioning, investigative interviewers should attempt to obtain a complete, chronological description of what happened, a complete description of the offender's appearance, the time and location of the events, and any other information relevant to the legal "elements" of the case, such as whether force, a weapon, or threats were used.[62,63,64,65]

How the interview is recorded can affect the case for better or for worse. Ideally, the interview would be recorded on videotape so that a public record exists of the types of questions asked and of the child's responses. Chaney[66] reports that showing the videotape to the suspect can be effective in obtaining confessions. Use of audio tapes or verbatim notes might be considered if video equipment is unavailable. Unfortunately, some investigators have run into problems with the use of such objective records. If, for example, the child has been threatened not to tell or feels uncomfortable with the interviewer, the child may at first falsely deny that abuse took place and only later admit that it did,[67] thereby producing an inconsistent report. In this case, the objective record is likely to be used later to try to discredit the child.

Perhaps due in part to the increased use of videotaped recordings, there has recently been increased legal focus on the issue of inconsistent statements. Impeachment of a witness's credibility by presentation of inconsistent statements made prior to the court testimony has been a standard legal technique.[6,68] Recently, some courts have permitted expert testimony in child sexual abuse cases concerning false recantations. For example, an expert can be permitted to explain that child victims frequently have ambivalent feelings towards the perpetrator, especially if the perpetrator is a parent and, consequently, the child may retract a previously made complaint or withhold information initially. Given such expert testimony, the jury might infer that the child's inconsistent statements enhance credibility rather than detract from it.[69]

Many mental health professionals believe that false recantation frequently occurs in incest cases. Various commentators[70,71,72,73] have described retraction as a coping mechanism employed when a child is confronted with a complex and disturbing situation. A look at the situation faced by many incest victims reveals why it is not surprising that retraction might frequently occur. When abuse is alleged by the child, he or she is asked about the distasteful details by various investigators, lawyers, therapists, and even media representatives. The child may have been removed from the family into the unfamiliar setting of a foster or group home, and have attendant adjustment difficulties. Alternately, the parent may have been incarcerated and the family may blame the child for a devastating loss of income. Other relatives, especially the offender's may be unable to believe that their loved one has violated the incest taboo and may press the child for a recantation.

SHOULD THE CHILD TESTIFY?

Once the investigative interview has been completed, the attorney must decide whether to call the child as a witness. Not all children who are potential witnesses should actually testify. The reasons for this exclusion fall into two broad categories: (1) if the anticipated result of the child's testimony would be detrimental to the effort to prove the case, due to such factors as the child's inability to demonstrate competency effectively, untrustworthy demeanor, hesitant or confused recital of facts, or a mental or emotional condition that suggests poor credibility; or, (2) if the stress of testifying would be inimical to the emotional health of the child. Therefore, the decision as to whether the child should actually testify should be carefully considered, and not be made casually or routinely, as is frequently the case, by a prosecutor, guardian *ad litem*, or attorney for the parent. Factors bearing on the decision of whether or not to call the child as a witness are discussed below.

Competency. The first general consideration is the child's competency to testify. Traditionally, children's competency has been thought of in terms of age. Due in part to the lingering effect of old common-law age requirements for criminal responsibility[74] and for testifying[75] and the continuing legal bias against children's credibility, lawyers generally presume that school-aged children can and therefore should testify, while preschool-aged children probably cannot qualify as competent witnesses. The more pertinent issue is the child's developmental level and memory, not chronological age. (A mentally retarded 12 year old, for example, may not be able to demonstrated competency while a developmentally appropriate 5 year old can.)

The test of witness competency for children is fairly standard[76,77] and relies on the child's ability to answer a series of questions in the strange and possibly intimidating setting of the courtroom. The requirement of a psychological evaluation of the child to aid in the determination of competency is under the judge's discretion. It has been our experience that psychological evaluation of the child to aid in the determination of competency is under the judge's discretion. It has been our experience that psychological evaluations are not typically obtained, especially if the child can demonstrate competency by answering questions posed in a pretrial hearing.

The child who is proffered as a witness must demonstrate that he or she has the ability to understand questions and to attempt to answer them responsively. This is shown through a few simple questions, for example: What is your name? Where do you live? How old are you? Who lives with you? The child must further demonstrate that he or she has memory of past events and the power of recall. This is shown by answering questions selected by the lawyer about past events in the child's life: Have you ever taken a trip with your family? Where did you go? What did you see? Did your school class do anything special last year? Did your family have any visitors, take any trips, have any special parties? Can you tell us about them? Did anything scary or unhappy happen to you last year?

The child must demonstrate an understanding of the difference between telling the truth and telling a lie. This ability is demonstrated by having the child answer questions that indicate concrete knowledge, such as: Has your mother or father ever talked to you about telling the truth or telling a lie? What did your mom say about it? Have any of your teachers talked about it? What did your teacher say about telling the truth and telling a lie? Do you think it is a good thing or a bad thing to tell the truth? Is it a good think or a bad thing to tell a lie? If you tell a lie, does your mother become happy, or angry, or sad, or not care? If I say this chair is a door, is that telling the truth or telling a lie?

Finally, the child must demonstrate an understanding of the obligation to tell the truth in court by answering such questions as: Do you think it is a good thing or a bad thing to tell a lie here in the courtroom? If someone tells a lie to the judge, does the judge become happy, angry, sad, or not care? Do you know what the judge could do to grown-ups who tell lies in the courtroom? Do you know what it means to promise to tell the truth? In all your answers so far, have you been telling the truth?

Can you keep on telling the truth, no matter who asks you the questions? No matter what? Will you promise to tell the truth? When we promise to tell the truth in court, we call it swearing to tell the truth; it's not like swearing *at* someone. It's a good thing. Will you swear to tell the truth? (Of course, in posing these questions, the language and sentence constructions used may have to be adapted to the child's abilities.)

Obviously, the lawyer proffering the child must know in advance of trial whether the child can answer these questions. There should be practices several times in advance of the trial, and the child's demeanor in answering them studied carefully. If the child has difficulty in answering these preliminary questions, there will probably be doubts in the minds of the judge and jury about the child's credibility. In that case, the child should not testify at all if there is an alternative means of presenting important evidence. Using these techniques, virtually all of the school-aged children who have been proffered as witnesses in felony trials in the District of Columbia Superior Court have been judged competent to testify. This may well reflect the effectiveness of the prosecutors' preparation of the children.

The issue of competency becomes extremely difficult with preschool-aged children, especially in sexual abuse or molestation cases where there may not be any other witness to the event(s) and there is usually no strong, corroborative medical or behavioral evidence. In such cases, the lawyer may have to prepare a pre-trial memorandum that will alert the judge to the difficulties young children have in meeting the artificial tests of witness competency, and stress that their testimony may be nonetheless reliable.

The results of a recent study may be helpful in preparing such a memorandum. Goodman et al.[22] surreptitiously videotaped children who were receiving standard medical inoculations. After 3 to 4 or 7 to 9 days, the children were asked to recall the event, to answer objective and suggestive questions, and to identify the nurse who gave them the shot from a 6-person photo lineup that included the nurse. Next, the children were asked a set of questions designed to mimic several of the questions asked in standard competence examinations. For example, each child was asked if she or he knew the difference between the truth and a lie, what happens if she or he tells a lie, and whether everything the child told the interviewer was true. The accuracy of the children's responses was then correlated with the accuracy of the children's memory. The "competence" questions were found to be largely unrelated to the children's accuracy of report.

Demeanor. A second factor is the child's demeanor. Juries are instructed to consider a witness's demeanor in assessing credibility.[6] If in practice sessions with the lawyer, the child appears evasive, distracted, over-rehearsed, mechanical in response, or too eager to please the questioner, it is probably better to avoid using the child if at all possible.

Similarly, the pseudosophisticated, truculent, or smug teenager may not be very convincing as an alleged victim of abuse or neglect. A child who is hyperactive may also be a troublesome witness because the overstimulating nature of most courtrooms will make it difficult for the child to maintain his or her attention to the question. It may be necessary to request the court's permission to take such a child's testimony by deposition in a room that can be arranged to minimize distractions.

Hesitant or confused recital of facts. A third factor is the manner in which the child relates the facts relevant to the case, since juries are instructed to consider this factor, too.[6] Most adult witnesses appear somewhat nervous and hesitant when testifying for the first time, and anecdotal evidence suggests that juries expect children to act similarly. However, when the child is so hesitant as to appear totally dependent on leading questions, it raises the concern that the content of the child's testimony is being suggested to him or her. Similarly, some confusion in a young child seems to be expected by jury members. But, if the child's account becomes thoroughly confused in practice sessions as well as during practice cross-examination, it is not likely that the child will be convincing during trial.

Mental or emotional condition. A fourth factor is the presence or history of a mental or emotional condition thought to affect credibility. It may be a denial of state or federal due process in a child abuse proceeding in family court for the attorney to conceal the fact that the child has been diagnosed as having a mental condition such as schizophrenia, which clearly is relevant to the issue of whether the child can recall facts accurately and truthfully. In particular, if a prosecutor proffering the child as a witness in a criminal or delinquency case knows of such a condition, failure to disclose this to the defense attorney after being requested to provide any exculpatory evidence is a denial of due process requiring sanctions, including a new trial or possible dismissal.[78] Such a situation may require full judicial review *in camera* of extensive mental health records of the child to determine which, if any, are relevant to the issue of credibility. (In some cases, the defense is aware of third parties who possess mental health records of the child, and may subpoena them, which would again necessitate *in camera* review.)

Trauma induced by legal proceedings. Even if a child can meet the test of competency and provide credible testimony, the child should not testify if she or he already has a mental or emotional condition that will be severely exacerbated by the stress of testifying in court.

To date there has been no reliable research that demonstrates the deleterious impact of a child's participation in legal proceedings as a witness. There are a number of reasons for this lack of evidence. First, most of the concern over children's courtroom stress has centered around victims of physical abuse, sexual molestation, or neglect, and it is difficult methodologically to separate negative effects of participation in court from those resulting from the child's original mistreatment. Second, if the child's mental health is evaluated prior to and following his or her testimony and this evaluation becomes known to the attorneys, the judge may order that the results of the evaluation must be made available to the opposing side. The evaluations may then be used to attack the child's credibility during the trial or in a motion to seek a new trial. This possibility exists in criminal cases because of the Sixth Amendment to the federal constitution; it may also exist in other cases as an element of Fifth Amendment due-process considerations. Third, there is anecdotal evidence that some children benefit from testifying against their victimizer, in that such testimony can serve as a cathartic vindication.[79] Fourth, a number of innovations in preparing child witnesses—using demonstrative evidence and providing emotional support—have been widely implemented and seem to reduce the stress experienced by the child.[79,80]

Nonetheless, it has been widely assumed[79,81,82] that children are victimized by the legal system in the course of their participation as a witness. To alleviate this presumed stress, it has been suggested and even permitted by new state statutes that children testify by closed circuit television; other states have enacted laws that will permit the use of the child's statements to others as an exception to the hearsay rule or the use of a child's testimony at a deposition in lieu of the child's testimony at trial.[80,83]

The constitutionality of such laws depends on the proceeding in which they are to be used. While they might pass muster against a due-process challenge in a family-court proceeding, any such innovations in a criminal or delinquency proceeding must not violate the defendant's constitutional right to confront and cross-examine witnesses.[84,85,86,87,88] The test for acceptability in the leading Supreme Court case of *Ohio v. Roberts*[89] is whether: (a) the witness is unavailable, and (b) the statement bears adequate "indicia of reliability," meaning that it either "falls within a firmly rooted hearsay exception" or "has particularized guarantees of trustworthiness." While there is some debate as to whether the second prong of this test can be met by these innovations, there is existing case law that defines "unavailability." It includes: the death of the witness; absence from the jurisdiction, despite attempts by the lawyer to secure the witness's attendance; and psychological unavailability.[85,86] This last ground, however, generally requires expert testimony by a psychiatrist or psychologist that the potential witness is suffering from a well-recognized diagnostic condition.[86] Thus, it appears that as a general rule children will not be routinely excused from testifying on the ground that it is harmful to them.

ARE THERE ALTERNATIVES TO THE CHILD'S TESTIMONY?

The lawyer considering the use of a child witness should weigh the foregoing factors against the specific need for the child's testimony. The lawyer should think creatively about the possibility of proving the case circumstantially or through innovative techniques. For example, in one prosecution for sexual molestation, the child victim was 4 years old and did not seem competent to testify even after strenuous practicer efforts. But, there was a 7-year-old eyewitness. The prosecutor merely had the 4 year old brought to the witness stand, state her name and age, and then excused her. The crucial testimony was presented by the eyewitness.

In child abuse proceedings it is common for the trier of fact to rely on the "battered child syndrome," a form of *res ipsa loquitur* (which means that the nature of the thing explains itself) that permits one to infer that the child was abused based on the nature of the injuries and, usually, also based on parental explanation inconsistent with those injuries.[87] Such an inference, presented through expert testimony of a physician (typically a radiologist and/or a pediatrician), shifts the burden of proof to the defense to come up with a plausible explanation. It has been suggested that there is a "sexually abused child syndrome"[88] that could equally apply in the family court. However, this suggestion has been criticized as unsupported by reputable research.[89]

Preparing Children to Testify

If it is decided that the child should testify, the child must be adequately prepared for the experience. The suggestions we offer below follow from our own and others' experiences in preparing children to testify.

ENVIRONMENTAL CONSIDERATIONS

As a first step, thought should be given to the setting for preparing the child for trial. It is generally helpful to interview the child in a playroom or an office that provides some indication that children are welcome there. At some point the child should be taken on a tour of an empty courtroom and be given the opportunity to sit in a judge's chair, the jury box, counsel tables, and the witness stand. At least one practice session using colleagues of the lawyer or other support people to interview the child should be held in the courtroom.

The time of day is also important, and the parent should be asked about the child's high and low points of energy during the day. Some children should not be interviewed, prepared for trial, or expected to testify during the early afternoon, since this can be a time of low energy. (When the child is called to testify, adapting to the child's schedule may require a shuffling in the order of witnesses!) Teenagers may prefer to have the session after school so that peers, teachers, and administrative staff are unaware of the court involvement. Actual practice sessions should be kept relatively short to make best use of the child's limited attention span.

CHILDREN'S UNDERSTANDING OF LEGAL PROCEEDINGS

Children's understanding of legal proceedings may influence their reactions to court. In preparing a child for a court appearance, it is important to have an appreciation for the child's understanding of what is to occur. The only completed study we know of on this topic was conducted in France by Pierre-Puysegar[91] who interviewed children about their understanding of such terms as "police officer," "attorney," "judge," and "prison." She found that the majority of 6 year olds could provide correct answers to questions about the role of police and prisons, but not about court, fines, judges, attorneys, juries, or witnesses. The majority of 8 year olds provided correct answers to questions about the role of the police, prisons, court, fines, and judges, but not about attorneys, juries, or witnesses. The majority of 10-year-old children gave correct answers for all of the terms listed above except for juries. Based on her findings, Pierre-Puysegar proposed three levels of legal knowledge. In the first level, the child only understands that when a person commits an offense, a police officer arrests him or her who, without recourse, goes to prison. At the second level, a rudimentary concept of a trial emerges, that includes notions of a judge and an attorney. The third level is much more elaborate and includes witnesses and a jury. A similar study conducted with American children about the American system of justice would be quite worthwhile. Of course, children who are immersed in the legal system may quickly learn more about it, but if they are young, they may start out with relatively little realistic knowledge about the people involved, their roles, or what to expect.

PREPARATION FOR DIRECT EXAMINATION

Preparation of the child witness is actually preparation of the attorney. If the lawyer can ask the right questions in the right manner, the child can provide useful information, but if the lawyer assumes that he or she can use the same language and concepts as one uses with an adult witness, the child will probably testify poorly. The lawyer must learn to think as the child does.

Preparation of the child witness begins with efforts to build rapport, as it does with an adult witness. This process may take longer with a child than an adult, requiring up to two or three visits. If possible, some of the visits should be just to develop rapport, with no effort to talk about the testimony.

The lawyer needs to explain what will happen and what the child is expected to do, occasionally asking questions to test the child's understanding. The lawyer must make sure the child knows, to the best of the child's abilities, the roles of the various people in the courtroom and why the child is testifying.

The attorney must have a clear sense of the child's developmental level and language abilities. Whenever possible, abstract questions should be avoided, (e.g., "What does it mean to tell a lie?") and compound questions should also be eliminated (e.g., "Were you in your room and then in your sister's or in your sister's first?) As mentioned earlier, questions with double negatives are troublesome for children. The attorney must, therefore, give careful thought to the particular terms used and to the concreteness of the questions posed to the child. Further, children may not have good recall of specific dates and times, and great effort may have to be spent on the use of "time markers," such as special events, TV shows, or mealtimes, to place events.

When practicing for testimony, the lawyer should vary the language of the questions and their order to reduce the rote, sing-song style some children adopt. This detracts greatly from a child's credibility, and prompts cross-examination about rehearsal (e.g., "You practiced this story with the District Attorney, didn't you? And he told you what to say today, didn't he?"). The practice questions should include those that will be used to demonstrate competency. If the child is going to be asked to identify photographs, objects, or drawings, or to use dolls, the entire procedure should be practiced. Good preparation also includes role playing to show how the child should deal with a loss of memory, with errors the child realizes and wants to correct, and with objections to the child's testimony.

PREPARATION FOR CROSS-EXAMINATION

The attorney must also prepare the child for the anticipated tactics of cross-examination. The arguments that form the basis of cross-examination of a child generally fall into one of four broad categories: (a) The child is honestly mistaken, and may have been manipulated by someone into error; (b) The child was manipulated by someone into lying; (c) The child chose to lie, especially to get out of trouble or to gain revenge against a strict parent; or (d) the child is seeking to gain attention. With each strategy, the attorney's questions may be devoted to extremely fine points of the child's memory. Again, the child must practice what to do when loss of memory occurs. With young children it may be better for a colleague of the lawyer to practice cross-examination so that the child is not confused as to whether the lawyer who will present the child now disbelieves him or her.

The child must be prepared to handle leading questions, especially those that attempt to gain the child's acquiescence in the hope of producing answers that will contradict the child's previous statements. Similarly, the child must be prepared for opposing counsel's attempts to appeal to authority or for feigned and exaggerated disbelief. The lawyer who presents the child must be prepared to make objections to prohibit the use of language that the child cannot understand or attempts to harass or intimidate the child, and the child must know how to handle objections and emotional upset.

Finally, the child must be prepared to acknowledge that he or she practiced the testimony with the lawyer. Occasionally the opposing counsel will try to make the child (or the jury) feel that such practice was improper, and that the child's testimony was dictated by the lawyer. One method to anticipate this is to tell the child. "I want you to tell in your own words what happened. I'm not going to tell you what to say, except I want you to tell the truth, no matter how it makes you feel or how it helps or hurts our plan to tell what happened. And, if anyone asks you if your lawyer told you what to say, you can tell them I told you to tell the truth."

Conclusion

The reliability or credibility of children as witnesses is being studied and understood to a greater degree as the importance of children's testimony has become more evident. Understanding the theory and practical steps necessary for effective presentation of a child's testimony, including the decision as to whether or not a child should testify, is essential for modern child protection team practice.

Notes

* Preparation of this article was supported in part by a grant to Gail S. Goodman from the Developmental Psychobiology Research Group, Department of Psychiatry, University of Colorado Health Sciences Center.

** In this chapter, we do not explicitly deal with children's actual court appearances. A discussion of children's courtroom testimony can be found in Goodman and Helgeson[90] and Goodman, Golding, and Haith.[52]

References

1.   Waters, T. "Girls' Testimony Blamed in Mistrial." *Los Angeles Times,* October 1985, pp. 1, 18.

2.   Malnic, E. "Bakersfield Torn by Horror Stories of Child Molestation." *Los Angeles Times,* August 4, 1985, Part I: pp. 3, 26-27.

3.   Baginsky as cited in G.M. Whipple. "The Psychology of Testimony." *Psychological Bulletin,* 8(1911):307-309.

4.   Gross as cited in A. Moll. *The Sexual Life of the Child.* New York: Macmillan, 1913.

5.   Lloyd, D. "The Corroboration of Sexual Victimization of Children." *Child Sexual Abuse and the Law.* J. Bulkley (Ed.), pp. 103-124. Washington D.C.: American Bar Association, 1983.

6.   Greene, H., and T. Guidaboni. *Criminal Jury Instructions, District of Columbia.* Washington, D.C.: Young Lawyers Section of the Bar Association of the District of Columbia, 1978.

7.   Binet, A. *La suggestibilité.* Paris: Schleicher-Frères, 1900.

8.   Stern, W. "Abstracts of Lectures on the Psychology of Testimony and on the Study of Individuality." *American Journal of Psychology*, 21(1910):273-282.

9.   Varendock, J. "Les temoignages d'enfants dans un procès retentissant." *Archives de Psychologie*, 11(1911):129-171.

10.   Small, M. "The Suggestibility of Children." *Pedagogical Seminary*, 4(1896):176-220.

11.   Berenda, R.W. *The Influence of the Group on the Judgments of Children.* New York: King's Crown Press, 1950.

12.   Costanzo, P.R., and M.E. Shaw. "Conformity as a Function of Age Level." *Child Development*, 37(1966):967-975.

13.   Rieff, P. (Ed.). *Sexuality and the Psychology of Love: Sigmund Freud.* New York: Macmillan, 1963.

14.   Masson, J.M. *The Assault on Truth: Freud's Suppression of the Seduction Theory.* New York: Farrar, Straus, and Giroux, 1984.

15.   Rush, F. *The Best Kept Secret: Sexual Abuse of Children.* New York: McGraw-Hill, 1981.

16.   Russell, D.E.H. "The Incidence and Prevalence of Intrafamilial and Extrafamilial Sexual Abuse of Female Children." *Child Abuse & Neglect*, 7(1983):133-146.

17.   Finkelhor, D. *Child Sexual Abuse: New Theory and Research.* New York: Free Press, 1984.

18.   Sporer, S. "A Brief History of the Psychology of Testimony." *Current Psychological Reviews*, 2(1982):323-340.

19.   Piaget, J. *The Moral Judgment of the Child.* New York: The Free Press, 1966.

20.   Nelson, K., and J. Gruendel. "Generalized Event Representations: Basic Building Blocks of Cognitive Development." *Advances in Developmental Psychology*, Vol.1. A. Brown and M. Lamb (Eds.). Hillsdale: N.J.: Erlbaum, 1981.

21.   Goodman, G.S., and R.S. Reed. "Age Differences in Eyewitness Testimony." *Law and Human Behavior* (in press).

22.   Goodman, G.S., C. Aman, and J. Hirschman. "Child Sexual and Physical Abuse: Children's Testimony." *Children's Eyewitness Memory.* S. Ceci, M. Toglia, and D. Ross (Eds.). New York: Springer-Verlag (in press).

23. Fivush, R., J. Hudson, and K. Nelson. "Children's Long-term Memory for a Novel Event: An Exploratory Study." *Merrill-Palmer Quarterly,* 30(1984):303-316.

24. Myles-Worsley, M., C.C. Cromer, and D.H. Dodd. "Children's Preschool Script Reconstruction: Reliance on General Knowledge as Memory Fades." *Developmental Psychology,* 22(1986):22-30.

25. Dent, H.R., and G.M. Stephenson. "An Experimental Study of the Effectiveness of Different Techniques of Questioning Child Witnesses." *British Journal of Social and Clinical Psychology,* 18(1979):41-51.

26. Goetze, H. "The Effect of Age and Method of Interview on the Accuracy and Completeness of Eyewitness Accounts." Unpublished doctoral dissertation, Hofstra University, New York, 1980.

27. Rudy, L. "The Effects of Participation on Children's Eyewitness Testimony." Unpublished paper, Department of Psychology, University of Denver, 1986.

28. Pear, T.H., and S. Wyatt. "The Testimony of Normal and Mentally Defective Children." *British Journal of Psychology,* 3(1914):388-419.

29. Loftus, E.F. *Eyewitness Testimony.* Cambridge, Mass.: Harvard University Press, 1979.

30. McCloskey, M., and M. Zarangoza. "Misleading Postevent Information and Memory for Events: Arguments and Evidence Against Memory Impairment Hypotheses." *Journal of Experimental Psychology: General,* 114(1985):1-16.

31. King, M.A. "An Investigation of the Eyewitness Abilities of Children." Unpublished doctoral dissertation, University of British Columbia, Vancouver, Canada, 1984.

32. Marin, B.V., D.L. Holmes, M. Guth, and P. Kovac. "The Potential of Children as Eyewitnesses." *Law and Human Behavior,* 4(1979):295-305.

33. Ceci, S.J., D.F. Ross, and M.P. Toglia. "Age Differences in Suggestibility." *Children's Eyewitness Memory.* S.J. Ceci, M.P. Toglia, and D.F. Ross (Eds.). New York: Springer-Verlag (in press).

34. Peters, D.P. "The Impact of Naturally Occurring Stress on Children's Memory." *Children's Eyewitness Memory.* S.J. Ceci, M.P. Toglia, and D.F. Ross (Eds.). New York: Springer-Verlag (in press).

35. Yuille, J.C., and M.A. King. "Children as Witnesses." Paper presented in M. Toglia (Chair), *Current Trends in Evaluation Children's Memory for Witnessed Event.* Symposium at the American Psychological Association Convention, Los Angeles, Calif., August 1985.

36. Malpass, R.S., and P.G. Devine. "Eyewitness Identification: Lineups Instructions, and the Absence of the Offender." *Journal of Applied Psychology,* 66(1981):54-76.

37. Bahrick, H., P. Bahrick, and R. Wittlinger. "Fifty Years of Memory for Names and Faces: A Cross-sectional Approach." *Journal of Experimental Psychology: General,* 104(1975):54-76.

38. Diamond, R., and S. Carey. "Developmental Changes in the Representation of Faces." *Journal of Experimental Child Psychology,* 23(1977):1-22.

39. Price, D.W.W., and G.S. Goodman. "Children's Event Representations for Recurring Episodes." Paper presented at the Society for Research in Child Development, Toronto, Canada, July 1985.

40. White, S., G.A. Strom, G. Santilli, and B.M. Halpin. "Interviewing Young Sexual Abuse Victims with Anatomically Correct Dolls." *Child Abuse & Neglect,* 10(1986):519-530.

41. Wells, G.L. "The Psychology of Lineup Identification." *Journal of Applied Social Psychology,* 14(1984):89-103.

42. Lindsay, R.C.L., and G.L. Wells. "Improving Eyewitness Identification from Lineups: Simultaneous Versus Sequential Lineup Presentation." *Journal of Applied Psychology,* 79(1985):556-564.

43. Chi, M.T.H. "Knowledge Structures and Memory Development." *Children's Thinking: What Develops?* R. Siegler (Ed.), pp. 73-96. Hillsdale, N.J.: Erlbaum and Associates, 1978.

44. Fischer, K. "A Theory of Cognitive Development: The Control of Hierarchies of Skill." *Psychological Review,* 87(1980):477-531.

45. Case, R. *Intellectual Development: Birth to Adulthood.* New York: Academic Press, 1985.

46. Undeutsch, U. "Statement Reality Analysis." *Reconstructing the Past: The Role of Psychologists in Criminal Trials.* A. Trankell (Ed.). Stockholm: Norsted and Sons, 1982.

47. Schooler, J., D. Gerhard, and E.F. Loftus. "Qualities of the Unreal." *Journal of Experimental Psychology: Learning, Memory, and Cognition,* 12(1986):171-181.

48. Johnson, M.K., and C.L. Raye. "Reality Monitoring." *Psychological Review,* 88(1981):67-85.

49. Miller, G.R., and J.K. Burgoon. "Factors Affecting Assessments of Witness Credibility." *The Psychology of the Courtroom.* N.L. Kerr and R.M. Bray (Eds.), pp. 169-196. New York: Academic Press, 1982.

50. Wells, G.L., and M.R. Leippe. "How do Triers of Fact Infer the Accuracy of Eyewitness Identification? Using Memory for Detail Can Be Misleading." *Journal of Applied Psychology,* 66(1981):682-687.

51. Yarmey, A.D., and H.P.T. Jones. "Is the Psychology of Eyewitness Identification a Matter of Common Sense?" *Evaluating Witness Evidence.* S.M. Lloyd and B.R. Clifford (Eds.), pp. 13-40. New York: Wiley, 1983.

52. Goodman, G.S., J.M. Golding, and M.M. Haith. "Jurors' Reactions to Child Witnesses." *Journal of Social Issues,* 40(1984):139-156.

53. Miller, A. *The Crucible.* New York: Bantam Books, 1959.

54. Hellman, L. *The Children's Hour.* New York: A.A. Knopf, 1934.

55. Timnick, L. "Children's Abuse Reports Reliable, Most Believe." *Los Angeles Times,* August 26, 1985, pp. 1-12.

56. Kleinsmith, L.J., and S. Kaplan. Paired Associated Learning as a Function of Arousal and Interpolated Interval." *Journal of Experimental Psychology,* 65(1963):190-193.

57. Schrivner, E., and M.A. Safer. "Repeated Testing of Eyewitness." Paper presented at the annual meetings of the American Psychological Association, Los Angeles, Calif., August 1985.

58. Labov, W., and J. Waletzky. "Narrative Analysis: Oral Versions of Personal Experience." *Essays on the Verbal and Visual Arts.* J. Helms (Ed.). Seattle, Wash.: University of Washington Press, 1967.

59. Menig-Peterson, C.L., and A. McCabe. "Children's Orientation of a Listener to the Context of Their Narratives." *Developmental Psychology,* 14(1978):582-592.

60. Sheehy, N. "The Child As Witness." Paper presented at the Conference of British Psychological Society, London, England, December 1980.

61. de Villiers, J.G., and P.A. de Villiers. *Language Acquisition.* Cambridge, Mass.: Harvard University Press, 1978.

62. Amidon, H.T., and T.A. Wagner. "Successful Investigations and Prosecution of Crimes of Rape: A Description Model." *Journal of Police Science and Administration,* 6(1978):141-156.

63. Inbau, F.E., and J.E. Reid. *Criminal Interrogation and Confessions,* 2nd edition. Baltimore, Md.: Williams and Wilkins Co., 1967.

64. Soderman, H., and J.J. O'Connell. *Modern Criminal Investigation,* 5th edition. New York: Funk and Wagnalls, 1962.

65. Swanson, O.R., Jr., N.C. Chamelin, and L. Territo. *Criminal Investigation.* Santa Monica, Calif.: Goodyear Publishing Co., 1977.

66. Chaney, S. "Videotaped Interviews with Child Abuse Victims." *Papers from a National Policy Conference on Legal Reforms in Child Sexual Abuse Cases.* J. Bulkley (Ed.). Washington, D.C.: American Bar Association, 1985.

67. MacFarlane, K. "Diagnostic Evaluations: Interview Techniques and the Use of Videotape." *Papers from a National Policy Conference on Legal Reforms in Child Sexual Abuse Cases.* J. Bulkley (Ed.). Washington, D.C.: American Bar Association, 1985.

68. Cleary, E. (Ed.). *McCormick's Handbook of the Law of Evidence,* 2nd edition. St. Paul, Minn.: West Publishing, 1972.

69. *State v. Middleton.* 294 Or. 427, 657 P. 2d 1215 (1983).

70. DeFrancis, V. *Protecting the Child Victim of Sex Crimes Committed by Adults.* Denver, Colo.: American Humane Association, 1969.

71. Goodwin, J., D. Sahd, and R. Rada. "Incest Hoax: False Accusations, False Denials." *Bulletin of the American Academy of Psychiatry and the Law,* 6(1979):269-276.

72. Sgroi, S., L. Blick, and F. Porter. "A Conceptual Framework for Child Sexual Abuse." *Handbook of Clinical Intervention in Child Sexual Abuse.* S. Sgroi (Ed.), pp. 9-37. Lexington, Mass.: D.C. Heath and Co., 1982.

73. Summit, R. "The Child Sexual Abuse Accommodation Syndrome." *Child Abuse & Neglect,* 7(1983):177-193.

74. Wigmore, J. *Evidence in Trials at Common Law,* Chadborn revised edition. Vol. 6. Boston, Mass.: Little, Brown, and Co., 1976.

75. Horowitz, R., and B. Hunter. "The Child Litigant." *Legal Rights of Children.* R. Horowitz and H. Davidson (Eds.), pp. 72-113. Colorado Springs, Colo.: Shepard's McGraw-Hill, 1984.

76. Goodman, G.S. "Children's Testimony in Historical Perspective." *Journal of Social Issues,* 40(2)(1984):9-32.

77. Melton, G. "Children's Competency to Testify." *Law and Human Behavior,* 5(1)(1981):73-85.

78. *Giles v. Maryland,* 386 U.S. 66 (1967).

79. Berliner, L. "The Child Witness: Progress and Emerging Limitations." *Papers from a National Policy Conference on Legal Reforms in Child Sexual Abuse Cases.* J. Bulkley (Ed.). Washington, D.C.: American Bar Association, 1985.

80. Whitcomb, E., E.R. Shapiro, and L.D. Stellwagen. *When the Victim is a Child—Issues for Judges and Prosecutors.* Washington, D.C.: U.S. Government Printing Office, 1986.

81. *Final Report of the Attorney General's Task Force on Family Violence.* Washington, D.C.: U.S. Government Printing Office, 1984.

82. *Final Report of the Attorney General's Task Force on Family Violence.* Washington, D.C.: U.S. Government Printing Office, 1982.

83. Bulkley, J. *State Legislative Reform Efforts and Suggested Future Policy Directions to Improve Legal Intervention in Child Sexual Abuse Cases.* Washington, D.C.: American Bar Association, 1985.

84. Coppel, K. "An Analysis of the Legal Issues Involved in the Presentation of a Child's Testimony by Two-way Closed Circuit Television in Sexual Abuse Cases." *Papers from a National Policy Conference on Legal Reforms in Child Sexual Abuse Cases.* J. Bulkley (Ed.). Washington, D.C.: American Bar Association, 1985.

85. Graham, M. "Child Sex Abuse Prosecutions: Hearsay and Confrontation Issues." *Papers from a National Policy Conference on Legal Reforms in Child Sexual Abuse Cases.* J. Bulkley (Ed.). Washington, D.C.: American Bar Association, 1985.

86. Lloyd, D. "Practical Issues in Avoiding Confrontation of a Child Witness and the Defendant in a Criminal Trial." *Papers from a National Policy Conference on Legal Reforms in Child Sexual Abuse Cases.* J. Bulkley (Ed.). Washington, D.C.: American Bar Association, 1985.

87. Mlyniec, W. "Presence, Compulsory Process, and pro se Representation: Constitutional Ramifications upon Evidentiary Innovation in Sex Abuse Cases." *Papers from a National Policy Conference on Legal Reforms in Child Sexual Abuse Cases.* J. Bulkley (Ed.). Washington, D.C.: American Bar Association, 1985.

88. Pierron, G. Joseph. "A Comparative Analysis of Nine Recent State Statutory Approaches Concerning Special Hearsay Exceptions for Children's Out-of-Court Statements Concerning Sexual Abuse with Emphasis on what Constitutes Unavailability and Indicia of Reliability under Ohio v. Roberts and Other Decisions." *Papers from a National Policy Conference on Legal*

Reforms in Child Sexual Abuse Cases. J. Bulkley (Ed.). Washington, D.C.: American Bar Association, 1985.

89. *Ohio v. Roberts*, 448 U.S. 56 (1980).

90. *State v. Wilkerson*, 295 N.C. 559, 247 S.E. 2d 905 (1978); Annotation, 98 *American Law Reports* 3d 306 (1980).

91. Pierre-Puysegar, M.A. "The Representation of the Legal System among Children from 6 to 10." Paper presented at the International Society for the Study of Behavioral Development, Tours, France, July 1985.

92. Goodman, G.S., and V. Helgeson. "Child Sexual Abuse: Children's Memory and the Law." *Papers from a National Policy Conference on Legal Reforms in Child Sexual Abuse Cases*. J. Bulkley (Ed.). Washington, D.C.: American Bar Association, 1985.

PART V

Specialized Teams

Section Editor: Donald C. Bross

26. Institutional Abuse Case Review Teams

Janet K. Motz and
Michael A. Nunno

Introduction

The issue of child maltreatment in out-of-home care (for the purpose of this article out-of-home care will include day care, foster care, and residential placements in a 24-hour care facility) has received increased attention during the past few years with the incorporation of a definition of institutional abuse in the "Draft Federal Standards for Abuse and Neglect Prevention and Treatment," priority spending on the federal level, and increased state regulatory and legislative concern in the field. Many states have placed the protection of children in out-of-home care squarely in the hands of child protection personnel whose traditional responsibilities have been the investigation of familial abuse and neglect; and other states must still address the question of which agency will provide independent oversight for children in placement. Assigning responsibility to child protective services for institutional abuse does not have the strong and widespread legislative clarity seen throughout the states in the child abuse reporting legislation movement of the 1970s; instead procedural and regulatory changes are typical.

Defining the Problem

Rabb and Rindfleisch's statement of the problem of institutional abuse is accurate and helpful:

> [References to] existing statutes and policies in many cases give the impression that institutional child abuse and neglect is covered under statutes written to deal with intrafamilial child abuse and neglect. This assumption systematically ignores the differences between institutional settings and familial settings.[1]

Compounding the problem is the lack of an accepted consensus between child care and the child protective professionals as to the scope of the problem and proper methods for identification, reporting, investigating, recommending corrections, and monitoring institutional abuse situations. Based on a survey, the same two authors concluded that:

> In general, the monitoring and investigative elements of the child protective system in each agency and each state had an *ad hoc* quality. The manner in which an allegation was identified and investigated varied widely even within each institution. The lack of clarity about what constitutes mistreatment and how it ought to be monitored and investigated contributed to this *ad hoc* quality. In some cases, conditions which were reportable did not reach the administrative level because staff "handled" it informally. When other conditions which were reportable reached the administration, they were frequently dealt with as failures in the performance of the worker [more] than as an infringement on the resident's rights. The issue was defined as a staff problem rather than as a problem of mistreatment. Even if administrators view them as child mistreatment, [they] were not reported outside the facility because the response from outside agencies was viewed typically as unpredictable.[2]

Nevertheless, some efforts have been made to standardize policy and procedure and establish practice standards for the investigation of child maltreatment in out-of-home care.[3,4,5] State and local agencies with the responsibility for the placement and protection of children in out-of-home care can assess and study the current status of the problem within their jurisdiction, partly by referring to these developing standards. In addition, states must clarify operational definitions of out-of-home care maltreatment, as these definitions affect each aspect of the response to institutional abuse.

Teams and the Response to Institutional Abuse

This chapter offers guidelines and a process for responding to institutional abuse. The approach offered incorporates a state-level policy or regulatory team similar to some of the community-based child protection teams described in this book. State institutional abuse teams, as described here, must be capable of reviewing cases of identified and reported child maltreatment in residential child care settings after the investigation is completed. This makes the state team distinct from a purely diagnostic or investigatory team. The team may make policy, define procedures, and recommend legislation regarding the scope of the problem. The team can lend assistance in defining institutional abuse and provide direction in identification and reporting procedures, investigation, corrective action, and plan monitoring. These teams can also help to determine whether the agencies involved in the investigation and treatment of abuse and neglect responded adequately and in a timely manner.

Although community-based child protection teams for familial maltreatment have been in operation for the past ten to fifteen years, the specialized institutional abuse review teams are a fairly recent phenomenon.* Based on the notion that the investigation of maltreatment in out-of-home care requires specialized knowledge and skill, it follows that teams reviewing these cases should also be specialized.

At least three states have a central state level review team for institutional maltreatment with at least a few of these functions (Colorado, Indiana, and North Dakota). A special advantage of the central state level teams is that they gain a perspective from reviewing all or a random sample of investigated cases. The development of a solid data base can be most helpful to the local and state agencies responsible for child protective and institutional program development, training, budget, and legislative initiatives.

REPRESENTATION

Effective membership of any review team is interdisciplinary and interagency. It is advantageous to have state and local representation with legislative, judicial, administrative, or programmatic responsibility for residential child care, licensing, child protective services, child placing agencies, and law enforcement.

Although this representation is optimal, all components are not essential for success. The interdisciplinary aspect is also important and thus the medical, legal, educational, social work, and law enforcement professions should be represented on the team or available for consultation. Preferably, a community representative will be included on the team to gain the perspective of the private citizen. It is important that team members have authority to speak on behalf of their agencies at team meetings and have access to individuals in their own agencies who can effect changes in agency policy and procedure when necessary. Knowledge regarding child abuse and neglect, special aspects of institutional maltreatment, legal and regulatory criteria for decision-making, efficient and effective case review, and functioning as a team member should be components of team orientation training.

It is essential for the immediate and long-term success of the review team to have clear written guidelines and a stated purpose, with administrative approval from each state agency represented. Equally important is the determination regarding the types and numbers of cases to be reviewed by this team, a consideration that is often dictated by the number of cases reported to the system. In some states over two thousand reports are made annually, necessitating a review of only a selected sample of cases, only certain types of out-of-home placements, or only some types of maltreatment. Other states receive only fifty or sixty reports per year, allowing for the review of all cases.

Case Review Factors

Since the team reviews the case after an investigation has been completed, it will receive a report that contains a determination by the investigator as to whether abuse or neglect has been found. The report must indicate the applicable legal and regulatory definitions, the corrective action recommended and the monitoring plan.

INDIVIDUAL PROTECTION AND SYSTEMS ISSUES

The team may consider each case from an individual as well as a system perspective and may make recommendation regarding the:

identification and reporting procedure
investigation of the specific incident
immediate and long term treatment of the child

corrective action recommended for the perpetrator, the
 supervisor, and the administrators and
monitoring of the corrective action recommendations.

ISSUES ANALOGOUS TO CHILD PROTECTION IN A FAMILY SETTING

Since systematic response to the problem of institutional child maltreatment in most states and localities is relatively new, basic aspects of the problem will probably have to be reviewed. Issues that have already been addressed in familial abuse can be studied in light of the dynamics of out-of-home care placement. Existing state and local identification, reporting, investigation, assessment, and decision-making criteria designed for familial maltreatment do not always provide clear guidance relative to the type of children in care, the environment of the out-of-home care placement, or the different standards of care for children in the custody of the state.[6,7,8]

With these considerations in mind, the state institutional abuse review team must decide first whether:

1. A state's statutory definition of child maltreatment is sufficient. (For example, does it take into consideration the type of children in care, the environment of the institution, and the differing standards of care for children in custody or at home?);

2. State and federal case law provide other definitions or insight into what constitutes unacceptable care;

3. The current identification and reporting system allows immediate and safe access to the child by staff, parents, the child advocate, the administration or any interested individual who might need to report;

4. Investigation procedures are timely and allow for
   (a) ensuring the immediate safety of the child and other children in placement,
   (b) removing the child,
   (c) transferring or suspending the alleged perpetrator,
   (d) closing the facility,
   (e) contacting law enforcement officials, as appropriate;

5. Assessment procedures take into account both the immediate and long-term effects on and needs of the child, the staff involved, and the child care agency;

6. Corrective action recommendations address the immediate incident and any systematic or administrative problems contributing to the incident;

7.   Monitoring and enforcement procedures ensure that the corrective actions recommended are carried through.

ISSUES MORE SPECIFIC TO INSTITUTIONAL ABUSE

The team should consider the following issues in a review:

1.   Interagency coordination and cooperation in the investigative process;
2.   Appropriateness of placement;
3.   Licensing violations;
4.   Previous incidents involving the facility and the child;
5.   Staffing patterns within the facility or investigation unit;
6.   Legal issues, such as current state labor law, civil service statute, employment agreements, and placement agreements;
7.   Law enforcement issues, including the due process rights of the staff and care facility;
8.   Medical and psychological issues;
9.   Child care agency hiring, orientation, training plans, and procedures.

Practical Considerations

An institutional abuse review team may not be able to limit itself to office or scheduled reviews. The review team may be confronted with an immediate and critical situation. Various jurisdictional and regulatory impediments, including geographic boundaries, may interfere with efforts to improve the handling of institutional child abuse. For example, a child protective unit investigating an incident in a child care facility, and the county in which custody of the child is vested, are often not the same. The determination of one county investigating abuse might be that the child is in immediate danger or inappropriately placed, while the custodial county and court might be reluctant to approve removal.

Because of the visibility of the state institutional abuse team, team membership, and the members' knowledge of and access to the power structures of the respective state and local units, the state team may be seen by a local agency as an appropriate means of overturning or redirecting a decision by another agency or authority. Early and appropriate response by the state team will establish credibility for future direct assistance in cases under active local investigation.

For the review team to decide that direct intervention in an active case is within its scope, however, clear and written policy should be developed and agreed upon by team members, their administrators and lawyers. More often and more within the scope of most review teams, the team primarily will consider problematic policies or procedures. Current policies and procedures may be impeding identification, reporting, investigation, corrective action, and monitoring. Current approaches may also prove detrimental to the rights of children, staff, or facilities. The review team must consider how urgently changes need to be made in policy and procedure, as well as which activities are justified by the state review team given the apparent urgency of the child's situation.

Program, Policy, and Procedural Recommendations

As discussed here, state review teams examine cases for questionable or illegal programs, policies, or procedures. Overstepping the mandate and purpose of the team can be detrimental to the overall usefulness of the team and may jeopardize its effectiveness in future case reviews. For example, the team might observe through case review that a facility is completing an internal investigation prior to making a report of suspected abuse or neglect—a clear violation of state law and procedure. Depending on its scope, purpose, and legal or regulatory mandate, the team may be able to make specific recommendations to that agency to correct this violation or it may only be able to note this violation and refer it to the proper officials. Whether the officials correct the violation may be subject to the review team's inquiry.

Because the team we have discussed here reviews cases from across a state system, the data on all or a sample of incidents can be collected and analyzed. Program, policy, and procedures can be based on real rather than perceived need. A state interdisciplinary and interagency team can gather objective data as well as sound, although subjective, impressions. With this background, the team can support or assist budget and legislative initiatives. Team members are in a good position to identify statewide training needs and to make recommendations regarding training for child care staff and investigative staff.

Experience demonstrates that recommendations from a multidisciplinary, multi-agency team regarding policy, program, training, budget, and legislative initiatives carry far more impact than the recommendations of one professional group or one agency.

Interagency Coordination and Cooperation

If the scope and purpose of the review team is clear, and the administrative procedures are agreed upon and supported by all concerned, then a state-level review team can assure coordination and cooperation between the state and local agencies charged with responding to child maltreatment in out-of-home care. As indicated earlier, an adequate review of each case will assure that interagency coordination and cooperation have also taken place during the investigative process. The review team might note, for example, that institutional staff in a given location failed to provide the local investigative staff with "confidential" information needed for the investigation. Conversely, the investigative staff may have failed to provide the institution with a report of its findings. The state team, if it is within their assigned scope of authority, may call or facilitate meetings between the local units to clarify procedures and legal issues concerning this identified problem.   The facilitation of improved communications is an invaluable role when there is a multi-county, multi-agency situation. Breakdowns in communications or misunderstanding by one or more of the agencies, on the other hand, are a primary source of potential liability.

The team is also in a position to actively promote cooperation of all involved agencies, support training, promote reforms, and testify before legislators. As an example, Colorado's state team is sponsoring a statewide effort to develop model procedures for the investigation of abuse in out-of-home care settings. Because Colorado's state level team is central in the area of abuse in out-of-home care, it is frequently approached by various agencies for mediation assistance in resolving interagency problems in the investigation of abuse in these settings. As another example, Indiana's review of cases established the need for training institutional staff in the therapeutic and safe handling of children in crisis.

Summary

The existence of a state-level review team heightens awareness of the problem of abuse in out-of-home care, assists in the identification and clarification of the problem, and encourages the reassessment of practice and procedures within the various responsible agencies. A review team can prompt needed policy change and legislative action. A state level team with clear, precise goals, and a regulatory or administrative mandate can be a powerful resource for communities trying to protect children in out-of-home care.

Note

* North Dakota established a specialized team in 1979.

References

1.   Rabb, J., and N. Rindfleisch. "A Study to Define and Assess Severity of Institutional Abuse/Neglect." *Child Abuse & Neglect*, 9(1985):285-294.

2.   Rindfleisch, N., and J. Rabb. "How Much of a Problem Is Resident Mistreatment in Child Welfare Institutions?" *Child Abuse & Neglect*, 8(1984):33-40.

3.   Smiles, G. "Institutional Child Abuse and Neglect in New Jersey: 1979 to 1980." Report to the National Center on Child Abuse and Neglect, New Jersey Division of Youth and Family Services, 1982.

4.   Nunno, M.A., et al. *Guidebook for the Investigation of Child Abuse and Neglect in Out of Home Care*. Residential Child Care Project, Family Life Development Center, Cornell University, 1985.

5.   Wilson, C., and S. Steppe. "Issues in the Investigation of Child Sexual Abuse and Day Care Centers." Unpublished manuscript, Tennessee Department of Human Services, 1985.

6.   Thomas, G. "Dimensions of the Problem of Child Abuse and Neglect in Residential Placements that Distinguish It from Child Abuse in a Family Context." Testimony before the United States House of Representatives, December 4, 1980.

7.   Harrell, S. "Institutional Abuse Is Different: Problems in Reporting, Investigation, and Disposition of Cases of Abuse and Neglect of Children in Publicly Administered Child Caring Institutions." Unpublished paper, District of Columbia Commission on Social Services, Washington D.C., 1980.

8.   Nunno, M. "Final Report of the Residential Child Care Project." Family Life Development Center, Cornell University, 1985.

27. Military Installation Teams*

Peter J. McNelis

Introduction

In the discussion of the military installation team, the reader will note many similarities between the organization and functions of military teams and several others presented in this book. There are significant differences as well. Some of the differences can be attributed to the unique mission and cultural characteristics of the larger organization within which the team operates.

Given that the Department of Defense may not be familiar to the reader, a brief overview of its people, purposes and special problems may be useful. By putting a discussion of teams into the military context, the reader can share the writer's perspective (and that of military colleagues) on the problems of, and approaches to, military family violence.

The Context of the Military Organization

What is currently known as the Department of Defense (DOD) evolved from an Act of Congress in 1789 which established the war department. The DOD has as its mission the maintenance of peace and, if necessary, the successful waging of war. It is a cabinet-level organization with an operational chain of command running from the

President to the Secretary of Defense through the Joint Chiefs of Staff, to the commanders of nine unified and specified commands (e.g., United States Pacific command).

Civilian oversight of the DOD is assured by Congress, which created the Office of the Secretary of Defense (OSD). OSD is staffed by civilians appointed by the President to manage the budget, establish policy, set standards and monitor the activities of the Military Departments, agencies and commands.

The Military Departments consist of the Army, the Navy (including the marine corps), and the Air Force. They are responsible for recruiting, training and equipping their forces, but operational control of these forces in battle is assigned to one of the unified or specified commands.

The Department of Defense provides the structure and mechanism for preserving the security of the United States of America and its allies.

THE MILITARY COMMUNITY

There are approximately 5 million individuals who serve on active duty in the National Guard and the Reserve Forces, and as civilian employees within the DOD. Of this total, 2.1 million serve on active duty in the three Military Departments, accompanied by some 1.2 million spouses, 1.6 million dependent children, and 73,000 dependent parents or others.[1] The active duty forces are assigned the major day-to-day responsibility of preparing for and carrying out the DOD mission. Most military health care and social services, including those that are the subject of this chapter, directly support active duty personnel and their families.

Active duty members of the military community are young (55% are 25 years of age or younger), healthy, and usually married. They and their families have a lifestyle different from that of the vast majority of their fellow countrymen. High-stress and high-risk jobs, frequent family separations and parental absences, overseas living and concomitant cultural shock, and a system whose needs have priority over individual needs, are all attributes of life in uniform. While these factors often are growth opportunities, their frequent presence sometimes threatens military family equilibrium. The military is aware of these factors and their potential impact on both the family and mission success, and it has responded by creating a sophisticated social service and health care delivery system. Several programs within the larger systems focus on the resolution of specific problems such as drug abuse, alcohol abuse, and family violence.

MILITARY FAMILY VIOLENCE

Family violence is one of the several problems that the military community is addressing. It is a problem that is no more severe than in the civilian community, but it is a significant problem. During fiscal year 1986 (1 Oct 85-30 Sep 86) there were a total of 7,904 established cases of child abuse and neglect and 11,318 established cases of spouse abuse among military families throughout the DOD. An established case is a substantiated incident of abuse and neglect; reports of family violence would obviously be much higher. The rate per 1,000 established cases of military child abuse and neglect in fiscal year 1986 was 5.0, and the rate per 1,000 for established cases of military spouse abuse during the same year was 9.72.

THE DOD FAMILY ADVOCACY PROGRAM

Following the passage of Public Law 93-247 (Child Abuse and Neglect Prevention and Treatment Act) in 1974, the Army, Air Force and Navy began developing separate programs to deal with this problem. Finally, in 1981, these separate programs were brought together under the guidelines of a DOD directive[2] which included spouse abuse as well as child abuse and neglect as an area of concern.

The DOD Family Advocacy Program is a comprehensive military family violence program of prevention, identification, treatment and rehabilitation, currently under the direction of the Assistant Secretary of Defense for Force Management and Personnel. To carry out his responsibilities, the Assistant Secretary has established an organization to develop and recommend policy and program guidance; set standards; prepare and submit budgets; assist the services in their efforts to develop their programs; and monitor program implementation. The organization is called the Military Family Resource Center; its director serves as the coordinator of the DOD Family Advocacy Program and as chairman of a joint-services Family Advocacy Committee. The joint-services Family Advocacy Committee comprises representatives from the Army, Navy, Air Force and Marine Corps, as well as from the offices of other Assistant Secretaries of Defense and the U.S. Coast Guard.[3,4] Details regarding service-specific issues, policies or programs may be best referred to the service program managers at their various headquarters; their names, addresses and phone numbers may be obtained from the Resource Center. Should information regarding a local installation program be sought or a case referral be necessary, the reader is advised to contact the Family Advocacy Officer at the military hospital or medical treatment facility located on that installation.

Each of the services implements the policies set by the Office of the Assistant Secretary of Defense for Force Management and Personnel in ways that best meet their mission requirements and the need of their own personnel. Since a sufficient number of manpower resources to undertake a comprehensive program is not currently available, the services have had to be administratively and organizationally creative in assuring that the program is operational, victims are protected, and families receive the assistance they require. If program funding continues to increase, this should be less of a problem in the coming years. Positive changes in program growth and development were evident as congressional funding increased considerably over several years.[5] This funding, often augmented by the services at the local installation level, has permitted the development of the preventive and rehabilitative thrusts of the Family Advocacy Program; the military installation teams that are the focus of this chapter have been one of the beneficiaries of increased funding.

The Teams

At military installations worldwide, all of the military services are responsibile for acting on cases of family violence. The titles given to these organizations vary somewhat, but their reasons for existence and methods of operating are quite similar. For this discussion, I will call them "case management teams." The following discussion of the nature and function of these teams implies a uniformity of design and universality of implementation throughout the Department of Defense. Although significant progress has been made toward standardization, availability of resources and organizational differences among the services tend to diversity. The following material should be read as representative, but not necessarily the standard, of team practice.

PURPOSE OF TEAMS

The case management team's purpose is to assure that the best possible decisions and dispositions are made regarding cases of family violence. It is believed that this purpose can best be served when a multidisciplinary team of invested individuals shares in data collection and analysis, makes a case determination based upon the findings, participates in a plan of action, and monitors the entire process until closure is achieved. All of the team's energies are focused upon the care and protection of the victim and the prevention of any recurrence of abuse or neglect.

COMPOSITION

Normally, a military case management team consists of one or more of the following: active duty military or Department of the Army civilian social workers, physicians (e.g., pediatrics, family practice), lawyers, law enforcement officers, chaplains, and a representative of the local command. Other personnel who are often included are nurses, military family service agency representatives, and local civilian child protection services workers. When their expertise is needed, additional professionals (e.g., psychologists, psychiatrists, radiologists) participate on a case-by-case basis. It must be noted, however, that military programs dealing with family violence are not yet fully resourced. Therefore, not all installation teams have available to them the aforementioned professionals. When the ideal membership mix is not available, local teams will call upon related or allied professionals (e.g., school counselors, Red Cross workers, other interested physicians, etc.) for assistance.

ORGANIZATION

The military medical treatment facility (MTF) commander of the local installation appoints the military members to the case management team. When membership includes individuals from the local civilian community, invitations to join are sent to the appropriate agency or individuals. The MTF commander retains responsibility for the activities of the team, but normally delegates chairmanship and responsibility for day-to-day operations to either the Chief of Social Work Services, the Chief of Pediatrics or the Chief of Hospital (i.e., Professional) services.

The chairperson of the team arranges and conducts the meetings, assures that a case manager is appointed for each case (often the chairperson is also the case manager, especially if he or she is a social worker), sees that team action is properly documented and that appropriate reports are forwarded to higher headquarters.

Since the Marine Corps receives its medical support from the Navy, cases of child abuse and neglect and spouse abuse among Marine Corps family members are referred to the Navy's Family Advocacy Representative (FAR) at their MTF. The Navy's FAR may or may not be the chairperson of their team, but he or she is the full-time person responsible for the overall management of the Navy's program at the MTF.

Case Management Process

REPORTING

As in most civilian communities, certain personnel are required to report incidents of suspected abuse or neglect. These include physicians, social workers, nurses, law enforcement personnel, school officials, and child support service workers. The services vary somewhat in requiring others to report incidents. For example, the Navy states that "all military agencies, departments and individuals" *shall* report; the Army on the other hand requires reporting for the first two groups while *encouraging* reporting by "military and civilian members of the installation community." The Air Force is less specific with regard to who must report, but a moral imperative to do so by anyone aware of a problem is implicit in the prevention and protection policies they have articulated.

The report of a case of abuse or neglect may be made to the individual designated by the MTF commander as the official point of contact (e.g., the Navy's FAR) for that installation or to the local military law enforcement agency. Depending upon the nature of the incident, either of these two choices is appropriate for those "required" to report. Whether the victim resides on or off the military installation should not affect this decision.

Regardless of who receives the initial report, the official "point of contact" shortly becomes involved, and he or she refers the case for action to the case management team. It is DOD policy that teams, in turn, notify their civilian counterparts concerning all child abuse and neglect cases with which they are involved, in accordance with laws governing reporting in the host state.

It should also be noted that when both the military victim and the individual reporting the incident reside in a civilian community, the local civilian child protection service agency often is their most expedient resource. The military Family Advocacy Program encourages contact with these agencies by the initial reporter under these circumstances. It is, however, in the victim's and their families' best interest if the initial reporter and/or the civilian agency notify the military point of contact as soon as possible after the initial report.

INVESTIGATION

The investigation that follows a report of child abuse and neglect and spouse abuse is a multi-pronged, multidisciplinary effort involving, ideally, all of the primary team members, the civilian child protection service agency, other medical professionals and the perpetrator's command.

No one agency or specialty area can provide an adequate investigation of all but the most simple of family violence cases. The reasons for this are: first, the investigation requires a full and complete exploration of the medical evidence to document the medical condition, its etiology and prognosis. Secondly, it requires an assessment of the psychosocial status of the victim, the perpetrator and the family to substantiate the abuse or neglect and to make recommendations regarding the rehabilitation potential of all concerned. Thirdly, an investigation by law enforcement personnel is required when any major offense is committed against a person to establish whether or not a prosecutable offense exists. Finally, the investigation should include evaluation of the perpetrator's past and present military performance, as well as his/her future potential, to arrive at conclusions regarding continued retention on active duty.

CIVILIAN INVOLVEMENT

The involvement of the civilian child protective service community is absolutely critical to the success of the entire DOD Family Advocacy Program. This fact is not well recognized by the civilian community, and is occasionally overlooked by some of the military personnel having responsibility for their installation's Family Advocacy Program.

The explanation for the essential role played by the civilian community in this family program is based upon the fact that although the military has considerable authority over its active duty personnel, it has little authority over families. The military has no authority to remove a child from a parent (except in cases of imminent danger to life or limb). The military cannot place a child in foster care. The military does not have family courts and it cannot require a non-active-duty person to participate in a rehabilitation program.

At best, the military can only indirectly influence the behaviors of family members by denying privileges to them (e.g., on-base housing) and by encouraging the active duty member to assure that his family member's misbehavior is corrected.

Because of these facts, open, two-way communication between those civilian and military professionals tasked with the responsibility of protecting the victim and preventing further episodes of family violence is essential. When the communication and cooperation does not occur, the victim loses again.

Although civilian community involvement is sometimes a problem within the fifty states, it is not so intractable to change, nor so prevalent an issue as in overseas areas where value systems, sophistication of social service delivery systems, and legal responsibility for U.S. service members and their families vary markedly. Often the disposition of choice is the return of the family members to the United States where they are once again subject to competent civilian jurisdiction. This action is costly, has a negative impact on military readiness, adds additional stress to the entire family, and does not address the problem of protecting the victim in the interim.

There is no question that the involvement, communication and cooperation of the civilian community, whether here or overseas, is critical to the development of military programs dealing with family abuse or neglect. The DOD directive governing the Family Advocacy Program, and each of the service's implementing instructions/regulations to their major commands, explicitly address this issue and task their program managers at all levels to enhance the civilian-military interface.

Case Conferences

Due to the need for immediate intervention in many, if not most, cases of abuse and neglect, several case management team members will be involved shortly after receipt of the initial report. Typically, the social work and pediatric members will act independently in their professional capacities, consult with one another and initiate the involvement of others by in-hospital consultation requests and referrals to outside agencies.

PURPOSE

Case conferences are called to coordinate activities, discuss findings, decide what is missing, make case determinations, establish a treatment, rehabilitation or administrative plan, and monitor ongoing cases. In most locations, the caseload is such that case conferences are held on a regularly scheduled basis, usually once a week. Sometimes, either because of a crisis to be confronted or the infrequency of referrals, unscheduled case conferences are initiated by the chairperson.

The focus of the case conference varies depending on whether the team is discussing a problem of child abuse/neglect or one of spouse abuse. In fact, if the personnel resources are available, it is generally the services' recommendation that two separate case management teams be established, one for children and one for spouse abuse. As stated in Army Regulations "the treatment goal for children is protection and services that help parents be better parents. The treatment goal for spouses is control of self and life circumstances."[6]

MANAGEMENT

Although team meetings do not stand on formality, they are conducted in a business-like manner with each participant presenting and discussing his or her findings or observations, and the entire team engaged in a consensus-seeking exercise regarding future courses of action. If the team is fortunate, they will have a secretary available to record the process; more often than not the minutes are taken by one of the members. The minutes are generally kept on a case-by-case basis, and then placed in the primary client's record.

Normally, the case discussion follows a standard outline such as SOAP (i.e., Subjective findings, Objective findings, Assessment, Plan) in order to keep team members focused. A separate summary sheet is kept by the chairperson, either by name or code number, on all active cases so that their status and required actions can be readily monitored.

As trends develop, community needs are identified, or policy issues arise, the team meeting may shift its focus to these other issues. The results of these discussions are channeled to the appropriate command level. Past results include local improvements, like hours of clinic and child care center operation, major policy and programmatic changes at the service headquarters level, and changes by the Office of the Assistant Secretary of Defense (with respect to money and manpower resources).

DECISION ALTERNATIVES

Among the most difficult dilemmas a case management team faces are decisions with administrative and criminal justice system ramifications for some or all of the participants. It is a dilemma dealt with daily by civilian child protective service workers, but one not normally faced by those clinically oriented members of the case management team who routinely work with more motivated, self-referred and less controversial clients.

The decisions made by the team should be based upon professional knowledge and experience, as social workers, pediatricians and others determine if abuse or neglect has or has not occurred, as well as what should be done about it.

Whether or not their judgment will ever get to, or be affirmed by, a court of law should not be the team's primary concern. When this concern becomes paramount, the team becomes immobilized and their decisions guarded, leaving a weak and unclear treatment or intervention plan. At these times, only a confession by the alleged perpetrator seems to suffice; in lieu of that and regardless of the medical and psychosocial evidence, a team may be reluctant to confirm their suspicions.

Certainly, the weighing of evidence by a court of law and the analysis of data by a case management team are not incompatible pursuits, but neither are they the same. The team's integrity is intact when it calls upon its clinical skills and its professional knowledge base and acts accordingly, regardless of whether or not their assessment is subsequently affirmed by a court of law.

After analyzing the available data, the team has three alternatives: they may decide that the incident of abuse or neglect did occur and declare that the case is "established"; they may decide that the incident did not occur and declare that the case is "unfounded"; or they may decide that there are reasons to believe that abuse or neglect may have occurred and declare that the case is "suspected."

Each of these basic decisions requires follow-up actions or decisions to be made. For example, once a case is:

(1) Established—a treatment/rehabilitation and/or administrative action plan must be decided upon for the victim, the perpetrator, and the family unit. If the civilian or military courts have not already been involved, this also needs to be considered. In addition, a decision needs to be made as to which of the team members will be the "case manager" for each case. The case manager is responsible for assuring that the team plans are coordinated and carried out, and for periodically reporting the case status at team meetings.

(2) Unfounded—case management team records regarding cases that have been unfounded are to be destroyed. Notification should also be made to that effect to the central registry at service headquarters; the registry should, in turn, purge its records of all unfounded cases.

(3) Suspected—A decision to classify a case as "suspected" should be based on a reasonable possibility that abuse or neglect occurred. The reasons for concern should be clearly articulated. Decisions must be made as to what specifically will be done to address each concern or question. Under normal circumstances, a case should not remain "suspected" for more than six weeks; within that time, and in the best interest of all

concerned, a determination should be made as to whether the case is "established" or "unfounded."

Reporting Requirements and Procedures

Each of the services requires that case information be transmitted to a central registry or repository maintained by the service's medical departments. Case information is retained in the service repository for case management, information maintenance, quality assurance, statistical analysis, and program development purposes, as well as for the facilitation of intra- and interservice case transfers. Additional information is forwarded to the central registry as it becomes available. Information reported may change the case status (e.g., from Suspected to Unfounded), provide notice of a transfer or closure, or document recidivism.

Records

Access to child abuse and neglect or spouse abuse records contained in the central registry is strictly controlled and monitored to preclude the record's misuse. Normally, central registry information is shared, if appropriate, with a local case management team inquiring as to a record of any past history on a new case they are investigating. The information may be shared with the service's military personnel center to assure that the family can remain where they are stationed so that treatment can continue. Information from the central registry may also be shared with the official, local county, or state child protection agency should it be determined that they have a legitimate need to know. The local civilian agency should request this information from the chairperson of the military case management team at the nearest military installation; the chairperson would, in turn, request that information from the central registry utilizing the procedures established by his or her service. If transfer cannot be avoided, information to the personnel center will assure that the family will be transferred to a site where treatment is available. The local case management team *must* report certain case information on active duty military personnel who are involved in the "Personnel Reliability Program" (PRP). The goal of the PRP is to ensure that military members having jobs related to nuclear weapons (e.g., bomber pilots, missile launch control officers) are reliable.

Each of the services either requires (Army, Navy, Marine Corps) or encourages (Air Force) reports of military child abuse or neglect to the state child protective services agency for the reasons cited. In fact, because the need for state involvement is so apparent to team members, this information-sharing with the state is rarely omitted from the action plan.

Information from the central registry may also be shared with the local county or state child protection agency should it be determined that they have a legitimate need to know. The local civilian agency should request this information from the chairperson of the military case management team at the nearest military installation; the chairperson would, in turn, request that information from the central registry utilizing the procedures established by his/her service.

Finally, reports containing aggregate statistics are prepared by those responsible for each of the service's central registries and forwarded to the Office of the Secretary of Defense for Health Affairs. These reports contain demographic information and incidence rates. They are utilized to analyze trends, programmatic issues, and resource requirements. The data collected by the DOD are currently being revised to make them more internally consistent and useful for service program managers as well as compatible, for comparison purposes, with data gathered by our civilian counterparts.

Follow-up Actions

Due to the many professional disciplines involved, as well as the several entities having a critical, vested interest in cases (i.e., the command, the state, the medical department), "follow-up" becomes the essential ingredient of a successful Family Advocacy Program. The case manager can assure that coordination of effort occurs by assertively following up on all aspects of the evaluation, treatment or rehabilitation plan that has been decided upon. There is too much room for cases "to fall through the cracks" if this responsibility is casually assumed.

When a case has been classified as "suspected," the actions needed to resolve the suspicions should have been recorded. These may include ordering and obtaining the results of lab tests, psychological evaluations, radiological examinations, home assessments, and similar procedures. Whatever is ordered or planned should be completed in a timely manner, or the reasons why this has not occurred must be justified. In the vast majority of cases, six weeks is considered to be more than enough time to resolve one's suspicions. Regardless of the resolution agreed upon, (i.e., "established" or "unfounded," a follow-up report must be forwarded to the central registry which will record the change.

On established cases, a treatment, rehabilitation or administrative action plan must be established. It is the case manager's responsibility to assure that the plan is carried out, to monitor its progress, and to arrange periodic follow-up reports to the team. As the case status changes through closure, transfer or recidivism, it is also the case manager's duty to see that reports of the changes are forwarded to the central registry or, if appropriate, to the state child protective service agency.

CRITERIA FOR SUCCESS

There are several ways to measure success in cases dealing with family violence and each of these has advantages and disadvantages. Nevertheless, criteria must be specifically stated so that quality assurance, cost effectiveness and even patient/therapist satisfaction measures can be instituted. For the Department of Defense, success is determined by the absence of any new reports of abuse or neglect for 365 days since the date of the last report. Regardless of the reasons for the success or the possibility that at some future date abuse or neglect may recur, a time-limited parameter has been set and it is proving to be reasonable and acceptable to those in the field.

CRITERIA FOR CLOSURE

Once a military family violence case has been established, it can only be closed for one of three reasons: success, transfer within the military from one installation to another, or discharge of the active duty member from the military.

When closure occurs, the case manager will make the appropriate notation in the record and notify the central registry of the change in status. In the event of a case closure due to transfer or discharge, the receiving installation (transfer) or appropriate civilian agency (discharge) should be notified of the family's arrival and made aware of the procedures to be followed for the transmittal of the case records.

Advantages of the Case Management Team

The case management team mobilizes the medical, law enforcement, social service and command resources of the military community and coordinates them with the activities of the civilian child protection agency. Because it involves so many professionals, it is a costly endeavor. But, it also addresses the problems of child abuse and neglect and spouse abuse effectively and efficiently.

Compared with other community-based family violence intervention efforts, the military case management team has unique aspects. All cases are routinely evaluated by the multidisciplinary team members and the team makes all disposition decisions. The specialized knowledge of each team member is needed. The inclusion of different types of specialized knowledge has a synergistic impact on the deliberations and ultimately enhances family outcomes.

Since similar teams are in place at military installations worldwide, a responsive resource/referral network has been created that could not be duplicated by the civilian community. In addition, with essentially the same Family Advocacy Program in place throughout the services, and coordinated organizational oversight coming from higher headquarters, the potential for improvements in policies, quality assurance and standards of care is greatly increased. Perhaps most importantly, the military family can expect at least a minimum level of services wherever they might be assigned.

Case Management Team Issues

Although the military is justly proud of the Family Advocacy Program it has developed, it is acutely aware of the improvements that are necessary and the issues that remain to be resolved.

RESOURCES

Despite the fact that there have been sizable increases in congressional appropriations for the DOD Family Advocacy Program over the past several years,[5] we are not yet at the point where adequate services can be provided at all military installations. Each of the services and OASD (FM&P) are, however, working hard to rectify this situation, and have been very successful to date.

There are currently about 723 civilian and active duty military personnel assigned full-time to this program throughout the DOD. This amounts to approximately two full-time people for every four U.S. military installations. Program coverage comes primarily from medical staff who have other full-time job responsibilities. Obviously, additional staff are required and are being sought. A significant increase in the total full-time strength of the services for these purposes is not anticipated, however. The DOD FAP is, therefore, moving aggressively into the contracts and contracting arena in an effort to purchase the services needed from competent professional civilian groups/agencies. Where contracting by the services has been done, it has proven to be a highly successful cooperative enterprise.

INFORMATION SHARING

For various reasons ranging from specific statutory proscription to uneasiness on the part of some civilian caseworkers regarding the military's use of case information, there has been a reluctance on the part of some states to share information on military child abuse and neglect cases with their counterparts at the local military installation. Many states, on the other hand, have amended or reinterpreted their existing laws or co-signed memoranda of agreement with the military, thereby enabling them to share this case information and work alongside the military case management teams.

Civilian-military cooperation is essential for a successful DOD Family Advocacy Program as noted previously, as well as being essential for the accomplishment of each state's responsibilities toward all individuals residing within its borders. The military family advocacy representative can enable the state child protection service agency worker to gain access to military medical, social service and law enforcement information that can have a significant bearing on the course of action taken by the state. Furthermore, the DOD Family Advocacy Program, although in need of additional resources, still has an impressive array of professional clinical resources available to it that can augment the services of the state. Most states and, therefore, most families can benefit from this additional support.

States must recognize that the military has a responsive and vast referral network at its disposal that is not matched in the civilian community. If a military family being followed for problems of child abuse or neglect by the state is reassigned and the military is not notified of the existence of the case, the odds are that there will be no adequate follow-up. If the military is notified, follow-up can be assured and the responsibilities of the state can be fulfilled. Ultimately, the local military case management team can be, officially or unofficially, viewed as state child protective agency "extenders," and team efforts can be directed toward complementing those of their host state.

JURISDICTION OVERSEAS

In overseas areas where local social services may not be as sophisticated, and where local responsibility and concern for military family violence may be non-existent, the limited capacity of the military command to intervene directly in cases of military family violence is even more of an issue.

If there is an immediate threat to life or risk of serious impairment, the military can and does intervene to remove the victim or constrain the perpetrator.   In all other cases, however, military intervention must be less direct. If the active duty member is unable or unwilling to stop the violent or neglectful behavior of his or her spouse, then the overseas command may request an early return of the family members to the United States. The command can curtail the assignment of the active duty member. Should the family members refuse to return to the United States, the overseas command may revoke their housing privileges and inform the host nation of their actions. In most instances, the individuals are no longer welcome guests in that country, and they ultimately return to the United States. The problem is the length of time it takes to complete this process, and the ongoing risks to the victim as the process unfolds.

A mechanism sanctioned by the Status of Forces Agreements (SOFA) and the laws of the host country is needed to clarify the jurisdictional issues involved. Such a mechanism would permit U.S. intervention in cases of family violence and other crimes of violence, vandalism, delinquency or similar criminal behavior of U.S. citizens overseas. For example, it might be appropriate to appoint a Federal Circuit Court judge to be responsible for covering crimes of this nature overseas.

JURISDICTION WITHIN THE UNITED STATES

The case management team is not just confronted with jurisdictional issues in overseas settings, however. There are some challenging problems to be faced in a number of states that have military installations within their borders. Depending upon when an installation was established, the legal opinions of the responsible state and federal parties at the time, and the particular mission assigned to that installation, a number of military installations operate under what is termed an "exclusive" jurisdiction. Basically, exclusive jurisdiction means that the federal government retains authority over and responsibility for all activities occurring within its boundaries. The state has no authority to intervene on-base unless or until intervention is requested.

Exclusive jurisdiction is not the typical military arrangement, but it creates special challenges for those involved in the Family Advocacy Program for the reasons cited above. The Department of Defense Directive governing this program[7] reflects an awareness of this issue and suggests a solution by advising the Secretaries of the military departments to "encourage local commands to develop memoranda of understanding providing for cooperation and reciprocal reporting of information with the appropriate civilian officials."

Another solution that has proven to be effective at many installations has been the use of a Memorandum of Agreement (MOA) between the state or county child protective service agency and the local military installation commander that permits state access to the installation and provides assistance to them, as appropriate, in the execution of their official duties. In effect, the signing of an MOA creates an exception to the exclusive jurisdiction status of the installation for this discreetly defined area of concern.

OTHER ISSUES

The three issues discussed are the most immediately critical to the success of the case management team, but there are other issues that must soon be addressed if the military Family Advocacy Program is to mature as a unique multidisciplinary effort. These issues can be subsumed under the heading of "accountability" since they deal with definitions, documentation, and the ongoing demonstration of the efficiency and effectiveness of the team's work.

While some excellent evaluations are currently underway, most notably at a joint-service family advocacy demonstration project on the cost-benefits of family advocacy programs, comparative studies of various treatment modalities with varying target populations. (e.g., batterers and high-risk groups) need to be undertaken. Some support for the Family Advocacy Program can be expected because the DOD agrees it is the right thing to do, but support will increase in direct proportion to the cost-benefit advantages demonstrated, especially with regard to the retention of service members and the readiness of military units.

There must be assurance that the professional services provided by the team are of the highest quality. Standards of care and the credentials of the care providers must be set and monitored. Team work must be documented and retrospective reviews of all cases should be a routine practice. It is good to know that much progress has been made in these areas, but the task is complicated by the diversity of team membership and the numerous offices and agencies necessarily engaged in this effort.

Summary

It has been barely a decade since the first case management teams were established by the services, and only about five years since the first funding for these teams was provided by the DOD. Yet, in this relatively short span of time, a worldwide, responsive, helping network has been established to deal with the very real problems of family violence within the military. The multidisciplinary team located on every installation will continue to be the key to the Family Advocacy Program's success as the services continue to improve what was recently begun.

Note

*   The opinions or assertions contained herein are the private views of the author, and are not to be construed as official or as reflecting the view of the Department of the Army or the Department of Defense.

References

1.   "Almanac." *Defense 86*, pp. 24, 31. Washington, D.C.: Department of Defense, September/October 1986.

2   "Family Advocacy Program." Department of Defense Directive 6400.1, 19 May 1981, revised 10 July 1986.

3.   The U.S. Coast Guard is part of the Department of Transportation, not the Department of Defense.

4.   Additional information regarding the DOD Family Advocacy Program may be obtained by writing the Director, Military Resource Center, 4015 Wilson Boulevard, Arlington, Virginia 22203 (Tel: 1-800-336-4592).

5. $0 in FY 81, $5,000,000 in FY 82, $7,500,000 in FY 83 and FY 84, $12,000,000 in FY 85, $12,000,000 in FY 86, and $15,000,000 in FY 87.

6.   Army Regulation 608-1, p. 7-5, 15 May 1983.

7.   Department of Defense Directive 6400.1 as amended 10 July 1986 at paragraph E2h.

28. State or Regional Consultation Teams

Donald C. Bross and Robert E. Cramer, Jr.

Introduction

The concept of a child protection team is very flexible: individuals with the perspectives and training needed to protect children formally associate in a cooperative effort. Thus it is not surprising that as additional needs have been recognized in the development of modern child protective services, new forms of child protection teams have been introduced in response.

Purposes of State and Regional Teams

Frontline professionals and local child protection teams can handle most cases reasonably well. However, the under-funding of positions is a concern. Every community cannot afford to pay alone for all the expertise that might be needed in every case; also, the overwhelming nature of some cases can exceed frontline resources. Case load standards for child protective services (hereinafter CPS) workers have been rationally established at under 25 cases per worker,[1] and ordered by at least one Federal court in Massachusetts.[2] Compliance with the standards by legislators and administrators, however, is rare.   This leaves workers outmanned.

In urban areas or other settings with special expertise available, CPS workers can be supported to some degree by the assistance of other professionals, a significant reason for local child protection teams.   In other counties or regions, there is limited expertise, and perhaps no local teams, for responding to unusually difficult diagnostic, treatment, or legal issues.   Where local teams exist, even local teams may wish to refer an especially difficult case.

Finally, as new developments arise in child protection, many practitioners have no incentive to learn quickly.   For example, one survey revealed that many frontline mental health, protective services and medical professionals were not keeping up with journal literature on child sexual abuse.[3]   State and regional teams can be a continuing source of information on new developments in child protection and can help assure equitable resource distribution, efficiency of resource distribution, support in depth, and accountability.

EQUITABLE RESOURCE DISTRIBUTION

The availability of a team of individuals with more extensive training or experience to help rural teams, to back up non-affiliated individuals on the frontline, and to assist even well-established and experienced services in particularly difficult cases, means that scarce expert resources will be available more fairly across a state or a region. Any community can face a child protection problem that is exceptionally difficult, often a type of case that is relatively uncommon.   A consultative service for a region assures that a case will not fail inevitably because of a lack of local resources, and reflects the realization that many difficult cases arise across a service cachment area that is sufficiently large.   A regional or statewide team assures that no county will be left without access to expert services.

EFFICIENCY OF RESOURCE ALLOCATION

Related to the problem of funding expertise is finding expertise. It is often difficult for a local individual or team to know how to gain access to specialists in medicine, social work, law, psychiatry, or other fields, especially if the expertise needed is outside one's own discipline. A state or regional consultation team can save considerable effort and expense by helping identify the type of expertise needed, as well as which individuals may fit the indicated criteria.   In one instance a pathologist may be better, in another, a pediatrician.   The varying indicators for a forensic odontologist, forensic psychiatrist, civil or criminal attorney must all be sorted out; and this can be done easily or with difficulty depending on the experience and support networks of those involved. In a sense the state or regional team should serve as a "registry" for experts.

SUPPORT IN DEPTH

In the same survey[3] that revealed that many frontline professionals were not keeping up with recent journal articles on child sexual abuse, Dr. Jean Goodwin and her colleagues found that the same individuals felt emotionally isolated, powerless, and even afraid in their work.[4] A back-up team has the potential for giving a second opinion, confirming or questioning the value of an approach, or bringing new resources to bear on a case. Any individual and any community can be overwhelmed by a difficult case when there is no back-up. With back-up, individuals can feel more comfortable with the position reached and be secure in the knowledge that others have become aware of the facts and will be available to step forward as needed.

ACCOUNTABILITY THROUGH SECOND OPINIONS, REVIEW, AND REFORM

When issues need to be addressed on a systemic basis, for example, with respect to institutional misconduct, a local program may not have sufficient authority to proceed. As discussed in Chapter 26, a state-wide team may be able to bring the necessary authority to bear when local efforts are not sufficient. A statewide consultation team can also identify systemic weaknesses, increasing prospects for an accountable system. By its continuing review of difficult cases, the consulting team should be in a good position to identify the need for reform and improvements.

Activities of State or Regional Teams

A variety of activities, including case staffings, are common for a state or regional team. Each of these activities is discussed in turn.

CASE CONSULTATIONS

The most directly valuable support a state or regional team can provide is clinical consultation in specific cases. When professionals seek assistance, it is likely that they are better-than-average practitioners, motivated to be thorough in their work and relatively unconcerned that they will appear less knowledgeable by having sought another opinion. Still, it is sometimes easier to seek advice from an outsider, presumably unaffected in judgment by local personalities or politics. The process of clinical consultation incorporates learning when each person involved is most open to learning. A specialty, for example, forensic odontology, that seems esoteric can offer a solution, e.g., interpretation of bite mark evidence or understanding of milk bottle caries. The broader scope of case consultation contributes to broader expertise and creates a larger reservoir of "institutional memory" for problems and their solutions.

TESTIMONY AND TRAINING

From the perspective of frontline professionals it is best if the regional team can provide direct evaluation and testimony in selected cases. Ideally, the local professional will be supported by the state or regional team to the point that local individuals will feel totally comfortable proceeding on their own. If a particularly technical diagnostic, prognostic, or legal issue is involved, the state or regional team specialist should be available to testify, to help prosecute, or otherwise be involved with "hands on."

Distance and scheduling conflicts may make it impossible for a specific team member to appear as a witness. The team can often refer the frontline professional to another qualified professional, providing ready access to a valuable referral network. As within most professional settings, but especially in child protection, because of the subtlety of some cases and the general lack of resources, the multidisciplinary nature of the team is essential for the "central exchange" or "switching function," the referral to appropriate experts within the state or nearby.

Just as with testimony, the state or regional team can provide direct, multidisciplinary training, or provide referrals to others with the background and educational skills needed. Training of an intact team should be preferred to individual-by-individual training, in order to increase the chances for institutionalized improvement and to enhance team relations. As already noted, however, training also takes place any time one or more professionals from a community share in a joint staffing of the state or regional team.

RESEARCH, TREND DETECTION, AND ANTICIPATION

Members of an experienced consultation team are likely to be able to recount many instances where, in a relatively short time, professionals have called them independently, from widely separated areas, about situations that first appeared as "novel" or "unique" cases. The experience of consultation teams shows that many such cases are "leading indicators" or a "tip of the iceberg," in the sense that many more cases exist that had not been previously recognized. Examples would be early referrals on what turned out to be Munchausen's Syndrome by Proxy cases, sexual abuse in preschool and school settings, and sexual abuse of very small children. In part just because it exists, the consultation team will often hear first about unique cases that later are seen as not unique. Multiple molestations by child care professionals and injuries of a series of infants by baby sitters are examples. An early experience and response to the "novel" case by the consulting team means that others referring to the team will be more likely to benefit from prior learning.

By their involvement with a wide distribution of individuals and agencies, state and regional consultation teams have the opportunity to experience new child protection challenges. Concomitant with the possibility for early failure is the possibility of early success, and the opportunity to carry out early research on new developments. Trends become evident sooner, and anticipation and planning are enhanced for consulting team members, other professionals, and agencies which employ the team.

Funding

A consulting team can be funded by many mechanisms demonstrated as suitable by any governmental, profit-making, or non-profit organization. In-kind contributions of services, appropriations, contracts, and case-by-case fees are all possibilities.

VOLUNTEERS AND IN-KIND SERVICES

If an agency has basic funding for child protection, as with a state or county child protection agency, it may attract many of the multitude of skills it needs with no monetary compensation. In Colorado, for example, child protection teams based in counties do not receive a state appropriation, yet in 1983 there were 42 county-based teams in

Colorado.[5]   The following lists show some of the agencies and professionals represented on the 42 teams:

Agencies Represented on Colorado Teams in 1983

Social services	42
Mental health	41
Public health	41
Schools	41
Law enforcement	40

Professions Represented on Colorado Teams in 1983

Social workers	42
Law enforcement officers	40
Nurses	40
Attorneys	35
Physicians	35
Psychologists	32

The presence of highly paid professionals, including lawyers and doctors usually not employed by agencies, demonstrates the possibility for extensive volunteer support. The presence of so many agencies documents the potential for in-kind services when a child protection team is organized and managed well. Some of the teams are "regional" within the state because they cover more than one county.

In exchange for providing a team coordinator, a meeting site, and a clear outline of duties and powers, the counties have attracted hundreds of hours of contributed support.

APPROPRIATIONS AND GRANTS

In some of the most developed multidisciplinary child protection programs, the state government funds the regionalization of child protection support. Louisiana has had regionalized child protection centers providing many of the services of traditional child protection teams since the mid-1970s. The State of Florida funds child protection teams with regional responsibilities.

State funds support three state-wide teams in Colorado as of this writing. A state institutional abuse review team operates within state social services. The University of Colorado Health Sciences Center child protection team responds to hospital cases *and* consults on an even larger number of cases referred from across the state. The state and regional forensic team (START On Crimes Against Children) based at the Kempe

National Center began operation as a pilot project with federal funding, and continues with contract and state victims' assistance funds.

CONTRACTS

Since 1979, the Kempe National Center has provided a WATS consultation service to client states by contract. One of the benefits of the service is the availability of team staffings on difficult cases of child abuse and neglect. These staffings have almost always taken place through the use of a speaker phone at the Kempe Center, with case professionals from the other state either using another speaker phone or joining the staffing through a conference call hook-up. Case records, X-rays, photos, videotapes, and other materials for review can often be shared in advance. On a few occasions, lawyers or evaluators have brought the case directly to the Kempe Center. Most of the states using the WATS system do so through a modest yearly retainer. One state sets aside a designated amount for fee-for-service. In 1986, the states supporting this system were Alaska, Arizona, Oregon, Idaho, Wyoming, Montana, Nevada, and South Dakota. The State of Colorado Department of Social Services has set aside funds for evaluation and court preparation in rural areas, and these cases are also frequently staffed at the Kempe Center by telephone. In criminal cases, the State and Regional Team on Crimes Against Children provides consultation, and in some jurisdictions and for selected cases, testimony and of-counsel assistance to prosecutors in court.

CASE-BY-CASE FEES

Rather than contracting by an annual retainer, a state can budget to a set amount, and pay for consultation to that limit on an hourly basis. This arrangement parallels the practice of many private divorce custody assessment teams, in which the partnership or corporation may consist largely of multidisciplinary team members. These private teams often attract referrals in complex domestic relations custody disputes much as child protection teams offer "one-stop" shopping for expert insight.

Variations in Team Sponsor,
Service Area, and Cases Staffed

Consulting teams can be categorized in many ways. For example, teams vary by the nature of the area served: rural or urban, region within a state, single state, multi-state. Referral teams can be categorized by the types of cases staffed and teams can be identified by the parent organization, agency, or site. These variations are discussed in turn.

SERVICE AREA OR CACHMENT VARIATIONS

The child protection team begun in 1958 by Dr. C. Henry Kempe is a prototype consultation team for a state. The University of Colorado Health Sciences Center Child Protection Team consists of a core staff of social worker, pediatrician, child health associate, and coordinator. Supported by adult and child psychiatrists, lawyer, nurse, and other individuals on a case-by-case basis, the team evaluates over 300 in-patient and out-patient cases annually as any ordinary child protection team would. Not by design but by evolution, the University Hospital Child Protection Team has become a resource for the entire state, with over 500 cases referred by consultation annually.

The demand for services reached the point that not all cases could be accepted. One result was the identified need for a team to specialize in criminal cases. The State and Regional Team (hereinafter START) On Crimes Against Children became active on July 1, 1985. The START serves Colorado and eight other states in difficult criminal cases involving children as victims or witnesses. In addition to the nine states served primarily, consultations were provided to five additional states in the first year of service.

CIVIL VERSUS CRIMINAL FOCUS OF CHILD PROTECTION TEAMS

Traditionally, the great majority of child protection teams have evaluated civil cases almost exclusively. The focus on civil proceedings is a result of many factors. There are a larger number of cases handled civilly than criminally. Almost every team in the past has been based in non-criminal agency settings, even though law enforcement officers and some prosecutors served on the teams. Many of those sitting on child protection teams have been uncomfortable with some aspect of criminal approaches to child protection. In the mid-1980s, a number of multidisciplinary programs began with a criminal focus.

The START is an example of such a program, a team specifically created to apply the expertise of multidisciplinary consultants to cases in which a child is a crime victim or witness to a crime. Because crimes against children are only a portion, but a special part, of the prosecutor's task, a specialized team of child-oriented experts makes practical sense. The START director is an experienced prosecutor. The team is also staffed by a social worker, pediatricians, and child psychiatrists. Available to the START are an adult forensic psychiatrist, a civil attorney with experience in child representation, and a psychologist. A crime scene detective is considered an important addition, and staffing options are being explored. The forensic aspects of criminal cases involving children can be so technical that many cases do not stand up because of early failures of evaluation, evidence gathering, or witness management. The name "START" illustrates concern with the early stages of the criminal process, as well as the state and regional "back-up" responsibilities of the forensic team. About half of the first year cases were from rural areas. The evaluators followed up on nearly 100 cases until the end of 1986 and all (100%) of the individuals contacted indicated they would use the START again.

A pioneering effort for prosecutors is the criminally focused National Children's Advocacy Center in Huntsville, Alabama. All steps necessary to document a child abuse case for prosecution, with input from law enforcement, social services, mental health, and medical professions, can be carried out in one comfortable setting.[6] As the team at the Children's Center has gained experience, it has begun to receive and respond to requests from other jurisdictions, both within and outside Alabama. The National Children's Advocacy Center shows that leadership by prosecutors can lead to the creation of significant resources and multidisciplinary cooperation for the protection of children.

AGENCY SPONSOR

Child protection teams, as contrasted to multidisciplinary teams in general, are usually found in county protective services agencies or hospitals. More mental health agencies and criminal justice agencies may become sites for CPTs in the future as their administrators realize the advantages of ensuring that all relevant disciplines contribute to case evaluation and dispositional issues.

CHILD PROTECTION AGENCIES

Whether created by statute or by administrative decision, the location of CPTs within social services assures ready access to different types and professional tools for child protection. The teams link social services not only to other individual professionals, but to the agencies and societies they represent. However, aside from institutional abuse review teams, only a few state protective services agencies have implemented expert "back-up" teams for an entire state or region.

HOSPITALS

In organ transplant centers, intensive care units, and emergency rooms, teams of different disciplines are common. Child protection teams are a variation on a common medical theme: maximize the data and skills that can be brought to bear on complex diagnostic and treatment problems. A referral system that permits moving from primary care, to secondary care, to tertiary care centers is common within medicine. Only a few hospitals, however, have recognized the need to support regional referral in child protection. As the logic of following referral patterns similar to those used in medicine, and to some extent in other professions like law, becomes more obvious, more hospitals can be expected to provide consulting team services.

CRIMINAL PROSECUTOR'S OFFICE

Unique at its inception in 1984, the Huntsville, Alabama, multidisciplinary child-focused approach to prosecution of crimes against children, by team staffing a center through the prosecutor's office, is now being emulated by other prosecutors. Children are victims and witnesses to large numbers of crimes in the United State every year, and leadership by prosecutors is a welcome development.

Summary

Taken together, the development of different types of regional support and consultation through specialized child protection teams, represents a necessary step towards a fully developed child protection system. Isolated professionals and local child protection teams can be linked and supported by state or regional teams with relatively rare or hard to obtain skills and experience. The advent of this referral structure will improve responsiveness to individual cases and create greater understanding about the cases that are the most troubling.

References

1.   Kawamura, G.E., and C.A. Carroll. "Managerial and Financial Aspects of Social Service Programs." *Child Abuse and Neglect: The Family and the Community*. R.E. Helfer and C.H. Kempe (Eds.), pp. 293-309. Cambridge, Mass.: Ballinger, 1976.

2.   *Lynch v. King*, 550 F. Supp. 325 (D. Mass., 1982) affirmed under the name of *Lynch v. Dukakis*, 719 F. 2d 504 (1st Cir. 1983).

3.   Attias, R., and J. Goodwin. "Knowledge and Management Strategies in Incest Cases: A Survey of Physicians, Psychologists and Family Counselors." *Child Abuse & Neglect*, 9(1985):527-533.

4.   J. Goodwin, letter and enclosures to D.C. Bross, July 10, 1986.

5.   Motz, J. *Colorado's Community-Based Child Protection Teams*. Denver: Colorado Department of Social Services, 1984.

6.   Cramer, R.E., Jr. "The District Attorney as a Mobilizer in a Community Approach to Child Sexual Abuse." *University of Miami Law Review*, 40(1985):1.

PART VI

Child Protection Team Development

Section Editor: Marilyn R. Lenherr

29. Stages of Team Development

J.M. Whitworth and
Carol C. Haase

Introduction

The beginnings of the child protection team concept in the State of Florida grew out of the combined dreams and idealistic musings of a small group of people across the state. These individuals had been working for a number of years to influence state government to address the issues of child protection beyond the designation of a responsible agency and the development of a state reporting system. What existed was an agency (Health and Rehabilitative Services—HRS) mandated to provide services, but which lacked the ability to access the variety of services needed to make rapid and multidisciplinary decisions. We had great confidence in the multidisciplinary team concept, but felt that a statewide and state supported system was necessary. This avoided a system supported only by local municipalities or counties which may be responsive to variable financial commitments and frequent political re-prioritization. The result was at least ten years of patient (and impatient) waiting with plan-in-hand for the right moment!

Development of a Statewide Team System

The plan was rather simple. It stated that the child abuse intake system needed support that was multidisciplinary and immediately responsive to agencies serving children on dependency issues. The team was to be consultative, as well as direct-service oriented and committed to community education.

FUNDING

Funding was sought for a pilot project to show that this concept would work to improve decision-making for the disposition of cases and improve the outcome of dependency actions that would serve to keep families together and help smooth entry into a therapeutic plan.

The state legislature decided to support such a pilot program and passed enabling legislation to provide funds from general revenue. Funds were administered by the Children's Medical Services Program Office. That first child protection team was organized in Jacksonville, Florida, in 1978. Based on the success of that team, four additional teams were funded in 1979, six in 1981, and three in 1985. The current budget for statewide child protection teams is $5.7 million for a system of eighteen major teams and eight small teams in less populous areas.

In this system, child protection teams are autonomous entities usually contracted to nonprofit corporations which makes it possible to use the best of the public and private sectors. Under this arrangement, the corporation agrees to provide specified functions to the state within a tightly controlled budget following state guidelines. Subcontracting with other agencies, which can provide existing services at a cost-saving when compared to development of a new service, is also utilized. This mechanism provides a means for control, but with incentives and support for innovative cost-saving programs and new service-delivery systems. In short, it is a matrix for effective community networking. If one uses the definition of networking as the process of joining agencies and agency people to reach consensus on a goal, in this instance to improve services to a client population by pooling resources, the multidisciplinary team is a natural focal point for this process.

RESOURCE AND PROGRAM EXPANSION

The original allocation of funds has stimulated resources far beyond the intent of the legislature. For example, it provided a laboratory from which new research projects are now developing. The system provided a new research tool for the expansion of information gathering and analysis with a population base larger than had ever been available.   Computerization of a standard data base is being accomplished at each location.

In addition, the state has funded more than 60 prevention programs and one full-time pediatric consultant to coordinate the activities of the child protection team system. The pediatric consultant also has the responsibility of developing new curricula for teaching about child abuse and neglect in all professional schools in the state. Further, the state has also recognized child sexual abuse as a major priority by establishing a state consultant position on sexual abuse, and is now carrying out a plan to implement statewide training and program networking of involved professionals in this area. At this time, the state funds in excess of 3.5 million dollars in prevention programs over and above traditional dependency functions.

PRELIMINARY PLANNING/TEAM DESIGN

"Prenatal" planning is crucial to the successful birth of a team. We used a medical model for a system of child protection teams. This model should not be intimidating, as the system was designed, first and foremost, to protect the integrity of professional entities while breaking down the traditional barriers created by turf and ownership. We clearly recognized the unique and special needs for input from every specialty, and tried to translate those needs into a family perspective.   The needs of the families served are almost overwhelming—to the family, the agencies, and individuals who serve them. Our service delivery systems depend on the blurring of roles and improving communication skills within the system.   We could no longer afford the luxury of being the isolated nurse, the isolated social worker, and the isolated pediatrician. Team effort, cross-training, and blurring of roles was required, but recognition and appreciation of individual skills and competencies was also necessary. Systems for utilization of skills were relatively easy to develop once the basis for sharing of skills was established.   If the employees of the team were full-time, shared loyalties did not interfere with this process.

Team design was a highly conscious endeavor and included everything from shared office space to carefully engineered professional interactions, including multidisciplinary staffings.   The model was designed to maximize interactions and minimize intrusions to help form a sense of team and family.

TEAM ROLES/RECRUITMENT

The full-time members of the team included a team coordinator who supervised a group of case coordinators made up of social workers and nurses. The special skills of each individual were recognized with dissimilar functions being minimized and like functions being maximized to facilitate role blurring. Vertical relationships were also blurred to reduce a feeling of administrative hierarchy and enhance a feeling of teamwork. This process was not easily accomplished as most new members of the team were veterans of an inflexible bureaucracy. Preservice training was scheduled along with informal exchanges designed to force constant interaction among team members.

Team recruitment provided a special challenge. The need for nursing expertise, as well as a social work expertise, was recognized. The market for nurses was broad, but pay scales were high. Recruiting became a challenge to find persons willing to take a salary significantly lower than available in the general market. In contrast, because social workers were underpaid, the market for them was broader. This meant drawing from the pool of professionals already providing services to the same general population. Only with constant communication with existing agencies could this be accomplished.

The intensity of full-time involvement with abused children and abusive families requires that every possible support system be in place for each worker with the team. As part of the interview process, an effort was made to ascertain home support, as well as the candidate's amenability to the support of the group. The ability of the individual to accept support was often more important than the ability to give it. Loners had a much more difficult task in coping with work stresses and often contributed little to group process necessary for a smoothly operating team. Interviewing was done both in an individual and group setting, and an evaluation of the individual was made by all potential co-workers.

THE PILOT TEAM

The first team had the true "pioneer spirit." This team was mandated to provide consultative and coordinative services to the Department of Health and Rehabilitative Services, to provide community education, as well as professional education, and to show the salutary effect of a multidisciplinary approach to abused children. We spent hundreds of hours training everyone in sight. Special emphasis was placed on training of protective service workers and medical personnel. (We had distinct concerns about the health ramifications of a steady diet of chicken and peas from talking at luncheon meetings of every service club in the area!) We laughed a lot, and the beginning of an "esprit de corps" was felt. This phase in development can best be remembered as the time of idealistic altruism and fond memories.

Since the first team was hospital-based, there was a rich patient population and no referral was turned down; a policy that would later come back to haunt us. If no referrals came in, clients were actively sought. Almost immediately, however, referrals came from the intake system which had labored for years without medical and psychological evaluation support systems, now available on an immediate basis. Just as quickly, problems in role definition began to emerge. By statute, the case manager's role in this system rested with the intake workers (HRS). By team design, the team case coordinator acted as a support system for the intake worker and the family to coordinate services and assist the family through evaluation, crisis counselling, disposition, and treatment. Power issues began to emerge. Division of labor and support became secondary issues as to who was the "boss." When there was division of labor, the division was often uneven. Constant input from a supervisory level was necessary to re-define roles and minimize interpersonal conflicts.

A variety of other internal issues became apparent during the first few months of operation. The training and orientation of various professionals differed significantly. For example, medical training is traditionally based on case analysis of those elements which were done improperly or could have been done better. If this approach was brought to team and group interactions, it was largely destructive. One group session in which the physician insists on pointing out all that was done wrong with a case is enough to interfere with all group interactions in the future. On the other hand, the physician has a unique perspective that, when couched in the proper terms, can provide information critical to group decisions. Similar interactional difficulties arose with other professionals, but were gradually solved by group process techniques.

The Developmental Process of Teams

We will now address the developmental aspects of team function based on seven years of observations with one team and the sequential development of other teams throughout the state. It is of interest that the development of these teams had remarkable similarities with predictable successes, failures, and frustrations. The dissimilarities were also largely predictable and usually reflected differences in community needs. The most significant variable was the community matrix into which the team was introduced. This led to differences in severity of problems and variability in length of time needed for solution. These factors will be discussed in more detail. Experiential data will also be discussed related to individual as well as team maturity.

In the community, the developmental process for teams was reminiscent of Erikson's Stages of Psychosocial Development:

Trust vs. Mistrust
Autonomy vs. Doubt
Initiative vs. Guilt
Industry vs. Inferiority
Identity vs. Role Confusion
Intimacy vs. Isolation
Generativity vs. Stagnation
Integrity vs. Despair

TRUST VS. MISTRUST

Trust and mistrust can be evaluated in terms of internal team dynamics and also the team's position in the community. If preliminary planning and training has been successfully completed, the team members should have the tools to begin building internal trust which helps protect them from external mistrust. These tools include a feeling of support within the team, a sense of team commitment, a strong sense of ego identity, a sense of equality, and the beginnings of good bonding with other team members. Internal mistrust needs to be identified immediately, as trust is central to future development.

Being the infant agency in town can be viewed with trust in some quarters and mistrust in others, and a team will be responsive to both. The team is entering into largely undisturbed domain and external mistrust is often manifested by the very agencies the team is designed to assist. The pilot team, for instance, received its strongest support from the medical community, and the strongest mistrust from the agency the team was designed to help. Many months of intensive daily work with this agency (HRS) was necessary to minimize the mistrust, and some individuals have not yet resolved this issue. There are no secret solutions to this problem; time, support, patience, and a proactive stance toward problem solving are required. Team members should always keep in mind that mistrust will always recur, as the population in other agencies is not static. This fact makes the development of a strong support system within the team even more essential.

AUTONOMY VS. DOUBT

In the second stage of development, a sense of autonomy should develop. Each team member must feel a sense of the autonomy of the team and team support to minimize feelings of doubt. This requires that the team be autonomous and be sufficiently supportive to its members to give each a sense of belonging. The importance of creating an environment so that the team has a real feel of family cannot be overemphasized. Constant formal and informal interaction with case sharing, sharing of frustrations, and a shared feeling of purpose is critical.

The team worker should now have experienced enough work with clients to have some mastery of skills and a need to master others. The worker continues to build on the trust from the first stage; cross-training within the team is now in full swing. There is a choice in casework as new skills provide a broader range of therapeutic choices with clients. Signs of trouble during this stage include role confusion, lack of flexibility, withdrawal, and the categorization of issues as black or white instead of gray. Resolution of these problems is to first recognize their existence and understand that resolution is possible within the group structure of the team. Formal and informal staff meetings, as well as retreats, are helpful. Supportive intervention with review of some of the earlier tenets of team development may be necessary.

INITIATIVE VS. GUILT

In the third stage, failure of portions of previous developmental stages becomes more apparent. The team or individual showing initiative will manifest real creativity with specialization, development of new programs, and expansion. Competence is now clearly internalized and a sense of confidence is ascending. This stage brings with it a sense of accomplishment, but this may be perceived by outsiders as a sense of superiority and must be shared with care. Seeing this growth of the team and of individuals by one who has not reached this stage generates a sense of guilt. The program may have become over-extended or may be fixed in an earlier stage. Demand may have outdistanced the ability to respond and burnout may be beginning. It is time for the team and the individual to re-evaluate priorities and goals for growth and team function. It may be time to learn to say no.

INDUSTRY VS. INFERIORITY

Industry with casework and within the team continues to develop confidence. Frustration during this stage often comes from workers in other agencies who have not had the time or support to develop similar skills. Again conflicts arise, and again the team worker must depend on the support of the team to rise above the conflict and commit to resolution.

Teams and team members may often begin research projects and publish papers in established journals, as well as present papers at national meetings. At this point, staff may begin to move on and the incorporation of new members offers a new challenge. Teams who have not met the challenge see others who have as being superior, and may become demoralized. Teams are often in a position of only existing. Staff may begin to leave, but leaving is more likely to be precipitated by boredom or frustration than by a vertical career opportunity.

IDENTITY VS. ROLE CONFUSION

Erikson refers to adolescence as the time for development of identity. Child protection teams often have a protracted adolescence. Role confusion is often the result of mixed messages from management, lack of a proactive stance by the team in the community, or the inability of the team to affect powerful existing forces. Identity of the program directly affects the identity of team members. Identity can be built by the commitment of the entire team, followed by careful planning and execution of that resolution.

A good way for the team to develop an identity is to do a needs assessment in the community. Nearly all communities have needs of children that are not being met. A needs assessment can readily be accomplished. Those areas which are compatible with the general goals of the team can be targeted with a plan to address those needs. There is nothing more powerful than an agency fulfilling a perceived need which is eventually seen as indispensable. The needs assessment then can be used by the team in developing programs that are needed to increase services in the community or community awareness. One example of such an area may be community education. A team can become highly visible and maintain that visibility by launching such a program while continuing to maintain basic program objectives. Approaching a community in this way gives a team time to become accepted, to be identified as an important resource, and to develop a sense of identity.

Another mechanism for the development of new programs is discovery of need by crisis. Although this method is more of a gambler's approach, it still may be very effective. For example, we discovered a small number of children hospitalized unnecessarily for up to 18 months due to parental inability to provide care. From this situation grew a medical foster care program. This program allowed these children to go to alternative placement, while the parents received intervention and training, resulting in the eventual re-unification of the family at a very significant cost saving. The program has been replicated in several locations and has given the team another basis for identity in the community.

It is critical to keep in mind that the process of role definition requires constant fine-tuning. This fine-tuning must reflect the changing roles of those programs with which the program interacts, the changing roles of individuals on the team, and the changing needs of the community. For example, sensitivity to the changing needs of the individual is essential to prevention of burnout. The professional must be given a role in the development of the program, and therefore, some control over his future. A sense of ownership of some portion of the program or program planning is essential. This does not mean that management should abrogate all decision-making, but as many decisions as possible should be shared. This leads to the beginning of a better defined vertical structure so that experience and service to the team can be rewarded.

INTIMACY VS. ISOLATION

Intimacy vs. isolation represent Erikson's alternatives for this period. It should be remembered that this stage may be reached very early by some teams and not at all by others. Because of poor planning and a lack of support, individual workers with the team may develop a sense of isolation. In addition, if appropriate community linkages and networking has not occurred, the team may be isolated. This is most often the result of the team's taking a position of being so expert that the goals and functions of other agencies are not considered and mechanisms of cross-support do not develop. The teams sit in a self-designed ivory tower and are under-utilized for that reason. Referrals decrease and those that are received are usually for specialized service which may not be available from any other source. The sense of team has been lost and the ability to provide a multidisciplinary approach to a case is non-existent. At this point, the team needs to re-define goals and objectives or cease to be a team. There is no point in pretending to be a community resource if the community does not perceive the team as such, and if the term "multidisciplinary" refers only to a loose association of professionals who remain isolated from each other and from the community as a whole. This problem is most likely to occur in university-based teams which tend to be segregated because of the inherent bureaucracy and demands of the institution.

Intimacy and commonality of purpose may become evident during this stage, however, if the proper groundwork has been laid. An important element of this groundwork is to approach each employee as a professional and to expect that he or she function as a professional at all times. This approach includes respect for the opinions of each employee, flexibility of work hours, adequate compensatory time off, assurance of continuing education opportunities, and creature comforts to support employees as they do their jobs.

Another important element in program planning is to design information flow and data gathering so that maximum time can be spent in service provision with a minimum of paper work. We have found it highly useful to schedule on-call periods, so that an employee can anticipate that every few months there will be a period when no new cases are received, providing some respite to catch up on existing caseload needs. With policies such as these, a sense of professionalism can develop and during this evolution, feelings of camaraderie can evolve into feelings of family and intimacy within the team. The task of administering the team then becomes an exercise in understanding and using techniques for family systems rather than agency administration.

GENERATIVITY VS. STAGNATION

The signs of generativity as compared to stagnation in a team can often be seen very early. Generativity characterizes the team which very early shows signs of developing new concepts and new methods to provide direct or community service and subsequently identifies new funding sources for these programs. The team becomes a community advocate for provision of new services and the improvement of existing programs. Prevention services are planned and networking becomes a reality rather than a concept. Grants and gifts are solicited with a view to local resources for continuation of funding on a local, state, or national level. Management of these types of programs is kept separate from the basic team and gives the corporation a broad community base.

This is often the stage that produces true research and papers for presentation at meetings. The individuals on the team become identified experts in the field. It can also be a time of intense mixed feelings in trying to decide whether the team, which is now an extended family, can continue to meet the needs of the individual, or whether a move to a more challenging and vertical employment opportunity is appropriate. It is a time when large portions of the team may be lost and a plan for re-starting may be necessary. If the plan takes into consideration the developmental steps outlined, the chances of success are great. Otherwise the outcome is unpredictable at best.

Early signs of stagnation are often manifested by an inability to look beyond the provision of after-the-fact services, a lack of proactive views in the community of providers, and an absence of involvement by the larger community. These events can actually occur at any stage.

Often teams will perceive low-quality services being offered by a given agency and will make perfunctory attempts at change. When these attempts fail, a defeatist attitude pervades the team and progress can halt. The teams which survive this experience are those with patience and the capacity to be creative in designing new systems or able to increase the effectiveness of other programs by intensive training and community advocacy.

INTEGRITY VS. DESPAIR

Integrity is the final positive stage of development for teams, and it is especially gratifying to note that several teams in our system have reached that goal. These teams are doing independent research, have survived the stresses of staff leaving for advancement, and provide services as an expert and valued agency in the community. We have been able to introduce the concept of primary involvement through tertiary involvement in child abuse and neglect cases depending on the stage of development of a given team. We are in the process of developing a research-based group of teams to address physical abuse, neglect, and sexual abuse across the state. However, it is critical to our design that no team is without a direct-service component. Our belief is that no component of the system can function without direct contact with clients. To do so would create the ivory tower which we assiduously seek to avoid.

Despair has been experienced in some of our programs. This set of circumstances is usually due to a lack of attention to the details outlined, but also may be due to the fact that a community is simply not yet ready to accept the team or its viewpoints. As much as one may believe in the team concept, it is not possible to change the world. Our approach has been to accept adversity, but to come back and try another time.

Summary

The State of Florida Child Protection Team Program has undergone an amazing metamorphosis in a period of seven years. The stages of this metamorphosis are both documented and predictable for other teams. The stages have been a positive influence on the child protection system, and continued growth is not only anticipated, but expected if based on this model.

Child Protection Teams Guiding Principles

1. Systems are people and are no better than the people involved.
2. Systems exist for the protection of the child.
3. When possible, integrity of the family system should be maintained by all other systems.
4. The child protection team system should always be supportive rather than confrontational or investigative to the family.
5. The child protection team system should provide linkages with the entire community for services for the family.
6. The child protection team system should provide advocacy for improvement or streamlining of services from various agencies in the community.
7. The child protection team system should provide adequate ability for staff to grow in positions of consultation, advancement, and job security to maintain expert staff.

References

1. Vander Zanden, J.W. *Human Development*. New York: Alfred A. Knopf, Inc., 1977.

2. Erikson, Erik H. *Childhood and Society*, 2nd ed., pp. 247-274. New York: W.W. Norton and Company, 1963.

3. Elkind, D. "Erik Erikson's Eight Stages of Man: One Man and His Time Plus Many Psychosocial Parts." *The New York Times Magazine*, April 5, 1970.

30. Training Models for New and Established Teams

Mary Caroline Kealoha and
Carol C. Haase

Introduction: Definition and Purpose

Training is an interactive process of sharing information between two or more people for the purpose of increasing knowledge and/or proficiency of the trainees. It is a means of closing a gap that exists between what should be and what currently exists. Careful assessment and planning are the key ingredients in *successful* training, and both require the time and expertise of a person familiar with the theory and practice of training.

Training is used to impart knowledge, to teach new or improve existing skills, to explore values, beliefs, and attitudes. It consists of two major components: the information to be exchanged, and the process employed to impart that information. The process may be likened to warp threads in a piece of woven cloth, which provide the framework through which the content material or woof threads are woven. Together they form the fabric of training, with both threads being essential and contributing equally to the overall design and quality of the finished piece.

Training Plan Components

At its best, training is the result of a comprehensive plan in which material is presented sequentially, with subsequent sessions building upon previously presented information. In this way, the level of knowledge of the trainees is increased in a logical and incremental fashion. Ideally, the plan begins with a careful needs assessment of the target audience to determine gaps or deficiencies in knowledge or skills (Appendix 30.1A, B, and C). This assessment must include a self-evaluation completed by the trainees to determine their *perceived* needs, and a more objective evaluation completed by the trainer. The objective evaluation can also include a job task analysis to determine the trainee's responsibilities, as well as soliciting information from other professionals who will work with the trainees.[1] Perceived training needs are usually more constricted than assessed training needs; however, they must be addressed if the trainee is to move forward and be receptive to new information.

After both perceived and objectively assessed needs have been identified, goals should be formulated and a training plan developed. From the training goals, *measurable* learning objectives can be written, a critical step in determining if training is effective and change has occurred (Appendix 30.2). After the objectives are determined, a review of the literature should be conducted, content area developed, and decisions made regarding the most appropriate training methods for transfer of knowledge (Appendix 30.3). Effective utilization of The Adult Learning Theory (Figure 30.1) is important in developing the training curricula.[2]

This illustrates that the more involved the trainee becomes, the greater the rate of retention. In designing training programs, those methods that lead to quality learning with maximum retention should be emphasized.

Following the implementation of training, an evaluation of the effort should be completed by the trainees. The evaluation should directly relate to the measurable learning objectives, address the scope and relevancy of the content material, and the training methods employed in presenting the material (Appendix 30.4). Based upon the results of the evaluation, the trainer can refine future training to make it as germane as possible.

What happens when a systematic approach is not used and these steps are overlooked or ignored? Frequently, decisions concerning who will be trained, the length of training, and the content material offered are decided without accurately determining problems or needs. Training should be the means of facilitating a measurable change. When an

Figure 30.1

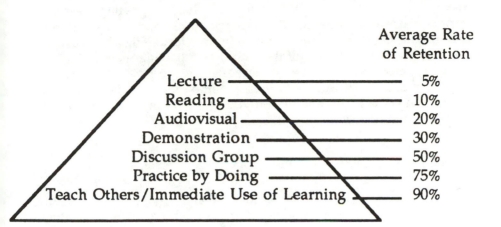

organized training approach is not taken, the application of the material presented is often unclear to the trainee. Neglecting these vital steps of needs assessment and developing a corresponding plan of action may negate the value of the entire training effort. When the costs for training, the lost work time of the employee attending the training, and travel expenses incurred by trainees are totaled, the effort may be expensive and yet "worthless." Thus, the importance of clearly defining training objectives, and not just providing interesting content material, cannot be overemphasized.

TYPES OF TRAINING

Training may be formal or informal and may occur individually, in small or very large groups. Formal training includes planned conferences, workshops, case reviews, pre-service or in-service training, and preceptorships. Informal training includes consultations, program staff meetings, work groups, multidisciplinary case staffings, brainstorming sessions, individual reading and observations of interactions, i.e., *shadowing*, of other professionals.

Each type of training is valid and helpful; however, the potential of informal training should not be overlooked as it provides an opportunity to transfer knowledge, explore attitudes and beliefs, and demonstrate problem-solving and group-process skills in a relaxed atmosphere conducive to learning. Such training can be planned and implemented as carefully as formal training to achieve the maximum benefit for all.

The atmosphere created by the trainer, in either formal or informal settings, is a major contributing factor toward the success or failure of the training effort. Learning involves change, and change involves letting go of a current belief, attitude or practice and developing a new or more expanded view. Learning is best in a setting of trust and acceptance in which the participants are encouraged to share through questions and discussion, without fear of ridicule or censure. If individual opinions, feelings and beliefs are respected, the learner feels validated, and group cohesiveness results fostering learning.

Training Role and Responsibilities of a Multidisciplinary Team

Multidisciplinary teams, through purpose and design, comprise experienced professionals from many disciplines. As individual professionals work together as a team, their knowledge and expertise regarding child abuse dynamics, intervention, and treatment issues increase, and their understanding of one another's roles and responsibilities expand. Each member is a link, a liaison between the team and his or her particular profession. Members become a conduit of specialized information about the field of child abuse and neglect, and will be called upon to educate their colleagues and the community, in both formal and informal settings. Multidisciplinary teams have a responsibility to train three distinct groups:

    a. team members
    b. community professionals
    c. the general public

Ideally, a skilled trainer should be hired and assigned the responsibility of developing and implementing a comprehensive training plan that addresses the needs of each group. Practically, one individual should be assigned responsibility for coordination of training, a role which may have to be carried out along with other responsibilities. Within the team setting, the absence of an assigned trainer, or at least a training coordinator, typically results in the diffusion of this responsibility among various team members. This results in no clear focus of responsibility, and training occurs in a reactive, haphazard fashion. When a team is without a trainer, the responsibility for coordinating training for the team and the community should lie with the team coordinator or another assigned individual.

If the team has a trainer on staff, the trainer is responsible, under the direction of the team coordinator, for all training developed for the team, community professionals and the general public. The trainer and team coordinator should agree upon an annual training plan and regular meetings should be scheduled to monitor implementation.

TRAINING CONTENT AND APPROACHES FOR NEW TEAMS

Training for new teams should be very comprehensive in both the depth and the breadth of material provided. Team members should be prepared to act as consultants and trainers of community professionals and the general public. This role requires that each team member be extremely knowledgeable and experienced concerning many different aspects of abuse and neglect. Usually as a team evolves, individual team members will develop additional expertise on specific topics, and as a result other team members will request consultation or refer questions regarding such matters to them. Specific expertise in a particular topic is typically the result of personal interest developed through a program of self-instruction. This includes reading the literature, attending conferences, gaining direct experience by applying the acquired knowledge to specific cases, and conducting training sessions. If such expertise is expected of team members, responsibility for *ensuring* its development resides with the *team coordinator*. Determination of the topic area and an individualized course of study, with timelines and tangible products (e.g., articles, presentations, monographs) can be part of the goals defined at each staff member's personal performance evaluation. Each individual should clearly understand that such study and growth is required. The team coordinator may schedule regular meetings with each team member to review progress; however, the responsibility for *acquiring* the expertise belongs to *each individual*.

ATTITUDES AND VALUES

Attitudes must be considered in training since they play an important role in how a person incorporates knowledge and skills. Positive attitudes, such as empathy, permit a person to implement skills in a nurturing fashion, while the absence of such attitudes often results in a very clinical, perfunctory professional manner that neglects the emotional needs of the client.

Attitudes grow out of personal values and may be defined as a posture or stance on a particular subject. An attitude influences an individual's emotional reaction to an event and ultimately the choice of response or action toward that event, object, or person. Clearly, values and resulting attitudes of team and community professionals will impact multidisciplinary case staffings and training provided by the team. Values and attitudes of team members can be explored in formal training sessions to raise personal awareness of how they can be analyzed, evaluated, and sometimes changed. The group facilitator at team case staffings should be very knowledgeable and alert to instances when personal attitudes interfere with the group process. Likewise, trainers must be aware of the same problem interfering with training sessions.

TEAM PHILOSOPHY

All professionals, regardless of their discipline, should have basic knowledge of child abuse and share a team philosophy to form a multidisciplinary team that functions cooperatively. This philosophy is the team's foundation, the focal point from which the roles and responsibilities of various team members evolve, and from which program policies, procedures, and practices develop. Congruence on these issues is imperative if the team is to operate cooperatively and productively. Misunderstandings among team members on these most basic issues frequently cause confusion, frustration and conflict, both with the team, with other professionals interfacing with the team, and with the community.

Due to the importance of all team members, understanding, accepting, and working within established guidelines, careful attention must be paid to training in these areas. New team members are usually interviewed to determine if their attitudes and style relate to the team philosophy. Too often, however, the required reading of program manuals containing team policies and procedures by the new team member is the extent of attention afforded to these pivotal issues. These philosophies and standards form the guidelines by which the team operates, and should be emphasized and reviewed on a planned basis by all team members. Staff meetings provide an excellent forum for new and existing staff members to review and reinforce program philosophy and goals.

SKILL BUILDING

Team and community professionals will be required to use many skills when working with abusive or neglectful families. Skills are a reflection of knowledge and the ability to implement that knowledge. They will be used in identification, investigation, intervention, and treatment of at-risk or abusive families. Specific expertise is needed for crisis counselling, documentation, court testimony, treatment, problem solving, decision making, and case planning. Administrative and management skills are also used by team members in supervision, community coordination, and program planning. Training facilitates the development of all these necessary skills; it is the bridge between knowing and doing. Training is also a skill that must be mastered by team staff who will be educating other professionals and the general public.

A job task analysis and a community training needs assessment will help identify specific skills required of each professional, so that training can be planned accordingly. The most critical issue about skill building is that trainees must have an opportunity to practice skills in a controlled setting provided by the training workshop. Practice sessions should be supervised by a trainer who is personally comfortable with the skill being taught (e.g., interviewing, testifying) and who can offer immediate reinforcement and feedback to the trainee. Analysis of the trainee's performance to identify strengths and weaknesses is essential. Instructions for improving weak areas provides encouragement, while criticism often interferes with learning by reducing the trainee's motivation. Videotaping is an excellent training tool to develop skills, as it allows the trainee to review his or her performance.

CPS POLICY/PROCEDURES

Next in importance for a new team member is a thorough grounding in the policies, procedures and practices of the child protective service (CPS) agency, and civil and criminal statutes that affect casework practice. Statutes and agency policies dictate the alternatives available when providing consultation, making recommendations, and developing service and treatment plans for children and families. Additionally, a new team member should be intimately familiar with CPS guidelines and framework to provide realistic training and consultation to CPS staff. Cross-training of CPS and team members by spending workdays with social workers to better understand their responsibilities and constraints would be a beneficial training experience for *every* professional on the team.

Case reviews at team staffings provide some of the most useful training opportunities. Case reviews reinforce relevant application of all available skills and knowledge. Community professionals can also better understand the limitations within which CPS works, both at case staffings and at formal workshops provided by the team.

New staff must familiarize themselves with these issues individually, and the team coordinator must be sure that staff casework reflects an appropriate understanding and utilization of this knowledge.

HUMAN GROWTH/DEVELOPMENT

Team members should demonstrate knowledge of normal human growth and development. To put abnormal or unhealthy development or lifestyles into perspective, one must identify abusive patterns and place them in a framework of what is and what is *not* normal child development and family dynamics. Consequently, professionals must make an effort to view client needs within the larger framework of what is normal and healthy, and make recommendations that assist families in managing their problems and stress in more positive ways. By utilizing a needs assessment, any areas of deficiency, such as lack of knowledge about human behavior, can be identified and training provided.

Information about the various forms of abuse and the dynamics occuring with each should be addressed in continuing, formal in-service training. Team members can be assigned responsibility for presentations on specific types of abuse. The presenter should be knowledgeable about books and literature considered to be classics in the field, as well as current literature. Staff should be encouraged to attend conferences and symposia featuring authors and practitioners noted for contributions in the field of child abuse. Again, case staffings provide an opportunity for training about dynamics, diagnosis, and treatment through sharing of knowledge and information, discussing cases, and formulating case plans.

COMMUNITY RESOURCES

Awareness of the multiplicity of community resources and how to access and utilize them is imperative. Multidisciplinary teams provide coordination as one of the primary team services. The efficient and effective provision of this service requires that team members not only be aware of community agencies providing services to abusive families, but also forge links with such agencies through sharing of knowledge and coordinating services with administrative and direct services staff. Contacts with direct service staff afford access to services, while connections with administrators offer the entree required when adjustment or expansion of services are necessary. Many communities have developed agency resource directories that should be available to team members.

Team members may become representatives to various community advisory boards or act as liaison for organizations and agencies. Interagency agreements, preferably written, form tangible links between the team and other agencies, clarify roles and responsibilities, and thereby promote a positive work relationship. Team members should also respond to requests for training from these organizations. Established teams can offer scholarships when possible to conferences conducted by the team for staff from other organizations unable to afford fees. This strategy promotes goodwill, increases knowledge and skills, and provides other agencies access to training.

GROUP PROCESS AND COMMUNICATION

Group process, problem solving, and decision-making skills are critical tools required for the healthy functioning of the team and the larger community system. Individually, human service providers should strive to be self-directed, healthy, integrated human beings. Since that is what is expected of our clients, expectations for ourselves should be no less. Group process skills are essential tools for effective communication, logical problem-solving, and consensus decision making that respect the needs of clients and providers alike. This process promotes a positive working atmosphere, productive group outcomes, and, as a consequence, the healthy growth of all participants. The heart of a team is the multidisciplinary case staffing, and the life force of such staffings is the group process. Therefore, knowledge and use of group process skills is especially important for teams. Members should receive formal training that can be implemented at case staffings by the group facilitator. Also, as various team members become comfortable with group process skills, there is often broader application in personal interactions and other settings as well.

Community professionals could also benefit from such training. However, the need is not as crucial since they will be exposed to these skills during participation in staffings. The team facilitator should provide a quick review of the staffing process whenever a new professional is in attendance. In this way, community professionals will receive informal group process training and will be able to better understand and participate in the case reviews.

Training for Community Professionals

Workshops for other professionals in the community are essential. The workshops should focus on identification of abuse and neglect, how to make reports and referrals to the appropriate agencies, and identification of available services. Time should be set aside during workshops to allow individuals to discuss feelings about reporting and how to advise the family. It is understood that personal feelings and prior bad experiences too frequently prevent case reporting. The training sessions will also "market" the team's existence and its functions. Therefore, a clear description of team purpose, responsibilities, and services must be provided. Any misperceptions about team role should be addressed at staff meetings so that the expectations of community professionals are accurate and realistic.

Training for the General Public

The general public is one of the first groups for which the multidisciplinary team provides training. Community groups such as PTAs, service clubs, and volunteer organizations often request speakers to address their audiences. The level of training required for such organizations should be very general and basic concerning child abuse and neglect issues. These engagements may allow a new trainer to become comfortable with both the subject matter and training skills in a fairly stress-free environment.

The general public should know about the scope of the problem, indicators that raise suspicion, the mechanics of reporting a suspected case, and have a general understanding of how the system responds to a report. In addition, information about dynamics of an abusive situation and the possibilities for improvement will sensitize the group to the problems of abuse in a family.

The trainer must be prepared to address any value or attitudinal issues that may arise during the discussion period following a presentation. Many myths abound concerning the "causes and cures" of child abuse and neglect, and a trainer will be required to provide comments and clarification at some time during training.

Relationship of Training to Stages of Team Development

As described in Chapter 29, teams move through predictable stages of development if they are progressing in a healthy and mature fashion. These stages can be loosely linked to Erikson's Stages of Psychosocial Development, and directly influence the types and level of training each team can provide at different times.[3] As team members gain experience, they bring an increasing maturity and depth of knowledge to training presentations, but, as the team gains credibility within the community, requests for team services will increase and less time will be available to respond to training requests. Both issues have an impact on training and must be addressed at the appropriate developmental stage.

STAGE I

During Stage I, which encompasses the conceptualization of the team and includes development of the internal structures (philosophy, policies, procedures, etc.) and external supports (funding sources, community support, interagency working agreements), informal training will be the norm and the trainers will be the team organizers. Each meeting and phone conversation is a source of training and a means of gaining support by informing various agencies of the team concept and the services provided. The "trainers" (team members) must be very clear about team functions and able to articulate this clearly and concisely. The underlying goal is to engender a sense of trust and acceptance within staff from other community organizations and professionals. This goal must be *consciously* nurtured. To overlook the issues of building trust may evoke a sense of threat, which often results in power struggles and territorial conflicts.

Also during Stage I, team members are recruited and receive pre-service and in-service training concerning the team's purpose, procedures, child abuse statutes, CPS policies, the dynamics of abuse and neglect, and each person's role and responsibility.

Group process training with team staff, CPS staff, and members of other agencies who may participate in staffings should be a part of pre-service training and occur before the first multidisciplinary case review. The success or failure of these conferences is a clear barometer of the acceptance and effectiveness of the team within the community. Therefore, considerable time and attention should be focused on training in this initial stage of team development. Overlooking this need, or minimizing its importance, will result in untold hours of conflict, frustration, and lost trust at later stages of team development. After the team is organized, staff hired and trained, and initial interagency training has been completed, the team is reasonably ready to begin taking referrals for training.

STAGE II

This stage includes the first 12-18 months of team operation. Referrals will typically come in slowly at first and the staff will "have time on their hands." During this period the team will be able to conduct many training sessions and can usually respond to any and all requests. Frequent training workshops will allow team trainers to become comfortable with the content material, to develop some standard agendas and materials (handouts, audiovisuals, etc.), and to become confident about their training ability. Early in this stage of team development, the major training audiences will usually include the general public, community organizations, and specific professionals who work as consultants with the team.

The team attitude is often very idealistic during this time because staff are able to provide hours to each case due to the low number of referrals. Team members may develop a critical attitude of the "poor quality" casework provided by CPS who often have an overwhelming number of referrals to investigate. They may also experience insecurity or inadequacy in relation to their new job which may be revealed by an egocentric point of view. Both the idealistic attitudes and the egocentric viewpoint appear to be phases through which new teams and team members must live. The key is to be aware and to deal with these developments as consciously as possible by acknowledging the influence of each on work relationships and casework. Team administrators must be very conscious of these dynamics in order to support team staff, to avoid conflict with other agencies, and to ensure that client needs are met. Training surrounding these issues will most frequently be informal, though a more formal discussion would be appropriate.

During this stage, team members develop more confidence. Towards the end of this stage, community agencies will also gain increasing trust in the team and its ability to work cooperatively and productively with others.

STAGE III

This stage spans the time from 18 to 36 months of team development. Trust in individual and collective abilities, which results from the experience gained during the first year and a half of operations, fosters a growing sense of autonomy for the team and its members. A feeling of confidence and pride in team accomplishments emerges, and egocentric perspectives should diminish. A realistic attitude toward casework develops as increased referrals result in less time for each case. Team staff develop specialty areas of expertise and exhibit individual initiative for projects during this time.

Training for community professionals becomes a major focus. The team has gained credibility within the community. The existence of a team invariably results in deeper recognition of the complexity of child abuse issues and the increasing need for a coordinated interdisciplinary response to the problem.

Towards the end of this stage, members begin to feel they are working to capacity and beyond, and training requests may seem overwhelming. However, training for community professionals should remain a primary focus to develop the expertise of staff from other agencies. This gradually increases the knowledge of others in the community who are then available to assist the team with training requests. Additionally, the development of a speaker's bureau is an excellent means to relieve the strain imposed by the increased requests for training.

The team's expertise and energy is most productively shared with other professionals and a proactive stance should be initiated regarding training. The team trainers should meet with supervisors from community agencies who have been accustomed to receiving training and explain that their requests will no longer receive automatic agreement due to increased demands. A schedule of training that incorporates the needs of all community professionals and covers a definite time span should be offered and circulated in the community. It is critical to gain the support and understanding of these agencies to avoid frustration and conflict that could be reflected in daily working relationships. This proactive, rather than reactive, approach to training can be achieved without damaging interagency relationships. Toward the end of Stage III and during Stage IV, the team will lose old members and gain new ones. This change in the original staff membership and increasing requests for team services may result in internal crises that demand immediate resolution. Attention must now be given to the "blended team family" and the training needs of the new and original staff must be recognized as the blending occurs. Soon, a new sense of identity will emerge through this reorganization process, if the team is provided proper nurturance.

STAGE IV

As the team moves into its fourth stage, the team coordinator (who has typically been responsible for clinical supervision of team cases, administrative functions of the team, and community relations) usually reaches a saturation point and will need to reassign responsibilities. This internal reorganization may involve assigning clinical supervision responsibilities to a qualified senior staff member, and administrative functions to an office manager. This allows the team coordinator to become more actively involved in community networking and child advocacy. This step is critical if the team is to continue to evolve and grow as a positive force within the community. By progressing through the previous stages, the team has built a bridge of trust with the community, gained autonomy and recognition for the quality of services provided, demonstrated initiative through its proactive stances with training needs, and is now able to move into a position of recognized leadership.

Training should continue to be provided on a scheduled basis rather than in response to requests. An annual training schedule should be printed and distributed to all interested agencies to apprise them of what is to be offered. Some flexibility should be built into the schedule to allow for training needs that may arise during the calendar year.

In conjunction with the extensive outreach and networking by the coordinator, the team may organize and participate in larger training efforts jointly sponsored by many agencies. Team members may also find themselves testifying before a local task force or state legislature and, though not technically classified as training, such presentations require the same considerations for preparation and presentation.

Summary

Training is the key necessary to open the door to knowledge, awareness, choices, change, growth, and renewal. It is a means of actualizing the information contained in this book. Training is needed to found a team, to nurture its growth through the many stages of development, to revitalize the energies of its members, and to foster their continuing growth. Caring team members form a caring team, and such a team can effect tremendous community response to the needs of children. Training must be viewed as an integral team service since it is the means of weaving knowledge, skills, and positive caring attitudes into the resilient, multidisciplinary fabric of a child protection team.

References

1.   Development Associates, Inc.   *An Instrumented Trainers Manual for Multidisciplinary Interagency Child Abuse and Neglect Training Teams.* National Center on Child Abuse and Neglect, U.S. Dept. of Health, Education, Welfare, 1978.

2   Knowles, M. *The Modern Practice of Adult Education: Androgogy vs. Pedagogy.* New York: Association Press, 1970.

3.   Erikson, E.H. *Childhood and Society*, pp. 247-274. New York: W.W. Norton and Company, 1963.

Bibliography

Beckhard, R. *Organization Development: Strategies and Models.* Reading, Mass.: Addison-Wesley Publishing Company, 1969.

Berne, E. *The Structure and Dynamics of Organizations and Groups.* New York: Grove Press, Inc., 1963.

Bradford, Leland P. *Group Development.* Washington, D.C.: NTL Learning Resources Corporation, 1961.

Burke, W.W., and R. Beckhard. *Conference Planning.* Washington, D.C.: NTL Institute for Applied Behavioral Science, 1970.

Dyer, W.G. *Modern Theory and Method in Group Training.* NTL Learning Resources Corporation (Ed.). New York: Van Nostrand Reinhold Company, 1972.

Jones, M.L., and J.L. Blesecher. *Trainer's Manual for Goal Planning and Permanency Planning in Children and Youth Services.* Millersville, Pa.: Millersville State College, 1979.

Mager, R.F. *Preparing Instructional Objectives.* Palo Alto, Calif.: Fearon Publishers, 1962.

Pfeiffer, J.W., and J.E. Jones. *A Handbook of Structured Experiences for Human Relations Training,* Vol. III. Iowa City, Iowa: University Associates Press, 1971.

Schindler-Rainman, E., and R. Lippitt. *Team Training for Community Change: Concepts, Goals, Strategies and Skills.* Riverside, Calif.: University of California Extension, 1972.

Appendix 30.1A

From: *Instrumented Trainers Manual for Multidisciplinary, Interagency Training Teams*. Developmental Associates, Inc.

ASSESSMENT OF TRAINING NEEDS

Needs Assessment

The process of examining a particular field or group to identify *problems*, their causes, and the resources or services needed to overcome those problems and eliminate their causes. *Assessment* weighs what exists against what is necessary, and identifies the difference as the *needs* of the target population. The trainer should address these needs to eliminate the causes of problems for the target group.

The Role of the Training Team or Trainer in Identifying Training Needs

The training team or trainer should meet with the trainee supervisor(s), agency, administrator(s), and any other parties with a significant vested interest in the training to be done, to determine the needs for training. This representation of all interested persons allows a broad range of tasks to be explored from varying perspectives.

The major product of this meeting is the development of specific staff performance standards necessary to achieve agency(s) goals. Estimates of training needed for trainees to achieve these performance standards can also be made. Final definition of training needs can then be made given input from trainees themselves.

It is this anchoring of the training enterprise in the ongoing welfare of the agency(ies) that is perhaps the most important service of the training team or trainer. Its capacity to commit the resources necessary to accomplish the training is essential.

Trainee Involvement in Identifying Training Needs

People learn what they want to learn. Trainees must have a strong vested interest in their own training if it is to be effective. They can develop this if they are directly involved in identifying what it is they need to learn in order to do what is expected of them as staff members at the conclusion of the training. This is done in a step-by-step process:

*   The trainer with the supervisor(s) establish agency goals in terms of services being provided by the agency or discipline.

*   The trainer with the supervisor(s) and trainees identify problems impeding attainment of these goals.

*   The trainer with the supervisor(s) and trainees define the tasks to be performed to solve the problems and achieve the goals. (Existing job descriptions and task data may be used as a reference point in these discussions but should not prevent posing of alternatives. They may, in fact, be modified as a result of trainee inputs defining what must be done to achieve goals.)

*   The trainer with the supervisor(s) and trainees identify what must be learned by the trainees to achieve the goals and solve the problems. (If trainees have sorted task statements into "have done," "have not done," etc. categories, this information can be used to identify what trainees need to learn. If trainees have not sorted the data but task statements exist, they could sort at this time. Regardless of the timing of the sort, however, task statements should not restrict identification of learning needs; such statements are not required to enable trainers to accurately identify their learning needs.)

At the conclusion of the above process, trainees will feel that the training they are to enter is truly for them and can equip them to do what they themselves have said they must do. They will be meeting their own challenges and not those imposed by the agency. Their learning experiences will be relevant because they will have already identified why they must learn. The training will help them learn what they want to learn.

Use of Needs Assessment Instruments

Various survey instruments may be completed by prospective trainees to indicate what they feel they want to learn in a given training experience. This approach is especially effective if prospective trainees are scattered geographically or if the time necessary to get inputs directly is unavailable.

This approach is limited, however, by the instrument's ability to set a complete context for the prospective trainee's reflection and judgment as well as by the prospective trainee's capacity to articulate clearly what he needs to learn.

A good survey instrument sets a clear context in which the prospective trainee identifies his training needs (i.e., agency goals and problems, job description the trainee fills). This is of necessity somewhat restrictive since the agency alone is setting the context but better than no context at all. The instrument should have a mix of multiple choice and open-ended questions so those who need structure will have it and those who can and wish to respond more freely as individuals can do so. Even a good instrument is, hence, a compromise in several ways.

Several hours of face-to-face communication will be almost always more fruitful than survey instruments, but well-designed instruments are much better than allowing the prospective trainee no opportunity to participate in identifying his training needs.

Conduct of the Needs Assessment

Step 1—Specify what the worker needs to know or be able to do to perform well on the job. This means describing the worker in terms of the duties and tasks he is responsible for and the knowledge and skills he needs to do them. This step can be done with the use of:

(a) *Job Descriptions*

It is obvious that accurate job descriptions are a good source of information about what those to be trained need to be able to do. They indicate, in general, the kind of knowledge, skills, and attitudes needed for the job. They are helpful as a guide in planning needs assessment meetings, interviews, or group sessions. It may be useful in some needs assessments to ask participants who already have experience to give the kind of detail job descriptions often leave out. Check this preliminary information with supervisors and experienced workers.

(b) *Questionnaires*

Two kinds of circumstances may suggest use of questionnaires, which should always be kept as short and simple as possible. First, when interviewees cannot be personally contacted during the needs assessment, they must be contacted by mail. A model questionnaire designed for such an unusual circumstance is very comprehensive.

Second, during a needs assessment, when time prohibits individual interviews or the trainer feels that he is not getting information he needs verbally, questionnaires may be written. Used this way, questionnaires can be checked by the trainer and immediately talked over with those who fill them out, but anonymity must be protected if the information you seek is sensitive (if you ask about participants' skills or attitudes, etc.).

Any questionnaire is dependent on the user's ability to read and express himself clearly in writing. There is also the problem of interpreting what is written. The amount of information you can obtain, and the accuracy of it, are very limited.

(c) *Observation*

It is often useful to observe participants on the job, in staff meetings, in the field, etc. This should only be done, however, when your role as a trainer is clear to those you observe and they do not regard your activities as evaluative and threatening. Make a list of the kinds of situations the worker must deal with, problems that arise, and duties performed on a typical day.

Step 2—Determine levels of knowledge and skills the trainees have at the start of the training. This means discovering the "starting points." If the trainer underestimates the participants, he will bore them. If he overestimates, he will confuse them. The needs assessment is an opportunity to discover how much the participants already know, what they need to have reinforced, what they need to "unlearn," and what new territory will need special attention.

(a) *Testing*

Testing is a useful way to determine how much accurate information participants have about a specific subject. Pre-tests have been designed for different levels of education and experience in family planning work. These tests can also be used after training (post-test) as an evaluation tool.

(b) *Role Play/Demonstration*

Each trainee is assigned a particular part to play in a typical work-related problem, or to observe and discuss the behavior of role-players.

(c) *Critical Incident Questionnaire/Group Discussion*

Describe a typical job situation that presents a realistic problem. The trainees work out a solution. An informal group discussion can be useful in analyzing solutions and can determine the level of communication and agreement on group issues among participants.

To assess levels of skill. Try to have trainee demonstrate the skill and have other trainees and a panel of "experts" rate the performance. If this is not possible, talk to supervisors and others who have observed the trainee's performance.

To assess levels of interest/attitude/values. Provide an experience by which the trainee can see this. Ideally the effect of the attitude demonstrated should be observed.

(d) *Reverse Role Play*

Example, a social worker plays the role of a judge and vice versa.

(e) *Drawing, Symbol Creating*

The group pictures others (clients, other organizations, etc.) and must explain why they pictured them as they did.

Step 3—Determine specifically what the trainees need or want to gain from the training. This step should be accomplished as much as possible by trainees themselves. Practically, as trainer and trainees go through Step 2 they should become aware of the differences between present levels of performance and what they will need to do the job well.

(a) *Interviews*

Individual Interviews—Regardless of any other procedures you use, talking with each potential trainee or as many as time allows, is always a good idea. It is often the best way to learn details about them or their jobs that do not surface in group discussions. *Group interviews* or an informal group discussion can be useful when time prohibits individual interviews.

(b) *Group sessions*

These differ from informal group interviews. They are structured meetings employing a variety of activities a trainer uses to encourage trainees to discover and articulate their ideas.

Ordinarily, they begin with a listing and clarification of goals or problems and proceed to a discussion of the training needs suggested by them. The series of exercises will need to be adapted and made relevant to the group or agency with whom the trainer is working.

Appendix 30.1C

TRAINING NEEDS ASSESSMENT

DATE_____

Name of Interviewee:_____

Staff Position/Title: _____

Name of Agency: _____

Type of Agency: _____

Instructions: Obtain a definite response for each of the items below and check *one* of three answers.

> "Much" for each item the interviewee feels he/she must learn more about.
> "Some" for each item the interviewee feels he/she would like to learn more about.
> "None" for each item the interviewee feels there is no need to learn about.

In which of the following topical areas related to services for abused and neglected children and their families would you like training?

	Response		
Topical Areas	Much	Some	None
Diagnosis and Identification ___			
Working Definitions ___			
-Abuse ___			
-Physical ___			
-Emotional ___			
Neglect ___			
-Physical ___			
-Emotional ___			
-Medical ___			
-Educational ___			
Sexual Abuse ___			
-Incest ___			

Topical Areas	Response		
	Much	Some	None
Treatment			
Case Management—Coordination of Treatment Modalities			
Treatment Modalities—Alternatives			
Attitudes			
-Sensitivity to parents' feelings			
-Awareness of own feelings—cultural biases			
Interviewing			
-Observation			
-Knowledge of Human Growth, Behavior & Child Development			
-Counseling			
-Keeping Case Records			
-Use of Courts			
-Rules of legal proceedings			
-Planning for the whole family			
Education			
-Review of reporting law			
-Mandated reporters			
-Definitions of abuse, neglect, sexual abuse			
-Confidentiality			
-Public awareness			
Topical Areas			
-Molestation			
Abuse			
-Symptoms/Indicators			
Neglect			
-Symptoms/Indicators			
Sexual Abuse			
-Symptoms/Indicators			

| | Response | | |
Topical Areas	Much	Some	None
Potential _____			
-Symptoms/Indicators _____			
Role and Responsibilities_____			
-Medical _____			
-Social _____			
-Legal _____			
-Community _____			

From: *Instrumented Trainers Manual for Multidisciplinary, Interagency Training Teams.* Development Associates, Inc.

FORMULATE SPECIFIC TRAINING OBJECTIVES

After the initial assessment of training needs, the development of the specific program translates these needs into objectives, on which a general training plan is constructed. From this the necessary training sessions are designed and resources are organized for the actual delivery of training.

1. *Recognize appropriate needs*

    It is important that the trainer determine which needs can best be met through training. An appropriate need is one which:

    *   a majority of the group requests;
    *   can best be met in a participatory group setting;
    *   deals with a desired change in skill level, factual knowledge, and/or attitudes;
    *   is job-related on an individual, departmental, or organizational level.

2. *Set priorities*

    Plan to respond to the most pressing needs first. If time is limited, meet those needs which trainees feel are urgent.

3. *Write training objectives*

    Each need is translated into a written statement which clearly indicates what is to be accomplished in training. This is called a training objective; written objectives provide the guideline which determines the training program. Generally, each need will produce at least one training objective and each training objective will describe the purpose of one training session.

    There are two types of training objectives. One is general. It is written from the trainer's point of view, stating what he expects to do or hopes to accomplish. For instance, where trainees need a better understanding of counseling, a general objective would be simply stated: To increase the trainees' knowledge of the counseling process.

Another kind of training objective is more specific. It is written in terms of anticipated change will be observed in the trainees' behavior. Such specific objectives are much more useful. Whatever difficulty is involved is well worth the effort and is generally a matter of breaking the conversion into components, in the following way?

Q. What will the trainees be able to do after training?
A. The trainees will be able to describe the counseling process.

Q. How well will they be able to do it?
A. They will be able to correctly list at least five steps of the counseling process and accurately describe their functions from memory.

Q. What will they need to do it?
A. A diagram of the counseling process.

The three components together would give a specific objective which might be stated: Given a diagram of the counseling process each trainee will be able to correctly list at least five of the steps and accurately describe their functions. This is to be done without the aid of notes.

Writing at least one specific objective for each session of the training helps the trainer to:

* *Focus on the actual needs expressed by the trainees.* A specific objective is more apt to be based on the trainee's proficiency level, insuring a program built on their skills and knowledge rather than covering standard material.

* *Develop and implement the actual training.* The design for delivering the training will flow from the stated objectives and provide concrete guidelines for what needs to be included in the delivery.

* *Identify the persons to be trained* in order to achieve the general objective.

* *Clearly describe what that person will be doing after training* that he was not doing before, or in other words, describe the *desired end behaviors* that will be observed and recorded.

* *Describe how well the person must be able to perform the behavior,* or in other words, describe the *acceptable level of performance.*

* *Identify the conditions for performing the behavior* by stating when and where the behavior will occur.

* *Provide a basis for evaluation.* A goal written in terms of the trainer makes the impact on the trainees difficult to measure. An objective in terms of specific trainee behavior can be measured either by testing or observation to ascertain whether it has been met. Such evaluation serves as an indication of what can be covered in subsequent sessions.

Not every training session will have a specific behavioral objective. The purpose of some sessions will be nearly impossible to state in behavioral terms. For instance, introductory and orientation sessions and those dealing with attitudes of one kind or another.

Avoid these words in writing objectives:

to know	to understand	to appreciate	to be acquainted
to remember	to comprehend	to recognize	to sympathize with
to perceive	to be familiar with		

Use these words in writing objectives:

to write	to recite	to identify	to differentiate	to list
to find	to solve	to construct	to demonstrate	to express
to state	to choose	to conduct		

It is worthwhile to note here that the power of training to reduce or resolve an agency's problems is often overestimated. It is the trainer's responsibility to make it clear that training is not the only solution or sometimes the most appropriate one. Some problems revealed in needs assessment can be alleviated by a change in procedures, a redefinition of policy, a reorganization of staff or the like.

Appendix 30.3

From: *Instrumented Trainers Manual for Multidisciplinary, Interagency Training Teams.* Development Associates, Inc.

DEVELOP LESSON PLANS

A lesson plan is a strategy for making the training subject matter work. It is a written plan for reaching your training objectives and it can be viewed as a textbook designed to fit a particular training need. All training sessions employ a lesson plan in some form. The advantage of thinking through the lesson plan, and writing it all down, is that in this process the trainers discover several ways to improve upon their ideas.

Another advantage is that each trainer, expert, or resource person can see exactly what each of the others is going to present or do, and all of the various sections of the training session can then be coordinated and sharpened to fit the objectives in a logical way. While some parts of the lesson plan can be developed individually by the trainer(s) responsible, the overall plan should be discussed and refined by a team and all training experts and resource persons. It is also very helpful for the training team and the support staff to review the lesson plan, familiarize themselves with it, and possibly suggest some corrections or additions.

The lesson plan, like the agenda, flows directly from the training objectives. In some ways, it is like an extremely detailed agenda, specifying exactly what will take place and in what manner within each section of the agenda. This is the point at which final decisions should be made about techniques to be used, and training personnel to be assigned to each section. Each section should be further broken down into smaller units of time and an outline developed showing who will do what and how in order to attain the objective(s) for each part.

A lesson plan is a highly detailed document specific to a particular training event. However, there are several components that are characteristic of good lesson plans.

Lesson plans should include the following characteristics:

(a) *The objectives for the session and a statement of the way in which they contribute to reaching the goal of the training session.* They are best when stated as behavioral—as opposed to conceptual—outcomes (e.g., notations on key words and concepts).

(b) *A description of the subject matter to be covered.* For example, if the objective of a particular section were to teach participants the differences between monitoring and evaluation, the description might include at a minimum: definitions of monitoring and of evaluation; the purposes of each activity; types of data useful for monitoring, for evaluation, for both; techniques for gathering and analyzing data; common problems in designing and implementing monitoring and evaluation systems.

(c) *The amount of time to be devoted to each topic or sub-topic.* If relevant, the time should also be broken out into smaller units required for specific activities within a particular session. For example, a two hour work-session devoted to critiquing a training evaluation plan might include: fifteen minutes for participants to read the plan; forty-five minutes to discuss and critique it; forty-five minutes to develop and discuss improvements; fifteen minutes to develop and discuss improvements; fifteen minutes to summarize the results of the work-session for presentation to a general session.

(d) *The trainers, resource persons, and/or staff who will participate in and be responsible for each section and/or each activity within it.* For instance, in the example above, one person might be responsible for leading the work-session critique and another for leading a discussion of improvements to the project evaluation plan.

(e) *A description of the methodology to be used in each section of the agenda.* This should be as detailed as possible. For example, the lesson plan should go beyond noting that role-playing will be used in a particular section. It should describe the role-play situation, actors, lesson, and so on.

(f) *A description of the roles various participants are to assume for different parts of the training event.* For example, if a work-session is designed to develop a project evaluation plan, whose responsibility is it to continually critique the plan as it is being developed—the trainer's? The trainee's? A resource expert in evaluation?

(g) *Expected session outcomes and follow-up procedures.* For example, if a particular session is designed to result in a series of recommendations regarding priorities for evaluation, procedures must be designed which specify who gets the recommendations, when, and how.

(h) *A listing and perhaps description of the background materials*, if any, with which trainers, staff, resource people, and/or trainees should be familiar prior to a particular session.

(i) *A listing of any special equipment, materials, handouts, etc., which will be used in a particular session.*

Lesson plans should be "personalized documents." That is, they should include and be in a format most useful to the particular trainer who will conduct the training session. Different trainers responsible for accomplishing the same objectives may therefore develop quite different lesson plans.

General criteria which can be utilized to judge the adequacy of a lesson plan are:

(a) *Relevance*

The subject matter is clearly related to learning needs felt by the trainees in the planning of the session and by introducing each lesson by pointing out to the trainees how the lesson relates to their learning needs and how it fits into the overall training goals and objectives. (This need not be "privileged information" for professionals.)

(b) *Prerequisites Considered*

Each portion of the lesson plan should include time for any prerequisite activities necessary to the success of that portion. This may simply be time for participants to talk with one another a while and open channels of communication. Or it may be time devoted to reviewing some subject not directly related to the task of a particular meeting but preliminary to it.

(c) *Relationship to Objectives*

Except for prerequisite activities, every portion of the lesson plan, no matter how small, should make a direct contribution toward the accomplishment of one of the training objectives. Hidden agendas and trivia have no place here.

(d) *Practice Experience Provided*

The lesson plan should provide an opportunity for active participation by the trainees in trying out the skill or using the information. Each trainee should have first hand experience with the subject. For example, if the subject is evaluation, the group should evaluate something.

(e) *Easy to Generalize*

Based upon the first hand experience and practice with the new skills and knowledge, trainees will need to generalize to their program responsibilities. If the subject is evaluation, the lesson plan should also demonstrate how evaluation is used in the case management, who is responsible, and how people can be involved.

(f) *Basis for Evaluation Provided*

The lesson plan provides both the basis and the opportunity for participants to review their progress towards the training objectives and, if necessary, to suggest revisions in the remainder of the agenda or the techniques.

Appendix 30.4

From: *Instrumented Trainers Manual for Multidisciplinary, Interagency Training Teams.* Development Associates, Inc.

EVALUATION OF TRAINING

In the field of training, evaluation has always been a problem. Those who pay for training want to assess their investment. Those who receive it are interested in determining what progress they have made. And those who deliver the program seek to ascertain whether the objectives were valid, understood, and achieved.

Basically, though, evaluation of the training effort will seek to measure four basic areas:

> -Trainee reaction to training session
> -Measure of learning
> -Measuring behavior
> -Measuring results

1.   *Trainee Reaction to the Training Session*

This measures the participant's likes and dislikes of a specific training session and should be done both during and after a program. The purpose is quite obvious, particularly during the course of a program. Training will not be very effective if it does not interest the trainees, or they do not accept the material presented.

There are a few important keys to measuring reaction:

(a) The measurement is best made in writing. This allows anonymity and encourages candid expressions of feeling by the participants.
(b) The measurement can be partially quantified by using a scaled system, asking participants to numerically express their reactions to specific aspects.
(c) The measurement should focus on three specific targets:

*   participants' feelings about the worth of the training;
*   how well they feel the training aligned with their needs;
*   their reactions to the trainer(s).

By using scaled responses to these aspects, reactions can be tabulated quickly, the trainer obtains information to help him revise the direction or approach if necessary, and improvements can be seen readily.

2.   *Measuring Learning*

It is important to distinguish learning (the increase of knowledge or skill) from behavior (how someone does his job).

It is most useful to measure learning as quantitatively and objectively as possible for comparison purposes. One way is to measure learning before and after training. This is done by a pre-test (administered before training) and an identical post-test (after) and the results are compared.

Another tool for evaluating learning is the "Session Evaluation Form," with questions or diagrams on a specific goal.

A check of learning accomplished in attitudinal sessions can be partially obtained through direct observation by the trainer and through reaction sheets and discussion (in which participants express what they felt they learned). A "General Evaluation of the Training Program" (or discussion) at the conclusion of a training program asks for trainees' opinions on the design and delivery of the training.

3.   *Measuring Behavior*

Although learning may be measured and found to be positive, there is no assurance that job performance and behavior will change to incorporate the new learning. In order for the benefit to take effect, several conditions are necessary:

(a) the trainee must have an opportunity to put the learning into effect and his supervisors must encourage him to use it;
(b) the trainee must realize that applying the new learning will make his job easier and more efficient;
(c) the trainee must be motivated to improve his job performance.

There are several factors to be considered when measuring behavioral change in staff due to training:

(a) Enough time must elapse after the training to allow the trainee to put the new knowledge into practice and for the change in behavior to be measurable.

(b) The measurement must be made by objective sources. One way to assure objectivity is to have various people do the measuring, including the trainee, his supervisor, his fellow workers, those he contacts (such as clients), and his peers.

(c) A comparison of behavior with that of other staff in similar jobs who did not receive training is also useful.

Essentially, changes in behavior following training can be measured by timing an evaluation of job performance at an appropriate interval to determine improvement attributable to training. Behavior is best measured several weeks following completion of a program.

The key to measuring both learning and behavior is the extent to which the objectives are actually met. If these are clear and specific, they provide a useful standard for evaluating the program. Any training will result in some learning achievement and some sort of behavior change. But only when these results are in line with the training objectives is the program successful.

4. *Measuring Results*

Results are perhaps the most important measurement in the eyes of those who pay for training but the most difficult to make:

(a) all results of the training need to be taken into account and these are not always easy to identify;

(b) only results attributable to training should be considered; training never takes place in isolation so other influences are difficult to eliminate.

The kinds of identifiable results to look for in a person who has attended training might include:

(a) better understanding of the overall goals of the agency;
(b) greater understanding of what is expected of the worker in terms of their specific duties and responsibilities;
(c) change in the caseload of the worker;
(d) change in the amount of time needed to process a client;
(e) change in the number of errors made by the worker in documenting a case;

(f) change in client follow-up procedures;

(g) better interaction, cooperation, and communication by the worker.

Other Analysis

A trainer should evaluate his own designing and planning. On completion of the program, the trainer can determine ways to improve later projects by reviewing certain cases.

(a) *Design of the Program*

-Were specific objectives developed?
-Were these objectives related to felt needs?
-Did program try to accomplish too much or too little?
-Was the scheduling realistic?
-Was the planning flexible enough to deal with problems and needs as they arose?
-Was enough information given?
-Were the specific objectives met?
-Did the plans focus on the involvement of the participants in developing the program as well as in the actual training?
-Was there a plan for evaluation of the program? Was it followed?

(b) *Plans for the Program*

-Were trainees properly notified of time, place, and location of training?
-Were the trainees properly oriented to the logistics of the training?
-Were the facilities adequate for the number of trainees?
-Was training room set up for use of audio-visual aids?
-Was ventilation and lighting good?
-Were training materials prepared and distributed beforehand?

31. Interdisciplinary Teams in Professional Schools: A Case Study

Donald N. Duquette and Kathleen C. Faller

Introduction

No single profession has the solution to the problems of child abuse and neglect. The skills and talents of many need to be brought to bear on the problem. One of the skills required is that of communicating clearly and accurately across disciplinary lines. Just as a lawyer needs to understand the concept of due process, a social worker a family history, and a pediatrician infection; each of these professions, to function well in an interdisciplinary setting, must understand and appreciate what the other disciplines can offer in addressing problems of child abuse and neglect. Understanding other disciplines includes knowing something of the *substance* of the others' expertise (e.g., that the law requires notice and an opportunity for hearing; that the radiologist's report of fractures in several stages of healing may indicate inflicted injury; that a family history in which the mother has been abused as a child is some cause for concern for her child), but also requires an understanding of the *process* by which various professions come to their judgments. Disciplines vary in their approach to gathering data and using that data to solve problems. A lawyer needs to ascertain specific facts and wants to know, "Who saw what, when? Who said what, when? How do you know that to be true?" A lawyer will fit the facts of the case into the statutes, rules, case law, and practices of the court. Physicians rely on a medical history and a physical examination of all the systems to come to a diagnosis. The mental health professional uses psychological testing, interviewing, or playing with a child to draw inferences about the child's functioning. Yet despite differences among professions in content and process, similarities abound and provide the common basis for working together.

Interdisciplinary education ought to be encouraged and rewarded by professional schools. As specialization increases, professionals, particularly academics, know more and more about less and less; and the place of the generalist or the person who can integrate the data and theories of many different perspectives and disciplines and apply them to the problems facing children and families, grows ever more important—and often more elusive. Many social problems require the integration of data and a team approach among various disciplines. Child abuse and neglect is one such problem.

The development of the Interdisciplinary Project on Child Abuse and Neglect (IPCAN) at the University of Michigan is presented here. The history of the project, its organizational development and contributions to easing the problems of child abuse and neglect and coping with the challenges of interdisciplinary collaboration are offered in the hope that others may benefit from our experiences.

The Beginning: The Importance of Private Philanthropy

A PRIVATE FUNDING INITIATIVE

A crucial factor in the development of IPCAN was the availability of generous funding from a private foundation. In 1976 the Harry A. and Margaret D. Towsley Foundation provided a three-year grant to the University of Michigan to support faculty from the schools of Law, Medicine, and Social Work. The foundation's intent was to create "a model program at the University of Michigan for education and advocacy for the abused and neglected child" and to create a body of expertise at the University on this troubling issue. The goals of the project as initially conceived were:

a. To advocate the use of interdisciplinary collaboration in the field of child abuse and neglect.
b. To train professionals to utilize interdisciplinary skills in a variety of contexts.
c. To advocate for policies which will improve services to abused and neglected children and their families.

d.   To conduct research and write for professional journals regarding child abuse and neglect.

The relatively generous funding allowed exploration of alternative means of interdisciplinary collaboration on cases of suspected child abuse and experimentation with various methods of teaching multidisciplinary content. Figure 31.1 represents the organization of IPCAN as it was in 1977-78.

COMPONENTS OF THE EARLY PROGRAM

a.   Law School Education
The Child Advocacy Law Clinic was developed by IPCAN and has been offered by the Law School for seven credits per semester since Fall 1976. In this specialized clinical law experience, eight to eighteen law students per semester handle actual child abuse and neglect cases under close supervision of clinical law faculty. Student attorneys appear in three legal roles: representing the county child welfare agency, children, or parents in separate Michigan counties. Class work and case consultation is provided by lawyers, social workers, pediatricians, and psychiatrists. Faculty-student ratio in the early years when the education model was first being developed was richer than at present. We are able to replicate the educational program more efficiently today. However, an interdisciplinary faculty continues to offer the law students training in traditional legal skills as well as seminars in medical aspects of child abuse and neglect, child development, interpersonal and family dynamics, and public policy issues raised by government intervention in the family.

As a result of IPCAN resources, child abuse and neglect materials were incorporated into non-clinical law school courses and a seminar on child abuse and neglect was developed and is taught each year.

b.   The Medical School
In the early years, IPCAN staffed the SCAN (Suspected Child Abuse and Neglect) Team at the University Medical Center. SCAN Team cases provided the initial learning lab for IPCAN faculty because, by attempting to provide high-quality service on cases, many of the difficulties of interdisciplinary collaboration were identified. These early experiences, and the opportunity to reflect upon them, provided the foundation for the development of curricula for the various university courses and the continuing professional education programs and spurred subsequent research and writing.

IPCAN faculty participated at many levels of the medical education curriculum to familiarize medical students with child abuse and neglect and interdisciplinary skills. Lectures from various

Figure 31.1 Interdisciplinary Project on Child Abuse and Neglect
University of Michigan

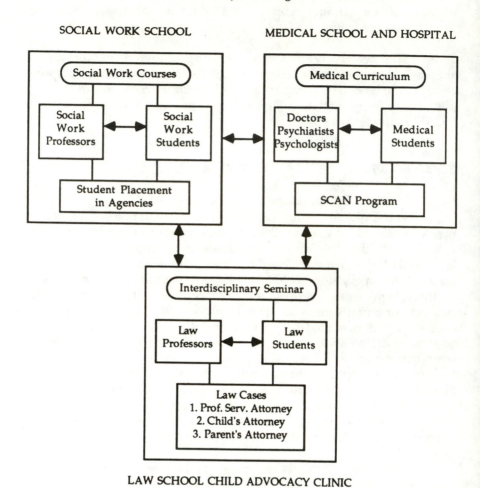

LAW SCHOOL CHILD ADVOCACY CLINIC

professionals on the IPCAN Team were incorporated into the undergraduate preclinical sequence; fellows, residents, and undergraduate clinical students participated in the SCAN Team, IPCAN seminars, community, and court intervention. Fourth year medical students were allowed to choose a 5 to 10 week experience working directly and intensively with IPCAN faculty and students from the other disciplines.

    c.   School of Social Work

    A student unit within the local department of social services was established as a clinical site for training social work students and a laboratory for testing innovative approaches to training and interventions with abused and neglected children and their families. Students were placed in protective services, foster care, and adoption and were co-supervised by agency and IPCAN social work staff. They attended a seminar series that provided multidisciplinary material on all aspects of child welfare. A multidisciplinary team including a social worker, psychologist, psychiatrist, and attorney from IPCAN was available every week for consultation with students and staff on cases.

    IPCAN also offered seminars in the School of Social Work which focused on child abuse and neglect. These multidisciplinary courses addressed such issues as identification, reporting, assessment, intervention, and legal aspects of child maltreatment. The seminars were widely attended and included students from other parts of the University, including the Psychology Department, the Law School, the School of Public Health, and the School of Nursing. The School of Social Work incorporated IPCAN child abuse and neglect materials into child welfare courses.

MULTIDISCIPLINARY, INTERDEPARTMENTAL COLLABORATION

    The early private funding of IPCAN allowed for full development of the clinical components. Faculty and students from clinical programs in the Law School, School of Social Work, and the Medical School worked together on cases, each performing the functions of his/her profession. Faculty collaborated on a select number of cases to explore the interdisciplinary process. They also supervised students from the three schools who worked together on cases. IPCAN faculty began producing written material that was used in continuing professional education and in university courses.

The Transition from Private Foundation Funding to Diversified Public and Private Funding

THE ADVANTAGES OF A UNIVERSITY-BASED PROGRAM

IPCAN's private funding allowed the faculty to experiment with different types of interdisciplinary collaboration, to advance substantive knowledge in the child abuse and neglect field, and to offer students a range of interdisciplinary learning opportunities.

However, in 1978, as the end of the three-year grant period approached, faculty were faced with the need to seek other support if this endeavor was to be continued. They began to seek commitments from the three schools and to investigate public sources of funding.

A project based in an academic institution has certain advantages as a source of service to the public. The first is the emphasis on academic rigor, specifically on the necessity for comprehensive knowledge in the substantive area under consideration (i.e., review of *all* the literature), and the recognition of the importance of empirical testing of interventions (research and evaluation). Second, because the academic institution has commitment to its faculty, a project such as IPCAN is not totally at the mercy of short-term funding sources. A sense of direction can still be maintained in a climate of changing priorities from funding sources. Thus it is in a better position to preserve its interests than programs totally dependent upon external funding.

Similarly, there are advantages to a university in having a rich clinical base for training professionals that is utilized as a laboratory for exploration of the broad range of issues presented both by child abuse and neglect and by interdisciplinary collaboration.

UNIVERSITY SUPPORT

The university assumed financial support for several IPCAN activities. University Hospital and the Medical School assumed the payment of salaries of the SCAN Team (now called the Child Protection Team), and that program has continued to grow. Presently the team has one full-time and one half-time social worker, two half-time pediatricians, and access to all the medical specialties, including psychiatry.

The School of Social Work eventually hired an IPCAN faculty member into a tenured position. The Law School extended hard financial support to the Child Advocacy Law Clinic and made a long-term commitment to the Director.

SHORT-TERM FUNDED PROJECTS

After the initial foundation funding, IPCAN sought and received funding from a number of public and private sources to support various short-term projects consistent with IPCAN's overall mission. Those projects include:

a.   *Children at Risk Study*: This project documented the extensive multiple agency involvement with 51 families on the active abuse and neglect caseload of the juvenile court. A mean of 7.9 agencies was involved with each family and many of the agencies were not aware of the others' activities.

b.   *Causes of Child Maltreatment*: Families referred to child protective services in a three-county area in Michigan were compared with a matched sample of families from the AFDC caseloads. Environmental stresses accounted for almost all the variance between the sample and comparison groups.

c.   *Guardian ad litem Study*: In an empirical study, children in child abuse and neglect cases were represented by trained groups of lawyers, law students, and lay (nonlawyer) volunteers under lawyer supervision. After comparing the performance of the three groups to one another and to a control group of attorneys who received no special training, the study concluded that training makes a significant difference in the process and outcome of child advocacy and that trained volunteer child advocates performed similarly to trained attorneys, although "better" than nontrained lawyers.[1]

d.   *Permanency for Children Legal Services*: The Child Advocacy Law Clinic contracted with several nearby counties to handle cases in which legal action was necessary to secure permanent placements for children in foster care. Handling primarily termination of parental rights cases, law students (under faculty supervision) provided a greatly needed service for the counties and the children; fees charged supported additional clinical legal education in child advocacy. Although medical education has traditionally charged for the value of services provided by their trainees, this was a significant new step for clinical legal education that could encourage expansion of this valuable, yet costly, component of law school.

e.   *Investigating Child Sexual Abuse in Day Care Centers*: IPCAN contracted with state licensing authority to assist in the investigation of allegations of child sexual abuse in several day care settings. Children were evaluated, videotapes were made of the children's statements, and subsequently used at administrative licensing hearings.

ONGOING FUNDED PROJECTS

IPCAN has been successful in obtaining long-term public funding for several activities, primarily from two sources. The U.S. Department of Education has provided partial funding to the Law School's Child Advocacy Law Clinic since 1979. The Michigan Department of Social Services has funded a Multidisciplinary Team Training Project administered through the School of Social Work since 1978; and the Family Assessment Clinic, a multidisciplinary diagnostic and assessment team in the University Hospital since 1985.

The Multidisciplinary Team Training Project warrants some elaboration here. Beginning in 1978, the Michigan Department of Social Services contracted with IPCAN to train multidisciplinary community based teams to assist the department of social services on abuse and neglect cases. To date IPCAN has trained approximately 60 such teams throughout the state. Additional training has been provided under this contract to protective services, foster care, and adoption workers, including instruction in multidisciplinary management of various types of child abuse and neglect cases, the legal aspects of child welfare, and multidisciplinary intervention in cases at risk for death or serious injury of the child. More recently, most of the training has focused on child sexual abuse, and during the current contract year IPCAN will train multidisciplinary community-based teams in the management of child sexual abuse cases. An additional service under this contract will include consultation to the Michigan Department of Social Services on policy and program development.

A concern of the department of social services has been that although several practice manuals have been developed under this contract, the workers do not have adequate skills, beyond the investigation stage, to assist families who abuse and neglect their children. To address this, IPCAN developed a manual that covers family intervention techniques that are both practical and consistent with the protective service role.

For the training of multidisciplinary teams, IPCAN has developed a series of discipline-specific resources. Manuals for lawyers, mental health professionals, nurses, physicians, protection services, foster care, and court staff include materials written by IPCAN faculty and other experienced professionals in the child welfare field.

Finally, IPCAN has developed a range of legal resource materials under this contract including: *Protective Services Law Manual*,[2] *Foster Care and Adoption Law Manual*,[3] *Michigan Child*

Welfare Law: Child Protection, Foster Care, and Termination of Parental Rights.[4]

Advocacy for Children: Social Reform

As the experience of the project grew, more and more people within the state of Michigan have looked to IPCAN as a resource. As a group and as individuals, IPCAN faculty are asked to speak, conduct workshops and training sessions, and to offer advice on specific cases and policy.   While most IPCAN activity is focused on teaching, clinical work, and research, the staff has also engaged in advocacy for children in the courts and in the legislature.   For example, when serious deficiencies were discovered in the workings of the Wayne County (Detroit) Juvenile Court, IPCAN provided further investigation and filed suit (*Virtue v. Wayne County Juvenile Court*)[5] as an original action in the Michigan Supreme court.   The Supreme Court ordered an independent investigation and assigned administrative personnel to the court for over a year to assist with resolving the problems.

The Child Advocacy Law Clinic worked with the Michigan legislature and a "blue-ribbon" committee was convened by a former Chief Justice of the Michigan Supreme Court to develop legislation to implement federal law P.L. 96-272, the Adoption Assistance and Child Welfare Act of 1980, and to address other obstacles to achieving permanency for children in foster care. That legislation drew upon the interdisciplinary perspective of IPCAN through incorporation of legal, psychological, and social work considerations and concepts.

Michigan, like other states, has wrestled with the problems facing child witnesses. IPCAN has developed a package of child witness protections, drawing from our several disciplines, research in psychology and child development, the work of national policy groups, the experiences of other states, and our own legal analysis. The legislature has considered these reports and we are working with the legislative committees to help develop legislation.

Interdisciplinary Knowledge Development

Over the years IPCAN has developed new approaches to many of the common and troublesome issues raised by child abuse and neglect.

Some of these have been described in publications and others have not. It is beyond the scope of this chapter to describe any of these in depth. However, material has been published by IPCAN faculty on the following topics: collaboration between lawyers and medical/mental health professionals in developing expert testimony,[6,7] decision-making in child sexual abuse,[8] and defining the roles of the child's advocate, agency attorney, and parents' attorney in the context of child protection.[9,10,11] In addition, a book entitled *Social Work with Abused and Neglected Children* with contributions from several IPCAN faculty was published in 1981.[12] To make the potential of the interdisciplinary processes more clear, one area of interdisciplinary knowledge development is outlined here.

Emotional Maltreatment

Emotional maltreatment has long been of grave concern to mental health professionals. At the same time, there is rarely any medical evidence of such insults, and lawyers have been sorely frustrated in their efforts to prove cases of emotional maltreatment in court. IPCAN has developed a strategy that integrates the mental health and legal strategies in emotional abuse and neglect.

DEFINITION

For a case to be defined as emotional maltreatment, professionals must be able to identify three components. First, there must be identifiable *parental behavior*. Second, there must be demonstrable *harm to the child*. Third, the mental health professional must be able to establish a *causal link* between the parental behavior and the harm to the child. In addition, for a case to warrant decisive interaction, professionals must provide proof of *chronic abuse* and *multimodality* (the parents emotionally maltreat the child in a number of different ways).

STRATEGY

Even though a case meets the definition criteria, professionals must pursue a conservative strategy. First, attempts should be made to involve the family in treatment on a voluntary basis. Such efforts may require several sessions with the family for professionals to communicate their concerns. Only if these efforts are unsuccessful and the case is considered very serious should coercive intervention be sought. Emotional maltreatment is a difficult concept for families and the court to comprehend. Thus, a posture of taking only clearcut cases to adjudication should be pursued. If jurisdiction is taken, interventions should be court ordered. The effects of intervention should be carefully monitored, and professionals need to exhaust all intervention possibilities, that is, all combinations of services that might alleviate the family problems. However, if none of these are successful, professionals must move decisively in the courts, so an alternative permanent home for the child can be sought. Mental health testimony that identifies parental behavior, its harmful effects on the child, causal link, and lack of response to services will be the key to successful termination.

Summary and Conclusions

The need for interdisciplinary professional education in child abuse and neglect remains, as does the need for further exploration of the interdisciplinary process. Among the risks inherent in a multidisciplinary team is the blurring of professional identity, so that the lawyer might make psychological assessments and a social worker might cite his/her understanding of a statute or court opinion. It is important that the spheres of expertise among the various professions be defined as clearly as possible and accepted by the other members of a team.

The potential of such programs in a university setting, both as a laboratory for developing new knowledge and as a ground for professional education, is substantial. The state and community in which similar programs are located may benefit from development of a resource to help improve practice and policy in protecting children and rehabilitating neglectful and abusive families. However, there are risks to programs that attempt to belong to the community and to several different departments within the university. In belonging to everyone, the program may belong to no one. If such programs are not attached to an individual school within the university, they may not receive high priority for funding. Stability and continuity of faculty and staff are essential to the success of an interdisciplinary program; however, faculty members run the risk that interdisciplinary expertise may not be given great weight in promotion and tenure decisions.

Similarly, state and local governments are always short of financial resources and may consider grants and contracts to the university program a lesser priority than maintaining existing staff.

The benefits of a program similar to IPCAN are worth the risks. Ongoing private funding, perhaps as an endowment, can ease some of the difficulties of such nontraditional enterprises. Certainly IPCAN would not have started nor would it have continued without the vision and support of the Towsley Foundation.

References

1. Duquette, D.N., and D. Ramsey. "Using Lay Volunteers to Represent Children in Child Protection Court Proceedings." *Child Abuse & Neglect*, 10(1986):293-308.

2   Duquette, D.N. *Protective Services Law Manual*. Lansing, Mich.: Michigan Department of Social Services, 1978.

3. Duquette, D.N. *Foster Care and Adoption Law Manual*. Lansing, Mich.: Michigan Department of Social Services, 1981.

4. Duquette, D.N. *Michigan Child Welfare Law: Child Protection, Foster Care, and Termination of Parental Rights*. Lansing, Mich.: Michigan Department of Social Services, 1984.

5. *Virtue v. Wayne Probate Court*, 407 Mich 1150 1979.

6. Duquette, D.N. "Collaboration Between Lawyers and Mental Health Professionals: Making It Work." *Foster Children and the Courts*. M. Hardin (Ed.), pp. 489-517. Toronto: Butterworth, 1983.

7. Duquette, D.N. "Mental Health Professionals and Child Custody Disputes: Are There Alternatives to the Adversarial Process?" *Infant Mental Health Journal*, 2(1981):159-175.

8. Faller, K.C. *Diagnosis, Case Management, and Treatment of Child Sexual Abuse*. New York: Columbia University Press (in press).

9. Duquette, D.N. "The Expert Witness in Child Abuse and Neglect: An Interdisciplinary Process." *Child Abuse & Neglect*, 5(1981):325.

10. Duquette, D.N. "Liberty and Lawyers in Child Protection." *The Battered Child*. R.E. Helfer and C.H. Kempe (Eds.), pp. 316-329. Chicago: The University of Chicago Press, 1980.

11. Duquette, D.N., and D. Ramsey. "Using Lay Volunteers to Represent Children in Child Protection Court Proceedings." *Child Abuse & Neglect*, 10(1986):293-308.

12. Faller, K.C. (Ed.) *Social Work with Abused and Neglected Children: A Manual of Interdisciplinary Practice.* New York: The Free Press, 1981.

32. The Prevalence and Characteristics of Multidisciplinary Teams for Child Abuse and Neglect: A National Survey*

Barbara B. Kaminer, Ann H. Crowe,
and Lisanne Budde-Giltner

Introduction

While the phenomenon of child maltreatment has been documented throughout history, attempts to address the problem and protect children from abuse and neglect are relatively recent. Kentucky was one of the first states to pass legislation in 1964 concerning child protection reporting. National legislation dealing solely with the reporting of child abuse, and related aspects of child protection, was not enacted until 1974. Thus, effective intervention strategies are still being conceptualized, implemented, and refined.

In 1982, the Kentucky Department for Human Resources entered into a contract with the Kent School of Social Work at the University of Louisville to develop multidisciplinary teams for child abuse and neglect in several communities throughout the state. The authors of this chapter were staff members of this project during its three-year duration.

For project purposes the following concepts of multidisciplinary teams were integrated into a working definition: a functioning unit composed of professionals and/or representatives of service agencies who work together to communicate, collaborate and consolidate knowledge from which plans are made, actions determined, and future decisions influenced.[1,2]

The very nature of child abuse and neglect requires the involvement of many community resources. Health care, legal and judicial services, law enforcement, and mental health interventions, as well as many others, are frequently required to provide protection and rehabilitation for the child and family. Most of these services are obtained outside the legally mandated protective service agency. Fragmentation of service delivery became a very real problem, as no single agency could provide the total array of services required. Since child abuse and neglect are complex problems, they need comprehensive and coordinated prevention, intervention, and treatment services provided by a multidisciplinary approach.

In recognition of this need, hospital-based multidisciplinary child protection teams were first developed in the late 1950s in Pittsburgh, Los Angeles, and Denver. These early teams generally consisted of a social worker, a pediatrician, and a nurse. These teams used a medical model approach to the management of the physical treatment and protection of the child. Community-based multidisciplinary teams came into existence a few years later and were generally under the leadership of the child protection services of the welfare department. Both hospital-based and community-based teams have increased in membership and psychiatry, psychology, law, and education are now usually added to the original disciplines of medicine, nursing, and social work. In some settings, still other disciplines are represented, such as law enforcement, the lay community, homemakers, the political arena, and others.[3,4]

Teams vary widely according to setting, functions, composition, sponsorship, and other factors. Each community or agency utilizing a multidisciplinary team develops a unique model based on community needs and resources. Functions of teams generally fall within four categories: treatment teams, case consultation teams, resource development or community action teams, and mixed model teams.[5,6] These models will be further defined and described with survey findings.

Survey Methodology

Throughout the project period, an extensive review of professional literature was undertaken. This search included a general survey of child abuse and neglect literature, with a special emphasis on collecting material about multidisciplinary teams. From this activity, project staff concluded that professional literature on multidisciplinary teams yielded little information and few guidelines for those wishing to develop teams. To better understand the options for team development, the project staff decided to undertake two national surveys to determine the number of existing teams and their general functions and policies.

The descriptive research method chosen for this study utilized mailed questionnaires which had the advantages of limited cost and easy accessibility. The first questionnaire (referred to as state questionnaire) was designed to obtain general information from each of the fifty states. This data included the numbers of functioning teams in the state; the models they represented; if they were mandated by law; type of authorization; state coordination and involvement in orientation and/or evaluation of multidisciplinary teams; presence of confidentiality waivers; type of funding; and future plans.

A contact in each state was determined through correspondence with each of the ten directors of the Regional Resource Centers for Children and Youth Services. A questionnaire and cover letter were sent to these state officials in the spring of 1983 and resulted in 39 responses (78%) from the fifty states. Another mailing to the remaining 11 states in January of 1984 brought five additional responses, increasing the total to 44 responses (88%). In December of 1984, the last six states were contacted and interviewed by phone. These three efforts resulted in a 100% response rate to the state questionnaire and resulted in the collection of sufficient data from all 50 states to allow for adequate comparison.

The state questionnaire asked respondents to identify existing teams functioning in their states. From this list, a mailing was compiled for the second questionnaire (referred to as team questionnaire). The team questionnaire was designed to obtain more specific information concerning individual teams rather than the broader areas covered by the state questionnaire. Through the team questionnaire, project staff wanted to collect such data as: main team function, length of team existence, disciplines represented on teams and their influence, characteristics of team meetings, funding, orientation and evaluation, and leadership issues.

Team questionnaires were originally planned to be sent to a maximum of four teams per state. As completed state questionnaires were received, up to four teams listed were mailed a team questionnaire and a cover letter. (Some states indicated they had fewer than four teams.)

Since responses varied from state to state, so did the number of team questionnaires sent. For some states team questionnaires were not sent because states did not provide a list of team names and addresses. Additionally, the last 6 states were contacted by phone in the final months of the project were not asked for team lists.   Therefore, representation of states in the team findings is varied.

A total of 150 team questionnaires was mailed from spring 1983 to spring 1984. Three of these were returned as undeliverable. Therefore, there were 147 possible respondents. Eighty-nine questionnaires were returned (two uncompleted) and two teams responded with information in letter form. This is a total of 91 respondents, a 62% response rate. Again, this can be considered adequate in evaluation of results.

Survey Results

Responses to the state questionnaire indicated that all 50 states had at least one functioning multidisciplinary team. The range was from one team to 100 or more. The total number of teams identified was 901, thereby making the average of 18 multidisciplinary teams per state.

Table 32.1 shows the states that indicated they have multidisciplinary teams, the number of teams existing, and if the teams are legislatively mandated.

A nationwide survey conducted by the American Humane Association in 1979, as reported by Pettiford in 1981, also found a growing trend in the utilization of multidisciplinary teams. These survey results indicated that more than one third (36.9%) of local reporting offices were utilizing multidisciplinary teams.[7]

The development and utilization of multidisciplinary teams has been encouraged by the passage of federal legislation (Public Law 93-247, The Child Abuse Prevention and Treatment Act). This act stipulates that states which receive federal grants under this legislation must have operational multidisciplinary programs and services to ensure effective intervention in child abuse and neglect cases.[8,9]

The National Professional Resources Center on Child Abuse and Neglect of the American Public Welfare Association conducted a survey in 1981 of nineteen teams in sixteen states. They found that two factors most frequently led to the development of these teams: community action and legislative mandate.[10] As indicated in Table 32.1, twelve states reported that multidisciplinary teams were legislatively mandated. For the remaining 38 states, respondents indicated the following types of sponsorship or authorization:

SPONSORSHIP/AUTHORIZATION RESPONSES*

Public Agency Sponsorship	18
Community Sponsorship	12
State Sponsorship	12
Hospital Sponsorship	10
Private Agency Sponsorship	4
Local/County Mandate	1
Other	4

*Most respondents indicated teams operated under a combination of sponsorships; therefore, responses total more than 38.

FUNDING

The survey also requested information on the funding mechanisms available to develop and maintain teams. Twenty-three states indicated that no funding was available. Of the remaining twenty-seven states, funding was reported from one or more of the following sources: federal funds (17 states); state funds (15 states); local/county funds (15 states); contributions/donations (8 states); private foundations (4 states); third party payments for services (2 states) and other (4 states). The team questionnaire yielded similar findings with 32% indicating a lack of funding for team development and operation.

TEAM MODELS/FUNCTIONS

Several models of multidisciplinary teams can be identified through the literature. These fall into four basic categories as described below:

Treatment Teams—A group of treatment experts who collaborate on the diagnosis and treatment of the child and/or family. This group of service providers shares responsibility with child protective service workers for case assessment, diagnosis, treatment plan development, referral to treatment resources, and case follow-up.

Case Consultation Teams—A group of experts who collectively provide opinions and advice regarding child protection cases. The team reviews cases in terms of case management and diagnosis, and serves in an advisory capacity to primary workers around treatment planning and critical decisions. Technical assistance and support to service providers are also functions of this team.

Resource Development or Community Action Teams—A group of service agency representatives, professional service providers, child advocates, and citizens who collectively work with local problems associated with child abuse and neglect. They address ongoing planning, coordination of services, community needs, community education/awareness, etc.

Mixed Model Teams—The combination of two or more of the above team functions by a single team; or two or more teams with different functions working within a central coordination mechanism.[5,6]

Respondents to the state questionnaire were asked to indicate which models could be identified in one or more teams in each state. The following list represents a total of more than 50 due to multiple responses: case consultation model (42 states, 85%); mixed model (31 states, 62%); treatment model (27 states, 54%); resource development model (26 states, 52%); other (9 states, 18%). (The models identified under the "other" category were: intake and closing screening, administrative case reviews, diagnosis only, public and professional education, investigation, state child protection team for institutional abuse cases, advisory group to state department of social services, public education.)

The random sample of individual teams was asked a similar question concerning the main team function on the team questionnaire. Of the 91 respondents, 48 (52%) reported being mixed model teams; 30 (32%) were case consultation teams; 7 (8%) were resource development teams; 1 (1%) was a treatment team; 1 (1%) and 4 (4%) respectively gave a response of "other" or gave no response.

Pettiford reports similar findings from a survey reported by the American Human Association in 1979. These data also indicated that case consultation is the most prevalent model of multidisciplinary teams utilized in child protective services. Of 461 local child protective services offices reporting that they used multidisciplinary teams, 58.77% indicated that their teams were advisory or consultative. Additionally, 22.6% reported their teams' functions as consultative, case review, and accountability in nature.[11]

Among the nineteen multidisciplinary teams surveyed by the American Public Welfare Association, all provided case consultation to child protective services personnel. The type of consultation provided was as follows: case assessment (19); case monitoring and review (18); and case closure (11). Along with these functions, 11 teams provided diagnosis and treatment, and two-thirds of the teams helped identify gaps and worked to develop or improve the service system in their communities. Public relations, education activities, and support for CPS personnel were cited as other team functions.[12]

TABLE 32.1 *Number of Teams and Legislative Mandates by State*

State	Number of Teams	Legislative Mandate Yes	No
Alabama	6		X
Alaska	5 (minimum)		X
Arkansas	4*		X
Arizona	undetermined		X
California	5*		X
Colorado	42	X	
Connecticut	25*		X
Delaware	3		X
Florida	21		X
Georgia	6		X
Hawaii	3		X
Idaho	5*		X
Illinois	30	X	
Indiana	92	X	
Iowa	35		X
Kansas	4*		X
Kentucky	4		X
Louisiana	10		X
Maine	10		X
Maryland	23		X
Massachusetts	11	X	
Michigan	13*	X	
Minnesota	67*	X	
Mississippi	1		X
Missouri	undetermined	X	
Montana	27*		X
Nebraska	6 (minimum)		X
Nevada	3 (minimum)		X
New Hampshire	10		X
New Jersey	undetermined		X
New Mexico	4*		X
New York	4 (minimum)		X
North Carolina	undetermined*		X
North Dakota	26		X
Ohio	21*		X
Oklahoma	2		X
Oregon	10 (minimum)		X
Pennsylvania	undetermined	X	

TABLE 32.1 *Number of Teams and Legislative Mandates by State (continued)*

State	Number of Teams	Legislative Mandate Yes	No
Rhode Island	1		X
South Carolina	56 (minimum)	X	
South Dakota	21		X
Tennessee	100 (minimum)	X	
Texas	23		X
Utah	14	X	
Vermont	14		X
Virginia	73		X
Washington	undetermined		X
West Virginia	5		X
Wisconsin	16		X
Wyoming	30	X	
	901 (minimum)	12	38

*Some respondents did not indicate the number of teams in their state, but the answer could be inferred from subsequent answers.

TEAM COMPOSITION/MEMBERSHIP

Three basic alternatives for composition of a multidisciplinary team were identified: by discipline, by agency, or by function. An example of each is listed below.

DISCIPLINE	AGENCY
Social Worker	Child Protective Service Agency
Physician	Medical Center
Psychiatrist/Psychologist	Mental Health Center
Attorney	Legal Services
Human Development Specialist	School System
Law Enforcement	Police Department
Nurse	Health Department

FUNCTION

Family Therapist (e.g., social worker, psychologist, etc.)
Community Organization/Social Systems/Resources
Casework Specialist (with child protective service experience)
Child Development Specialist (e.g., educator, nurse, child psychologist)
Physician (e.g., pediatrician, family medicine)
Legal/Court System (e.g., attorney with knowledge of dependency docket, child advocacy experience, etc.)
Law Enforcement Officer

On the team questionnaire respondents were asked to identify team composition only by disciplines represented. Table 32.2 shows the number of respondents indicating each of the following disciplines included in their team composition.

Table 32.2
Disciplines Represented

Social Worker	86
Psychologist	65
Nurse	64
Physician	63
Lawyer	54
Educator	53
Public Health Representative	52
Law Enforcement Representative	52
Judicial Representative	38
Psychiatrist	23
Lay Representative	23
Developmental Specialist	20
Day Care Worker	11

Homemaker	11
Minority Representative	8
Politician	2
Other (clergy—7, clients—3, etc.)	32
No Answer	5

Every team that answered this question (N=86) has social work representation. Other disciplines/professions that are represented by at least half of the respondents are psychologists, nurses, physicians, lawyers, educators, law enforcement, and public health representatives. In the 1981 survey by the American Public Welfare Association, the following eight major professions were identified as team disciplines: social workers/case workers, psychiatrists/other mental health personnel, nurses, physicians, attorneys, police officers, educators/teachers, judges/court staff. All but judges/court staff were reported to be on at least half of these teams.[13]

The survey also included two rating scales to ascertain the various disciplines' impact upon two hypothetical situations. The respondents were asked to rate each discipline by its level of impact (always, usually, seldom, never). The following tables show the breakdown of the reported influence by each discipline in discussions of returning children to their home environment after temporary placement.

Table 32.3 addresses the short-term impact while Table 32.4 addresses the extent of impact of each discipline on discussions of long-term treatment plans for the physically abused child.

Upon close examination the two grids show minimal variation. In dealing with returning a child to the home the legally based disciplines (lawyer, judicial representative) appear to have more influence. In the situation involving long-term treatment for the physically abused child, the physician appears to have greater impact. In both cases, however, the social worker ranked first in influence. The ranking of most other disciplines also remained comparable.

LEADERSHIP

The reported influence of each discipline does not necessarily reflect the leadership of a team. For each meeting a leader is needed to facilitate team discussion. This leader may be the same person each time or may be rotated on a meeting-by-meeting, monthly, or some other basis. Teams also have various methods of leadership selection. A two-part question on the team questionnaire dealt with leadership. Thirty-eight respondents stated the position was a permanent one as opposed to 18 indicating a rotating position. Only three answered that there was no identifiable leader.

TABLE 32.3 *Impact of Disciplines on Decisions to Return a Child Home*

Discipline	Always	Usually	Seldom	Never
Social Worker	30	18	4	—
Lawyer	16	21	12	4
Psychologist	15	28	11	3
Nurse	12	20	16	5
Judicial Representative	11	16	8	9
Physician	11	27	12	5
Psychiatrist	11	9	19	7
Public Health Representative	10	17	15	3
Educator	8	10	20	9
Law Enforcement Representative	6	15	21	5
Lay Representative	5	2	11	18
Politician	2	4	7	22
Developmental Specialist	1	18	13	8
Homemaker	1	7	17	9
Day Care Worker	—	3	16	15
Minority Representative	—	1	7	22
Others				
Mental Health	1	1	—	—
Clergy	—	—	1	—
Clients	1	2	3	—
No Answer	13			

TABLE 32.4 *Impact of Disciplines on Long Term Treatment Plans for a Physically Abused Child*

Discipline	Always	Usually	Seldom	Never
Social Worker	49	19	5	1
Physician	24	26	11	1
Psychologist	24	26	7	1
Nurse	17	19	24	3
Psychiatrist	15	10	16	4
Lawyer	14	25	13	4
Public Health Representative	14	23	15	4
Judicial Representative	11	24	9	6
Educator	7	22	22	3
Law Enforcement Representative	7	16	24	6
Lay Representative	5	7	13	19
Homemaker	4	4	23	8
Developmental Specialist	3	18	18	6
Politician	3	3	5	24
Day Care Worker	1	7	21	12
Minority Representative	—	4	9	22
No Answer	12			

In ascertaining the method used in choosing leadership, the most frequent answer was being elected by the team (24). The other choices were natural evolvement (14) and appointed from outside (6). This question was obviously incomplete since 20 respondents wrote in answers including appointed by sponsor (10) and employed (3).

OPERATIONAL FACTORS

The team questionnaire also considered operation mechanisms of teams. It is important to consider the time and other constraints of volunteer members in determining the length and frequency of meetings. A meeting of 2 to 2 1/2 hours is generally as long as people can be expected to work intensively and productively. On the team questionnaire, most teams (71) stated they have a limited time period for team meetings. The following table shows the answers received.

Table 32.5
Meeting Length

Usual Length of Meeting	Responses
One hour or less	21
1 to 1 1/2 hours	20
1 1/2 to 2 hours	26
2 hours or more	4

Meetings may be scheduled in a variety of ways including weekly, biweekly, monthly, or as needed. Respondents to the team questionnaire indicated that 83 of the teams meet on a regular basis while only three do not. In terms of frequency of meetings 41 (48%) meet monthly, 17 (20%) meet weekly, and 16 teams (19%) meet twice monthly. Additionally, one team reported meeting every two months, one team meets quarterly, and one hospital team meets three times weekly. There were also three respondents who stated they meet when needed. The range here varies from three times weekly to four times yearly. The most frequent answer, however, is monthly for nearly half the teams responding.

Realistic expectations of work to be accomplished at these meetings must be established for the team. A minimum of 30 minutes is usually needed to present and discuss a case. For new teams, 45-60 minutes may be needed for each case review. Respondents to the team questionnaire were asked to report how many cases were presented and/or reviewed at each meeting. Most answers corresponded to the length of the meeting (the longer the meeting, the more cases discussed). The following table gives the numbered responses.

Table 32.6
Number of Cases Presented/Reviewed at Team Meetings

Number of Cases	Responses
1 - 5	30
6 - 10	18
11 - 15	9
16 - 20	4
21 - 30	4
31 - 40	1
41 - 50	1
51 - 60	1
Over 61	2
No Answer	17

According to this information, the most frequent pattern of team meetings from this sample involves a 1 1/2- to 2-hour meeting held once a month to review 1 to 5 cases.

The team questionnaire also requested information on team attendance. Seventy-six respondents indicated all members are expected to attend the regular meetings. Nine teams have other attendance patterns. For example, one has a "sub-team" that screens all cases presented and chooses only a limited number for the whole team to review.

CONFIDENTIALITY

Several questions regarding policies and procedures for team functioning were asked on both questionnaires. Respondents to the state questionnaire were asked to report on confidentiality policies and procedures. State laws concerning confidentiality in child abuse and neglect cases may or may not specifically address the issue of multidisciplinary team involvement. Table 32.7 summarizes responses to the question of confidentiality. Twenty-three of the states confirmed that a confidentiality waiver is in effect. The remaining 27 states gave five alternatives employed by various teams:

signed release by clients (11 responses)
confidentiality agreements signed by team members (8 responses)
coding case names/anonymity (6 responses)
teams under state sanction/agents of the state (6 responses)
no policy regarding this matter (3 responses)

Since only 24% of the nation mandates multidisciplinary teams, but 46% of the states provide such confidentiality waivers, it can be hypothesized that most of these waivers are generic in nature.

The survey conducted by the American Public Welfare Association in 1981 indicated that just over half (10) of the 19 teams surveyed operate under legislation which empowers them to handle confidential information.[14]

ORIENTATION/TRAINING

The authors of this chapter found, through experience in multidisciplinary team development, that it is important that all involved understand the functions and responsibilities of both team members and referring workers. Clarification and definition of terms and procedures are also important. Team members must understand the importance of openness, trust, and mutual respect for colleagues for the team to operate effectively. One approach to accomplishing this is the provision of initial orientation and/or ongoing training for teams.

Through the team questionnaire it was found that not all teams have a formal orientation process. Twenty-nine teams responded that members receive a formal orientation while the majority, 54 respondents, stated it was not available. Of the 20 that offer an orientation program, 26 are either responsible for the process themselves or their sponsoring agency is responsible. Thirteen of the teams state they have an orientation program at initial team development; eleven indicate they have a program for the entire team when a new member joins; eight hold orientation for the new members only; and seven indicate they have some orientation process at regular intervals. Methods used in orientation included informal sharing of information by team (23); formal presentation (15); recommended readings (15); simulated conferences (9); and audiovisual resources (8).

Eleven respondents to the state questionnaire indicated that formal orientation is provided at state level. Most of the states that reported some involvement related that it was on an informal basis. This included the provision of some written materials or state personnel participation with or representation on teams.

TEAM EVALUATION

Evaluation of a multidisciplinary team provides for the measurement of its effects against the goals it set out to accomplish. This contributes to rational decision making concerning team maintenance or

TABLE 32.7 *Confidentiality Policies*

State	Waiver		Comments
	Yes	No	
Alabama		X	Signed release forms and coding case names.
Alaska		X	Signed release forms and coding case names.
Arkansas		X	Team members sign confidentiality agreement.
Arizona		X	Confidentiality statutes cover those contracted by the state.
California	X		
Colorado		X	Teams are sanctioned by statute and have access to pertinent information regarding cases.
Connecticut		X	Release forms.
Delaware		X	Signed release from client.
Florida		X	Team members considered agents of the state.
Georgia		X	Client signed releases.
Hawaii	X		
Idaho	X		
Illinois	X		Some teams have own waiver forms.
Indiana	X		
Iowa	X		
Kansas		X	Signed release forms.
Kentucky		X	Team members sign confidentiality agreement/release forms.
Louisiana		X	Team members become agents via confidentiality law.
Maine	X		
Maryland	X		
Massachusetts	X		Members considered employees of state.
Michigan	X		
Minnesota	X		
Mississippi		X	Team members are professionals providing services to child and/or family.
Missouri	X		
Montana	X		
Nebraska		X	Signed release.
Nevada		X	Team members sign a confidentiality agreement.
New Hampshire	X		

TABLE 32.7 *Confidentiality Policies (continued)*

State	Waiver		Comments
	Yes	No	
New Jersey	X		
New Mexico		X	
New York		X	Coded case names.
North Carolina		X	
North Dakota	X		
Ohio		X	Some use coded names; others release form signed by client.
Oklahoma		X	
Oregon		X	State personnel can share information between agencies.
Pennsylvania		X	Sign confidentiality form/cases presented anonymously.
Rhode Island		X	Federal regulations do not require specific waiver.
South Carolina	X		
South Dakota	X		
Tennessee	X		
Texas	X		
Utah		X	No specific policy regarding issue.
Vermont	X		Some also used release forms.
Virginia	X		Also teams encouraged to sign confidentiality agreement.
Washington		X	Agreement from team members.
West Virginia		X	Signed agreement by team members/cases presented anonymously.
Wisconsin		X	Release forms; DHSS has introduced legislation which would give permission for information sharing among team members.
Wyoming	X		

adaptations. Both formal and informal approaches to evaluation can provide valuable data.

Respondents to the team questionnaire indicated that thirty-two teams (35%) indicated they do have some form of evaluation. They stated that the team is most often responsible for this process (22 responses). Other answers regarding responsibility for the evaluation were team sponsor (10), state (5), and other (6).

In describing the various types of evaluations the most common answer was informal, ongoing evaluation (12 responses). Ten teams reported annual evaluations, some of which were verbal, some written. Only five reported having formal evaluations performed and these were by the teams' sponsors.

The team questionnaire also addressed the issue of team longevity. Responses ranged from six months to 15 years. Table 32.8 shows the distribution of teams by years of operation. As would be expected, the oldest reported team in this survey is a hospital-based team in a state children's hospital.

Table 32.8
Team Longevity

Less than 1 year	2
1 year	10
2 years	12
3 years	10
4 years	12
5 years	12
6 - 10 years	23
11 - 15 years	2
No answer	8

The average length of team existence was 4.3 years.

Summary

The results of these surveys have provided some basic descriptive data on currently functioning multidisciplinary teams for child abuse and neglect. Findings indicate that teams exist in all fifty states with the majority providing case consultation. Team composition varies widely, but usually consists of social workers, mental health professionals, physicians, nurses, lawyers, educators, and law enforcement officers. The most frequent pattern of team meetings involves a 1 1/2 to 2 hour meeting held once a month to review one to five cases. Team sponsorship is most often provided by public agencies. Over one-half the states provide some form of protection for teams regarding confidentially issues.

While this information appears to be the most comprehensive data on multidisciplinary teams available to date, there are many areas that warrant further study. Particularly, it would seem, more evaluative efforts need to be undertaken, including: analysis of types of cases referred to teams; comparisons of these to general caseloads of child protective services; outcomes of cases reviewed by teams as compared to similar cases not referred; whether or not the referring workers learn from team consultation and generalize the problem-solving approaches and recommendations to other cases, and whether or not team efforts strengthen community involvement in addressing the problem of child abuse and neglect.

The experience of these authors in developing and utilizing multidisciplinary teams demonstrated the value and effectiveness of such teams. It is highly recommended that efforts be continued to develop, maintain, and utilize multidisciplinary teams as an adjunct to the service system for child abuse and neglect. Development and utilization of multidisciplinary team approaches can also be adapted for use in other service settings or with other target populations. For example, consultation, treatment, or resource development teams could be creatively modified for use in the area of foster care, institutional child care, or adult protective services.

Note

* This study was supported in part by a contract from the Kentucky Cabinet for Human Resources with the Kent School of Social Work, University of Louisville, Louisville, Kentucky.

References

1. Brill, N.I. *Teamwork: Working Together in the Human Services.* Philadelphia: J.B. Lippincott Company, 1976.

2   *Child Abuse and Neglect: The Community Team, An Approach to Case Management and Prevention*, Vol. 3. DHEW publication No. (OHD) 75-30075. Washington, D.C.: Government Printing Office, 1975.

3.   Schmitt, B.D. *The Child Protection Team Handbook: A Multidisciplinary Approach to Managing Child Abuse and Neglect*. New York: Garland STPM Press, 1978.

4.   Pettiford, E.K. *Improving Child Protective Services through the Use of Multidisciplinary Teams*. National Professional Resource Center on Child Abuse and Neglect, American Public Welfare Association and National Association of Social Workers, pp. 2-3, June 1981.

5.   Chamberlain, W.A. *Multidisciplinary Child Abuse and Neglect Team Manual*. Athens, Ga.: Regional Institute of Social Welfare Research, Inc., November, 1978.

6.   Pettiford, E.K. *Improving Child Protective Services*, p. 4.

7.   Pettiford, E.K. *Improving Child Protective Services*, p. 5.

8.   Selinske, J. *A Survey of the Use and Functioning of Multidisciplinary Teams in Child Protective Services*. Washington, D.C.: National Professional Resource Center on Child Abuse and Neglect, American Public Welfare Association, 1981.

9.   Pettiford, E.K. *Improving Child Protective Services*, p. 3.

10.   Selinske, J. *A Survey of the Use and Functioning of Multidisciplinary Teams*, pp. 5-6.

11.   Pettiford, E.K. *Improving Child Protective Services*, p. 5.

12.   Selinske, J. *A Survey of the Use and Functioning of Multidisciplinary Teams*, p. 7.

13.   Selinske, J. *A Survey of the Use and Functioning of Multidisciplinary Teams*, pp. 7-8.

14.   Selinske, J. *A Survey of the Use and Functioning of Multidisciplinary Teams*, p. 10.

PART VII

Trends, Expansion, and Funding

Section Editor: Richard D. Krugman

33. The Influence of Child Protection Teams on the Development of Community Resources

J.M. Whitworth, Michael W. Lanier,
and Carol C. Haase

Introduction

As awareness of child abuse has increased around the country and more individuals have been sensitized to the needs of children, the number of groups identified as multidisciplinary child protection teams has undergone a parallel increase. These teams have emerged in many forms ranging from (1) volunteer professionals who review cases with little or no client contact, (2) more formalized groups of professionals that provide consultative services, to (3) full-time, direct-service provider teams.[1] The influence of child protection teams has been impressive in the development of other community resources which, in turn, have a profound effect on improving needed services for abused children. Why is it that some teams have far greater positive impact on their community than others? This chapter will discuss some of the reasons.

Development of Teams

In a community, a multidisciplinary child protection team usually develops in one of three basic forms. Originally, teams were developed by members of the community who wanted to improve basic services to abused and neglected children. They formed committees and selected individuals to form volunteer groups to assist the community and existing agencies to improve services to children. They also reviewed cases, but had little or no direct contact with the family. An additional purpose was served by increasing community awareness of abused children.

Second, an agency within the community may receive seed money or a grant to support the organization of a group of professionals into a team. This type of group typically takes its focus from whatever agency received the grant and is therefore more dependent on the agency that has the funding. This type of team usually meets weekly or bi-weekly to review cases and make treatment recommendations, with input from professionals of several disciplines, some of whom may have evaluated the family directly.[2]

Third, in the last ten years, many multidisciplinary child protection teams have been fully funded through federal, state, and local dollars to serve as an adjunct to child protective service agencies and provide many direct services to abused and neglected children. These services typically include medical diagnosis and evaluation, psychological evaluation, case coordination, multidisciplinary team staffings, and short-term treatment.[3] Any of these types of teams can have tremendous influence on community development depending on a variety of factors.

PERSONALITIES (THE HIDDEN VARIABLE)

When a team is newly established, the community's initial response will depend on the way the team was formed, the amount of original community support in the formation of the team, and the personalities within the team itself. If a team director (usually medically oriented) appears as a "superman to clean up the town and rescue the poor abused children," the team can surely expect negative backlash, resentment, and a defensive posture from the agencies already in the community. Individuals who are cooperative and nurturing and who seek creative solutions to gaps and problems within the community will no doubt fare better than those teams that are out to expose vulnerabilities of the system. Team members who tend to emphasize the deficits within agencies will find that they confront, and indeed create, a defensive and guarded community posture.

GREAT EXPECTATIONS

Newly formed teams often become disappointed in their ability to correct deficiencies in the community as quickly as they would like. Realistic goal setting in the first few years of a team's development is critical to prevent the team, and the community, from becoming disillusioned. Slow and deliberate planning and execution of plans are hallmarks of a growing team. Unrealistic expectations of other agencies lead to a sense of failure and interfere with team growth.

PSYCHOLOGICAL POSITION OF THE TEAM WITHIN THE COMMUNITY

How the team is perceived by the community will enhance or retard the team's influence and ability in developing community resources. Just as individuals have a self-image, so does a team. Many working in this field have experienced the feeling of being "God's gift to child abuse." The illusion is shattered when it is discovered that such people are perceived by us as a pain in the neck. A multidisciplinary team must present an image of supportive professionalism at all times if it is to maintain credibility in the community. If credibility is lost, a team is severely handicapped in the development of other services for children. There will be a cautious stance taken by other community members and agencies, and there will be a hesitancy to affiliate with a team that has a questionable or ill-defined image. The team must become part of the community rather than a watchdog over it to be truly effective.

Community Assessment

WHAT IS NEEDED

After a team has been established, it has time to develop a sense of its own position within the community. An awareness of obvious gaps and needs will be identified quickly as the team attempts to develop realistic treatment plans for abusive families. This process can be referred to as "needs assessment under fire" and is the first step in developing further community resources. Before team members begin plans for development, a careful assessment of the community's history is also critical when considering new services.

Knowledge of the evolution of existing agencies and community support groups will keep a multidisciplinary team from attempting to re-invent the wheel or working to gain support from individuals or groups not interested in or even antagonistic to the project.

Agencies are a product of the people within them. For example, a prosecuting attorney's office can be uncooperative one year and highly supportive the next simply because the staff has changed following an election or a new appointment. If a team experiences difficulties with an agency, the director should quickly identify the individuals who are in conflict, not immediately assume the agency is the problem. This same type of personal orientation is helpful in terms of cross-support and networking. Therefore, in conversation one should never refer to the "mental health center." Rather, one should refer to "Jane Smith at the mental health center." Basically, the mental health center does not exist if Jane Smith and her other staff members are not there. Therefore, a personal orientation is critical in identifying support within the community to develop new resources for abused children.

WHAT/WHO DO WE NURTURE FOR THE FUTURE?

A multidisciplinary team should make conscious efforts to determine not only who the support figures are in the community, but what services are worthy of team support. For example, it is our experience that there is far more community support for a treatment program for sexually abused children than there is for a treatment program for sexual offenders. While both are essential services, the team can find itself running into many difficulties if they have not identified what will or will not be accepted by the community. Showcasing the acceptable and minimizing the less acceptable, has served us well in developing a variety of programs.

Community development is evolutionary in nature. One program will beget another. Historically, child protection teams have nurtured the development of prevention programs, medical foster care, and incest treatment programs in communities.

THE FOUR REALMS OF RESOURCES

The four realms of resources that are available in a community consist of: power, expertise, funding, and service. These terms are self-explanatory and represent areas that a team can tap for assistance in developing resources in the community. It is rare that the head of an insurance company or bank will have expertise in child sexual abuse or that the mayor of the city is a former child protective services worker. On a board or task force, all four areas must be represented in order to catalyze the establishment of new community resources.

Community Directions

The multidisciplinary team should be looked upon as the vanguard of expertise and professionalism in the realm of child abuse and neglect. By anticipating the next client need, the team can make better use of resources and energy. In our community, as all over the United States, child protective services and the child protection team experienced a great increase in sexual abuse cases in the early 1980s. As a result, law enforcement was inundated with cases. The prosecuting attorney and juvenile and criminal court systems had a similar and parallel experience. Every challenge should be anticipated at every point in the continuum of service. There may be no worse disservice to a client than to offer a service that does not lead to resolution or improvement in status. The need for networking is absolute.

THE REVOLUTION/EVOLUTION TRAP

Another way to see the importance of the continuum is to recognize that with any action, there is a reaction. For instance, there is a tremendous amount of information concerning child sexual abuse and the dynamics that exist within the sexually abusive family. In turn, this has created increased numbers of reports of child sexual abuse that most agencies have not been able to handle effectively. In communities where agencies have been able to catch up and successfully deal with the onslaught of child sexual abuse cases, we are now seeing a similar success by the long-term mental health treaters of children and families. More cases are successfully being brought to the attention of child protective services and child protection teams in the community. As knowledge has expanded, more cases have successfully gone through juvenile and criminal courts. Therefore, more cases are now finding their way into the therapist's office for court ordered or voluntary treatment. Thus, we have a cycle of action/reaction that continues to expand. One must always look at sequellae and anticipate how any new community service or information will impact on other existing services or even create new needs.

THE CRISIS

There is a place for reactive positioning with a team, in that many solutions occur during a crisis situation. The Chinese symbol for crisis has two characters: the first character represents danger; the second represents opportunity. With this philosophical perspective in mind, a team can capitalize on a crisis or a dangerous situation. When the news media reveal the terrible state of emergency shelter care for sexual abuse victims, the team can go to the media and tell the public about the plight of child abuse victims. An appeal to the community to help with the problem is seen as a cooperative effort and honesty rather than a defensive posture or cover-up. With this approach, any sensationalistic leak of negative information can be turned around by the agency to mobilize the community to develop solutions.

Practical Examples of Community Resources
(The Cookbook of Cases)

The following are some practical observations of program development in a state-funded direct-service oriented child protection team in Florida. This team began as a pilot project in 1978 in the State of Florida and has become integral in the development of community resources for abused children and their families.

PHYSICAL ABUSE/MEDICAL FOSTER CARE

This program is an example of reactive development of a community resource rather than proactive development. After a year of existence, the child protection team had two particularly haunting cases. Both children were essentially growing up in the hospital because of their abuse-related medical difficulties. One child had extensive burns and the other had an esophageal constriction secondary to swallowing lye. The parents of both children were marginally competent and although able to care for a healthy child, lacked the skills and ability to care for a child with these medical problems. Foster care had no placement facility for these children, and as a result, they remained in the hospital. Their attending physicians agreed that these two children did not need hospital care.

Medical foster care developed from this need and is a program that recruits and trains nurses or other individuals with medical expertise to become foster parents.[4] Each home cares for one child and works along with the team psychologist. The goal is to return this child to the home once the injuries are resolved and the parents demonstrate readiness. This program was relatively easy to fund since medical foster care costs approximately $600 per month as compared to hospital care, which costs approximately $10,500 per month. Although this specialized type of program served relatively few children, children received better care, families were reunited, and the saving to the state in terms of dollars was tremendous.

SEXUAL ABUSE

In 1978, this child protection team reviewed 26 cases of sexual abuse and over 500 referrals for physical abuse and neglect. The following year, over 280 cases of sexual abuse were referred to the same team. This increase in reported sexual abuse cases to the team was the result of heightened community awareness of the problem, and also a perception by the community that the team possessed skills to deal with these difficult cases. The team was overwhelmed by this ten-fold increase in referrals. As team members and other professionals in the community learned how to deal better with these children, cases were also successfully brought to the court. After adjudication, it was found that psychological treatment resources were scarce. Therapists in the community had not been trained in dealing with the complex set of dynamics that sexually abused children and their families present. This gap in knowledge forced us to find creative solutions.

The reaction to the crisis was to seek out a clinical psychologist who had experience in the prison system with sex offenders. We contracted with him to start a small pilot program to treat incestuous families.[5] Two members of the team with therapy backgrounds joined the psychologist and began a treatment program for sexual abuse victims and their families. The initial program has resulted in a well-established treatment program now in its fourth year of operation, with locations in two counties. Over 270 families have been served to date by highly qualified therapists in the community, all of whom have been trained locally. At present, every treatment agency dealing with children in this community has therapists on staff trained in the treatment of sexual abuse victims.

MEDICAL DIAGNOSIS AND EVALUATION

As the referral rate of child sexual abuse cases increased, the problem of obtaining competent medical examinations of these children became apparent. In the past, when individuals were sexually assaulted in our community, they were examined at the city morgue by the medical examiner. Later, the venue was changed to the county hospital emergency room, which was still less than ideal for these examinations. Subsequently, examinations were done in a treatment room on the psychiatric floor of the hospital, which was *still* inappropriate. Finally, with the cooperation of the OB/GYN department, the child protection team, the medical examiner's office, and the sheriff's office, a separate facility was established for the examination of adults and children who were victims of sexual assault. Child protection team staff assisted medical personnel in interviewing and evaluating these children in a cooperative effort.

POLICE/SEX CRIMES

While the number of sexual abuse cases was continuing to climb, law enforcement responded in similar evolutionary fashion. Originally all sexual assaults on children or adults were handled by the homicide division. These individuals were experts at handling murder cases, but usually untrained in dealing with sexual abuse. Law enforcement was targeted as a group to train in the dynamics of child sexual abuse, as well as the handling of adult rape victims. As a result of that training and a heightened awareness by law enforcement, a sex crimes unit was established within the sheriff's office. This is a small group of individuals who have been highly trained and work cooperatively with other social service and protective service agencies dealing with child victims.

THE PROSECUTING ATTORNEY'S OFFICE

The prosecuting attorney's office experienced the same quick evolution over a period of about four years. At one time, cases with charges associated with physical or sexual abuse were randomly assigned for trial to each of the assistant prosecuting attorneys. Child protection team staff suggested joint management on several of these cases, and the prosecuting attorney's office became aware that a specialized division was needed for these complex cases. As a result, the family justice division was formed and became a critical element in deferred prosecutions, probation agreements, or jail sentences for sexual abuse offenders. The prosecuting attorney's office has been a model of cooperation with the sexual abuse treatment program. The family violence division later created another division and assigned a special prosecutor for all child sexual abuse cases. This special prosecutor meets with the team on a weekly basis to discuss cases that have been reported the previous week.

THE JUDICIAL SYSTEM

A child protection team can have a tremendous influence on the judges in its community. This is a delicate scale to balance, however. Judges must maintain a certain distance to make fair and impartial decisions in abuse cases. However, the judicial branch can avail itself of education and training to understand the dynamics of child abuse and how the law can most successfully impact on abusive families. At times there are beneficial spinoffs from a cooperative interaction with the judicial branch. If the judicial and law enforcement branches hold a team in high esteem, it makes case management work go that much easier. Their support is critical.

ATTENDING TO DETAIL

Special recognition of members of the community who have been particularly helpful goes a long way in cementing bonds of cooperation and good fellowship. Activities such as an honorary breakfast or dinner, a special plaque, or simply a note of appreciation can be of tremendous benefit in establishing a bond with fellow professionals in the community. Some may compare it to a courtship, but a better term for this special appreciation would be a "nurturance" of individuals who are trying to do the same difficult job as the team.

Cautions: Gaps and Traps

HOLIER THAN THOU (PROBABLY SMARTER, TOO)

The omnipotence factor can be a deadly trap for an individual; however, it is encountered with great regularity, especially with the development of new programs in a community. Child protection teams are a collection of talented, experienced individuals. It is important that these individuals be developed as professional helpers rather than all-knowing, all-seeing experts on abuse. A newly formed multidisciplinary team will sometimes run into skepticism from established agencies. The veteran child protective service worker who is suddenly confronted with a child protection team may feel threatened. Resentment can build in such a situation. However, if team personnel take the stance of professional helpers such resentment can be kept within limits.

EGO NEEDS OF THE CHILD PROTECTION TEAM (INDIVIDUAL AND COLLECTIVE)

The ego needs of the child protection team and its individual members have been interesting to witness as teams develop. Many child protective service workers have complained that some child protection teams do little actual work on a case and seem to receive all the glory and attention. Multidisciplinary child protection teams appear at times to have a great need for recognition and deference. One way to avoid falling into this trap is to take a proactive stance in the support of the child protective service workers in the community. Being supportive of pay increases and good pre-service and in-service training will go a long way toward maintaining the cooperation of a child protective service worker. Teams that are case review or consultation teams only and do not provide direct services should be especially humble and realistic when making treatment recommendations. Nothing alienates a direct-service provider quicker than to be handed a list of glittering treatment recommendations that are totally unrealistic.

MY EYES HAVE SEEN THE GLORY (I WAS LOOKING IN A MIRROR)

Some individuals in a multidisciplinary child protection team may develop the "I am the only one who can do it right" syndrome. This syndrome is clearly identified and may cross all disciplines on any given team--"I am the only one who can do the proper medical exam"; "I am the only one who can interview these young sexually abused children properly and get a good story"; "If those people out there get this case, they will screw it up. I am keeping it"; "If only we could get a decent attorney in the juvenile system besides me, everything would be great." The above statements may be foreign to you, but likely they are familiar and have been heard at one time or another from someone in the community. It is a deadly trap into which individuals can fall. They begin to hoard knowledge rather than distribute and share it. This is similar to the Prometheus legend in Greek mythology where the gods jealously guarded their secret of fire. When Prometheus gave it to man, the gods chained him to a rock. No one is omnipotent, no one is the only one who can do it right, everyone has an obligation and a duty to share the knowledge gained from experience and training with others. Often it is difficult for a professional to let go of a special niche. It is nice to be the only pediatric expert on child abuse in a community and it is also nice to be the only therapist who can deal with pre-adolescent sexual abuse victims. However, the sheer number of cases mandate that individuals with special expertise share knowledge with others, even though they will make mistakes along the way. It is critical to provide support and encouragement for other individuals and programs to help them successfully deal with these complex cases.

POWER BALANCES

Of all the problems a family can experience, child abuse is probably the one arena that brings in so many diverse individuals and agencies attempting to protect the child and family. The orchestration of the various individuals within these agencies is critical and requires a subtle appreciation of the delicate balances of power that exist. If any one agency attempts to maintain control or power over others, the entire system can break down. If an agency persists in attempting to monopolize control, often the rest of the system simply goes around them.

Engagement

THE DORMANT INTEREST IN CHILD ABUSE

After several years treating abused and neglected children, the authors have observed one common factor—the dormant interest everyone seems to have in child abuse. Be it doctor, lawyer, or citizen, everyone seems to have a spark of interest, and if approached in the correct manner, will respond. Essentially, this is a four-step process that begins with gaining the interest of an individual. Once the individual's or agency's attention is focused, it is possible to educate them not only in the dynamics of abuse and neglect, but also about efforts in their community to better the lives of children.

One important factor that comes into play is safety. Individuals need to feel safe when approached. They need enough information so they can feel comfortable with the topic with which they are dealing. Directors of agencies tend to shy away from the treatment of sexual abuse as an uncomfortable and complicated realm that will require their therapist to attend numerous court hearings and get entangled in endless law suits. Individuals in law enforcement, when not familiar with the dynamics of abuse and neglect, tend to dismiss it as something for which people should be jailed and feel that it is the best and only cure for abuse. Then there is the physician who is hesitant to report because he will lose the family from his practice. He fears he will suffer legal hassles, with lawyers and social workers dragging him into court. All of these are legitimate concerns of professionals. However, with the right approach and proper information, they can be brought to a more informed view of abuse and neglect, for example, treatment efforts that are being successfully utilized.

THE STRUGGLE CONTINUES: CONFLICT IN TEAM COMMUNITY RESOURCE DEVELOPMENT

Any time highly educated, well-trained, experienced individuals from several disciplines come together, there will be a natural clash of emphases, priorities, ideas, and ideals that will affect the team direction. A nurse or a physician on the team will need more medical clinics, the psychologist will push for more treatment of the emotional scars of abuse, the case worker will emphasize basic community resources such as shelter and transportation for these individuals. Social workers have accurately argued that the biggest barrier to psychological care is that the client cannot reach the therapist's office because of lack of transportation and no agency to provide it. These complex dynamics must be dealt with within a team. One of the best administrative directions for this is the same approach we take with abusive families: to assess the dynamics, respect the current belief systems and experiences of these individuals, and come up with common goals and a collective direction that will ultimately provide a better network of services for children.

This same conflict is created on a broader scale within the community. Everyone is looking for funding and support for similarly worthwhile children's projects in the community. However, it is a convincing and supportable argument that if a young child is brought up in a nurturing and caring environment from the beginning, many other programs will be less necessary.

Summary

These issues are not easy to resolve. Often it is difficult to know the best direction and priority to follow. The realm of child abuse and neglect in some ways remains in infancy. Research into this area on an empirical basis is still far from conclusive. There are likely as many demonstration projects in the country as there are multidisciplinary child protection teams, each one having a different emphasis and focus. It is not likely that any one particular system or approach will prove superior over another. There are many roads to Rome. Indeed, it is the individuals within that agency and the connection between them and the community, and between them and their clients that ultimately make the difference. The influence of child protection teams on the development of community resources can be profound and widespread. It is likely that the critical variable is the personalities within each team, and their own personal commitment to better the world for abused children and their families.

References

1. Schmitt, B.D. *The Child Protection Team Handbook*, pp. 29-36. New York: Garland STPM Press, 1978.

2. Helfer, R.E., and R. Schmidt. "The Community-Based Child Abuse and Neglect Program." *Child Abuse and Neglect: The Family and the Community*. R.E. Helfer and C.H. Kempe (Eds.), pp. 229-266. Cambridge, Mass.: Ballinger, 1976.

3. Whitworth, J., M. Lanier, R. Skinner, and N. Lund. "A Multidisciplinary, Hospital-Based Team for Child Abuse Cases: A Hands-On Approach." *Child Welfare*, 60(4)(April 1981):233-244.

4. Davis, A., P. Foster, and J. Whitworth. "Medical Foster Care: A Cost Effective Solution to a Community Problem." *Child Welfare*, 63(4)(July-August 1984):341-350.

5. Giarretto, H. "A Comprehensive Child Sexual Abuse Treatment Program." *Child Abuse & Neglect*, 6(1982):263-278.

34. Family Outreach

Paula Rosenstein

Introduction

Family Outreach is a program that seeks to prevent child abuse and neglect by offering one-to-one counseling services and parenting classes to parents experiencing child related problems. Information and referral services are also offered as well as speakers and media presentations for community groups. Family Outreach has existed since 1973 when the first center opened in Richardson, Texas, as a joint effort of the Texas Department of Human Resources (now the Texas Department of Human Services) and the National Council of Jewish Women, Inc. There were few community efforts toward prevention of abuse and neglect and none that made an extensive and effective use of trained volunteers, thus Family Outreach began as a truly innovative program.

By 1986 this program model had been replicated 24 times in two states. At each location the local branch of the state agency responsible for the investigation of referrals of abuse and neglect joined with a local volunteer organization to sponsor the program (e.g., in Lubbock, Texas, the volunteer group is the Junior League; in Abilene, Texas, it is the Seroptimists). Eventually, the volunteers formed a separate corporation to sponsor the center. Each Family Outreach center offers service to families including: (1) taking telephone calls from families needing information or crisis counseling; (2) regular home visits to families at risk of abuse or neglect; (3) classes for parents and children to enhance parenting and communication skills; and (4) speaking engagements for the general public on abuse and neglect. All services, including home visits, are provide by trained volunteers under the supervision of a professional caseworker from the responsible state agency. Funds to pay the salary of the casework supervisor are provided by the state agency. Since services are provided by volunteers, large numbers of families can get help at relatively little expense to either the state agency or the corporation. In 1985 the 19 (4 less than 1 year old) reporting centers handled more than 10,000 callers and the volunteers donated more than 83,000 hours of service. There were approximately 31 volunteers at each center.

Program Goals, Objectives

To accomplish the broad goal of prevention, four objectives were adopted: (1) to inform the public about child abuse and neglect and create an awareness of community responsibility; (2) to create a corps of paraprofessionals trained to establish one-to-one relationships with families identified as potentially abusive or neglectful; (3) to offer parent education classes to a variety of parent groups; and (4) to assist the state agency with foster/adoptive home recruitment. The public education program is conducted both in the media and by offering speakers to community groups on a variety of subjects related to parenting and child abuse or neglect. Presentations are done to recruit volunteers to the program, to encourage the reporting of abuse or neglect incidents by the public, and to generate funds for the Family Outreach programs. These presentations also encourage families needing assistance to call for help for themselves. Forty-seven percent of the families at risk served each year self-identify.

Each center presents parenting classes with objectives that meet specific needs in that community. The classes are generally open to both the current client population and other parents. Thus, the classes not only generate clients for the program, but further the team approach by getting assistance to current clients from additional paraprofessionals.

Project Responsibilities

Project responsibilities are designated by the sponsoring groups in a statement of purpose and agreement and in the bylaws. The state-mandated agency provides a full-time caseworker whose duties are to investigate those cases referred to the Family Outreach program, assign cases to the volunteers, supervise the training of the volunteers, and supervise the casework of the volunteers. In some cases, additional agency staff time is provided for supervision of the caseworker, for assistance with volunteer training and to serve on the board of directors.

One of the aspects of this program that makes it unique is the degree of responsibility accepted by the volunteer corporation. In most private agencies, paid staff are responsible for the recruitment of volunteers and the administration of the programs. In Family Outreach the volunteers agree to do the recruiting and the maintenance of volunteer staff. They also provide volunteers to conduct the parenting class programs, administer the public awareness campaigns, maintain the office and accomplish the fund raising. The volunteers elect a project chairperson or president who then appoints chairpersons to see to each of these tasks. Fund raising for all monies other than the salary of the professional caseworker is done by the volunteer corporation. Sources of funds may include the following: (1) donations from individuals and businesses; (2) in-kind services such as allocation of shared office space; (3) grants from private and governmental sources including the United Way; (4) product sales or fees to fund raising events; and (5) membership fees.

A board of directors of volunteers and state agency representatives is designated as a review and policy-making body. This board meets frequently to assess program objectives, procedures and progress.

In 1981 the Family Outreach volunteer corporations formed an umbrella organization called Family Outreach of America, Inc. This group wrote guidelines for the establishment of Family Outreach centers. A service mark has been secured by Family Outreach of America to the name Family Outreach giving Family Outreach of America, Inc., the exclusive right to license the name to groups wishing to replicate the model. A complete set of requirements can be obtained from Family Outreach of America. Provisions in these requirements include the following: (1) that Family Outreach of America reserves the right to monitor centers with regard to continuing use of the name Family Outreach; (2) that the center must have as its purpose the prevention of child abuse and neglect; (3) that it must provide casework services to families by volunteers who have primary responsibility for delivery of services to the family; (4) that the casework be supervised by an employee of the state agency mandated by law to investigate referrals of abuse and neglect; (5) that there be a core group of volunteers responsible for administrative functions, and (6) that the board of directors have a majority of its votes from volunteers.

Role of the Paraprofessional

The paraprofessional caseworker fills the temporary role of nurturer to the family. She first allows the parent to become dependent upon her for the kind of nurturing support generally provided in a healthy family by the other adult family members. To be nurturing is to provide a "safe place" for someone to talk about feelings and fears. By creating a non-judgmental atmosphere, the paraprofessional can teach the parents how to trust and be trusted. It is also in this role that the paraprofessional will begin to help the client change her self image from negative to positive. The success of this approach will depend to a large degree upon the willingness of the paraprofessional to set limits and expectations for the parent that he or she can reach, to assist in the accomplishment of these goals, and then to reward these accomplishments.

Secondly, the paraprofessional serves as a family advocate in the community. She assists the clients in identifying their needs; guides them in the exploration of realistic alternatives, and then, in a very concrete and direct way, leads them to the community resources or programs that best meet these needs. Often this may include advocating with the agency on behalf of the family and interpreting agency policy and instructions to the clients. The paraprofessional becomes coordinator of a treatment team on behalf of the client family.

Her third role is that of teacher. She will slowly and specifically teach parents, through repetition and modeling, and by example, new ways to care for and discipline the children. She must be careful to be patient and reward any positive efforts toward change. In addition to specific parenting skills, there are two things that the paraprofessional will be teaching over and over again: (1) the difference between feelings and behaviors, especially with regard to anger; and (2) a problem-solving method.

The fourth role of the paraprofessional is to provide relief of isolation. Polansky speaks of treating loneliness as the most important aspect in making progress with neglectful families.[1] The paraprofessional is particularly suited to this role. As a volunteer, her very presence in the family projects a message of caring. Treating loneliness takes time and time is what the paraprofessional has to offer. Dr. Polansky's studies show that consistent, short visits over an extended period of time are necessary. The volunteer, because of a limited, small caseload can fill this need.

Training

The training programs for the paraprofessionals have been designed to teach the following skills: (1) listening and responding; (2) identification of family needs; (3) parenting techniques; and (4) casework skills, including goal setting and case recording. The initial phase of training varies in length from center to center but generally includes (a) an orientation to the program; (b) skill-building sessions; (c) at least one supervised session on the telephone; and (d) a private interview with the casework supervisor. Some of the topics covered in the 18-40 hours of skill-building sessions are: characteristics of abusive and neglectful families; family dynamics; child development; telephone intake procedures; telephone counseling techniques; and how cultural differences affect families. Volunteers are introduced to the philosophy of the program, are given information about the sponsoring organizations, and explore their own feelings about abuse and neglect.

The ongoing phase consists of a three-hour training session each month during which the volunteers get an opportunity to practice skills learned during the initial phase, listen to guest speakers from other agencies or role-play client situations. Care is taken to see that client confidentiality is maintained at all times. Volunteer candidates must complete the initial phase of training to qualify for active status. Two categories of active status are available: family consultant volunteers do casework and community consultant volunteers limit their client contact to telephone intake and telephone crisis counseling.

It is important that potential volunteers come to the program with life skills that prepare them to deal with the feelings that are triggered in potentially abusive or neglectful situations. The person who believes in the ability of others to change and who understands the need for, and who can utilize, emotional support systems is likely to be "naturally therapeutic." Efforts are made to recruit volunteers who are receptive to new ideas, who have respect for the feelings of others, and who are mature. It is also helpful if the potential volunteer has the following qualities:

-awareness of his/her limitations
-acceptance of value systems differing from his/her own
-acceptance that no one will change completely to the volunteer's liking
-realization that he/she is not responsible for the actions or decisions of others
-stability during upsetting situations
-a sense of humor

-dependability
-honesty about his/her feelings
-confidentiality

The experienced volunteers and the casework professional will be watching for these characteristics during the training of the new volunteers.

The casework professional is responsible for the design and implementation of both the initial and ongoing phases of the training. She will teach many of these sessions, but will be assisted by professional counselors in the community who volunteer their time to teach sessions in their areas of expertise. The state agency provides specialists to assist in the training, and experienced volunteers also participate in some sessions. These volunteers are especially helpful during discussions of volunteer expectations and in role playing. Several centers have had client panels as part of training during which former clients are invited to tell the new volunteers about their involvement with Family Outreach. Handled carefully, this can be a powerful learning experience for both the client and the new volunteers.

Many centers ask the volunteers to sign a one-year commitment to work a specified minimum number of hours per month. The Corpus Christi, Texas, center, for example, has a 12-hour per month minimum requirement, including two hours per month spent in ongoing training. Family consultant volunteers are asked to fill the remaining time with one telephone shift and their casework. Community consultant volunteers are asked to do two telephone shifts and are encouraged to fill the remaining time with committee work.

Publicity and Public Education

As mentioned, the publicity and public education programs have been designed to serve more than one purpose. The volunteers who have been trained as speakers use a variety of audio visual aids and program outlines to present programs on abuse and neglect, on specific aspects of parenting and on the services of the Family Outreach center.

Many of the centers offer parenting classes that are pre-scripted and sold in kits. Several of the most often taught courses are: Systematic Training for Effective Parenting (STEP); STEP TEEN for parents of teenagers; How To Talk So Kids Will Listen and Listen So Kids Will Talk; and We Help Ourselves (WHO). Several centers have also sponsored Parents Anonymous groups. At other centers volunteers have developed their own parenting programs. Several examples of these are Safety Through Assertive Response (STAR); Mothers Offer Mutual Support (MOMS); several Teenage Moms Support Groups; New Directions for Divorcing Families (NDDF). In addition, centers have begun Car Seat Loaner Programs. Descriptions of the various programs offered at all participating centers can be obtained from Family Outreach of America, Inc.

Other volunteers specialize in conducting media campaigns for volunteer or client recruitment. Special brochures have been designed on Outreach programs. Articles for newspapers, public service announcements and interviews on TV "talk shows" have all been used to publicize the Family Outreach programs. Team building and publicity for the program are accomplished by having volunteers represent Family Outreach on community and state coalitions. This networking process also facilitates access by Family Outreach clients to the programs of other agencies. The credibility of the total program is enhanced by these efforts.

Client Population

Early intervention is the key to successful secondary prevention. The Family Outreach client population has been defined to maximize the possibility of identifying families before any debilitating injuries have been incurred. The goal of direct services is the same as that referred to by Gray and Kaplan when they said, "We hope this early intervention can modify the parents' child-rearing patterns and thus help prevent abnormal parenting practices."[2]

Families are referred to Family Outreach from a variety of sources some of which are: (1) families referring themselves for help; (2) relatives; (3) interested individuals; (4) school or day care facilities; (5) medical or health care agencies; (6) police; and (7) state child protective services units. Self-referrals, at 47 percent, are the most common source of clients. The program was carefully designed to encourage self referrals as it was surmised that the self-referred client population would allow the program access at the earliest intervention point possible and at a time of maximum motivation to change.

As an employee of the state mandated agency, the Family Outreach casework supervisor does the intake investigations on all cases referred directly to the Family Outreach office in the following categories: (1) family conflict; (2) school problems; (3) borderline neglect; (4) financial problems not requiring placement of children; (5) deficient parenting skills; (6) lack of supervision; (7) pre-delinquency; (8) truancy; (9) borderline abuse; and (10) all self-referrals.

All calls reporting abuse, abandonment, exploitation, sexual abuse, severe medical neglect, severe physical neglect, the need for child placement and/or court action, and severe mental illness of parent and/or child are referred to the child protective services unit for investigation. The volunteers have learned as a part of their training course which cases to turn over to child protective services. The child protective workers are advised by an intake agreement which cases they may pass on to Family Outreach. The consistent interchange of cases enhances the team effort.

CASE STUDY I—MRS. M. AND DANNY

Mrs. M. called for help for herself after learning about the program from a neighbor. The volunteer who spoke with her listened carefully, gave crisis counseling and took the information down for the casework supervisor to review. During the investigation the supervisor learned from Mrs. M. that she had had a difficult pregnancy with this child, age three, and that Mrs. M. was concerned that "something is wrong with Danny." Mrs. M. described Danny as ill, uncontrollable and unresponsive. His activities included climbing the kitchen cabinets and playing with knives which he would use to stab at the walls when he was frustrated. Mrs. M. was desperate for help. The caseworker also noted that Danny's language development was delayed to approximately the level of an eighteen-month old. After explaining the relationship of Family Outreach to the mandated agency, the worker offered Mrs. M. the services of a trained volunteer to help her and to visit her regularly.

The next visit was from the volunteer who had accepted the assignment. As Mrs. M. and the volunteer got to know each other during weekly visits they worked out a case plan together, and the volunteer made regular notes on their visits. Both the case plan and the notes were submitted for review by the casework supervisor. Some diagnostic tests were performed to test Danny's intellectual abilities and a medical exam was conducted to check for illnesses. For each exam, the volunteer accompanied Mrs. M. and Danny, helping Mrs. M. understand the results and reinforce the comments of the examiners. Major changes began to occur when Mrs. M. was encouraged to see that her son was a healthy, intelligent child capable of learning and responding to her. The volunteer helped her learn how to work with him on his language development. During these sessions, the volunteer would model the skills with Danny and then help Mrs. M. to do them also. With praise and encouragement Mrs. M. changed her perception of the child and was able to make many changes in the way she treated him. During this time the volunteer was learning of other problems in the family, some having to do with the relationship between Mrs. M. and her husband and others involving the other two children. Mrs. M.'s self image was improving as she was assisted in working out these matters. Her attitude toward herself and her family was changing from feelings of isolation and helplessness to a more positive outlook. In helping this family, the volunteer made use of no less than four community resources including a school system diagnostic center, the medical community and a speech clinic. Services were provided by Family Outreach to this family for seven months. Mrs. M. told the volunteer, "Your being with me has helped me so much. When you first came I wanted Danny to be able to love us. I wanted him to be able to settle down and be with us. I wanted him to stop using knives and stop being wild and I knew something was wrong with him. Now he can be part of our family."

CASE STUDY II—MISS J. AND KAREN

Miss J., a first-time mother at age 30, was referred to Family Outreach by the local children's hospital. Miss J. had returned to the well-baby clinic with Karen concerned about a "cold" she felt the child had. The clinic staff found no evidence of a cold but confirmed that the child had constipation. They also noted that, though Karen was four months old, she was only one pound over her birth weight. The hospital suspected non-organic failure to thrive. However, they noted Miss J.'s concern for Karen and her willingness to follow their instructions. Her response to the infant was good, so the staff suspected inadequate feeding, most likely from ignorance. The case was referred to Family Outreach. The casework supervisor followed the intake procedure and assigned the case to a volunteer. On the first visit the volunteer noted two things were happening that proved to be the major cause of the lack of weight gain. First, though Miss J. had a rocking chair, and was able to hold the baby comfortably, she reported that she most often fed Karen by propping her bottle in her mouth while she was still in bed. Secondly, Miss J. was letting Karen sleep through many night feedings. Karen was a placid baby and seemed to tolerate her mother's sleeping through her feedings but her nutrition was suffering. Miss J. was eager to learn and the necessary changes came quickly. During the second visit, Miss J. told the volunteer, "I did what you said about holding the baby and she is much better. I hope you can come back next week." The volunteer and Miss J. were able to set some goals and Miss J. was very pleased with herself when she saw the baby gaining weight. Meanwhile, the volunteer encouraged Miss J. to come to the Family Outreach group for mothers with infants and pre-schoolers where she could socialize with other mothers and get some time away from the baby. They also made frequent visits back to the hospital well-baby clinic to weigh the baby and check on her general health. The volunteer showed Miss J. how to prepare formula for Karen, instead of using "ready to feed" and as Karen grew, how to select baby foods and feed her with a spoon. At each visit they discussed what Miss J. might expect from Karen as she learned to sit and then crawl and then walk. The volunteer also helped Miss J. enroll in the WIC program. (Miss J. was already on AFDC.) The volunteer also noticed that Karen might need a brace, as she seemed to have one leg turned in too far. This resulted in a referral to an orthopedic hospital clinic and a foot brace for Karen. At the end of six months, Karen had grown to an age-appropriate weight and the case was closed.

Both of these cases illustrate how trained volunteers can be used to serve families who would otherwise go unserved by the "system." They also demonstrate how the volunteer can become the coordinator in a service team for a family to which services, if provided at all, might have been haphazardly and possibly inappropriately assigned. The volunteer has also assisted the family to identify needed resources.

Number of Families Served

Table 34.1 shows the number of families assisted by the 16-19 Family Outreach centers reporting services to Family Outreach of America, Inc. for the years 1982 through 1985.

Studies of Prevention Programs

Several studies have been conducted of demonstration programs which include paraprofessionals. A 1974-1977 study conducted at the University of California at Berkeley by Cohn and Miller of eleven three-year projects concluded among other factors: "It would appear that child abuse and neglect services are maximized if: the program utilizes more high trained, experienced workers as case managers, but stresses the use of lay services and self-help services as part of its treatment offerings, as well as 24-hour availability. . . ." All the programs in this study used volunteers as some part of the service team, one of the programs being SCAN. The study found also that, while each client

TABLE 34.1

	1982	1983	1984	1985****
# of Volunteer Hours	60,322	84,519	73,536	83,524
# Hours Direct Service	32,956	49,720	38,584	46,752
% Direct Service	55%	59%	52%	56%
Speeches Given	478	551	725	1,368
Persons Attending	14,034	16,864	26,787	(unreported)
Average # of Volunteers per Center	44	38	33	31
# of Families Served*	10,847	15,218	12,029***	10,855
# of Case Referrals (investigated)	1,951	2,112	1,443**	1,689
# Cases Open to Volunteers	952	691	768	981
% of Self Referrals	59%	57%	47%	(unreported)

*Includes all those served with telephone counseling, information and referral to other programs, those served in parenting classes and those referred for casework services.

**13 centers reporting   ***14 centers reporting   ****19 centers reporting (4 less than one year old) contact by the professional cost $14.74, contacts by the volunteers cost as little as $7.25 each.[3]

Another study conducted over a three-year period starting in 1979 by Ellen Gray for the National Committee for the Prevention of Child Abuse also looked at eleven demonstration programs. All these programs were community-based and they were all either primary or secondary prevention programs. Gray concluded that "education can be effective in altering parenting attitudes." And, further, that "it is essential to realize, however, that in every case this education was dispensed within a supportive relationship; and in most cases, it was a one-to-one relationship. In any case, it is the naturalness, the meeting of several needs simultaneously, the reciprocity of benefit for mother and volunteer that seems to be the successful factor in this prevention method."[4]

Several other studies have been conducted which included Family Outreach programs. In 1983, David Brock of the Texas Department of Human Resources (TDHR) conducted a study of the Priority III Case Recidivism Rates in TDHR in Dallas County. TDHR includes in this category all cases in which findings show that the family is in need of continuing contact "to help the situation from deteriorating into abuse or neglect," but for which services should be provided by TDHR only if resources allow such services. Brock checked three groups of Priority III referrals, a group of previously investigated, a group of uninvestigated and a group referred for services by Family Outreach. He found that 14.9% were "referred again as a Priority I or II abuse/neglect complaint." However, he found that the recidivism rate for those served by Family Outreach was 2%. He concluded that "at risk families receiving services from such centers (meaning Family Outreach) have chances of re-referral in one out of fifty cases. Such services are beneficial to the protective services delivery system and funding in the area of Family Outreach services is probably well spent."[5]

Another study which included a Family Outreach center was the Self-Referral Demonstration Program Collaborative Research Effort conducted by Cicchinelli, Keller and Fox at the University of Denver, Denver Research Institute, Denver, Colorado, April 1982. This study was not designed to show "the relative success of the five demonstration projects," nor to study the effectiveness of paraprofessionals. Only two of the programs included volunteers in the treatment plans, Family Outreach and the Voluntary Intervention and Treatment Project. The purpose was to come to an understanding of the "nature of self-referred cases" and to explore beneficial services to offer these clients "within the confines of public agencies." Therefore, like all Family Outreach centers, all these programs were part of a public agency.

Four of these projects, including Family Outreach, offered what the authors called "parent education/therapy" which, they noted, was not provided by the public agencies to other clients. The authors noted that, "not only did self-referrals benefit from the addition of this service, but anecdotal evidence from some sites suggests that CPS clients also participated in these sessions." Further, the results of this study suggested that programs that attract self-referrals are effective in "involving the at risk population in social services."[6] None of the Family Outreach centers limits services to self-referring clients. However, publicity has always been slanted toward attracting self-referrals. The average self-referral rate at Family Outreach centers is 47 percent of the total case population. By implication, it can be assumed that Family Outreach is attracting the "at risk" population it has intended to serve.

Summary

In the thirteen years since the first Family Outreach center opened in Richardson, Texas, the program has seen steady growth and expansion. By 1978[7] there were twelve centers. At this time, there are twenty centers open in three states and eight other communities are working to set up centers that will most likely open within this year. The Family Outreach program is a unique and effective model of a team effort between a public agency and a private, nonprofit group to prevent child abuse and neglect. Co-sponsorship with the state agency mandated to investigate instances of abuse and neglect ensures that casework services will be carried out within the laws of the state in which the center is located. Such co-sponsorship provides protection for the volunteers and gives the state agency an opportunity to serve families it otherwise would not have the time or funds to serve. This is especially true of the Family Outreach program since direct casework services are reserved for families identified as being "at risk" for abuse and neglect.

The program is designed and implemented with the co-sponsors working together. From the first step of implementation in any location, it is a joint effort in which both parties take part in the decision making. The volunteers are involved in all administrative aspects of the program including policy making, evaluation, and management. The volunteers will continue to be responsible for all aspects of the program other than the investigation, supervision and assignment of the casework and their own training.

The training program for the paraprofessionals is comprehensive and prepares them to be the primary caseworkers responsible for the delivery of family services. However, responsibility for the investigation, assignment and supervision of client services remains with the casework professional to ensure that only potentially abusive and neglectful families are served by the program.

References

1.   Polansky, N., M.A. Chalmers, E. Buttenwieser, and D. Williams. *Damaged Parents*. Chicago and London: University of Chicago Press, 1981.

2.   Gray, J., and B. Kaplan. "The Lay Health Visitor Program: An Eighteen-Month Experience." *The Battered Child*, 3rd Edition. C.H. Kempe, and R.E. Helfer (Eds.), pp. 373-378. Chicago and London: University of Chicago Press, 1980.

3.   Department of Health, Education and Welfare. "Evaluation of the Joint Office of Child Development and Social and Rehabilitation Services National Demonstration Program in Child Abuse and Neglect." Public Law 93-247, 1974-1977.

4.   Gray E. "What We Have Learned About Preventing Child Abuse? An Overview of the 'Community and Minority Group Action to Prevent Child Abuse and Neglect' Program." Chicago, Ill.: National Committee for the Prevention of Child Abuse, 1979.

5.   Brock, D. "Priority III Recidivism Study." Dallas, Tex.: Texas Department of Human Resources, 1983.

6.   Cicchinelli, L., R. Keller, and P. Fox. "Self-Referral Demonstration Program Collaborative Research Effort Final Report." University of Denver, Denver Research Institute, Social Systems Research and Evaluation Division. Denver, Colorado: National Center of Child Abuse and Neglect, Administration for Children, Youth and Families, Office of Human Development Services, Department of Health and Human Services, 1982.

7.   Rosenstein, P. "Family Outreach: A Program for the Prevention of Child Neglect and Abuse." *Child Welfare*, 57(1978).

35. Building Resources for Prevention Programs

Anne H. Cohn and Thomas L. Birch

Introduction

Why should child protection teams be concerned with prevention? Child protection teams typically have child abuse identification, diagnosis and treatment as their primary concerns. And yet, the only way the United States can reduce significantly the amount of child abuse is to enlist the support of everyone in *prevention* efforts. This includes child protection teams.

The Need for Prevention

The numbers are never easy to comprehend. One million children are abused and neglected each year. Deaths are estimated at 2,000 to 5,000. The nation's response and indeed the role of child protection teams to date had been to deal with the problem *after* it occurs: to identify suspected cases of abuse, to conduct investigations, to take cases through court systems, and to provide punitive and therapeutic intervention. Over $2 billion a year is spent responding *after* the abuse or neglect has occurred. The best studies to date suggest this approach is successful less than half the time. And, studies show that even as families are in treatment, reincidence rates of serious abuse and neglect may be as high as 30%.

The long-term consequences of abuse are costly. Studies show that the majority of juvenile delinquents, teenage drug addicts and alcohol abusers and teenage runaways report that they are running away from abuse. We know most parents who abuse had troubled childhoods themselves, typically characterized by serious abuse or neglect. Child abuse can be characterized as the linchpin of many other social problems. By preventing child abuse, we can save our nation tremendous social upheaval, pain and expense.

How Can Child Abuse Be Prevented?

Our knowledge, while not complete, offers guidance on promising ways to prevent child abuse. Child abuse is a community problem, lodged in the values and mores of diverse geographic, economic, cultural and ethnic groups. Prevention programs must take account of these differences and be tailored to individual communities—child abuse cannot easily or accurately be predicted; we do not know in advance who will and who will not abuse. Thus, prevention programs must be directed to *all* families, all parents and children, even if on a voluntary basis. Because of the complexities of the child abuse problem and the variety of underlying causes or factors, no one approach to prevention is adequate; a variety of approaches is needed. A comprehensive community-based approach to prevention would include programs that:

-help new parents get off to a good start by providing close and healthy bonds with their new babies, and with information about child care and child development.
-help parents develop good parenting skills by making parent education readily available.
-help families better manage stress during times of crises by making available helplines, hotlines, crisis nurseries, drop-in centers, and crisis caretakers.
-help parents find periodic relief from the heavy and continuous responsibilities of child care with adequate, quality day care.
-help children learn how to protect themselves from abuse by making prevention education programs readily available.
-help eradicate the scars of abuse and break the cycle by providing therapeutic services to children at the time of the abuse and in the ensuing years.

Table 35.1
Comprehensive Approach to Prevention*

PRENATAL PROGRAMS
The purpose of prenatal programs is to prepare individuals for the job of parenting by building on existing prenatal medical programs to educate about-to-be parents in child development, parent-child relationship, and adult relationships. Information should be provided in the community on resources available to new parents about infants and children. In supplying information and in teaching skills for coping with the challenges of being a parent, special emphasis should be placed on developing, through group activities, a social network among new parents, thereby creating peer relations and peer support. While such programs should be available to all parents, special attention should be paid to first-time parents, teen-age parents, and single parents.

PERINATAL BONDING PROGRAMS
A perinatal bonding program's focus is on making available care that enhances the parent-child attachment. Childbirth procedures involving both parents, rooming-in, and unlimited visiting privileges for parents with their infants are all important. Hospital procedures should facilitate opportunities for families to get to know their newest member.

PROGRAMS IN INTERACTING WITH INFANTS
As a continuation of the prenatal program and to complement the perinatal program, all new parents should have an opportunity to participate in a program that would increase their skills in caring for a new baby. The programs should be directed toward creation of social networks, through new-parent groups or by pairing first-time parents with experienced ones, and toward continuation of instruction in child care and child development. Such programs should also offer well-baby and well-parent health and development checkups at regular intervals after the family leaves the hospital. These checkups might become the first activity of the home visitor program.

PROGRAMS FOR PARENTS OF INFANTS IN NEED OF EXTRA SERVICES
To reduce the additional stress created for parents by infants with special problems following birth (premature babies, sick babies, babies with abnormalities or defects), special programs would focus on group support from parents with similar children. The programs would educate parents about the particular needs of their child and how to deal with

those needs in a family environment. Every attempt should be made to furnish supports that would minimize distortion of the parents' perception of their new child. Separating newborn babies from their families to provide intensive care can require a special adjustment for parents, and they should receive help that is sensitive to this unique stress.

HOME VISITOR PROGRAMS

As in ongoing source of support and information for parents, the home visitor programs include periodic visits to the home following childbirth until the child begins school. These visits should be made by a trained home health aide who would provide information and advice to parents on child care, nutrition, and home management and would also carry out routine health checkups on young children. When indicated, the aide would refer parents to needed social and health services in the community. In some communities the services of the home visitor might just as effectively be rendered through a local well-baby program.

MUTUAL AID PROGRAMS

The overall intent of mutual aid programs is to reduce the isolation experienced by many parents through the development of peer support systems. Beginning with social networks created through parent groups in the prenatal and perinatal programs, a variety of opportunities should be offered for parents to participate in group activities or establish social contacts. Examples include foster grandparents programs, and Parents Anonymous or comparable problem-oriented self-help or support groups. The mutual aid programs would also focus on the development or strengthening of neighborhood-based natural helping networks.

CRISIS CARE PROGRAMS

To provide immediate assistance to parents in times of crisis, crisis care programs should have available on a 24-hour basis for all families in the community the following services:
 -a telephone hot line
 -crisis caretakers
 -crisis babysitters
 -crisis nurseries
 -crisis counseling
Parents facing immediate problems could, through the programs, receive support to alleviate the stresses of a particular situation. Help would be available over the phone or through face-to-face counseling. The

programs should offer parents the option of having someone come into the home on a temporary basis to assist with child and home care or of taking the child to a crisis nursery. The concept of crisis care is temporary and short term. Crisis care programs would be equipped to refer parents to long term services as needed.

CHILD CARE PROGRAMS

The purpose of child care or day care programs is to furnish parents with regular out-of-home care for their children. While it is a necessity in households where all adults are employed, such a service is also beneficial for parents who do not work but who find continuous child care responsibilities very stressful. These programs could also identify instances of child abuse and provide an opportunity to involve, teach, and counsel parents.

PREVENTION EDUCATION FOR CHILDREN PROGRAMS

The purpose of these programs is to equip children and adolescents with interpersonal skills and knowledge that will be valuable in adulthood, especially in the parenting role. Educational classes or supports should be provided throughout the school system. Skill and knowledge building should be stressed in areas of child development, family and life management, self-development, self-actualization, and methods of seeking help. For adolescents in particular, education in sexuality, pregnancy prevention, and issues related to parenting should be provided. Young children should be taught how to protect themselves from abuse.

PROGRAMS FOR ABUSED CHILDREN

To minimize the longer term effects on children who have been abused, age-appropriate treatment services should be available to them. The programs should be through diagnosis of developmental (social, psychological, and emotional) and physical problems. Comprehensive therapeutic services should be offered to alleviate identified problems. Assistance should be rendered on the basis of an individual child's needs and should include individual and group services as well as an enriched day care program.

What Role Can Child Protection Teams and.
Individual Team Members Play
in Prevention?

Given that child abuse is a community problem, it is argued that child abuse can only be prevented if *everyone* gets involved. There are a variety of options for involvement—particularly for child protection teams and their members.

1. *Identifying Prevention Needs*: Child protection teams can serve the community by identifying needed prevention programs. Just as such teams have historically served to identify needed treatment programs in a community, because they network with existing services in the community, so they can play the central role in flagging gaps in prevention services.

2. *Serving on Prevention Coordination Committees*: Just as there is a need to coordinate treatment services on a community basis, so there is a need to do the same with prevention services. Unlike treatment services, however, involving professionals alone is insufficient for coordination since prevention must involve everyone. The corporate, civic, and lay communities must be involved as well. Thus, child protection teams could expand to become the local prevention coordination committee or individual members could serve on such a committee.

3. *Setting Up Prevention Programs*: Child protection teams and their members can be most influential in planning, developing, implementing, and helping to operate prevention programs. Whether they are serving as volunteers after hours or as part of their own jobs, child protection team members have skills that are important in the prevention area.

4. *Educating Public About Prevention*: Child protection teams often serve as the community's child abuse speakers' bureau; even if the team doesn't, individual members do. Given the public's awareness and knowledge of the child abuse program in general, an important challenge now faces those who give speeches and engage in other public education activities to help the public move beyond awareness, toward actions that will prevent abuse. Child protection teams and individual members have an important role to play in educating the public how to prevent abuse.

5. *Advocating for Prevention Dollars*: Resources for prevention—as described in this chapter—exist in large part because of the concentrated efforts of a variety of individuals and organizations. Child protection team members are credible advocates; their involvement in

advocating for prevention dollars is needed to assure a growing funding base in this area.

6. *Reaching Out to Family and Friends*: Perhaps the work of a given child protection team itself is so all encompassing that a team or its members do not have the time to become actively involved in the five types of prevention-oriented activities described above. There remains one role which anyone can play and everyone should—that of reaching out to families, friends, or neighbors who are under the kinds of stress that can lead to abuse. Tending to your sister's new baby for an afternoon, telling a neighbor about the local crisis nursery, suggesting a friend take a parenting education program for new parents are all actions which each of us can take to help prevent abuse.

Funding Prevention

GENERAL PUBLIC DOLLARS: FEDERAL AND STATE TRENDS IN SUPPORTING PREVENTION

As a resource for preventing child abuse, the potential for dollars from public agencies is enormous. As a foundation for financial backing, public support offers a basis from which to attract private dollars. As a constant source of funding, however, public money is unpredictable. Because the availability of public assistance depends upon the political climate, funding from the public sector is liable to rise or fall dramatically.

Identifying the total amount of federal and state dollars spent on preventing child abuse is difficult. Money available from one source for prevention may also go to support treatment and other services after a child has been abused. Definitions of prevention vary, so that funds may go to stop child abuse from recurring, as well as to prevent it from happening initially. It is possible, though, to identify the sources of public dollars, both federal and state, that are available for funding child abuse prevention efforts.

NATIONAL CENTER ON CHILD ABUSE AND NEGLECT (NCCAN)

In 1974, Congress enacted the Child Abuse Prevention and Treatment Act (Public law 93-247) establishing the National Center on Child Abuse and Neglect as the focal point for federal efforts to address this problem. The federal program serves as a catalyst to mobilize professionals, volunteers and citizen advocates to address the abuse and neglect of children. During its first ten years, NCCAN funded over 500 projects nationwide to improve knowledge about preventing, identifying and treating child abuse and neglect.

NCCAN has contributed to our expanded awareness of and knowledge about the child abuse problem. Through its support of programs to educate the public about child abuse and neglect, NCCAN has helped to increase public awareness of the problem and developed a better understanding of what can be done to combat child abuse. In a Harris poll conducted in 1981 for the National Committee for Prevention of Child Abuse, more than three of every four Americans rated child abuse as a serious problem, and one in which the government should take a major responsibility.

By supporting public awareness efforts, NCCAN has opened the door to families in trouble. People now know that help is available. Through its program of grants to states, NCCAN has helped states improve their child abuse laws and programs to prevent and treat child abuse.

The federal involvement in child abuse through NCCAN highlights child abuse as a critical concern for state governments. NCCAN's state grant program shares information among states about successful efforts approaches and models that can be duplicated elsewhere. States have used their money for a variety of innovative programs—hotlines, public information campaigns, and established special clinics.

All fifty states now have statutes requiring the reporting of child abuse and neglect. NCCAN has helped states establish effective protective services with better trained staffs. Federal grants have supplemented state funds for child abuse services with seed money to support special treatment programs for abused children and their families.

Assistance from NCCAN to state and local organizations has also worked to leverage funds in support of child abuse services. Professional services worth dozens of times over the initial federal investment have been volunteered. Money has been used as a catalyst to form local programs of volunteers working with parents and abused children. Funds to state agencies interested other public and private agencies to sponsor programs for treating and preventing child abuse. State funds have been appropriated to carry forward support for programs that were seeded with federal funds from NCCAN.

Federal appropriations to NCCAN have never been large. The highest level of funding before 1981 was $22.8 million for discretionary research and demonstration grants and for state grants. In that year, NCCAN's budget was cut (though the agency was not eliminated as the administration had proposed) and annual funding remained at $16.2

million until 1985. Through the efforts of the National Child Abuse Coalition, Congress raised authorization for NCCAN to $26 million and more thereafter.

Still, there is much more that needs to be done. In 1980 the Government Accounting Office (GAO) reported that NCCAN had devoted little to prevention and called for "continual national focus on child abuse from the federal government." It suggested that NCCAN "identify and disseminate information about practical and effective programs or approaches for preventing child abuse and neglect and help states and localities implement such approaches."

In 1984, again at the suggestion of the National Child Abuse Coalition, Congress amended the Child Abuse Prevention and Treatment Act to direct more NCCAN support to prevention efforts. In testimony to Congress, the coalition advised that "30 percent of NCCAN funds directed at prevention efforts would be an appropriate beginning. States should be encouraged to use a portion of their NCCAN grants for prevention activities."

TITLE XX—SOCIAL SERVICES BLOCK GRANT

Title XX of the Social Security Act, signed into law in 1975 as a "consolidate program" of federal financial assistance to the states, is the principal federal funding source for the full range of social services and the major federal program of support to services for abused children. Assistance under Title XX grants is made on the basis of population, but the law requires that services be directed toward five goals: (1) self-support; (2) self-sufficiency; (3) prevention and remedy of neglect, abuse or exploitation of children or adults and the preservation of families; (4) prevention of inappropriate institutional care through community-based programs; and (5) provision of institutional care where appropriate. Examples of services range from care for a child in a day care program while the parent is at work, through training for a disabled adult provided in a rehabilitation center, to homemaker services for a frail, elderly person living alone.

In 1981, Congress at the urging of the Administration cut Title XX funding by 21 percent, from $2.9 billion to $2.45 billion. (In terms of dollars, Title XX funding has actually decreased every year except one. Because the program has not kept pace with inflation, states report difficulty in absorbing funding reductions while retaining essential services.)

At the same time, the Department of Health and Human Services (HHS) stopped requiring the states to report on how Title XX grants were spent. Consequently, no comprehensive information has been available on the kinds of services provided with Title XX funds, the number of persons receiving services and the amount of money expended on designated services. Prior to 1981 all states used part of their Title XX allotment on protective services—indeed, approximately 62 percent of the funds were expended for services to children and their families. Yet, in 1983, HHS reported that according to a state-by-state analysis of reports on proposed Title XX expenditures, only 11 states showed a service known as "prevention and intervention" in addition to protective services. Protective services and prevention programs, including day care, seem to be receiving less attention. Partial restoration of money cut from Title XX raised the funding level to $2.7 billion in 1985. Also, in 1985, Congress added special funding to Title XX for one year in an attempt to stem the abuse and sexual exploitation of children in day care programs. An extra $25 million in social services block grant money went to states to train day care staffs, state licensing officials, and parents in the prevention of child abuse in day care programs. States receiving this money had to establish procedures for checking employment histories, backgrounds and criminal records of all day care employees and staff in juvenile facilities.

TITLE IV-B

Child welfare services are supported by grants to states from Title IV-B of the Social Security Act which may be used to (1) prevent or remedy family problems resulting from child abuse, neglect or exploitation; (2) protect homeless, neglected or dependent children; (3) protect the welfare of children of working mothers; and (4) promote the welfare of children by strengthening their own families or providing adequate care for children away from their homes in family foster homes, day care or child care facilities. Any child is eligible for Title IV-B services regardless of economic status. The services states provide with these funds include protective services, family counseling, emergency shelter, health care, homemaker services and subsidized adoptions. The Adoption Assistance and Child Welfare Act of 1980 (Public Law 96-272) made changes in Title IV-B to help states find permanent homes for children in their care. The 1980 statute mandates statewide preventive and reunification services. Programs can include emergency shelter, day care for special-needs children, homemaker services, temporary housekeeping services, and parent training. In fact, according to research from the American Bar Association's Foster Care Project, very few services are actually provided, services are unevenly distributed within states and specific types of services are often available sporadically.

Funding for Title IV-B in 1986 stood at $207 million. However, when P.L. 96-272 was enacted in 1980, a more rapid growth rate in appropriations was expected for Title IV-B (and for Title XX), one of the reasons explaining why states have had difficulties in fully developing the preventive and reunification programs mandated by the law. P.L. 96-272 anticipated that by 1986 approximately $1.2 billion in total funds under the Title IV-B child welfare services program would already be available to the states and that states also would have had $15.5 billion in Title XX social services funds available for child welfare services. Instead, $841 million in Title IV-B funds have been provided, 29 percent below the anticipated amount, and $13.2 billion in Title XX, a 14 percent decrease from what was anticipated. The impact of the cuts of federal service dollars on state child welfare agencies came at a time of increased service demands on agencies resulting from escalating reports of abuse and neglect.

OTHER FEDERAL PROGRAMS

In addition to the resources provided by the federal programs just discussed, with emphasis exclusively or substantially on addressing the abuse of children, agencies with a different focus may also support activities whose aim is preventing abuse. For example, funds available under the Community Services Block Grant may go to ameliorate underlying causes of child abuse by helping low-income families to obtain adequate housing, health care, or suitable employment. Money can be used on an emergency basis to provide food to poor children and their families suffering starvation or malnutrition.

Alcohol and drug abuse have been linked to incidents of child abuse. Federal funds from the Alcohol and Drug Abuse and Mental Health Services Block Grant may support services that prevent substance abuse, alleviating circumstances that contribute to violent behavior. Grants also support community mental health centers with services to mentally ill adults and children that can help to treat the abused and abuser, and prevent the recurrence of abuse.

Services to mothers and children who are without good health care are supported by the Maternal and Child Health Block Grant. States receiving funds may provide medical services to battered children as well as to those who may be at risk of abuse because of inadequate attention to their health.

The Adolescent Family Life Program, Title XX of the Public Health Service Act, supports demonstration projects in communities providing care and training to pregnant teenagers and adolescent parents. The program also seeks to reduce the incidence of adolescent pregnancy by providing prevention information to young people before they become sexually active.

Indian Health Service Programs have identified stress and violent behavior prevention as a priority. Consequently, multidisciplinary screening committees for abuse and neglect have been established and support goes to primary prevention programs such as parenting classes and child drop-in centers.

Research on the causes, prevention and treatment of child abuse receives support from the National Institute of Mental Health. Grants have gone to develop a screening instrument identifying personality traits that are characteristic of abusive and neglectful parents; to prevent sexual assault by focusing on the early identification and treatment of sexually abused boys who may become high risk for committing sexual abuse later in life; and to develop information on the process of juvenile entrance into prostitution.

In 1984, Congress enacted legislation creating the Child Abuse Prevention Challenge Grants, a program of federal matching funds for states that set up trust funds for child abuse prevention activities. The special state funds have been created with money generated from surcharges on marriage licenses and birth certificates or by checkoffs on state income tax returns. Support goes to a broad range of community programs, including education programs in schools on sexual abuse prevention, respite child care for children under stress, and training volunteers to teach child-rearing skills to new parents. The Child Abuse Prevention Federal Challenge Grant program provides incentives for states to establish funds to support child abuse prevention projects, money that has been historically lacking because of the need to direct limited resources toward treating the increasing numbers of children already abused. For every $4 states make available in prevention funds, the federal government will provide $1 in matching support.

ANSWER AT THE STATE LEVEL: CHILDREN'S TRUST FUNDS

The first reliable, widely available source of state funding support to programs for preventing child abuse has come through the Children's Trust Fund. Revenues to build the Children's Trust Funds are generated by surcharges on marriage licenses, birth certificates or divorce decrees, or by specially designated refunds of the state income tax. Grants from the funds go to preventive programs for child and family abuse, and the distribution of the grants is supervised by an advisory group of individuals with an interest in preventing child abuse.

By 1986, advocates for abused and neglected children had worked toward the passage of legislation in 38 states that created new sources of funds for preventive services. In an era of diminishing governmental budgets and scrutiny of public responsibilities, the Children's Trust Funds emerged with a unique funding solution to boost programs for preventing child abuse.

Understandably, the Children's Trust Fund bill has been especially attractive to state legislators. This approach presents legislators an opportunity to fund programs they have traditionally neglected—those for the prevention of child abuse and neglect—and even though depressed state economies or deficits of revenue might inhibit the creation of new ventures, in a way that is apart from the question of appropriations and safe from cuts in state budgets.

The Children's Trust Fund approach is flexible. Each state that has enacted the legislation differs in geographic size, population, demographics, economics and political ideologies. Yet, each has taken the Children's Trust Fund and adapted the concept to suit its own constituency. The field is rich with models that might suit any state's situation.

Virginia and Rhode Island, for example, have increased the fees for marriage licenses, adding five to ten dollars to the cost of a license to benefit the Children's Trust Fund. The money in most states is deposited directly in the state treasury for this specially designated fund. Laws in Wisconsin and California have put a surcharge on copies of birth certificates: two dollars and four dollars respectively. The State of Michigan took a different approach, one followed later by other states, which enables taxpayers to designate a portion of their state income tax refund to the Children's Trust Fund. Missouri makes additional provision for a donation through the income tax return. The money collected from the income tax checkoff goes into a separate fund in the Michigan Department of Treasury. Half of each year's receipts to to fund programs. The rest is invested and earnings are credited to the trust fund. The refund checkoff in Michigan will be halted when the fund's endowment reaches $20 million. After that, programs will be financed from the interest on the money in the account.

Typically, the money is located in a separate fund in the state treasury. In some states, though, policy prohibits establishing a specially designated fund of state money. In those cases, like Virginia and Iowa, the extra fees from marriage licenses go into general revenues and are then automatically passed along through appropriations to the Children's Trust Fund advisory boards for grants to support preventive programs in child abuse.

Through the advisory boards which direct and administer the Children's Trust Funds, a public and private partnership has developed important new links to address the prevention of child abuse. States include on their boards statutorily specified heads of governmental agencies which are, or should be, working to prevent abuse—education, social services, health, mental health, law enforcement, and criminal justice.   The advisory boards' public members are appointed by the governors and legislative leadership of the states.

The responsibilities of boards vary from state to state, but they generally include both advisory and administrative duties.   In administering the Children's Trust Fund, a board may: hire staff to run the program; develop a state plan for the Children's Trust Fund; establish priorities for projects to be funded; develop eligibility criteria for grantees; review proposals; approve the awarding of grants; monitor expenditures of the trust fund; evaluate the effectiveness of the Children's Trust Fund; and submit an annual report to the legislature and the governor.   As appointees of the governor and the leadership of the legislative and executive branches of state government, board members are in a unique position to act as advocates for the prevention of child abuse.

In most states, the advisory board is attached to the department of social services for administrative support, but in some states, the Children's Trust Fund council is an independent agency.   The Alabama Child Abuse and Neglect Prevention Board, for example, administers a fund supported by a state income tax checkoff, and was created as an independent agency paying its own expenses out of money collected.

The Kansas Children's Trust Fund began in 1981, receiving about $170,000 a year.   Since the marriage license surcharge was first enacted in 1980, the Kansas fund has been supplemented by increased fees from birth certificates passed by the state legislature in 1984, and direct legislative appropriations have increased the Children's Trust Fund to almost $300,000 a year.   In Kansas, attention has been focused on prevention to show how it works.

Grants, limited to $15,000 each, provide seed money for community-based preventive projects and education programs, and communities have assumed financing after the grants have terminated. Applications run well above the numbers of programs that can receive grants.   Funding has gone to a play program for children who have been under stress because of violence at home.   Other money has gone to train volunteers as advisers to new parents.   A coalition for developing primary prevention services has been helped, and assistance was given to a self-care educational course for elementary school-aged "latch-key" children.

Aside from the number and variety of programs that have been assisted by the Kansas Children's Trust Fund, advocates cite as one of its prime accomplishments the positive attitude generated toward the prevention of child abuse.   Prior to establishment of the trust fund, resources in Kansas were scarce for preventive programs.   That has changed now as dollars have become available, along with a belief by legislators and agency staff that prevention works.

Virginia's Family Violence Prevention Program began awarding grants in the fall of 1982 from the $400,000 generated yearly by a marriage license surcharge. As in other states support must be matched with local money and grantees must demonstrate an ability to continue the program after Children's Trust Fund support ends. Here are some examples of projects that have been funded.

The planning Council of Norfolk received support for its Pride in Parenthood Project. Six hundred "at risk" mothers and their husbands or boyfriends received eight weeks of child rearing education and support during pregnancy and following delivery to develop nurturing and coping skills. The Lynchburg Department of Social Services launched a program with Children's Trust Fund support to develop parenting skills training for mentally retarded parents. The community services board in Charlottesville was awarded a grant to sponsor a project for the prevention of violence in families of learning-disabled children, educating families about appropriate ways for both parents and children to cope with the increased stress this disability presents.

In Washington, the Children's Trust Fund, which receives about $400,000 annually from a $5 surcharge on marriage licenses, is looking at additional funding mechanisms to build toward the goal of a self-sustaining fund that will provide ongoing support for local projects. Washington's statute, like that of most other states, allows the Children's Trust Fund to accept "contributions, grants, or gifts in cash or otherwise from persons, associations, corporations or the federal government," and with that authority the Washington council has begun efforts to generate additional income.

Solicitations are made to individuals and corporations. Public service announcements have been televised asking for contributions to the Washington Children's Trust Fund. Long-range giving has not been overlooked. Packets of informational materials have been developed for attorneys and accountants who work in estate and tax planning. Information on the Washington Children's Trust Fund is available to pass along to their clients who seek advice on charitable giving.

A unique effort to generate money for child abuse prevention through private enterprise has brought together a group of designers, business advisers and child abuse prevention experts. This group develops a line of products for marketing, with the objective of raising the public awareness of child abuse prevention and the Children's Trust Fund, and generating revenue for the fund. Children's furniture is now being manufactured for marketing, with the proceeds from sales going to the Washington Children's Trust Fund.

Indeed, the Children's Trust Fund has proven its value everywhere. The variability of the legislation is one of its prime strengths. It presents a model for support of programs to prevent child abuse that is easily adaptable to the political demands of a state.

Children's Trust Funds have passed in states with governments across the political spectrum, conservative as well as liberal.

Children's Trust Fund takes the pressure off the regular state social services budget to fund often neglected preventive services. In a time of limited funding the Children's Trust Fund has been advanced as a significant means to achieve the goal of preventing child abuse.

Through an emphasis on community-based programs selected by a citizens' advisory board, the Children's Trust Fund fosters the creation of local programs to prevent child abuse and shift some of the responsibility for planning to the local level.

With solid support going to preventive efforts, often for the first time because of the Children's Trust Fund, attention can be focused on prevention. Administrators of public agencies and state legislators can be educated about prevention and regular appropriations can increase the support for prevention engendered by a Children's Trust Fund.

PRIVATE RESOURCES FOR PREVENTION

Private dollars and other resources for prevention became more readily available during the early and mid-1980s but on neither the scale nor with the predictability of federal and state prevention funds. Yet, corporations and foundations, service groups and individuals have each played a role in helping to support prevention activities.

Corporations and Foundations: The most common source of private support is that provided by corporations, corporate foundations, and foundations. Contrasted with the 1970s when a common response to any child abuse solicitation, particularly those with a focus on prevention, was "not interested," the early 1980s saw a growing awareness in the corporate community about the full implications of child abuse. "Our employees may include those with child abuse problems. And, when our employees have problems at home, like child abuse, they don't do as well at work. Even if our employees aren't abusing their children, their children may be at risk of being abused." With this awareness came an interest in helping to respond to the child abuse problem both for the community at large and within the corporate structure. Not only did corporations begin to develop preventive services for their own employees—day care, parenting classes, flexible working hours, shared jobs, stress management—but they also began to provide preventive services to the community. McDonald's carried prevention tips for children on the paper place mats covering food trays; several public utility companies did the same through their advertising campaigns; and suppliers of children's products carried prevention messages through their products such as a Marvel comic book featuring the Amazing Spider Man which tells children how to protect themselves from sexual abuse.

In addition, funding from the corporate and foundation sector for prevention programs grew.

Grants from corporations and foundations are typically modest in contrast with federal and state grants. A gift of $1,000 or $2,500 is usual, with the rare grant of $10,000 or more. The smaller gifts are often renewable year after year; the larger ones usually are not.

Despite the growing numbers of corporations and corporate foundations which are supporting child abuse prevention activities, by 1985 there was still no foundation dedicated completely to child abuse prevention.

Service Groups: A growing number of service groups have taken on child abuse prevention as their philanthropic focus. The National Exchange Clubs expressed interest in this area in the late 1970s and sought to raise funds for parent aide and lay therapy programs across the country. A number of sororities have joined the Exchange Clubs—notably Kappa Delta and Sigma Delta Tau—and the American Contract Bridge League took on child abuse prevention in the mid-1980s as its philanthropic issue. Each of these service groups has sought to raise funds and to recruit volunteers for child abuse prevention organizations. The funding from year to year is unpredictable, albeit welcome.

Individuals: The American public has become an enormously important resource for prevention. Whether reached through direct mail appeals, invitations for special events, or opportunities to give through work-related programs (such as the Combined Federal Campaign or Employer Matching Programs), the public has become increasingly generous in donating to child abuse prevention programs. And, the public's concern about child abuse is seen not only in cash donations but in the volunteer time of literally thousands of individuals. Prevention programs by and large depend heavily on volunteers to carry out the services.

Prevention resources from the private sector include important dollars but extend beyond funds to include actual prevention programs and volunteer services.

Summary

Child protection team members are part of a societal effort to reduce child abuse and neglect. Through knowledge of program alternatives and funding options, team members will be able to inform colleagues, the public, and opinion makers of important methods for reducing child abuse. With the development of prevention resources, referral options will increase and abuse and neglect will be reduced.

Note

*The table was adapted from "National Committee for the Prevention of Child Abuse Community Plan for Preventing Child Abuse," National Committee for Prevention of Child Abuse, 1981.

36. Future Challenges for Child Protection Teams: Research, Education, Advocacy

Richard D. Krugman

Introduction

The field of child abuse and neglect has progressed significantly, whether one looks back over the three decades since the development of the first multidisciplinary child protection teams in Pittsburgh, Los Angeles, and Denver, or whether one looks back over a century to the first descriptions of physically and sexually abused children by Ambroise Tardieu, Professor of Legal Medicine in Paris.[1] During this time, we have come to recognize that there are many forms of child abuse and neglect, that each of these forms has its own body of knowledge, and that the best approaches to recognition, treatment, and prevention of all forms of abuse and neglect are multidisciplinary. Child abuse and neglect is neither a medical problem, a legal problem, nor a social problem. It is a child's and a family's problem and relies on professionals from all disciplines to work together to recognize, treat, and prevent it. This chapter will review briefly what we know and what we don't know about the various forms of child abuse and neglect, lay out an agenda for action by multidisciplinary child protection teams, and suggest approaches to dealing with ten major challenges to the provision of multidisciplinary services in communities.

Physical Abuse

We have learned a great deal about the recognition of physical abuse of children. We now know how to differentiate accidental from non-accidental injury; we know a great deal about multidisciplinary approaches to treatment; and the literature is increasingly filled with evaluations of approaches to prevention of physical abuse. The reported incidence of physical abuse of children has remained relatively stable over the past decade. There are fluctuations in communities with variations in employment rates and economic conditions, but overall it appears that progress is being made in the area of physical abuse. Clinically, it is now unusual to see children with the appearance of the "battered child" reported by Kempe and his colleagues in 1961. While there are nearly two million reported cases of abuse and neglect nationwide, less than 3% of this total represents serious physical abuse. Part of the reason for the decline in the numbers of battered children may be that the community recognition and reporting mechanisms have led to earlier intervention in cases of abuse and neglect. In addition, there have been many prevention efforts at the local level that have led to an increased awareness and an increased level of support for young families who are at higher risk for physical abuse. Crisis nurseries, hotlines, home visitor programs, the provision of therapeutic preschools and day care centers and mental health services for children and families have all combined to have impact on the reduction of severe physical abuse of children.

What we don't know about physical abuse represents a challenge to those working in the field to provide the research data necessary to answer some significant questions. We don't yet know all of the long-term consequences of physical abuse of children. While it has been known for some time that most, if not all, physically abusive adults have been inadequately nurtured and the overwhelming majority have been abused the way they abuse their children, it is not clear what percentage of abused children grow up to repeat that cycle. Neither is it clear what relationship abuse has to other problems, such as alcoholism, substance abuse, and teenage pregnancy. Nor has there been enough research into the biological and neurophysiologic aspects of abusive and neglectful behavior.

Sexual Abuse

Sexual abuse has been defined as the engaging of a child in sexual behaviors which the child does not comprehend, to which the child cannot give informed consent, and/or which violate the social taboos of our society. Over the past decades we have learned a great deal about the recognition of sexually abused children and the varying offenses that occur. The efforts of Finkelhor who has developed a four preconditions model for sexual abuse occurrence,[2] of Summit who has described the child sexual abuse accommodation syndrome,[3] and many others who described the behaviors and physical findings of children who have been sexually abused either within the family or in an extrafamilial setting, have contributed greatly to our understanding. The long-term and short-term outcomes for sexually abused children have been deduced by studies done on adults who had been sexually abused and later reported numerous difficulties in their relationships and everyday lives. Yet with the great increases in knowledge of sexual abuse have come enormous problems in dealing with false allegations and false denials of the occurrence of sexual abuse by children. Because sexual abuse, unlike physical abuse, is uniformly a criminal offense, the pressures to accumulate evidence, as well as to fight allegations, carry much higher stakes than in the usual cases of physical abuse that are dealt with by the child protective services system.

As with physical abuse, there is a great deal that we do not know about the long-term outcomes of sexually abused children. Adults who were molested as children (survivors) have only recently begun to form groups for mutual support. Further research with this group may help elucidate some of the long-term outcomes and risks to children of being sexually abused within and without the family. Data are accumulating on the effectiveness of child sexual abuse prevention programs. Some have demonstrated cognitive gains in children, a few have demonstrated behavioral changes in children, but the overall effectiveness of these programs and for whom they are effective, and by whom should they be done are questions that still need to be answered. Also needed are evaluation studies of the outcomes of the varying forms of treatment ordered by courts for children who have been sexually abused within their families. Further, the relative usefulness of civil and criminal court efforts in cases of sexual abuse still needs to be addressed.

Nonorganic Failure to Thrive

We know what failure to thrive is: it is first a disorder of parent-child interaction that leads secondarily to a failure to gain weight appropriately because of an inadequate caloric intake. We know that the mortality for hospitalized failure-to-thrive children who have been followed for up to five years ranges from 4 1/2 to 15 percent, depending on the study. We know that the morbidity of these same hospitalized failure-to-thrive cases is substantial, with the majority of children having developmental, behavioral, and neurologic deficits on follow-up. We know that a substantial portion of failure-to-thrive children will either be physically abused or conversely that some physically abused children will develop a nonorganic failure to thrive syndrome.

And yet here, too, there is a great deal that we don't know. Primarily, we really don't know very well how to treat nonorganic failure to thrive. Our treatment efforts in physical abuse and sexual abuse are a great deal better. Perhaps this is because we can be more successful in treating abuse, which is an active event and a behavior that may be amenable to change; failure to thrive is a form of emotional neglect that implies an inability to provide nurturance and love to children, and teaching individuals how to love and nurture children when they themselves have not been loved or nurtured may be too difficult a task. We also do not yet know how to prevent failure to thrive in children.

Other Forms of Abuse and Neglect

Emotional abuse, which is perhaps the most prevalent form of abuse of children and the one with the least intervention, physical neglect, which is the most reported and the one with the most intervention, and medical care neglect, which is only recently being understood, are all areas in which less is known than in the areas of physical abuse, sexual abuse, and failure to thrive. Garbarino[4] and others have contributed greatly in this area, helping classify the forms of psychological maltreatment: rejecting, isolating, criticizing, ignoring, and terrorizing behaviors by adults toward children.

It is probably because emotional abuse is so hard to document and physical neglect is so easy to document that these are the least and most reported interventions by child protective services systems in the United

States. Yet some of the same issues remain and raise the same research questions, namely, what are the determinants of being a casualty or a survivor of this form of child maltreatment.

Systems Issues

High on the list of questions that are being asked in the 1980s is whether or not the child protective services system and the system of mandatory reporting by professionals is effective. On one hand one could state that the mandatory reporting system is effective if one looks epidemiologically at what appears to be a reduction in the numbers of "battered children" (as seen by Kempe et al. in 1962) over the past 20 years. But, it also needs to be said that since so few child protective services agencies follow up cases or publish results of their interventions (many claiming confidentiality of information as a smoke screen), one cannot really say with certainty that the CPS system works. Political and economic pressures will probably lead to an increase in this type of study over the next decade.

Role of Child Protection Teams

While only a few studies document the impact of multi-disciplinary child protection teams throughout the United States, it is clear that the growth of these teams from the original three in 1958 to the present 1,000 teams has contributed greatly to the understanding we now have of child abuse and neglect. These teams have not just functioned on a case-by-case basis. Many have been the nucleus for the development of community-wide or even statewide child protection councils. These councils have taken an advocacy role in the community adding bankers, educators, major corporations, and other concerned citizens and lay people to the team. They have banded together in national groups such as the National Committee for the Prevention of Child Abuse, to form potent advocacy groups that have changed laws, increased funding, and pushed for community treatment and prevention programs throughout the United States. Without diminishing the importance of volunteers, it is clear that professionals, preferably with experience on a multidisciplinary child protection team, must be the nucleus or primary resource of such a group. No lay or community group can effectively develop advocacy efforts in child abuse and neglect without the knowledge that professionals working in the field bring to the issue, any more than efforts to combat polio or AIDS can succeed without a partnership between citizens and specialists.

It is these community and statewide child protection councils that will, over the next decade, tackle the difficult issues facing those working in the field of child abuse and neglect. Among these will be whether abuse should be dealt with as a criminal issue or as a civil issue, a social problem or a disease, and whether society will take a punitive or a therapeutic approach to those individuals who abuse children. These groups deal also with the difficult economic issues of fiscally supporting a system that is developed to protect a few hundred thousand children and now is faced with trying to protect millions. We do not yet know how big the problem of child abuse and neglect really is, how costly it is, what the long-term economic effects of abuse and neglect of children are, and how pervasive the economic impact of the problem is. To help teams develop these approaches in a rational way, the following ten steps are suggested as a reasonable way to start.

(1)   Recognize that complex problems do not have simple solutions. There are two ways to try to solve a complex problem. One is to spend many years devising the perfect complex solution. The other is to break the complex problem down into its multiple parts and implement many simple solutions. There is probably no one way for a community to prevent all forms of child abuse and neglect. For progress to be made in the next decade, the problem needs to be divided into its many component parts. Multiple simple solutions need to be implemented at the federal, state, county, local, agency, and individual levels.

(2)   Responsibility for providing solutions must be placed where it belongs. Multidisciplinary child protection teams and community child protection agencies must fix responsibility for appropriate efforts at the federal, state, county, professional, agency, and individual levels. We cannot expect the federal government to solve local problems any more than we can expect individuals to deal with local, state, or federal responsibilities. Thus, the federal government must be held responsible for providing core support for new directions in the research and training of professionals in abuse and neglect. State and county governments must provide the services needed to support children and families. They must collect the data on the county or statewide level to assess problems and implement necessary programs. Each profession must take responsibility for educating its members as well as monitoring their competence, and each agency must take responsibility for evaluating its programs and employees. Each individual must continue his or her education

and keep up to date in the field so that the best services can be provided to children. (Note: this list is not meant to be all-inclusive, but merely a guide.)

(3)   There must be ongoing evaluation of all programs that deal with abused children and their families. This is true for teams, CPS agencies, mental health, law enforcement, district and county attorneys, and judges. It includes prevention and treatment programs.

(4)   The multidisciplinary approach must be enhanced and supported. The existing 1000 multidisciplinary child protection teams should be organized into regionalized networks, similar to the existing systems for the delivery of care to premature high-risk infants. No front-line social worker or law enforcement officer should lack access to expert medical, legal, psychiatric, or social work advice if it is not available in the community.

(5)   There needs to be a greater focus on prevention. Existing prevention efforts are somewhat random and haphazard, depending on the interests of individuals and communities. Prevention should be undertaken for physical abuse, sexual abuse, and neglect. An important component of prevention is the provision of treatment services to abused children. The treatment of abused children today may well prevent the repetition of the cycle of abuse in the next generation.

(6)   There must be a dramatic increase in manpower training for all professions involved in the multidisciplinary team. A team is only as strong as its weakest link. It does no good to have expert medical advice, sensitive social work, and good law enforcement only to have a county attorney who will not file a case or a judge who will not listen. We need to stimulate manpower education and training in all of the professions involved in the multidisciplinary assessment and treatment of child abuse and neglect. This should be a federal responsibility.

(7)   We need to increase dramatically the number of treatment facilities. The community mental health system in the United States in the early 1980s has been overwhelmed with caring for the chronically mentally ill who were deinstitutionalized in the late 1970s. Chronic funding shortages have left this system unable to cope with the dramatic increase of families who have been harmed by abuse or neglect. The continued increase in the recognition of children who are being abused and neglected, without provision for the treatment of these children or their families, will only exacerbate the problem.

(8)   To accomplish each of these tasks, we must have an increase in funding, from either public or private sources. But there must be a concerted and coordinated effort to obtain this funding.

(9)   There must be a dramatic increase in political awareness and activity on the part of all those who work in this field. Federal, state, county, and local political efforts to obtain public appropriations must be accompanied by concerted private efforts including business, corporate, and service club fund raising activities. Media awareness is essential, not just of terrible death cases or highly publicized sexual abuse cases, but as part of an ongoing education effort. The media must help the public be aware of the complexity and the pervasiveness of the problem of abuse and neglect, and ways in which the problem can be attacked.

(10)   Those working in this field must have realistic expectations. The abuse and neglect of children have been present for centuries. Our efforts of the past 25 years, while spectacular in many of their achievements, do not guarantee that the problem will be eliminated within the next generation. Lest those working in the field become disenchanted, because it is their perception that by not eliminating the problem nothing has been achieved, it is important to set realistic goals. Working to eliminate child abuse and neglect is analogous to standing on the beach with a number of buckets and trying to bail the ocean. There are at least two dangers to standing in the beach and bailing the ocean. The first danger is that one will start bailing at high tide and six hours later leave feeling very pleased with one's efforts in dropping the ocean by two to three feet. Those who work only in the intake process or those who do not provide ongoing services to children and families over the years that they need us may suffer from the feeling that they have done very well in a short period of time. Conversely, the second danger in trying to bail the ocean is that after two to three years of effort one might get depressed if one continues to look at the waves crashing in on the beach. That is the time, however, for one to turn around and look behind and see, because of the two to three years of bailing, the large pool behind us, each bucket representing a child or family who has been helped by our efforts. If we maintain this perspective, we will all be here for the third edition of *The Child Protection Team Handbook.*

Good luck.

References

1.   Masson, J.M. *The Assault on Truth*. New York: Penguin Books, 1985.

2.   Finkelhor, D. *Child Sexual Abuse: New Theory and Research*. New York: The Free Press, 1984.

3.   Summit, R.C. "The Child Sexual Abuse Accommodation Syndrome." *Child Abuse & Neglect*, 7(1983):177-193.

4.   Garbarino, J. *The Psychologically Battered Child*. San Francisco: Jossey-Bass, 1986.

Index